Paul Klee,
*lenkbarer Grossvater
(The Docile Grandfather)*,
1930. Pen and ink,
height approximately
24 inches.

MANAGEMENT:
A Modern Approach

The Harbrace Series in Business and Economics

Editorial Advisory Board

MANAGEMENT:
A Modern Approach

Martin K. Starr

Columbia University

Harcourt Brace Jovanovich, Inc.

New York   Chicago   San Francisco   Atlanta

© 1971 by Harcourt Brace Jovanovich, Inc.

ISBN: 0-15-554681-3

Library of Congress Catalog Card Number: 73-141609

Printed in the United States of America

To Christopher H. Starr and Loren M. Starr

At every management level myths exist to answer questions that no one has thought to ask. Myths reflect imagined constraints and objectives chosen by habit. The perceiver of myths discovers in them unexpected opportunities to create the future.

Preface

The fundamental objective of this book is to familiarize students with the field of management as it exists today—that is, to bring to the teaching of management the important new ideas that have reoriented the practice of management over the last twenty years. Most instructional material concerning management derives from the work of the 1930's, 1940's, and 1950's. Yet since those years four related developments have radically changed the concepts and practices of managers.

The first is a significant improvement in quantitative techniques. We try, in this book, to reflect these new analytical capabilities (although we confine ourselves to high-school algebra and simple matrix forms) and to foster an understanding of their potential for management. The second development has been that of computer technology, which allows on-line, real-time information management. Third is the concept of systems, with its profound psychological effect on the manager. The systems approach emphasizes the interconnectedness and interdependencies of any system, which in turn require analysis and synthesis to be understood. Fourth, because of new communication and transportation technology, information flows have increased in number and in rate of flow. The result has been greater interconnectedness, with increasing sensitivity to delays and decreasing stability of systems' performance.

In meeting the challenges posed by these developments, managers more and more are giving up reliance on arbitrary rules of thumb and common sense. There are now rational principles they can utilize and there is the ability to interrelate such principles so that a theory of management begins to emerge. For example, words such as "planning," "controlling," and "policy-making," which have been used ambiguously for years, have now been defined and related to one another. This is not to say that any single theory of management exists, any more than it can be said that a theory of marketing or a theory of production exists. Yet, increasingly, both marketing and production are taught with a theory base, and in management also the approaches of reasoned analytic thought, model-building, model-solving, and model use can provide a unifying structure.

Theory-building is a self-fostering attitude. And, for management, theory is more important as an attitude than as a basis for rigorous explanation of complex phenomena, because management itself is largely an attitude—a willingness to debate issues and resolve them, an acceptance of appropriate techniques and procedures for applying or rejecting solutions. Because of these dialectic properties, apprenticeship as a way of "learning to manage" is less economical than well-designed instruction in management theory.

There remain, of course, substantial areas of management that are scarcely touched by principles and for which theory is only incipient. For example, apprenticeship may be the only operational way to train "the company president" because present theory is not satisfying when applied to top management levels. Nevertheless, the basis for a "theory attitude" exists, and this book pulls together from many sources the ingredients for that basis. For those who are accustomed to using cases, this book will provide ample evidence of the advances that have been made in analyzing decision-making, planning, controlling, and organizing. Those who prefer to use the framework of managing as a basis for instruction will observe that the management-science view synthesizes developments in many fields *related* to managing—that is, a variety of significant economic, behavioral, and organizational materials.

The essence of the approach used by this book (which began as classroom notes and has been evaluated and refined in classroom use) is based on the concept of modeling management. First, we develop a classification and taxonomy of management activities. Then, *model-building, model-solving,* and ultimately *model use* are explained and shown to be the strongest means by which to consider *decision-making,* which can in turn be viewed as the gateway to the more complex management functions. For example, an understanding of *planning* is developed in terms of the basic decision structure, and the various types of planning model are explained fully. Then the planning function is contrasted with *policy-making* and *control*. We next weave the management of information systems into the fabric of these considerations, which allows individual behavior, group behavior, and *organizations* to be discussed in terms of the model-building, decision-making, planning, policy-formulation, and control notions developed in earlier sections of the book. We continually connect knowledge obtained from the behavioral sciences with the quantitative approaches of management science, thus approaching a synthesis of the functions of management. But these functions cannot be fully understood unless management is seen, finally, as a whole process. We therefore must consider both the interacting systems that are the parts of the firm as well as the systems outside the firm such as the marketplace, the economy, and legal and societal directives.

My interest in management was first kindled by the work being done in the early 1950's by Professors Robert T. Livingston, David B. Hertz, and Sebastian B. Littauer of Columbia University, and especially by the emphasis placed on communications and information. With Professor Al Rubenstein and Dr. David Sachs, we conducted a variety of experiments about interactions, connections, and dependencies within and between systems. Hundreds of hours of informal discussions clearly delineated the growing importance of the management function. I therefore must express my gratitude to all of the above. In addition, I thank Professors Anees Hussain and Bill Frey for their critical reading of my manuscript and the excellence of their criticisms. Professor Barry Dumas read several sections of the book that relate to his research and gave me helpful comments. Judith L. Dumas managed all the manuscript logistics and typed it into existence, for which I am grateful.

MARTIN K. STARR

Contents

MANAGEMENT:
A Modern Approach

Chapter 1
The Framework of Managing

Management's self-understanding is a fundamental part
of the framework of managing. The same is true
of management's sense of purpose, its goals,
and its language—all of which reflect management's
complete acceptance of its *responsibility* to provide
rational means to achieve desired ends.

Chapter 1

THE FRAMEWORK
OF MANAGING

In the winter of 1650, I was going into the city of Chiaochuan from the Little Harbor, accompanied by a boy carrying a big load of books, tied with a cord and strengthened with a few pieces of board.

It was toward sunset and the country was covered with haze. We were about a mile from the city.

"Will we be in time to get into the city before the gates are closed?" I asked the ferryman.

"You will if you go slowly. But if you run, you will miss it," replied the ferryman, casting a look at the boy.

But we walked as fast as possible. About halfway, the boy fell down. The cord broke and the books fell on the ground. The boy sat crying. By the time we had retied the package and reached the city gate, it was already closed.

I thought of that ferryman. He had wisdom.[1]

How do you react to the word "management"? Does it have some good and some bad connotations for you? It probably has both, for the management function is a part of many different life patterns, some of which are sought after and some of which are not. Managing certain things is a burden; managing others, a pleasure.

---

[1] Chou Yung (1619–79), quoted in R. G. H. Siu, *The Man of Many Qualities—A Legacy of the I Ching* (Cambridge, Mass.: M.I.T. Press, 1968), pp. 19–20.

1

Although individuals may differ about the specific connotations of *management,* the word, in its best sense, brings to mind responsibility for the achievement of objectives that are valued highly.

Some people are better managers than others. In addition to having natural abilities, the better manager has usually studied what managing entails. There is no guarantee that one can learn to be a good manager, but it is evident that many individuals have learned to be better managers. Moreover, the things to learn have been changing; they are not the same now as they were twenty years ago. The framework of managing has been incorporating more science, and the view of that framework has been clarified as a result. It will be our purpose to use these newer views in exploring the question, "What does management entail?" We will build on many fundamental concepts, and this takes time.

Great managerial ability is now recognized as being essential for the good of society. Certainly, in absolute numbers, people today are better educated and have greater resources to purchase the products of a continually improving technology. According to many of the accepted measures of how we are doing, things are better than before. But the evidence of our current history warns us that the old measures are no longer valid. We have crossed some thresholds, and new measures of how we are doing are needed. Only by altering our view of the manager, by respecting that job and supporting it in transition, can we hope to be able to cope with the existing situation and prepare promising futures for ourselves and those who follow. It seems unlikely that mere adequacy in managerial ability will be enough. We must prepare to be excellent in it. Will we be able to do so? As the ferryman said, "You will if you go slowly." The professional manager cannot be trained in haste. The profession of management needs time to find its direction and to set its standards.

MANAGEMENT PROVIDES RATIONAL MEANS TO ACHIEVE ENDS

Management requires the judicious use of means to accomplish prescribed ends. Judiciousness is a chain concept that is no more effective than its weakest link. Consider the means-end chain in Figure 1–1. If any link in it is faulty, the achievements from that point on are defective.

It is not an easy matter to be prepared for the long-term consequences of each stage in such a chain of effects. And, in fact, the chain never really stops. Managing is a continuous function extending well beyond an immediate set of means and ends.

To handle such situations, *management must proceed rationally to use the resources it owns in order to accomplish the objectives it has,* especially when the implications of failure are serious. For each specific situation, it has to determine the particulars concerning means and ends. From the chain concept,

Figure 1–1   A Means-End Chain

NOTE: "Each subordinate end must be justified as a good means toward a broader, or more basic, end. Once such ends have been accepted, their fulfillment becomes a desired 'value.' "

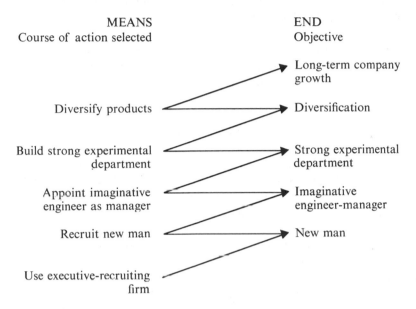

MEANS	END
Course of action selected	Objective

SOURCE: William H. Newman, Charles E. Summer, and E. Kirby Warren, *The Process of Management,* 2nd ed. (Englewood Cliffs, N.J.: Prentice-Hall, 1967), p. 383.

we see that ends at one stage become part of the means of the next stage. The rational use of means is not, therefore, a one-step activity; it is a continuing dynamic process. Repeatedly, the manager must *allocate* his resources to meet demands in accordance with his objectives. Over and over again, he must evaluate the *configuration* of his resources in their organized patterns to reach decisions about plans and policies and to exercise control over the system in accord with his objectives.

The *conversion* of resources from one basic type to another (such as money to material or materials to energy) is part of the management of means-end chains. For example, the decision to use manpower instead of machines involves a sequence of appropriate actions, such as hiring and training, that are very different from the actions that would have been required by an investment in machines. The conversion process makes for changes at all stages, right through to the final products and services.

The precise forms of management that parallel the design and operation of the physical system can be described, in a general way, as *model-building, de-*

cision-making, planning, controlling, and *organizing* (the five sections of this book). As thousands of words about managing flow past the reader's eyes, he becomes familiar with this generalized terminology, which is characteristic of all management systems. He recognizes that management can be viewed without taking into consideration organizational particulars—that is, specific goods or services, production, financial or marketing issues, industry or government interests. Highly general management fundamentals, reflected by a broad and nonspecific terminology, can be applied to all variants of specific cases. And there is *high transferability* of management know-how, which enables a good manager to operate effectively in many different situations.

The Framework of a Rational Approach

We have referred to model-building, decision-making, planning, controlling, and organizing. These are the major components of the management framework. They are usually treated in management literature as separable, indeed independent, components. It is our intention, however, to analyze these management functions as interrelated, as integrated into a single structure, for recent technological and methodological developments have shown them to be so.

Significant modifications are now taking place in the way these fundamental management terms are viewed as a result of a change in the meaning of "rational approach." It is no longer construed as being merely common sense and systematic procedure. To portray rationality as a form of common sense activity[2] does our efforts to understand management a distinct disservice. To say that systematic procedure is what the rational approach is all about is not much different from saying that sound is that which is audible to the ear. The ultimate description of rationality is the existence of a *theory* that fully explains "judicious use" in terms of means and ends. The development of a theory of management requires consideration of how to balance interactions between all the framework concepts. The need for a theory of management is tied directly to the lack of principles for describing when something is rational and when it is not.

THE PROBLEM OF CHOOSING ENDS

Our interest in this section centers on the goals (or ends) valued by management. As a generalization, we can say that ends are subjective elements and

---

2 As Stuart Chase said, common sense is "that which makes us think the world is flat."

means objective ones (see Figure 1–2). But since ends are often means to other ends (see Figure 1–1), this fact limits the generalization. It is also limited in another way. Rationality *seems* to imply that a totally objective form of reasoning will be used in deciding on the means to employ—that is, that no

Figure 1–2   Objective Selection of Means Related to Subjective Ends

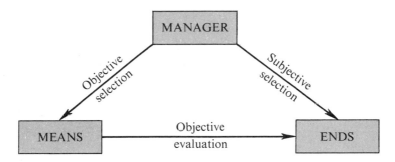

subjective intuitions of managers will be allowed. But this point of view has been modified substantially in recent years to allow subjective reasoning to be considered as a form of information that can be treated objectively. In other words, subjective reasoning can be embodied in objective analyses, so the generalization is weak here also. We should be careful, however, to distinguish between subjective forms of means analysis and the subjectivity involved in choosing ends. The former can usually be replaced by objective procedures, but the latter has no substitute.

Subjective Values

The personal *values* that account for chosen ends (such as profits, sales, clean cities) are obviously *subjective*. But the nature of such values is not readily understood. And we cannot simply decide to study this behavioral aspect of management, for the choice of personal values is not open to rational analysis. In the management process, values are a beginning point; they are basic premises that every management program accepts as given. Such values are the major part of what we mean by the philosophy of management. We have no quarrel with discussions concerning the philosophy of management; how they reflect social values, historical incidents, and so forth, can be fascinating. Nevertheless we feel impelled to caution against the failure to distinguish between management theory, on the one hand, and management values, on the other. Difficulties arise when, as so often happens, the two are indiscriminately mixed in descriptions of management principles.

Culture and society determine the norms for acceptable objectives. These objectives can differ greatly, depending on the value system of each particular culture.[3] This is one of the reasons for the current emphasis on studies of international business. The aim of the effort is to become acquainted with the values of others. But it is not to change these values. Because of gaps in understanding the nature of values, more than one United States firm has lost business in Latin America, Asia, and the Middle East. Europe may be less of a problem because of similarities of Western values, but even it poses difficulties.

Different values exist as well between business, government, and other institutional managements operating within a single culture. Such dissimilarities lead to many problems. One need only consider the past history of dealings between the United States government and the steel, telephone, automobile, or computer industries to grasp the extent of value divergence that can exist. To complicate matters further, values everywhere, and at all levels, are changing rapidly and dramatically with respect to individual status, personal power, social leisure, competitors' roles, company size, profit, prestige, and so on.

Values differ even among the closest participants in the same organization. In an actual decision situation, the president and executive vice president of a large industrial company discovered that they fundamentally disagreed on what they wanted the company to achieve. The president (in effect) said, "Thinking back, I guess we never agree—that's why I don't ever take his advice." A check made several years later indicated that these men remained in identical positions. This fact raises some questions. Is there an advantage in having different values represented at approximately the same management level? In spite of social pressure to think otherwise, we can point to reasons why this may not be advantageous. When there is disagreement, consistency in direction can be obtained only if one view overrides the others. Value consensus, by definition, does not occur by using reason, so disagreement is likely to persist. Value differences are wasteful of both energy and spirit. Somewhere in the system, the effects of the opposing views must clash. Often this will occur at levels where those responsible cannot even observe it. In the case cited above, of course, the president may not care about his disagreement with the vice president because he can simply ignore his advice, and he may feel that the vice president does a good job just carrying out instructions. He evaluates his subordinates in terms of objective matters only. This is neither unusual nor to be condemned. However, the value difference between these managers cannot be shown to help either of them or the organization.

---

[3] See, for example, the discussion concerning potlatch, pp. 245–46.

Objective Evaluations

No treatment of ends would be complete without a discussion of the role of objective approaches. We have previously noted that values are not arrived at objectively. However, the way in which resources are used to satisfy management's purposes *can* be judged objectively in terms of consistency and efficiency. A peculiar paradox emerges, because ends can be viewed as means to other ends. By changing the viewpoint, the appropriateness of subjective and objective approaches is altered. The longer the chain of means and ends, the more objectivity that can be brought to bear. But, at the end of the chain, there will be a subjective goal.

There is a significant difference between the treatment of the domain of value selection, on the one hand, and that of resource use, on the other. Because of this division between subjective and objective judgment, management must be considered part *art* and part *science*. Recently, science has been playing an increasingly important role. Although its usefulness is limited to its own sphere of evaluating means, the achievements of science have an effect on management's selection of ends, for the new methodologies permit ends to be achieved that were previously unreachable. This point should be kept in mind throughout the book—particularly because it allows longer chains to be considered.

Managers tend to assume that they share the same value system. Perhaps they do for long chains, where the more fundamental values are involved, but differences become apparent regarding shorter ones. In any case, where managers actually do share the same values, differences between means (based on objective evaluations) can be discussed and resolved. Where they do not, care must be taken to avoid confusing value disagreements with discrepancies in the objective measures of the system's performance.

Consensus

Given an unambiguously rational world, science can be expected to produce solutions with which all participants can agree. Since this kind of world does not exist, the ability of science to provide consensus must be questioned. Still, by using science, at least some of the confusion can be cleared up. We could isolate differences of opinion due to subjective values if we could apply science to explain and remove differences uncovered by objective evaluation. But the objective methods must be examined to determine whether they are really free of personal biases. If they are not, steps can be taken to separate resource utilization from ultimate goals or, in other terms, means from ends. The confusion of means and ends, as we have previously pointed out, can occur because they are separable only on an artificial basis. So, if this approach of separation will not work, we can start with subjective questions rather than objective ones. A variety of behavioral studies can be utilized to determine how similar the value systems of several individuals really are. We do not need to include all managers in such a study, only those whose opinions will count—that is, those whose purposes control the managerial process. Then, we must determine whether those managers have sufficiently common goals in mind. If they do not, the health of the organization is questionable.[4] Good organizational health is difficult to define, even though poor health is easily identified. Both for humans and organizational systems, the combinations of factors that signify good health are too many and too complex to enumerate. But in this case, we can say that a sign of poor health exists when the managers cannot agree on ends to be pursued.

With the ideal of goal consensus before us, let us consider what usually occurs when managers differ markedly about values and therefore about specific goals. Although the gap is clear enough between what two managers think "ought" to be done, seldom are the managers' premises brought into the open. The managers assume that the means analysis is at fault. They are not aware that each might be arguing rationally for his own value system. This is a situation in which expectations and realities diverge. If the managers believe wrongly that their expectations are the same, they are bound to accuse the realities of being unreal and of accounting for their differences. Awareness of expectations is, therefore, essential if realities are not to be distorted or misinterpreted. Moreover, it is the first step in achieving consensus, for, with an awareness of the lack of consensus, managers can use scientific abilities to clarify the issues. And, with such a focus, it becomes conceivable to repair organizational consensus by influencing those factors that are related to it. This may take the form of new assignments, consulting a third and higher authority to judge a winner, and so forth.

MANAGING INTERRELATED BUT DIFFERENT GOALS

The overall objectives of organizations are composed of the subobjectives of many different individual and group goals. For the broadest kind of cut at these management relations, we can consider the "division-of-interest" schematic

---

[4] "Textbooks usually define health as the absence of disease, and vice versa. The two conditions are alleged to be opposites of each other. Is this really so? Are they not rather different only in degree . . . ?" Hans Selye, *The Stress of Life* (New York: McGraw-Hill, 1956), p. 221.

Figure 1–3   Managerial Multigoal Relations

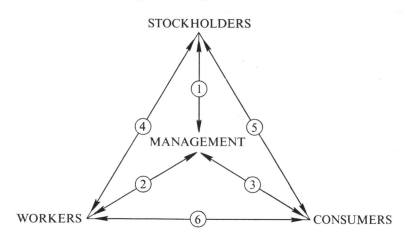

shown in Figure 1–3. Variants of this diagram have appeared in management literature for many years. Formerly, they were intended to identify the different points of view that are present in all management activities; more recently, they have been used to study the conflicts inherent in the interrelations of the various goal systems.

In recent years management has become concerned about unresolved conflicts, whereas previously it had simply accepted them as inevitable. Much management activity now accents the resolution of divisive forces. Conflict resolution takes on many different forms, including theoretical formulations of game playing and behavioral theories for negotiating and compromising. Participative management, which encourages all of the vertex roles to engage in some management activities, is intended to achieve conflict reduction by having all participants share the conflicts. In Figure 1–3, the special polarity of the manager's role is apparent. One approach, therefore, is to reduce this polarity of the manager; another approach is to enable him to use it to maximum benefit.

Management is the hub relating stockholders, consumers, and workers with the enterprise. Communications flow both *from* and *to* management. Thus, line 1, connecting management and stockholders, is primarily the concern of financial management. Stockholders invest capital in the company and vest authority in executives to manage it. In turn, management reports regularly to the stockholders and tries to return dividends, stock appreciation, and growth potentials.

The second line, 2, connecting management and workers, represents a combination of what is generally called the industrial relations and personnel area. Aspects such as motivation, leadership, and loyalty characterize this domain, along with the somewhat more measurable items of wages and productivity.

The relations of line 3, representing management and consumers, are readily identified with marketing management. The dual relationship between buying and selling requires consideration of the complex composed of distribution, pricing, advertising, and so forth. It should be noted that lines 4, 5, and 6, which connect workers, stockholders, and consumers in different pairs, are also real relations. Many possible patterns of communications between managers, workers, stockholders, and consumers therefore exist, though some are more common than others.

Figure 1–3 can be also interpreted in another way, with the connecting lines representing the same person having multiple roles. One individual can be a stockholder and a worker; another person might be simultaneously a manager, a stockholder, and a consumer. Much interest has begun to center on such mutual roles because they occur with increasing frequency and because they are having profound effects on management's fundamental relations—1, 2, and 3.

There are $2^4 - 1 = 15$ different combinations of roles for Figure 1–3. The value of one is subtracted because the case of no roles at all is a meaningless arrangement. Thus, where M stands for manager, S for stockholder, W for worker, and C for consumer, we have:

M	*MS*	*MSW*	*MSWC*
S	*MW*	*MSC*	
W	*MC*	*MWC*	
C	*SW*	*SWC*	
	SC		
	WC		

Four of the arrangements have no interrole connection (e.g., the manager alone); six of them necessitate one connection (e.g., manager-stockholder); four require three connections (e.g., manager-stockholder-consumer); and the total set of roles uniquely uses all six of the links shown in Figure 1–3.

A large part of managerial awareness has to do with recognizing that only the manager is concerned with both the roles and communications in the six-link system. In our view of the manager, he is always dealing with the three direct links, 1, 2, and 3, and the results he achieves are continually affected by the additional three forms of intercommunication, 4, 5, and 6. Nevertheless, in many situations the manager *acts* as though only one connection is operating. He does this because his job description accents a single vertex of the triangle. While he is usually well aware that all goals affect his performance, he assumes that his job has not positioned him to deal with the larger system. Of course, traditionally, this is true, but it is a tradition that is changing. Each manager is concerned with more roles and their goals than ever before.

This does not mean that even top management will ever be able to obtain complete goal consensus between all roles. Nevertheless, although it may not be any one manager's goal, it is management's purpose to find a balance be-

Figure 1–4   Vector Resolution of Two Opposing Forces

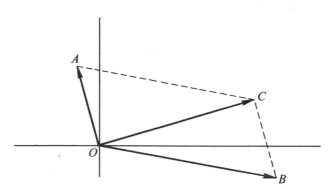

tween them. By thinking in terms of a resultant effect, management can view the aggregate of individual value structures as reflecting the enterprise's objectives. For example, Figure 1–4 depicts a vector resolution, *OC*, of the two forces *OA* and *OB*.[5] To amplify this point, let us assume that *up* means more cash on hand and *down* means less; further, that the left direction signifies reducing product-line variety and the right means increasing it. If the resultant, *OC*, satisfies the participants, *A* and *B*, as a reasonable compromise, then consensus is well on its way to being achieved. But real problems are seldom so simple. The inclusion of many participants and additional group interests complicates the notion of such a resultant effect. Community involvement, legal and social affairs, tax matters, and even broad cultural and ethical effects that extend across national to international boundaries have severely complicated the interrelations of management and surpassed simple ideas of resultants. What is more, complex dimensionality is not the only problem. There must be human behaviors that support such a model of value resolution. If there are, they are certainly not universally applicable. The study of management demands far richer viewpoints.

Pareto's Criterion[6]

The concept of resultant consensus as a guide to management is at least augmented by that of Paretian optimality. Pareto's criterion suggested that each

---

[5] Vectors are good descriptors of a system's properties, having both magnitude (in length) and (angular) direction, and there are strong mathematical methods for dealing with them.

[6] Vilfredo Pareto (1848–1923) was an Italian economist and sociologist. His chief work, *Mind and Society*, was written in 1916.

Figure 1–5   As a Result of Any New Policy Each Person Must Obtain a Zero or Positive Increment of Benefit

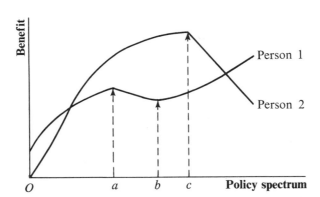

person's needs be met as much as possible without decreasing the degree of achievement of any other person. Look at Figure 1–5. Our objective is that no one experience a decrease in benefits as a result of someone else's gaining benefits. Therefore, policies between *a* and *b* are eliminated because they decrease Person 1's benefits; policies beyond *c* are eliminated because they decrease benefits for Person 2. This leaves as acceptable policies between the origin and *a* and between *b* and *c*. We can readily substitute managers, workers, stockholders, and consumers for Persons 1, 2, 3, and so on.

However, without a high level of consensus, Pareto's criterion would produce a low level of resultant satisfaction, for almost no policies could be found that would not be destructive of some group's benefits. The question must then be raised: How similar are the goals of the different groups with which management deals? The answer is that there are many strongly shared goals at the end of long means-end chains and far fewer shared goals for intermediate means (so readily viewed as ends). We find a reason, therefore, for encouraging management to think in bigger terms; and we point out again that developments in scientific methods have substantially increased management's ability to contend with longer means-end chains.

Let us now use one such method to achieve a more precise view of the relationships shown in Figure 1–3.

Matrix Representation of Management Roles

Books on management can be characterized by the time and attention devoted to each of the links, 1 through 6, described above in connection with Figure 1–3. Certainly, therefore, it is relevant to ask: What proportion of our discussion should be devoted to each area for the proper consideration of the management field? Whose value system should predominate? The answers to these questions are important.

Scientific developments dictate that every component that affects the achievement of objectives be included in the analysis. Managers, workers, stockholders, and consumers are all participants in the management process. And, for any real system, all participants will affect and be affected (to some extent) by the choice and achievement of the objectives. Therefore, the entire triangle of relations must be considered at the start of any management study, although reasons for not including all goals may emerge later. Some group may seem unimportant, but before it can be dropped from consideration, the longest reasonable means-end chain should be examined. A Paretian type of criterion can be used to determine whether the group in question is really unaffected and, consequently, unaffecting. Such examination requires detailed analysis of the interrelations of roles and expectations.

It is necessary to understand that the managerial links consist of two-directional flows—that is, both *to* and *from* management. Awareness of these relations can be expanded by replacing the triangular representation of Figure 1–3 by a matrix format. What, then, is a matrix? It is a construction that we shall be using in literally dozens of different ways throughout this text. It is based on the classification of information in terms of two different scales (such as *before* and *after, to* and *from, speed* and *weight, marketing cost* and *production cost, sales volume* and *profit*). If one scale is assigned to rows and the other to columns, the resulting array of ordered cells is called a matrix. Some matrices have no particular order of row and column in which they should be read. For example, if length and width are assigned to row and column, respectively, they can be multiplied in any order to produce the intersection values of each row and column that are areas. More often, matrices represent sequence. For example, the matrix in Table 1–1 is a *to* and *from*

Table 1–1   Matrix Representation of Managerial Relations

→	To: Stockholders	Workers	Consumers	Management
From: Stockholders	7	4'	5'	1'
Workers	4	8	6'	2'
Consumers	5	6	9	3'
Management	1	2	3	10

translation of Figure 1–3. The arrow in the upper left of the matrix indicates the direction in which the matrix should be read—namely, from row class to column class.[7] So 2' represents that which originates with workers and flows to management, whereas 2 originates with management and flows toward workers.

The matrix draws attention to several points that were obscured in Figure 1–3. First, it shows that two-way flows can and should be systematically separated. Second, the diagonal of the matrix forces recognition of some new relations—indicated by numbers 7 through 10. These have real enough meaning: 7 might be stockholder associations; 8 labor unions; 9, consumer groups from which growing pressure is felt; and 10, communication between executives as well as the self-awareness of management. By self-awareness we mean the manager as he sees himself; we also mean the study of management practice, executive programs, and research on management functions and capabilities.

Expanding the information content of the role matrix. We have organized sixteen cells of participating relations, each of which has its own unique identity in the total management process. But this is not yet a sufficient picture. We must expand the matrix to approach an adequate representation of management. For instance, external factors (frequently called exogenous) can be added (see Table 1–2). These might include the state of the economy, competition, vendor relations, and a variety of other environmental considerations that apply to any specific situation. So the matrix grows quickly from sixteen cells to twenty-five, thirty-six, or more.

In each cell we would describe the forces (appropriate to that cell) *that affect the enterprise.* For each organization the particulars that portray the situation would be different. The matrix of such expanded descriptions con-

---

[7] When the arrow is pointing down ($\downarrow$) the matrix should be read from column class to row class. Direction here is simply a convention. Any matrix can be written in either way. The standard appearance of a square matrix would be:

$$
\begin{array}{c|ccccc}
\rightarrow & i & j & k & \ldots & n \\
\hline
i & R_{ii} & R_{ij} & R_{ik} & \ldots & R_{in} \\
j & R_{ji} & R_{jj} & R_{jk} & \ldots & R_{jn} \\
k & R_{ki} & R_{kj} & R_{kk} & \ldots & R_{kn} \\
\cdot & \cdot & \cdot & \cdot & & \cdot \\
\cdot & \cdot & \cdot & \cdot & & \cdot \\
\cdot & \cdot & \cdot & \cdot & & \cdot \\
n & R_{ni} & R_{nj} & R_{nk} & \ldots & R_{nn}
\end{array}
$$

where $i, j, k, \ldots n$ are the factors that produce the results $R_{ii}, R_{ij}, \ldots$ and so forth. For row i and column j, the result R_{ij} is obtained; whereas for row j and column i, the result is indicated by R_{ji}.

Matrices do not have to be square, and the row factors can be entirely different from the column factors. The key is that each matrix should be a useful representation of the problem being studied; in this case, the interrelationships of goals.

Table 1–2

→	Stockholders	Workers	Consumers	Management	Externals
Stockholders	7	16	17	18	19
Workers	4	8	20	21	22
Consumers	5	6	9	23	24
Management	1	2	3	10	25
Externals	12	13	14	15	11

stitutes an approximation of the system that concerns management. The matrix provides a useful classification system for organizing the relevant information.

One can concentrate on any cell or set of cells of the matrix above. Some cells are (by tradition, if nothing else) more common to the traditional study of management than others. For example, 2 and 21, dealing with workers and management, will be found accented in a majority of management texts that have long been in use. A more recent trend to treat 10 in depth can also be noted.[8] The study of fields—for example, marketing management—will be seen as concentration on the submatrix

9 23

3 10

The discussion of problems can also be assisted by this type of framework. However, with such an approach, the submatrix must be free enough of involvement with the matrix of the total system to enable a useful solution to be obtained by considering only the submatrix. In other words, the submatrix must capture the essence of the problem. Problems, when viewed objectively, are seldom that free of involvement. Consequently, with the total matrix before us, we see why the management science approach can be most useful when it spans many of the cells of relations.

THE NATURE OF RATIONAL MEANS

The framework of managing begins to fall into place once we know *whose* values are involved in setting objectives and recognize that each *means* chosen produces intermediate ends with many consequences. This indicates that de-

---

[8] This includes comparative management (comparing the management function in different cultures) and psychiatric views of management.

cisions, plans, and policies are dramatically affected by the manager's value viewpoint. The use of rational means takes hold in different ways, at various stages, in direct response to this viewpoint. But once the goals are set, there is no ambiguity about what is rational and what is not.

The results of rational analysis are not independent of the values that are held, although the methods of rational analysis are. Rational method interprets the interaction of values and events. A set of facts will convey different meanings, depending on what the underlying laws are assumed to be. That knowledge is fundamental to the practice of law.

> Each week the courts decide hundreds of cases which purport to turn not on disputed "questions of fact" but solely on "points of law." If the law is unambiguous and predictable, what excuses can be made by the lawyers who lose their cases? They should know in advance of the decisions that the rules of law are adverse to their contentions. Why, then, are these suits brought or defended?[9]

Jerome Frank explains the reason: "The law is in doubt." That is why rationality does not provide unambiguous answers to complex legal or management questions. But rational method itself is not in doubt.

Rational method is objective in the sense that problems are stated clearly in terms of goals and that solutions are examined and tested systematically and critically. Numbers, as measures of performance, provide the clearest route to rational method, but one can still be rational even if quantification is lacking. Rationality should not be confused with the rationalism of eighteenth-century philosophers, who rejected empirical evidence and contended that truth could be obtained solely by reasoning from (so-called) self-evident premises. Rationality, as we mean it, is sometimes called the experimental philosophy. It combines reason and observation in the systematic pursuit of verifiable truths. Scientific method is the product of these ideas. Throughout the book we subscribe to the use of rational method, and we develop it in application to management goals.

The Development of Managerial Rationality

In the early 1900's, great efforts were made to develop rational management views. Progress was evident, but nowhere were great strides reported. Changes came slowly because old ways always seemed to work well enough when judged against the potential penalties of untried alternatives. However, there were numerous contributors to the effort to rationalize management. One of the most impressive was Frederick W. Taylor (1856–1915). In 1898, Taylor,

---

[9] Jerome Frank, *Law and the Modern Mind* (New York: Brentano's, 1931), p. 8.

who had worked as a patternmaker's apprentice, discovered with a colleague a new method of tempering tool steel. He realized the generality of his method of discovery, which involved the systematic reduction of uncertainties through analysis. Taylor systematized metal-cutting and then began studying ways of improving the efficiency of workers at other jobs. Eventually he expanded his notions into a broad "theory" of scientific management. Taylor's books, *Shop Management* (1903) and *Scientific Management* (1911), emphasized the managerial benefits of rational method. His beliefs commanded serious worldwide attention when, during a court hearing, the railroads were unable to override his position that lower rates could be achieved through greater efficiency. The so-called efficiency expert was born from these beginnings. Taylor's students and colleagues included Henry L. Gantt and the Gilbreths (Frank and Lillian), all of whom received international recognition for their efforts to replace existing subjective procedures with rational methods.[10] For many years Taylor's concepts dominated the ideas of management rationality, but gradually they began to be absorbed and transformed by larger views of systems and by the infusion of behavioral elements that could not be reduced to mechanistic forms of rational analysis.

There were other contributors, such as Henri Fayol, Chester Barnard, and Mary Parker Follett, who dealt more with the philosophy of management than with rational method.[11] Their interest converged on affecting managerial behavior by changing value systems, from which changes would follow for methods and means. For example, emphasis was placed on the division of labor and work specialization (terms whose meanings are self-evident). This rationalization of means directly reflected the values of that time, just as participative management, job enlargement, and feedback follow from today's values. (The latter terms may not be self-evident but will be examined at appropriate places in the text.) Unfortunately, these early management pioneers seldom clarified the distinction between subjective values and rational method. As a result, a management language grew up that mixed means and ends together.

---

[10] The Gantt chart is well known in industry for scheduling work and projects. Therbligs (which are almost Gilbreth spelled backwards) were tiny units of the motions used by workers to accomplish their jobs. These units provided a framework for work simplification and job analysis and led to great interest in and reliance on time and motion studies by industry.

[11] The choice of these particular individuals should not obscure the fact that there are at least another twenty-five vitally important contributors who could have been included here. A glance at the writings of these three will, however, justify their inclusion in this special group. See, for example, Henri Fayol, *General and Industrial Management* (New York: Pitman, 1949). (The book was originally published in French in 1925 by Dunod.) See also Chester Barnard, *The Functions of the Executive* (Cambridge, Mass.: Harvard University Press, 1938), and H. C. Metcalf and L. Urwick, eds., *Dynamic Administration: The Collected Papers of Mary Parker Follett* (New York: Harper & Row, 1941).

The Language of Management

In savage lore, as John Dewey points out, to manipulate names is to master their objects.

> The delight that children take in demanding and learning the names of everything about them indicates that meanings are becoming concrete individuals to them . . . savages attach a magical efficacy to words. To name anything is to give it a title, to dignify and honor it by raising it from a mere physical occurrence to a meaning that is distinct and permanent. To know the names of people and things and to be able to manipulate these names is, in savage lore, to be in possession of their dignity and worth, to master them.[12]

Management words, even when held to their simplest definitions, tend to have overlapping meanings. For example, the word *directing* interacts with *coordinating* and is part of what is involved in *organizing.* Similarly, *planning, decision-making, policy-making,* and so forth, are used by managers in ways that obscure the specific character of what is intended. It is our intention to explore the words that are special to management and, if possible, to improve their usefulness. This requires removing their ambiguities. Then we can begin to articulate them in terms of viable structures for studying managerial behaviors. By following such a course, the science of management becomes possible.

In management, as elsewhere, the names by which "things" are called often represent classifications that become crucial to understanding. For example, why do we name management activities as we do? We classify functions of management as marketing, finance, production, research and development, and so on. And we can find divisions in companies according to these lines and courses in schools to match the industry practice. Is this organizational practice in the best interests of management? As another example, what has led us to examine management's performance by means of the standard accounting categories rather than in some other way? Are there more fundamental reasons for the standard approach than convenience in preparing tax returns? The same type of question can be raised about the labels for management positions in the organizational hierarchy. Are these labels relics from tribal days, or are they real organic components in the organization, as the heart and brain are in the individual? Who decided on chairman of the board, president, vice presidents, and controller?

To understand the nature and effects of classification and category names, we must begin by examining classification in general—that is, *taxonomy,* which means the scientific (systematic) classification of subjects.

---

[12] John Dewey, *How We Think,* rev. ed. (Boston: Heath, 1933), pp. 173–74.

Management Taxonomy

One basic motivation for classification is to reduce uncertainty by controlling the amount of variety that must be handled. Without any classification scheme, each item in the system must be treated as unique. With classification, individuality is sacrificed to achieve a reasonable number of groups. Classification reduces variety, but when used solely for such purpose it will often lead to confusion, misassociations, and, ultimately, erroneous views. On the other hand, classification for the purpose of expanding understanding is another matter. The key here is the design of the grouping rules. If the underlying hypotheses capture the properties of the system that are useful to the manager, then the taxonomy is founded on rational premises and is a first step toward the construction of management principles and theory.

In general, principles represent greater variety and uncertainty than does theory. It is useful to differentiate between principles and theory. For our purposes, we will define them as follows: A *principle* is a fundamental truth or basic law that is believed for *intuitive* reasons, whereas a *theory* is a *scientifically acceptable* principle. The distinction is most relevant because classifications can be developed that resist scientific approaches but lend themselves to intuition.

The study of management took its first step toward the development of comprehensive theory in the early 1900's with the creation of a basic taxonomy. Over the intervening years, the old taxonomy has been followed to the limits of its usefulness. New directions have now appeared, growing out of the old ones with an assist from recent scientific developments.

The earliest investigators of management emphasized *static* taxonomy— that is, straightforward classification, lacking information about the effects of interaction of one category with another. This tended to block theory-building, although it encouraged the construction of useful principles. These pioneers in management taxonomy were concerned with the identification and naming of critical managerial functions. They assumed that hierarchical managerial levels could be classified in terms of the major components of different managers' jobs. The emphasis on *hierarchical structuring* was derived from the approach of natural scientists, who had long preempted the field as experts in taxonomy.

The intensive study of classification systems began with botany and can be traced to roughly 300 years before Christ. At that time, Theophrastus wrote *A History of Plants,* which classified some 500 species employed at that time in the treatment of diseases, in terms of the uses of the plants in such treatment. Andreas Caesalponus (1519–1603) of Florence, Italy, later classified plants according to the distinguishing characteristics of each plant's fruit. Other systems evolved related to different hypotheses, such as the external or internal forms of plants, useful functions performed by the organism, geographic distribution at different points in time, and, eventually, stages of plant development, or morphology. This last system, morphology, came closest to satisfying the needs and expectations of the botanists of that time. But botanists are still, after hundreds of years, searching for better answers.[13] Therefore, the present, unsatisfactory state of management classification is hardly surprising considering the short time that it has been the subject of investigation. In the earliest days of botanical research, the opportunities for classification and the criteria by which one system was chosen over another were not obvious. The *same* conclusions were applicable to the development of management taxonomy, but since 1950 some important forces for change have been at work.

New Directions

Static classification can lead to management principles, but it cannot go much further than that. It stops short of theory because management is too complex to be treated in static terms. We must not lose track of the fact that a *satisfactory* classification system is defined by the purposes to be served.[14] It is not

---

[13] The most famous name in the field of botanical taxonomy was Linnaeus, the name given to Carl von Linné (1707–78), a Swedish botanist. Yet the well-known Linnean system provided, at best, a convenient form of *static* grouping. Antoine Laurent de Jussieu of France (1748–1836) developed a superior taxonomical system, which supplanted the Linnean system and lasted for a considerable time. But even now, most botanists claim that the present system of taxonomy is unsatisfactory (because it remains essentially static), and efforts are being expended to extend botanical classification into multiple dimensions that interact with one another. We will call this *dynamic* taxonomy. For a relevant and up-to-date discussion of taxonomy in the natural sciences see Robert R. Sokal and Peter H. A. Sneath, *Principles of Numerical Taxonomy* (San Francisco: W. H. Freeman, 1963).

[14] For example, we can rapidly classify oranges, apples, marbles, and bananas in a number of different ways.

   a. Oranges, apples, and bananas belong to the class of fruit; marbles belong to the class of nonfruit.
   b. Oranges, apples, and marbles belong to the class of spherical objects; bananas belong to the class of nonspherical objects.
   c. Oranges, marbles, and bananas belong to the class of seven-letter words; apples belongs to the class of six-letter words.
   d. Together, all belong to the class of things.

Each of these approaches may have utility for some purpose. That is what W. T. Calman had in mind when he stated: "It should be clearly realized that, although classification of any sort demands some system of nomenclature, the latter is no more than one of the tools of the classifier and has no importance in itself provided it fulfills in adequate measure the purposes he has in view." *The Classification of Animals* (London: Methuen, 1949), p. 25.

the same for all interests. For managing to be properly understood, we need to approach the subject by means of a dynamic taxonomy. What hope is there for a rational, dynamic classification of management activities?

There is a lot of hope. A look at the field of model-building (which is the focus of Part I of this book) will support this contention. *Models are representations of systems that can be studied in rational ways.* Model-building provides a powerful approach to the development of dynamic taxonomies. This is epitomized by decision models, which are the central topic of Part II.

We will find that decision-making analysis does an excellent job of raising the information level of the taxonomical system. Decision classifications are rich and dynamic. They provide the basis for planning and control classifications, which are treated in Parts III and IV. Planning and control models are dynamic and comprised of many forces. Nevertheless, the taxonomies for planning and control have begun to simplify as a result of conscientious study of these activities. The process of moving from complex explanations to simpler ones typifies an advancing science. The effort is not surprising since the planning and control functions encompass so much of what management does; they synthesize and integrate a great range of managerial activities. Finally, when we reach organizing, the topic of Part V, we realize that we have reached an apex. The taxonomy falters because there are gaps we cannot close. Rationality gives way to intuition; means and ends begin to look alike; value judgments are not easily separated from rational ones. The approach to theory is befuddled by behavioral complexities, but, still, the sense of a total structure remains.

SUMMARY

This chapter has described the current framework for management thinking, providing some of the background that has led to the present state of management's understanding of itself. This includes its sense of purpose, the variety of its goals, and its language. We observed that management is responsible for providing rational means to achieve desired ends. Using the concept of a means-end chain, we examined the difficulties of choosing goals and then the way in which these goals affect the rational process of selecting means. The nature and desirability of goal consensus was discussed. This led to an expanded view of goals as they are held by managers, stockholders, workers, and consumers. Value resultants and Paretian optimality were introduced as possible criteria for resolving goal differences between participants. Matrix representation of interrelated goals, we saw, permits far more precise views of the complex goal system.

Assuming the structure of the participants' goals as given, we explored the character of rationality, including some history of its development in the management sphere. Rationality was shown to be intimately associated with classification systems, or the science of taxonomy. By recognizing the existence of classification models, consciously working with them and trying to improve them, management begins to include science in its framework. New directions assert themselves because scientific method, as discussed throughout this book, has begun to raise the level of taxonomy from a static (noninterrelated) one to a dynamic (interrelated) one. The key notion is that of models, which are defined as representations of systems that can be studied in rational ways. In Chapters 2 and 3, we will go on to provide a close examination of model-building, model-solving, and model-using, applied at many levels.

EXERCISES

1. Does the concept of management apply equally well to hospital administration, military systems, government, manufacturing organizations, and the management of one's own affairs? Comment on your answer.

2. Why is the distinction made between a theory of management and principles of management? Comment on the validity of this distinction as you see it.

3. Find in the work of various students of and contributors to management (e.g., Henri Fayol, Chester Barnard, and Frederick W. Taylor) some quotations that define such primary management functions as decision-making, controlling, planning, organizing, and so forth. Compare these definitions with each other. How consistent do you find them? Discuss the comparisons you have made.

4. What significance does a means-end–chain analysis have for management? Give some examples of how this approach can be used to set up an entirely new department to answer consumer queries and complaints.

5. Distinguish between subjective *values* and objective *evaluation*. Why might it be said that the selection of values is not part of what we mean by a theory of management?

6. What can be done when two executives are known to disagree about what they want the company to achieve? Are such differences of opinion advantageous or disadvantageous?

7. Change the division-of-interest triangle on page 9 into a division-of-interest *square*. Place each of the following, in turn, at the fourth vertex.
   a. vendors (i.e., suppliers of the organization)
   b. the community
   c. government
Using a matrix form of analysis, explain the new relations that develop for each case. Then describe circumstances that would make the inclusion of each fourth vertex a meaningful addition.

8. Give an example of how the criterion of Paretian optimality might be applied in a realistic situation. Do you think that this criterion is, in fact, often used?

9. Give an example of how the resultant of vectors can be used to describe a group's value system. Discuss the strengths and weaknesses of this approach to value resolution.

10. In the text, a good deal of attention is given to the subject of taxonomy. Do you think that managers would benefit by having some knowledge of taxonomy? Explain.

11. Distinguish between static and dynamic taxonomies. Why is dynamic taxonomy of critical importance to an understanding of management?

12. What classification scheme might account for the following sets?
   a. [B, C, D, G]   [A, E, F, H]
   b. [1, 2, 6]   [3, 7, 8]   [4, 5, 9]
To whom could such classification have relevance?

Part I

MODEL-BUILDING
AND MODEL USE

The Framework of Managing

PART I
MODEL-BUILDING AND MODEL USE

Models are the crux of rational management. They are simplified
representations of the complex realities with which management
deals. In order to use models to advantage, management must
recognize that model-building and model use are
entirely interdependent.

Models are "representations of systems that can be studied in rational ways." Based on this definition, "models" can be described in many different ways, and Chapters 2 and 3 are concerned with giving detailed definition to this term. Can a model be built to study any system? Can the model always be used effectively? Part I addresses itself to answering such questions. First, however, the background for understanding the role of science in model-building and model use should be examined.

Poor decisions, bad planning, and control failures—all organizational inadequacies—are anathema to managers who have strong professional views about doing the best job possible. Consequently, management has turned to model-building because there is definite evidence that objective ("scientific") models can improve its performance. On the other hand, managers know that model-building and use are in a formative stage. How far models can penetrate the inner sanctums of the enterprise is not yet known.

Action taken in the name of science is hardly a guarantee of success. Use of models for their own sake is an ever-present danger. Like medicine, models can help if used as prescribed but can harm if used incorrectly. And some types of model, like some medicines, are still experimental. Although they hold promise, they will not be widely used until tested and approved. What is more, the testing is often vulnerable to error, since in many cases we do not yet know how to set proper standards for evaluating the results.

There are risks in model use, but there are also risks in disregarding models. The nature of the penalties to be suffered by following one or the other course must somehow be estimated—by intuition if necessary. To accomplish this, the manager must understand models and be able to evaluate their believability or applicability in each situation.

The believability of the model-building approach varies with the nature of the circumstances. Believability is responsive to many factors—for example, (1) how much is being invested in the study and who is doing it (which will affect its consistency and completeness); (2) how available and how accurate are the relevant data; (3) how stable is the system, and (4) what evidence is there that scientific method can cope with such problems?

Let us attend to the fourth point, which is highly relevant to our present discussion. It is essential to know the degree to which scientific theory is supported by pragmatic evidence. Proof that something works can be obtained through repeated trials of well-designed experimental studies. But pitted against believability is the *urgency* for solution. A manager may accept a solution simply because he needs an answer, even though he may lack confidence in the correctness of his solution. This is a problem that cannot be ignored, for it occurs often.

The problem of validity raises two further questions: How can managers recognize when their models are applicable in their own field? Should managers or scientists be the arbiters of the validity of science when it is applied to enterprise and institution? Our answer to the latter question is unequivocal—management must make the final determinations. But this *new responsibility* of management requires that we answer fully the first question concerning the applicability of science. This we will do in the two chapters that follow.

While the scientific position is critical in building models, it has no parallel in the application of these models. The successful user must be both artist and scientist. In the past, art and science have formed at best a colloidal mixture—that is, they have never blended homogeneously. No neat aphorisms have been developed about how art and science can cooperate to become synergistic. The future undoubtedly holds a more harmonious art-science relationship than now exists. What is required is a *synthesis* of art and science in pursuit of management excellence.

To understand this relationship, we must emphasize the distinction between *analysis,* taking apart, and *synthesis,* reassembly ("and all the King's horses and all the King's men couldn't put Humpty Dumpty together again"). Many children, curious about how a clock works, are led to take a clock apart. By studying the pieces they learn a great deal, but usually not enough to put the clock together again in working order. The complexity of the system of parts raises beyond the feasible limit the amount of information required to achieve reassembly. Model-building and model use require both analysis and synthesis. This places such demands on the manager that the end product may fall short of his expectations. In this regard, he is in good company.

An art dealer (this story is authentic) bought a canvas signed "Picasso" and travelled all the way to Cannes to discover whether it was genuine. Picasso was working in his studio. He cast a single look at the canvas and said: "It's a fake."

A few months later the dealer bought another canvas signed "Picasso." Again he travelled to Cannes and again Picasso, after a single glance, grunted: "It's a fake."

"But *cher maître,*" expostulated the dealer, "it so happens that I saw you with my own eyes working on this very picture several years ago."

Picasso shrugged: "I often paint fakes."

—From Arthur Koestler, *The Act of Creation* (New York: Macmillan, 1964), p. 82.

The Framework of Managing

MODEL-BUILDING AND MODEL USE

Chapter 2
Building Management Models

There are many ways to classify models. The situation
to be modeled determines the type of model that
can be built. The variety of model forms matches the
needs of reality sufficiently for management to have
accepted the model-building function as an essential
part of its work.

Chapter 2

BUILDING

MANAGEMENT MODELS

His Majesty's Ministers, finding that Gulliver's stature exceeded theirs in the proportion of twelve to one, concluded from the similarity of their bodies that he must contain at least 1728 (or 12^3) of theirs, and must needs be rationed accordingly.[1]

WHAT IS A MODEL?

A model is a *simplified representation of some part of reality*. It is usually simplified because reality is too complex to copy exactly and because, for the modeler's purposes, much of the complexity is irrelevant. For example, you do not have to specify the color of the seats in an airplane prototype to examine its in-flight performance. On the other hand, the model must have a level of complexity sufficient for the use to which it will be put. If you intend to study the performance of a management team, an organization chart is too simple a model of the relationships among the members of the team.

---

[1] Jonathan Swift, *Gulliver's Travels*.

Why Has the Conscious Use of Models Grown?

The idea of modeling is hardly new. The earliest astronomers had models of the universe as they saw it. Engineers probably modeled their aqueducts, architects their cathedrals, and generals their military campaigns. Galileo (1564–1642) developed some very general principles of similitude. He indicated that, based on fundamental structural properties, a maximum size existed for ships, buildings, and living organisms. Isaac Newton (1642–1727) studied principles of physical modeling and set them down as laws of dynamic similitude. Although less evident, considerable precedent also exists for non-physical models. For example, merchants in Renaissance Italy developed bookkeeping models; economists (such as Walras and Keynes) created economic ones; and Lewin, Korzybski, and others set down behavioral models. What might be called new, however, is the *recognition* that models are being used to advantage and that, in consequence, the *extent* of their use is growing —particularly as applied to other than physical systems.

Three main reasons can be cited for this growth. One is that the *manipulation of real entities* (such as people and organizations) *is now socially frowned upon and in many instances outlawed.* At the beginning of the twentieth century, captains of industry (known for direct action and lacking models of specific enterprises and of the economy as a whole) did not hesitate to operate on reality. Today stockholders, unions, and the laws of the land are formidable guardians against managerial *experiments* on reality. It is essential to students and managers alike that a clear-cut distinction be made between operations on reality and those on a modeled image of it. In fact, steps to move from the model to reality place some of the most difficult burdens on present-day management.

A second reason for the expanded use of models is that the *amount of uncertainty with which management must deal has been increasing rapidly,* and along with this has come an increase in the consequences of errors. The uncertainty level has risen as product life has become shorter, technology more dynamic, and societal factors more forceful. The cost of errors has grown with national distribution of products, tighter profit margins, and increasing social penalties.

Uncertainty has always been an anathema to management, and, before accepting the inevitable conclusion that decisions must be arrived at in terms of uncertainty, management characteristically tries to remove its causes. Uncertainty with respect to the performance of blue-collar workers was a prime factor leading to industry's high level of mechanization. Attempts at price-fixing, the use of contract agreements, and the replacement of white-collar workers with computer systems all owe their existence in some part to management's efforts to reduce uncertainty. These developments have taken place because associated with uncertainty are the real costs of being prepared for something that does not happen and not being prepared for something else that does happen. Such costs must be included in any decision-oriented computation that compares the benefits of alternative systems. And, since management has found itself decreasingly able to experiment with systems, and in that way to lessen uncertainty, it has turned, not unreasonably, to model-building as a means of evaluating new strategies designed to master the consequences of existing uncertainty.

Third, *the ability to build models that are good representations has improved dramatically.* During the Second World War, the military invested heavily in operations-research work aimed at tackling logistical problems, and this work markedly improved model-building abilities. Simultaneously, computer capabilities showed real promise and their further development received widespread support from both government and industry. A majority of new models owed their strength to the interaction between these methodological and computer developments. Under such favorable circumstances, management acceptance of the model-building framework was inevitable.

Model and Theory

Previously we have said that what management needs is a theory of management. We shall define *theory* as a systematic, generalized explanation of some part of reality that is scientifically acceptable, and we shall try to show how theory and models, though different, are intimately related.

When we compare models and theory, we note first that a model is a simplified representation, whereas a theory is a broad, systematic explanation. Second, theory is generalized to include all specific cases, whereas models seldom include more than a few specific situations. Third, a general community is the group that determines the acceptability of a theory, whereas a particular management decides on the acceptance of its own models. Fourth, models with a strong foundation in theory are always preferable. And, fifth, model-building supports theory development.

But the relationship between models and theories is more complex than the preceding discussion would seem to indicate. In the process of managing, a number of specific models are designed to treat different parts of a given system. The models, in turn, embody various parts of the body of theory. For example, management makes use of inventory theory, waiting-line (or queuing) theory, and replacement theory. The theories have captured general principles and laws that form the pattern for many different specific instances. When we observe a company utilizing a particular inventory model for specific items whose characteristics of demand, price level, allowable outage rate, and so forth are listed, we can understand why a model is said to be an exemplification of some part of theory.

And, just as we can work from theory to models, we can work from models to theory. If we can generalize from aggregates of specific subsystem models to broadly useful principles, we succeed in developing theory.

At present management theory can be described as a system of loosely knit specific models that range across decision-making, planning, controlling, and so forth. Undoubtedly the weakness of management theory today lies in the lack of ties between behavioral models and those of physical process. Yet some formidable bridges are being built. The ability to include in objective models the subjective evaluations of executives is one aspect of the closing of this gap. Another is the inclusion of mechanisms for dialogue between the manager and the model.

BASICS OF MODEL-BUILDING

Let us now examine the various types of model. Some contribute more than others toward the development of management theory, but all play a part in helping to improve management's effectiveness.

First Stage

Primitive models are simply lists of factors (variables and constants) that are relevant to some unspecified list of outcomes supposedly related to objectives. A shopping list, for example, is a primitive model designed to increase the family's happiness. It might include variables like "soap," with an unspecified brand, and fully specified constants like "brand X coffee." Happiness is some composite of price, taste, shopping convenience, and so forth. Objectives, such as happiness, are usually unspecified and purely intuitive. Suppose, for example, that the individual's purpose is to reflect an organization's objectives. What these objectives are is always a matter of conjecture, to be resolved only by some set of personal opinions. In fact, when objectives are to be specified, the personal opinions are themselves open to some doubt. Even if you specify exactly what you want from life, both friends and psychiatrists will question what you say. Objectives *can* be made "hard" (i.e., specified) if a principle is used. The often-used hypothesis of the rational, economic man, for example, leads to specific objectives, and the principle of least effort in human behavior describes a clear-cut goal.[2] Strong individual preferences have similar effects of specifying objectives unambiguously.

---

[2] See the discussion of Zipf's work, Chapter 14, pp. 617–19.

In all models, including primitive ones, the variable factors are capable of changes in amplitude or intensity, whereas the constants are fixed. The factors are assumed to combine somehow, producing outcomes that affect the achievement of objectives. Primitive models ignore the system—that is, they do not consider the *way* the outcomes are produced by different arrangements of the factors (see Figure 2–1). In the earliest stages of the application of the

Figure 2–1

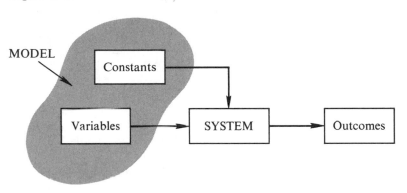

scientific method, such models are quite typical. In any case, no further steps in modeling can be taken until one achieves the *knowledge of how the variables are relevant to the outcomes*. Such knowledge allows one to proceed to the second stage.

Second Stage

The second stage in model-building requires specification of *relationships* so that the values of the relevant variables and constants (or parameters)[3] fully explain the values of the totally specified list of outcomes. This is shown in Figure 2–2.

The mathematician captures some of the nuances of Figure 2–2 by writing a functional equation such as $y = f(x_1, x_2, \ldots)$, which states that the value of an outcome (y) is a function (f) of the value of the variables (x_1, x_2, etc.).

---

[3] *Parameter* is defined as "an arbitrary constant or variable in a mathematical expression, which distinguishes various specific cases. Thus, in $y = a + bx$, a and b are parameters which specify the particular straight line represented by the equation." G. James and R. C. James, eds., *Mathematics Dictionary*, 2nd ed. (Princeton, N.J.: Van Nostrand, 1959), p. 282.

Figure 2–2

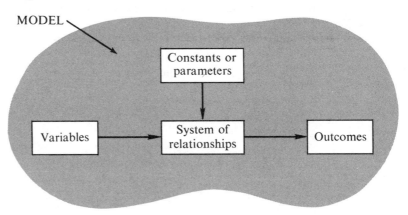

Function is simply the mathematician's way of stating the relationships between the outcome and the variable factors that affect it. When he writes a specific equation, such as $y = a + bx$, he details the exact relations and identifies the parameters. If the mathematician misses a relevant variable, or parameter, or assumes the wrong specific function, his model is quite as mistaken and potentially as misleading as that of the individual who reasons on the basis of incorrect information.

Third Stage

At the third modeling stage the relationships among the variables, the parameters, and the outcomes, as illustrated in Figure 2–3, are more difficult to discern and specify, and an understanding of such systems may grow slowly. Here the outcomes (through what is called *feedback*) alter the values of the variables and also change the relationships. The feedback effect accents the importance of time and, depending on transmission rates and delays, can cause the system to behave in complex ways. (Many situations that managers face embody this kind of complexity, and systems of this kind will be treated in detail as we proceed.)

The effect on the mathematical model builder is that the equations of the model must now include time (t), or sequence, as well as the feedback effect of y on x. So $y = f(x, t)$, and $x = f(y, t)$.

The fact that the next outcome will be influenced by some combination of past outcomes can also be written in functional form, where t is just preceded by $t - 1$, which is just preceded by $t - 2$, and so forth.

$$y_t = f(y_{t-1}, y_{t-2}, \ldots, y_o)$$

Figure 2–3

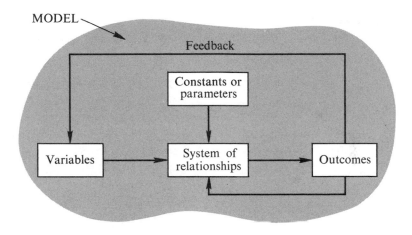

In Summary

The basics of model-building are straightforward. For first-level models, attempt to specify the outcomes that are of interest and identify the relevant variables and constants. For second- or third-level models, fully specify the outcomes, relevant variables, and parameters; then isolate the pattern of relations between the variables and the outcomes. At the third level, consider feedback effects.

These guidelines are seemingly uncomplicated, but when we attempt to apply them as logical steps in the modeling of reality we discover incredible diversity confronting us at every turn. As a result of this diversity many forms of models must be employed; in addition, by examining this diversity a great deal can be learned about both management and model-building.

INFORMATION MODELS

Accounting Models

According to our explanations, words and sentences (whether written out or simply thought about) qualify as primitive models. We should not dismiss this notion as trivial, since the source of all models is in mental activity, and their construction involves some profound interaction of intuition with linguistics. The *structure of language* is involved at the most basic level of model construction.

Part of the present-day language of management is reflected in accounting models. The accounting language operating at the first stage of model-building has not found ready translation into second- and third-stage models—but this is changing. Management has recognized accounting's unique role in handling information and has recently broadened its responsibility to include *capabilities of communication* about second- and third-stage models concerning all parts of the management process.

Computer Models

The need for dynamic changes in management language has been emphasized by the growing importance of computer linguistics. Model-builders, managers, and accountants have all had to learn something about the new computer languages such as BASIC, FORTRAN, COBOL, and ALGOL. Such languages are actually based on just a few fundamentals—for instance, the ability to ask "Is $a > b$?" and the knowledge that multiplication, division, subtraction, exponentiation (e.g., e^{ax}), logarithmic transforms, and so forth can be achieved through variations of addition. The linguistic characteristics of these computer languages are embodied in the methods (of numerical approximation) used to achieve a broad set of capabilities from a few fundamental operations.

The effects of computer modeling are widespread throughout all levels of management. And management, accounting, and management science have had significant influence, in turn, on the form of developments in computer linguistics—within the degree of freedom that computer technology allows.

Data-Handling Models

Accounting models that represent the state of the firm (such as the balance sheet) and its performance over time (such as the profit and loss statement) are only part of management's arsenal of information models. Throughout the firm, sales, finance, production, personnel, and so forth, engage in data collection as a primary activity. Indeed, many new sources are almost too readily found, their discovery being encouraged as much by underutilized computer facilities as by a sense of need. So much information is available that the management of information has become a new managerial function in many firms—especially those for which computer facilities have increased the throughput of *somehow relevant* data.[4] The need to say "somehow relevant"

---

[4] *Throughput* is the total volume of information that can flow through the system in a given period of time, at varying rates. One of the goals of information management is to remove irrelevant and marginally useful information from the throughput; see p. 521.

follows from the fact that useful intelligence must be extracted from the total volume of information—just as pure metal must be refined from its ore. To the manager, unrefined information is worse than useless. It carries the costs of collection and storage and often the highest penalty of all—wasted time— if the manager feels compelled to study pages and pages of unrefined data. To carry the analogy one step farther, we can say that some ores are better than others, for with them, less refining produces more results. In informational terms, there is more immediately relevant information for the manager in some reports than in others, and the more relevant the information is, the less analysis is required to prepare it for use.

To cope with a growing information deluge the manager turns to information reduction and compression models. For example, thirty daily sales are averaged, with the resulting effect of what might be called data compression of $30:1$.[5] Graphs, pictures, and diagrams are models for information display that frequently save many words of explanation. In keeping with our description of the basics of model-building, we should note that the relevance of information to managerial objectives is critical. And what is more, the *distribution* of information must have *directed relevancy*—that is, *informational needs should be matched with information flows.*

The importance of managing information is widely recognized, but the means of managing it through the use of new technology and methodology is vague. An adequate background in models and their use must be built before understanding is possible. Information models exist as inputs to individual executive judgment, but they are also incorporated as a part of larger models for decision-making, planning, controlling, and organizing. The following discussion of taxonomical models sheds additional light both on model-building per se and on the implications of managing information systems.

Taxonomical Models

In its simplest form taxonomy provides the equivalent of a set of labels for separate containers. The labels describe the contents of these containers, differentiating them according to specific characteristics that they possess—for example, red paint, blue paint, and so forth. The characteristics should be those that are primary with respect to the objectives for which the taxonomy was set up. We need only consider the difference between a thesaurus, a dictionary, and an encyclopedia to recognize that differences in objectives lead to quite different methods for classifying information.

In general the taxonomical model signifies more than a list of relevant

---

[5] Formally, we call such compression *homomorphic transformation;* see pp. 59–60.

variables. At the most basic level it is an ordered list. For example, we have the well-known hierarchical arrangement in the natural sciences:

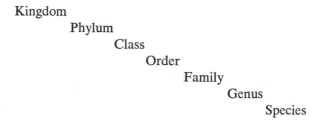

Usually, a set of individual labels can be grouped into larger classes—for example, boys and girls are both instances of children. The nature of such hierarchical properties, where one class subsumes several others, is the basis of many studies in the taxonomical field.

Figure 2–4   A Partial Taxonomy of Numbers

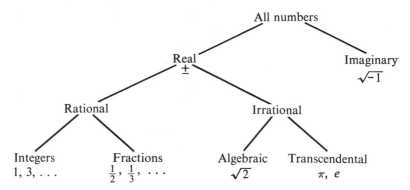

Let us consider the taxonomy for numbers shown in Figure 2–4. It is a map or a catalogue that allows us to do two things: first, to find out what a number is, and, second, to find out what it is not. Thus, the $\sqrt{2}$ is algebraic, not transcendental; irrational, not rational; a real number, not an imaginary one. The $\sqrt{2}$ is a member of a very specific set,[6] and our taxonomical model has unambiguously located that set on the hierarchical tree of number properties.

Trees and matrices. As we have seen, a major property of taxonomy is hierarchy (precedence or antecedence). The levels of management (top, middle, foremen, etc.) lack exact definition but do reflect information about

---

[6] A *set* is a group whose members are related by specific common properties, such as a set of red objects or a set of even numbers.

hierarchical rank that lends itself to tree representations of the types previously shown.

Trees can be changed to matrices (and vice versa), as illustrated in Figure
2–5, where D represents requests for information that are flowing down and U
represents reports from lower ranks moving upward.

Figure 2–5

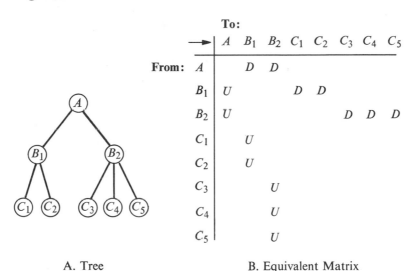

From:	To: A	B_1	B_2	C_1	C_2	C_3	C_4	C_5
A		D	D					
B_1	U			D	D			
B_2	U					D	D	D
C_1		U						
C_2		U						
C_3			U					
C_4			U					
C_5			U					

A. Tree   B. Equivalent Matrix

Both the matrix and tree formats succeed in organizing information, but their
individual characteristics recommend them for different jobs. The tree has
advantages for organizing information visually, while the matrix lends itself
more readily to analytical manipulations. Many kinds of matrices can result
from tree maps having different structures and purposes.

Compacting the matrix—homomorphic models. If the information
level is too great in the taxonomy, it is possible to compress information by
reducing the size of the matrix. The matrix of Figure 2–6B is a *homomorph*
of the one given in Figure 2–5B.[7] An equivalent reduction in the tree complexity of Figure 2–5A is shown in Figure 2–6A.

An *isomorphic* model of a system is simply an equivalent representation of
that system. There is no information compression. Every element of the

---

[7] The term "homomorphic" is first used in the footnote on p. 39.

Figure 2–6

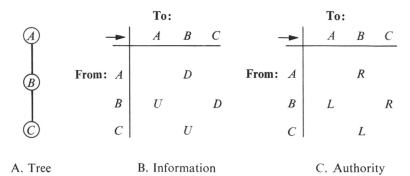

A. Tree   B. Information   C. Authority

original system has a unique and exact translation in the model; consequently, the level of complexity of the system is the same as that of its model. There is no difficulty in translating the model back into the terms of the original system (as there would be in the case of a homomorphic model). Similarly, an isomorphic transformation of a model is an equivalent representation of that model in different terms. See, for example, the tree and matrix models of Figure 2–5. As another example, an isomorphic representation of 2–6B is obtained in 2–6C by substituting R for D and L for U. Say that R stands for authority and that L represents allegiance. Then the second model depicts authority relations rather than information flows as the first model did. The matrix size remains unchanged with respect to information, but a model with new *meaning* and potential utility is achieved.

Critical to the homomorphic construction is the question of what bases were used for the original classification and for the principles of reduction. The original model in Figure 2–5 differentiated between departments (B_1 and B_2) and the managerial levels (C_1 and C_2) within these departments. After transformation of the model to a smaller size, intradepartment information was lost. This instance shows clearly, as we have noted, that without additional information it is impossible to work backward from the compacted matrix to the larger one.

Causality and correlation. Underlying all taxonomy is the *implication* of causality. Management's ability to run the enterprise is enhanced if it can discover causal relationships that explain which factors affect the performance of the enterprise. Often, however, only tenuous guesses can be made concerning causal relations. Taxonomy is a first step in the discovery process, for there must be some unique set of properties that can explain why two things are different from one another yet are related in a hierarchical

Figure 2–7   An Assembly Taxonomy

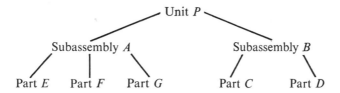

structure. In the assembly taxonomy shown in Figure 2–7, the fact that a set called A is differentiated from a set called B is caused by the fact that they are different units requiring unique manufacturing procedures. They are joined to P in a hierarchical tree because, when assembled, together they make up the finished product. Thus, in a real sense, $A + B = P$. It is also quite correct to say: $P = f(A, B)$. Similar statements can be made about $C, D, E, F,$ and G.

It will be noted that a tree representation of the taxonomy of probability distributions (Figure 2–8) is also helpful as a descriptive model. But here the implications of causality are difficult to determine, as they would be for the number taxonomy (Figure 2–4).

Although "continuous $\dashv$ discrete $=$ all distributions," the conviction of causality is lacking. In large part the reason for this is that when constants are related in a hierarchical tree—as in Figure 2–9A—the taxonomy is static and

Figure 2–8   A Partial Taxonomy of Distributions

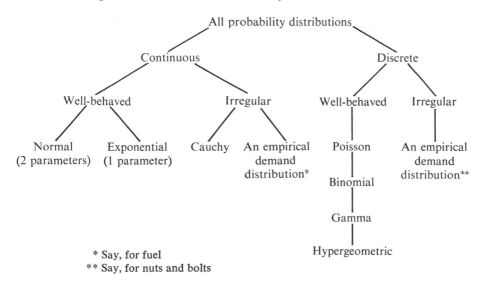

Figure 2–9

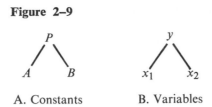

A. Constants   B. Variables

primarily concerned with definition. If variables appear—as in Figure 2–9B—the taxonomy is dynamic, and causality, real or imagined, can be inferred. For example,

x_1	x_2	y
width	length	area
unit price	unit cost	unit profit
scope of job	salary	morale

The knowledge of "what causes what" is crucial to management control. If causes that relate to performance are found and understood, management can control its operations and successfully plan its future. Knowledge of causality is particularly weak when it comes to behavioral systems, and with such systems it is difficult to discover even primitive taxonomies that can help to point out causal factors. Leadership, for example, remains a vaguely defined, yet highly valued quality.[8] The causes of creativity are similarly misty. Thus, the creative individual is most frequently identified by his prior history of being creative (or, with less success, by "being different" from the noncreative social norms).[9] Because of the lack of causal explanations for it, the marketplace remains a source of uncertainty even in communist countries, where it is under jurisdictional control. Even though causality is difficult to determine, hypothetical taxonomies can nevertheless be created by means of correlational methods. This is the major importance of correlation, which is one of the most advanced techniques for building taxonomies.

Taxonomical models can be created through (1) observation, e.g., the subassembly tree; (2) logical reasoning, e.g., width $\times$ length = area; (3) definition, e.g., an organization chart; (4) conjecture, e.g., morale = f(salary, scope of job); and (5) correlation, e.g., relating stock-market prices to sunspot activity. Objective correlational methods can include both diagrammatic and statistical approaches. There are generally many factors that might explain some particular phenomenon. A primary purpose of correlational analysis is

---

[8] See the discussion in Chapter 15, pp. 644–47.
[9] See Chapter 6, pp. 209–13.

to spot those factors that are most closely associated with the occurrence of the phenomenon in question. It is hoped that the association found in this way can be shown to be causal. Frequently, however, there is no way to establish which, *if either,* is the cause of the other, and we must be careful not to mistake correlation for causality.

For example, studies have shown that stock-market prices are strongly correlated with sunspot activity, but it would not be profitable to discuss which is the cause of the other. Therefore, lacking any reasonable explanation for the correlation, one must dismiss the implied relationship between sunspots and market behavior as spurious. In another (though far less dramatic) example, large-scale analyses have indicated that television ratings are highly correlated with certain factors such as preceding program, time of day, cost of talent, network, and so forth. The assumption is then made that these factors are causative of television ratings. Undoubtedly ratings are related to these program factors through causal mechanisms, but exactly how this fabric is woven is not well understood. The difficulty begins because there are too many variables and too little knowledge of how they contribute to ratings. And even if we think we know the important variables, we do not know how to set them, since we do not know how the variables affect one another. Moreover, the strengths of the correlations that reflect these patterns of interrelations will change over time. Some of the variables will become more highly correlated, others less. In many instances the patterns of relations between the variables will shift significantly, and because the factors that contribute to this shifting are unknown, sufficient causal knowledge cannot be claimed. Consequently, the correlational study does not provide as much information as the manager would like to obtain in order to improve his control of the situation.

Correlation is used for two primary objectives. The first, which we have been discussing, is to try to identify those variables that are relevant to the outcome. The second is to determine what patterns (or functions) relate the variables to one another. These steps, as we have previously stated, are the fundamental requirements of model-building. But, whereas correlations may help with these model-building purposes, they guarantee nothing. Causal relations will provide high correlations, but high correlations can occur for many reasons that will not assist management in its quest for an understanding of causal relations, and, thereby, for greater control over its performance. Often correlational models are used to *organize* information, which can then be subjected to further testing. When meaningful associations can be made, a model can be built to represent that part of reality which is tied to the manager's objectives.

Many years ago, John Stuart Mill set down a systematic line of reasoning that he called the "Canons of Induction." We shall not attempt to give more than a brief view of the structure of the Canons, but for those who are interested in pursuing the topic we recommend C. West Churchman's *Theory of Experimental Inference*. Essentially the Canons were concerned with determining relevant variables and the relationships of independent to dependent variables. The investigation into many factors to uncover associations likely to be causally related is generally recognized as the necessary first step in all scientific effort. Quoting from Churchman, "The Canons of Induction are a set of methods for inducing the most important types of nature's laws, those of causality." [10] Mill developed his five Canons as follows:

Canon 1: The method of agreement. Assume that the same event occurs in two environments that are totally different except for one common factor. Then that common factor and the event are causally related, although which causes the other is often unknown. Furthermore, there is nothing to assure us that an unperceived third or fourth factor is not present in both situations and is the real causal factor.

Canon 2: The method of difference. If an event occurs in an environment and then does not occur in the same environment from which only one factor has been removed, then the event and the factor that was removed are causally related. (The same objections that were stated for Canon 1 exist here too.)

Canon 3: The joint method of agreement and difference. An event continues to occur in a changing environment in which only one factor remains constant and at the same time does not occur in any environments in which that constant factor is not present. Then the event and the constant factor are said to be causally related.

Canon 4: The method of residues. All aspects of a given event, except one, can be explained by the environment in which it occurs. If one part of the environment is not included in the previous explanation of causality, then the unexplained aspect of the event is causally related to the unincluded part of the environment.

Canon 5: The method of concomitant variations. If an event changes in direct response to a change that is made in one factor in the environment, the event and the factor are causally related.

We observe that in Canon 5 a means is introduced to begin to determine a pattern of relationship between variables. For example, in Figure 2–10 a series of points is plotted relating x and y. The points fall along and around what appears to be a straight line. The equation of that straight line can be determined; and the functional relationship, or pattern, between these two identified variables has then been established. A correlation can be assigned on a strictly visual basis in terms of the plot. A variety of statistical methods

---

[10] C. West Churchman, *Theory of Experimental Inference* (New York: Macmillan, 1948), pp. 91–95. Quote is from p. 91.

Figure 2–10

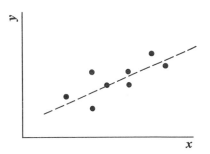

also exists for assigning a functional relationship, either linear or nonlinear, to a scattering of points. It will be observed that a fundamental sense of this assignment is to remove as much variability as possible between the hypothesized relationship (the equation of the straight or curved line) and the observed scattering of points. Correlational models are available that far surpass the first primitive efforts of Mill. They constitute a highly developed form of information model. Both in determining associations between variables and in assigning functional relationships, or patterns, the correlational technique removes uncertainty by providing a hypothesis to explain what might otherwise be considered random variation of the observations.

Computer programs for running correlational studies are readily available. If properly used to search for relevant variables and patterns, the programs can greatly reduce the burden of information analysis. On the other hand, if such analyses are assumed to *prove* the existence of the relationships, they can be misleading and harmful. Formerly, an executive would not tolerate the collection and presentation of all "somehow relevant" information. He couldn't handle it. So he approached the specification of what he would like to see with a good deal of incisive thought, including a determination of what he would not like to see. Correlational methods (even with such imposing names as regression analysis, serial and auto correlation, analysis of variance, factor analysis, and multivariate correlation) are not substitutes for wisdom but merely aids to it.

CLASSIFICATION OF MODELS

By categorizing models we can learn a great deal more about what they are and what they can do for management. The tree-map in Figure 2–11 shows that an initial division of models can be based on the distinction between subjective and objective structure.

Figure 2–11   Tree of Models

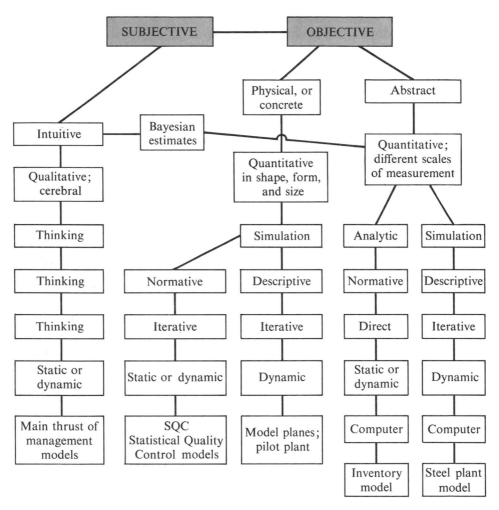

Subjective and Objective Models

Subjective models play a large part in the management process, and it is the managerial art to think about systems subjectively. However, little can be explicitly stated about subjective models. They all begin with intuition, and, as we have said before, even first-stage taxonomical models of the thinking process are difficult to develop. The most important distinction of the subjective branch of the model tree is the *lack of formal methods,* but experience interacting with mental skills is somehow fundamental to it. This is hardly an operational statement, however, and studies of thinking are in a rudimentary stage. If we were to catalogue the talents required for subjective model-building, it might be reasonable to emphasize the ability to provide total pictures, or gestalts, through synthesis, rather than detail through analysis. The contribution of science in objective models has been primarily in terms of analysis. Only recently have we begun to record successes in seeing things as wholes and treating total systems. (More will be said about this in Chapter 3 and later as well.) Put another way, the generalist is more evidently needed for subjective modeling than the specialist. This dovetails with the fact that subjective models have increasing applicability as the managerial level is raised. Such notions are critical in the selection of executives.

Physical and Abstract Models

In moving down the objective-models branch of the tree, the first main distinction is drawn between physical models and abstract ones. By "physical" we mean concrete and material; models of planes, ships, and automobiles are the most apparent, but a pilot plant or an experimental production run fits the bill as well.

By *abstract* we mean mathematical—at least 90 percent of the time, for there are some other forms of (symbolic) logical representation that might not be called mathematical in the strict sense of the term. In all cases a rigorous language of representation (as mathematics is rigorous, with rules for symbolic manipulation and interpretation) is essential. Thus, $y = mx + b$ is an abstract model that serves to identify those variables that affect the dependent variable, y.

It is interesting to note that in science and technology the use of physical models is being reduced and the use of abstract ones is being increased. For example, the Wright brothers had to fly with their model to see if it would go, and generations of fearless test pilots, whose job it is to be part of the model, have followed. With growing sophistication in the knowledge of aeronautics, however, engineers made wind tunnels to test scale models. This still involved the use of a physical model, but it was not as dangerous as actually going up with the plane. Then abstract models appeared. The modelers learned how to write equations to represent airfoil design, and wings could be "flown" through varying conditions by programming the appropriate mathematics for the computer. Nevertheless, the wind tunnel and scale models remain for viewing the larger system, and test pilots continue to be required, in the last analysis, in order to observe the airplane as a whole, performing entity. This is because pilot performance, which is an essential part of present-day systems, cannot be simulated by the computer or in the wind tunnel. Consequently, strict testing rules under actual flight conditions that may require several years are required for government certification of the plane's design. (See the discussion of large systems, pp. 537-39.)

To an extent, pilot-plant operations can be abstracted. Great savings can be realized when six- and seven-digit investments can be bypassed in favor of an abstract model. Much work remains to be done in this area, but much work *is* going on. Some physical phenomena, however, resist abstracting, and in certain cases the transformation may be impossible. Towing tanks filled with mercury continue to be used for testing ship design. The prediction of performance resists interpretation in purely mathematical terms. Similarly, criteria for visual appearance and the aesthetic process itself are such great unknowns that physical prototypes of cars and buildings may never be replaced.

Level of measurement. All objective models, whether physical or abstract, must be constructed with measurable dimensions or scales. Here we shall identify five different scales. The first of these we can call a *subjective scale*. It is qualitative and, being strictly internalized, belongs largely in the realm of psycho-physiological phenomena. Individuals may have different subjective scales, and each individual's scales may be inconsistent and biased in unknown ways. We cannot represent a subjective scale because as soon as we do it becomes objective. But we can try to convert subjective scales into objective form by using rank-order methods or the approaches of utility theory (as described in Chapters 7 and 14). We can never be sure, however, that we have pictured the subjective scale accurately.

Let us now turn our attention to objective scales. Figure 2–12 is based on objective scales with and without a natural origin and on objective scales that do and do not have distance measures associated with them. A natural origin exists when a zero quantity of a particular dimension makes sense. We can have zero dollars of money or zero tons of sulfur on hand—but we really cannot have zero amounts of preference for one design over another or zero amounts of hunger. The advantage of a natural origin is implicit in the mathematical importance of a zero quantity, which permits a total comparison to be made between two quantities and allows a mathematical model to be built that can examine *differences* between performances and *ratios* of outcomes. Accordingly, in physics, though it is difficult to visualize having zero amounts of temperature, nevertheless absolute zero is predicated as a base point, or natural origin, from which all measurements can be developed. From theoretical physics we know that all molecular and atomic motion ceases at absolute zero on the Kelvin scale. If we were to use this Kelvin scale, then something that is 40°K would be twice as hot as something that is 20°K. The same would not apply to the Fahrenheit or Centigrade scale; a temperature of 60°F is not twice as hot as one of 30°F.

Distance measures are equally advantageous. Lacking distance measures, we can only rank a series of outcomes, whereby we establish a numerical order

Figure 2–12

NOTE: The value of x is transformed into the value of y. For the ordinal scale, all we can say is that increasing values of x are associated with increasing values of y, but we do not know exactly what the values of y are. When a natural origin is added to the ordinal scale we know that x and y have one point in common, namely zero. For the ratio scale, the zero point also exists, and, in addition, specific values of y are associated with specific values of x. In this regard the interval scale is the same as the ratio scale, but there is no zero point in common.

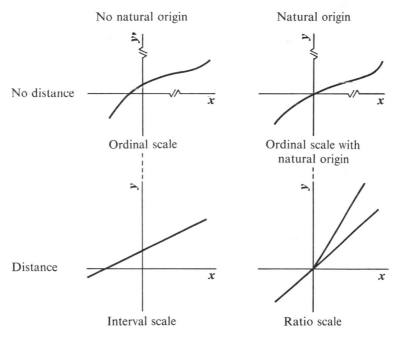

SOURCE: Based on a diagram from Warren S. Torgerson, *Theory and Methods of Scaling* (New York: John Wiley & Sons, Inc., 1958).

such as 1, 2, 3, 4, 5, and so forth. But the distance between the ranked items may vary greatly, as shown in Figure 2–13. If, in addition to having a natural origin, we know the distance that separates the descriptive numbers, then we are in a position to have a *ratio scale,* which permits averages, subtraction, division, and many other arithmetical operations. The *interval scale,* lacking a natural origin but providing measures of distance, is typified by temperature scales of the Fahrenheit and Centigrade type. Averages may be taken, but subtraction and division of quantities measured on the interval scale are not possible. Most of the complicated (but necessary) behavioral scales are of the

Figure 2–13

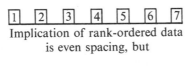

Implication of rank-ordered data
is even spacing, but

reality may have uneven spacing
and clusters.

interval type—for example, preference, satisfaction, intelligence, and loving-ness. Many physical processes have a natural origin and therefore permit the use of ratio scales or *ordinal scales with a natural origin.* The latter occur when distance measures are not feasible—for example, the perception of light in-tensities.

The weakest scale, that of ordinal rank, permits few arithmetical operations. Not even averages are possible. Nevertheless, if we lack something better, it can provide us with at least some vital information. But there are occasions when even ranking is difficult. Not everything can be ranked—for example, colors can be ranked according to either their intensity or their wave length or their hue because each of these characteristics lies along a single dimension. However, ranking the colors themselves in terms of all three characteristics would raise questions concerning the role of each dimension in the ranking process. It is for this reason that complex objectives cannot easily be ranked. If we were to ask an executive to rank several plant locations, he might be hard-pressed because each location could have an advantage over the other in some respect. This situation can produce what is called a breakdown in *transi-tivity*—that is, when A is preferred to B, which is preferred to C, which in turn is preferred to A.[11] Given the problem of ranking a set of strategies with mul-tiple objectives, the individual can rank them in pairs to determine whether or not his sequence of choices runs counter to transitivity. If it does not, then there is a chance that the dimensionality of the problem is internally consistent and harmonious. At least the individual is able to relate the dimensions so that they work together in his model.[12]

Types of scales can vary greatly for different models. One of the major problems in the behavioral field is the difficulty of developing strong and con-sistent scales that have refined measures of distance. The manager must be aware of the scaling and measurement problems that inhere in the *type of problem* he tackles. He should be careful not to ask more from the types of

[11] $A > B > C > A$ (where $>$ stands for "preferred to").

[12] For further treatment of these matters, see pp. 273–84.

scales he has—or attribute more to them—than they can deliver. The significance of these remarks is threefold; first, with respect to the data obtained from objective studies; second, in the construction of specific models; and, third, concerning the validity of intuitions based on weak scales and poor distance measures used to describe the information sources.

With respect to the third point, how much better is an advertisement with a noting score[13] of 40 than another with a noting score of 20? Certainly it cannot be assumed that the first advertisement is twice as good as the second except with respect to noting. Pin-up art may have a high noting score, but it may also produce a hostile response from many readers—say, housewives. In other words, how does one relate noting to sales dollars? The manager must supply that answer, in most cases, purely by intuition—hopefully, however, not without wondering how valid the noting score is and how sensitive its measure of distance. As another example, consider merit raises based on an index comprised of years with the company, present salary level, absentee record, and supervisors' ratings. How does such an index number get turned into salary dollars? We must be wary of intermediary measures such as noting and also of index manipulations, in which multiple factors are combined to produce an intermediary measure that is then used to derive our result (say, dollars of profit or dollars of pay). In model-building far more subjectivity is often involved than the formal procedures tend to indicate.

Analytic and Simulation Models

To the untrained eye a series of equations designed for simulation purposes may look very much like those intended for analytic studies. They are basically different, however. Simulation equations are like instructions, whereas analytic equations are intended to be reduced and solved. Simulation models require highly detailed descriptions of transactions and information flows that occur in their specific systems. A flow diagram is the key to simulation studies. The equations are written to describe the flow of information throughout the system. Figure 2–14 is illustrative of a particular simulation. The model applies to an inventory problem concerning how much stock to order of two interdependent items and when to order it.

In Figure 2–14 we observe that Customer A, for example, could order 0, 1, or 2 units of Item 1. If the demand is for 1 or 2 units, this lowers Item 1's stock on hand (S.O.H.$_1$) and produces a calculation to determine whether the reorder point has been reached. If it has, then stock on hand plus stock

---

[13] *Noting* is the measure of the percentage of individuals reading a particular publication who have seen a specific printed advertisement. It does not mean that these individuals recall what the advertisement said. (Recall, however, is another fairly typical measure of advertising effectiveness.)

Figure 2–14

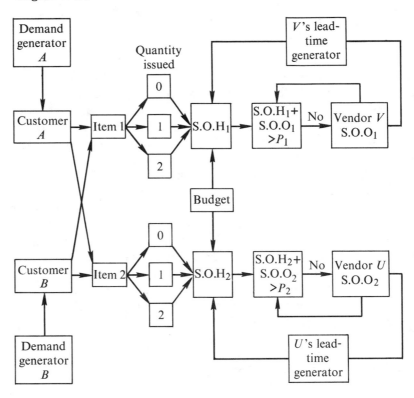

S.O.O.$_j$ = stock on order for jth item

S.O.H.$_j$ = stock on hand for jth item

P_j = reorder point for jth item

SOURCE: Martin K. Starr and David W. Miller, *Inventory Control: Theory and Practice* © 1962. By permission of Prentice-Hall, Inc., Englewood Cliffs, New Jersey.

on order (S.O.O.$_1$) is not greater than P_1, the reorder point (i.e., the answer to S.O.H.$_1$ + S.O.O.$_1$ > P_1 is "No"). Therefore, vendor V is sent a new order. V's lead time generator[14] indicates how long it will take for the order to be delivered. Meanwhile, the budget for shared inventory levels of Items 1 and 2 cannot be exceeded; accordingly, the order quantity must be adjusted. If the

---

[14] We use the term *generator* (for demand levels, lead times, etc.) to indicate that values for these factors are being artificially "generated," which is the only way that "simulation" could proceed.

rules for adjustments to budget, reorder points, order quantities, and so forth are not sound, then the customers may find no stock on hand to supply their needs when they place an order. This is the way these simulation flow charts can be read. Of course, specific rules exist concerning what numerical quantities of stock are to be ordered.

This problem is complicated by the fact that the inventory policies (or rules) for treating each item affect the inventory levels obtained for the other item because two large customers order both items. In this simulation, the rules (which are not shown) for the demand generators reflect the fact that each customer is affected by the service he gets. So if Customer A is unhappy about not receiving Item 1, he is likely to cease ordering Item 2 as well. And the same is true for Customer B. A simulation run is shown in Figure 2–15 for the stock on hand for each item, after introducing specific policies and generating demands and lead times, upon which this simulation is based. The first part of the simulation—say, through week 10—shows the readjustment from the old policies to the new ones. The problem would be very difficult to treat analytically—that is, in a mathematical model. Such assumptions as the interdependencies of customers and items often prove intractable to mathematical analysis. The simulation, however, is not significantly complicated by these conditions.

Figure 2–15   Two-Item Simulation

NOTE: After the first ten weeks, the effects of the initial stock on hand conditions disappear and the inventory levels of both items tend to stabilize. But a long simulation run would be required to observe how the system responds to the great variety of conditions that might arise.

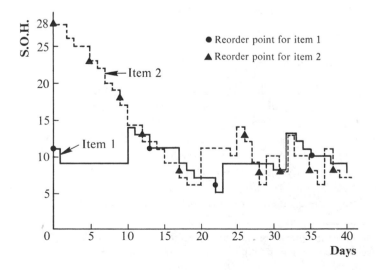

Causality is difficult to trace in simulation models, for there is a very long chain of events, and each event leads to others. In contrast, the analytic model is a statement of causality, describing unambiguously the way in which the outcomes change as the relevant variables in the system are altered. With an analytic model it is necessary to write equations that specify the behavior of all the variables in the system. As a result, it is often possible to determine in what combinations these variables will produce optimal values for the outcomes.

In the case of the simulation example we have used, such equations, with the outcomes fully specified in mathematical terms, would be exceedingly difficult to write and probably impossible to solve. On the other hand, by using simulation the various elements of the system are brought together in a flow network configuration. Demand and lead time are derived on the basis of the random number generators[15] (shown in Figure 2–14) that are placed at appropriate points in the network. Other variables in different situations can be represented in similar fashion. Consider, for example, the question of designing a good air-traffic control system. In spite of schedules, planes take off and land irregularly. Furthermore, because of multiple objectives it is difficult to determine which characteristics of the system should be optimized.[16] Simulation would permit a variety of the performance characteristics of the system to be observed, and the manager could then judge the various performance measures in this complex contest between alternative configurations.

In short, simulation is useful when it is not possible to determine optimal conditions because of a lack of relevant information, conflicts in objectives, irregular patterns of random variables, and so forth. Conversely, with simulation it is not possible to discover optimal conditions, whereas, when analytic formulations apply, the optimal configuration generally can be determined. Put another way, simulation permits improvements to be made for systems that are simply too complex to be handled analytically.

Prescriptive and Descriptive Models

The most important distinction that can be drawn between models lies in this category. Almost all simulation models are of the descriptive kind. Descriptive models can be used to study the performance of a complex system, which makes them very useful even though they do not specify the optimal behavior of the system. They can also help to determine the best possible systems configuration—but only through the mediation of the manager's judgment.

Prescriptive, or *normative,* models embody the criteria and *means* for determining the configuration that will produce an optimal solution. Being

---

[15] The operation of random number generators is explained on pp. 363–68.
[16] See the discussion of multiple objectives in Chapter 7.

essentially mathematical, normative models are less dependent on intuition and personal managerial contact than are descriptive models (although they are not independent of these factors). However, the abbreviated technical language of analytic prescriptive models tends to discourage managerial rapport with them. On the other hand, the greater detail of descriptive models tends to overinvolve the manager. Although little is known about the reactions of managers who are faced with a prescriptive format as compared with a descriptive one, there is a real psychological difference in the way management approaches both types of models and in the degree to which management participates in their construction and use. Some managers basically prefer the analytic detachment of abbreviated, technical language in prescriptive models, whereas others prefer the burden of detail and its corresponding level of involvement in descriptive models.

When prescriptive models are used properly, management will not feel that the answer derived from the model *must* be followed even though the model's result is unambiguous. *Sensitivity analysis* (which is discussed further in Chapter 4) is one way to get rid of the notion that one *ought* to follow the model's recommendation, for, by probing the prescriptive model, the manager in effect asks a series of "what if" questions. His intention is to determine whether changes in some of the variable values will effect a change in the model's solution. Such probing and testing (sensitivity analysis) bring analytic models and simulation models closer together.

Some problems (for example, many involving scheduling and inventory) lend themselves readily to a prescriptive format that can succeed in optimizing a *subsystem*. The use of this approach is beneficial, however, only if the subsystem can properly be isolated from the larger system. In other words, when it is reasonable to treat one or a few items at a time, or some segmented portion of the total system, then the analytic prescriptive formulation is often advantageous. Alfred North Whitehead succinctly characterized the problem of analytic mathematical models when he said that they are attenuated. Nevertheless, these models allow us to determine a solution rapidly. When speed is desirable the assumption of an independent subsystem may be warranted, even though it will lead to suboptimization. (In Chapter 3 we will examine the nature of conditions that permit subsystems to be separated from the total system and treated individually.)

In general, then, for highly researched and understood areas, the prescriptive approach results in efficiency and rapid solution. When such problems are known to be repetitive and sufficiently independent of the rest of the system, the prescriptive format can be modeled, programmed, and placed in the computer, where it can then provide solutions without further managerial attention.

For complex questions concerning investment, plant location, and other areas of upper-management concern, however, a descriptive format seems more appropriate. Although simulation is one of the major approaches to descriptive models (and this includes the use of scale models, such as planes in wind tunnels), there are viable alternatives, including the use of a descriptive analytic format. The analytic model should be classified as descriptive when the necessary equations can be written but the optimizing criterion cannot. The basic form of a descriptive model is such that the manager can request information about how one or more factors change as a result of changes in the other factors. Analytic modeling, though usually employed in a normative fashion, often lends itself to useful descriptiveness as well when, because of multiple objectives, a straightforward solution of a single problem in the system is not available.

Direct and Iterative Solutions

Analytic formulations can, in general, be treated by direct manipulation, in the full mathematical sense of algebraic and calculus operations. Frequently simulation requires iterative procedures, whereby a cycle of computations is made, producing a result (number) that is then returned to the system and reworked in a gradually converging series of approximations. Many search techniques proceed on an iterative basis. In this way a particular set of conditions required for solution is approached by stages. The iterative approach applies in well-known models such as linear programming and the transportation method.[17] It also characterizes many of the numerical techniques utilized by computer programmers to allow the computer to make complex mathematical computations based on simple arithmetic operations that converge to the solution.

It is apparent, then, why the direct approach to solution is rapid, whereas the iterative one consumes a great deal more computer time. Frequently, however, iterative methods are the only ones that can be used, and, when they can converge to a satisfactory solution in a reasonably short time, their use is particularly recommended. Although both analytic and simulation models can use either the direct or the iterative approach, the analytic form is usually direct, and the simulation form usually iterative.

Static and Dynamic Models

By *static* we mean here that no time parameter appears in the equations or model.[18] The dynamic model, on the other hand, uses time as one of the

---

[17] See pp. 284–91 and pp. 656–60.

[18] The terms "static" and "dynamic" were used in a seemingly different sense with respect to taxonomy. A little thought, however, will show that the terms as used here are a special case of the former reference—namely, time is the interrelating variable.

fundamental parameters, or variables, in the system, concerning itself with changes over time or with delays and lags. Generally, if a model provides a starting time and initial state and a closing time and ending state, it is considered a dynamic model. Simulation utilizes the dynamic form as a general rule, since the temporal factor is implicit in the idea of systems flows, which is at the core of simulation. Of course, because of the artificial nature of simulation it is possible to speed up such flows and to represent many years of time in an extremely short period. For example, in a matter of minutes of computing time we could have generated *years* of performance for the inventory system shown in Figure 2–15. Time can also be compressed when it is properly shown in analytic form. And in a given system it may well be one of the factors to be optimized—for example, time minimization.

The use of time effects in models is important. Managers must notice the way time is incorporated in their models and should, as a general rule, proceed with great caution when time is not represented in the structure of their models. It may be that in some cases time is an unnecessary factor; in most of the decision models represented in Chapter 4 time is only *implicit*. But the fact is that implicit time can produce misleading results, because it is not really what the manager had in mind.

Furthermore, since the planning horizon is not stated when time is ignored but implicit, inconsistencies can easily arise. Some parts of the model will generate results that are based on longer term effects than others. By *planning horizon* we mean the interval, or period, between the initial state and the end state of the model. In planning terms, it is how far ahead consideration of cause and effect is carried. If the model does not include time, we may assume that cause and effect are relatively immediate, and a static model will suffice. When a change in the planning horizon produces a basically different answer, signaling that a different approach should be used, it is a clear sign that a dynamic model is critical. On the other hand, in a satisfactory static model, as time passes and a longer period is involved, the results will merely change in proportion to the extra time allocated, and the same approach will continue to be used. The advantage of static models over dynamic ones is that they are less expensive and easier to understand because they are simpler to handle.

Isomorphic and Homomorphic Models

We have already had occasion to mention homomorphic models—those that compress information about the system. As we mentioned (see p. 42), the original model cannot be reconstructed from the homomorph, since the compression results in loss of detail. Isomorphic models, on the other hand, utilize a transformation from which the original model *can always be retrieved*. For instance, changing inches to feet is an isomorphic transformation.

The purpose of homomorphic transformations—for example, transforming a series of numbers to an average—is to cut down on the information load for the manager so that he can cope with it and thus perceive the pattern of the system. Put another way, an insightful homomorphic transformation removes the excessive variety from a system and allows the basic pure pattern to be seen. As a greater amount of exact detail of the system is required, an isomorphic rather than a homomorphic model is chosen. The need for detail is related to a lack of theory and the fact that severe penalties can be incurred if the system under study is too grossly approximated by homomorphic modeling. Theory provides a pattern for explaining the behavior of the system, and the variables that describe that pattern generally remove the need for a great deal of extraneous information, so homomorphic models are advantageous. It should be noted, however, that models with a strong theoretical framework are isomorphic in terms of basic behavior of the system but homomorphic in terms of extraneous detail and peripheral factors that might otherwise be watched with care. Marketing is a good example of an area that lacks a strong theoretical framework. Many data about consumers are collected, ranging from demographic statistics through psychological psychographic profiles and information on television-viewing, eating, and sleeping habits. The marketing models are isomorphic to detail because a lack of theory does not permit homomorphic models to be used with respect to that detail.

EXAMPLES OF MODELS

Throughout this text we shall have numerous opportunities to examine a variety of prescriptive, descriptive, analytic, and simulation models. At this point, however, we wish to illustrate, by the use of several examples, the fact that having a *taxonomy for models* enables managers to think far more clearly about the role of models in management.

Simulative-Descriptive: Statistical Samples

The oldest type of model is the scale model, objective and physical. Despite its age, however, the twentieth century has made an important contribution to it. We have in mind statistical surveys in which the sample is intended as a model of the population (*ergo,* a simplified representation of some part of reality). Surveys, polls, and the like may turn out to be among the most influential models invented in this century.[19]

---

[19] Objective sampling theory can be said to have started with R. A. Fisher in 1920, although significant work was done by others as well at that time.

Many kinds of sampling models exist, and each type has its own advantages. There is also a substantial body of theory concerning how to take, interpret, and use samples. The polling of real people qualifies as a simulation of the actual electorate, marketplace, and so on. The simulated performance of a plane in a wind tunnel is a sample of its behavior under actual flying conditions. The performance of a product or a package under various marketing conditions may be simulated in a test market. The capabilities of such models are only descriptive; there are no prescriptive properties that can tell the marketer or the plane designer how to optimize his performance, and he can only choose the best of the alternatives he has brought to the test situation. In the test market, for example, the purpose of the model is to describe consumer responses to alternatives, not to derive the characteristics of an optimum marketing system.

Analytic-Prescriptive: Inventory Models

One of the first areas that was successfully approached using the analytical form of abstract models was that of inventory control. In 1928 a Western Electric engineer named Harris created the (so-called) economic lot-size model, which fully qualifies as an analytic-prescriptive model. These early efforts predate operations research work, which, starting in the 1940's, developed elaborate analytical models for planning and controlling inventories. Eventually, the level of understanding was sufficient to say that a theory of inventory existed. The key to this theory is that equations can be written for the total costs of carrying different amounts of inventory under various circumstances. Thus, total cost, TC, is the relevant outcome variable, and it is what management desires to minimize. In the economic lot-size model there is only one other relevant variable—x, the quantity ordered from the vendor. The parameters that are considered include

z: the monthly demand or usage rate
C_1: the cost of placing an order
C_2: the dollar cost of carrying a unit of inventory for a month

Then

$$TC = \frac{z}{x}C_1 + \frac{x}{2}C_2$$

Though the value of x that provides the minimum TC is readily obtained by mathematical means,[20] a simple graph will show how TC varies with different values of x (see Figure 2–16).

---

[20] Simply set $\frac{z}{x}C_1 = \frac{x}{2}C_2$ and solve for x; or set the derivative $\frac{dTC}{dx} = 0$ and solve for x.

Figure 2–16

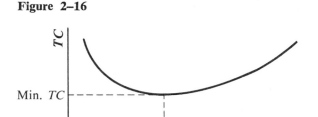

It will be found that the function always has a minimum where

$$x_o = \sqrt{\frac{2zC_1}{C_2}}$$

Consequently, this is a *normative,* analytical, abstract model, since it tells us what we *ought* to do about x.

Simulative-Prescriptive: Fault-Location Model

The next model is an unusual one and its use, as reported, is said to be true. It is an ingenious example of an objective physical model with simulation properties that produce a *prescriptive* result.

As the story goes, during the Second World War a new type of bomber that had begun to fly numerous missions was suffering unusually high losses. Because of the deep urgency of the situation, there was no time to undertake an elaborate test program to determine the fault, for such a program might have taken six months to a year. An operational research group (as OR is called in Britain) was formed. They postulated that planes that did not return had been hit in some critical area by antiaircraft fire and, conversely, that all planes that returned had not been hit in the unknown vulnerable spot.

A prototype of the plane was available. After each mission all flak marks on the returning aircraft were drawn on the prototype. Eventually a pattern, such as that shown in Figure 2–17, revealed the weak spot as the place where thin armor left the fuel lines relatively unprotected. Planes hit in the unmarked area, it was surmised, never returned. The fuel-line area was redesigned and all planes converted. After that, only expected numbers of losses occurred. A more traditional (physical) investigation would have taken many months longer than did this approach—and time was of the essence.

Figure 2–17

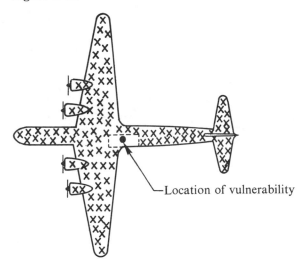

—Location of vulnerability

Model-Building by Analogy

Many models are developed through reasoning by analogy to the successful applications of models in other fields. The absolute importance of analogy to model-building for management becomes evident to anyone who studies the history of various forms of application of similar techniques.

It is said that the dramatic speed-up in finding the solution to the problem in the preceding example resulted in analogous models being used to solve other problems. For example, the war had called up individuals with many special skills, and this had an adverse affect on industries that required unusual talents. Leather-goods manufacture was one of these industries.

Skins of animals contain abrasions, cuts, scars from fighting, and so forth. The skin-cutter lays out a pattern of wallets, belts, purses, and so on, in order to avoid the imperfections of the particular skin concerned. However, the wartime shortage of cutters made it impossible to continue giving each skin such individual treatment. So skins were grouped by types and sizes, and, using the aircraft fault-location analogy, a prototype for each class of skin was marked up by studying a number of samples of each class. It was found that imperfections clustered in certain areas of the skins, and that there was a high probability that none would be found in other areas (see Figure 2–18). Based on this, a generalized pattern for cutting each skin class was set up, and automatic machinery was used to cut the skins to the preset pattern.

Of course, every now and then an imperfection did appear on a cut part, but this was removed by inspection before further operations were wasted.

Figure 2–18

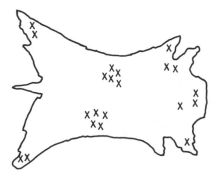

Inspection had much lower skill requirements and consumed fewer man-hours than the job of laying out the cutting pattern. In fact, great skin utilization could be expected, since a close to optimum cutting pattern would result from studying each class of skin and, additionally, since the cutting patterns could be related to the overall production requirements of the company.

We have now examined another *prescriptive simulation model,* this one obtained by analogy.

A MODEL DESIGN

Throughout this book a variety of models, formal and informal, objective and subjective, are discussed. How does management choose its modeling style? The answer is that while management can select a model, it does so within certain constraints dictated by circumstance and logic. This becomes apparent when we recognize that the manager must perceive the problem before he can select the model. He chooses the model with the intention of finding a useful solution to the problem.

The model that is used will depend on how simple or complex the problem is perceived to be. Very complex problems may be treated with very simple models because they are too complex to be treated satisfactorily with any other known form of model. The relevance of human behavior to the solution, especially individual human behavior, usually increases the complexity of the problem. Often, for very complex problems, a first-stage model alone will be used. Top management is most likely to turn in this direction. Problems of average complexity, on the other hand, are likely to be treated with second- or third-stage models because they are understood well enough to be handled in this manner.

Model choice will be affected by the assets at stake in the problem's solution. If the potential worth of a solution is large, higher modeling expense (and complexity) can be justified. Model selection will also depend on how much the manager knows about the problem situation. Depending on his experience in the problem area, he may either accept or discard normative solutions obtained from second- and third-stage models.

In other words, while each situation is unique, model design nevertheless will be affected in understandable ways by the type and complexity of the problem, the manager's knowledge and experience with the problem, the capabilities and costs of different types of model, and the potential worth of the problem's solution. (The subject of model choice will be discussed again in Chapter 6.)

SUMMARY

This chapter attempts to give a concise picture of what models and model-building are all about. It starts with a broad definition of a model and explains some of the factors that account for the increase in the conscious use of models. A distinction is drawn between the meanings of model and theory and an explanation given of why the increasing number of models used by management provides a growing basis for management theory.

The basic stages of model-building are described, starting with primitive (first-stage) models, which do not have normative (or optimizing) capabilities. These models list important factors but do not describe how outcomes are produced by different arrangements of the factors. Second-stage models, which can be normative, relate the factors to the outcomes with functional descriptions. Third-stage models can also be normative. They embody feedback effects, which make it essential that time or sequence be considered.

A major class of models—those dealing with information—includes accounting models, computer models, data-handling models, and taxonomical models, each of which is briefly described. The use of trees and matrices to present information in an ordered form is explained. By means of homomorphic models, information can be compressed and the size of the problem under consideration thereby reduced. There is no such reduction when an isomorphic model is used. Both have advantages and drawbacks. Causality must be considered as an important factor in the interpretation of information models, and in this regard correlational methods are examined and interpreted. Mill's Canons of Induction are presented to illustrate the essential nature of reasoned thinking about causality and the relations between variables.

Models used by management can be classified in a number of different ways. A tree of models is offered as a means of identifying the significant attributes by means of which it is possible to categorize models. Although dichotomies are used, it is quite clear that for many categories, combinations of the properties can appear together. For example, the first classification pair discussed is subjective and objective models, but most systems are studied using both in varying proportions. Subjective models are readily identified with a lack of formal methods, and objective ones with explicit analysis.

Second, physical and abstract models are treated. Physical models are concrete, abstract ones essentially mathematical. Both kinds of model must be constructed with measurable dimensions or scales. Five different levels of scaling are examined—namely, subjective, ordinal, ordinal with natural origin, interval, and ratio.

The third classification pair is analytic and simulation models. Analytic models are usually mathematical models that express causality and can be solved for optimal conditions. Simulation models bring together interacting elements in a logical flow network. The simulation of flows under varying conditions provides different descriptions of how the system performs.

The fourth classification pair is prescriptive (or normative) models and descriptive models. Normative models are designed to specify what ought to be done, whereas descriptive models present a kind of map for the manager to study. This distinction is critical and appears repeatedly throughout the remainder of the book. Another recurring theme, that of sensitivity analysis, also is introduced.

The fifth classification is based on the difference between direct and iterative solutions of the models. Iterative solutions require cycles of computations that gradually converge on the solution.

The sixth classification distinguishes between static and dynamic models. Simply stated, the static model does not explicitly include a time parameter, whereas the dynamic model does. The way in which time is used in the manager's model can be of crucial importance.

The seventh classification is based on the difference between isomorphic and homomorphic models, which can be distinguished by the way they translate information.

The chapter concludes with examples of four different kinds of model, which are briefly described in order to indicate the real variety that exists among models management can use. In particular, an example is cited in which, through reasoning by analogy, a model for one problem was converted into a form suitable for a different problem. Finally, some of the factors that influence model selection and design are examined. They include problem complexity, managerial knowledge, and model capabilities.

EXERCISES

1. How is it that you were able to use models before you knew consciously that they existed? When would you say that model-building began? What forces prompted the increase in conscious use of models? Do you expect these forces to continue to grow in strength? Think carefully about this question, since opposing forces may exist that do not support increased use of models.

2. Relate management model-building to management theory. What do you think is the present state of development of models and theory in
    a. aeronautical design
    b. financial operations of the government
    c. medical treatment
    d. operation of a petroleum refinery

3. Give some examples of
    a. first-stage, primitive models
    b. second-stage, functional models
    c. third-stage, feedback models
Discuss the need for each type of model. Do you think that all first-stage models develop eventually into third-stage ones as a result of experience and sophistication with models?

4. Give an example of a data-compression model. Explain why too much and too little information are both undesirable, and comment on whether they are equally so. What is meant by the statement that "the *distribution* of information must have *directed relevancy*"?

5. Compare the common properties of trees and matrices for presenting information in an ordered form. Describe the conditions under which you would prefer one form to the other.

6. Give an example of a homomorphic transformation. Explain what an isomorphic model is by comparing it with a homomorphic model, and evaluate the usefulness of each form under varying conditions.

7. Why is the knowledge of "what causes what" crucial to management control? In that regard, why do behavioral components in a system make it difficult to achieve real control of that system?

8. Give an illustration of each of Mill's five Canons, and explain what the strengths *and weaknesses* of such reasoning might be. How can these Canons be considered as precursors of correlation methods?

9. Using the tree of models on page 48, locate on it:
   a. the model of a ship in a towing tank
   b. a normative, economic-lot-size inventory model
   c. a national economic planning model
   d. management's plant-location model
   e. management's diversification and merger models

10. What kind of scaling problem is involved in the measurement of how well a group of workers get along? How about the measurement of a consumer's response to a new package?

11. What advantage does a scale with a natural origin possess? Give some examples of dimensions with and without natural origins. What advantages does a scale with distance measures have? Give some examples of dimensions with and without information about distance.

12. Make a list of ten books, movies, television shows, and so forth. Then, taking them in pairs (1 and 2, 1 and 3, 2 and 3, etc.), choose the member of each pair that you prefer. There are forty-five such paired comparisons that you can make. (You will save time by developing a method to do this.) After this process is completed, check yourself for consistency. Have you said, for example, that 3 is preferred to 6, that 6 is preferred to 9, and that 9 is preferred to 3? If you find a lack of consistency in your results, such as described above, then transitivity has been violated. Explain what this means, what caused it, how to interpret such results, and what to do about them.

13. What is meant by "we must be wary of intermediary measures"? Why has this particular significance for management?

14. Discuss the advantages and disadvantages of normative and descriptive models. Give some examples of when you would prefer to use one or the other. For instance, which would you choose to treat a problem of military strategy, a plant expansion decision, the selection of a restaurant to take some out-of-town friends to, the number of tubes of toothpaste to buy at one time?

15. Give an example of an iterative solution to a problem. Does the model of a pendulum help? Consider the path of an airplane landing under an automatic guidance system.

The Framework of Managing

MODEL-BUILDING AND MODEL USE

Building Management Models

Chapter 3
Using Models

The characteristics of a system must be defined before the system
can be modeled. Even then, there are many ways in which the
model can be created, and only a few of these will produce a useful
solution that can be implemented successfully. The size and complexity
of the system as well as the degree to which people are involved
will play a crucial role in determining what should be done.

Chapter 3

USING MODELS

The centipede was happy quite
   Until a toad in fun
Said, "Pray which leg goes after which?"
That worked her mind to such a pitch,
She lay distracted in a ditch,
   Considering how to run.[1]

Certain questions that management can ask will help improve its performance; others will tend to paralyze it. In the case of the centipede, the reflexive behavior of walking was natural, but analysis began to transfer the walking function to the conscious plane, where it was too complex to be coordinated. The same kind of difficulty can be experienced by management, although different managers react in different ways to analysis.

The kind of organization within which the manager works also has a bearing on the effects of following various lines of reasoning. One pertinent factor, for example, is the size of the system about which questions are being asked. In general, the larger the system a question pertains to, the harder it becomes and the longer it takes to answer the question. If answering requires tinkering with the system, additional troubles frequently develop, for the process of answering may confuse what is already being accomplished.

---

[1] Mrs. Edward Craster, *Pinafore Poems,* 1871.

Moreover, some systems are more complicated than others, having a greater number of connections and feedback links. Where more detail is necessary, the questions are harder to ask and harder to answer.

In modeling, this becomes clear. To model the centipede's walking, perhaps only one leg, or maybe two, would be necessary. Or two on each side of the body might provide a sufficient model of the system. A model of more legs might break down, creating more confusion than understanding. From this example we can begin to realize that models should be built to help us understand and improve the system, not to make us admire the size and complexity of the model.

WHAT IS A SYSTEM?

We can begin to answer this question by observing the following relationship: A map is to its chosen terrain as a model is to its system (map/terrain = model/system). This relationship between a model and its system should not be confused with the higher-level comparison: system/reality. Reality is strictly a *concept* of everything that exists. It can be known only as it is perceived in terms of systems. The focus of perception on some part of reality produces a system. We define a system, therefore, as a chosen part of reality that is observed or sensed in specific ways.[2] Consequently, concrete thinking begins with the definition of a system.

Any objective description of a system is a model of it. And it should be emphasized that many models can be proposed to map out a particular system that is under study. Using our map analogy, we need only observe how many kinds of map exist—showing roads, altitude, rainfall, navigation aids, weather, and so on—to understand that there are many different ways to model a system. Always, a model depicts only a part of the system; the rest of one's perceptions of the system are not included. But that does not mean they are necessarily forgotten. Executive intuition and judgment, which somehow synthesize all the individual's perceptions of the system, are used more often than not in conjunction with a formal model.

A graphic way to depict a system is shown in Figure 3–1. The arrows that cross the boundary of the system, moving both in and out, provide the criterion for our definition—namely, that a system is so founded that all the major effects are included within its domain. In other words, the boundary is drawn so that all effects that are *relevant* to the system are included. However,

---

[2] In the case of a map, note that a geographic selection process, delimiting reality, takes place as soon as we choose the specific boundaries of the terrain. Choice is an important element here, and much of this chapter is concerned with the role of choice in delineating a system.

Figure 3–1

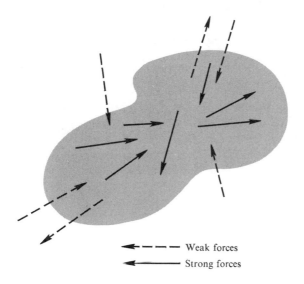

not all these forces can be included in any model, and therein lies one of the major difficulties encountered in making a *usable* model of the system.

Identifying a System

Because it is a *perception* of reality, a system can take on meaning only through the observations, interpretations, and *values* of the persons defining it. Whether they use verbal expression or mathematical symbols, their translation of reality will always be incomplete. But incomplete does not mean unsatisfactory. Each system is identified for a particular purpose, and, even though perfection is impossible, the purpose may be satisfied by far less than perfection.

Systems identification is a highly personal affair. Great latitude exists concerning the observation and reporting of the properties of the "real" world. Who is to say what is relevant or how the system works? There is ample evidence to show that witnesses to the same event will report on it differently[3]

---

[3] The movie *Rashomon,* a Japanese film classic, was based on a story illustrating how witnesses to a tragedy testified with remarkably different views that were conditioned by their roles and values. In role-playing—where, for example, an executive and a foreman are asked to interchange their usual roles in the context of a given situation—it is well known that unexpected insights occur to each participant about the other's point of view.

and that even twins will disagree about the character of their home life. Psychiatrists have testified that individuals project views of varying degrees of distortion in describing their personal life-systems.

If the executives of a company disagree about the nature of a particular system, then any specific model of all or part of that system is likely to be misleading and destructive, for the model will not represent the system and reality as they are viewed by some of the managers. This will inhibit, or even prohibit, coordination in the use of the model. It is therefore essential that management have a communality of views concerning its systems. This is not the same as having agreement about what model to use or what the solution is to a problem; it is more like agreement about the nature of the problem.

Modeling a System

Management is responsible for agreeing on the definition of the system. Management's analysts, model-builders, and scientists are responsible for providing an operational model of that system—that is, they should use good economic sense in neither overmodeling nor undermodeling. Furthermore, it is essential that they keep management apprised of the systemic elements not included in the model and that management intuition must augment technique when the model is used.

Scale of modeling (how fine or how gross the model's categories are) can be as critical as the choice of variables to be included in the model and the method of representing their relationships. The choice of model type is of paramount importance in this regard. For example, simulation models often provide far more categories, but less fine measures within the categories, than do normative models. In choosing between the two, one must bear in mind that a simulation is likely to cost more than the benefits it produces. In such a case, there is no reward for the manager; he has succeeded only in overmodeling his system. On the other hand, a simple normative model built for a highly interdependent system probably will not be used or will be discarded rapidly as an instance of undermodeling the system. Understanding such relations is critical to model use and is frequently referred to as the *implementation problem*.

For the manager, the trust generated by one or another type of model construction will be determined by the *way* in which the model "captures" the system. If the formal model is small in relation to the system being studied, intuition may have to play a larger part than if all the variables are included in the model. There is, therefore, a distinct advantage in making sure that the system is large enough to enable management to exercise some form of control over all the relevant factors. Herbert Simon developed the phrase *bounded rationality* to describe the notion that total rationality in modeling was a myth.[4] By "bounded rationality" he meant that the factors to be considered in any model, and their interrelations, are intuitively reduced in number before the remaining alternatives would be considered rationally. If management has failed to determine the full extent of the system that influences its objectives, it is likely to engage in many small modeling studies, none of which is operationally useful. Without an adequate view of the system, even the most advanced mathematical or simulation modeling ability is pointless, and the overall result is likely to be degenerative rather than helpful. This is particularly important because frequently more than one model is used to study a system—for example, when separate inventory and scheduling models are employed for a single production system. A systems framework must prevail to coordinate the results of these models.

An example of a system. Assume that management has asked the operations research and systems department to study the scheduling of production. The production manager is upset by this decision because he believes he has already developed the necessary policy for satisfactory production runs in his department. Whether or not he has used a formal model, the production manager is confident that he has already solved the scheduling problem; he knows that he runs an efficient shop.

When management made the request, however, it probably did not intend that the solution be narrowed to production efficiency; we can assume that it had in mind a larger system. An inner-directed production-model approach ignores inventory-level effects on marketing (e.g., those that delays in delivery might have), and it is usually insensitive to the financial manager's other uses for money or unaware of new opportunities for investment and the changing conditions of the money market. The production manager's optimal runs and full utilization of equipment are only one part of the story. Should the production manager have chosen a larger view of the system and solved his problems so as to optimize the combined performance of production, marketing, finance, and so forth? Even if the production manager had tried (which is unlikely), it would have been hard for him to do and likely frowned upon by the marketing and finance managers. If nothing else, the production manager would have been unable to trace the effects of implementing his solution throughout all areas of the company. Figure 3–2, which shows a small (static) organization chart, contrasts a strictly production-oriented systems study (3–2A) with the *problem-oriented* view of the larger system (3–2B). The description of the problem, as is clearly shown here, must originate at a level high enough to call forth adequate modeling of the system that actually affects the company's performance.

---

[4] See Herbert A. Simon, "A Behavioral Model of Rational Choice," *Quarterly Journal of Economics,* Vol. 69 (February 1955), pp. 99–118.

Figure 3–2

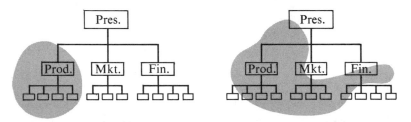

COMPLEXITY AND SIMPLICITY

A model is a simplified representation of reality, but the degree of simplification is bounded by the complexity of the systems view. Once we recognize this relationship, we can begin to assign problems to different systems categories, such as those of varying levels of organized complexity.

David Hertz has listed in his book the categories of simplicity, disorganized complexity, and organized complexity, pointing out that organized complexity is the most demanding to deal with.

> Problems may also be defined in terms of the complexity which they exhibit, requiring various classes of method for their solution. Warren Weaver has described problems of "simplicity," "disorganized complexity," and "organized complexity." Simple problems are those of only a few variables and relate particularly to mechanical problems in the physical sciences, such as were solved with such outstanding success in the seventeenth, eighteenth, and nineteenth centuries. Problems of disorganized complexity are those in which the solution must be obtained in terms of random-ordered sets by means of statistical techniques. . . .
>
> Problems of organized complexity are those in which the variables exhibit the essential features of organization; i.e., the variables studied are dependent upon individual and mass psychological effects, as well as purely physical ones. They are the "unknown middle ground" for present methods of problem solving.[5]

Using this taxonomy, we can relate problem areas and systems categories with the appropriate management level. We would expect that as we move up the hierarchical scale the systems considered will become larger, and the manager

---

[5] David B. Hertz, *The Theory and Practice of Industrial Research* (New York: McGraw-Hill, 1950), p. 28. Hertz is quoting Warren Weaver, "Science and Complexity," *American Scientist,* Vol. 36 (October 1938), p. 542.

a greater generalist. Though detail will be lost, the organization of complexity will become more demanding. The manager will treat larger aggregates over longer time spans. Thus, the character of useful models will change markedly as we move from foreman concerns to those of the president.

Some History

When it comes to dealing with complexity, science can claim a long tradition dating back to William of Occam, a Franciscan friar of the fourteenth century. Occam held that the *simplest* explanation that satisfies observation should be the basis for accepting a theory. This "principle of parsimony," known as Occam's Razor, has influenced the course of science to the present time.[6] Although its greatest effect was in the nineteenth century, when scientists believed that the ultimate perfection of understanding was shortly to be achieved, this principle is still applied widely, many times *unconsciously,* because it has been woven into the fabric of scientific thought.

Perhaps this explains why many managers (not being parsimonious perfectionists or believing in simplicity) find it difficult to establish rapport with their scientific staffs. Many management scientists are parsimonious-model oriented, whereas the manager is systems oriented. Parsimonious views of systems of organized complexity, as reflected by simple models, make little sense to the manager, for application of Occam's Razor to complex systems problems leads to highly attenuated models. We all admire the indisputable strength of mathematics for describing certain types of problem, but we should also recognize that it does not properly describe others.

Intellectual literary tradition is strong in its opposition to parsimony. For example, Henry Adams felt impelled to write that "simplicity is the most deceitful mistress of all." At the turn of the twentieth century, when scientists came to realize that simple, unified theories would not explain everything, they began to rely on quantum mechanics and statistical theories to describe situations of disorganized complexity. The "young Turks" of science, by advancing statistical interpretations of reality, disturbed men such as Einstein, who said, "God does not play dice." Nevertheless, prevailing scientific theory began to reflect the "new simplicity" of probabilistic statements. The conflict between the literary camp and the scientific one continued, for it was recognized that probability was in fact a parsimonious explanation of reality. When C. P.

---

[6] In his own time, this maxim led Occam to question the laws of motion set down by St. Thomas Aquinas. Thereafter, scientists such as Copernicus, Galileo, Kepler, and Newton, in arguing their advances in astronomical models, followed a tradition based on the criterion of parsimony.

Snow developed his notion of the two cultures,[7] he was bitterly attacked by F. R. Leavis (a literary critic) for extolling the superior role of rationalism (which Leavis interpreted as scientific simplicity) in governing the affairs of mankind.

But science continues to change. The quantum mechanics rebels are now "the establishment," and a new group of "young Turks" has arisen in response to the latest challenge of complexity. They question whether direct observation alone can be used statistically to predict behavior, challenging classical statistical attitudes and championing the use of subjective measures. They are called Bayesians, after Reverend Bayes,[8] who enunciated related principles in the eighteenth century but whose work was largely ignored or discredited in the years that followed. Recently, the Bayesian influence has begun to have an effect once again. And it is a strong effect, for the Bayesians have found a means for the manager to express his opinions and for these subjective measures to be represented in a quantitative formulation. Because these are such important notions, we will have the occasion to discuss them in greater detail in subsequent pages.

Crisis Management

Any charge of oversimplification is critical in the present age of large systems. Because they are also complex, today's systems run a greater risk of failure than yesterday's simpler ones. At the same time, the consequences of failure

---

[7] C. P. Snow, *The Two Cultures and the Scientific Revolution* (The Rede Lecture, 1959) (New York: Cambridge University Press, 1961). Consider, for example, the following quote from page 15 of the book. ("The other side" is the literary, or nonscientific, culture.)

> But what about the other side? They are impoverished too—perhaps more seriously, because they are vainer about it. They still like to pretend that the traditional culture is the whole of "culture", as though the natural order didn't exist. As though the exploration of the natural order was of no interest either in its own value or its consequences. As though the scientific edifice of the physical world was not, in its intellectual depth, complexity and articulation, the most beautiful and wonderful collective work of the mind of man. Yet most non-scientists have no conception of that edifice at all. Even if they want to have it, they can't. It is rather as though, over an immense range of intellectual experience, a whole group was tone-deaf. Except that this tone-deafness doesn't come by nature, but by training, or rather the absence of training.

One does not have to read between the lines; the scientist is acutely aware that the intellectual accuses him of oversimplifying his solutions for complex systems; and the scientist counters by faulting "traditional culture" for its lack of understanding.

[8] See pp. 227–30.

are also greater. New York City, as well as much of the eastern sections of the United States and Canada suffered a major blackout in November of 1965, and similar blackouts have occurred in other places; air-traffic control studies report many near-collisions; airport congestion has become critical at many major airports; overload in stock-market paperwork has caused early closings and four-day weeks; monumental auto traffic jams have come to be accepted as common; telephone lines are jammed beyond capacity; population surges ahead of food supply. The list is far from complete, and the future undoubtedly holds even more striking possibilities. Such inability to manage a system's complexities results in what can be called *crisis management*.

The critical question for management is: How large a system should it consider in a given study? Each system requires its own answer. Some systems are more crisis-prone than others, and such susceptibility will affect the manager's decision concerning the appropriate size of the system to study. Usually crisis conditions arise because of interrelationships that exist at detailed levels. For example, bridge-building requires that the total span be designed as a whole, yet delineated in terms of the utmost detail. The left half and the right half cannot be designed separately; nevertheless every component must be treated in detail because one error in detail can cause failure of the whole system. Numerous interdependent models are therefore used to treat the total system. Ample safety factors are added, since safety is the overriding objective. Whatever is well known and tested in the theory of bridges is used. Invention is kept to a minimum (as it is in shipbuilding) so that unknown factors do not creep in to create crisis potential. On the other hand, for systems in which behavioral factors are important, the answer to our question is more difficult to arrive at. Large behavioral systems cannot fall back on established theory, but the tendency to treat smaller systems as though they were independent has been recognized to create crisis conditions with increasing frequency and severity.

LARGE SYSTEMS

Because of technological and social changes, and an awareness of the increasing probabilities of crisis conditions, management has recognized the growing need to be concerned with large systems.[9] In fact, management has been recognized as a large systems topic, of which the small system is only a special case. The need for the large systems view is real because interconnectedness and dependency among systems components have increased greatly. There is more

---

[9] Chapter 13 addresses directly the problems of dealing with large systems. Other chapters treat decision-making, planning, controlling, and organizing for large systems.

communication among an increasing number of components, and the components are more educated and more sensitive to effects of the communication than ever before. The change is, therefore, a result of cultural adaptation to new technology, increased population, more information, and so forth.[10]

Seldom does a machine, job, or person any longer receive the isolated attention of the manager. Machines aggregate with people, creating communication patterns that exceed departmental lines, and departments operating together become more than divisions. That is why we must emphasize that model-building can be fruitless if it is carried out on too small a scale.

System Size Distortions

By crossing functional boundaries, seeing problems as having their own uniquely defined areas (rather than limiting problems to traditional areas), infusing analysis with an awareness of competition, and sensing the dynamics of the marketplace and the economy, the manager has augmented his accustomed telephoto view of the enterprise with a wide-angle one. But certain information distortions occur when the manager shifts his attention from small to large systems. In photography, where each type of lens has special uses for which it is particularly well adapted, the photographer knows that both types have characteristic distortions. The wide-angle lens, which gathers in more information than can properly be represented on a flat surface, bends straight lines to make them fit onto the rectangular sheet of film. The telephoto lens foreshortens, elongates nearer points, and eliminates much of the surroundings. As the manager moves from the magnification of the small system to the wide-angle compression of data in the large system, he must recognize how reality is being "bent" in order to allow greater spans of information to be encompassed.

Grouping more information into the same number of classes to describe a larger system leaves the same number of variables to be studied. This can be contrasted with the approach of increasing the number of classes so that each contains about the same amount of information required for a small systems study. We shall discuss the apparent natural limit on the number of variables

---

[10] The intelligentsia play an important part in determining the stability of cultural patterns. Eric Hoffer, in his book *The Ordeal of Change,* supports Stalin's comment that no ruling class can endure without its intelligentsia. And there is considerable evidence that the intelligentsia's interest has shifted in favor of the large systems view. Teilhard de Chardin, a Jesuit priest, has written extensively about the growth in man's relations from small to large systems. (See, for example, Pierre Teilhard de Chardin, "The Planetisation of Mankind," in *The Future of Man,* translated from the French by Norman Denny [New York: Harper & Row, 1964], pp. 129–44.) Ultimately, Chardin states, a "noosphere" of total interconnectedness will result from the continuation of present trends.

that a person can consider at one time. This physiological limit influences the differences in treatment of large and small systems studies. As a result, the concept of "gestalt" becomes critical as a requirement for viewing large systems without distortion.[11]

The large systems view contains man. It does not eliminate him by means of selective telephoto effects nor distort his complexity—for example, to a static box on an organization chart. This is of such importance that in a later section we will discuss *systems membership,* emphasizing the way in which people aggregate in clusters. We do this because the large system also includes the group. And we will see later how complicated is the problem of getting undistorted measures of people's participation in systems affairs. Since purely objective *rational* approaches cannot contend with the unpredictability inherent in larger systems, new approaches that blend subjective and objective methodology are required. A basis for a dynamic theory emerges. This basis invokes recognition that "things" change, that they are not fixed for all time. The first precept for such a theory of management is that what the system is today will be the major determinant of what it *can* be tomorrow. Management must see itself as a dynamic entity, not only in step with, but influencing the changing rhythms of the system it manages. This dynamic view forces enlargement of the system because it includes the additional variable of time in all its considerations.[12] To ignore time often produces major distortions in how the manager views the systems with which he works.

The effect of technological change on the selection of a system of appropriate size is marked. Communication satellites speed our progress toward Chardin's "noosphere."[13] Mach 2 jet velocities assist the growing belief in the correctness of existentialism as a philosophy, which maintains that all mankind is interdependent. That men walked on the moon in 1969, while the Wright brothers first flew a plane at Kitty Hawk in 1903—and that men talked to the earth from the moon, while Bell invented the telephone in 1876—might help to explain why we say that the size of an adequate system for study has been

---

[11] The *Columbia-Viking Desk Encyclopedia* (New York: Dell, 1964, p. 694) defines *gestalt* as "a school of psychology which interprets phenomena as organized wholes rather than as aggregates of distinct parts and which maintains that the whole is greater than the sum of its parts. The term Gestalt was coined in Germany by Christian von Ehrenfels."

[12] If we assume that there is a natural limit to the number of variables in any system that can be viewed and understood by man (pp. 598–99), then adding a variable will cause some other variable that is presently used to be subsumed within a larger class. It is even likely that by adding time to all studies of the system, an entirely *new set* of variables will emerge. Cybernetic studies often introduce new variables that measure rates of change in the system rather than absolute conditions. This viewpoint alone may alter substantially the set of modeling variables.

[13] See footnote 10, p. 80.

increasing geometrically. Yet decisions continue to be based on the conventional wisdoms of the familiar small systems, resulting in distorted solutions that produce social unrest.

The number of bits of information received by all persons, the number of contacts made, the miles traveled are moving upward so rapidly that some natural limit must be reached soon to change this course of events.[14] It is quite possible, of course, that we may find ways mentally to shut off the bombardment or to restructure it by a new taxonomy so that it is not perceived as being above a reasonable level. For example, say that a person can deal with only ten units of information in a given interval of time. If forty units arrive he can aggregate them into ten subsets of four. But he will need new methods to deal with the aggregates.

A major difference between present-day scientific efforts and those of earlier periods is that formerly only *simple* systems were studied, whether they were small or cosmically large. Today, systems of organized complexity occupy the center of the stage. New approaches by science and new theoretical structures are required if advances are to be made in understanding systems of organized complexity.

SYSTEMS MEMBERSHIP

The crucial question of how to define the system as to size, components, levels of information detail, period of time, and so forth, must be examined before we can discuss fully management's use of models. Toward this end, we observe that different principles for bounding systems will produce different configurations and sizes of system. Also, by including people and their behavior in our definitions, we increase the size of the system. The study of both criteria for and representation of systems membership is therefore essential.

Management can begin, of course, by visualizing the universe of all relations as the system that affects its decision-making and planning. The existentialist philosophy previously mentioned holds that each man is part of *all* systems; each entity has universality. Although such a philosophical point of view

---

[14] We are accustomed to think of science as growing exponentially, but every scientist ought to know that exponential growth never goes on for very long, for if it did, there would be only one thing left in the universe. There is, therefore, a non-existence theorem about exponential growth, as all great processes must eventually reach an equilibrium. Not even science is exempt from this fundamental scientific principle.

Kenneth E. Boulding, "The Specialist with a Universal Mind," *Management Science,* Vol. 14, No. 12 (August 1968), p. B649. See pp. 476–78 of Chapter 12.

exceeds the operational needs of management and the actual abilities of management science, the idea poses important questions concerning the allocation of personal time and energies to job, community, politics, family, friends, and fellow employees. These are a few of the competing commitments and loyalties that all people share. It is reasonable to ask (though difficult to answer): What systems do you belong to? Cosmic creature, citizen of the world, nationalist, company man, family man, loyal alumnus, stockholder, member of the Elks, churchgoer, Boy Scout, country-clubber, and so on?

The memberships are vastly greater in number than one tends at first to suppose. They are not easily represented or visualized. *Venn diagrams* (such as the one shown in Figure 3–3) are helpful, at least, in depicting the nature of

Figure 3–3 A Venn Diagram of Management's Political Affiliations

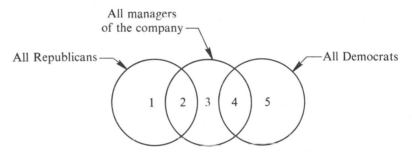

overlapping systems memberships. The managers of a particular company are represented by the center circle, which is the sum of (2) Republican managers, (3) independent managers and those of other parties, and (4) Democratic managers. The remaining areas are (1) all Republicans who are not managers of the company and (5) all Democrats who are not managers of the company. Clearly, with additional groups the combinations of overlaps become complicated measures of large systems.[15]

The city is a fine example of a system of many parts. It can be studied as a collection of municipalities; in terms of functions such as education, road-building and maintenance, and garbage collection; in terms of individuals grouped according to their respective tax brackets, age, sex, and other characteristics. The church is another complex system with many overlapping sets. The military establishment and the university are additional examples.

Perhaps one way to approach an understanding of systems membership is

---

[15] We note that the set of all Republicans did not overlap the set of all Democrats, indicating that joint membership was impossible. If it had been allowed, there would have been seven classes to consider instead of only five.

to try to understand what behavioral factors influence it. We may note, for example, that some people seem to like to belong to as many systems as possible; others tend to move to the largest systems; still others (hermits, for example) prefer the fewest and smallest systems. Managers differ, not only in their preferences for dealing with various sizes and numbers of groups, but also in their abilities to do so. Overlapping memberships can produce conflicts and anomalies. The president of a company is not the president of his family. The manager may be asked to answer a consumer survey at the same time that he is planning his own company's survey for others to answer. Concurrently, the manager has problems caused by the anomalies of his own overlapping memberships, as well as by those of the people he has to deal with—that is, employees, consumers, fellow managers, and so on. And we should bear in mind that membership is not always by choice and fellow members not always of one's choosing. The draft illustrates the former and the proverbial "mother-in-law jokes" accent the latter. The motives for membership can range from the aim of implementing an integrated plan for accomplishment to the simple desire to spend time with a good friend.

From management's point of view, the organization of the company is a design for overlapping systems memberships within the company in a beneficial way. Since the organization chart does not succeed in representing the overlapping systems, some other means must be developed to depict the relations that are to be included in models. This is difficult because of behavioral complexities. In an all-machine system, the interrelations of the system's members are arranged. Specifying the system's membership to make a diversification plan work is quite another matter. But some steps must be taken to ensure that proper systems-modeling needed for useful implementation *can* occur.

Membership Clusters

The existence of membership clusters can be identified to assist management's thinking. By a *cluster* we mean a highly interrelated grouping of entities. Clusters can be specified as either formal or informal aggregations that have been observed to occur. Put another way, clusters are groupings of entities that are dense with respect to one or more dimensions of membership association. If all consumers were homogeneous in terms of the variables that determine purchasing behavior, then there would be but one dense cluster of consumers. On the other hand, if consumers were distributed more or less evenly across the critical dimensions that affect buying behavior, then there would be no clustering of types. Figure 3–4A portrays two distinct clusters in a two-dimensional field; Figure 3–4B shows no real cluster configuration; and Figure 3–4C can be viewed as one cluster having no potential variety.

Figure 3–4

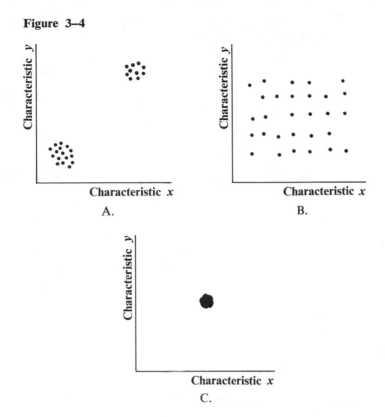

Roderick Seidenberg predicts an eventual reduction in the number of clusters and an increase in the membership of each cluster.[16] Thus, Figure 3–4B, which has the most clusters with the fewest members per cluster, becomes like Figure 3–4A, which, in turn, reduces to Figure 3–4C, the single cluster that contains all members. Seidenberg explains that a high-level of homogeneity is the ultimate state of man because, he says, a mental state of complete rationality is inevitable. He sees such rationality as a uniform state wherein everyone has the same objectives and chooses the same ways of achieving them. Whether or not Seidenberg is correct,[17] managers frequently

---

[16] Roderick Seidenberg, *Post-Historic Man, An Inquiry* (Boston: Beacon Press, 1957).

[17] It is possible to develop an argument to counter Seidenberg, whose viewpoint is as likely to be fallacious as Taylor's (see p. 86)—though it is applied to thinking rather than physical work. As the Seidenberg effect is felt, it may well become rational *to be irrational* in order to avoid the "undesirable" state of being in the same cluster with everybody else. We should recall, in this regard, our previous footnote describing Boulding's remark concerning the nonexistence theorem for exponential growth.

act as though his hypothetical state has already come to pass. By defining a job and then searching for a "qualified" worker, the "irrational" characteristics of the worker are removed from consideration. A fully automated system can be viewed as one cluster. It is like a single machine. Only by accepting the fact that the worker continually modifies the job—that is, that there is job-worker interaction—can we obtain the view of several clusters such as in Figure 3–4A or many individuals as in Figure 3–4B. Managing many clusters (or individuals) is definitely more demanding of the manager, and it is understandable that he would prefer to cope with a single cluster.

Frederick W. Taylor's notion of the "one best way" to do any job, and his belief that a worker can be trained to be machinelike and be given incentives to become "best" (in a mechanistic way), may be recognized by today's managers as unrealistic—but their preference still lies in that direction.[18] When there are too many clusters of low density (i.e., when a high level of variety exists in the system), the manager, if he can, will substitute machines for workers. In this way he can devote himself to dealing with the requirements of the job without worrying about the variabilities of the workers. We should note that a set of identical machines would correspond well to Seidenberg's conception—that is, to the single cluster of Figure 3–4C. Later, when discussing control theory, we will see why it is that the more dispersed the clusters, the more complex and costly is the task of controlling.

Industry tends to cluster densely in its own right so that greater control can be exercised. Consider oligopoly (where only a few major companies are competing with one another) or monopoly (which is epitomized by Figure 3–4C). The free and open market of many competitors (such as portrayed in Figure 3–4B) leads quickly to mergers. Though each merger can be explained in specific economic terms, in general they are caused by the disadvantages of many-clustered systems. In the same sense, pressure to cluster is brought to bear on consumers. Advertising can have this effect, as can consumer protection groups when they recommend a best buy. Consumer clusters can range from many independent and individualistic ultimate consumers, to a few industrial markets, to monopsony (where only one purchaser, such as the government, exists). Monopsony is usually considered undesirable by suppliers, but of course the single consumer likes it because of the control he can exercise.

Measures of set propensity. Using a matrix form, we can establish some measures of the extent to which human and machine entities associate with one another in different cluster patterns. (This approach could also be used to define formal or informal sets of membership relations; it would be

---

[18] Frederick W. Taylor, *The Principles of Scientific Management* (New York: Harper & Row, 1911).

harder to acquire the kind of data that we need in the informal case.) We shall call the various measures we obtain *set propensities* because they describe an individual's degree of association with various overlapping groups. They allow us to define the *interrelatedness* of a variety of components that communicate with one another. We will also attempt to test the density of the numerous clusters to which an individual or an entity belongs. But the interpretation of set-density measures will depend on our interests and on the variables that we choose to reflect them.

It should be emphasized that the concepts of set propensity and set density have relevance for management because they relate to the modeling of some part of a system. The notion of bounding a system, which is an important criterion for model-building and model use, is implicit in these measures. Management, to be effective, must use its models in the systems context. But systems are complicated to define because definitions determine which clusters will be found. The concept of set-propensity measures emphasizes this kind of complexity as it applies to the man/machine systems with which management must deal. In none of our discussions need we specify whether "individuals" are men or machines. Measures of relations can take on many forms: for example, the levels of communication between individual entities; or, in a sociometric sense, the expressions of preference of individuals to work with one another; or the amount of time that individuals spend with themselves and with one another. Different measures will create different matrix conditions, which stand for unique situations. We can deal with only a few cases, but the potential for further applicability and invention should not be overlooked.

It is not really possible, of course, to assign "individuals" to membership in clusters on the basis of such simple measures as those just described. Yet measures of who speaks to whom, who prefers to work with whom, and who spends his time with whom can be closely related to the *purpose* of association that underlies the membership structure and to the resulting cohesiveness or homogeneity of a group. For any particular situation, one or more chosen measures of association will be best able to capture the spirit of membership. Part of the manager's task, whether or not he uses formal methods to define his system, is to find appropriate dimensions for relating the system's components. If he cannot find objective measures (based on questioning and counting) to describe the character of group clustering in the system, then he must use subjective (intuitive) ones. The key notion, no matter what the approach used, is to determine which factors are critical in defining and setting the size of a system. Such knowledge bounds the system so that one or more models can be developed to study it.

According to the Venn diagram of Figure 3–3, each manager could belong to only two sets at the same time: first, the group of managers and, second, one political group. But each individual normally belongs to many groups and therefore has a variety of multiple-group propensities, as represented by the size of the lettered intersection areas in Figure 3–5.[19]

Figure 3–5   An Attempt to Map Systems Membership

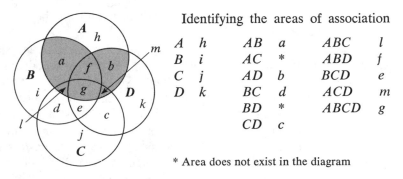

Identifying the areas of association

A	h	AB	a	ABC	l
B	i	AC	*	ABD	f
C	j	AD	b	BCD	e
D	k	BC	d	ACD	m
		BD	*	ABCD	g
		CD	c		

* Area does not exist in the diagram

Let us question the way in which individuals relate to others in this figure. For example, is membership as strong in *ABC* as in *BCD*? If we judge just by the size of the areas, the answer would be no. Now, assume that *A*, *B*, *C*, and *D* are departments of the company having different numbers of individuals as members. Do departments *B* and *C* form as dense a cluster as, say, *A* and *D*? We cannot tell because we do not know how areas relate to numbers of individuals and how these individuals differ in their intensities of association. The diagram is not sufficient to tell us what we would like to know. Therefore, let us turn to a different example using a matrix form of representation.

For our first matrix example, we will measure the proportion of time that an individual spends in his own and in other people's offices. The numbers in the matrix in Table 3–1 are a hypothetical example of such information. We can read the matrix as follows: person 1 spends 57 percent of his time at his own workplace, meeting with others and, when he is alone, perhaps reading, writing, or doing research. We observe that 2, 3, 4, and 5 spend a total of .41 (.15 + .09 + .07 + .10) with person 1. Since some of this time may be joint time (e.g., 2 and 3 visit 1 together), we cannot automatically derive the time that person 1 has to himself. He has been observed to spend 13 percent of his

---

[19] We should not lose sight of the fact that the clusters we identify are *evolving* at some rate. Because they reflect *ongoing* dynamics rather than static prescriptions of "what should be," they must be examined for stability over time. Although, for simplicity's sake, the analysis that follows depicts a static situation, appropriate steps for introducing dynamics can be developed.

Table 3–1

spends in the column person's office

		1	2	3	4	5	Σ
The per-	1	.57	.03	.13	.16	.11	1.00
centage of	2	.15	.47	.15	.08	.15	1.00
time that	3	.09	.06	.55	.15	.15	1.00
the row	4	.07	.01	.14	.64	.14	1.00
person	5	.10	.05	.14	.19	.52	1.00

time in the office of person 3. Note that persons 1, 2, 4, and 5 spend a total of 56 percent of the time with person 3, who is in his office only 55 percent of the time—a clear example of the fact that during some portion of the time, pairs of individuals are together with 3.

Now let us choose a propensity rule such as: If the members of a subgroup of individuals (say, 1 and 2) spend a greater percentage of their time with *all* of the remaining individuals in the system (3, 4, and 5) than these other individuals (3, 4, and 5) do with them (1 and 2), then the latter (3, 4, and 5) are a cluster and the former (1 and 2) are not.[20] The underlying notion of this rule is that the cluster attracts individuals from nonclusters, whereas the members of the cluster are not, in turn, attracted to the noncluster individuals. It is only one of many possible rules and is purely hypothetical and speculative. Specifically, 1 and 2 spend with 3, 4, and 5 the sum of the submatrix

	3	4	5
1	.13	.16	.11
2	.15	.08	.15

which totals to .78. Also, 3, 4, and 5 spend with 1 and 2 the sum of the submatrix

	1	2
3	.09	.06
4	.07	.01
5	.10	.05

which totals to .38. So 3, 4, and 5 possess our defined properties for a cluster, while 1 and 2 do not.

---

[20] An exception would be a tie result, and the rule could be extended to include this possibility.

There are fifteen different grouping situations for this five-by-five matrix, and for each one there will be one cluster and one noncluster.[21] All the combinations can be represented by the fifteen lines shown in Table 3–2.

Table 3–2

Cluster membership	Sum of time spent with noncluster	Noncluster membership	Sum of time spent with cluster
2345	.41	1	.43
1345	.15	2	.53
3	.45	1245	.56
4	.36	1235	.58
5	.48	1234	.55
345	.38	12	.78
13	.66	245	.75
14	.56	235	.76
15	.70	234	.75
145	.50	23	.77
135	.64	24	.80
134	.50	25	.81
34	.52	125	.85
35	.64	124	.82
45	.51	123	.80

We find that the individuals represented by the points 1 through 5 exhibit varying degrees of propensity to engage with their neighbors. Table 3–3 summarizes the number of clusters to which each individual belongs. The set-propensity measures are obtained from the ratio

$$\text{set propensity} = \frac{\text{number of clusters}}{\text{number of clusters} + \text{number of nonclusters}}$$

---

[21]Simple combinatorial math tells us this. Where C_r^n is read as the number of combinations of n people taken r at a time, we find

$$C_1^5 + C_2^5 + C_3^5 + C_4^5 = \sum_{r=1}^{n-1} \frac{n!}{r!(n-r)!} = 30$$

C_0^5 and C_5^5 are not included since they represent an empty set of no people or a set that includes all the people in the system. Then, since C_1^5 and C_4^5 are equivalent, as are C_2^5 and C_3^5, we divide thirty in half producing fifteen different situations to be evaluated $(n! = (n)(n-1)(n-2)\ldots(1); 1! = 0! = 1)$.

Table 3–3

| | Individual: | | | | |
	1	2	3	4	5
Clusters	7	1	9	9	10
Nonclusters	8	14	6	6	5
Set propensity	.469	.067	.600	.600	.670

When the individual enters the maximum number of clusters, set propensity $= 1$; when he finds no clusters, set propensity $= 0$. Person 2, finding only one suitable cluster, has a distinctly low set propensity; he will probably be singled out for study. In any case, management obtains a new way to view this system of five individuals. Appropriate models can be developed for each cluster. For example, cluster 1345 is very dense (as we will show in the next section). It should be treated as a system and modeled as a whole, since looking at only part of it would be unrealistic. Individual 2 can be studied in isolation; if, however, we desire to interrelate individual 2 with the rest of the organization, any pair of individuals of which 2 is a member would seem a reasonable place to start.

Set density. With each cluster we can associate a density measure, ρ. This value can be calculated by first finding the difference between the number of individuals entering into a specific cluster and the total time the group spent with the noncluster and then dividing that difference by the number of persons entering into the specific cluster. In equational terms:

$$\rho_i = \frac{(N_i - S_i)}{N_i}$$

where N_i is the number of persons in the ith cluster, and S_i is the sum of the proportion of the ith cluster's time that is spent with its noncluster group.[22]

Note that the maximum value of S_i is N_i and that when S_i is at its maximum (clearly, typical of a noncluster), $\rho = 0$. If $S_i = 0$, the ith cluster spends no time with its noncluster, and its density measure is then one. This would be the "perfect" cluster. The above relations are acceptable intuitively and, when applied to the various cluster configurations, provide management with additional information about the system under study. The appropriate ρ measures for our example are presented in Table 3–4. We note that persons 3, 4, and 5 are involved in the three top-ranking (i.e., densest) clusters and that 3 and 4

---

[22] For example, consider the cluster 3, 4, and 5; $N_i = 3$, $S_i = .38$; therefore $\rho = .87$.

Table 3–4

i	Cluster (i)	ρ_i	Density rank	i	Cluster (i)	ρ_i	Density rank
1	2345	.90	2	9	15	.65	11
2	1345	.96	1	10	145	.83	4
3	3	.55	13	11	135	.79	5
4	4	.64	12	12	134	.83	4
5	5	.52	14	13	34	.74	7
6	345	.87	3	14	35	.68	9
7	13	.67	10	15	45	.75	6
8	14	.72	8				

are part of the four top-ranking clusters. Management may benefit by turning its initial attention in that direction, but study of the data that have been presented will reveal additional possibilities.

Systems decomposition. For example, the large system can be decomposed into smaller systems when the cluster and noncluster are essentially unrelated to each other. If, in Table 3–2, the sum of time spent with noncluster and the sum of time spent with cluster are both below some reasonable limit (such as .10 or .05), then the cluster and noncluster might be treated as two independent subsystems.[23] Suppose that instead of 3, 4, and 5 spending .38 with 1 and 2, they had spent only .03, and that instead of 1 and 2 spending .78 with 3, 4, and 5, they had spent only .04. Then, the five-by-five matrix would decompose into a two-by-two matrix (for 1 and 2) and a three-by-three matrix (for 3, 4, and 5). The parts of the five-by-five matrix that are removed are treated as approximating zero.

The extreme situation for the five-by-five matrix would be one in which each individual is essentially a separate system. In this case, after matrix decomposition, only the diagonal values remain. Five separate subsystems result. It is critical to note that a faulty decomposition occurs if interrelations are incorrectly observed. For example, assume that the measure of relations is visits and that the five individuals never visit one another; if, however, they are in constant communication by telephone, essential relationships exist that have been missed. Such errors in decomposition are caused by oversights, by the overlooking of basic patterns of coordination and interchange. Some of these relations may be latent. In these terms, leadership may be viewed as the discovery of latent connectives and the ability to activate them. It should be

---

[23] This assumes that the small amount of time spent together does not include any critical interchanges. If it does, a different dimension for grouping should be used.

evident by now why the size of a system is not determined simply on the basis of convenience but is instead a fundamental organizational property.

Another example. It is not difficult to obtain measures of the actual amount of communication between all pairs of individuals and in this way to determine an alternative measure of set propensities. The example that follows presents yet another option. It will be based on expressed preferences for associating with other individuals in the system. We will assume that the information shown in Table 3–5 has been collected using sociometric techniques,

Table 3–5   Matrix of Expressed Preferences Converted into Probabilities

		with column individual:					
		1	2	3	4	5	α
Row	1	x	.18	.14	.03	.05	.40
individual's	2	.12	x	.07	.03	.08	.30
preference	3	.05	.04	x	.03	.03	.15
to work	4	.01	.02	.03	x	.04	.10
	5	.01	.02	.01	.01	x	.05
		.19	.26	.25	.10	.20	1.00

which are methods developed by the social sciences for measuring attitudes and behaviors. Clearly, the diagonal should be crossed out, although many individuals may well prefer themselves alone for an associate. The sum of all numbers in this matrix must equal one. Each row can sum to a different value —equivalent row sums would obscure the fact that no two people are likely to have the same strength of preference. The α column indicates the relative strength of individual preferences. Person 1 has the strongest preference; he cares about with whom he works eight times as much as person 5 does.

In this case, the hypothesis concerning set propensity (*SP*) can be based on the ratio:

$$SP = \frac{\text{within-group preference}}{\text{outside-group preference}}$$

If $SP > 1$, then the group is a cluster; if $SP < 1$, then the group is a noncluster. Consider, for example, the *decomposition* of the system into the groupings 12 and 345. As shown at the top of page 95, group 12 prefers to work with group 345:

Table 3–6

A	B	A for B	B for A	A for A	B for B	SP ≥ 1
1	**2345**	.40	.19	0	.41	$\dfrac{.41}{.19} = 2.16$
2	**1345**	.30	.26	0	.44	$\dfrac{.44}{.26} = 1.69$
3	**1245**	.15	.25	0	.60	$\dfrac{.60}{.25} = 2.40$
4	**1235**	.10	.10	0	.80	$\dfrac{.80}{.10} = 8.00$
5	**1234**	.05	.19	0	.76	$\dfrac{.76}{.19} = 4.00$
12	**345**	.40	.15	.30	.15	$\dfrac{.15}{.15} = 1.00$
13	245	.36	.25	.19	.20	
14	**235**	.46	.25	.04	.25	$\dfrac{.25}{.25} = 1.00$
15	234	.39	.33	.06	.22	
23	145	.34	.40	.11	.15	
24	135	.35	.31	.05	.29	
25	134	.25	.36	.10	.29	
34	**125**	.19	.29	.06	.46	$\dfrac{.46}{.29} = 1.59$
35	124	.16	.41	.04	.39	
45	**123**	.10	.25	.05	.60	$\dfrac{.60}{.25} = 2.40$

	3	4	5	
1	.14	.03	.05	
2	.07	.03	.08	Total = .40

Conversely, 345 prefer to work with 12:

	1	2	
3	.05	.04	
4	.01	.02	
5	.01	.02	Total = .15

And preferences internal to 12 are $.18 + .12 = .30$; those internal to 345 are equal to .15.

Table 3–6 has been constructed on the same basis as the above calculations, using A to stand for the smaller partition and B to stand for the larger partition of the matrix. The groups indicated by heavy type are (preference) clusters according to our definition whereby preference internal to the group is equal to or greater than the preference of the group for nongroup individuals. The strongest cluster is 1235. By interchanging person 4 for person 5, the ratio measure is cut in half. We observe further that person 4 has the lowest set propensity, followed by person 1. (See Table 3–7.) It is difficult to say whether

Table 3–7

	Individual:				
	1	2	3	4	5
Clusters	6	7	7	5	7
Nonclusters	9	8	8	10	8
Set propensity	.400	.469	.469	.333	.469

person 4's low measure presents a problem. After all, someone must have the lowest measure. Maybe all individuals are associated sufficiently well in this system so that no remedial action is called for. On the other hand, if we assume that person 4 has been cut out, then managerial effort might pay off if it resulted either in finding means to reestablish person 4's communication with the others or in transferring person 4 to a situation more congruent with his personality and substituting for him a new member who would fit better into the group and improve its performance.

Again, many kinds of invention are possible. Cluster definitions of systems properties should reflect managerial aims and shed light on such concepts as leadership, authority, and responsibility.

THE PROCESS OF IMPLEMENTATION

The implementation of solutions obtained from models of large systems is a matter of great concern to the manager. We emphasize large systems because the implementation process is not normally difficult with small systems. The fact that managerial perceptions of systems sizes have been changing accounts for the recent focusing of attention on implementation.

The set-propensity and set-density concepts that we have just examined illustrate that the definition of a system is highly variable. The model that is built for the system, on the other hand, is very specific. An excellent model built for the wrong system represents a futile exercise, and the manager must fail in trying to implement any solution obtained from such a model. There is no point in building a model that has no useful application or instructive base. Often, however, the manager finds it politic (because he does not have jurisdiction over a particular issue or because he wants to cover himself against a charge of not having used every possible approach) to let the model-builders work although he knows that their work does not relate properly to the system that he has in mind. Later, by faulting the model, he can have it set aside. Could the manager help in such a situation to make the model-building successful? Often he may not know how he can help, or he probably would. Providing the systems framework is usually too complex a task because the set relations are multiple and devious. But the underlying problem is that there are a number of critical phases involved in the process of model use that must be seen distinctly to facilitate the process.

Phase 1: Model-building. Its success is dependent entirely on an awareness of phases 2 and 3.

Phase 2: Manipulation or transformation of the model to a solution form. This is usually accomplished mathematically or by simulation; in any case, some form of change or transformation of the model must occur, or it would have been pointless to build the model.

Phase 3: Implementation. The original system that was modeled is altered in line with the solution or guidelines developed by the phase 2 transformation of the model.

These three phases are shown in Figure 3–6. We can see that the size of the system is related to the conception of what part of "reality" is relevant to the manager's interests. An aspect of the system is then modeled, the model solved, and (hopefully) the solution implemented, phases 1, 2, and 3, respectively. In Chapter 2, where we examined some characteristics of model-building, our major purpose was to provide a taxonomy for thinking about models. Now we have broadened this view to include model transformation and implementation. The three, when coordinated, add up to model use.

Figure 3–6

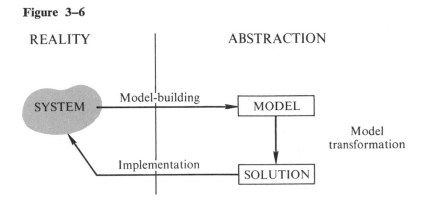

Theory or Practice

Another aspect of the implementation problem is revealed in a story told by Nikos Kazantzakis in his book *Journey to Morea*. He describes certain travelers who come upon two doors. One is marked "Paradise" and the other "Lectures on Paradise." The travelers choose the door marked "Lectures on Paradise." In so doing, they exemplify one of the major problems that characterize the implementation process—namely, that model-building or model transformation or both frequently overshadow the ultimate purpose of studying the system. Managers work with many individuals who prefer the door marked "Abstraction" to the one marked "Reality"; but the manager himself works on the reality side by choice.

Implementation, being the third phase in the sequence, requires the full participation of the first two phases, but there must be a return to reality (or practice) if implementation is to be successful. Awareness of all modeling phases from start to finish, or from theory to practice, is essential. There is no point in investing in the development of elaborate models that cannot then be returned to the system for operational implementation.

Model transformation is highly specialized work. It embodies the skills of mathematicians and the abilities of all technicians who, for example, know how to "fly" planes in wind tunnels or run programs on computers. The technical ability is abstract and removed from the specific problems that models actually treat.[24] The desire to *build* complex models or to use great technique to *trans-*

---

[24] A famous mathematician at Columbia University is said to have stated that a (pure) mathematician is like a tailor who may design suits for people with three arms and who believes firmly that it is someone else's problem to find a client with three arms. In other words, it is the "suit" that interests him and not the wearer. The applied mathematician, we may note, is more interested in "two-armed" suits and often is enlisted by the "wearer" to solve his specific problems of fit.

form them is reflected in Susan Ertz's telling comment that "millions long for immortality who do not know what to do with themselves on a rainy Sunday afternoon."[25] William Colihan has described the same attitude in a different way by characterizing our present society as "cruise oriented." "What the new customers want," he says, "is experience rather than result, the sense of journey rather than destination. . . ."[26] Since management does not have this cruise orientation and many scientists do, rapport between them is not achieved. Yet, because of the nature of managing, cruise-type talents can be put to good use if they are integrated with the rest of a team. Management's knowledge of how to use specialists is no different in this case of converting theory to practice than in many another situation more familiar to organizational life.

Schools of Management Thought

From this discussion of the implementation loop it is evident that personal differences of line managers (responsible for making decisions and getting work done) and staff project personnel (responsible for giving advice) will often differ as to where attention should be focused—that is, which model should be built. Mathematicians will tend to accent transformation; researchers will favor the abstracting process of model-building; and managers responsible for operations can be expected to concentrate on the final user's end of the loop, which we have called implementation. A "new breed" of individual, balanced and able in all three areas, may develop. Such research-oriented manager-technicians may be able to harmonize these varied aspects of model use but it will never be an easy task. Different personality traits seem to be required for each of the three phases.[27] In any case, communication and coordination among cooperating individuals must be emphasized if all three phases are to be balanced.

Unbalanced attention to any one area results from the way that responsibilities are assigned to managers, model-builders, and mathematicians. It is therefore no surprise that schools of thought about managing have tended to become polarized, indicating a preference for one or another approach to the

---

[25] Susan Ertz (b. 1894?), American novelist and short-story writer, in *Dictionary of Humorous Quotations,* Even Esar, ed. (New York: Bramhall House, 1949), p. 72.

[26] William J. Colihan, Jr., then Executive Vice President, Young & Rubicam, Inc., "Three Thoughts for the Future," a talk given at the Association of National Advertisers' 5th Annual Advertising Management Seminar, September 11–16, 1966, Princeton, N.J., p. 20.

[27] Various studies of the traits of different kinds of professionals have been published. It would be unreasonable to single out any one of them, but it is useful to note the often-mentioned comparison of the introversion of the scientist to the extroversion of the manager.

treatment of the phases. Differences of opinion exist about how to teach (i.e., pedagogy) and what to teach (i.e., phase emphasis). Furthermore, the solutions arrived at by the various schools tend to be different for each functional area. The reasons are apparent when we recognize the various roles played by human behavior in the different fields—for example, behavior is a critical variable in marketing but seldom crucial to production. In order to understand this better, let us examine some of the attributes of model-building, model-solving, and model-using.

Model-building accents creativity, tends to shun behavioral problems, stresses what can be modeled, and for obvious reasons is inclined to ignore what cannot be modeled—though this is changing slowly because of the Bayesian developments previously mentioned. In any case, it accepts mathematical attenuation as inevitable, highlights inductive reasoning,[28] and leans toward normative conclusions.

Model-solving demands a special kind of creativity; it is indifferent to behavioral or functional problems and is concerned only with formal problems of mathematics, logic, and computer programming. In many instances, creativity in model-solving produces generalizable model-solving routines from which technicians can then derive the formats for handling specific problems.

Model-using emphasizes behavioral problems, turning on the individual level to psychology (and the kind of material discussed in Chapter 14) and on the group level to sociology (and the kind of material presented in Chapter 15). It favors intuition derived from experience; often stresses what is not in the model, rejecting or compensating for attenuation; highlights deductive[29] reasoning; and leans toward descriptive use of models, interpreting even normative models in a descriptive fashion.

It is apparent that model-building and model-solving talents and ability have much more in common than either has with model-using, and a distinction is usually made that pairs the first two against the last. Although such polarization is undesirable, it exists. Its causes are inherent in the different work needs of model-builders, model-solvers, and model-users, in their different life styles and talents, and in the character of the methodology available to each. To achieve a balance between these polarities requires a view of management that is total—and authority to match. It is probably neither possible nor desirable to homogenize life styles and talents—to look for the same characteristics in a model-solver as in an operating manager or to draw no distinction between line responsibilities of the manager and the staff behavior of the model-builder.

---

[28] Inductive reasoning is working from facts to laws. In other words, discerning patterns from many specific instances, we might also say the direction of thought is from complexity to simplicity.

[29] Deductive reasoning is described as working from laws to facts—or, by our parallel (used in the footnote above) the direction of thought is from the simple to the complex.

Therefore, the answer would seem to be for everyone concerned to develop considerably more understanding of the function of coordination.

In Chapter 1 we used the triangle of relations to show how emphasis could be placed on functional areas of marketing, finance, labor, and production. We spoke about self-awareness in terms of managers studying management and also about the field of human behavior, which reaches out from management in several major directions: to the employee, the consumer, the stockholder, the vendor, and so forth. Here, too, an arbitrary segmentation of the management field appears, and polarization follows.

The reasons become readily apparent on closer examination. (1) In the *production* area, operations research and management science play a vital role. This is because the production function is visible, measurable, and highly determinate. The same considerations apply to logistical problems of distribution, maintenance, and replacement. Emphasis is on model-building. No matter how elaborate these models may be, their critics see them as examples of what Weaver called situations of simplicity (see p. 76). (2) On the other hand, statistical experiments, surveys, and individual interviews (whose antecedents were in such fields as psychology and education) are widely used in marketing, because preference is a personal expression whose causes are not visible. Preference is difficult to measure, not because it is stochastic, but because its basic dimensionality is hardly clear and observations of it are of doubtful stability. Stress is placed on analysis or model-solving. Without much effort, we can recognize the strong similarities to what Weaver called situations of disorganized complexity. (3) The nonstatistical behavioral approach (with developments in group dynamics, applied anthropology, economics, and sociology) finds its focus on interpersonal and organizational relations. For example, employer-employee relationships are interpreted as issues of morale, motivation, needs, and incentives. Such terms are part of the language of a cultural system that widely employs psychiatry, recognizes the importance of two-way communication links, treats the motivations of consumers (rather than their reactions, as in (2) above), and establishes union-management grievance and bargaining procedures. Implementation is at the core of these discussions, which deal with situations that Weaver termed organized complexity.

Reflecting these distinctions, blended with the three phases of model use, different approaches to the study of management have evolved.

1. The *case method* attempts to model total situations; that is, all three phases—model-building, transformation, and implementation—are included. Case studies, especially the renowned Harvard cases, have played an influential role in business education throughout the world. The student is, theoretically, given the opportunity to exercise critical judgment over all the stages in terms of the (good and bad) results that were achieved in each specific case.

He is then supposed to be able to generalize these specific "experiences" so that they can benefit him later when he is faced with comparable situations. To help him do so, work is given in comparative studies whose object is the determination of similarities in a variety of particular situations. Under these circumstances, model-building, in particular, tends to be diffuse. The empirical approach, characterized by the case method, has the many advantages of focusing on the total system, but it lacks the emphasis on theory development that has become increasingly rewarding in recent years. Since cases are necessarily homomorphic models of total systems, much of the surrounding reality that affects the total systems performance is missing, and, say the critics, the gestalt that is obtained is far too incomplete to serve educational purposes successfully.

2. The *management-science school* of managerial education places primary emphasis on model-building and model-solving techniques, especially, in most instances, on the former. Some schools favor more rigorous training of transformation techniques than others, but rarely are real creative abilities in mathematical model-solving expected. Instead, total competence in the range of existing model-solving routines is taught. Similarly, it is rare that really creative model-building is pursued; a routine research orientation is usually followed. Successful implementation is not assumed to be a problem, and so the nonstatistical behavioral area receives little attention. In the usual case, the fundamental notion is advanced that standard models (such as those of linear programming, queuing theory, inventory theory, game theory, information theory, etc.), if properly understood by managers, can organize their most serious problems by classifying these problems according to technique types. In the less usual case, the manager/technician approach to education replaces technique classification with problem classification and emphasizes the importance, not of finding problems for routine models, but rather of finding unique models for nonroutine problems. Although such an approach is more philosophical than technical, it has tended, because of the generally attenuated nature of mathematical models, to neglect the large system concept attempted by the case method. However, recent emphasis on simulation and on (statistical behavioral) Bayesian procedures has been reversing this effect, making management-science schools increasingly pragmatic and closing whatever gap might be said to exist between quantitative methods and behavioral approaches.

Some classifiers of these educational positions believe that proponents of the classical decision-theory approach (of the type that we treat in Chapter 4) constitute a separate school. In fact, however, underlying all management-science techniques (whether normative or descriptive) is the assumption of a decision-maker and a theory of decisions. It does not have to be recognized as such, but it exists nevertheless. Furthermore, as we explain in Chapter 6, a nonclassical decision-theory approach that utilizes (Bayesian) subjective estimation has been incorporating increasing amounts of statistical behavioral considerations into the classical approach.

3. A third approach to management education might be called the *organization-theory and human-behavior school*. Often these two subjects are treated as being allied but separate. But there seems to be no advantage in separating them because the community of interest between them is apparent, extending from the behavior of the individual, through that of informal groups, to that of formal organizations. Whatever its particular antecedents—whether sociology, psychology, anthropology, or even physiology—this approach clearly differs from the two previously mentioned.

The key concept of the human-behavior approach is that effectiveness in working with people can be taught, a tenet based on a mixture of scientific knowledge about behavior and principles of cause and effect in human behavior. Organization theory extends this tenet to group behavior and the interpersonal relations that lead to such terms as *leadership, authority,* and *responsibility.* Another aspect of this behavioral-science approach to studying management is its emphasis on the organization as an organism embedded in a particular culture.

It should be readily apparent, even from this brief discussion, that none of these schools can succeed ultimately without the others. How can we integrate these three approaches? We must postulate a fourth approach, which, despite some claims to the contrary, does not yet fully exist.

4. Let us call this fourth approach the *operational school*. It is predicated on the notion that management is multifaceted and requires the use of any considerations that facilitate development of a greater understanding about the management process. The fundamental notion of the operational school is that at any point in time a manager should be trained in terms of everything that is then known about managing. Cases can be used, behavior introduced, and mathematical models employed as seems desirable, allowing for as complete a distillation of experience and knowledge as possible. And it is only through recognition of the three-phase implementation loop that this school believes it can succeed.

Advocates of the operational school trace its beginnings as far back as those of any of the other schools. Its approach has been attributed to Henri Fayol and also to Frederick W. Taylor, but perhaps looking at it this way may be misleading. In fact, it is more reasonable to say that Taylor was a precursor of the management-science school. Fayol comes closer to representing the operational point of view, since he had a broad outlook, but the knowledge about managing that was available in his time was far less complete than it is today.

Those of the operational persuasion also point to the school's dynamism; more than any of the other schools, it is said to have continually adapted its philosophy over time. The reason for this is apparent. Since it is viewed as a synthesis of other fields, the operational school has assimilated new specializations as they have come from other schools of management.

Philosophically the operational point of view is the most acceptable, but in actuality it has turned out to be a smattering of unintegrated materials. The most important claim it can presently make is that persons educated by its method are broadly aware of developments and not committed to single positions. The likelihood is, however, that at some future time it will absorb all the subset schools in such a way as to permit research to continue along each of the various lines of thought, while providing a more ready assimilation of materials into a synthesis of management as a whole. Specialization, after all, has its customary utility if it can be *coordinated* through generalization.

The implementation concept provides an interesting basis for a deeper understanding of the various schools of management. The case method addresses implementation, but generally it by-passes complex, formal model-building and the transformation of the model through sophisticated technique. So the implementation achieved is highly artful and weak in theory. Case methodology is good in concept but too homomorphic in practice. The real essences of model-building, solving, and implementation are lost. The management-science method falters at the implementation stage but covers its tracks by assuming that a good manager can always utilize the clarity afforded by formal technique. It overlooks that large segment of phenomena dealing with human behavior. Behavioral science, while critical for implementation, does not deal with the issues of what logical model to solve and then use. All three approaches taken independently are less than one might hope for. The operational school, finally, is acceptable as a notion, but it must be made into a reality. One of the purposes of this book is to show that it can be supported if it ceases to rely solely on words and instead starts using the developments of which it speaks: the integration of the behavioral sciences with the three-phase abilities of quantitative methods viewed in as total a system as is feasible.

The Computer Effect

When we discussed measures of set propensity, we said it would not matter to us whether men or machines were participating. And that is still largely true. But computers have some special effects on model implementation that should be noted.

The computer has become one of the most active sources of communication, destinations for information, and participants in dialogue. Model-building often leads to computer programming; model transformation is greatly expedited by the computer. In some cases, interaction with the computer is essential (e.g., large simulations). Consequently, we need to modify our previous implementation model (Figure 3–6) to indicate that in most cases, in moving from the system to the model, an *interface* with the computer must be passed. Also, after model transformation has been accomplished, the implementation phase must again pass through the computer interface as the transformed model is brought back to the reality side. Thus we arrive at Figure 3–7.

Figure 3–7

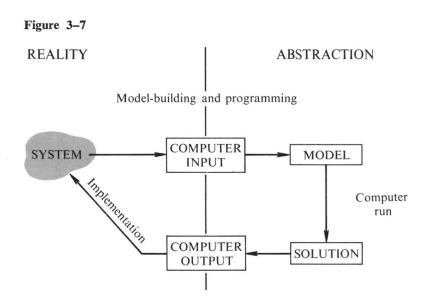

The computer speaks a simple language, rich in neither vocabulary nor syntax. But computer language is intensely logical; therefore, what is logical, even if it is highly complex, can be translated into this language with no difficulty. The language cannot, however, accept or render feelings or emotions, and these, consequently, must be converted to logical statements before the computer can be used. But this is no different from formal model-building. What is different is the linguistic distance, or lack of structural rapport, between the computer language and normal spoken language. The latter produces associated images—it encourages a gestalt—and the former does not. Benjamin L. Whorf brings up the example of a watchman who might smoke if he has been told that the gasoline drums by which he is surrounded are empty. *Empty* has two potential meanings to this watchman. One is "void of content," and the other is "not dangerous."[30] The gestalt of multiple meanings and ex-

---

[30] See Benjamin L. Whorf, *Collected Papers on Metalinguistics* (Washington, D.C.: Foreign Service Institute, Department of State, 1952), p. 27.

perimental associations becomes highly attenuated or lost entirely when the model is translated into computer language, where *empty* would be represented as a zero-valued variable. At the output end of the computer sequences, the model has been changed, and in the process of solution certain linguistic transformations may have taken place that are not recoverable. Thus, the computer's linguistics may have its own effect on what can be understood about the system. In a larger sense, there is reason to believe, from the existing knowledge of logic and linguistics, that use of the computer is influencing the structure of organizations, the nature of models, the role of management, and the implementation of solutions. This is particularly critical because most of management's difficult problems are such that computer participation in their solution is essential. Consequently, it is crucial that management examine its entire systems dialogue to determine the computer's effects.

Age of Systems

One important determinant of what will be the most useful design for the three model phases is the age of the system with which the manager is dealing. One aspect of systems age that has long commanded interest is reflected by the so-called growth curve (also known as an S-curve), which is shown in Figure 3–8. It was once thought that eventually such a model could be used to explain a great variety of systems phenomena in a relatively deterministic way, but the great expectations have been tempered with time. Nevertheless, strong insights about systems evolution are available from this model.

We have divided the curve into three stages: (1) early growth, which starts slowly but continually accelerates; (2) continuing, but decelerating, growth,

Figure 3–8   Three Systems Stages Represented by an S-curve

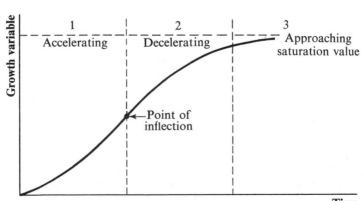

which occurs after the point of inflection is reached; and (3) very slow growth, which tapers off toward an asymptotic or saturation value. Many systems are in stage 2 for most of their existence. Implementation for a systems study in one stage will be different from that for a system in another. Compared to later stages, larger risks can and usually must be taken in the first stage. Model-building is difficult in this stage because there is minimum experience with the system. In second-stage systems, strong model use is possible to reduce risks and to perfect efficient procedures for obtaining the best possible results. In third-stage activities, only minor adjustments are generally required, and only small investments can be tolerated. Managers are averse to making any changes, since they are likely to produce only downturns. In general, the attitudes of managers toward model-building and model use are critically different in each stage for the general reasons given above. As a result of these attitudinal differences, the size of the system to be studied and the level of detail to be used in the model will vary according to the system's stage. To illustrate: new product introduction usually takes the system through stage 1 quickly, but intensive modeling has preceded the introduction. Most companies attempt to get triers for the new product rapidly to build high repurchase rates quickly. There is little time to solve new problems at this stage. But before the product is released, an estimate could have been made for the position of the inflection point. If the actual inflection point is too low, the product is usually withdrawn. Once the point of inflection is reached, the system can be called a maturing one. Model-building can begin again to bring about improvements and to maintain momentum against competitive forces. An established system, in stage 3, has lost momentum, but it may instead have achieved a reasonable level of stability. If it has, control systems based on appropriate policies frequently can be designed for stage 3. A fourth, or downturn, phase could also be added to the curve. Most business organizations try to get out of the system before these downturns occur. There are usually ample warning signs, but the implementation phase of model use in stages 2 or 3 should lay the groundwork for spotting stage 4 in time.

Previously we dealt with system size in terms of the number of entities encompassed within the system's bounds. Now another way has appeared to make a system larger or smaller for study. That way is temporal bounding, reflecting the stage at which a system exists in its development, the number of stages that it has yet to pass through in its morphology, and, accordingly, the length of the planning horizon that is incorporated in the models (i.e., how much of the future the models take into account). Clearly, implementation requirements are markedly different for young and old systems.

Another critical factor is stability. In highly stable systems (young and old), it is possible to plan far ahead, but it makes no sense to implement solutions that will be affected by the erratic and unpredictable conditions of unstable systems. Consequently, when we talk about the need to study larger systems, we must look to the possibility of stabilizing a system's behavior before attempting implementation based on an expanded planning horizon. In any case, temporal characteristics are certainly as influential in determining the appropriate size for a system as are the operating factors of marketing, production, finance, and so on.

IMPLEMENTATION THEORIES

A number of conclusions can be drawn about the how's, when's, and where's of implementation. For example:

1. If a solution can be implemented gradually, there is less risk than if it is implemented all at once, since the implementation can be stopped, if that seems desirable, before all resources have been committed. (By *gradually* we mean that one portion of the system is treated at a time, in a serial sense, rather than many portions being partially completed, in a batch sense.)

2. If steps can be reversed as they are taken, then implementation can proceed faster because there are relatively few sunk costs.[31] Given gradual implementation abilities and/or reversible steps, one can attempt implementations involving higher risks and do so with less faith in the adequacy of the solutions on which they are based.

3. Gradual transition from the use of simple models to that of complex ones may be another desirable implementation strategy. Marginal analysis (which is based on the effects of making small, incremental changes) can help to indicate the appropriate upper level of model complexity. The speed at which complexity should be increased will be sensitive to many other systems factors, but it can be adjusted in line with experience.

4. Another interesting implementation strategy is to run the present system and the proposed system simultaneously. If the proposed system turns out to be superior, then the present system is switched over to the new configuration. Such parallel implementation schemes can relieve insecurity, but one must expect to pay for this insurance with increased costs of model use.

5. The risks of implementing strategies are lower in decentralized organizations than in centralized systems, because decentralization usually makes for gradual implementation (gradual in the sense of point 1). On the other hand, the advantage of centralization is the efficiency that comes with being able to locate all information and management systems in a single place.

---

[31] By definition, sunk costs are irretrievable.

Participation and Managerial Style

Current theories of implementation are contradictory. Some say that the manager should participate in the entire loop of activities, others that the manager be brought in only at the final phase, the implementation stage, and then only if necessary.

The style of the manager will be important in this regard. For example, among the many distinctions that can and have been made are the ability to deal with details as compared with gestalts, the ability to keep an item separate from its background or to embed it in an appropriate context, analytic talents as opposed to synthetic ones, the facility to handle stress or avoid it, the visual orientation versus the cerebral one, and so forth. Subjects of this kind have received research attention, and a considerable literature exists, although it has hardly been exploited as yet in an effort to understand how the participants in a managerial situation can work together to achieve successful implementation. Churchman and Schainblatt, in a paper[32] that gave rise to later commentary,[33] talk of four different manager/researcher implementation modes.[34] These are the separate-function position, the communication position, the persuasion position, and the mutual-understanding position.

> The *separate functionalist* thinks of management and research as essentially separable functions. For him, implementation consists of designing the operational solution, which is a specification of the physical changes that must take place in the organization in order for it to be able to accommodate the optimal mathematical solution.
>
> The *communicator* emphasizes the need for creating more understanding on the part of the manager, i.e., for creating better lines of communication. While it is vital that the scientist appreciate this need for communication, a detailed understanding of the manager is not required in order to have the manager understand the scientist. That is, communication is a fairly direct process which is independent, for the most part, of the personality of the manager.
>
> In contrast to the communicator, the *persuader* views the implementation problem in terms of the manager's personality. Here the problem is not to provide for the manager's complete understanding of

---

[32] C. West Churchman and A. H. Schainblatt, "The Researcher and the Manager: A Dialectic of Implementation," *Management Science,* Vol. 11, No. 4 (February 1965) pp. B69–70.

[33] "Some Commentary on: The Researcher and the Manager: A Dialectic of Implementation," *Management Science,* Vol. 12, No. 2 (October 1965), pp. B3–B39.

[34] Churchman and Schainblatt define the problem of implementation as the determination of "what activities of the scientist and the manager are most appropriate to bring about an effective relationship between the two."

the scientist—since the former is too busy—but to ensure that the scientist understands enough about the manager so that the scientist can overcome managerial resistance to change *per se,* alter specific managerial attitudes, or persuade managers to accept recommendations.

Finally, the *mutual understander* takes a synthetic position which embraces the positive aspects of the previous positions in the effort to bring about the successful union of managers and researchers. The mutual understander argues that science and management cannot be separated; if science is to become a method of managing, then management must become the method of science.

Clearly the word which is central in displaying the contrariety of the four positions is "understanding." And we indeed mean something quite precise by the term. An individual understands a stimulus if he responds to the stimulus in an efficient manner relative to his ends. For example, the assertion "the manager understands the researcher" means that the manager reacts to what the researcher is trying to do in a manner that improves the manager's chances of attaining a purpose empirically assigned to him.

In another paper[35] Churchman describes the way in which differences in cognitive style affect the adoption of a research recommendation. He calls adoption without understanding *acceptance.* Persuasion is frequently used to gain acceptance. Adoption with understanding Churchman calls *implementation.*

In a different mode, Jan Huysmans identifies two ways of managerial reasoning—analytic and heuristic—and two corresponding types of implementation. The first is *sustained implementation,* where the manager expects the researcher to provide continuous support during implementation. The second is *autonomous implementation,* where the manager does not expect continuous support. Huysmans then offers the following observation based on laboratory experiments.

> When the cognitive-style propensities of operations researcher and manager do not agree, the manager may discard the operations researcher completely as a source of information: A research recommendation will not be implemented, no matter how persuasive and intuitively appealing the operations researcher's arguments may be, simply because the manager has no serious intention of considering it in the first place.[36]

---

[35] C. West Churchman, "Managerial Acceptance of Scientific Recommendations," *California Management Review* (Fall 1964), pp. 31–38.

[36] Jan H. B. M. Huysmans, "The Effectiveness of the Cognitive Style Constraint in Implementing Operations Research Proposals," *Management Science,* Vol. 17, No. 1 (September 1970), pp. 92–104. Quote is from p. 101.

Perception and Creativity

"Who told thee that thou wast naked?" —Genesis 3:11.

The system is *perceived* reality, and our perceptions are circumscribed in many ways by what we know about ourselves. The system and the application of a model's solution to it are separated only by the three-phase implementation loop, yet that can represent a very great distance. Implementation demands creativity or, often, improvisation; the manager must be open to opportunity. Implementation requires perception abilities; an unstable system can easily shift and so render a formerly acceptable solution no longer acceptable. Added to all of this, management must be fully aware of the costs of implementation.

Churchman's reference to *mutual understanding* (previously mentioned) is closely related to managers' and scientists' appreciation of communication and, in turn, to their educability. Much will be decided by who talks to whom, when, and how.[37] In fact, is any communication possible? Can the manager talk science? Can the scientist talk management? The key to these problems seems to lie in the ability of the manager to communicate his needs to the model-builders and then to be able to understand and evaluate the utility of the solutions for the system. Managerial *learning* is an *indirect* form of implementation that can be achieved.

Now we come to a third variant of our implementation loop model—namely Figure 3–9. Here implementation is not direct. Instead, the manager is

Figure 3–9

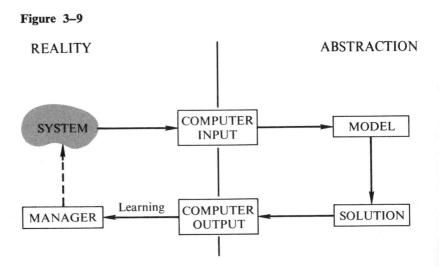

REALITY   ABSTRACTION

---

[37] See pp. 633–37 and pp. 656–60.

changed; his perceptions are altered, and as a result the system is changed.[38] However, whether the solution succeeds directly by changing the system or indirectly by changing the manager is immaterial; in either case, implementation has been achieved.

The New Breed of Student

The communication problem may never be fully solved, but it may simply disappear. Schools are now trying to teach the same individual both managerial and scientific know-how. Although the implementation phase is strongly management oriented and model-building and model-solving strongly science oriented, the new student can at least recognize the function of all parts of the loop to obtain the closure required for analysis and synthesis. Executives who are strong on experience and now are trained in the new methodologies can also play an important role in this transition to effective model use.

On the other hand, there is evidence that mathematical and computer-science training, when overemphasized, can produce shallow, technocratic behavior. Managers so trained tend to become introverted and specialized in the roles assigned to them by the organization. Hopefully, recognition of and exposure to behavioral sciences will overcome the deficiencies inherent in being known best as a well-trained quantitative or computer type. But it is far from certain that one person *can* embody simultaneously intuition, action orientation, mathematical reasoning, computer programming and language aptitudes, and the other abilities implicit in achieving successful model use. Even so, any steps taken in this direction should prove entirely rewarding.

SUMMARY

The third chapter focuses on the importance of defining and identifying the characteristics of a system. In this sense, models are related to systems and systems to reality. The system is explained as a perception of reality and the model as one of many possible perceptions of the system.

Model use, which is called the implementation problem, begins with an attempt to model the system and is completed when the model's solution has been applied to the system to change it in accordance with the manager's objectives. Inability to define the relevant system can prevent adequate imple-

---

[38] Remember that we stated (p. 73) that the system is a perception of reality.

mentation; even if a credible model has been built, it will have been constructed for the wrong system. A model of insufficient scope can cripple the implementation effort.

The size and complexity of the system, as viewed by the manager, are translated into the adequate complexity of the model. The managerial level at which particular problems are tackled, as well as managerial style, affect the design and ultimate use of the model. Some background is given concerning the history of choices that have been made between complexity and simplicity. Then the point is made that technology and new social forces have pushed management to recognize larger and more complex systems than before. The questions of how large a system must be studied by management and in how much detail are approached in several ways, including consideration of the fact that certain systems breakdowns produce crises that can be handled only through comprehensive large systems management.

The definition of specific systems becomes especially difficult with the introduction of human behavior. Systems membership is examined, and several measures (such as set propensity and set density) are introduced to explain the overlapping systems configurations that coexist. Depending on the particular measures of association that are used, individuals (men and machines) will appear to aggregate into different groups. Implementation will be more readily achieved with some of these models of the system than with others.

As we have said, to achieve implementation, the relevant system must be selected for modeling. This selection and model-building are called phase 1 of the implementation loop. The second phase is the (essentially mathematical) transformation of the model to provide a solution. And phase 3 sees the actual implementation of the solution as it is applied to the original system. The various approaches used to study management and to educate managers are shown to accent certain of the three phases. The major schools of thought that are treated are the case method, the management-science school, the organization and human-behavior approach, and, finally, a fourth point of view, the so-called operational school which attempts to integrate the various positions. We show that only through recognition of the three-phase implementation loop can the operational approach hope to succeed.

The introduction of people into the systems definition and the relationship of men and machines lead to a reformulation of the implementation loop. In this more complex view, the computer is added as part of the model-use cycle. Questions of computer language arise, and they must be taken into consideration if successful implementation is to be achieved.

Another aspect of the implementation process is related to the age of the system to be modeled. It is explained that different approaches arise according to the system's age because age affects what information is available about the system, how stable the system is, what managerial attitudes are likely to be, and so on.

In concluding the chapter, we advance a number of theories about implementation. They are related to speed and scope of implementation as well as management's perceptions and creativity. Great demands are placed on management, which, it is hoped, a new breed of student, versed in all phases, could cope with. Since there are reasons to doubt that any such new type of manager will actually appear (although steps in this direction will occur), an indirect implementation effect of learning on the part of the manager should greatly assist in the improvement of model use.

EXERCISES

1. As the size of a system increases, it becomes harder to study or manage. Would this reasoning apply to studying a city system as compared with a state system or a federal system? Explain your answer and give some examples of your own.

2. In what way does the system to which a production scheduling model applies relate to the marketing of the production output? How does this reflect the problem-oriented view of a larger system?

3. Is it true that effective crisis management cannot be achieved unless the system is modeled on a scale large enough to encompass all the critical interdependencies? Discuss this notion and speculate about where in the organizational hierarchy responsibility for such matters should be vested.

4. Explain how technological and social changes have forced the manager more and more to perceive larger systems as being relevant to his needs.

5. When people are included in a system, various overlapping views of that system emerge. Explain why this effect occurs and give some examples of overlapping membership clusters. Describe some of the membership clusters to which you belong. Set up a matrix of relations for any one of them. What measures of association would you apply?

6. What matrix relations would you expect for the crew and captain of a sailboat? For a teacher and the members of a class?

7. Analyze the matrix shown below for its set-propensity and set-density characteristics.

	A	B	C	D
A	.02	.06	.08	.84
B	.06	.08	.84	.02
C	.08	.84	.02	.06
D	.84	.02	.06	.08

What kind of situation might this matrix describe?

8. The three-phase implementation process can be applied to such a mundane subject as a shopping list. Explain this and describe the difficulties at all phases. (Note that the system you choose for modeling your shopping list will not be obvious and requires total description, which will not come easily.)

9. Describe the different schools of management thought. Explain your preferences and then, taking a step back, explain how you think a unified approach that can be subscribed to by all positions can be developed. Do you think that such a school can emerge?

10. What relationship does the age of a system have to the manager's view of the workable size of that system for modeling?

11. Various theories of implementation have been suggested for successful model use. Comment on these, describing the situations in which each of these theories might be effective.

12. Do you believe that a new breed of manager can emerge, synthesizing the capabilities of the three phases of implementation?

Part II

DECISION-MAKING

The Framework of Managing

MODEL-BUILDING AND MODEL USE

PART II
DECISION-MAKING

Each major management function (planning, policy-making,
and organizing) has a decision basis. Decisions are the
foundation, the unit structures on which all management
activities are dependent. We can define planning as
a special configuration of decision model and policy-making
as another particular set of decision circumstances;
so a rational approach to management theory
must begin with the decision-making concept.

In treating decision making as synonymous with managing, I shall be referring not merely to the final act of choice among alternatives, but rather to the whole process of decision. Decision making comprises three principal phases: finding occasion for making a decision; finding possible courses of action; choosing among courses of action.

—From Herbert A. Simon, *The New Science of Management Decision* (New York: Harper & Row, 1960), p. 1.

Decision-making is the root process of all managing. It is *the* generalized activity—common to all management. While this point is unlikely to produce disagreement, there is some question as to the extent to which the manager can use scientific methods in reaching his decisions. The question is often asked: Is normative decision-making what is meant by rational managing? One major school of management says it is; but another says it cannot be, because intuition based on descriptive model use is the ultimate basis for decision-making.

We do not believe that one point of view tells the whole story. We can accept the fact that managing involves the whole spectrum, proceeding from the "mathematical school" through the intuitive approach to decision-making. With this in mind, we have made decision-making Part II of this book. We refer to decision-making not in the narrow sense of techniques for reaching mechanical solutions, but in the larger sense that encompasses realistic criteria for making decisions that satisfy managerial practice and needs. Decision models, in this wider sense, are to managing as roots are to a tree, as the foundation is to a building. Thus, planning, controlling, and organizing—dealt with in Parts III, IV, and V, respectively— are not readily understood without decision-making; neither are they decision-making. They are dependent on it, as language is on vocabulary and syntax; yet we must not forget that it takes a Shakespeare to transform language into great literature.

The Framework of Managing

MODEL-BUILDING AND MODEL USE

DECISION-MAKING

Chapter 4
The Decision Behaviors of Management

The structure of decision models should be examined
in detail. Controllable variables interact with uncontrollable
variables to produce results that are related to management's
objectives. The type of decision model that can be used
depends on the nature of the forecast that can be made for
the uncontrollable factors. For each type of decision model,
different criteria have been developed to permit a rational
decision to be made.

Chapter 4

THE DECISION
BEHAVIORS
OF MANAGEMENT

Making decisions is not the only thing that management does, but it is surely one of its most fundamental functions. We can make a simple flow chart of management's roles as in Figure 4–1.

Figure 4–1

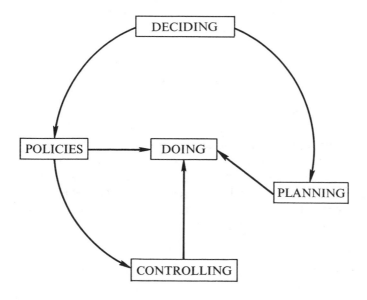

First, let us treat deciding; then we can expand our horizons to include policy-making and planning; finally, controlling will be spelled out. Doing is the target of all these activities. Its presence as the end of a means-end chain will be implicit and often explicit throughout our discussions. These broad functions include many other management activities, such as organizing, coordinating, staffing, and leading—all of which are related to deciding. In fact, organizing can be interpreted as setting up the actual structure of components to provide the flows shown in the figure.

SCIENCE AND DECISIONS

Science helps us take a close look at management's decision-making function. Science is playing an increasingly important role in developing objective decision methods, which can be ranked along a continuum by their level of involvement with *theory* and scientific procedure. At one extreme is the totally objective, scientific approach to decision-making; at the other, intuition, experience, and subjective knowledge take over the decision process.

To achieve *actionable* decisions for *real* problems, a mixture of these two extremes is generally used. Still, there can be no doubt that the subjective-judgmental approach has dominated decision-making in the past and continues to do so (although less than formerly). The manager seldom can explain perfectly the basis for his hunches, but he can make remarkable inroads in this direction. The notions of heuristics[1] coupled with utility theory[2] have recently brought the manager closer to science. Economists, econometricians, social scientists, sociometricians, and management scientists are increasingly motivated to probe the nature of individual as well as institutional and organizational decision-making. Although they have approached the problem in many different ways, a model has emerged that all concede is useful. It constitutes a body of *objective* decision methods that can parallel and reinforce intuitional approaches to complex problems, thus reducing reliance on strictly intuitive decision-making.

The new decision methods have roots that can be traced at least as far back as Aristotelian logic. A substantial contribution came from the work of Bertrand Russell and Alfred North Whitehead (in their *Principia Mathematica* of 1912). Later developments in symbolic logic, as reflected in the work of Carnap, Rosenbloom, and others (circa 1930), were also critical. These approaches stressed linguistic logic, which (as Russell, among others, later noted) can be converted perfectly into mathematical descriptions of the same

---

[1] Pp. 437–38.
[2] Pp. 170–71.

problems. Gradually the search for "ideal" forms of objective, logical expression yielded to the logician's ultimate weapon, mathematics, with increasing success. Matrices, for example, are one of the most convenient methods of representing logical statements. They also facilitate the bounding of systems into logical sets and subsets. Consequently, the matrix form is widely used for understanding the structure of management decisions—and, necessarily, the concepts of matrix construction are critical for our purposes.

Because middle and lower management levels are so heavily involved with information processing, reliance on the computer has also become increasingly evident. The almost simultaneous development of computing systems and the mathematics of decision models is not surprising. For example, it is interesting that George Boole in the mid-nineteenth century (about 2,200 years after Aristotle) created a form of mathematical logic that built on Aristotelian logic in an ingenious way necessary for both the design of systems models and the construction of appropriate computing systems. The existence of high-speed computers has been accompanied, in turn, by new forms of logical, objective methods. It is clear that these new methods are not discovered (or created) as independent events but are part of an evolutionary process that is motivated by the strong desire of managers to improve the decision process.

Management level. The decision-maker's involvement with science varies according to the management level of the decision. Lower-level decision-making lends itself to scientific procedures (for reasons that are fairly obvious but which we will detail, nevertheless, as we proceed). Reduction in the use of intuition is less characteristic at the upper decision levels of the organizational hierarchy, since formal methods do not seem to work as well there. Therefore, although the direct use of scientific method has grown over all phases of the decision-making process, it has begun to affect upper-level decision processes primarily in indirect ways.

As the validity of applying scientific decision methods to enterprise problems has become apparent, managers have provided support and encouragement for these methods. Nevertheless, the role of decision theory in the business context is recognized to be in its infancy. The real significance of these methods, operating at different managerial levels, is yet to be understood; the nature of the methods to be applied, especially at the upper hierarchical levels, is still to be evolved; the characteristic problems of each level have not yet been classified; and the extent of the various payoffs is unknown. Perhaps one of the most important effects on every level of management is the extent to which these new methods modify the situations that exist and create new values, new objectives, and new configurations. In other words, decision methods not only solve existing problems in new ways but change the nature of problems that exist. In response, the profile of the manager's job is changing at all levels.

A Paler Shade of Gray

Right or wrong exists in logic and in mathematics—but *only* in terms of the internal correctness and consistency of the method employed. A real-world problem can seldom be resolved strictly within such an either/or framework. External factors keep intruding, and the model is always incomplete. Answers must be interpreted, not believed literally. So real problems have to be defined with a sense of integrity for reality, which means that, as much as possible, *all* relevant factors and relations must first be identified and then made explicit. These are always the minimum requirements for model-building.

The manager, at any level, cannot take the isolated position of the logician. For him there are degrees of right and wrong; correctness is not simply a question of internal consistency. The manager's actions may be either/or, but his reasons for taking action will almost always be a blend of opposing forces and complex values. Before he can utilize decision methods, the manager must establish these values. It is possible too that he may ultimately reject the use of decision models. And suitable decision models may not even exist to cope with the type and complexity of many real situations. The manager may prefer objective methods to subjective decision approaches—but only so long as they provide him with superior help in reaching a decision, never when they bully him through pretense or stymie him through their inadequacy.

THE STRUCTURE OF DECISIONS

Decision-making is *always* a normative process. Clearly, for a decision problem to exist there must be choice based on at least one pair of alternatives. Decision theory is an objective, analytic approach utilizing normative properties of decision models to indicate which alternative "ought" to be used. There are no shades of gray until the manager exercises his overriding judgment.

Decision theory provides a base by means of which *any* problem can be represented in an entirely abstract or generalized manner. The components of a generalized decision are the strategies and environments that produce results.

Strategies

Strategies are composed exclusively of *controllable factors*—that is, a strategy is an arrangement of those variables in the system that are *entirely* under the control of the manager. For example, assume the existence of a control panel with a given number of knobs. Each knob can be used by the manager, and each knob setting affects the results the manager will get. Any particular configuration of these knob settings is called a strategy. We call the ith configuration of these factors (or knobs) the ith strategy, or x_i.

Environments

Environments are composed of *uncontrollable* factors in the system. Assume that another panel exists with a given number of knobs but that the manager *cannot* reach these knobs; he cannot influence their settings, and frequently he has no advance notice of what settings will appear.

We must go further. The environmental knobs are under no intelligent control, not that of our manager nor that of any competitive entrepreneurial force.[3] They are set at random in accordance with patterns imposed by natural events. We call the jth arrangement of these factors (or knobs) the jth environment, or z_j. We could also call such environments states of nature (e.g., the jth state of nature). The name is appropriate since it properly implies the existence of natural phenomena that are exogenous to the enterprise—phenomena that are independent of the manager's tools and the technology of the enterprise.

Although he lacks control over the z_j's, the manager can at least attempt to predict the likelihood that any specific environment will occur. We should note, however, that it is not at all unusual for the manager to have no idea about the *nature* of the unreachable (i.e., uncontrollable) environmental knobs. This, of course, makes predicting infinitely more difficult. Clearly, the implications of these distinctions for decision-making are of enormous importance.

Results

R, the result, is an outcome that will be observed when a given x and a specific z appear together. For example, x_i and z_j will yield the result designated R_{ij}.

Sometimes *several* kinds of *result* (e.g., sales volume, brand share, and profit) must be considered in reaching a decision. For these cases, a multidimensional specification of results is required. The dimensions used to specify the results are *dictated by the manager's objectives*. He observes only those outcomes that are relevant to his objectives. In the same sense, he considers only those strategies and environments that can affect the results he is concerned about.

Let us return to the control panel for a moment. The manager has controllable knobs and, in addition, one or more dials from which he can read

---

[3] We shall ignore the competitive factor until Chapter 5. Many decision problems are not sensitive to it, but, for those that are, it is of sufficient importance to warrant our devoting an entire chapter to decision-making under competition.

results of various knob settings. (See Figure 4–2.) So he can manipulate the knobs until the dials show the outcomes that reflect his objectives.[4]

Figure 4–2   A Representation of the Decision Factors That Produce an *Actual* Result

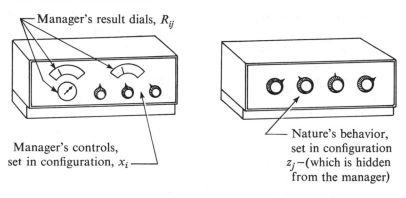

Manager's result dials, R_{ij}

Manager's controls, set in configuration, x_i

Nature's behavior, set in configuration z_j –(which is hidden from the manager)

ANALYTIC DECISION MODEL

We can write a general equation to describe the relationships we have just been discussing. It is:

$$R_{ij} = f(x_i, z_j) \tag{1}$$

This equation states that the result, R_{ij}, is a function of the ith strategy and the jth environment. Since the function is unspecified, it is indicated by $f(\ )$.

We can also represent this generalized decision system by means of a decision matrix—for example the one in Table 4–1.

Table 4–1   Matrix of Results

Environments:

	z_1	z_2	z_3	z_4
Strategy x_1	R_{11}	R_{12}	R_{13}	R_{14}
Strategy x_2	R_{21}	R_{22}	R_{23}	R_{24}
Strategy x_3	R_{31}	R_{32}	R_{33}	R_{34}

---

[4] We will consider the problem of multidimensional results in Chapter 7. Until then, only a single result will be treated in our discussions.

Problem-Solving

At the intersection of a given pair of i and j configurations, there is a specific result. This intersection outcome, R_{ij}, is sometimes derived by means of direct observation. At other times, a (costly) experiment might be required. And at still other times, if theory exists in specific mathematical form, such as $R_{ij} = ax_i + bz_j$, then that model can be used to generate all the intersection values for the total array.

These approaches are readily identified with scientific method. There is no reason, however, to require that the intersection values of the decision matrix be generated exclusively by objective or scientific methods. Since such methods may be impossible or infeasible to use because of exorbitant cost, the array of results can be guessed at or estimated by the manager on the basis of a minimum amount of pertinent information. The combination of the rational decision framework with intuition and judgment to complete the decision matrix is another example of a "gray" area that is not destructive of either the intuitive or the objective approach. On the contrary, it utilizes the best elements of each approach to achieve a new synthesis.

Each decision model is associated with some specific *period of time;* consequently, every result, R_{ij}, is a cumulative outcome. In other words, an end result is achieved over a period of time during which the strategic variables and the environmental variables are allowed to interact with one another. The decision period, especially when informal methods are used, can play a critical role in distorting the situation. For example, the periods for evaluating can differ, resulting in a meaningless comparison, or the wrong basic period can prevail. The formal approach helps to highlight such discrepancies. In either case, the period must be chosen so that a meaningful result can occur and an adequate forecast be developed.

Forecasts[5]

We cannot see the settings on nature's control panel, but we can at least try to surmise what settings will occur. To do so, we require likelihood measures to describe the probability that one or another environment will exist. Let p_j represent the probability that the jth environmental configuration (z_j) will

---

[5] Forecasting becomes one of management's most difficult problems as the significance of the problem and the level at which the decision must be made increase. The uncontrollable factors are of two types: competitive, which are under the intelligent manipulation of the opponent; and environmental, such as the forces of the economy or nature, as represented by weather and earthquakes.

occur.[6] There is a p_j for each environmental configuration (z_j) such that the Σp_j across all possible environments, $j = 1, 2, \ldots$, will equal one—that is, $\Sigma_j p_j = 1$.[7]

The ability to predict the occurrence of z_j's is dependent on what is known about the system of uncontrollable factors. When the decision problem is not unique, many historical precedents may exist. And if the system is also of a stable sort, then meaningful forecasts generally can be made. Since problems tend to be more stable at the lower managerial levels, they are also more amenable to forecasting at those levels. Such stability is particularly true in the realm of technology—that is, of machine, instrument, and process systems.

The reliability of forecasts begins to deteriorate as the problem involves more behavioral factors and its level rises on the managerial ladder. Nevertheless, correlation and other predictive models can sometimes uncover stable patterns to aid in forecasting behavioral and other complexities, even at higher managerial levels. A variety of forecasting models exists. Many of them are so sophisticated in the mathematical sense that they give a false appearance of providing "truth." If nothing else works, management can at least forecast on a hunch basis—it does so all the time, and the only difference here (i.e., where a formal decision model is being used) is that we request objective statements. (We shall continue at a later point with this discussion; see pp. 222–26.)

DECISION CRITERIA

A fundamental rule is required for reaching a decision—that is, for selecting the optimal strategy from a set of alternatives. The rule will differ according to the type of decision problem to be resolved. Consider the decision matrix of Table 4–1. It was written in totally abstract terms—with R_{ij}'s, x_i's, and z_j's. And we have now added p_j's. There can be many sets of numbers for these variables and unlimited variety in the size of the matrix used. But the variety can be categorized, and, as will be explained shortly, there is only a limited number of types of decision problems that may be encountered. Each type has associated with it a different decision criterion.

Decision models can be described and classified in terms of the *conditions*

---

[6] The letters i and j, as we have been using them, are called "dummy" designations, which means that they are totally general and can represent any specific i or j value, such as $i = 1, 2, \ldots$ or $j = 1, 2, \ldots$.

[7] The Greek symbol Σ (sigma) is used to represent the mathematical operation of summing. $\Sigma_j p_j$ thus means $p_1 + p_2 + \ldots + p_n$, for all values of the dummy of summation j (here $j = 1, 2, 3, \ldots, n$) that apply.

of the decision components—for example, the x_i's, z_j's, and so forth—but a decision problem cannot be classified until the forecast of p_j's is specified as (1) being unknowable, or (2) consisting of only partial information, or (3) being based on a given, *believable* set of values.

Let us turn our attention for the moment exclusively to the third situation, where a believable forecast exists. Assume that the set of p_j's has been derived and provides a probability distribution that is believed to be relatively *accurate* as well as sufficiently *stable. Under these specific circumstances,* it can be shown that the *maximum expected value* (defined below in Equation (2)) is the appropriate decision criterion to use. (We use the maximum value when the results are given in units of benefit, the minimum value when the results are stated as costs.)

Utilizing matrix form, we can now set down systematically the total decision structure for a problem with i strategies and j environments, shown here in Table 4–2. The expected value is simply an arithmetic average, so for the ith strategy:

$$EV(R_i) = p_1 R_{i1} + p_2 R_{i2} + p_3 R_{i3} + \ldots + p_j R_{ij} = \Sigma_j p_j R_{ij} \qquad (2)$$

Table 4–2   Matrix of Results

Forecast of likelihood:	p_1	p_2	p_3	$\cdots$	p_j	
Environments:	z_1	z_2	z_3	$\cdots$	z_j	Expected Values
Strategy x_1	R_{11}	R_{12}	R_{13}	$\cdots$	R_{1j}	$EV(R_1)$
Strategy x_2	R_{21}	R_{22}	R_{23}	$\cdots$	R_{2j}	$EV(R_2)$
.	.	.	.		.	.
.	.	.	.		.	.
.	.	.	.		.	.
Strategy x_i	R_{i1}	R_{i2}	R_{i3}	$\cdots$	R_{ij}	$EV(R_i)$

Thus, the decision matrix is compressed by the expected value criterion so that each row is converted into a single value and the total array into a single column of expected values. The complete decision criterion is: select activity i such that *max* $EV(R_i) = $ *max* $(\Sigma_j p_j R_{ij})$ is obtained.

Accordingly, the manager can now search the single column of expected values for the maximum (or minimum) expected value. He will then select whichever strategy is associated with this value—so long as he can accept the model of the decision problem as a realistic representation. Should this not be the case because some considerations are faulty or lacking (e.g., missing variables, incorrect inferences or distorted measurements), then human judgment will intervene. The model will then be corrected if possible, and if not, the manager will override it with justification.

Example 1: The Make Versus Buy Decision

After careful study, a large manufacturer has determined his payoff matrix (Table 4–3) for a make versus buy decision on a subassembly part. The relevant environments have been stated to be

z_1: There will be available manpower to do the job.

z_2: Some extra manpower will have to be recruited.

z_3: All the necessary manpower will have to be recruited.

Table 4–3   Decision Matrix of Costs (in thousands of dollars)

	z_1	z_2	z_3
x_1: Buy	100	100	100
x_2: Make	60	110	125

The environmental manpower classifications, while arbitrary, presumably were chosen to represent specific conditions that might be expected to exist depending on certain contractual demands that may be made on the company, the product demand that results, labor turnover conditions, and so forth.

The managers knew that determining the probabilities of these environments was not going to be an easy matter. Therefore, they assembled a panel of experts (from among themselves) to estimate the probabilities. The panel's results were as follows: $p_1 = .25$, $p_2 = .35$, and $p_3 = .40$. It is worth noting that they first agreed to rank the environments by their relative likelihoods. This resulted in total consensus that $z_3 > z_2 > z_1$ (where $>$ indicates "is more likely than"). After this, they worked out the set of values above by averaging the group's individual estimates and correcting them so that they would sum to one. The decision matrix computations were

$$EV \text{ (buy)} = 100$$

There is no need to compute this average since one of the advantages of the "buy" strategy is its invariance to the environments.

$$EV \text{ (make)} = .25(60) + .35(110) + .40(125) = 103.5$$

Since the objective is to minimize the cost of the part, the company would be obliged to *buy* this part.

However, many reasons may exist for overriding this normative model solution. For example, it may have been impossible to represent properly in the model the cost of losing the chance to gain know-how through making the part, the lower degree of control over delivery and quality that comes from buying the part, and so forth. Management not only retains the right to override the normative solution it has in hand, but it has a responsibility not to accept that solution at face value. Only after the model has been appraised and understood for what it is and what it is not can management blend its subjective evaluations with the objective solution to reach a proper managerial decision.

SENSITIVITY ANALYSIS

An extremely important tool of management is sensitivity testing. It is really a modeling concept rather than a specific analytical technique. Its purpose it to determine how much change can be made in various estimates before a change occurs in the indicated solution. Alternatively, it is a way of finding out which estimates are "sensitive" (i.e., will, when changed only slightly, cause the solution to change) and which ones are not. Since sensitive estimates are solution "swingers," they deserve careful attention.

Sensitivity analysis can be applied to the forecast estimates, p_j's, to the results, R_{ij}'s, or to both, depending on the manager's view of what in the system is sensitive. Consider the "make or buy" example just given. First, the cell entries of the matrix are potentially sensitive estimates, and therefore worth analyzing; second, the probabilities for the environments are also candidates for sensitivity analysis. Thus, sensitivity analysis accepts as correct the model (variables and relations) but not the numbers assigned to parameters, variables, and results. We should note that although sensitivity analysis can be applied to any one specific change in an estimate, its real strength lies in the mapping out of all regions of stability and of change.

We will illustrate the change in a single estimate first. What if, we ask, the probabilities were in fact: $p_1 = .28$, $p_2 = .30$, and $p_3 = .42$? Answer: the EV (make) would be 102.3, which is not very different from 103.5. In this case, the sensitivity probe does not change the solution, and although this result is useful, broader generalization is really required. Therefore, let us consider the concept of sensitivity mapping. What does shake things up? If nothing does, then the solution is reasonably invariant to estimating errors. To map out the sensitivity characteristics of this system,[8] let us use some simple algebraic and geometric considerations. First, note that $p_3 = 1 -$

---

[8] For more general considerations, see Martin K. Starr, "A Discussion of Some Normative Criteria for Decision-Making Under Uncertainty," *Industrial Management Review*, Vol. 8, No. 1 (Fall 1966).

$p_1 - p_2$. Second, the point at which the decision for make or buy can change either way (i.e., the *point of indifference*) is when *EV* (make) = *EV* (buy). With these observations in mind, let:

$$p_1(60) + p_2(110) + (1 - p_1 - p_2)(125) = 100$$

then,

$$60p_1 + 110p_2 + 125 - 125p_1 - 125p_2 = 100$$

whence,

$$25 = (125 - 100) = 65p_1 + 15p_2$$

Figure 4–3 shows this line of indifference. All space to the right of the line is equivalent to a *make* decision; all to the left is *buy*. Next, note the diagonal line connecting $p_1 = 1$ and $p_2 = 1$. All points on this line and to the left and below it are valid—that is, $p_1 + p_2 + p_3 = 1$. Roughly half of this area results

Figure 4–3

* NOTE: p_1 must be changed by .07, holding p_2 fixed, before the point reaches the switch line. On the other hand, p_2 must be changed by .23, holding p_1 fixed, to have the point reach the switch line.

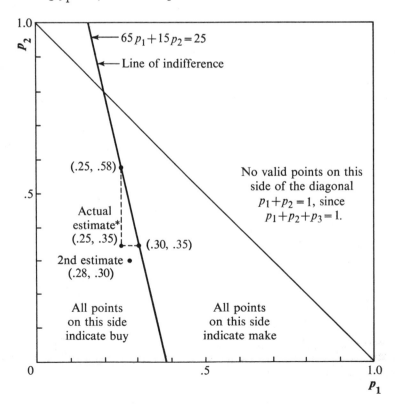

in a make decision. If it had turned out that, say, 90 percent of the area resulted in a make decision, the manager's thinking about the problem would have been different. Certainly, such lower sensitivity concerning the make decision would have increasing significance for the manager as his degree of belief in the likelihood of estimates *decreases*.

The estimate in our example and its revision are also shown on the diagram. They are both very close to the "switching" boundary. This means that *certain kinds* of error in the estimates, even if minimal, can change the indicated solution from buy to make. In this case, compare the effect of equal changes in p_1 and p_2. Figure 4–4 is an enlarged detail of the previous figure.

Figure 4–4

NOTE: For point A, the original estimate for p_1 is increased by .05, and the solution shifts from buy to make.

For point B, the original estimate for p_2 is increased by .05, and no change occurs in the solution. As can be seen from the figure, no change would occur, even if p_2 had been increased by .15 to .50.

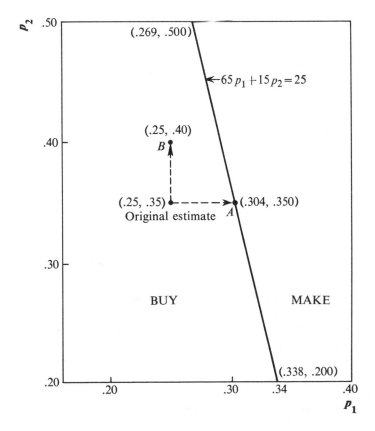

It shows how a change in p_1 results in a switch, while the same absolute change in p_2 does not. So, for this case, p_1 is much more sensitive than p_2.

Comparable charts could be constructed to include p_3 and determine its sensitivity.[9] However, such charts cannot be drawn for all cases, nor need they be. Sensitivity testing can be carried through successfully, without recourse to visual maps, by using well-programmed analytical subroutines that were designed at an early stage, at the time of model-building.

Once sensitivity of various elements has been tested, how do we apply the results of our analysis? In the present example, we have learned that investments in information to improve the critical p_1 estimates would be sensible, whereas expenditures to improve the p_2 estimates would be less useful. In other words, sensitivity analysis tells us which information is critical, and therefore should be refined, and which is not. Similar applications of analysis are possible to other types of data in the decision model. Each sensitivity analysis is its own case and demands innovative model architecture. As part of implementation responsibilities, the sensitivity system should be built in at the inception of the model-building phase.

Example 2: Stock-Market Speculation

Here we offer a simple decision model—and a criticism of it. The model is intended to typify the kind of problem that faces the day-to-day trader in stocks, who sees each decision as being independent of the next. We will assume that he buys as the market opens in the morning and sells just as the market closes. The current problem is then one in a sequence of decisions that our matrix analysis makes possible. The major advantage of such a model may be, not its answers, but what the manager can learn about the process (through the operation of the educational-implementation link).[10] In any case, the prospects for useful results are uncertain. Presumably the data entries for the matrix are based on analyses of historical records. We shall detail this as we proceed.

Let us *assume* that correlational studies have shown that the four stocks listed (as strategic alternatives) in Table 4–4 change their dollar value with changes in the Dow Jones Index as specified in the matrix. Of course, the correlation is not perfect. Rather, a scattering of points is observed such as that shown in Figure 4–5. If the correlations are fairly close—that is, the dispersion of the scattered points around the hypothesized functions for the stocks is not too great—then this matrix might be used with some confidence. The correlations do not have to be formal statistical derivations; satisfactory

---

[9] Similar analysis, assigned in Exercise 3 following this chapter, shows that p_1 is even more sensitive when compared with p_3.

[10] For a discussion of this topic see pp. 110–11.

Table 4–4   Matrix of Changes in the Dollar Value of $100 of the Named Stock as a Function of Changes in the Dow Jones Index

Dow Jones environments:

Range of Dow Jones point changes:	$(> +1.5)$	$(+.5:+1.5)$	$(+.5:-.5)$	$(-.5:-1.5)$	(< -1.5)	
Environmental probabilities:	.10	.20	.50	.15	.05	Expected values:
Stock A	+5	+3	0	−2	−3	+.650
Stock B	−2	−1	0	+1	+2	−.150
Stock C	+4	+2.5	−.5	−2.5	−4	+.075
Stock D	+3	+2	+.5	−1	−2	+.700

visual groupings are frequently used in similar situations. (*Sensitivity testing* could be employed at a later point to explore the significance of dispersions that seem too large.)

The probabilities describing the relative likelihoods of the changes in the Dow Jones Index might have been obtained simply by studying the historical record—that is, the daily Dow Jones Index changed by more than 1.5 points in 100 out of 1,000 days, and the same reasoning applies to the other categories of change in the Dow Jones Index. However, such an approach is not likely to be used. The day-to-day trader would probably change the environmental probabilities with each successive Dow Jones outcome. In other words, the probabilities for the Dow Jones environments are likely to be influenced by what happened most recently. Trends in stock values (epitomized by bears and bulls) are widely published, and they make us question whether suffi-

Figure 4–5

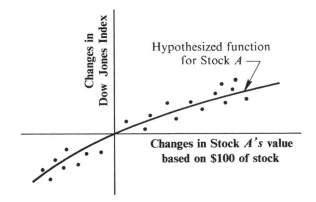

ciently good correlations between the price movements of individual stocks and changes in the Dow Jones Index (which is a composite measure of a sample of "typical" stocks) could be obtained without taking these trends into account. Many additional criticisms could be made of a nonsequential, historical approach, which suffers from being too simple an explanation of a complex system. For example, business and world news can affect the market's performance. Reports of security analysts and the actions of mutual funds can be influential. Nevertheless, for purely illustrative purposes we will construct this simplistic view of the problem.

Dominance. It should be noted that we do not have to work with the entire matrix as it has been conceived by the model-builder. A condition of dominance exists that enables us to cross out the third row (Strategy C); Stock A is better than Stock C for every Dow Jones condition. The result is that the size of the decision problem is reduced. *Dominance is an important management concept.* In its objective, written-out form, it consists of striking out one or more row strategies (as described above) or striking out columns that are identical to other columns across all rows.

Because of dominance, there are certain things that management just does not have to think about. This same reasoning applies to the subjective as well as to the objective aspect of the model. But subjective dominance is not visible or subject to checking because it happens in the manager's mind. It is a clear example of bounded rationality[11] in action.

The day-to-day trader will buy Stock D *if* he believes in his cell-entry estimates and, above all, in his probability assignments for the environments. If they are accurate, then, for the day, with each $100 the trader will obtain .7 percent, or $.70. If the same type of situation is repeated day by day, using $100, then in a thirty-day month the trader will earn $21 (less brokerage commissions).[12]

DECISION TREES

Any decision matrix has an alternative form of representation, the decision tree. For the trader's problem, Figure 4–6 shows the tree configuration. (Part

---

[11] See Chapter 3, pp. 74–75, for a discussion of bounded rationality (the reduction of considerations before the rational examination of alternatives).

[12] Say that the brokerage commission would be $44 if the stock was worth $50 per share and 100 shares were traded. The expected profit from this trade would be $50 \times .70 = \$35$, so the trader would take a net loss unless he was able to trade without commission or at a lower rate. Also, if higher-priced shares were traded, the net profit would improve.

Figure 4–6

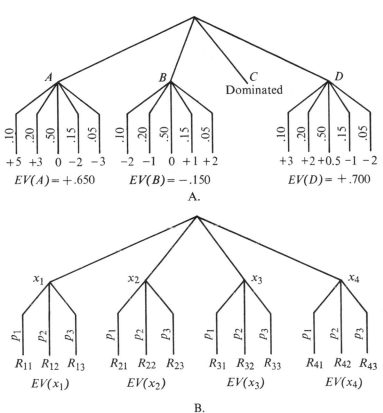

A.

B.

B is a more generalized version of Part A.) It is used in the same fashion as the decision matrix. That is, $EV(x_1) = p_1R_{11} + p_2R_{12} + p_3R_{13} + \ldots$. However, the tree becomes increasingly advantageous as the decision situation becomes more complex, since it permits an organized approach to the problem and has the distinct advantage of sorting out what is going on in the decision process.

Strategy: probability interactions. A more complex situation occurs when each strategy is associated with its own set of probabilities. This is not at all unusual. In many cases, the strategy affects the probabilities of the states of nature because the strategy shifts the entire system so that it operates under a different environment. (For an illustration, see "Example 3: Alternative Packaging Strategies," which follows.) When such a situation exists, the decision matrix is raised to a higher level, as in Table 4–6.

Table 4–6

	z_1	z_2	z_3	$\cdots$
x_1	p_{11}	p_{12}	p_{13}	$\cdots$
	R_{11}	R_{12}	R_{13}	$\cdots$
x_2	p_{21}	p_{22}	p_{23}	$\cdots$
	R_{21}	R_{22}	R_{23}	$\cdots$
x_3	p_{31}	p_{32}	p_{33}	$\cdots$
	R_{31}	R_{32}	R_{33}	$\cdots$

Example 3: Alternative Packaging Strategies

Consider the following situation: Environments, z_j's, are demand levels; strategies, x_i's, are packaging varieties;[13] the results, R_{ij}'s, are profit measures. We can then set up a matrix as shown in Table 4–7.

Table 4–7   Matrix of Profits (in millions of dollars)

	Demand levels:				
	z_1	z_2	z_3	z_4	EV
Demand probabilities x_1:	.2	.2	.3	.3	+1.4
round package	−2.0	0	+2.0	+4.0	
Demand probabilities x_2:	.2	.3	.3	.2	+1.6
square package	−1.0	+.5	+2.5	+4.5	

This form of matrix rapidly gets cumbersome as the number of possibilities increases, but the size of its tree representation remains unchanged. The probabilities on the tree branches simply differ according to which strategy trunk is represented. For example, p_2 for $x_1 = .2$, while p_2 for $x_2 = .3$. Reference to Figure 4–6 will help to illustrate these remarks. It is suggested in Exercise 6 of this chapter that the appropriate tree be developed for this matrix and the problem resolved on the basis of this tree form of representation.

Interactive sequences. In most real management situations, once a decision has been rendered, the conditions for the next decision have been changed. In other words, previous results alter future opportunities. The tree

---

[13] Substitute product-line configurations as well.

form of representation is most suitable to indicate this state of affairs and to resolve such decision problems. A simple case (where the sequence of decisions consists of repeated choices from the *same* strategic alternatives —e.g., x_1, x_1, x_2, x_1, ...) is illustrated in Figure 4–7.

Figure 4–7

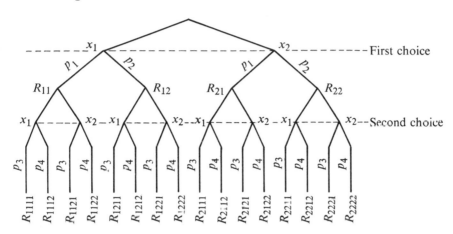

It is useful to point out that in some cases p_3 might equal p_1 and p_4 might equal p_2. But such equality is not essential; in fact, each of the probabilities can differ from all the others. And the sequential interactions could affect the results as well as the probabilities. We always label the tree with the best available numerical descriptions of reality.

Probably the most significant advantage of the tree lies in the fact that, with no conceptual difficulties and not much additional labor, as many decisions can be strung in sequence as is desirable for the analysis. For the example shown in Figure 4–7 the expected values would be

$$EV(x_1, x_1) = p_1(R_{11} + p_3R_{1111} + p_4R_{1112}) + p_2(R_{12} + p_3R_{1211} + p_4R_{1212})$$
$$EV(x_1, x_2) = p_1(R_{11} + p_3R_{1121} + p_4R_{1122}) + p_2(R_{12} + p_3R_{1221} + p_4R_{1222})$$
$$\vdots$$
$$EV(x_2, x_2) = p_1(R_{21} + p_3R_{2121} + p_4R_{2122}) + p_2(R_{22} + p_3R_{2221} + p_4R_{2222}).$$

Example 4: Artichokes or Stringbeans

We shall exemplify the sequential decision tree with a story about Farmer Jones, whose quandary is whether to plant crop A, artichokes, or crop S, stringbeans, to maximize his profits. He knows that weather is the crucial environmental factor. Let us assume that artichokes grow very well in good weather but grow poorly in bad weather, while stringbeans are relatively unaffected by weather. The farmer considers only two types of weather, good (G) and bad (B). The probability for G has been determined as .4; accordingly, for B it is .6. These probabilities are assumed to be stable over successive seasons and were determined from the records of past weather.[14] We will further complicate the case by assuming that if artichokes are planted in the same field for two successive seasons, then the second season's crop will not be as good as the first. And we will assume that stringbeans do not require crop rotation.

Let us look now at the sequential decision tree for two consecutive seasons as shown in Figure 4–8.[15] The farmer's strategies are: AA, AS, SA, and SS; and the expected values, in thousands of dollars, are:

$$EV(A, A) = .4[40 + .4(20) + .6(0)] + .6[5 + .4(40)$$
$$+ .6(5)] = 33.6$$
$$EV(A, S) = .4[40 + .4(15) + .6(12)] + .6[5 + .4(15)$$
$$+ .6(12)] = 32.2$$
$$EV(S, A) = .4[15 + .4(40) + .6(5)] + .6[12 + .4(40)$$
$$+ .6(5)] = 32.2$$
$$EV(S, S) = .4[15 + .4(15) + .6(12)] + .6[12 + .4(15)$$
$$+ .6(12)] = 26.4$$

The tree does not have to be this big. Insight tells us that $EV(A, S) = EV(S, A)$ under the present assumptions, so only one of these branches need be calculated. Also, frequently, some branches that are dominated can be removed—although not in this case. Dominance can be recognized in trees by observing that all the *final* end-points of one trunk are superior to those of another. Because of the interactive relations that may exist in a sequence of decisions, it is not possible to reach a decision based on the superiority of any one trunk at an intermediate level. In fact, some of management's worst mistakes are made in this way.

---

[14] Exercise 7 in this chapter introduces the additional complication that the probability of a weather trend is high and should be used to modify successive weather probabilities in the tree. This is an interactive sequence, not in the sense that strategies affect the probabilities, but in the sense that *actual* states of nature affect the probabilities of future states of nature.

[15] It will be well worth the reader's time to examine the architecture of this tree. Tree-reading must be learned, but, with practice, facility can be developed rapidly. Once he understands the generalized construction of a tree, the manager can begin to build his own. He has thereby gained a new means to express objectively a great variety of situations. Decision trees may well become for management what blueprints are for engineers.

Figure 4–8

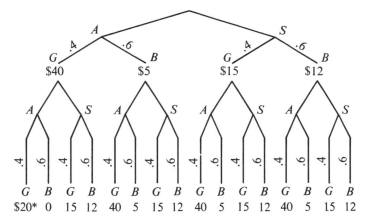

* All results in thousands of dollars.

WHAT IS KNOWABLE ABOUT ENVIRONMENTS

Let us say that for a given problem we consider j environmental configurations; each j represents a unique environment. How can we know that all relevant environments have been recognized, let alone considered? Furthermore, under what circumstances is the extent of our knowledge about environments likely to be important?[16]

It is reasonable to expect that as the decision level moves upward and toward more complex, less well-known, and increasingly crucial problems, it should become harder and harder to state with confidence what the relevant environmental conditions might be. In traveling to Sirius by spaceship, we expect to encounter conditions that are as yet unknown (and more or less unguessable). Even in so-called controlled economies it is not possible to be certain of the behavior of all the forces that can affect the system's behavior. For example, the consumer may not respond as planned to the goods that are offered in the marketplace. And, no matter what the level of social controls, events such as hurricanes, earthquakes, drought, flood, blight, and pestilence cannot be predicted by the planner. It is unreasonable to expect that each decision problem will include all possible states of nature. In fact, many extreme situations will not even be thought about until they occur.

Practically, then, it is unreasonable to attempt to enumerate all the states of nature that could possibly be relevant, let alone to predict with reasonable

---

[16] See Chapter 6 for some particular aspects of this question that emphasize cost.

accuracy which of them will occur. Upper-managerial problems, such as those concerned with bond issues, plant investments, and major organizational changes, are particularly vulnerable to these kinds of difficulty. Yet it is precisely here that the pressure to *know* is greatest, because *the higher the decision level, the more sensitive the system becomes in terms of penalties for errors of environmental omission.*

To whatever extent possible, therefore, we attempt to deduce environments that *might* occur and influence the attainment of our objectives. This is surely the best that can be done. We emphasize that the theoretical requirement is to identify *all relevant* factors not under our control. Practically, we must somehow choose the right ones to take into account. But we cannot make a choice unless we are *aware* of what might be done. We can ignore factors not relevant to the systems being studied, but we err when our ignorance is bliss and we do not ignore by choice.

Occasionally circumstances permit us to eliminate a large group of conditions (rather than one condition at a time) simply because all members of the group possess a common characteristic—such as being mutually dominated— that renders them irrelevant. Market segmentation uses this kind of thinking —for example, we begin the definition of the market for feminine products by excluding males. We can call this method *identification by negative characteristics*. On the other hand, direct, positive identification is more frequently employed and requires that we recognize and enumerate specific environmental factors of importance. Such creative capability is no less a part of the process of innovation than is the ability to design beneficial strategies. This relationship between creating strategies and identifying environments has become more evident now that the decision model has been developed.

How, in general, does the manager go about this process of environment identification? The answer would seem to be that he employs deduction based on some purely subjective model of the situation. This informal model encompasses his total set of experiences and in various ways is able to provide reference to situations analogous to the one being analyzed. As a formal process, such deduction would be far too tedious and demanding if, in fact, it could be carried out. No one would recommend it, but, alternatively, the value is apparent of a manager who can *use* his experience rather than be *subject* to it.

CLASSES OF DECISION PROBLEM

Decisions Made Under Ambiguity (DMUA)

At any organizational level in the decision-making process (even at some low levels), there may be no way of determining all the relevant environmental conditions. For example, when we inspect the output of a machine, we know that variation (designed to be within tolerance limits some stated percentage of the time) *must* occur. The chance cause factors responsible for this variation are essentially unknown and *unknowable*. They are related to manifold atomic and subatomic phenomena that affect the exact interpositioning of the machine's parts. It is hardly surprising that we are unable to specify *all* such elusive phenomena, less so that we have no control in these domains.

What can the manager do when he finds himself unable to identify all relevant environments? No matter what the decision level, when the manager lacks knowledge about relevant environments, then his decision can be said to be rendered under conditions of *ambiguity*. In such cases, he is forced to look at his problem in a somewhat different way. Let us transform the conventional decision matrix previously shown into one that conveys far less information but is compatible with the manager's knowledge of the situation and amenable to the data that are available and obtainable.

We shall call this an *outcome state matrix,* since in place of the environments, z_j's, along the top of the array we substitute the full range of possible *results, R_m's,* that can occur.[17] Having replaced environments with results, we now specify that the intersection values of the matrix should be measures or estimates of the likelihood of the results, p_{im}'s. These describe *the probability that any possible result will occur as a function of the strategy that is used.* Such likelihood measures frequently can be obtained by observation. They are often available when the forecast of p_j's for the environments is not. An outcome state matrix is shown in Table 4–8.

Table 4–8

	R_1	R_2	$\ldots$	R_m
x_1	p_{11}	p_{12}	$\ldots$	p_{1m}
x_2	p_{21}	p_{22}	$\ldots$	p_{2m}
.	.	.	$\ldots$	.
.	.	.	$\ldots$	.
.	.	.	$\ldots$	.
x_i	p_{i1}	p_{i2}	$\ldots$	p_{im}

By using this *model,* we have by-passed the need to name all relevant uncontrollable factors and the configurations they can create. Our outcome state matrix retains the controllable variable configurations—that is, the strategies, x_i's; however, it replaces the uncontrollable environments, z_j's, with the spec-

---

[17] Note that whereas each R_{ij} is a unique result associated with the *i*th activity and the *j*th environment, R_m is the *m*th result falling along the scale of *all possible results.* There may never be an activity that can ever produce this result.

trum of all possible results, $R_1 \ldots R_m$, and converts the likelihood estimates for environments, p_j's into likelihood estimates for results, p_{im}'s.

By transforming a regular decision matrix into an outcome state matrix, we have foregone consideration of *causal relations* that could help to explain how the various results might arise. Instead, we have chosen to use statistical procedures that by-pass the underlying relations. Usually the outcome matrix is used because the causal type of information could never have been known. But we can still observe the frequency with which the different results occur when the various strategies are utilized. (Note that a particular strategy might yield a given result under several quite different environments.) And the probability estimates are representative of the system's overall behavior, which is, after all, one of management's prime concerns.

Some managers are inclined to think causally, whereas others characteristically reason with odds on results without studying in detail the causes of these odds. This distinction may well be critical for job assignments—there being an advantage in placing managers in situations in which the available information is best handled by their pattern of reasoning.

Decisions Made Under Instability (DMUI)

A further distinction now appears as a function of the decision level. We recognize that the manager's ability to supply believable predictions for the total spectrum of results diminishes markedly as the decision level rises. *At low levels* it is generally possible to derive the appropriate probability distribution of results because situations tend to recur often enough to provide a stable historical record of relative frequencies. Using statistical quality control (SQC) methods, the underlying system frequently can be rendered statistically stable[18] and then monitored (see pp. 440–50) to ensure that it remains so. This is possible even though we do not know which particular environments are responsible for the actual, observed results. SQC methods require the identification and removal of assignable causes of variation—that is, causes of variation that can be identified by statistical methodology. Once assignable causes are identified and removed, the system is left with those myriad chance causes that belong to the physicist's "quantum" world of unidentifiable random variations.

Control systems, on the other hand, provide an important method for dealing with instability when the environments are known. Monitors feed back information concerning the system's behavior and trigger corrective control

---

[18] Statistical stability is imperfect evidence that "true" stability exists. However, since managerial intuition in assessing stability appears to be weak, statistical methodology has had a major impact on evaluating this critical condition.

actions. The environments are not rendered stable, but it is important to know what they might be (not how often they might occur) in order to be able to have appropriate corrective actions available. Such matters are treated in depth in Part IV.

Let us examine *higher decision levels,* where it is usually impossible to obtain the required probability distributions for either the outcomes or the environments. The outcome matrix cannot be completed largely because the historical record either is irrelevant or is too skimpy to provide a basis for overcoming ambiguity. Furthermore, the stability of the systems under consideration is in doubt. The kinds of environmental factors that influence upper-level results are quite likely to be unknown to begin with and, even after study, not amenable to being brought into a stable predictive state. A control system cannot be designed because of ambiguity as to what can occur. Under such circumstances, present scientific approaches to decision problems are of little avail.

While acknowledging that this is so, one may still wonder exactly how useful intuitional methods are when the system is apt to be ambiguous and unstable. Our conclusion must be that when such conditions exist, luck alone controls our destiny. Sometimes, however, dependence on luck becomes so exasperating that great research efforts are made, and technology succeeds in gaining a degree of control over the situation.

A Background for Classifying Decision Models

Before we go to decision problems in which the relevant environments *can* be named, we should note that a major consideration in defining a decision model relates to whether ambiguous or nonambiguous conditions exist in combination with stable or unstable environments. Thus, with ambiguity about environments, statistical quality control methods can often be applied to remove instability, resulting in a decision model of outcomes. Once stability is achieved, then the expected-value measure is an appropriate criterion for decisions. Lacking the power to achieve stability, however, nothing can be done.

Given the condition of nonambiguity, a strong classification of decision problems becomes possible. In this case, all relevant j environments are known. The estimates of their likelihood can be specified, at least in abstraction, as the *set* of relevant p_j's.

We discover that the *fundamental character* of a decision problem is revealed by the form of its p_j values. Four different categories emerge and will be discussed later in this chapter. They describe variations concerning what is known about the p_j's and what configurations the values of the p_j's take on.[19]

---

[19] It is not difficult to relate each of these four categories to a particular decision level; see Chapter 13, pp. 580–84.

Table 4–9   What Is Knowable About Environments

		All j's are known: Ambiguously	Nonambiguously
The p_j's are known to be:	Stable	Outcome matrix Process control	Decision models with environments
	Unstable	Planning models	Feedback-type of policy control models

Stable nonambiguity is the basis for rational use of the decision matrix. Stable ambiguity is the result of successful SQC, which is a method that can convert unstable systems to stable ones even though environmental ambiguity exists. The statistical reasoner turns to the outcome form of the decision matrix with a feeling of its adequacy—if not with a sense of relief—once the (unknown) underlying system has been rendered stable. Unstable nonambiguity leads to the development of feedback-type control systems that can override but not alter the instability—for example, an automatic pilot. But what happens to managerial attitudes under confirmed ambiguity and instability? The manager's mind turns to planning, which is the subject of Part III of this book. The matrix of Table 4–9 summarizes these points. Figure 4–9 shows the same categorization in tree form.

Neither the matrix nor the tree provides the whole story, but they do provide a valuable basis for explaining why managers do one thing or another—and, in the converse sense, for specifying where decision-making, planning, and both process and policy control (as shown in the matrix) apply. The strength of this taxonomy will become apparent later, when, for example, we look at planning models. We shall see in Part III how instability and ambiguity are treated by different classes of planning model; and in Part IV we will examine policy control models.

Management attitudes and systems types. Perhaps the alternative tree arrangement of Figure 4–10, which lets stability conditions precede those of ambiguity, will shed additional light. This breakdown groups decision and outcome models together and planning and policy control models together. It is more appealing than the prior tree because *the attitude of the manager will depend primarily on the interaction of his native characteristics with what he knows about the system (stability) and secondarily with what he knows he knows about the system (ambiguity).* Put another way: *Stability is a property of the system; ambiguity is what is known about the system and is therefore a property of the manager.* These are entirely separate concepts, yet they are often confused. Figure 4–10 is closer to the way the manager groups his use of

Figure 4–9

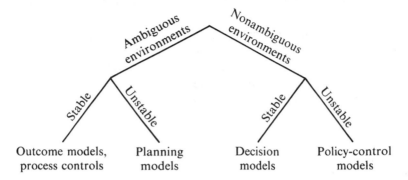

models than is Figure 4–9. The unstable side of the tree of Figure 4–10 tends to be supervised by upper management, the stable side by a lower level.

Much time could and should be spent on the way managers react to conditions of ambiguity and instability in the systems with which they deal. There is reason to believe that great individual differences exist. Presumably, those who like to plan enjoy the lack of security and the need for conjecture on their branch of the tree. Policy-making is more jurisdictional than planning, yet not as secure as decision-making under stable conditions. Ambiguity is usually anathema to an accountant; uncontrolled instability is intolerable to an engineer. Promotion and placement of personnel are affected by the individual's sense of risk-taking. Comfort with risk could be matched with the reactions of the manager to the amount and nature of the information available to him. In general, the sufficiency of information can be ranked as below, from the most to the least secure situation for the manager.

Figure 4–10

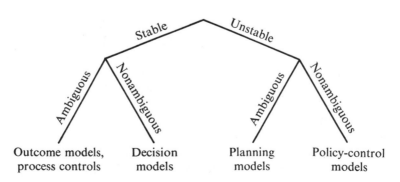

1. *Outcome matrix, process models, input/output systems*[20] (*stable, ambiguous*). There is no need to identify the environments (z_j's) or to forecast the environmental p_j's.

2. *Policy control models*[21] (*unstable, nonambiguous*). There is no need to forecast the p_j's because the control system overrides the instability. However, when ambiguity arises because the policy does not cover a particular occurrence, the sense of security dissolves.

3. *Decision models* (*stable, nonambiguous*). It is necessary to *assume* that all relevant environments have been identified; it is necessary to forecast the p_j's on the *assumption* that the system is stable.

4. *Planning models* (*unstable, ambiguous*). It is necessary to assume ambiguity and instability and, nevertheless, to decide what to do.

No matter what the point of view, the simultaneous occurrence of ambiguity and instability accounts for the major challenge to upper management. This is primarily because the relevant system cannot be observed for results, since no one knows exactly how to define or bound that system. Is it unreasonable, under these circumstances, for managers to isolate that part of reality which is nonambiguous and stable in order to permit the use of decision models? If they do so, how, then, can they work back to reality? For example, a careful, fully rational study for an airport location ignored the political issues that might be expected to arise. The result pinpointed an area whose residents immediately mobilized to prevent that area from being selected as a site. Should more than just the physical aspects of the problem have been included in the study? The issue involved is not one of values in conflict with rationality. There is a behavioral, attitudinal problem, and a systems modeling problem. First, the manager must be willing to extend his thinking beyond limited results, back to reality. Then, he must understand the nature of systems to know how to accomplish this end. Much discussion throughout the book is devoted to such questions.

Decisions Made Under Certainty (DMUC)

Decision-making under certainty occurs when there is only one environment that is relevant to the decision problem. The word "relevant" is critical. An astute observer might contend that many different environments were being lumped together and treated as one. But such lumping is permissible, and in fact desirable, as long as the differences are ones that do not affect the results. What we mean by the condition of certainty is that the *results* of employing various strategies *are unchanged by* any possible form of *environmental vari-*

---

[20] See Chapter 13, pp. 539–42.
[21] See Part IV, pp. 440–47, for detailed definitions.

ety; in other words, the results are invariant to changes in external factors. Therefore, environmental variety is of no consequence to the decision problem, and only one environment can be said to exist. Each strategy produces only one outcome. The decision matrix has as many rows as the number of strategies, but it has *only one column*—for example,

$$z_1$$

$$
\begin{array}{cc}
x_1 & R_{11} \\
x_2 & R_{21} \\
\cdot & \cdot \\
\cdot & \cdot \\
\cdot & \cdot \\
x_n & R_{n1}
\end{array}
$$

Somewhat surprisingly, such unicolumnar decision tableaus can be found to occur in practice at *all* decision levels, although the frequency of their use decreases as we move upward in the hierarchy.

Managerial attitudes are critical in the practical implications of assuming certainty. Problems such as work-scheduling or the procurement of materials are quite often treated as being completely indifferent to variations in environmental conditions. Everyone knows that this is an approximation—but it is not generally understood that it may be unwarranted. On another front, we would have expected process problems (those dealing with the *physical* transformations performed by machines, facilities, etc.) to lend themselves most readily to the unicolumnar construction associated with DMUC. But here an anomaly is encountered. Manufacturing tolerance limits, which are entirely characteristic of process operations, reflect a multiplicity of relevant environmental states that cannot be observed and must be transformed by means of the outcome state matrix. So many managers regard the process level of decision as one of the least tractable of all decision levels with respect to the theory of DMUC. Practically, however, the effects of each of the many environments are small and tend to cancel out one another, with the result that certainty may be a reasonable position to take. Surprisingly, the assumption of certainty can often be made with far more convenience at high decision levels than at lower ones, but the conviction of the validity of such an approach is likely to be weakest at the higher levels.

Many situations exist where multiple relevant environments are known to characterize the decision problem and where, in spite of this, the condition of certainty may be employed. When the variation in results caused by the different environments is extremely small, the system can be described as *insensitive,* and environmental differences can reasonably be ignored. Alternatively, even when environments can cause significant (but not disastrous) differences in the results, such environments can be eliminated from consideration if the probability that they will occur is *very* small. The use of certainty approximations can be disastrous, however, if one of the results associated with an unlikely (but not impossible) environment is catastrophic. Only when the improbable results are not extremes can they be ignored with a degree of sanguineness.

If DMUC is accepted as the form of the decision problem, then the single, relevant environment is considered to have a probability equal to one (i.e., $p_1 = 1$), and a variety of mathematical and logical methods is available for handling very complex unicolumnar problems. (Their efficacy depends, of course, on whether the assumption of certainty is accurate.)

Once the unicolumnar matrix is constructed, all row values in the single column must be considered so that the most desirable row result can be discovered. Some of the most efficient *search methods* operate in accordance with a procedure that first bounds out of the system large blocks of unwanted characteristics before beginning to search through those that remain. Such identification by negative characteristics is involved in bounded rationality. Frequently, a combination of search procedures is used. Speed of solution is often the critical factor, and the speed with which the most desirable result is found is a function of the method used and the number of items that must be examined.

When the decision model for search under certainty is fully accepted, then the decision is made as soon as the strategy that produces the optimal result is found. Usually the strategy is selected because it produces either a maximum or minimum value for the result. When the required value is a middle-range value, some form of transformation is usually available—for example, the column of values can be transformed by subtracting all entries from the goal value so that a minimum absolute value exists that represents the preferred solution (i.e., the value of zero is the best possible result).

Various strong methodological approaches exist for locating maximums and minimums. For example, we can apply mathematical reasoning, utilizing (from calculus) the derivatives of a function.[22] The plotting of curves and the visual searching of columns of numbers are approaches that are often used. So-called cut-and-try methods, which are based on guessing where the solution exists and then testing the guess, are frequently used with success. Unicolumnar search procedure characterizes linear programming (LP), which we will discuss later. For many LP problems the single column of results can have millions of row entries—each representing a unique strategic variant. In Chapter 7 we will examine the method and implications of LP with respect to managerial objectives.

Problems treated under conditions of certainty are considered difficult only

---

[22] Thus, we obtain the first derivative of the function $y = f(x)$. Setting it equal to zero $dy/dx = 0$, a maximum or minimum of the function can be determined, if it exists; see pp. 261–62 for text discussion and clarification.

because of the size of the search. That is, so many strategic possibilities exist (even after bounded rationality, negative identification, etc., are applied) that a formal method must be used to search for the optimal value.

The assumption of certainty, if it is a poor approximation, can create serious problems. We would hardly wish to use an advanced mathematical model designed for conditions of certainty when a single activity seems able to produce a range of results—some of which entail sizable penalties. On the other hand, when only small penalties are expected and the cause can be corrected as the decision is repeated over time, or when in a series of repetitive decisions the errors tend to cancel each other out, then substantial savings can be gained *by refusing to overcomplicate* the decision analysis. While the assumption of certainty appears to be most generally acceptable at the process level, its convenience value at any level must be balanced against the degree of its believability, to estimate the consequent utility of a solution under certainty.

Decisions Made Under Risk (DMUR)

When there are several *relevant* environments, which means that the results will vary according to which environment actually occurs, we have DMUR. Accordingly, to the j environments we assign appropriate p_j's.[23] The decision criterion for this case, which is the *expected value,* has previously been discussed.

Certainty is a special class of risk problems wherein a single state of nature has a probability of one of occurring—that is, if $j = 1$, then $p_1 = 1$. The single column for the only environment under conditions of certainty is functionally equivalent to the single expected-value column that is derived from the more general type of risk problem. This is another aspect of the practical meaning of approximations of certainty.

Once the *average* result for *each strategy* has been obtained in the risk case, the decision matrix is compressed to a unicolumnar array, which is then searched by the same procedures used for conditions of certainty. Thus, methods that seem to be restricted to certainty have often been applied to expected values. This is probably the best rationale for the use of linear pro-

---

[23] As was previously noted, the sum of all p_j's equals one. This is equivalent to saying that the area under a probability distribution must equal unity (or encompass 100 percent of all occurrences). Specifically, given n different environments, each of which is observed to occur with frequencies of $f_1, f_2, \ldots, f_n$, then the sum, $f_1 + f_2 + \ldots + f_n$, will be equal to the total number of observations made. Calling this total N, we have

$$f_1/N = p_1; \quad f_2/N = p_2; \quad \ldots; \quad f_n/N = p_n; \quad \text{and} \quad \sum_1^n p_j = \sum_1^n f_n/N = 1.$$

gramming and other unicolumnar models when environmental variety is known to exist. The manager can believe that he has estimated subjectively the "correct" expected values. He may, indeed, have done a good job.[24]

The methodology characteristic of DMUC is fundamentally less complex and less costly than that required for DMUR. Risk-modeling requires everything DMUC does, and in addition it involves statistical analysis and data compression to obtain EV's. The use of formal statistical methods is predicated on the existence of sufficient information as well as a stable system. Neither an historical record nor proof of stability is characteristic of the upper decision levels. In such situations approximations of certainty may be out of the question. As we shall see shortly, upper-level problems can be treated (reluctantly) as decision-making under conditions of uncertainty (DMUU). On the other hand, by the utilization of experimental methods, these problems frequently can be transformed to come under conditions of partial uncertainty (DMUPU) and sometimes under conditions approximating risk (DMUR).[25]

The manager can generally expect to find that DMUR is applicable to the tactical problems of middle management.[26] For such problems it is usually safe to assume that the environmental probabilities are likely to be believable. By this we mean that the manager's degree of belief in the likelihood estimates is sufficiently high for him to be at ease using them in the decision algorithm. (A decision algorithm is any systematic *procedure* used to reach a decision.) Only information of a causal nature could modify the analysis, because for DMUR the distributions of the probabilities are fully known, including *all basic parameters and the shapes of the distributions*. In the event of discrete distributions that lack a well-known form, it is necessary that the probability for each event that can occur be completely specified. And, of course, for nonambiguity, we should be able to name all the relevant environments.

Decisions Made Under Partial Uncertainty (DMUPU)

When the shape of the distribution of probabilities (such as normal, Poisson, or binomial) is not known but some information is available about the

---

[24] How managers go about approximating certainty and their style in using the results of such approximations provide a good example of the kind of research areas that are beginning to receive attention because they combine human behavior and quantitative methods.

[25] To avoid confusion, we define uncertainty as the *total* inability to *assign* values for the p_j's. A risk situation occurs when there is a *believable* set of estimates for the p_j's. Partial uncertainty is defined as a situation with a set of p_j's developed by methods of inference working from *incomplete data* about the p_j's.

[26] For a definition of *tactical*, as it comes under strategy, see pp. 581–82.

parameters and/or character of the distribution (such as averages, modes, medians, or various measures of symmetry, skewness, and dispersion), then a decision can be reached using only this partial knowledge. Decision methods applicable to partial uncertainty are found in nonparametric and distribution-free techniques that have been highly developed.[27]

For the manager these methods do not answer a pressing operational need. They have arisen because of their mathematical interest and potential for analyzing tests and experimental results. The manager prefers not to be uncertain. He will authorize expenditures to collect information, or he will supply his own intuitive estimates, rather than be forced into using decision methods based on a high degree of uncertainty. At the root of the difficulty is the manager's respect for perfection in the abstract and his rejection of it in practice.

It is true that the notion of partial uncertainty brings to mind the possibility that more information about the distribution might be purchased for a reasonable expenditure. Chapter 6 is concerned with the value of obtaining additional information by such means as test markets, scale models, and pilot plants. It addresses the question of how much can be spent for additional information without exceeding the gains that are likely to be derived from that information. And it is also true that, as the decision level increases and situations of partial uncertainty are more likely to occur, the manager can be expected to turn more and more to his intuition.

Still, there is something to be said about the line of reasoning used in partial information methods. Generally, the properties of an incomplete set of data are developed to show that it can be described by means of inequalities such as $p_j > k$ or $k_1 > p_j > k_2$. The approach signals a certain "style" of perception and reasoning that appears to be related to intuition. Perhaps these ideas are simply a technician's concern rather than that of a manager, for equivalent results can usually be obtained through sensitivity analysis, with which the manager is more at home. Using sensitivity analysis he gains a greater feel for the system, whereas with methods of partial uncertainty he is dealing with an isolated analytic technique.

Decisions Made Under Uncertainty (DMUU)

The last category of decision problems that we shall consider is that of decision-making under uncertainty. Here we know the environments but *nothing whatever* about the probabilities associated with those environments. This condi-

---

[27] See Sidney Siegel, *Non-Parametric Statistics for the Behavioral Sciences* (New York: McGraw-Hill, 1956).

tion represents one extreme of the partial-uncertainty dimension. Forecast information has reached the zero limit, and, as a result, many decision options are available. At the opposite extreme of partial uncertainty we find DMUR (not DMUC, which is itself a special case of DMUR).

For DMUU we assume total ignorance of the relative frequencies with which each environment is likely to occur, although we are not ignorant of which environments apply. The next point that comes to mind is whether or not this unknown distribution of environmental likelihoods is a stable one. It might be changing (either continuously or sporadically) over time, but, unless a stable pattern holds, decision models are pointless. Therefore, DMUU *assumes stability*—and this is a vital consideration. We see that DMUU is based on two kinds of information, stability and nonambiguity. Whenever conditions of DMUU exist, it appears essential to ask: How much should we spend for information to convert our problem into a risk-type decision system? Once the probability distribution is obtained, we might find that it appears to be unstable. Then we can institute a statistical quality control program with the hope of stabilizing the system, and if we succeed we will have achieved DMUR.

It is worth noting how the formal aspects of decision matrices illuminate the underlying essentials of real management situations. The concept of decision classes brings useful structure to a highly complex area. The classes relate reality to what is actually known about a decision situation and to what remains to be found out. The theory of decisions turns out not to be just an interesting construct. On the contrary, it has substantial utility for examining familiar management approaches. In subsequent chapters it will become evident how well these decision classes also serve for discovering further classes that can be applied to planning, controlling, and organizing.

Let us consider now three kinds of decision criteria for DMUU. (Further aspects of these criteria and of a fourth one will be treated in Chapter 6.)

The pessimist's criterion. First, let us consider a familiar military decision criterion called the Wald minimax.[28] The Waldian procedure is quite simple.

1. Select the least desirable result associated with each strategy (row) of the decision matrix. This is *Min* R_{ij} for each *i,* if the matrix is expressed in profits; it is *Max* R_{ij}, if the matrix is expressed in costs.

2. Choose the strategy that produces the most desirable result from among all of the previously chosen, least desirable results. This would be that activity for which, in terms of profits, *Max* (*Min* R_{ij}) is true—hence, *maximin.* In

---

[28] Named for Abraham Wald, who suggested its use. The military application is explained in detail in Chapter 5.

Table 4–9

	z_1	z_2	z_3	z_4	Min R_{ij}	Max R_{ij}
x_1	2	8	6	3	2	8
x_2	5	4	1	7	1	7*
x_3	9	6	4	5	4*	9

terms of costs the best of the worst would be *Min (Max R_{ij})*—which explains the term *minimax*.

Table 4–9 provides an example of a decision matrix for which the above steps can be used. If the matrix has been written in terms of profits, then the maximin solution is the third strategy, x_3, with a value of four. Conversely, if the matrix has been used to express costs, then the minimax solution is the second activity, x_2, with a value of seven.

The Waldian criterion ascribes a kind of malevolent intelligence to nature. That is why it is also called the pessimist's criterion. At high decision levels, when one mistake may be the last, the notion of getting at least the best of the worst appears to be quite tenable. At lower decision levels the pessimist's approach has little appeal.

Note that the pessimist's criterion succeeds in converting consideration of a problem under uncertainty into consideration of a problem under certainty —that is, it is assumed that the worst possibility will occur. This is a strange form of certainty because it is based, not on predicting which specific environment will appear, but on the fact that each such environment will always produce the worst possible result for each strategy. Although this is a strange form, it is nevertheless the condition of certainty. In this case, the single column required for certainty is achieved by using the worst case in each row. Engineers call this the fail-safe approach, and it is traditional in military thinking as well.

The rationalist's criterion. The second decision criterion we shall explore is based on the so-called principle of insufficient reason. The problem of reaching decisions under conditions of uncertainty has for many years captured the interest of philosophers, mathematicians, and logicians. The Reverend Thomas Bayes (1702–61) suggested that if the relative likelihoods of a system's environmental states were *truly* unknown, then in no sense could any one state be expected to occur more frequently than any other. This viewpoint, which was published posthumously, is called Bayes's Postulate. The Marquis Pierre Simon de Laplace (1749–1827) considered all of Bayes's work to be important and both supported and further developed it.

According to the principle of insufficient reason, with n possible states, each should be assigned an equal likelihood; thus, $p_j = 1/n$. When applied to the matrix of Table 4–9, the Laplace-Bayes criterion produces the following result:

Laplace-Bayes Value
x_1 19/4 = 4.75
x_2 17/4 = 4.25   (Select if matrix of costs.)
x_3 24/4 = 6.00   (Select if matrix of profits.)

While in this case both the Waldian and the Laplace-Bayes criteria produced the same result, it is not always certain that they will do so. (See Exercise 12 in this chapter.) Many decision criteria exist for conditions of uncertainty that are quite capable of providing divergent results. The quandary is in part a philosophical one, although we prefer to identify it as a behavioral-attitudinal problem. In this regard, we have called the Laplace-Bayes criterion the rationalist's criterion because it takes no sides. Uncertainty is expressed in a completely rational way. The pessimist, on the other hand, has an obvious attitude (that he is unlucky), as does the optimist described below (that he is more or less lucky).

The manager generally elects to avoid expressing personal attitudes in his decision studies, but he is hard-pressed to do so when the problem is really one of uncertainty. Given a formal approach, the manager prefers to accept less believable approximations of the probabilities so that he can use DMUR. Therefore, he is willing to take a position based on personal preferences, supplying his own "personalistic" probability estimates and thereby converting his problem from the distasteful conditions of DMUU to the more palatable ones of DMUR. This quasi-intuitional approach has more adherents than opponents, but the opposition is both influential and vocal.

The entrepreneur has still other recourses that he is apt to prefer since they do not require arguing about the validity of his subjective estimates of likelihood. The first of these is to call upon sensitivity analysis; the second is to spend additional sums of money for experimentation and information collection. A third approach requires technological abilities to be embodied in the design of a control system so that it can override the environmental factors. A fourth assumes research to convert uncontrollable variables into controllable ones. We will have more to say about these options in Chapter 6.

Coefficient of optimism. Still another decision criterion was suggested by Leonid Hurwicz. For each strategy, the best or most desired result is multiplied by a coefficient, chosen between zero and one and called α. It is intended to measure, in a relative sense, the manager's optimism. Correspondingly, the worst possible result is multiplied by $(1 - \alpha)$. When $\alpha = 1$, the manager is completely optimistic. When $\alpha = 0$, he is completely pessimistic—

exactly equivalent to the Waldian pessimist. The α-level between zero and one expresses different degrees of optimism. Using the matrix

	z_1	z_2	z_3	z_4
x_1	4	8	6	3
x_2	5	4	1	7
x_3	9	6	2	5

Table 4–10 illustrates the results obtained for different values of α. (The selected strategy is indicated by an asterisk.) We see that the cost type of

Table 4–10

$\alpha = 1.0$	For Costs	For Profits
x_1:	$(1)(3) + (0)(8) = 3$	$(1)(8) + (0)(3) = 8$
x_2:	$(1)(1) + (0)(7) = 1^*$	$(1)(7) + (0)(1) = 7$
x_3:	$(1)(2) + (0)(9) = 2$	$(1)(9) + (0)(2) = 9^*$

$\alpha = .8$		
x_1:	$(.8)(3) + (.2)(8) = 4.0$	$(.8)(8) + (.2)(3) = 7.0$
x_2:	$(.8)(1) + (.2)(7) = 2.2^*$	$(.8)(7) + (.2)(1) = 5.8$
x_3:	$(.8)(2) + (.2)(9) = 3.4$	$(.8)(9) + (.2)(2) = 7.6^*$

$\alpha = .6$		
x_1:	$(.6)(3) + (.4)(8) = 5.0$	$(.6)(8) + (.4)(3) = 6.0$
x_2:	$(.6)(1) + (.4)(7) = 3.4^*$	$(.6)(7) + (.4)(1) = 4.6$
x_3:	$(.6)(2) + (.4)(9) = 4.8$	$(.6)(9) + (.4)(2) = 6.2^*$

$\alpha = .4$		
x_1:	$(.4)(3) + (.6)(8) = 6.0$	$(.4)(8) + (.6)(3) = 5.0^*$
x_2:	$(.4)(1) + (.6)(7) = 4.6^*$	$(.4)(7) + (.6)(1) = 3.4$
x_3:	$(.4)(2) + (.6)(9) = 6.2$	$(.4)(9) + (.6)(2) = 4.8$

$\alpha = .2$		
x_1:	$(.2)(3) + (.8)(8) = 7.0$	$(.2)(8) + (.8)(3) = 4.0^*$
x_2:	$(.2)(1) + (.8)(7) = 5.8^*$	$(.2)(7) + (.8)(1) = 2.2$
x_3:	$(.2)(2) + (.8)(9) = 7.6$	$(.2)(9) + (.8)(2) = 3.4$

$\alpha = 0$		
x_1:	$(0)(3) + (1)(8) = 8$	$(0)(8) + (1)(3) = 3^*$
x_2:	$(0)(1) + (1)(7) = 7^*$	$(0)(7) + (1)(1) = 1$
x_3:	$(0)(2) + (1)(9) = 9$	$(0)(9) + (1)(2) = 2$

analysis would be invariant to the degree of optimism, whereas, if the matrix represented a profit system, a switch does occur somewhere between $\alpha = .6$ and $\alpha = .4$. Figure 4–11 is helpful in illustrating these points. For the cost

Figure 4–11

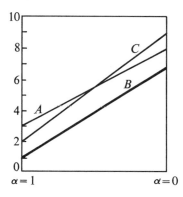

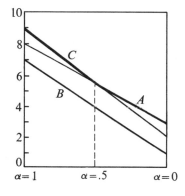

For the cost matrix

$A \quad 3\alpha+8(1-\alpha)=8-5\alpha$

$B \quad \alpha+7(1-\alpha)=7-6\alpha$

$C \quad 2\alpha+9(1-\alpha)=9-7\alpha$

For the profit matrix

$A \quad 8\alpha+3(1-\alpha)=3+5\alpha$

$B \quad 7\alpha+(1-\alpha)=1+6\alpha$

$C \quad 9\alpha+2(1-\alpha)=2+7\alpha$

matrix, the line of minimum values is always given (across all values of α) by B. No switch ever occurs from the second strategy. On the other hand, for the profit matrix a switch does occur when $3 + 5\alpha = 2 + 7\alpha$—that is, at $\alpha = \frac{1}{2}$. This is shown for the maximum values of C(from $\alpha = 0$ to $\alpha = .5$) and A (from $\alpha = .5$ to $\alpha = 1$).

Decisions and Managerial Attitudes

The decision format can be very antiseptic in spite of its persuasive logic. At every level we can show how most human managerial behaviors interact with the simplistic perfection of the decision theory format. In the manager's measurements of a system's properties there are divergencies from the real system's characteristics, and there are even more direct influences of management attitudes in the estimates for factors that cannot be measured. Thus, for DMUC there is the question of what is an acceptable degree of approximation to certainty; for DMUR there are the issues of when a system can be considered stable and how to ascertain the believability of a forecast; for DMUU there is the question of when it is reasonable to assume complete uncertainty, and then there is the choice of an acceptable decision criterion, which the manager must recognize as being conditioned by his attitudes.

Attitudes pervade the entire subject of decision-making. To believe otherwise is to fall under the spell of methods quite apart from the problems they are intended to cope with. Let us concentrate on DMUU in order to examine the kinds of behavioral interaction that exist. Consider the following decision problem: The manager's strategies in reaching a decision under uncertainty are the various decision criteria that we have previously discussed. In other words, in terms of Table 4–11, which attitude should the manager take (assuming that he can control his choice)?

Table 4–11   Matrix of Profits

		The manager's choice is:	
		Right	Wrong
The manager chooses one of these strategies:	Optimistic, $\alpha = 1$	R_{11}	R_{12}
	Pessimistic, Wald, $\alpha = 0$	R_{21}	R_{22}
	Rational $p_j = 1/n$	R_{31}	R_{32}

Whatever values are entered in the matrix, estimates of the probability of being right and being wrong are essential. If they cannot be obtained, then the problem continues to be one of decision-making under uncertainty. But if the estimates could be given, then the problem never was one of uncertainty. So, we must dismiss that possibility or else admit that the manager had had, in fact, subjective feelings about being right or wrong that permitted him to select one of these strategies.

We should note, then, that the only strategy that does not imply some knowledge of what would happen is the Laplace-Bayes criterion. That is why we call it the rationalist's criterion. At the same time, it is completely impractical because the manager (having much experience that relates in one way or another to the problem) is seldom, if ever, impartial. The rationalist's criterion is the last one that we would actually expect to be used. The uncertainty in Table 4–11 reflects whatever uncertainty existed in Table 4–10. If another decision matrix were constructed to try to resolve the questions raised in connection with Table 4–11, it would suffer from the same flaw. With real uncertainty it is possible to design an infinite sequence of decision matrices and impossible to resolve any of them. It is much like a hall of mirrors; we cannot determine how to decide to decide to decide to . . . until information or attitudes unbalance the system and free its paralysis.

SUMMARY

The main emphasis of this chapter is on the fundamental structure of decision models. The major steps for constructing a decision model are the following:

1. Identify the controllable variables. Taken together, they constitute the manager's *strategies,* called x_i's, to obtain his *objectives.*

2. Discover all the uncontrollable variables. Taken together, they are the *environments,* called z_j's, that affect the manager's achievement of his *objectives.* If all the environments cannot be identified, then the problem must be treated as one of decision-making under *ambiguity* (DMUA), in which case the decision problem cannot be resolved properly until the ambiguity is removed.

3. Determine the *result,* R_{ij}, that arises when a specific x_i and a particular z_j occur together. That is: $R_{ij} = f(x_i, z_j)$. Each R_{ij} is an intersection value of the decision matrix, which has i rows and j columns. R_{ij}'s should reflect directly the manager's ability to achieve his *objectives.*

4. A *forecast* of the probabilities for the likelihoods of the environments, called p_j's, is required. When the forecast indicates that only one environment exists, then the decision problem is categorized as decision-making under *certainty* (DMUC); if several environments should be considered, then decision-making under *risk* (DMUR) is indicated. Sometimes the forecast is incomplete, and *partial uncertainty* is involved (DMUPU). When no forecast information can be obtained, the problem is classified as decision-making under *uncertainty* (DMUU). The stability of the environmental system is critical. If the forecast changes in unknown ways, then the decision problem cannot be resolved using the matrix model.

5. A variety of decision criteria exists. For DMUC, the quest is for the "best" value in the single column of the matrix. When DMUR exists, first an *expected value* is obtained for each strategy, and then *search* procedures are used, as in DMUC. For both of the above situations, there are no alternative procedures. However, the probability distribution for DMUR must be *believable,* and, if DMUC is postulated, the *approximation* of certainty must be realistic. Often the manager will not allow DMUU conditions to prevail, but if he does, a variety of decision criteria can be applied. The choice of the criterion (pessimistic, optimistic, rational, etc.) is greatly influenced by the manager's attitude.

Much more remains to be stated about the decision model and its inter-action with the human decision-maker. In this chapter the fundamental structure of the decision matrix has been developed. Succeeding chapters will present a far broader view of the decision process.

EXERCISES

1. Develop a specific matrix example of a decision problem (coming as close to reality as possible) in terms of strategies, environments, results, and probabilities of the environments. Explain problem-solving in the context of your example; discuss the relevance of the decision period; and describe in detail the forecasting problem that you face.

2. Set up a "make versus buy" decision problem using your own numbers. Solve your problem and apply sensitivity analysis to illustrate its importance. (Remember that sensitivity analysis can be applied to any of the estimates that contribute to the solution.)

3. The "make or buy" example, developed on pp. 128–29 of this chapter, examined *sensitivity mapping* for the values of p_1 and p_2. Work out the analysis for p_1 and p_3 in the example. (See footnote 9 on p. 132.)

4. Refer to the example of the day-to-day stock-market trader (pp. 132–34). What would his net profit be if he bought and sold in lots of 1,000 shares? (Take commissions into account. A call to your neighborhood broker will get you the prevailing commission rate.) Suggest an improved model for the trader based on the stock's closing prices on the previous day. Get some actual data for a few selected stocks and determine what the results would be for your system. Try to choose stocks that have high daily variability.

5. In Exercise 1 you developed an example of a decision problem and cast it in decision-matrix form. Convert the representation of this problem to a decision-tree format. Show all the branches of the tree and the way in which you would interpret and apply this model. Now assume that each strategy is associated with its own set of probabilities and analyze the problem in this way.

6. For the matrix on p. 136 describing alternative packaging strategies, develop the appropriate decision tree and resolve the problem by means of the tree representation.

7. Using the structure and data of "Example 4: Artichokes or Stringbeans" (on pp. 137–39), determine what happens if we make the following change: If the weather has been good (G), then the probability that the weather will continue to be good is .90; if the weather has been bad (B), then the probability that it will continue to be bad is .70. Resolve this problem using the decision-tree format. (Note footnote 14 on p. 138.)

8. Consider what might be relevant *environments* for the following decision outcome measures:
   a. The safety of a new drug
   b. The stability of a newly designed jet air-bus
   c. The success of a city renovation program
   d. The probability that a new high-speed train can compete successfully with airlines on a 500-mile route

9. Soapy, Inc., is developing a new soap that is intended to be as alkaline as possible. Alkalinity and acidity are measured on a pH scale, where a pH of seven is the neutral point. When the pH is less than seven, the substance is acidic; when the pH is greater than seven, the substance is alkaline (or basic). A mathematical model has been developed to describe the pH that will result from adding an ingredient x, in quantities from .1 to 1.0, namely:

$$pH = 50x - 40x^2 - 3$$

Treat this as a decision problem under certainty, where the strategies are values of x between 0.1 and 1.0. What value of x will be found to produce the optimal result? Show how this result appears in the single column format of DMUC. Is the result satisfactory?

10. The decision matrix below is said to have believable p_j's, and the results are measures of satisfaction. Which strategy should be used?

$p_j = .10$	.30	.20	.40
z_1	z_2	z_3	z_4

	z_1	z_2	z_3	z_4
x_1	6	10	5	9
x_2	7	2	2	15
x_3	8	8	8	8

What kind of decision problem is this? To what situation might it apply? If the environments are weather conditions and the strategies are different vacations (swimming in the Bahamas, skiing in the Alps, etc.), why is this decision matrix incorrect? Explain.

11. A particular decision problem has four environments, and none of the probabilities is known. Then the additional information is obtained that $p_1 = p_4$ and $p_2 = p_3$. How does this new knowledge convert the problem from DMUU to DMUPU? Could the additional information affect the manager's decision? Explain.

12. For the matrix in Exercise 10 assume that the probability estimates have been rejected by the manager. He intends to use the pessimist's criterion instead. What strategy will the manager choose on this basis? What reasons might have led him to this choice?

a. If the rationalist's criterion had been used, would the result have been different?

b. Assume that the manager asked for resolution of the problem based on a coefficient of optimism of .5. Would this result differ from those obtained by the two previous criteria? What might a coefficient of optimism of .5 mean to the manager?

The Framework of Managing

MODEL-BUILDING AND MODEL USE

DECISION-MAKING

The Decision Behaviors of Management

Chapter 5
The Effects of Competitive Behavior

Competitive decisions require a game-theory basis. The
concepts of game theory are applicable within the organization
as well as in the marketplace. These concepts illuminate
some profoundly rational aspects of managerial behavior in
a competitive situation, while, at the same time, they
call attention to the realistic complexity introduced by human
behavior. Planning, policy-making, and organizing cannot
be discussed adequately without appropriate appreciation of
the competitive structure of decision-making.

Chapter 5

THE EFFECTS
OF COMPETITIVE
BEHAVIOR

Some forty years ago, Alexander Meiklejohn pointed out the difference between tennis (in which one leans over backward to be strictly honest and generous to one's opponent) and baseball (in which anything goes if one does not get caught at it—and razzing is part of the game). He was complaining that "We are receiving a tennis education for a baseball world." [1] In computer-based competitive management games, occasionally one team will direct its attention to "beating" the computer program rather than trying to apply good business sense within the system. The logic of this approach is indisputable. Nevertheless, it causes complaints from competing teams, who want to pretend that the computer program is the "real world."

UBIQUITOUS COMPETITION

Competition is indeed everywhere and in everything. Even self-competition exists, an inner-directed prod to each individual to

---

[1] Quoted by Charlotte E. Mauk in a letter to the editor of *Science,* Vol. 151 (January 7, 1966).

move along in his development.[2] In many fields studies have been made of the extent to which competition is a part of man's nature. Freud pointed out that aggressive competition is inherent in the organism. Anthropologists have examined primitive cultures and described competition ranging from potlatch gifts among the Kwakiutls to the headhunting of the Jivaro Indians in the Amazon and the bargaining in Eastern bazaars. Nikolaas Tinbergen, famous for his studies of instinct,[3] has stated that man has changed in no obvious way since the days of his Cro-Magnon ancestors, thousands of years ago. He goes on to make the point that competitiveness is a fundamental trait of human behavior (an instinct?) and apparently not susceptible to education.

Studies of the drive to own territory (see Chapter 14, pp. 605–06) reveal behaviors that seem to affect all animals, including our simian cousins. In human society, group territorialism manifests itself in competition between teams, departments, divisions, and companies, as well as in struggles over national boundaries. Certainly the implications of territorialism on a national scale are of immediate importance to the *survival* of man, but the relevance of territorialism for smaller groups is equally important to the *condition* of man. There has been an upsurge in research efforts at many levels and concern for the study of conflicts and their resolution.[4]

Competition is a *force for change* and is at the root of both balance and imbalance. The balance that is achieved is a dynamic one; new competitive forces are arising all the time to cause imbalance and the search for a new equilibrium. The balance may be of the *open systems* type,[5] wherein partially specified multiple forces can change and adjust to one another in some unknown way to keep the system (such as an economy) on a stable track. Competition may, on the other hand, produce balance, or equilibrium, in a *closed system.* For example, the mongoose was brought to St. Croix in the Virgin Islands to control the snake population, which it did with great effectiveness. After the snakes had been wiped out, the mongoose remained to plague the island's inhabitants by finding other means of survival, which included raiding family garbage cans. Thus a new problem of balancing forces arose as the inhabitants attempted to kill off the mongooses. The seven-

---

[2] As a reflection of this, a personal philosophy known as Couéism was based on the saying: "Every day, in every way, I am getting better and better." This was a major movement in France in the early twentieth century; it was so appealing that it spread quickly to the United States and elsewhere.

[3] Dr. Tinbergen's work is discussed in Chapter 14.

[4] Another new name has been coined, illustrating the scientific interest in this topic. It is *polemology.* There is an Institute of Polemology in Paris and another in the Netherlands. There are also various publications, such as the *Journal of Conflict Resolution.*

[5] In a *closed system,* all influencing factors can be observed; in an *open system,* some factors, at least, cannot.

year visitations of locusts are another example of a balanced closed system. So is the situation of tent caterpillars, which at times become so numerous as to cause their predators to overbreed. When the caterpillars are almost wiped out, the predators, lacking a food supply, diminish in number until the caterpillars can gradually rebuild their population. This is an example of *oscillation* in a closed system. Prey-predator systems typify the ubiquity of competition in nature, where it is rare that the numbers of either side are ever totally exhausted.[6]

Organizational Competition

Some individuals appear to possess, inherently, a high quotient of personal loyalty to an organization, no matter what organization it is, whereas others do not readily identify themselves with any institution. For example, there is considerable evidence that many persons with strong "leftist" political orientations switch to "rightist" orientations and maintain the same avidity. The constant seems to be zealousness, not issues or context. In terms of competition, it is clear that deep affiliation to an organization, for whatever reason, leads to real and not trivial competition. (This is all the more interesting since changes in an individual's affiliations can occur overnight.) *Real* competition is distinguished by a lack of clear-cut rules such as exist in cases of *trivial* competition (e.g., games of Monopoly or cards).

Turning to organizations themselves, we observe two major forms of organizational competition. First, there is *internal* competition, such as that between fellow employees for advancement or between project groups for a share of the budget; second, there is *external* competition for sales volume, brand share, brand loyalty, prime time, executive talent, and so forth. While the classroom (as an organization) does an incomplete job of reflecting either type of competition, the internal form of competition is more easily seen there (in the competition for grades, class standing, and extracurricular positions) than is the external form of competition. However, the recent use of computer games between fictitious firms is at least a first step toward embodying some of the external forms of competition.

Values

Discussions about the merits of competition are known to produce rancorous, emotion-filled disputes, and no single argument has yet prevailed that either

---

[6] Although it is rare, it is not impossible, as the mongoose-snake relationship illustrates. Usually, there is great reluctance to influence prey-predator relations because the new equilibriums often have unexpected and undesirable ramifications.

entirely supports or entirely denies the benefits of competition. The real issue seems to be that both "healthy" and "unhealthy" competition exist, in business and industry as well as elsewhere.

But the characterization of "good" and "bad" competition is a matter of judgment and degree—varying both in time and between societies. Is a particular form of competition good for one system and not for another? Is competition beneficial only if supported by a system that believes it to be beneficial? Is competition a theological issue? In theory at least, communism rejects the advantages of marketplace competition and instead substitutes control. Capitalistic concepts of competition appear to be either good or bad according to one's value system. Developments in recent years in the United States and in world business show signs of a change in values—though possibly not in the directions that had once been thought of as the only alternatives. The world press reflects on social and economic value systems; its attitudes, depending on which publications you read, range from fierce antagonism to total support for free enterprise and even for a capitalist system (of the 1920's) that no longer exists.

It is not our intention to become involved with such issues here. We should resist the temptation to confuse our personal preferences for degrees and forms of competition with the development of understanding for actual competitive situations. Changing existing standards may be one form of mission—but it is not the one to which we shall address ourselves. Because the determination of "good" and "bad" competition is a matter of value, it is to us a personal and nonoperational issue for examining the theory and principles of management.

This is not to say that each manager as a person must not arrange his thoughts on these subjects, nor is it to say that there are not some aspects of the issue that he must consider operationally. In our society a line is drawn between "rough" competition and "gentlemanly" competition. Governmental legislation substitutes control for some types of competition and at the same time attempts to encourage other types of competition. And social morality, although it allows that many forms of competition are desirable, does not encourage verbalization of loopholes in the law or circumvention of ethical considerations. In a classroom it is difficult to provide much focus on such matters, but they are concerns with which managers must learn to cope. (We will discuss ethical problems at some length in Chapter 7.)

Alternative Forms of Competition

The government looks with disfavor on companies that decide between themselves not to compete on price but to agree on it. (This is particularly true if they control the supply and agree on a high price.) To the extent that cooperation can be substituted for competition, some form of regulation is usually required. Therefore, control may be considered an alternative to competition. In fact, however, the competitive essence continues to exist. It simply has been transformed to a new condition—that is, that of control, where the regulatory agreements permit competition to operate under less variable conditions. Competitive efforts are then directed by some to change the control policy and by others to maintain it. Governmental lobbying is an example of both positions.

According to Seidenberg, in his study *Post-Historic Man,*[7] all individuals will eventually *agree* because of their complete rationality. Agreement, however, will not end competition where two or more competing parties must divide a fixed amount of resources and each is striving to get the largest amount possible. In other words, agreement will not remove conflicting objectives. Thus, Seidenberg is not proposing that rationality will end competition; what he really means is that it will end disagreement. Competition persists in spite of agreement. Control and cooperation may be substituted for outright competition in agreeing on how the resources should be divided. But these are simply alternative forms for resolving competitive issues. Competition operates under specific rules and at a higher level to determine the rules for proportioning resources; without such rules, individuals will fight to earn a reasonable share for themselves. (The concept of "a fair share" is a commentary on particular individual and social ethics.) Given rules for proportioning, historically, men will try to change the rules through their wits and strengths and by waiting for pure chance events to intercede in the balance of forces. It is hard to believe that rational men would do otherwise. An invention or a new idea will alter the competitors' shares. Rational men will not engage in irrational conflict; they will accept the new basis for division.[8] Problems of competition are increased by the fact that the size of the kitty is variable and usually is affected by what all the competitors do. Thus, not only are companies competing with one another, but together "as a system" they are competing with the external world that surrounds them.

Competition persists, as we have said, long after disagreement has been removed. (The most fundamental game theory model, which we will discuss shortly, demonstrates this point perfectly.) But agreement and disagreement are attitudes that can affect the nature of competition in several ways. First, disagreement can cause one or more players to depart from whatever rational

---

[7] Roderick Seidenberg, *Post-Historic Man, An Inquiry* (Boston: Beacon Press, 1957).

[8] A prophetic science-fiction theme portrays the computers of two nations examining a state of war. Instead of sending real men onto the field, the computers simulate the optimal battle strategies, and the loser acknowledges defeat just as if real battles had been fought. The obvious goal for each side is to keep the situation balanced until it finds a new technology, strategy, or the like, that cannot be matched by the opponent.

procedures apply because they are angry, annoyed, indifferent, and so forth. Such departures are *never* beneficial to the sole irrational player. But the penalties will vary if the irrationality becomes widespread. Second, in competitive situations where more than two opponents exist, coalitions can be formed, based on personality compatibilities and individual abilities to agree. Third, a competitive system can be converted to a noncompetitive one by methods that are not usually considered "fair play"; this occurs only when there is disagreement. Espionage, for example, which is as familiar to industry as to the military, can remove all competitive advantage from one opponent. In one sense, this is equivalent to invoking new rules in order to win. If each side uses espionage and knows that the other side does too, then espionage becomes part of the competition. From this brief description, we can see that attitudes of agreement or disagreement can play a powerful role in the determination of what will happen to the total system, which often includes many noncombatants (such as consumers) as well as the opponents.

GAME THEORY

Management models in the competitive sphere are usually termed *game models*. By studying game theory, we can obtain substantial insight into management's role under competitive conditions, even though much of game theory is neither directly operational nor implementable. In other words, the relation of the game theory model to the real world is weak, and, since the manager operates in the framework of reality, the game model becomes less useful to him in the normative sense.[9] Its main advantages are conceptual and educational. It helps the manager move closer to the kind of awareness that is essential for implementation. Consequently, we will spend some time on the details of game theory.

To begin, certain terminology will be helpful. First, we must contrast *zero-sum* and *non-zero-sum games*. In a zero-sum game, when the amounts won by one and the amounts lost by the other are totaled, the sum is zero. For example, P_1 wins \$5, which is paid to him by P_2, so

$$P_1 \text{ wins } +5$$
$$P_2 \text{ loses } -5$$
$$\text{Sum} \qquad 0$$

All resources in these systems are conserved; they are merely reapportioned.

---

[9] Among all management science models, competitive ones, as a class, probably have the least direct applicability. Since competition is so critical to organizational decision-making, the lack is particularly unfortunate.

The above arithmetic does not work for non-zero-sum games. P_1 could win \$5 while P_2 loses \$2. A positive sum always occurs when two competitors increase the total size of the market, say as a result of an intensive advertising duel. Advocates of advertising believe that such positive effects occur frequently. The sum could just as well be negative, however. As an example, in a military game where P_1 destroys a P_2 tank, the sum would be $- 1$ (tank).

Second, we classify games by the *number of opponents*—for example, two-person, three-person, n-person games The only competitive situations that can be handled directly by normative modeling are two-person, zero-sum games. When more than two players are involved, coalitions can and usually do spring up. The form of such collusion must be described as erratic (not just variable), for the participants' roles in the collusion are, at best, only as predictable as the knowledge of human behavior will allow. Few real competitive situations are simple, determinate affairs.

Third, the amount of *information available* about each opponent's strategies sets the type of game. There might be *total ambiguity* about what any opponent will do—that is, even the potential strategies that could be used are unknown. *Complete uncertainty* could also exist, in which case the strategic alternatives would be known but no estimates of the probabilities of their use would be available (except through the logic of the model, as we shall soon see). On the other hand, by means of information collection methods (including espionage) it becomes possible to *know* to some degree what will occur. Such knowledge can *range* from just a glimmer to total and exact detail. We can readily understand why any manager would like to have believable information about his opponent's intentions. Such information might be translated into a probability distribution and the competitive situation changed from a zero-sum game to a (risk) decision problem that can be handled by the methods described in Chapter 4. Surprisingly, when no probability information can be obtained—that is, in the case of complete uncertainty on the part of all opponents—the logical approach of zero-sum games can be used. This converts the situation to one of no uncertainty, of *complete determinancy*. Let us see why this is so.

Competitive Decision Matrix

The decision analysis that is available for competitive systems shares many elements with decision-making under uncertainty. But there, it will be remembered, no definitive decision criterion could be unequivocally recommended. Let us replace, for the moment, the states of nature, z_j's, with a *new* set of *controlled* variables, c_k's. These variables are controlled by one or more opponents, each of whom has motivations and is able to act with intelligence in pursuit of his objectives. The competitive strategies, c_k's, are certainly unlike the chance variable systems of environments.

The matrix of Table 5–1 describes a two-person, zero-sum decision situation. For convenience, we shall call one player the "entrepreneur" and the other player the "competitor." The entrepreneur must lose exactly what the competitor wins (and vice versa). The x_i's represent entrepreneurial activities; the c_k's are competitive activities; and the matrix is written from the entrepreneur's point of view. Payoff estimates must be identical for both the entrepreneur and the competitor; in other words, they must agree completely as to what will happen when any specific x_i encounters any particular c_k. For the zero-sum condition only one matrix is required, although from the standpoint of "whose payoff" there are two. The competitor's matrix is obtained by multiplying all entries in the entrepreneur's matrix by -1, in order that the sum of the two matrices, competitor's plus entrepreneur's, be zero in keeping with the zero-sum criterion.

Table 5–1

	c_1	c_2	c_3
x_1	6	6	5
x_2	-5	8	-3
x_3	7	-2	0

Utilities and non-zero-sum situations. When non-zero-sum conditions exist, we cannot derive the competitor's matrix from the entrepreneur's, for both parties to the competition will stand to gain different amounts by utilizing the various activities that are available to them. In effect, the outcomes reflect the creation or destruction of wealth. This is equivalent to hypothesizing that a third player (perhaps the marketplace) exists and functions as both a source and an absorber of wealth.

Such complications also arise when the opposing managers place different *utilities* on the payoff values. Variation in utilities for, say, money can arise from many sources, the most usual being a difference in company size and assets. One of the parties may represent a powerful and wealthy company, while the other may possess a lesser amount of assets. The latter clearly will be prone to value an additional dollar of profit more highly than the former. Often, moreover, the accounting measures that are available for payoffs misrepresent the situation for both players. When dollar measures are suspect, the concept of *utils* is handy. Utils, in this case, are units of the managers' utilities for dollars, and they are substituted for direct dollar measures. When the number of utils (for one or more payoffs) are not the same for both managers, the game format necessarily changes from zero to non-zero sum.

Running counter to this kind of setback is the fact that through clever transformations it is sometimes possible to convert non-zero-sum situations into zero-sum situations. The use of brand-share information instead of sales volume in a payoff matrix is a good example. In this case, when the entrepreneur loses a certain percentage of the market, the competitor must gain that same percentage, and the sum of gain and loss then equals zero. There are, however, complications. Since brand share converts sales volume to a percentage, it represents a homomorphic transformation, and some information is lost. An expanding or contracting market might not be noticed in share analysis. In a shrinking market, for example, the entrepreneur and the competitor might both lose, while the brand shares could remain unchanged. Clearly, in a rather unstable market, with considerable fluctuations in total sales volume, share analysis can lead to erroneous conclusions. Nevertheless, the ability to use zero-sum treatment may be worth some loss of information.

Approximations. The loss of information inherent in moving from sales volume to brand share is representative of the loss of information experienced in approximations of other kinds, many of which are required in converting a complex competitive situation into a simple zero-sum game. For example, in constructing a zero-sum game, we assume that the entrepreneur and the competitor reason in an identical fashion—an assumption that is at best an approximation. However, do managers, in fact, not tend intuitively toward such an assumption? Doesn't the entrepreneur visualize the competitor much as he visualizes himself? There are indications from the behavioral sciences that people have a difficult time perceiving that others might feel differently from themselves. In line with this, we can generally assume that each manager's view of the typical competitive situation will tend to discount differences and thereby move him conceptually closer to the zero-sum approximation.

A more specific aspect of this approximation is the assumption of the *perfect rationality* of all competitors. Since all parties to the competition have the same payoff matrix and are expected to know what it is, each is in a position to reason out what activity to use with full knowledge of what activity he would use if he were the competitor. The manager is likely to believe in his own rationality. If his tendency is to think that the competitor is like himself, not only does he assign the same measures of utility to the competitor's payoff matrix but he endows him as well with his own rationality.

When taken together, the imposition of two-person systems ("me" and "the others"), the use of zero-sum utility measures, and the requirements of complete rationality and full knowledge of the payoff matrix create a highly artificial situation. Competitive models that are far more elaborate than two-person and zero-sum ones are required for practical analytic benefits in most "real" situations, but these more elaborate conditions are not readily put into a formal, analytic model. Experiments and simulations of competitive systems often are more effective, but they are costly and still open to criticism concerning the realism of their behavioral components. In consequence, extensive research is going on in this area. However, although we can predict significant advances will come, operational benefits are presently slim. It is in the conceptual realm that the modeling of competitive systems makes its greatest contribution.

Now that we have presented some of the issues that should be kept in mind when studying competitive systems, let us explain the solution to the simple game given above. The discussion is straightforward because of the determinate nature of the model—that is, there are no probability distributions or expected values, and there is a straight line of reasoning that must be followed.

Solution Waldian

Both managers *must* use the Waldian criterion; maximin for the entrepreneur, minimax for the competitor (who prefers negative matrix entries). Thus, in the light of Table 5–2, the entrepreneur selects activity x_1, which is associated

Table 5–2

	c_1	c_2	c_3	Entrepreneur's minimum:
x_1	6	6	5	5 ←MAXIMIN
x_2	−5	8	−3	−5
x_3	7	−2	0	−2
Competitor's maximum:	7	8	5 ←MINIMAX	

with a payoff of 5; the competitor selects activity c_3, also associated with the value of 5. Five is then called the *saddlepoint* value of the game because it provides a zero-sum solution.[10]

Consider what would happen if one party uses his Waldian solution and the other one does not. Let us say that the entrepreneur uses x_1, but the competitor does not use c_3. The entrepreneur stands to gain the difference

---

[10] The mathematical definition of a saddlepoint for a game is such that the value of the minimax equals that of the maximin. It is possible that no cell entry of the game matrix can provide such a result, in which case mixed strategies (as described shortly) must be used.

between 6 and 5. Similarly, if the competitor uses c_3, but the entrepreneur does not use x_1, the competitor can gain either ten or seven points. Consequently, if one player uses the Waldian approach, then the other party will be obliged to use it also. What motivates these players to turn to the Waldian criterion in the first place? Aside from the logic of minimaxing or maximining, one party is driven directly to use it by the fact that random choice is the other alternative. If both parties together can choose any of the nine pairs of $x_i c_k$ as if they were equally likely, then the expected value for the entire matrix would be $\frac{22}{6} = 3\frac{2}{3}$. This would be good for the competitor but not for the entrepreneur, who can get 5 by using the maximin. Therefore, the latter would prefer to use his maximin, and our initial reasoning prevails.

If the result had indicated different values for the entrepreneur and the competitor, then a *mixed strategy* would be required. In this case, one or both parties would use a mixture of activities. The choice of which strategy to use is determined by a *random* selection process based on the determination of relative frequencies for the potential activities. This will be fully discussed shortly, when we consider the far-reaching implications of mixed strategies for management.

In the example we have used, the best that the competitor can hope to do is to *lose* five units at each play. If the competitor can invent another activity, c_4, he may yet improve his lot.[11] As things stand, however, he is a *loser*.[12] And the Waldian criterion *must* be used when the assumptions that we have enumerated hold; it is the only possible criterion that can be employed. Consequently, if the competitor cannot invent a successful strategy, c_4, he might try to find a "disconnect" type of strategy—that is, one that would enable him to quit the game.

Competitive information. If the entrepreneur learns that the competitor is not rational, then he knows that his opponent will not use the Waldian criterion. This promises the entrepreneur a larger return on his maximin strategy. However, if he finds out just how the competitor is going to act—for example, that a stable probability distribution describes the competitor's behavior—then the entrepreneur could improve his payoff by using this distribution and treating the problem as DMUR.[13] Whenever there is additional information available about the competitor, the entrepreneur may be able to use it to improve his performance. When the entrepreneur knows *exactly* what the competitor will do, he simply uses his best choice.

---

[11] For example, a successful c_4 would be -5, -6, -7.

[12] See the discussion on p. 190. Refer also to Warren Weaver, *Lady Luck* (New York: Doubleday, 1963), Chap. XIII: "Rare Events, Coincidences and Suprising Occurrences," pp. 278–303.

[13] See the discussion on the value of information, pp. 220–30.

For example, the entrepreneur may learn that the competitor will use c_1. Because he possesses this special information, the entrepreneur will employ his activity x_3 and thereby obtain a payoff of seven points instead of the six that the Waldian choice of x_1 would produce. The additional payoff of one unit is a measure of the value of the special data obtained by the entrepreneur. The cost of information should, of course, never exceed its value. Test markets, surveys, and industrial espionage are examples of information sources that are used to determine a competitor's strategy when the situation appears to lend itself to risk analysis or to the perfect prediction of DMUC.

Mixed Strategies

When a saddlepoint result does not occur in the matrix—that is, when the minimax and the maximin solutions have different values—it is necessary to obtain a solution by manipulating combinations of strategies. There is a fundamental theorem in game theory that assures us that some mixture of strategies will always provide a saddlepoint result and that, given the rationality of both parties, this is the optimal solution. For the matrix of Table 5–3, the mixed-strategy situation will now be demonstrated.

Table 5–3

	c_1	c_2	c_3	Entrepreneur's minimum:
x_1	6	−5	7	−5
x_2	−4.5	2	−1.5	−4.5 ←MAXIMIN

Competitor's maximum:	6	2	7

$$\uparrow$$
MINIMAX

We observe in the table that the game matrix is not square; and there is no reason why it should be square, for frequently one opponent will have more options available than another. Since here the maximin is −4.5 and the minimax is 2, there is no obvious saddlepoint. We cannot even tell at this point whether it is the entrepreneur or the competitor who is the winner of this game. All we know is that the final solution must fall somewhere between 2 (the entrepreneur is a winner) and −4.5 (the competitor is a winner). The diagrams in Figure 5–1 provide the answer. The entrepreneur is the loser because the saddlepoint value of the game is −.6. This is obtained when the

Figure 5–1

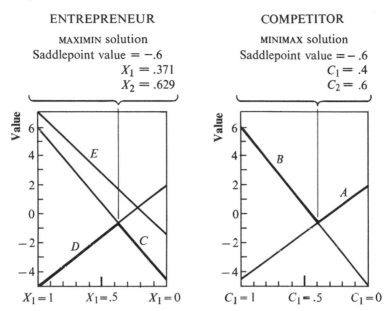

ENTREPRENEUR

MAXIMIN solution
Saddlepoint value = −.6
$X_1 = .371$
$X_2 = .629$

COMPETITOR

MINIMAX solution
Saddlepoint value = −.6
$C_1 = .4$
$C_2 = .6$

entrepreneur uses his x_1 strategy 37.1 percent of the time and his x_2 strategy 62.9 percent of the time. The competitor, being entirely rational, will use his strategies as follows: c_1, 40 percent; c_2, 60 percent; and c_3, 0 percent.

The graphic method of solution that has been used can work only for an opponent who has two strategies. A three-dimensional figure could extend graphic capabilities by one additional strategy, but that would be the limit. Usually such problems are solved by algebraic means. It is not our intention to discuss these methods at great length, because our purpose is to convey the sense of a mixed strategy and not its derivation. Nevertheless, since we can quite readily explain the basis of the geometric solution by using algebra, we shall do so. First, it should be noted that the competitor's strategy c_3 will never be used because for the competitor 6 is better than 7, and −4.5 is better than −1.5. We say that c_1 *dominates* c_3, and this reduced the game matrix to a two-by-two size, thus:

	c_1	c_2
x_1	6	−5
x_2	−4.5	2

If the entrepreneur uses his pure strategy x_1, then the value (V) of the game to the competitor will be: $V = 6c_1 - 5c_2$. Since $c_1 + c_2 = 1$, we can rewrite our equation: $V = 6c_1 - 5(1 - c_1) = 6c_1 - 5 + 5c_1 = 11c_1 - 5$. On the competitor's diagram, this line is plotted as B. Line A is derived for the condition in which the entrepreneur uses his pure strategy x_2. It is $V = -6.5c_1 + 2$. As the use of c_1 changes from being a pure strategy, $c_1 = 1$, to never being used, $c_1 = 0$, the upper surface of these lines maps out all maximums. The point of intersection, where $V = -.6$, is the minimax. The same reasoning applies to the entrepreneur's diagram. His equations are: for strategy c_1, $V = 10.5x_1 - 4.5$ (marked C); for strategy c_2, $V = -7x_1 + 2$ (marked D); and, for strategy c_3, $V = 8.5x_1 - 1.5$ (marked E). The entrepreneur traces along the bottom surface of the lines to find the maximum of these minimums —where $V = -.6$. To achieve these maximin and minimax results, each opponent uses the indicated mixtures of his strategies.

The selection of a strategy is on a random basis, so neither opponent can be sure of which strategy his opponent will use next. Any procedure for achieving such randomization is satisfactory—even the simple idea of thoroughly mixing thirty-seven chips marked x_1 and sixty-three chips marked x_2 in a bowl and drawing one chip out at random each time that a strategy is to be used. If either opponent learns in advance of the other's selection, the Waldian approach ceases to be sensible.

It is worth pointing out that mixed strategies convert the determinate, pure-strategy game into an artificial risk situation. When probabilities are introduced into the formulation of the mixed-strategy game, the strategies of each opponent become states of nature for the other, and the solution is based on equalizing the players' expected values, which is the explanation of the saddle-point characteristics of the game. Still, the result of such competition is fully determinate—that is, everyone knows who is going to win how much in the long run.

Adding complexity. Part of the function of management is to introduce uncertainties into competitive systems, even when the situation is viewed as essentially determinate in form. In terms of games (whether of the casino or industrial type), it is desirable to invent elements that can remove the determinacy from the competitive situation in order to make the games interesting. First, we can allow outside random events to occur—for example, in bridge, the hands dealt are not predetermined. Second, we can increase the size of the game and thereby its level of complexity—for example, in chess or the game of go, there are so many possible moves that the mere fact of determinacy does not dampen the player's interest. For additional variety, the number of competitors could be increased. More than two players can produce complicating relationships, as epitomized by shifting coalitions. Third, bluffing can be used, as in poker, in which some players try to project mis-information and the others try to judge its validity. In other situations, information that reduces uncertainty can be obtained gradually (e.g., knowing which cards have been played). In this sense, the character of random events can change over time, and the efficient competitor will track that information.

All these issues for simple and complex games have their counterpart in the managerial situation. When it does not cost too much, the manager wishes to reduce uncertainty for himself and to increase the uncertainty with which others must deal.

COMPETITION AND ENVIRONMENTS

Competitive structure frequently coexists with environmental risk conditions, z_j's. Furthermore, competitive decisions can be associated with environmental conditions whose likelihoods run the gamut from certainty through risk to uncertainty. Problems of this kind can be viewed in terms of a set of decision matrices, as shown in Figure 5–2.

Figure 5–2

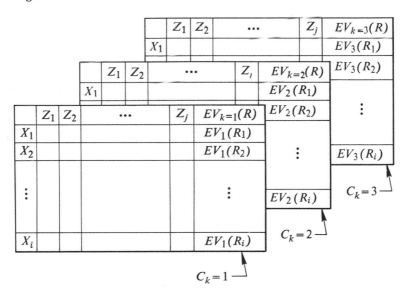

As before, the x_i's are the entrepreneur's strategies; the c_k's are the competitor's strategies; and the z_j's are states of nature. The cells of the matrix are filled with the payoffs, or results, R_{ijk}'s. Each matrix is associated with an index, k, such that each setting of k represents one specific (pure) strategy of the competitor. For any given number of competitive conditions, $k = 1, 2,$

3, . . . , we would have that number of decision matrices. There could be quite a large stack of cards, although only three are shown in the figure.

How do we resolve this kind of situation? Each risk matrix, $k = 1, 2, 3,$ . . . , can be collapsed into a single expected-value column. This column is identified by the competitor's index number, k, and has as many rows as there are strategies available to the manager. Such a set of expected-value columns, when regrouped, gives us a new competitive decision matrix, as shown in Table 5–4. Each column of *expected values* must be identified by the appropriate k, as described above.

Table 5–4

		Competitive strategies:				
		$c_k = 1$	$c_k = 2$	$c_k = 3$		$c_k = k$
Entrepreneur's	x_1	$EV_1(R_1)$	$EV_2(R_1)$	$EV_3(R_1)$	$\ldots$	$EV_k(R_1)$
strategies:	x_2	$EV_1(R_2)$	$EV_2(R_2)$	$EV_3(R_2)$	$\ldots$	$EV_k(R_2)$
	.					.
	.					.
	.					.
	x_i	$EV_1(R_i)$	$EV_2(R_i)$	$EV_3(R_i)$	$\ldots$	$EV_k(R_i)$

By collapsing the three-way array, we have now derived a single competitive payoff matrix that can be handled by the Waldian criterion applied to game theory. However, the variability within each cell is not fairly represented. After all, each $EV_k(R_i)$ could have been derived from a set of numbers that are almost the same or, conversely, from a set with an extreme range. (Five is the average of 4, 5, and 6 as well as of 1, 5, and 9.) Again, we have resorted to the kind of approximation that could raise questions about these game theory procedures. Sensitivity testing might be used where there is doubt as to the correctness of the approximation. The key would be to determine whether a shift occurs in the indicated strategies of both the entrepreneur and the competitor when some of the expected values are raised or lowered by a reasonable amount.

Whether he uses formal, objective models or informal, subjective ones, the manager's decision problem is still concerned with the same factors, the same kinds of approximations, the same use of transformations, and the same reflections of decision criteria. Often he proceeds informally. But if he turns to model-building, then a formal picture is presented, based on the decision theory of how managers reason. One of the most critical questions is: Does the manager, without a model, intuitively simplify his problems in this same way? If the answer is yes, then the formal model will always be able to serve as a check on the manager's intuitive conclusions. If the answer is no, then another question must be raised: Would the manager like to simplify his problems in this way? If the answer to this question is yes, then theory and practice have come together. If the answer is no, then the manager has to decide whether the model can still assist him as a guide, formulated for his use to tell him what information to get and what situations to avoid. Reasoning along such lines, we observe that a theory of management makes use of charts that show shoals and obstructions, as well as the channels to be navigated, and that point out what other information it might be useful to obtain.

The Game Tree

The game tree is a helpful device. It can show where randomness occurs, the nature of that randomness, information availability, and so forth. Above all, it details the strategy options and records the consequences of various sequences of alternative strategies. An illustrative tree is shown in Figure 5–3. Repetitive games, where a series of moves by both opponents is involved, require complex and dynamic forms of analysis, which a tree permits. It allows

Figure 5–3

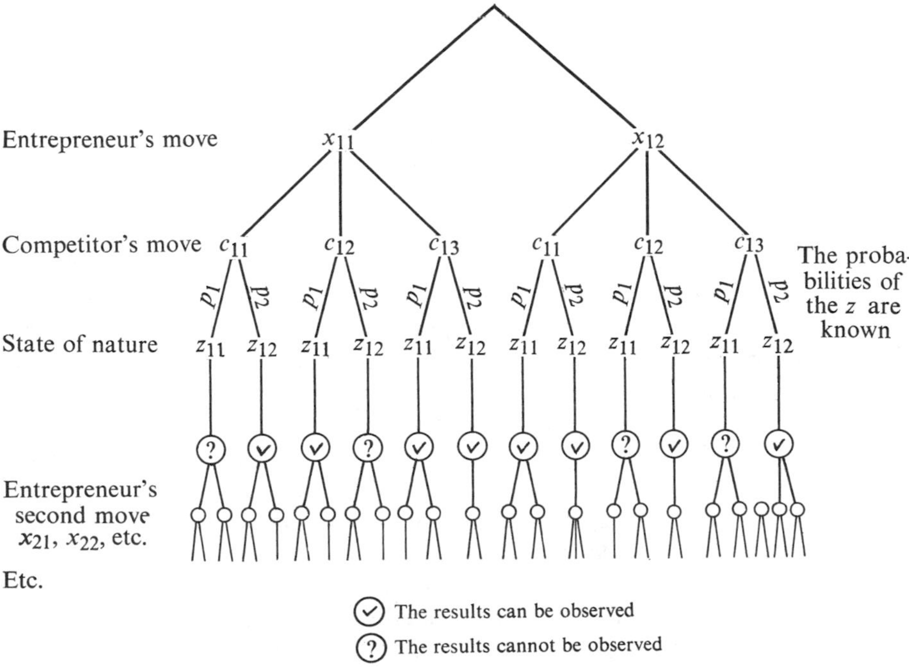

Entrepreneur's move x_{11} x_{12}

Competitor's move c_{11} c_{12} c_{13} c_{11} c_{12} c_{13} The probabilities of the z are known

State of nature z_{11} z_{12} z_{11} z_{12} z_{11} z_{12} z_{11} z_{12} z_{11} z_{12} z_{11} z_{12}

Entrepreneur's second move x_{21}, x_{22}, etc.

Etc.

⊘ The results can be observed

? The results cannot be observed

a clear image of a complex reality. If all the end-points of the tree are determined, a normative solution can be found.

Trees are thus helpful in analyzing highly complex systems, but at some point of complexity they break down. Most often the reality is too complex for the tree to represent it. For example, no one would try to draw the complete tree of chess moves. The reader will benefit if he works out the tree analysis for some simple, well-known game (such as rock-scissors-paper or two-finger Morra). Such an analysis will help to illustrate why competitive systems of business cannot be resolved by means of formal models. But it will underscore as well the fundamental characteristics of competition that are open to generalization, and it will increase awareness of the manager's role under competitive conditions. An advantage of trees is that they can be *simulated*. Therefore, quite complex aspects of competition, which cannot be resolved analytically, may be studied by simulation methods (assuming that the necessary information can be obtained and that the complexity does not exceed reasonable bounds).

Gaming of this sort (of which both military gaming and the case method of study are examples) is often used in the training of managers. It is related to, yet fundamentally different from, the normative methods of game theory. Many times, heuristics, which are far closer to principles than to theory, are used by the designers of such games. This fact always leaves in doubt the value of the training that the student is receiving. Gaming can withstand criticism when it accents problem-solving method rather than specific facts and relations.

BEHAVIORAL ASPECTS OF COMPETITION

We have noted that control can sometimes be substituted for competition— and that one of the most fundamental forms of competition (i.e., two-person, zero-sum games) is totally deterministic. The addition of new sources of randomness, increased size, and bluffing, more than just enlivening competitive situations, can be basic strategies in complex systems. For example, consider the situation shown in Table 5–5. (The matrix is written in terms of A's profit.) Company B is at a disadvantage from which it cannot escape as long as it wishes to stay in business. B will continue to lose between three and four units with every repetition of the competitive activities. Since B cannot get out, he will try to change the rules, add random factors, and increase the size and the degree of complexity of the competition. As a last resort, he might attempt to mislead A into playing A_1 by supplying incorrect information to indicate that B_2 is a certainty, when, of course, he intends to use B_1. This last strategy might work if very high stakes go with each game. Otherwise, A is not likely to be tricked more than once into giving up his maximin strategy. We see that there

Table 5-5

	B_1	B_2	B_3		
A_1	-2	4	3	-2	
A_2	6	3	5	3	← MAXIMIN
	6	4	5		
		↑			
	MINIMAX				

are game strategies and strategies *about* game strategies. The latter are clearly as important as the former and are deeply involved with behavior.

The behavioral aspects of competition are so relevant that few managers can bring themselves to accept formal game models that ignore behavioral variables—even though managers often rely on economic models that either ignore or discount the behavior of consumers under competition, and even though they treat many systems as stable without knowing whether they are in fact stable. Such inconsistency in management's demands and expectations can be explained, in part, as follows: The manager accepts those practices that predate him sufficiently for him to treat them as traditional. Also, major economists have contributed time and attention, with some results, to the problems of including behavioral components in economic theory, and although not much of this theory has found its way into practical management analysis, it has lent credibility to economic models in general. Another reason is that management never deals directly with economics, while it deals constantly with competitors. More fundamentally, it seems fair to say that we are "conditioned" to expect *game*-playing to depend on the opponent's behavior because we are conditioned by the games we have played all our lives.

Unstable Competitive Systems

Nothing adds as much to the confusion and complexity of the gaming situation as the introduction of unstable systems. Assume that the rules change from time to time, that the environmental factors are highly unstable, that the utilities of individuals participating in the competition shift unexpectedly, and that as a result the nature of the mixed strategies for optimization undergo continual alteration. In such a world, game-playing becomes, for some, a source of pleasure in itself. The game is played as much for the sake of playing as for the wealth or power that can be obtained. (For others, the situation is frightening, and they call for a return to stability.) Next, add two other contemporary ingredients: an onus on wealth and a reduction in the effectiveness of whatever power can be won. Is our present society adjusting to effects such as these? Perhaps these effects are transitory (or merely illusory, a creation of the press). In any event, the manager must allow such considerations to play a part in his analysis of the competitive systems that affect his organization.

Consider the role and effect of behavior in a competitive game such as the stock market. We can see, for example, the institutional buyer in competition with the individual investor. Because institutions have much greater leverage as a result of their asset base, the large institutional buyer can control many swings of stock value to which the individual investor can only respond. The individual, lacking the information of the institutional buyer, acts as though he were dealing with a chance-cause system, when in fact it is, in part, a deterministic one. (The effect of regulation by the SEC can and should be examined in the light of individual behavior under such competitive conditions of buying and selling.)

Predictable Behaviors of Competitors

Behavior is discountable only when it is predictable. Because much competition is based on emulation, and because few want to desert the pattern to run the risks of the real innovator, competition can be said to tend toward average, or expected, performance rather than unique, or extreme, performance. Great chess players dislike playing novices because of the latters' unorthodox positions. For management, accepting competition that involves unexpected behaviors can raise the levels of uncertainty beyond tolerable thresholds. Therefore, seeking collusion—through trade associations, price-fixing, and so forth—is a totally rational response to competitive uncertainty.

Some interesting questions arise that game models and trees could help to resolve. For example, what might the effects be if efforts to create unusual strategies replaced cautious adherence to traditions; if rewards were developed for innovative competition and the acceptance of occasional large losses (similar, perhaps, to tax advantages offered for speculative investments in petroleum prospecting); if the present patent law were altered to provide greater motivation for truly original new-product development?

Prisoners' dilemma. Even though some formal aspects of competitive behavior might be dictated by rationality, this is not always so. A well-known example is the conceptual model of the prisoners' dilemma. It is a good example of educational benefits derived from model-building, although not even prisoners could hope to use this model for operational purposes.[14]

---

[14] Recent Supreme Court rulings concerning the rights of arrested individuals invalidates its use for prisoners.

First, the story. Two men are arrested by the sheriff on suspicion of robbery. The sheriff wants to obtain a confession, so he separates the prisoners, promises each one leniency (say, a sentence of only one year) if he is the first to confess, promises to throw the book (say, a sentence of ten years) at the one who has not confessed, and then strongly intimates to each prisoner that the other is about to confess. Table 5–6 depicts the matrices of both prisoners; A's payoffs appear above the diagonal in each cell, while B's payoffs are below.

Table 5–6   Combined Prisoners' Matrix

	B confessess	B does not confess	A's MINIMAX
A confesses	5 5	1 10	↓ 5
A does not confess	10 1	0 0	10
B's MINIMAX	⟶ 5	10	

Note that if neither confesses, they both get off (i.e., the 0 entry), whereas if both confess, neither leniency nor "the book" will prevail, and both will get a sentence of, say, five years.

The Waldian criterion calls for mutual confession, yet this runs counter to common sense. With a simple prior agreement based on *trust*, both prisoners can get off scot-free. But they do not trust easily, since each knows that the other can gain great advantage if he sees himself as independent. Each is fearful that he might resist temptation whereas the other will not. Therefore, under the sheriff's persuasion the coalition falls apart. This theoretical result is borne out empirically in laboratory experiments. All of which supports the notion that non-zero-sum games (even of the two-person variety) are severely complicated by behavioral factors.

Dominance. Again, in competitive situations, intuition threatens to be misleading. Perceived complication appears to increase with the data size of the problem and with the number of variables, variable sets (rows and columns), and functional relations. Yet large competitive situations often turn out to be far simpler than they seem to be at first sight. With objective analysis, dominance relations can be found that are not likely to be spotted subjectively. The reason they are not easily spotted is that the removal of a strategy that is dominated by another one often uncovers a number of other dominances that could not have been spotted before the first reduction. Illustration will save many words.

The matrix below is written in terms of S's profits.

	C_1	C_2	C_3	C_4
S_1	0	+7	+14	−12
S_2	−6	−8	−8	−4
S_3	−14	+8	0	−20
S_4	+12	−1	+20	0

Strategy S_4 is everywhere better than strategy S_2. Aside from this, no other dominances exist, so we can reduce this competitive matrix by one row and no more. Doing this, we obtain

	C_1	C_2	C_3	C_4
S_1	0	+7	+14	−12
S_3	−14	+8	0	−20
S_4	+12	−1	+20	0

Now we observe that C_4 is everywhere better than both C_1 and C_3, dominances that were not apparent before. The reduced matrix is

	C_2	C_4
S_1	+7	−12
S_3	+8	−20
S_4	−1	0

The matrix has been reduced from sixteen entries to six.

Dominance relations, such as the ones described above, are strongly related to the notions of bounded rationality developed by Herbert Simon (see pp. 74–75). In a noncompetitive (normal) decision matrix, it is relatively easy to uncover dominance conditions. By using intuition the manager might be able to spot these row relations and remove the appropriate rows. But, in the case of the *interlaced* competitive payoff matrix, dominance conditions can tie into one another in such a complex way that we have good reason to doubt whether the manager is able to achieve such reduction by purely subjective thinking.

If bounded rationality is not effective in competitive situations, this would help to explain why managers consider it reasonable to drop competitive situations from their analysis—and why a great deal of management analysis does not include the competitive factor. But then, nature would have to be dropped from the manager's point of view in order to get the classic zero-sum payoff matrix. One cannot help but wonder how important these juxtapositioned types of approximation are in determining managerial performance.

ESTIMATING COMPETITIVE PAYOFFS

Appropriate measures of payoff (that is, measures that truly reflect the individual's utilities) may not be easy to derive. Under many circumstances, some form of estimated rank-order measure is reasonable. To exemplify this important concession to practicality, we present two military examples. They are particularly relevant because military use of game theory concepts (whether formal or not) is probably the most advanced application of competitive reasoning in managerial problems.

Simple *objective* measures of competitive payoffs are seldom available in the military case. However, the competitive element is so overpoweringly real that it is impossible to treat the problem as if it were a straightforward decision matrix situation. As a result, *subjective* estimation often is employed under these circumstances to describe payoffs. Managers, of course, can try to supply meaningful estimates for the interaction of their strategies with those of competitors and can use them in the same way that military estimates are used here for the matrix analyses of the battles of the Bismarck Sea and the Avranches Gap. At the end of the chapter, we shall follow the two military examples with an illustration of a competitive business problem.

Battles of the Bismarck Sea and the Avranches Gap

The Bismarck Sea battle (1943) resulted from the strategy decision of General Kenney, who was commander of the Allied forces in the Southwest Pacific, and that of the commander of the Japanese forces. Through intelligence reports Kenney learned that a Japanese troop and supply convoy was being assembled at Rabaul to unload at Lae. Figure 5–4 is the map that O. G. Haywood presents in his excellent article, which forms the basis of our example.[15] The convoy could sail by either of the two routes shown. General Kenney's problem was how to distribute his reconnaissance so as to have the best chance of finding the convoy. Haywood has provided us with Kenney's five-step "Estimate of the Situation":

Step 1.   The Mission

General MacArthur as Supreme Commander had ordered Kenney to intercept and inflict maximum destruction on the convoy. This then was Kenney's mission.

---

[15] O. G. Haywood, Jr., "Military Decisions and Game Theory," *Journal of the Operations Research Society of America,* Vol. 2, No. 4 (November 1954), pp. 365–85.

Figure 5–4   The Rabaul-Lae Convoy Situation

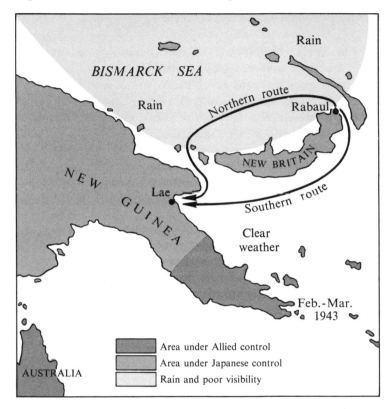

SOURCE: O. G. Haywood, Jr., "Military Decisions and Game Theory," *Journal of the Operations Research Society of America,* Vol. 2, No. 4 (November 1954), p. 366.

Step 2.   Situation and Courses of Action

The situation as outlined above was generally known. One new critical factor was pointed out by Kenney's staff. Rain and poor visibility were predicted for the area north of New Britain. Visibility south of the island would be good.

The Japanese commander had two choices for routing his convoy from Rabaul to Lae. He could sail north of New Britain, or he could go south of that island. Either route required three days.

Kenney considered two courses of action, as he discusses in his memoirs. He could concentrate most of his reconnaissance aircraft either along the northern route where visibility would be poor, or along the southern route where clear weather was predicted. Mobility being one of the great advantages of air power, his bombing force could strike the convoy on either route once it was spotted.

Step 3.   Analysis of the Opposing Courses of Action

With each commander having two alternative courses of action, four possible conflicts could ensue. These conflicts are pictured in [Figure 5–5].

Step 4.   Comparison of Available Courses of Action

If Kenney concentrated on the northern route, he ensured one of the two battles of the top row of sketches. However, he alone could not determine which one of these two battles in the top row would result from his decision. Similarly, if Kenney concentrated on the southern route, he ensured one of the battles of the lower row. In the same manner, the Japanese commander could not select a particular battle, but could by his decision assure that the battle would be one of those pictured in the left column or one of those in the right column.

Kenney sought a battle which would provide the maximum opportunity for bombing the convoy. The Japanese commander desired the minimum exposure to bombing. But neither commander could determine the battle which would result from his own decision. Each commander had full and independent freedom to select either one of his alternative strategies. He had to do so with full realization of his opponent's freedom of choice. The particular battle which resulted would be determined by the two independent decisions.

The U. S. doctrine of decision—the doctrine that a commander base his action on his estimate of what the enemy is capable of doing to oppose him—dictated that Kenney select the course of action which offered the greatest promise of success in view of all of the enemy capabilities. If Kenney concentrated his reconnaissance on the northern route, he could expect two days of bombing regardless of his enemy's decision. If Kenney selected his other strategy, he must accept the possibility of a less favorable outcome.

Step 5.   The Decision

Kenney concentrated his reconnaissance aircraft on the northern route.

Vulnerability to bombing was the main performance measure used by both commanders. In fact, it was a basis only for *ranking* the utility of each outcome, not for measuring the actual results that would occur. But it did offer a strong ranking measure. Such *intermediary* variables, when used to represent the final payoff measure, should be viewed with suspicion; but in this case, at least both commanders appear to have agreed on the choice of the intermediary variable. (This kind of consensus is most frequently available when some form of technology is the dominant factor.) Therefore, this competition

Figure 5–5   Possible Battles for the Rabaul-Lae Convoy Situation

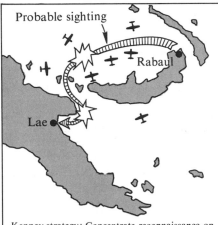

Kenney strategy: Concentrate reconnaissance on northern route.
Japanese strategy: Sail northern route.
Estimated outcome: Although reconnaissance would be hampered by poor visibility, the convoy should be discovered by the second day, which would permit two days of bombing.

TWO DAYS OF BOMBING

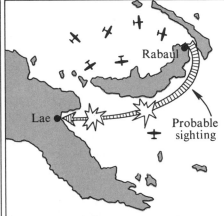

Kenney strategy: Concentrate reconnaissance on northern route.
Japanese strategy: Sail southern route.
Estimated outcome: The convoy would be sailing in clear weather. However, with limited reconnaissance aircraft in this area, the convoy might be missed on the first day. Convoy should be sighted by second day, to permit two days of bombing.

TWO DAYS OF BOMBING

was treated as a two-person, zero-sum problem—what was good for one side was equivalently bad for the other.

Using game-matrix form, the decision problem can be set down as in Table 5–7. The matrix entries are days of bombing; the K strategies are those of Kenney, the J strategies those of the Japanese commander; and the maximin and minimax strategies are found to be equal at the saddlepoint value of 2. Both commanders, using accepted military procedure, followed the indicated saddlepoint strategies, K_1 and J_1, the Japanese convoy sailing on the northern route and Kenney concentrating his reconnaissance on the northern route.

What actually transpired? The Japanese convoy was sighted about one day out of Rabaul, and bombing began. Although the result was a Japanese defeat, the Japanese commander cannot be faulted. Properly, he wanted to minimize his exposure to bombing. Furthermore, an earlier convoy had succeeded, the Japanese need was urgent, and the Japanese commander was unaware that Kenney had perfected a new low-level bombing technique. No error occurred, and yet a serious loss resulted for one side. For management, the message is clear: *In some competitive situations, the best that can be done is to lose less badly than one might have otherwise.*

Now let us turn to the Avranches Gap situation, which presents a somewhat

Figure 5–5 (continued)

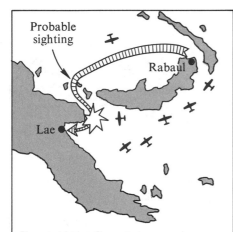

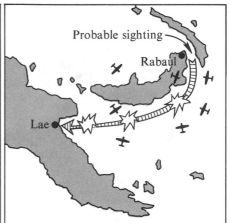

Kenney strategy: Concentrate reconnaissance on southern route.

Japanese strategy: Sail northern route.

Estimated outcome: With poor visibility and limited reconnaissance, Kenney could not expect the convoy to be discovered until it broke out into clear weather on third day. This would permit only one day of bombing.

ONE DAY OF BOMBING

Kenney strategy: Concentrate reconnaissance on southern route.

Japanese strategy: Sail southern route.

Estimated outcome: With good visibility and concentrated reconnaissance in the area, the convoy should be sighted almost as soon as it sailed from Rabaul. This would allow three days of bombing.

THREE DAYS OF BOMBING

SOURCE: O. G. Haywood, Jr., "Military Decisions and Game Theory," *Journal of the Operations Research Society of America,* Vol. 2, No. 4 (November 1954), p. 368.

Table 5–7

	J_1	J_2	Worst for K:
K_1	2	2	2 ← MAXIMIN
K_2	1	3	1
Worst for J:	2	3	
	↑		
	MINIMAX		

more complex measurement situation. In the European Theater, in August 1944, General Omar Bradley's forces faced General von Kluge and the German Ninth Army, as shown in Figure 5–6.[16]

---

[16] *Ibid.* General Omar Bradley discusses his estimate of the situation in his *A Soldier's Story* (New York: Holt, Rinehart and Winston, 1951).

Figure 5–6   The Avranches Gap Situation

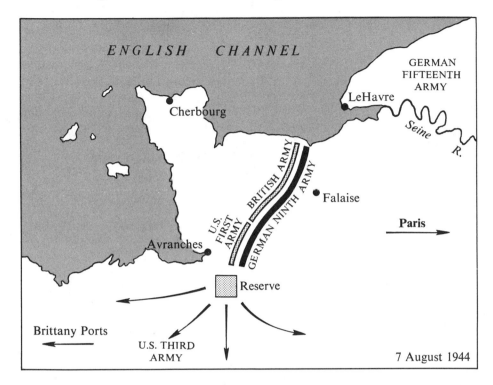

SOURCE: O. G. Haywood, Jr., "Military Decisions and Game Theory," *Journal of the Operations Research Society of America,* Vol. 2, No. 4 (November 1954), p. 372.

Again, we are using Haywood's diagram of the situation and his report of the steps taken and their results.

Bradley's *mission* was to destroy enemy forces in the field. The *situation* was that the Allies had broken out of their beachhead through the Avranches Gap, thus exposing the west flank of the German Ninth Army. As a result, von Kluge had two choices; either he could *attack* toward the west to reach the sea, secure his west flank, and thereby cut off Bradley's forces south of the Gap, or he could *withdraw* his forces to the east, taking a more defensive position near the Seine River. (We shall call these strategies K_1 and K_2 respectively.) Bradley's Third Army, commanded by General Patton, had slipped through the Avranches Gap; his First Army was holding the German Ninth by a frontal attack. Bradley had to decide how to use his reserves of four divisions, which were south of the Gap and not yet committed. He could order his *reserves back* to defend the Gap; he could send the *reserves east* to harass the German army and possibly cut off their withdrawal; or he could keep the *reserves in place* to have uncommitted forces that could be moved either to the Gap if needed or else to the east if the Gap proved defensible without reinforcements. (We shall call these strategies B_1, B_2, and B_3, respectively.) So von Kluge had two choices, and Bradley had three. These are shown in Figure 5–7.

In this case, there was no single measure (such as days of bombing) that could be used. Both generals had to (1) perceive the same alternatives, (2) determine that the same outcomes would occur in each of the six situations, and then (3) express the same preferences for these outcomes. Otherwise, the two-person, zero-sum game analysis would not hold. Yet, because of the military-technological constraints that existed, it is not inconceivable that the two generals, without any consultation, would have come to reasonably similar estimates of the situation and preferences for the outcomes. Bradley's rank ordering of preferences, from best to worst, was:

1. Gap holds; there is a possibility of encircling the German army.
2. There is strong pressure on German withdrawal.
3. There is moderate pressure on withdrawal of the German army.
4. There is weak pressure on withdrawal of the German army.
5. The Gap holds.
6. The Gap is cut.

and von Kluge's would have been the reverse.

The game matrix, using these rank-ordered preference payoffs, would be as indicated in Table 5–8, where the B_i's are Bradley's strategies and the K_j's are von Kluge's strategies, as previously defined. The minimax and maximin strategies are found *not* to be equal. Since there is no saddlepoint value in the matrix, a *mixed strategy* is indicated. Of course, it does not have to be used. Bradley, by using the pure strategy B_3, could assure that nothing worse than 3 would occur; von Kluge, by using K_2, could at least eliminate the possibility of the outcome associated with the preference measure of 1. Using a mixed strategy, the saddlepoint payoff value lying between 2 and 3 would be obtained, *if* the situation were to be repeated over and over. But a single battle hardly fits that situation.[17]

What actually happened? Von Kluge decided to withdraw (his K_2 strategy), but Hitler overrode this decision, insisting that von Kluge attack the Gap. Bradley, following the B_3 strategy, had held his units in place. The result was

---

[17] Still, according to Haywood, "At the end of the last war in Europe, the United States had some 600 battalion combat teams on the European continent. Had each commander used mixed strategies to accept a risk for an expectation of gain, the probability that an overall loss would have resulted becomes negligible." This raises some very ticklish questions concerning a commander's responsibility to his men. The issue is unclear and debatable on many levels.

Figure 5–7 Possible Battles for the Avranches Gap Situation

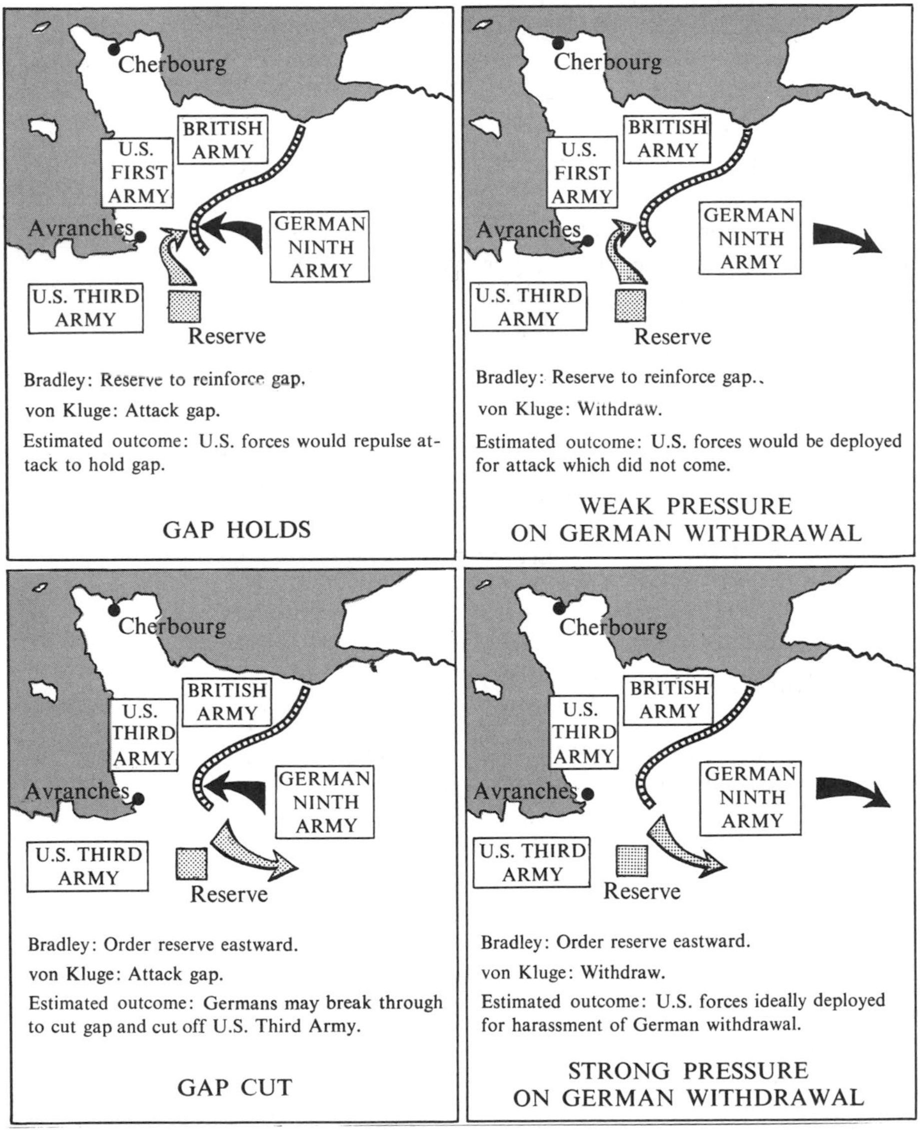
Cherbourg
BRITISH ARMY
U.S. FIRST ARMY
Avranches
GERMAN NINTH ARMY
U.S. THIRD ARMY
Reserve
Bradley: Reserve to reinforce gap.
von Kluge: Attack gap.
Estimated outcome: U.S. forces would repulse attack to hold gap.
GAP HOLDS
Cherbourg
BRITISH ARMY
U.S. FIRST ARMY
Avranches
GERMAN NINTH ARMY
U.S. THIRD ARMY
Reserve
Bradley: Reserve to reinforce gap.
von Kluge: Withdraw.
Estimated outcome: U.S. forces would be deployed for attack which did not come.
WEAK PRESSURE ON GERMAN WITHDRAWAL
Cherbourg
BRITISH ARMY
U.S. THIRD ARMY
Avranches
GERMAN NINTH ARMY
U.S. THIRD ARMY
Reserve
Bradley: Order reserve eastward.
von Kluge: Attack gap.
Estimated outcome: Germans may break through to cut gap and cut off U.S. Third Army.
GAP CUT
Cherbourg
BRITISH ARMY
U.S. THIRD ARMY
Avranches
GERMAN NINTH ARMY
U.S. THIRD ARMY
Reserve
Bradley: Order reserve eastward.
von Kluge: Withdraw.
Estimated outcome: U.S. forces ideally deployed for harassment of German withdrawal.
STRONG PRESSURE ON GERMAN WITHDRAWAL

B_3, K_1: The German Ninth Army was surrounded, and, after von Kluge succeeded in withdrawing a badly battered army, he committed suicide.

Thus, even if the commanders in these situations did not use formal decision theory, their procedures were equivalent. With our knowledge of game theory, a concise explanation is available. The vital requirement of using the Waldian criterion when the opponent is rational is dramatically evident in this example.

Figure 5–7 (continued)

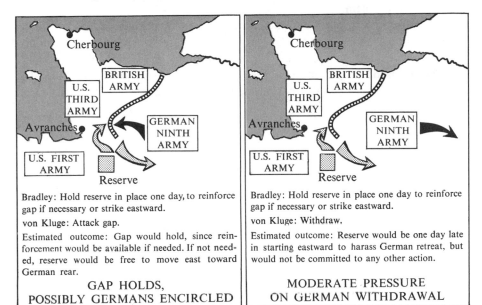

Bradley: Hold reserve in place one day, to reinforce gap if necessary or strike eastward.	Bradley: Hold reserve in place one day to reinforce gap if necessary or strike eastward.
von Kluge: Attack gap.	von Kluge: Withdraw.
Estimated outcome: Gap would hold, since reinforcement would be available if needed. If not needed, reserve would be free to move east toward German rear.	Estimated outcome: Reserve would be one day late in starting eastward to harass German retreat, but would not be committed to any other action.
GAP HOLDS, POSSIBLY GERMANS ENCIRCLED	MODERATE PRESSURE ON GERMAN WITHDRAWAL

SOURCE: O. G. Haywood, Jr., "Military Decisions and Game Theory," *Journal of the Operations Research Society of America,* Vol. 2, No. 4 (November 1954), p. 374.

Table 5–8

	K_1	K_2	Worst for B:
B_1	5	4	5
B_2	6	2	6
B_3	1	3	3 ← MINIMAX
Worst for K:	1	2	
		↑	
		MAXIMIN	

A Business Problem

Competitive management situations can be *approached* in much the same fashion as our military examples. Frequently, however, payoff measures based on rank ordering of intermediary (and especially preference) measures will not be equivalent for both opponents. In spite of this difficulty, it is worthwhile for us to consider a simple example of the use of rank-ordered data for a management problem.

Two major industrial organizations are highly competitive. Alpha has about 60 percent of the market, and Beta has the remaining 40 percent. Both companies are considering announcing a longer guarantee period for their products. Let *PG* represent the present guarantee period and *LG* the longer period. The game matrix (Table 5–9) is constructed using preference measures of rank

Table 5–9

		Alpha (60 percent):		Worst:
		PG_α	LG_α	
	PG_β	4	3	3
Beta (40 percent):	LG_β	5	4	4 ← MAXIMIN
	Worst	5	4	
			↑	
			MINIMAX	

order (that indirectly reflect share of market) to represent Beta's payoffs. Because the rank-order measures are tied to market share, a zero-sum situation is approximated. It must be assumed that both companies would agree about the size of the preference measures that have been set down by Beta's management. Because this is Beta's matrix, larger numbers are expressions of greater preference. The reverse interpretation is held by Alpha.

Let us see what reasoning might have been used. Beta's manager has indicated that *measuring from the present situation, PG_α, PG_β,* Beta would be at a disadvantage if the longer guarantee period was adopted by Alpha alone, LG_α, PG_β. On the other hand, if Beta was the first to announce the new policy of longer guarantee, PG_α, LG_β, it would be likely to obtain a number of Alpha's customers. For both Alpha and Beta to switch to longer guarantees would create a standoff situation in terms of market share, but both organizations would be incurring additional costs that could be offset only by a sufficient growth of the market (responding to the more attractive guarantee period).

This competitive dilemma is not unlike the prisoner's dilemma in one respect. Prior agreement *not* to extend the guarantee period would produce the best result for both companies. However, in this case, not only is trust necessary, but such a prior agreement is legally vulnerable. Therefore, a saddlepoint solution of 4 is found with LG_α, LG_β, indicating that both companies should move to the more costly policy of longer guarantees, even though it produces a status quo result for both companies with respect to market-share ranks. It is doubtful whether either company likes that result, but without collusion neither can do anything about it. Whether or not we agree with such reasoning, it does illuminate the fact that under certain circumstances rank-ordered data can be used to determine optimal competitive strategies.

SUMMARY

The importance of competition to the manager may vary, but it never disappears. It is therefore unfortunate that competitive decision models are more useful conceptually than they are practically. In spite of this drawback, however, the concepts of game theory illuminate many aspects of organizational significance and, for this reason, have definite value for the manager.

Chapter 5 develops the most basic game model, the two-person, zero-sum game. In this game model, the Waldian (pessimist's) decision criterion must be used by both opponents to choose their strategies. The conclusion will not hold, however, if either party knows that the other is not rational in his game-playing. Nor will it apply if the players have different values (utilities) for the game's payoffs. Lacking similar utilities, a non–zero-sum game model must be used. With more than two opponents, the two-person game format cannot be used. As soon as there are more than two parties involved, collusion and deals can arise, and a variety of special value problems concerning cooperation, controls, and the effects of attitudes might be expected to influence the results.

The basic game model requires mixed strategy solutions when the so-called saddlepoint solution cannot be obtained by using pure strategies. These mixed strategies are determined randomly, yet the game remains an essentially determinate decision structure.

Game theory models are extended to conditions where environmental conditions apply. In this way, the decision matrix of Chapter 4 is itself extended to include competitive effects. The notion of a game tree is introduced, and its ability to represent a variety of realistic situations is indicated. The simulation of the game tree sometimes permits more complex situations to be studied than do analytic game theory models. Finally, some behavioral aspects of competition are treated, including the prisoner's dilemma model and the effects of dominance.

EXERCISES

1. Coué is said to have observed, "When the imagination and the will are in conflict, the imagination always wins." How can this abstract conflict between "will" and "imagination" be explained by the concepts of a two-person, zero-sum game? Discuss your answer.

2. In what way is competition "a force for change"? Does the competitive behavior of a two-person, zero-sum game support this notion?

3. How does the change in the dimension of the payoff from sales dollars to brand share alter the nature of the game theory problem? Can you think of another transformation that produces the same effect? What does this discussion have to do with utilities?

4. How does "lobbying" represent a competitive effort? Would it usually lend itself to the two-person, zero-sum form of model?

5. Resolve the following two-person, zero-sum game, written in terms of x's profits.

	c_1	c_2	c_3
x_1	25	18	30
x_2	18	18	18
x_3	20	24	12
x_4	24	0	−6
x_5	16	−2	2

   a. Discuss your solution.
   b. Would the indicated strategies change if all of the values in the matrix were divided by two?
   c. What might explain why x has more strategies than c?

6. Is it possible to create an example of a (two-by-two) zero-sum game matrix in which no dominance relations between rows or between columns exist and the saddlepoint occurs for pure strategies? Discuss your answer.

7. It was stated that "people have a difficult time perceiving that others might feel differently from themselves." What implications does this remark have for the task of building a payoff matrix and completing a game analysis? How does the utility concept relate to this point?

8. The payoff matrix of profits (*written for the manager* whose strategies are the x_i's) is the following:

	c_1	c_2	c_3
x_1	-1	0	0
x_2	-9	$+2$	-11
x_3	-6	-8	$+1$

The manager is not constrained to engage in this particular competition. Should he stay in the game? Explain.

9. What happens to a game theory model if a constant amount is subtracted from each entry in the payoff matrix?

10. Develop the matrix to describe the first and second players' potential moves, *and the results,* for the following game: When the hand is held in a fist, it symbolizes the rock; the flat of the hand stands for paper; two fingers held out in a "V" signify scissors. Each player holds one hand behind his back, and, on the count of "three," each shows his hidden hand signal (for rock, paper, or scissors) to the others. The *rule* that is used is: Rock breaks scissors $(+1)$, paper covers rock $(+1)$, and scissors cut paper $(+1)$. Solve your matrix and interpret the results. (Ties are scored zero.)

11. For the game described in Exercise 10, build a tree diagram that represents all the potential strategies for one move in depth by player A followed by one move in depth by player B. Now build a tree to indicate that when standoffs occur, a new rule calls for a coin toss to determine the winner $(+1)$.

12. Does the prisoner's dilemma model fit the following case? Two companies have a present product-line and are known to each other to be contemplating substantial redesign. Each would prefer not to make any change but is afraid that the competitor will do so and catch him unprepared to follow suit.

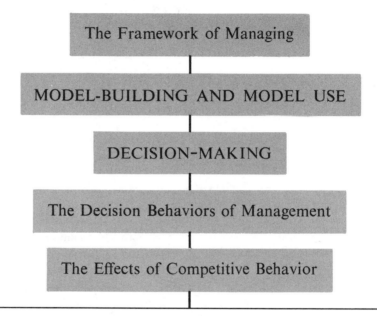

The Framework of Managing

MODEL-BUILDING AND MODEL USE

DECISION-MAKING

The Decision Behaviors of Management

The Effects of Competitive Behavior

Chapter 6
"Predecisions" and the Value of Information

Managers are always making decisions, some immediately, some
with study. On which decisions should the manager concentrate?
Should the manager allocate his decision-making funds on: creating
strategies, learning about environments, improving forecasts, reducing
error in measurement, or gaining control over environments? This
is the *predecision* area, which is vital to rational management
but is frequently overlooked. It requires a measure of the value of
information against which alternative allocations can be judged.

Chapter 6

"PREDECISIONS"
AND THE VALUE
OF INFORMATION

Management lacks procedures for assessing its own efficiency. Still less can it evaluate its effectiveness. And an efficient manager is not necessarily an effective one. A manager who saves costs efficiently may not contribute to profit effectiveness. For example, in the days of the Model A Ford, being efficient about buggy-whip production might actually have delayed recognition of a significant market shift; the inefficient manufacture of a horn would probably have been a more effective alternative.

Management's ability to account for its performance is notably weak. The fact that a company is profitable does not offer a clue as to how much more profitable it might be. Accounting should be helpful, but it places much of its emphasis on allocating administrative costs to the overhead category, a procedure of dubious meaning. And it treats as unmeasurable administrative performance that is not reflected by costs. Perhaps this is unavoidable, given the present state of the art of managing such information. But the demand for change is growing, and science holds more than just a superficial promise of being able to help evaluate management's decisions, plans, and policies.

199

THE PREDECISION PROCESS

Management has generally accepted the idea that it can improve its ability to render *particular* decisions by studying the decision process in abstraction (as described in Chapters 4 and 5). An impressive array of methods and techniques exists for categorizing decision problems, for manipulating decision elements, and for choosing between decision alternatives. Much less attention has been given to the predecision process, which every decision situation entails.

Predecisions are conclusions that are required to convert decision abstractions into operational terms. The predecision area is epitomized by three questions: (1) At what point in time should a decision be made? (2) How much should be invested in reaching the decision? (3) How should that budget be allocated to the various components of the decision problem?

At the present time, management's general approach to predecisions is essentially hit or miss. In many cases, management is not even aware of the predecision area. It is one thing to ignore a complication, quite another not to perceive it. The way an executive assigns time and budget in resolving a particular decision problem is usually based on intuition. The factors that influence him include

1. The importance of the problem, as it commands top management attention. This factor is responsive to the percentage of total assets involved, whether the problem is receiving competitive attention, and so forth.
2. The complexity of the problem and its resistance to solution.
3. The availability of time and budget when awareness of the problem first occurs. Interesting questions are: *when* to decide on resource allocations, how *irreversible* such decisions are, and how to *predict* future demands for both time and budget.

Although they rely on the intangible element of *good judgment,* managers usually ask for specific information that they believe is required to reach a decision. This request, in turn, implies the level of expenditures needed for the collection of such information. An obvious question is: How precisely do managers know what it is that they need to know? Do managers usually settle for less than they can use because of the cost of information or their inability to handle more than a certain amount of information?

In this process of deciding how to decide, rational management would be delighted to have some handles to grab onto (especially in the rarefied upper-management regions of decision-making). It would like to have procedures for a relatively honest self-examination of its functions. To achieve this, some means of accounting for the costs and *values* of decision-making is required.

Normative *methods* for determining how much should be spent to make a particular decision should be substituted for guesswork whenever possible.

Ideally, the effectiveness of a manager's performance would be measured by comparing his *actual* achievements with his *opportunities* for achievement. But this is far easier to state than to accomplish. Another approach would be to rate the manager on how he makes decisions. His effectiveness might be related to the qualities and quantities of information that he directs his staff to collect—and then to how, in fact, he uses it. Designing a project schedule and then meeting or missing it is another observable factor that might be important. The rates at which data are collected, transformed, put in storage, and subsequently updated affect the age of the information and its timeliness at the moment of decision. But there are problems with this approach to evaluating effectiveness, too. For example, it might influence the manager to avoid unusual performance, even though performing according to standards (or a list of principles) would not do the job as well. It is only in general that we can state which qualities and quantities of information are appropriate. In specific situations we expect the manager to do what is needed and not to conform to an arbitrary job description.

Undoubtedly, the use of intuition is currently the most popular approach to the predecision problem. Management allocates its available executive time and study funds by some subjective ranking of what it "feels" needs to be done. We are recommending that the intuitive process be opened to conscious examination, for if the manager lacks that kind of awareness, what is to prevent predecisioning from being random? Perhaps more decisions are triggered in accordance with a random pattern (such as results from the toss of a coin or the throw of a die) than most managers would like to believe.

Net Benefits

Each approach to a decision is a unique decision problem in its own right, implying different costs and values. We have called this *designing* of decision models "the predecision process." Predecisioning constitutes an area of acute management vulnerability, but management is usually unaware of this fact—or is indifferent because it believes it has no way of learning how far it has strayed from the mark.

The ability to avoid improper allocation of funds for decision-making is central to predecisioning. The ultimate criterion for determining how management should allocate its resources to reach a decision is the maximization of *net benefit*—that is, total benefits (or gross value) derived from a particular predecision strategy less the total costs of using that strategy. Although the specific composition of a net-benefit calculation will change as the particular details of the situation are modified, the objective still holds. Improper allocations of a correct total budget or incorrect total investments in the decision process, either too much or too little, produce less net benefit than could otherwise have been achieved. And, because patterns of decision-making become *habitual,* such losses are likely to be multiplied by repetition.

Even more important, the penalties of overinvestment are not canceled out by subsequent underinvestment and are therefore cumulative. Figure 6–1

Figure 6–1

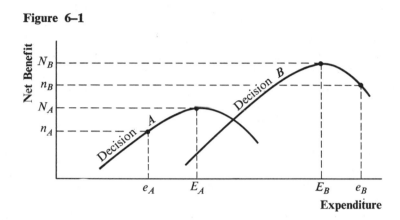

illustrates this notion. It is important that the computations of net benefit *include* the investment expenditures for the decision process. Optimal net benefits for decisions A and B (which are independent of each other) are N_A and N_B. Total net benefit that could be derived is $N_A + N_B$. The total net benefit actually obtained is $n_A + n_B$. Both n_A and n_B are less than their respective optimums, even though the actual expenditure, e_A, for decision A is less than the optimal expenditure level, E_A, while the actual expenditure, e_B, for decision B is greater than the optimal expenditure level, E_B. In this way, the penalties for over- and underinvestment are cumulative: $(N_A - n_A) + (N_B - n_B) + \ldots$.

If management lacked a framework for structuring and analyzing the costs, values, and net benefits of its decision behaviors, it would be pointless to speak about spending the right amount on any particular decision situation. But such a framework does exist in the form of measures of the value of information.

The term "information," as we shall use it here, is intended to mean what is *known* about the decision system. We shall also use the term "control" to describe the decision-maker's ability to manipulate the decision system—that is, his ability to make it unnecessary for management to require certain kinds of information. For example, by signing a contract, the manager can gain control over uncertain sales demand; by building a greenhouse, the horticulturist removes the risk factor of weather; by having visits by appointment, the dentist controls the otherwise uncertain number of people in his waiting-room. Proper measures for predecisioning should permit us to determine the net benefit of obtaining more or less information and of exercising greater or lesser control.

Imperfect models. In theory, we can discover the optimal decision alternative by using the correct decision model. In fact, we seldom produce models so nearly perfect as to give us such results, and we never produce a perfect model of a richly complex system. Even if it were possible, the cost of doing so would far exceed the value of the model.

There is no such thing as one "right" model. Many kinds of representation exist at a variety of levels of accuracy. The range stretches from the purely intuitive to the totally objective. Most often, model construction falls some-where in between. The level of elaboration of the model is a matter of man-agement option and is another critical aspect of what we mean by the pre-decision process.

Investment Patterns

An organization's investment in decision studies cannot be designed to mini-mize the total cost of all such activities. (The *minimum* minimum would be zero.) Decision investments must be designed to maximize the organization's *total net benefit.* Though the concept is simple, the realization of the objective is not. In fact, the exact determination of the appropriate investment level for a specific decision problem is likely to be more complex than any example that may be given here. However, we can begin to explore this issue by placing it in the context of the various decision categories discussed in Chapter 4.

Decision problems under certainty, for example, do not require investments for forecasting. Conversely, problems classified as totally uncertain will prob-ably require unorthodox data collection procedures and ingenious experiments to produce even a crude fix on the information required to convert the situ-ation to one of risk. Accordingly, the judgment of what constitutes an appro-priate decision investment is clearly related to the category of the particular decision problem.

It is understandable (but not necessarily reasonable) that management *tends to emphasize investments in decision studies in those situations where conditions of certainty exist.* The average investment per project is smaller than for other types of problem, and the net benefit is less difficult to calculate. Risk problems, for example, require forecasting expenses. In addition, there is the cost of completing the expanded risk-type decision matrix. It is hardly surprising that proposals to undertake the proper analysis of risk systems meet with some noticeable degree of management reluctance.

A popular gambit is to solve problems demanding risk considerations as if they were in fact problems resolvable under certainty. Such approximations, however, may be a serious mistake; they are not likely to maximize net benefit for the enterprise unless they are based on good reasons. But the net benefit measure, because it is less visible than the measure of investment costs, can be more easily overlooked, even when it is negative (i.e., a penalty). On the other hand, there are many circumstances when approximations are entirely warranted and perfectionism is reprehensible. Too often, however, what is done is a result of a characteristic attitude of the individual manager rather than a reflection of the situation. Some managers are noted for their "compulsive" desire for perfection. They study fewer problems more thoroughly than managers at the other extreme, who follow what is known as the "buckshot" routine of treating many problems at minimum depth. This difference is apparent in many managerial situations. In fairness to the managers' rationality, various factors—such as their respective systems, bosses, employees, personal abilities—could reasonably account for such different patterns of behavior. But here we wish to supplement the idiosyncrasies of reality with an objective decision-theory basis for insight.

Problems characterized by conditions of uncertainty are most easily relegated by management to its own intuition. This is equivalent to assigning such problems to overhead (i.e., managerial salaries) and making a zero investment with respect to variable costs. It is rare, however, that this accounting actually takes place. Here, too, we cannot be surprised by this omission, even though the study of such problems is likely to provide an enormous range of potential gross benefits. The payoff matrix for a problem classified under uncertainty can be expected to include some very large and some very small payoffs. Nevertheless, problems of uncertainty are often ignored, overlooked, and even consciously deferred.

Timing

The mention of deferral brings us to our next subject—timing. At what point in time should a decision be made? A decision cannot be made unless a choice exists.[1] However, an always present alternative is to defer making a decision. Deferred decisions (see below) require zero investments, but they do involve opportunity costs, which are the penalties incurred for not having done the best possible thing in the sense of net benefit. Executives are continually making decisions, most of which call for deferral. On the other hand, the fact that

---

[1] Hobson's choice, which is explained on p. 616, has frequently been used to illustrate this situation.

the greatest part of such a continuous sequence of decisions is based on un-conscious behavior raises doubt concerning the usefulness of the concept of continuous deferral. Therefore, let us rephrase our question: At what point in time should an investment that is greater than zero be made in the decision process?

Various situations are known to trigger a decision. One of the primary triggers is *threat*. We need only consider such words as predicament, plight, quandary, and dilemma to illustrate this point. The *threat* motivation for reach-ing a decision is based on the existence of a set of threshold conditions. When a threshold is violated, by either outcomes or environmental conditions, a de-cision is called for. (Later, we shall recognize this as a parallel to the activities of a control system. It makes sense that in a control system the predecision conditions have been worked out so that the system can function in a relatively automatic fashion. Such a control system requires a vigilant observer to detect those conditions that trigger the need for decision.)

Although it can be said that management may be motivated to reach a decision by the breaching of threshold conditions, the line of demarcation of the threshold is frequently vague—either undefined or a matter of opinion. Using reports such as the profit-and-loss statement, the balance sheet, inven-tory ledgers, and production records, a manager may perceive conditions that he believes warrant action; another manager may disagree. Generally, the vagueness allowed in threshold demarcation decreases as the likelihood of bankruptcy or other catastrophes increases.

Deferred decisions. It is often said that a necessary attribute of the dynamic executive is his ability to reach a decision without delay. "Undecided" is a negative term; to be indecisive is to deserve condemnation. This attitude is common throughout most of the world, and there is even a colloquial saying: The patient died while the doctors were deciding. Similar opprobrium clings to the concepts of deliberation, procrastination, and delay. The speed with which world events now occur and are reported may account for the cult of the decisive. But, journalism notwithstanding, somewhere along the line the fundamentals of the issue seem to have been lost. A rational position would not discredit procrastination, deliberation, or delay, for they are not intrin-sically bad; it would employ them freely when they are useful in producing optimal results. When to procrastinate, how long to deliberate, and, especially, how to deliberate are legitimate issues for management to consider.

Let us then delineate some of the more profound underlying reasons for deferring decisions. Management might be dissatisfied with all the available strategies, in which case an investment in research and development would be preferable to an investment in the decision model. Or management may believe that more information should be obtained before it attempts to reach a decision; in this case, an investment in tests, experiments, and surveys, or a search for experience and talent would be warranted.

Another criterion for the deferred decision follows from the fact that it represents a zero investment. Deferral is justified when the cost of designing, constructing, and using a decision model promises to be greater than the gross value that can be derived from the use of the model. But this net benefit evaluation can change when additional experience with the system is acquired, when payoff conditions improve, or when innovation in methodology alters the costs. The predecision concerning the amount to invest in the decision study is clearly related to the expected *returns* for the amount invested. With limited study funds and a scarcity of executive time, the most promising decision problems—that is, those promising the greatest net benefits from a decision investment—would be chosen first. In other words, certain decision problems will repay care and attention better than others, and it is management's responsibility to determine an appropriate priority list based on a comparison between various alternatives, each of which is evaluated at its optimal investment level.

Allocation

The problem of determining the optimal investment level for a specific decision area is likely to be highly complex. It necessitates the discovery of an optimal allocation pattern for each aspect and phase of the decision study.

Timing and investment level are interrelated, as we have said. What constitutes an appropriate investment level will differ, depending on the timing that is followed. Optimal timing for the organization's decision studies will not necessarily minimize the total investment in such activities, but it should maximize the *present worth of net benefit*. Discounted cash (or benefit) flow analysis is required so that adequate comparisons can be made between alternative time and investment plans.[2]

If there are no budgetary restrictions and no shortage of executive time, then the investment in each decision study can be determined independently of investments in other studies. This assumes that the studies are completely unrelated with respect to interactions, informational ties, and decision procedures. On the other hand, if we assume interrelations between problem areas (i.e., dependent relations), then net benefit must be figured in the sense of the *total* system, wherein all restrictions, interactions, and dependencies are defined as enclosed by the system. Such problems become very intricate. It is likely that only simulation procedures (as described in Chapter 2) would possess sufficient flexibility to cope with really complex systems.

---

[2] See pp. 275–76.

TYPES OF PREDECISION PROBLEM

Predecision Components

We can gain insight by examining the predecision components of a single decision area. These are the operational issues of predecisioning that must be resolved (whether intuitively or objectively) *before* any decision model can be used. A representative list of such components must include (at least) the following determinants of cost, value, and net benefit:

1. *Creation of strategies:* determining the appropriate number, average quality level, and distribution of quality of strategies that should be designed before attempting to choose a best one. This component includes predecision (timing) strategy concerning *when to decide.*

2. *Identification of environments:* determining the number of environmental conditions necessary to describe the problem area fully. This refers to the level of refinement of the system of classification as well as to the scope of the investigation in terms of the range of environmental conditions included. Together, these determinations will directly affect the size of the study.

3. *Reduction of error:* determining the extent of use of procedures to verify estimates, as well as the appropriate level of expenditure for data collection.[3] (Errors of commission and omission follow from the design of the data-collection method.) This determination must take account of the cost and benefit of obtaining valid information suitable in both precision and age.

4. *Improvement of forecasts:* determining the appropriate forecasting model and the amount and nature of information that is required by the model. This includes considering the use of experiments, tests, surveys, and information-recovery systems in conjunction with methods for analyzing economic time-series data. Related statistical techniques to establish the stability of the systems to be forecast are also essential.

5. *Employment of control systems:* determining a reasonable level of investment for the design, construction, and operation of control devices, which can be used either to override or to by-pass the effects of environmental conditions.

Other decision components exist, but the five that we have listed are the most important parts of the decision-investment problem. They are the major consumers of time and money invested in the decision process.

If we assume that the costs and values of the pertinent decision components are relatively independent of one another, the equation below can be a guide

---

[3] The data are frequently obtained as a sample of the total information that is available. Selecting the appropriate sample size is a problem familiar to all managers.

to finding investment patterns that improve total net benefit. If we also assume that no budgetary constraints exist on the total amount that may be invested, then the overall maximum net benefit can be obtained by maximizing the individual net benefit of *each* component.

overall maximum
net benefit = maximum (value − cost) of strategy options
+ maximum (value − cost) of environment options
+ maximum (value − cost) of error options
+ maximum (value − cost) of forecasting options
+ maximum (value − cost) of control options

The order in which these decision components have been presented is not meant to indicate their relative importance, but there might well be a ranked order for particular types of decision problem. For example, strategy options might rank first for advertising, brand image, and diversification decisions; environment options might rank first for medical and pharmaceutical decisions; error options might rank first for auditing and military decisions. Perhaps forecasting options would rank first for inventory, scheduling, and new-product development decisions, while control options might rank first for nuclear power plants and rocket-probe design decisions. Rankings of those considerations following the one assigned first importance could be used to further describe types of problem by their predecision characteristics. If ranking relations yielded an accurate picture of classes of decision problems, they would provide a useful guide for decision-investment *policy*.

A large-systems problem occurs when the investment decisions for predecision components interact with one another. For example, if the results produced by strategy options are dependent on the number of environments considered, or if the best error option is not discernible apart from consideration of the kinds of control system that are technologically feasible, then the investment problem must be treated in the context of a larger system. The same conclusion applies when budgetary constraints exist, because the investment funds are insufficient to permit "ideal" allocations to each decision component. In other words, we could make no move without considering its effect on the remaining components of the system.

To represent the larger-systems equation, we take one maximum for all the terms on the right-hand side of the equation, thus:

overall maximum
net benefit = maximum (value − cost) of [strategy options
+ environment options + error options
+ forecasting options + control options]

The resolution of interdependent systems problems is more difficult than that of independent systems problems. Nevertheless, a total system can be studied by using various techniques and procedures of systems analysis and synthesis. Most managers, however, if they consider the predecision problem objectively at all, would prefer the subjective approach for the larger system. It is simply that investments in objective studies grow disproportionately great as the size of the recognized system increases.

Competitive considerations further complicate the picture, producing additional investment options, but to include detailed considerations of competitive or interdependent systems in our present discussion would introduce severe complications.

A Discussion of Strategy Options

Innovation and imitation. The essence of strategy development can be reduced to one of two categories: either imitation or innovation. Probably nothing more perceptive has ever been written about the nature of imitation and the surprising forms it can take than Gabriel Tarde's *Laws of Imitation.*[4] Tarde argued convincingly that being "just like" or "as exactly opposite as possible" are both forms of imitation, whereas progress comes from principles that *evolve* from previous conditions and thereby represents a new pattern—an innovation.

Conforming imitation has advantages. Much information is available about the results of using similar strategies under a variety of environmental conditions. Strategies that are "known to work" lower managerial risk levels, although at the same time additional use of them may "wear out" their utility. Imitative wage scales and the use of the "human behavior approach" to generate enthusiasm and maintain worker morale are examples of such strategies. When conforming strategies are used in opposition to each other (as in competitive marketing), division results more often than multiplication (i.e., the competitors are more likely to share the market than to increase the total market size). As practiced, nonconforming imitation, or "doing the opposite," is probably not as drastic as it might at first sound. The "opposite" characteristics are limited to only a few dimensions of the overall pattern. Nonconforming imitation has the advantage of appearing to be innovation and picking up untapped market segments, while at the same time enjoying many of the previously mentioned benefits of conforming imitation.

Innovative forms of creative behavior are not obvious. Consider the following quote of Charles Schulz, the creator of "Peanuts." Is Linus innovative or simply imitative in a nonconforming sense? Is Charlie Brown a conforming imitator?

---

[4] Tarde was a French jurist who published his *Laws of Imitation* in the 1890's. He attempted to show that asocial and criminal behavior were forms of "opposite" imitation.

"Incidentally, Snoopy wasn't in the most popular strip I ever did, the one I've had the most mail on. That was the one where the kids are looking at the clouds and Linus says, 'See that one cloud over there? It sort of looks like the profile of Thomas Eakins, the famous portrait painter. And that other group over there—that looks as though it could be a map of British Honduras and then do you see that large group of clouds up there? I see the Stoning of Stephen. Over to the side I can see the figure of the Apostle Paul standing.' Then Lucy says, 'That's very good, Linus. It shows you have quite a good imagination. What do you see in the clouds, Charlie Brown?' And Charlie says, 'Well I was going to say I saw a ducky and a horsey, but I've changed my mind.' "[5]

Innovation is the product of creative mentality. Although little is known about creativity, it has been studied, and various approaches to understanding its nature have been suggested.[6] The special character accorded to "being creative" is due in large measure to the way that people feel about it.

Many years ago T. S. Knowlson gathered examples of various stimulating sensory conditions with which the creative workers provide themselves. Some of these seem bizarre indeed: "Dr. Johnson needed to have a purring cat, orange peel and plenty of tea to drink. Balzac wrote all night stimulated by constant cups of very strong black coffee. Zola pulled down the blinds at midday because he found more stimulus for his thought in artificial light. Carlyle was forever trying to construct a sound-proof room, while Proust achieved one. Schiller seems to have depended on the smell of decomposing apples which he habitually kept concealed in his desk." Poincaré agreed about black coffee. Stephen Spender cites his reliance on tea and notes that Auden must have coffee and tobacco. . . .[7]

Quality array. We can also examine the role of *search* in the innovative process. It seems reasonable that a distribution of quality will result from efforts to create successively a number of strategies. In other words, just as height is distributed in the population, there would be a range of qualities from the creative effort.

On the one hand, if "practice makes perfect," then as more strategies are

---

[5] Barnaby Conrad, "You're a Good Man Charlie Schulz," *New York Times Magazine,* April 16, 1967, p. 33.

[6] For example, the synectic approach suggested by William J. J. Gordon. See William J. J. Gordon, *Synectics: The Development of Creative Capacity* (New York: Harper & Row, 1961).

[7] Harold Rugg, *Imagination: An Inquiry into the Sources and Conditions that Stimulate Creativity* (New York: Harper & Row, 1963), p. 15. Rugg is quoting from Peter McKellar, *Imagination and Thinking, a Psychological Analysis* (London: Cohen and West, 1957), p. 124.

Figure 6–2

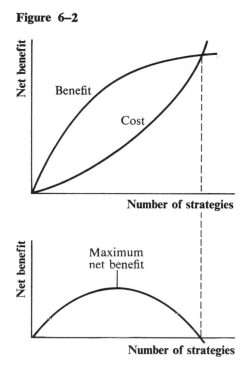

created the quality of later strategies should be higher than that of earlier ones. However, the increase in value will be offset at some point by the growing cost of producing the strategies. Cost growth is linear or even geometric, while benefit additions are marginal. (See Figure 6–2.) Consequently, at some given number of strategies, the creation of yet another one will produce a decrease rather than an increase in net benefit.

On the other hand, if no learning occurs as a result of practice, then each new strategy can be treated as if it were obtained at random. Under such circumstances, there would be an average quality level for the strategies, with variation of some degree around this average value. The quality of any particular strategy would be a matter of chance. Having been produced under random conditions, some strategies would be poorer than average, while others would be better. The array of qualities for a given number of strategies would be distributed in accordance with the characteristics of the relevant probability distribution. It is important to note that the probability of extremes of either kind would increase as a greater number of strategies were created.

If it were possible to develop a reliable method of evaluation, then the poorer-than-average strategies could be discarded and a new and improved distribution of qualities obtained. This evaluation ability would reduce the size of the decision problem. The saving, however, might be offset by the cost of developing and using the evaluation procedure.

Searching for Quality. The issues we have been discussing focus on a basic question: How many strategies should be created in order to have on hand a sufficiently good set of strategies for any specific decision problem?[8] This is, in large part, a question that lends itself to a quantitative formulation of measures relating to creativity. In this regard, there are several things to consider—for example, Eureka-type strategies.

Eurekas are those rare events whose patterns of occurrence fall outside the descriptive province of the statistical methods of expected values (with which we ordinarily deal). Some, like the patterns associated with contest winners, record flood crests, old age, and airline accidents, are best described by the statistical methods of extreme values. Others, like technological breakthroughs, are runaway strategies that signal a system's change and a shift to new terms. For example, Alexander the Great cut the Gordian knot instead of attempting to untie it as his predecessors had. Columbus supposedly solved the puzzle of how to stand an egg on its end by gently bashing the shell. He was somewhat less inventive but more courageous in finding a new route to the Indies. Tarde would have called all such happenings "innovative."

Some creative results can be attributed to serendipity[9]—in effect, to chance. It sometimes happens, for example, that when an individual is looking for the solution to one problem, he stumbles inadvertently upon the solution to another. Creative solutions are found in other cases because certain people have special innovative abilities in one or more decision areas and can generate superior distributions of strategic quality. But investments in such creative talent are in conflict with investments for decision-making talent. Expenditures for testing procedures to identify creative abilities are yet another available investment option. These fundamental investment issues clearly are concerned with the design of an organization and its personnel.

Another aspect of this problem is related to facility investments. A decision might be deferred because suitable strategies are lacking and because it is felt that research could provide important new directions. When funds are invested for the purchase of (creative) research, talent, and supporting facilities,

---

[8] Irving Gross, on p. 7 of his Advertising Research Foundation paper of March 1964, indicated that under some highly particular conditions, an insufficient number of advertisements are prepared for testing. "If the variation in advertising quality causes anything like the range in profit return assumed in the analysis, then it would probably pay for advertisers to devote much more attention than they have in the past to generating a larger number of genuinely different ads and campaigns."

[9] The term was coined by Hugh Walpole after the princes of Serendip (now Ceylon), who encountered a succession of pleasant events in the course of travels intended for other objectives.

other decision components can be affected. For example, the research effort could succeed in producing a Eureka strategy, which might even obviate the need to construct a decision model, since the preferred strategy would be immediately obvious. This situation could produce savings by removing the need to collect information and to provide a forecast. In other words, the investment in research alone would have resulted in a solution to the decision problem. Such possibilities are inherent in the decision framework for both product and process development. And the investment problem arises whenever there is good reason to suspect that superior strategies could be developed if the effort were made. Investment funds must then be divided between the cost of creating new ideas and the cost of testing their effectiveness before reaching a decision. A rational manager, of course, will attempt to allocate his investment budget in such a way as to yield maximum net benefit.

Mathematical models can describe search procedures that reflect innovation. They can provide a rough means for approximating the cost and value of generating different numbers of strategies. Although far from specifying instructions for action (they provide insight rather than solutions), they do offer legitimate guidance concerning the investment of funds in the strategy option. In the Appendix to this chapter we have developed some models of creativity. These models highlight such questions as: What is the effect of the ability to learn to create? How does the potential of the field for discovery affect creativity? What number of feasible strategies should be created and what are the related costs? In model form such issues help to structure the creative problem in ways that words alone could never succeed in doing. At the same time, these models clearly are treating complex areas in attenuated ways. They are subject to the same pros and cons that we continually experience with respect to the use of models.

Still, although such models may be simplistic, they demonstrate the advantage of having a rich area to search (that is, an area that contains many more feasible strategies than the number that must be created). Also, any investment that improves the executive's ability to *learn* how to create superior strategies can be seen to warrant serious consideration.

In the light of the above discussion (and the material in the Appendix), we can ask: Is management spending the right amount on strategy options? The answer will depend on the nature of the creative process that is applicable to the situation. Some systems permit learning, while in others discoveries are random; in some the amount of variation from the average that can be expected is large, while for others it is negligible. The answer will also depend on the value to the enterprise of extremes, as well as the likelihood and cost of creating such extremes. When the decision framework is used, data that are relevant to these issues can be collected. Knowledge of the system's properties can be developed over time. At least an adequate perspective is available for framing questions and for phrasing answers.

A Discussion of Environment Options

The problem of finding important environments is similar in many ways to that of searching for creative strategies. It has, however, some special attributes. For example, the search for significant states of nature is likely to be one of diminishing returns for the efforts expended. We would expect that the average time required to discover some given number of environmental conditions would increase either linearly or at an accelerating rate (as shown in Figure 6–3).[10] This is especially true as the number identified approaches the

Figure 6–3

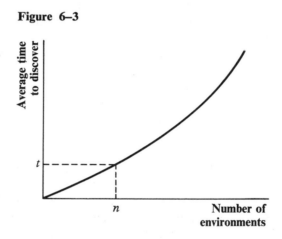

total number of environments that *could ever* be discovered. Such search characteristics can be built into quantitative models, which then can be studied to provide crude policy guides. As was the case for strategies, mathematical formulations can be designed to help evaluate the effort that will be required to search for environmental options.

Basic differences between discovering environments and creating strategies can be revealed by such models. Even our word models, "discover" and "create," reflect a distinction. While there are times when it seems reasonable to talk about "discovering strategies," the same does not apply to "creating environments." Our primary purpose, however, is to use the logic of the decision model as a basis for determining an intelligent environmental investment policy.

---

[10] The linear case is exemplified by one of the models for strategy creation, called variant *C,* found in the Appendix.

There are situations in which the penalty for overlooking a relevant environment can be catastrophic. Under such circumstances, it is crucial that any potential ruin environments be discovered. The first need is to recognize that intensive search is warranted. Two examples will serve to reinforce this statement. First, a well-known drug was not tested under enough environmental conditions. Disastrously, a critical environment (namely, that of a certain stage of pregnancy) was not included. An unexpected interaction occurred between strategy (the drug) and environment (the pregnancy), with tragic results. Second, a large bridge, reputed for its handsome proportions, had been designed with safety factors appropriate for all potential environments save one. The span was entirely stable except for a set of environmental factors that produced resonant vibrations. When these occurred, the bridge was destroyed.

The extent to which environmental options are modeled is a function not only of the number of dimensions (such as pregnancy or resonance) used but of the scaling of the dimensions. Consider, for example, a system where temperature conditions form the relevant states of nature. To begin with, temperature can be divided into *unit* degree classes. There can be hundreds or thousands of such classes, depending on the range to be covered. On the other hand, the same range of temperatures can be grouped into sets that span, say, twenty degrees per class—for example, 0–20, 20–40, 40–60, and so forth. If the system's response is sensitive to minute gradations of temperature, then the refined scale is warranted—and perhaps even the unit degree classes are too crude. Consumer perceptions of taste and color are other measurement situations that might require refined scales. In such cases, the lack of properly refined categories means the loss of important information. However, the reverse condition of overrefinement is probably a more common fault.

The level of refinement of a scale may appear at first to be only a matter of degree—that is, to produce small incremental changes in the manager's selection. But this is not so. Scale interval design is totally related to the proper definition of environments. The size of the intervals can adversely affect the implementation of a solution when it does not match the operational requirements of the system. At other times, the model can produce incorrect results because it is *sensitive to scale,* by which we mean that the decision can change when only the scale of measurement is modified. The implications for management are evident. Often, because of tradition, the kind of information that the manager receives may lead him astray even though he is entirely consistent in dealing with the information he gets. The correct scale is, therefore, always susceptible to a sensitivity criterion applied to all phases of the implementation process. For some problems "inches" or "cents" may be required for precision, whereas for others "feet" or "dollars" would do. This issue is especially pertinent to the observation of environments because they are the part of the system that is not under the manager's control. Perhaps, as a result, there is a compelling tendency to think that forecasting environmental likeli-hoods is a self-defining problem that can be turned over to technicians whose specialty is forecasting. But this is not warranted until the forecasting problem is fully defined and the interval sizes specified.

To demonstrate the relationship of decision-model sensitivity to the scale of measurement, consider the three parts of Table 6–1. Assume the decision criterion is to select the strategy with the greatest average value. We note that fundamental changes occur in the manager's decisions *because* of the way he defines the environments (in this case, the interval size). To understand this result, let us examine the construction of these matrices.

Environmental values have been determined in accordance with the relative frequencies of appearance of the environments. That is, when the smallest intervals are used:

	z_1	z_2	z_3	z_4
Probability	.05	.20	.25	.50
Value	1	2	3	4

Consequently, when z_1 and z_2 are seen as one environment and z_3 and z_4 as another, we find:

$(z_1 + z_2)$	$(z_3 + z_4)$
Probability: (.05 + .20) = .25	(.25 + .50) = .75
Value: $z_1 = 1$ occurs .05/.25 = .20	$z_3 = 3$ occurs .25/.75 = .33
$z_2 = 2$ occurs .20/.25 = .80	$z_4 = 4$ occurs .50/.75 = .67
Therefore:	Therefore:
(.20 × 1) + (.80 × 2) = 1.8	(.33 × 3) + (.67 × 4) = 3.67

And, when $z_1 + z_2 + z_3 + z_4$ are seen as one environment:

Probability of $(z_1 + z_2 + z_3 + z_4) = 1.0$
Value: (.05 × 1) + (.20 × 2) + (.25 × 3) + (.50 × 4) = 3.20

As for the outcome values for this hypothetical case, we have indicated in the matrices that:

Strategy 1 outcomes: $O_{1j} = .8z_j{}^2$
Strategy 2 outcomes: $O_{2j} = 24/z_j$
Strategy 3 outcomes: $O_{3j} = 18 - 3z_j$

where O_{ij} is the outcome for the *i*th strategy and the *j*th environment, while z_j is the value of the *j*th environment

In the first matrix, the scale is refined. Four environments have been iden-tified with values of 1, 2, 3, and 4, respectively. The second matrix represents

Table 6–1

	z_1	z_2	z_3	z_4		
Value of environment z_j:*	1	2	3	4	Average	
Forecast:	.05	.20	.25	.50	value	Rank
Strategy 1: $.8z^2$	.8	3.2	7.2	12.8	8.80	(1)
Strategy 2: $24/z_j$	24	12	8	6	8.60	(2)
Strategy 3: $18 - 3z_j$	15	12	9	6	8.40	(3)

INDICATED ACTION: Choose strategy 1.

	z_1, z_2	z_3, z_4		
Value of environment z_j:**	1.8	3.67	Average	
Forecast:	.25	.75	value	Rank
Strategy 1: $.8z^2$	2.592	10.755	8.720	(1)
Strategy 2: $24/z_j$	40/3	72/11	8.242	(3)
Strategy 3: $18 - 3z_j$	12.6	7	8.400	(2)

INDICATED ACTION: As before, choose strategy 1, but note that the ranked order of strategy 2 and strategy 3 has shifted.

	$z_1, z_2, z_3,$ and z_4		
Value of environment z_j:***	3.2	Average	
Forecast:	1.0	value	Rank
Strategy 1: $.8z^2$	8.192	8.192	(2)
Strategy 2: $24/z_j$	7.500	7.500	(3)
Strategy 3: $18 - 3z_j$	8.400	8.400	(1)

INDICATED ACTION: The choice has shifted from strategy 1 to strategy 3.

---

* For example, the value of $z_2 = 2$.
** The values of z_1 and $z_2 = 1.8$ and z_3 and $z_4 = 3.67$ are derived in the text.
*** The values of $z_1, z_2, z_3,$ and $z_4 = 3.2$ are derived in the text.

a less refined scale. Environments 1 and 2 are observed together, as are environments 3 and 4. The values of these combined environments might have been taken as the averages, that is $(1 + 2)/2 = 1.5$ and $(3 + 4)/2 = 3.5$, but the more general case is the one we have shown where the probabilities of the environments have been taken into account. In the third matrix, all information about environmental variability has been lost. There is only one environment. The problem has been transformed to one of decision-making under certainty. Again, the value of the single environment could have been computed as an average value—that is, $(1 + 2 + 3 + 4)/4 = 2.5$. However, the use of averages in this example is not as reasonable as the approach we have used (even though it is conceivable in practice), and, in this case, the resulting sensitivity to scale would not change.

We observe that when the scale of measurement is highly refined (as in the first matrix), the manager would select the first strategy. If he is unable (or unwilling) to sense such refined environmental categories and uses instead the two-environment matrix, the manager probably will not be aware of the switch in rank order of the second and third strategies. However, should our manager approach the situation as one of certainty (as in the third matrix), for reasons of reducing costs or because he cannot do any better, then strategy 3 would be the indicated choice. Because it is based on *less* information than the choice arising from the first two matrices, this decision would be an error. How bad such a mistake might be is not clear in this example, for our intention is merely to illustrate the relevant theory and the concepts behind it. But one thing to note in this regard is that the third strategy is invariant to scale changes because it is linear, whereas the other two strategies are not. The same expected value is obtained for linear strategies whatever scale is used for the states of nature. In fact, the expected-value calculation simply follows a different order of processing the numbers when combined states of nature are employed, but this is not true of the nonlinear payoff functions of strategies 1 and 2. It is apparent that knowledge of linearity of the payoff function *and what that means* could afford substantial savings. The manager might find it worthwhile to go directly to the third matrix, which has the lowest modeling costs, once he has observed that all the payoff functions are linear.

This example illustrates a situation where the choice of strategy switches easily as the level of refinement of the environmental measuring scale is altered. When changes of this kind do not take place readily—for example, in this case, strategy 3's linear system—the model is described as insensitive. Since, generally, any increase in the refinement of measurement also increases the cost, refinements are a total waste when the system is insensitive.

Another aspect of environmental effects can be pointed out. The cost of completing the decision matrix for some given number of strategies will increase as additional environments are considered. If there are M strategies, then M additional tests and related computations must be performed for each additional environment that is treated. But, as we have previously indicated, this fact does not mean that accounting procedures can be used to enumerate environments. Some of the most interesting management situations warrant limiting emphasis on creative strategies so that stress can be placed on environmental analysis.

A Discussion of Error Options

The notion of sensitivity can be applied beneficially to errors of estimation and measurement as well as to the degree of refinement of environmental categories. Sometimes even one mistake can cause a wrong decision to be made, or a number of minor discrepancies in data treatment can produce a wrong decision. It is worthwhile to avoid such penalties when the cost of doing so is less than the penalties.

Error avoidance requires investments in particular predecision procedures that promise improvements in net benefit. With budget limitations, expenditures for error avoidance and for error-detection systems are justified, of course, only when they produce an increase in net benefit that is competitive with amounts invested elsewhere in the predecision process. This is most likely to occur when the system is both *susceptible* and *vulnerable* to error—in other words, when it is error-prone and when errors may produce serious systems failures and aberrations. The worst type of error is the one that threatens ruin. But we must also consider the possibility of error contagion, where the appearance of an initial error increases the probability that further errors will occur.[11] Such systems, because they have interdependent parts, become increasingly susceptible and, ultimately, vulnerable.

Management can usually afford to evaluate the reliability of its measuring tools for those scales that supply vital decision information.[12] If the data sources are error-prone, then verification procedures can be employed—on either a 100 percent or a sample basis. Often the quality of either the data source or the measuring tools can be improved. As before, the guiding rule requires that a balance be found between the costs of error prevention and the penalties associated with the occurrence of error.

Most frequently, the reduction of error to a reasonable, predetermined value is sufficient. Sometimes, however, it is necessary to push as close as possible to the *absolute* prevention of error. Duplication of equipment, though

---

[11] For example, an error in air-traffic control puts great pressure on everyone participating in the system and thereby may increase the likelihood that another error will be made. This behavioral form of dependency is not unfamiliar to managers.

[12] We differentiate between reliability and validity, the latter being an intrinsic model-building problem—i.e., is the model correct?

costly, is often employed for this purpose. For this reason multiengine planes are designed to fly on fewer engines than they actually have. Similarly, two altimeters for planes and back-up electronic switching equipment for telephone centers can be justified. Equipment redundancy rises as both the probability and the cost of critical failures increase. To achieve its purpose, the design of redundant equipment should be such that each unit and its duplicate will be as independent as possible of each other's errors.

Various mathematical models have been developed for analyzing the reliability of systems that utilize error-prevention or detection facilities.[13] These facilities are not restricted to mechanisms. Management is entirely familiar with (but not adroit in) the use of human inspectors, and people are frequently employed to replicate work that requires verification. Redundancy is often difficult to build into human systems, where interactions occur and interdependencies exist that will not be encountered in the relations of machines with one another. While human and machine systems each pose their own problems, they offer particular advantages in combination. Further issues arise when we draw the distinction between cooperative and duplicative relations of human and machine systems. Probability theory and the more recently developed information theory have made significant contributions in these areas. Models fashioned in logical and quantitative terms permit us to estimate the reduction in errors that can be achieved with given verification procedures. Knowing the costs of errors as well as the costs of removing them permits a net-benefit calculation to be made for various alternative error-reducing methods.

There are many important aspects of the related problems of preventing errors before they occur and removing them once they occur. Technological design factors, the diagnostic procedures of systems analysis, experimental designs based on the replication of tests, the selection of proper samples, and the determination of a system's stability are all relevant. Failure analysis (used in conjunction with reliability models) is essential for the economic design of error procedures. Over- and underspending for these procedures can be costly.

A Discussion of Forecasting Options

A large percentage of management's total investment in the decision process is normally channeled into forecasting and predicting activities. These attempts to foretell the future can be handled in many different ways and at various levels of cost and degrees of confidence. When predictions are derived solely by means of entrepreneurial wisdom and managerial intuition, *real* costs

---

[13] See pp. 515–18, for example.

exist for the use of this talent, even though they tend to be lost in the accounting for overhead. The variable costs of information collection and statistical analysis are more visible. Reasonable cost estimates, therefore, are available for most circumstances and can be analyzed to determine whether management is spending the right amount on the forecasting function.

The words "forecast" and "prediction" are generally used interchangeably. But there is no advantage in having two words that mean the same thing. Supported at least in part by our dictionary, we will draw a useful distinction between these terms. *Forecasting* connotes conjecture. In practice, we can take this to mean the derivation of a distribution of likelihood measures for a spectrum of possibilities. (For example, the probability that it will rain tomorrow is 60 percent, and the probability of no precipitation is then 40 percent.) On the other hand, we make a *prediction* that a specific event will occur (e.g., that it will rain tomorrow). Predictions arise from an *inferential* process. They are based on fundamental relations that imply suppositions of causality. Both forecasts and predictions have their place—determined by the way the problem characteristics affect the criterion of maximum net benefit.

Forecasts can be derived by analyzing the frequencies of occurrence of past events. Descriptive methods of statistics and correlation procedures have been employed with success. Probability theory, describing systems of interdependent relations, can be built into model form. Purely subjective assignments of probability distributions have been receiving increasingly favorable attention.

When a perfect prediction can be made, there is no need for a forecast. Perfect predictive ability is equivalent to omniscience. Of course, few predictions (not fixes) are perfect. At different levels of accuracy, predictions are achieved in various ways: by knowing what environment will occur next because of special information; by using the mode (or state) associated with the highest value of the distribution; by using the average or expected state; by projecting trends discovered in data collected from tests, experiments, and surveys; and by weighing the believability of the evidence. Betting on a particular horse, for example, is equivalent to making a prediction. The stated odds are the forecast. If the bettor thinks that the race is fixed, he can use this special information; if he bets on the horse that won most frequently, he is using the mode. By assessing many factors, such as track condition, jockeys, and so forth, the bettor can make his prediction by weighing the evidence and its believability.

Let us consider the net benefits of forecasts and then of predictions. Outcomes can be translated from either costs or profits into *opportunity costs*. These costs have been defined previously as the difference between the outcome that would result if a specific strategy is chosen and the best outcome that could have been obtained under the circumstances. Accordingly, for *each* state of nature there is at least one strategy that can deliver a zero opportunity

Table 6–2

States of nature, z_j's:

	1	2	3
Strategy 1	5	4	3
Strategy 2	1	5	6

Matrix of Profits

States of nature, z_j's:			(Row maximums)
	1	2	3	Worst cost:
Strategy 1	0	1	3	3 Best of worsts
Strategy 2	4	0	0	4

Matrix of Opportunity Costs

cost. Table 6–2 demonstrates this kind of conversion for a hypothetical decision problem in which the objective is maximum profit. The largest profit *in
each column* is assigned a zero value; all other column entries are obtained by
subtraction from the largest profit. Strategy 1 provides the *best of the worst*
opportunity costs (a value of 3). This is the minimax opportunity-cost value.
We observe that (as in the case of competitive models) an entrepreneur need
never accept a larger opportunity cost than the minimax value, since if he uses
whichever strategy yields the *least worst* result, he is protected from experi-
encing any greater penalty than the minimax value.[14] A measure of information value begins to emerge: *The use of either forecasts or predictions to improve decision-making results, cannot be justified if the cost of forecasting or
predicting is greater than the minimax opportunity-cost value.*

Assume that the manager has only a hunch concerning the forecast values.
He can act on the basis of this subjective forecast, or he can ignore the hunch
and use the minimax criterion, or he can attempt to obtain evidence to justify
his hunch. If he decides to use his subjective forecast, he does so by obtaining
the average opportunity cost for each strategy. Table 6–3 shows this calculation for an executive's subjective forecast. It shows a situation of decision-
making under risk, with a hypothetical, subjective forecast and the profit
matrix converted to an opportunity-cost matrix. If he believes in his forecast,
the manager will select the strategy associated with the minimum expected

---

[14] When an opportunity-cost matrix is used in this fashion, whether it is derived from a
cost or profit matrix, it is applicable to decision-making under conditions of uncertainty.
The minimax of opportunity costs identifies the strategy to be used. This is called the
Savage Regret criterion because L. J. Savage, who developed it, called the opportunity
costs "regrets."

Table 6–3

States of nature, z_j's:	1	2	3	Expected Opportunity Cost (EOC):
Subjective forecast:	.2	.5	.3	
Strategy 1	0	1	3	1.4
Strategy 2	4	0	0	.8 Best (minimum EOC)

opportunity cost (minimum EOC). Now let us assume that the manager does not believe in his forecast. He can turn to sensitivity analysis as a means of improving his belief level. Instead of a single set of forecast values, he now has a range. The broader the band of values the manager takes, the greater his belief that the correct forecast falls within the range. For example, using our previous numbers, the manager might specify the following range:

States of nature:

	1	2	3
First bound	.1	.4	.5
Subjective forecast	.2	.5	.3
Second bound	.3	.6	.1

Table of Probabilities

The expected opportunity costs can be derived quickly, following the same pattern of calculations shown in Table 6–3 but using the appropriate probabilities. Thus

	Strategy 1	Strategy 2
First bound	1.9	.4
Subjective forecast	1.4	.8
Second bound	.9	1.2

Table of Expected Opportunity Costs

The extreme values for the minimum expected values are .9 and .4, meaning that the expected opportunity cost could reach as low a figure as .4 and is not likely to be higher than .9.

The question of how to use such results is more personal than definitive. A cautious manager would say that since he has a good deal of belief that costs can be reduced to at least .9, he can afford to spend

$$\text{minimax} - .9 = 3.0 - .9 = 2.1$$

to validate his forecast. At the other extreme, a more optimistic manager might state that

$$\text{minimax} - .4 = 3.0 - .4 = 2.6$$

sets an absolute upper limit to what he can afford to spend to obtain the forecast. A third position, based on the manager's initial forecast, would be to compute

$$\text{minimax} - \text{minimum } EOC = 3.0 - .8 = 2.2$$

and use that value as the maximum amount to spend on the forecast.

In this way, at least a reasonable range of values for investments in forecasting is derived—that is, from 2.1 to 2.6. We might note that even in a Parkinsonian, work-expanding world, the manager will not be willing to spend the entire amount (of potential savings) that he chooses to view as his maximum expenditure level (such as 2.2) because he wants to do more than break even. And another useful fact emerges—namely, if the minimax opportunity criterion and the minimum EOC criterion both indicate that the same strategy should be chosen (which they did not do in this example), then it is probably unreasonable to allocate any funds for validation of the subjective forecast. In our example, only the second bound result selected the same strategy as the minimax criterion. Since the minimum EOC strategy of the initial subjective forecast, as well as the first bound result, chose a strategy other than that of the minimax, it is quite reasonable to allocate some funds for developing the forecast, if such procedures are feasible within the acceptable investment bounds.

If good predictions can be obtained for about the same cost as an accurate forecast, the manager will prefer to invest in predictions. To begin with, the value of providing an accurate forecast cannot be larger than the value of predicting *exactly* which environment will occur. Of course, it is not often that perfect predictions can be obtained. Investments in tests, experiments, and surveys for predictions of any given quality must be more than offset by the resulting improvement in the net-benefit basis for making decisions. Mathematical methods exist that permit us to combine subjective forecasts with predictive tests of varying quality. When tests are used, the selected prediction reflects the results of the tests. In this situation it is possible to determine what value *various* test procedures have. Strong tests (i.e., those that provide correct results most of the time) can be too costly, and less expensive tests are frequently warranted. Managerial *compulsiveness* for large samples, tight criteria, and rigorous methods is often encountered where the manager lacks net-benefit information. His tendency is to "do it right or not at all." This attitude is unlike management's usual investment behavior and stems presumably from a sense of technical inadequacy. The manager at his ease will select the test that is best suited to his needs—or even decide to ignore tests entirely if he judges that to be best.

We have shown that investments in predictive methods should cost no more than the minimax opportunity-cost value—given that no reliable forecast exists. This idea can be extended easily to the case where a *believable* forecast is already on hand. Then *the manager should not spend more than minimum EOC for the development of predictive methods.*

These results, which are entirely general, epitomize the kind of investment guideline that decision theory makes available with respect to the value of information. When such simple and abstract rules are presented as a guide for complex situations, caution is warranted. For example, if the manager decides to invest heavily in his forecast option, he should be fully aware of the possibility that the forecast he develops can, in turn, influence other factors in the environment. Illustrations of this kind of interaction can be cited with respect to forecasts for GNP and for the behavior of the stock market. Predictions may exercise even greater leverage. This accounts for present-day concern with preelection polls and with early computer predictions of election results.[15]

A discussion of Bayesian options. Bayes's Theorem[16] was published posthumously by the Royal Society in 1763. Since that time, the ideas he formulated have produced much philosophizing and speculation. Perhaps Bayes's most noteworthy advocate was the Marquis Pierre Simon de Laplace, but for a long while after Laplace died, Bayes's work was forgotten. Following the development of classical statistics in the first half of the twentieth century, there has been a widespread renewal of interest in Bayes's Theorem[17] for use as a practical management tool.

One of the most attractive aspects of the theorem is that it enables the manager to combine his formal knowledge with his intuitions. The essence of the method is that it provides a relationship for combining two kinds of input information to produce one kind of output information. These components are described in Table 6–4.

Table 6–4

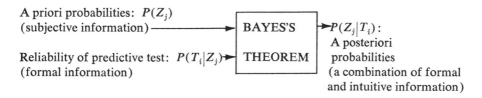

A priori probabilities: $P(Z_j)$
(subjective information) ⟶ BAYES'S ⟶ $P(Z_j|T_i)$:
A posteriori

Reliability of predictive test: $P(T_i|Z_j)$ ⟶ THEOREM   probabilities
(formal information)   (a combination of formal and intuitive information)

---

[15] For further discussion of these points, see the treatment of the voting model, pp. 490–94.

[16] Not to be confused with the Laplace-Bayes criterion discussed earlier (pp. 153–54).

[17] Bayes's Theorem is
$$P(Z_j|T_i) = \frac{P(Z_j)P(T_i|Z_j)}{\sum_j P(Z_j)P(T_i|Z_j)} = \frac{P(Z_jT_i)}{P(T_i)}$$

$P(Z_j)$ is the probability that the jth environment (Z_j) will occur. Using the notation previously developed in Chapter 4, we would call this p_j. Next, $P(T_i|Z_j)$ is the probability that the ith test result (T_i) will occur—given that the true state is Z_j. We have not had the occasion to use this notation before. It is called a *conditional probability statement*—the factor to the right of the vertical line is the condition and the factor to the left of the vertical is the event dependent on the condition. Thus, T_i is the event based on the condition Z_j. We are interested in the probability that T_i will occur, given that Z_j exists for various i and j configurations. To exemplify this, if Z_1 is male and Z_2 is female and T_1 is color blindness, then $P(T_1|Z_1) = .065$ and $P(T_1|Z_2) < .01$ because it is known that about 6.5 percent of men, but less than 1 percent of women, are color-blind. Finally $P(Z_j|T_i)$ is the conditional probability that the jth environment, Z_j, really exists if the ith test result, T_i, was observed. This description will take care of explaining the notation, but the interpretation still must be clarified. Using the example of color blindness, $P(Z_1|T_1)$ is the probability that a color-blind person is male, and $P(Z_2|T_1)$ is the probability that a color-blind person is female.

The Bayesian method can be applied in the following way. The manager will reach different decisions according to the probabilities that he assigns (as forecasts) to the environmental conditions, Z_j's. Based on his experience, he is encouraged to develop intuitive estimates—the a priori probabilities, $P(Z_j)$'s.

We can present a simple example by allowing only two environmental conditions, Z_1 and Z_2. To begin, let us presume that when the manager is asked to estimate the probabilities of the environments, he says, "As far as I am concerned, you can toss a coin." Consequently, following the Laplace-Bayes criterion, $P(Z_1) = P(Z_2) = \frac{1}{2}$. The manager does, however, have an experiment that he can use to test for the next environment. Naturally, he wishes to discuss the reliability of this test. We can represent reliability in the matrix form shown in Table 6–5. This predictive test, we observe, is strong in spotting Z_1 (correct eight out of ten times) but not so good for spotting Z_2 (correct only six out of ten times).

Table 6–5   Matrix of Probabilities that Test Result T_i Will Occur When the True Condition Is Z_j.

		on the condition that the actual state is	
		Z_1	Z_2
Probability that the	T_1	.8	.4
test result will be	T_2	.2	.6

NOTE: In conditional-probability form, each entry in the table is a value of $P(T_i|Z_j)$.

By following Bayes's Theorem, we can derive a new matrix, each term of which is $P(Z_j)P(T_i|Z_j) = P(Z_jT_i)$. In other words, all these table entries are joint probabilities of the form $P(Z_jT_i)$. For example, $3\frac{1}{4}$ percent of all people are both male and color-blind. This assumes that half the population is male—that is, $\frac{1}{2}(.065) = .0325$. Applying similar reasoning to the manager's problem, we get

	Matrix of $P(Z_jT_i)$		$P(T_i)$
	Z_1	Z_2	
T_1	$.8(\frac{1}{2}) = .4$	$.4(\frac{1}{2}) = .2$	$.4 + .2 = .6$
T_2	$.2(\frac{1}{2}) = .1$	$.6(\frac{1}{2}) = .3$	$.1 + .3 = .4$

We have calculated $P(T_i)$ by summing the values in each row of the matrix of $P(Z_j|T_i)$. The a posteriori probabilities are now obtained by dividing each row entry by its respective row value of $P(T_i)$. Thus

	Z_1	Z_2
A priori probabilities	$\frac{1}{2}$	$\frac{1}{2}$
A posteriori probabilities[18] if T_1 occurs	$\frac{.4}{.6} = \frac{2}{3}$	$\frac{.2}{.6} = \frac{1}{3}$
A posteriori probabilities[18] if T_2 occurs	$\frac{.1}{.4} = \frac{1}{4}$	$\frac{.3}{.4} = \frac{3}{4}$

Bayes's Theorem has combined the a priori probabilities with the test's characteristics and formed the a posteriori (also called inverse) probabilities. The manager can now measure the influence that the test information can have on the value of his decision. Knowing the cost of the test, he can determine the net benefit of employing this predictive device.

Our test would have been useless if its ability to recognize the true condition had been 50–50, for in that case the a priori probabilities, whatever they were, would not be changed by testing. Let the a priori probabilities be $P(Z_1) = \frac{1}{4}$ and $P(Z_2) = \frac{3}{4}$. We then have this result:

	$P(T_i|Z_j)$		$P(Z_jT_i)$		$P(T_i)$
	Z_1	Z_2	Z_1	Z_2	
T_1	$\frac{1}{2}$	$\frac{1}{2}$	$\frac{1}{8}$	$\frac{3}{8}$	$\frac{1}{2}$
T_2	$\frac{1}{2}$	$\frac{1}{2}$	$\frac{1}{8}$	$\frac{3}{8}$	$\frac{1}{2}$

The a posteriori probabilities if T_1 occurs and Z_j exists equal those when T_2 occurs and Z_j exists: for Z_1, $\frac{1}{8} \div \frac{1}{2} = \frac{1}{4}$; for Z_2, $\frac{3}{8} \div \frac{1}{2} = \frac{3}{4}$. This is the same

---

[18] Note that the a posteriori probabilities $P(Z_j|T_i) = P(Z_jT_i)/P(T_i)$.

for both T_1 and T_2, and represents a final result that is the same as the initial a priori probabilities.

Now let us see how the information derived above can be used to determine whether a *particular* predictive test is worthwhile. We return to the opportunity-cost matrix that was the basis of our previous computations (see Table 6–3). The subjective forecasts were .2, .5, and .3. The characteristics of this *particular* predictive test will be hypothesized as

	$P(z_j)$	.2	.5	.3
			$P(T_i\|z_j)$	
		z_1	z_2	z_3
T_1		.9	.2	.0
T_2		.1	.7	.1
T_3		.0	.1	.9

Then, the matrix of $P(z_jT_i)$ and $P(T_i)$:

	$P(z_jT_i)$			$P(T_i)$
	z_1	z_2	z_3	
T_1	.18	.10	.00	.28
T_2	.02	.35	.03	.40
T_3	.00	.05	.27	.32

This gives the final table of results:

	z_1	z_2	z_3
I. A priori probabilities:	.2	.5	.3
II. A posteriori probabilities if T_1 occurs:	18/28	10/28	0/28
III. A posteriori probabilities if T_2 occurs:	2/40	35/40	3/40
IV. A posteriori probabilities if T_3 occurs:	0/32	5/32	27/32

Each result is now applied to the opportunity-cost matrix. The expected values for I were previously derived as 1.4 and .8 (see p. 223). It is essential to note that the probabilities for II, III, and IV occurring are $P(T_1)$, $P(T_2)$ and $P(T_3)$ respectively—that is, .28, .40, and .32. (See Table 6–6.) Consequently, *with the predictive test,* the minimum expected opportunity cost would be

$$.28(10/28) + .40(8/40) + .32(0) = .18.$$

This is a definite improvement over the minimum *EOC* of I, which was .8.

Figure 6–4 may be helpful in visualizing the significance of these results in terms of those previously developed. We can see that it would be wasteful to spend more than $.80 - .18 = .62$ for this particular predictive test, assuming that the forecast that produced the .80 result is entirely believable to the manager. (Of course, the scale of .62 units might represent a test cost of $62, $620, or $62,000.)

Table 6–6

II.   If T_1 occurs: $P(T_1) = .28$

	18/28	10/28	0/28	EOC	
S_1	0	1	3	10/28	Minimum, use S_1
S_2	4	0	0	18/7	

III. If T_2 occurs: $P(T_2) = .40$

	2/40	35/40	3/40	EOC	
S_1	0	1	3	44/40	
S_2	4	0	0	8/40	Minimum, use S_2

IV.   If T_3 occurs: $P(T_3) = .32$

	0	5/32	27/32	EOC	
S_1	0	1	3	86/32	
S_2	4	0	0	0	Minimum, use S_2

Figure 6–4

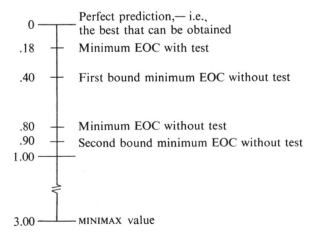

OPPORTUNITY COSTS

0 ——— Perfect prediction,— i.e., the best that can be obtained

.18 —+— Minimum EOC with test

.40 —+— First bound minimum EOC without test

.80 —+— Minimum EOC without test
.90 —+— Second bound minimum EOC without test
1.00 ———

3.00 ——— MINIMAX value

It is not essential to use opportunity costs to determine the value of information. Similar computations can be performed using profit and (direct) cost matrices. But the rules for the opportunity-cost transformations can be applied to both profit and total-cost analyses in the same way, and the opportunity-cost transformation has the additional advantage of placing a zero value in each column against which everything less good can be measured.

Previously we have used tree forms, and it would be appropriate to do so again. For the example just explained, the tree is shown in Figure 6–5.

Figure 6–5

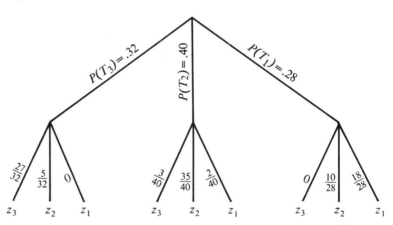

A Discussion of Control Options

The minimax value as it was previously defined is an upper threshold for investments only so long as no control exists over the environments. (Remember that this absence of control is a fundamental condition for environments when viewed in the decision-theory context.) Suppose, however, that a technological change occurs that suddenly permits control to be exercised over the previously uncontrollable environments. Air conditioning, artificial illumination, cloud seeding, and irradiation are examples of technological developments that *allow states of nature to be converted into strategies.* It is reasonable to ask first: How much should be spent on research to develop the required control technology? And then: How much can the manager afford to spend to implement such control?

Let us consider, in Table 6–7, the profit matrix previously used in Table 6–2. The value 3 is the best of the worsts (i.e., the maximin). The value 6 is the best of the bests (i.e., the maximax). At least one particular combination of a strategy and an environment will always produce a maximax result—

Table 6–7 Matrix of Profits

	States of nature, z_j's:			Minimums (worst):	Maximums (best):
	1	2	3		
Strategy 1	5	4	3	3	5
Strategy 2	1	5	6	1	6

that is, the best possible result that can be obtained from the system. In our example, the use of strategy 2 in conjunction with the third environment produces the maximax value of 6. This decision matrix also has the maximin value of 3. The maximin is the profit equivalent of the minimax value that applies to costs. It can be demonstrated that the largest justifiable investment to obtain complete control over a system's environment must be given by the difference of maximax − maximin. For our example, this is $6 - 3 = 3$. It cannot be sensible under any circumstances to spend more than this amount to develop and implement environmental controls. In fact, if the manager has additional information, such as a believable forecast, then the maximum amount to be spent for perfect control will probably be even less. This is shown below in equational form, using the familiar notation ($\leq$) to mean "equal to or less than."

$$(\text{maximax} - \text{maximum expected profit}) \leq (\text{maximax} - \text{maximin})$$
$$\textit{Forecast exists} \qquad\qquad \textit{No forecast exists}$$

The amount that should be spent to achieve control may be still less if the manager already possesses the ability to render an accurate prediction. For example, if the forecast .2, .5, .3 holds, then, with perfect predictive ability, the manager will use his first strategy when z_1 is predicted, producing a profit of 5; and he will use his second strategy when z_2 or z_3 is predicted, producing a profit of 5 or 6 accordingly. We then calculate the expected profit under conditions of perfect prediction as

$$.2(5) + .5(5) + .3(6) = 5.3$$

It follows that $6 - 5.3 = .7$ is the maximum amount to spend for environmental controls, given that a system providing perfect predictions is already available.

When we consider control, opportunity costs can no longer be defined in column isolation. The entire matrix is involved—not just the columns that confine each of the environments. Control over environments breaks the (column) boundaries imposed by nature. The concept is significant for management theory, for the way of thinking is different when control potentials exist. The convenience of partitioning systems into separate environmental states is replaced by the necessity for a larger-systems view. On the other hand, control changes the decision problem from a probabilistic framework to a deterministic one. As an aside, we should note that when prediction is involved, a form of determinism is also achieved. That is, it is always known what result the use of a specific strategy will produce. But such determinism is achieved only at the cost of carrying an inventory of strategies to meet each predicted condition. The implementation procedures involve additional costs of a systemic kind that should be considered in conjunction with the value of information and the net-benefit concept.

Returning to the idea that there is at least one strategy and one environment that combine to produce the best overall result from the system, we recognize that the maximax value of 6 is the basis for determining the zero opportunity cost for the control case. It is the point from which all other matrix values are subtracted. When subtracted from itself, it becomes the minimin value of the total opportunity-cost matrix—that is, $6 - 6 = 0$. Similarly, using the figures from Table 6–7, we subtract each value from the maximax value of 6. We note that columns are no longer used as separate partitions for determining a set of opportunity costs; only one value in the entire matrix is the basis of the determinations for the total-opportunity-cost matrix. Table 6–8 represents

Table 6–8   Matrix of Total Opportunity Costs

	States of nature, z_j's:			Maximums (worst):	Minimums (best):
	1	2	3		
Strategy 1	1	2	3	3	1
Strategy 2	5	1	0	5	0

the transformation. In it, the value 3 is the best of worsts (i.e., the minimax), while the value 0 is the best of bests (i.e., the minimin). All these terms, in this case, refer to *total* opportunity costs.

The minimin must necessarily be zero. The difference

$$\text{minimax} - \text{minimin} = 3 - 0 = 3$$

measures the largest permissible investment for control. The equality shown below will always hold in determining the largest permissible investment for control.

For profit matrix   *For total-opportunity-cost matrix*
$$(\text{maximax} - \text{maximin}) = (\text{minimax} - \text{minimin}) = (\text{minimax})$$

We see why a redefinition of opportunity costs into *total* opportunity costs is required when circumstances permit control to be exercised. The maximax value of the profit matrix can appear in any column. The calculation of maximax − maximin cuts across column boundaries of the profit matrix. Therefore, only the total-opportunity-cost concept can be applied to the control evaluation. Also, as in the other cases we have examined, the amount of investment that can be justified for control will depend on what is known initially about the system. If no forecast or predictive ability is available, then the minimax (of 3) is the most that should be spent. If a believable forecast exists, then the appropriate value of minimum *EOC* (in total opportunity costs) is the upper limit. If a *perfect* test for prediction exists, then the amount to spend on control is further decreased. In our example, it could not exceed 1. Note that with perfect prediction the manager would use his first strategy if z_1 will occur, yielding an outcome of 1. Otherwise, he uses his second strategy. Then, if z_2 occurs, the outcome will be 1, and, if z_3 occurs, the outcome will be zero. In no circumstances, then, should the manager spend more than 1 to obtain complete control. According to our previous calculation, derived from the profit matrix, .7 is the maximum amount that can be spent for environmental control. This result is in agreement with the constraints we have just derived from the total-opportunity-cost analysis. Thus, as anticipated, the value of the control system to the manager decreases as his knowledge about the system increases.

A great deal more can be said about the value, costs, and net benefits of employing control under various conditions. For example, the effects of delay and of aging information can be important. Control strategies may be depleted as they are employed (in the sense of an inventory), or they may be self-replenishing. These and many more issues remain of major interest to the enterprise. They can be best understood when viewed as part of a theory of management rather than as a subject too complex to grasp in any way but intuitively.

DIFFERENTIATION AT THE ENTERPRISE LEVEL

The decision-investment problem is sufficiently important and complex to warrant special attention. Decision theorists are not even close to synthesizing the total problem area, but the methods they have developed (some of which have been reported here) do represent significant inroads. In conclusion, therefore, let us consider a few overall observations that appear to be cogent.

Benefits are measures strictly related to the decision-maker's objectives— a fact that enables the decision structure to provide differentiation between companies of dissimilar sizes. What constitutes a substantial benefit to a small company may be too insignificant for a large company to bother with. Therefore the question of size must somehow be reflected in the decision model. Often, the values of the outcomes are transformed to relate to the asset base of the company. The decision matrix, when properly used, should reflect other dissimilar circumstances of decision-makers. For example, it should distinguish between organizations that are embedded in unlike international settings. And although the same decision may be called for in different companies, often it will be for different reasons. All factors (economic, geographic, social, etc.) must be embodied in an adequate decision model and their varying significance in individual circumstances accounted for.

Variations in company objectives and in their basic conditions produce diversity in the way a problem is framed. According to the situation, emphasis may best be placed on the creation of strategies or the extent of the search to discover environments, on the accuracy and precision deemed to be necessary, on the investments for forecasts and tests for predictions, or on the design and construction of suitable control systems.

We would not expect an inventory problem to be solved by the same kind of model in a country with mounting inflation as in a country with a stable currency. Predecision investments will differ according to economic conditions such as the supply and relative cost of labor and skills. The optimal variety for new-product strategies will respond to market conditions. In all cases, differentiation between the small and the large, the affluent and the growing to affluence, the stable and the dynamic, the predictable and the nonpredictable, the controllable and the uncontrollable is introduced by management in the options it chooses for investments in decision components. And, for such reasons, decision models for essentially the same types of problem will differ markedly between companies and over time within a single company.

Predecision considerations shed new light on the manager's job. So much of his responsibility is allocated to the way he goes about reaching decisions that the questions we have raised here are frequently taken for granted. The predecision tree shown in Figure 6–6 should help to accent these options for managerial emphasis and serve as a guide for the manager who wishes to check out whether his thinking has touched all bases.

SUMMARY

It is essential to recognize that there are a variety of ways in which managers can go about making a decision. We call these methods the predecision process, because a great many subdecisions must be considered before the major one can be made. Most of these subdecisions are reached without any awareness that they have been made.

Figure 6–6   A "Predecision" Tree

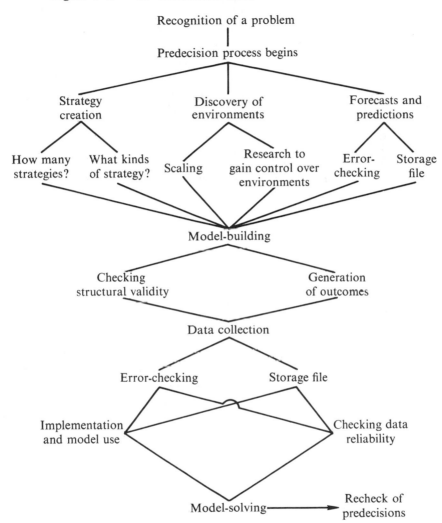

It is suggested that a rational criterion be used to determine the allocation of funds to the various components of the decision model—namely, that the net benefit be maximized, where net benefit is measured as the total value minus the total cost of a particular decision approach. Time is required to prepare all the information on which a decision is based. Delays can cause managerial indecisiveness, which is not the same as a strategy to procrastinate. The timing of a decision affects the net benefit obtained. The manager might increase his benefit by deferring a decision. For example, the day after the decision has been made, a new and superior alternative might appear.

This chapter concentrates on five essential predecision areas. These are the creation of strategies, the identification of environments, the reduction of error, the improvement of forecasts, and the employment of control systems. Each is examined in turn for some of the critical elements that determine what benefits can be gained by investing more in that particular area and how much must be spent to obtain those benefits. In the strategy-creation area, the nature of search is explored. With respect to environmental identification, issues of sensitivity of the outcomes are treated. A substantial discussion of Bayesian decision methods, as they can be applied to improvements of forecasts through testing, is presented. Throughout the chapter, the concept of the value of information is developed, so that the reader will come to think in this way about the entire decision process.

APPENDIX

Strictly for the purpose of illustrating the kind of model-building that might be applied to the problems of creativity, let us consider an example. Assume that a large set of technological possibilities can be searched for feasible strategies. Our purpose is to determine the average time, T, to find (or, better yet, create) k strategies. When we attempt to build a mathematical model that adequately represents this situation, we discover that not enough is known about the creation of technology to allow us to come up with a single model to explain what takes place. As a matter of fact, it rapidly becomes evident that various situations can exist. Consequently, in this case we have constructed three different models. Their equations are shown below, and the three variations are graphed in Figure 6–7.

$$T(A)_{Q,k} = \sum_{i=1}^{i=k} \left[\frac{1}{1 - \left(\frac{q}{i}\right)^{K+1-i}} \right]$$

$$T(B)_{Q,k} = \sum_{i=1}^{i=k} \left[\frac{1}{1 - q^{K+1-i}} \right]$$

$$T(C)_{Q,k} = k \left(\frac{1}{1 - q} \right)$$

We are concerned here less with the specific mathematical derivation of these models than with the interpretations of their relevant variables and the

Figure 6–7

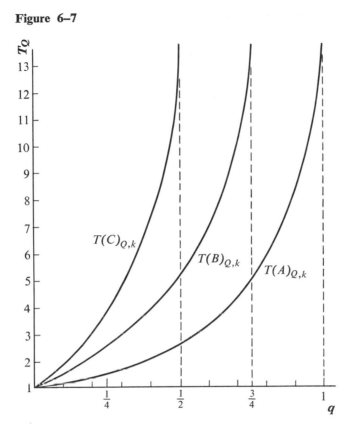

way in which they account for the differences in the manager's creative process. First, let us explain the terms that appear in these models. We define *feasible strategies* as those that possess a quality level greater than some minimum amount—say, a threshold value of Q. There is a probability, p, of finding or developing such a feasible strategy in some given period of time. The probability of not discovering a feasible strategy in that same period of time will be called q, so $p + q = 1$. In other words, p and q are related measures that describe how easy or difficult it is to create feasible strategies for the particular kind of situation to which they apply. K is the total number of feasible strategies that could be found if the search were continued indefinitely—it is therefore a measure of the potential richness of this area for creative work; k is the number of strategies to be created; and i is a dummy variable representing the number of times that each term has to be summed to account for all k strategies.

To understand these equations, let us first examine the results when $k = 1$, meaning that only one strategy is to be created. We find that the average time to create one strategy (of quality Q or better) would be

With numerical conditions: $q = \frac{1}{2}$; $K = 3$

$$T(A)_{Q,1} = \frac{1}{1 - q^K} = \qquad\qquad 8/7$$

$$T(B)_{Q,1} = \frac{1}{1 - q^K} = \qquad\qquad 8/7$$

$$T(C)_{Q,1} = \frac{1}{1 - q} = \qquad\qquad 2$$

Every area of study has its own level of potential for discovery. We have used K to symbolize this potential. For our example, the A and B variants produce the same results, which are smaller than that of the C variant. This is because K must be assumed to be only one feasible strategy in the case of the C variant, whereas it is 3 for the A and B variants. Since $K = 3$ for A and B, the expected time to find one feasible strategy is less. (Of course, if $K = 1$, all the above equations will be identical.)

Now let us look at the situation when two feasible strategies are to be created. In the case of the C variant, two different fields of concepts and conditions must be searched, so its value is simply doubled.

With numerical conditions: $q = \frac{1}{2}$; $K = 3$

$$T(A)_{Q,2} = \frac{1}{1 - q^K} + \frac{1}{1 - \left(\frac{q}{2}\right)^{K-1}} = \qquad \frac{8}{7} + \frac{16}{15} = 2.21$$

$$T(B)_{Q,2} = \frac{1}{1 - q^K} + \frac{1}{1 - q^{K-1}} = \qquad \frac{8}{7} + \frac{4}{3} = 2.48$$

$$T(C)_{Q,2} = \frac{1}{1 - q} + \frac{1}{1 - q} = \qquad 2 + 2 = 4$$

In this case, variant A is less than variant B because learning has taken place. The potential of the field for discovery is one important factor; the ability to learn how to create is another. With respect to the latter, the probability, q, of not discovering a second feasible strategy has been reduced by learning to $q/2$ (i.e., it is the second trial and $i = 2$). We note that in general, $T(A)_Q \leqq T(B)_Q \leqq T(C)_Q$, as shown clearly in Figure 6–7. Variant A promises the least average time whenever more than one search is involved. But this does not mean it produces the lowest cost for generating k strategies. That will depend on the cost of search, which might be either large or small for any specific A-type problem. Variant A's average time decreases as k increases. It presumes that a learning function exists, such as q/i, which means that the likelihood of discovering a new feasible strategy improves as a result of previous experience. Variants A and B are both based on the assumption that no more than K feasible strategies could *ever* be found, while K always equals one for variant C.

It would not be easy to figure out how to estimate K precisely, although approximations of its size might be reasonable to obtain. Variant C, on the other hand, reflects the existence of k separate problem areas, each of which must be explored if k strategies are to be created. For this reason, variant C will require the greatest expenditure of time. It may be viewed as an upper boundary for the time that may be needed to create k new strategies.

A tree representation of the search procedure of variant C might be helpful and is shown in Figure 6–8. The average number of steps required to achieve the first success is:

$$T(C)_{Q,1} = \bar{n} = \sum_{n=1}^{\infty} nq^{n-1}p = (1)q^0p + (2)q^1p + (3)q^2p + \ldots + (n)q^{n-1}p$$

This series has a well-known mathematical form, namely:

$$\sum_{n=1}^{\infty} nq^{n-1}p = \frac{1}{1-q}$$

which is the expression we previously used for variant C.

Figure 6–8

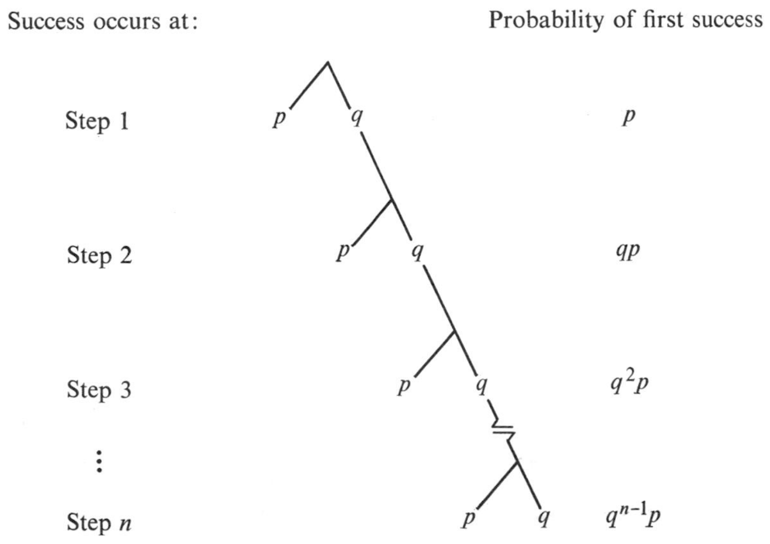

Success occurs at:		Probability of first success

Step 1 p q p

Step 2 p q qp

Step 3 p q q^2p

⋮

Step n p q $q^{n-1}p$

EXERCISES

1. Describe fully the nature of the predecision process. Is there a *pre*-predecision process?

2. How does the importance of a given problem affect the kind of predecisions that a manager is likely to reach? What about the complexity of the problem and its resistance to solution?

3. How does timing relate to the following kinds of decision problem?
   a. the selection of a new plant site
   b. the production of a new product design
   c. the choice of a new president

4. The project manager has been asked to develop a new miniature tape recorder and has been given a fixed budget to achieve this objective. What predecision problems must he resolve? How much of his job is concerned with predecisions and how much with a decision? What decision is involved, and how will it usually be made?

5. Determine the point of maximum net benefit where the number of strategies created is n. The value of N strategies is $20 \log_2 N$. (See p. 508.) The cost of each new strategy is c (and $c = 10$), and the cost of n strategies is cn. What value does an approach such as this one serve?

6. Discuss the importance of discovering critical environments. Give some examples of where such investments in discovery have been too small and have, as a result, decreased net benefit.

7. In what sense is sensitivity important for predecisions concerning investments for the discovery of environments? Were you a manager of a food company, how would this reasoning affect your point of view?

8. The manager of a drug company has stated that the error option is his major concern. Why might this be so?

9. Describe the distinction between forecasts and predictions that is given in the text. How do you feel about these definitions?

10. Given the profit matrix below, determine the value of information for all options that might apply.

	z_1	z_2	z_3
x_1	5	2	7
x_2	12	6	3

The probabilities are believed to be: $p(z_1) = .20$, $p(z_2) = .30$, and $p(z_3) = .50$; at least, that is what the manager has estimated.

11. The manager decides to use a test procedure for the matrix in Exercise 10, above. The test that he can buy is said to have the following characteristics:

	z_1	z_2	z_3
T_1	.5	.5	.1
T_2	.3	.5	.3
T_3	.2	0	.6

Should he use this test? (Use a tree form in your description.)

12. We are told that a person applied for a job involving color-matching and was turned down because of color blindness. What is the probability that the applicant was male? (Use the data given on pp. 226–27, and for simplicity assume that exactly 1 percent of all women are color-blind.)

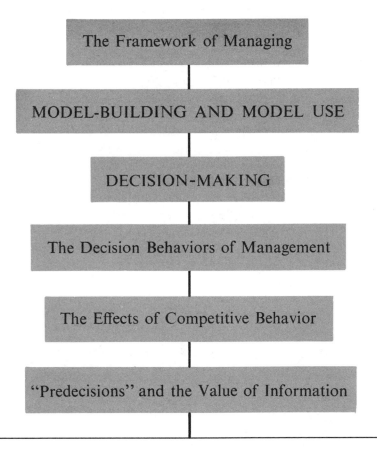

The Framework of Managing

MODEL-BUILDING AND MODEL USE

DECISION-MAKING

The Decision Behaviors of Management

The Effects of Competitive Behavior

"Predecisions" and the Value of Information

Chapter 7
Managing Systems with Complex Objectives

The problems of management are seldom resolved in terms of a
single objective. Instead, managers want to achieve several
goals with each decision, and different managers often place varying
stress on the same objectives. As a result, none of the essential
functions of management is clear-cut. Issues of management ethics
are a fundamental part of the complexity of multiple objectives.
Three basically different models can be used to show diverse ways
of rationally approaching the problem of managing systems with
complex objectives. Without the concepts derived from these models,
planning, policy-making, and organizing cannot be studied.

Chapter 7

MANAGING
SYSTEMS WITH
COMPLEX OBJECTIVES

Plus ça change, plus c'est la même chose.

Every system has a certain content and structure, which the manager relates to his organization's objectives. Although the content and structure can change, the basic objectives of organizations have a fundamental stability. There are only a few major types of organization—profit-motivated, service-oriented, military-competitive, and so on. Across many cultures, business contexts, and service configurations, the basic objectives are remarkably similar and stable, reflecting the core of human values shared by mankind.

Yet change is an apparent reality of the contemporary scene, and the manager is forced to view the system as including many more elements, seen in finer detail than if the system were stable. The potential for such complexity has always been present, but the need is recent. It is called forth by the physically greater interconnectedness of systems components, which has overthrown the good sense of isolated objectives. The manager now needs to consider complex objectives instead of simple ones.

The simultaneous consideration of multiple objectives is one apparent form of complex objectives. But we mean more than that by the term "complex objectives." We mean that while the specific nature of management's objectives may be stable, their treatment is not. The set of multiple objectives to be simultaneously considered is a modeling problem, the solution of which can change.

And the importance of the objectives with respect to one another is also a dynamic variable. The solution of one problem provides the basis for the next unsolved problem. In many cases, the act of solving alone gives rise to new conditions. So we can define complex objectives as being more than multiple objectives, as being objectives that do not stand still, that react to their own resolution. Moreover, they are never entirely clear because they are so inter-related—with themselves, with the environment, and with the values of the people who seek their achievement.

THE NATURE OF OBJECTIVES

What are organizational objectives? There are many different kinds, but they are best defined generally as the aggregate of all participating individuals' purposes. A charter of organizational purpose will be meaningless unless, in one way or another, individual purposes combine to underwrite the charter. Every manager has to deal with multiple objectives because each employee's objectives do not coincide exactly with those of other employees, with the manager's, or with the organization's. However, in their multiplicity, individual objectives do overlap to create an area of communality, as illustrated by the Venn diagram of Figure 7–1. The organizational roles of each individual occur in the shaded area; the remainder is the organization's social environment.

Conflicting Objectives

How long do objectives last? How permanent are they? As we have pointed out, fundamental objectives appear to be highly stable, but less basic objectives that are directly concerned with material benefits are transitory and even evanescent. The answer must depend therefore on the societal level of the

Figure 7–1

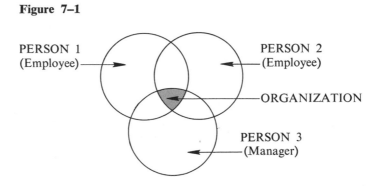

objectives and on circumstances. The organization's lesser objectives may be altered rapidly by the forceful operation of society on most of the material goals of the interacting individual participants. And, of course, the important question is not only how many goals are being acted on but which ones they are (vis à vis holders of power and influence). A nonoverlapping area in the Venn diagram may include objectives that are independent of the nonoverlapping objectives of the other members, or these areas may encompass highly conflicting purposes. The system of objectives is likely to be far more dynamic (or unstable) in the latter case, which is one of conflict, than in the former. This is especially true if the power balance in the conflict is shifting.

An excellent illustration of the rapid changes that can take place when conflict occurs is the complete change that the Kwakiutl Indians of British Columbia underwent as a result of their interactions with the Canadian settlers.

> The civilization of the Kwakiutl . . . was one of the most vigorous and zestful of the aboriginal cultures of North America, with complex crafts and ceremonials, and elaborate and striking arts. It certainly had none of the earmarks of a sick civilization. The tribes of the Northwest Coast had wealth, and exactly in our terms. That is, they had not only a surplus of economic goods, but they made a game of the manipulation of wealth. It was by no means a mere direct transcription of economic needs and the filling of those needs. It involved the idea of capital, of interest, and of conspicuous waste. It was a game with all the binding rules of a game, and a person entered it as a child. His father distributed wealth for him, according to his ability, at a small feast or potlatch, and each gift the receiver was obliged to accept and to return after a short interval with interest that ran to about 100 per cent a year. By the time the child was grown, therefore, he was well launched, a larger potlatch had been given for him on various occasions of exploit or initiation, and he had wealth either out at usury or in his own possession. Nothing in the civilization could be enjoyed without validating it by the distribution of this wealth. Everything that was valued, names and songs as well as material objects, were passed down in family lines, but they were always publicly assumed with accompanying sufficient distributions of property. It was the game of validating and exercising all the privileges one could accumulate from one's various forebears, or by gift, or by marriage, that made the chief interest of the culture. Everyone in his degree took part in it, but many, of course, mainly as spectators. In its highest form it was played out between rival chiefs representing not only themselves and their family lines but their communities, and the object of the contest was to glorify oneself and to humiliate one's opponent. On this level of greatness the property involved was no longer represented by blankets, so many thousand of them to a potlatch, but by higher units of value. These higher units were like our bank notes. They were incised copper tablets, each of them named, and having a value that depended upon their illustrious history. This was as high

as ten thousand blankets, and to possess one of them, still more to enhance its value at a great potlatch, was one of the greatest glories within the compass of the chiefs of the Northwest Coast.[1]

Potlatch, as this socioeconomic game was called, was an entrenched pattern of competition in which wealthy members could give all too generously and thereby break both the spirit and body of the ill-fated receiver of the gifts. Potlatch was not necessarily more severe than our own form of competition, but it was certainly unfamiliar to those accustomed to European traditions. Ruth Benedict goes on to say that the economic system of these Indians was "in many ways a parody of our own economic arrangements." It is precisely that parody that created conflict. For the Kwakiutls and the Canadians, the incompatibilities at the intersection were created primarily by the conflicts between their nonoverlapping objectives.

The Canadian government outlawed potlatch as well as other customs (such as dances) by legal action backed up by efforts on all levels, including law enforcement—although many thoughtful observers disputed the correctness of or need for these measures. The Kwakiutls, as a group, did not adapt to this change. They drifted apart, lost their renowned energy, and waited listlessly for whatever forces might eventually arise.

Environments and Objectives

The nonintersection objectives (and roles) in Figure 7–1 constitute the social environment for the intersection group or organization. When conflict exists between nonintersectional social environments, a strong influence can be exercised at the intersection to modify one or more sets of objectives of the participants. From the above story, it is evident that with respect to model-building and implementation (which is always an activity at some intersection), the nonoverlapping objectives can play an influential role. In other words, they create the *environment* for the solution and can spell the difference between success or failure. The Kwakiutl problem was to model a mutually acceptable relationship and to implement it under a Canadian jurisdiction. The conflict was too great, and the procedures too emotional (rather than rational), for a mutually acceptable solution to emerge.

It should be emphasized that these solution environments are not simply the *decision* environments of Chapter 4, which deal with payoffs that result if a given strategy is used. Rather, they are the social and economic environments of the entire decision process and the roles of the people involved.

---

[1] Ruth F. Benedict, "Anthropology and the Abnormal," in *Personal Character and Cultural Milieu,* 3rd rev. ed., Douglas G. Haring, ed. (Syracuse, N.Y.: Syracuse University Press, 1956), pp. 189–90.

Individuals and Objectives

Since organizational objectives are composed of and affected by individual objectives, we should note some of the characteristics that typify the latter. First of all, one seldom holds to objectives he *believes* to be unobtainable. Second, people have a strong tendency to think that their objectives are far simpler than they really are. Third, people generally lack an awareness of how highly interconnected their own objectives are. Fourth, an individual frequently chooses objectives for superficial reasons—such as tradition or the desire to maintain his position by courting favor or, conversely, not "crossing" those who hold the balance of power. Fifth, even if considerable effort is put into comparing individual and organizational objectives, little thought is given to the need to differentiate between the intensities with which individuals wish to satisfy these objectives. Sixth, multiple objectives that do not conflict in an obvious manner are often so intertwined that they are not recognized as being several. This may result in the wrong problem being solved, and it is likely at the least to produce communication difficulties.

Multiple Objectives

This sixth point concerning objectives is well illustrated by *The Monkey's Paw,* a play written by W. W. Jacobs and produced at the Haymarket Theater in London on October 6, 1903.[2] The story concerns a middle-class English family, who obtain the use of a talisman, a monkey's paw, that has the magical power to grant three wishes to each of three owners. The family possesses the third and last set of three wishes.

We are told: "But, mark you, though the wishes was granted, those three people would have cause to wish they *hadn't* been." (The second owner, the Sergeant, is speaking.) "The first owner had his three . . . . I don't know what his first two were . . . but the third was for death." The Sergeant unwillingly turns the monkey's paw over to the family, indicating that he has had nothing but trouble from the wish-fulfilling powers of the paw.

There should be every reason to suppose that the three owners of the monkey's paw would be among the luckiest people on the face of the earth. But that does not turn out to be the case. The father wishes for enough money to clear the mortgage on his house.

MRS. WHITE: How could two hundred pounds hurt you, eh father?

MR. WHITE: Might drop on my head in a lump. Don't see any other way.

---

[2] (London: Samuel French, 1910.)

But the wish is soon granted in the form of compensation for their son's death, which was caused by an industrial accident. The skein of interrelated multiple objectives is readily demonstrated here. The desire for money was not the only objective. It was imperative that other objectives—many taken for granted— be stated *simultaneously* to protect the family against the almost infinite variety of disastrous means that could account for bringing them a fortune.

The same difficulty of interdependence is encountered in the later wishes of this story. The mother uses the talisman to request that her son be returned to the living. But this is cancelled by the father's third wish, since he realizes that the possible side effects of the second wish are beyond his understanding.

In the mythology of granted wishes, the results are seldom what had been anticipated, for no *if*'s, *and*'s, or *but*'s are allowed. If the family had set down a whole list of conditions under which they should receive the money, that list undoubtedly would have been ruled invalid. The literary trap is based on single minded purpose, and any reasonable wish can be attained only in conjunction with unexplored effects on associated objectives. This condition, though an artificially imposed stricture in the fictional situation, is all too often characteristic of real situations, and those of us who use single-objective decision models (described in Chapter 4) without regard for further interpretation should not fail to take this into account. Before seeking simple objectives, one must think carefully about the total system of effects. In a system of interconnected multiple objectives, as one objective is perfectly met, outcomes along other dimensions change. What is more, these parallel phenomena are more likely to be destructive than constructive because of the conflicting nature of objectives.

We recognize that value systems come into play in the definition of objectives. This means that all individuals do not necessarily want the same things— and that, in fact, conflicts arise even among the various objectives of a single individual. For example, the objectives of profit and survival are tightly tied together and have a tendency to be inversely proportional. An experiment that increases wages to improve morale for the long-term survival of an organization is at odds with the goal of immediate profit; yet it might eventually have a greater profit payoff than a strategy aimed at paying minimum wages. An acceptable strategy can usually be found somewhere between minimum and maximum wages. What is apparent here is the *need to compromise* and to balance the expectations for conflicting goals.

Spurious Objectives

Organizations are no freer of spurious objectives than are individuals. The desire for growth, for example, stems in large measure from the notion that the lack of growth is equivalent to going backwards (especially when other, similar, organizations are growing). It is also related to value judgments embedded in our culture concerning the importance of progress. Growth for the sake of growth has such a positive appeal that reasons, real or spurious, will be found to justify it. In fact, however, growth cannot be said to be either good or bad until specific issues are explored. In the same sense, few organizations would consciously allow "competition for the sake of competition" among their primary objectives; yet "keeping up with the competition" is an often-held spurious objective.

If a contention, such as that growth is good, is accepted without proof, then that contention must be treated as *dogma*. Management commonly accepts many dogmatic statements. How many present-day objectives are related more closely to superstition than to logic, or more directly to personal pride than to organizational benefit? The answer depends heavily on the frequency with which single objectives motivate the actions of management, for awareness of multiple objectives reduces the likelihood that dogma is guiding the system. And the only possible way of becoming aware of multiple objectives is to recognize how values and objectives interact and to question whether stressing certain objectives can actually deliver the desired ends.

MANAGEMENT ETHICS

Ethics are a curious matter. Many of them are so deeply embedded in our culture, so "traditional," that they change very slowly if at all. Yet a variety of structural forms can be erected on the foundation of tradition. One of the main questions management faces is what, if any, part it should play in the design, construction, and preservation of ethical structures. Should management, for example, be expected to introduce and support gradual social change? Or should it uphold the status quo? Does it have a responsibility to its employees, to consumers, and to society at large as well as to its stockholders? Management behavior is a reflection of the ethics of the prevailing social system, and today that system holds management responsible for business' participation in and contributions to society—at least in a general way.

If, then, management by and large accepts such responsibility, how does it go about defining and fulfilling its ethical objectives? This is not a matter of a straightforward dollars-and-cents calculation; many problems and conflicts arise. For example, when there is only minor conflict in a society with respect to values, management may have little trouble defining its ethical objectives—but how does management fare when society is divided as to what its own aims should be? In addition, the corporation is itself a transitory cultural phenomenon. It must evolve to meet social, political, and technological changes. At the same time, one of its multiple objectives is to remain consistent with its own traditions, logic, and history. And always it must cope with the other social institutions that are intrinsically concerned with the evolution of ethics. These institutions, like the corporation, tend to be self-protective and growth oriented, and this is a reality that management must recognize. Such considerations as these make clear why management cannot always discern a straightforward, ethical course of action.

The foresighted members of society see many ethical principles as transient, but they understand that this is true only if a long enough planning horizon is used. For day-to-day decisions and short-term plans, the present ethics, as they are interpreted, are the vital determinants in any real system. Bearing this in mind, let us proceed to discuss some of the more specific managerial concerns with ethical issues as they relate to the formulation of objectives.

Ethical Objectives for the Consumer

The obligations of the enterprise to the consumer have been highlighted somewhat through government intervention. Claims of consumer organizations also tell us something—but not all. Organizations such as better business bureaus have grown up to provide a mechanism for serving consumer needs and for hearing consumer complaints, but such organizations exercise only minor pressure on businesses to provide promised quality and service. The greatest pressure comes from management itself.

The essence of a management ethic implies self-monitoring. There is no doubt that the majority of organizations seriously assume responsibility for the objectives of fairness to and protection of consumers. Yet there are exceptions, and in some fields the exceptions cannot be tolerated. For example, deficiencies in the purity or character of food and drugs can have such disastrous results that the federal Food and Drug Administration was created and endowed with strong regulatory powers. Similarly, the Civil Aeronautics Board determines the air-worthiness of aircraft. Even if we disregard the exceptions and consider business organizations generally responsible, there are many "gray areas," where ethical objectives are not generally agreed on and where, consequently, an industry's position does not correspond to that of the more adamant consumer groups. Nevertheless, for at least twenty years the trend has been consistently in favor of consumer protection, and it continues to gain momentum. The courts today process a great variety of complaints pertaining to many product and service areas. The number of such cases continues to increase rapidly, for the complaints no longer relate only to major hazards. There is also more and more generalized public and governmental pressure— to wit, the growing attention being paid to such problem areas as tobacco hazards, automobile safety, truth in packaging and labeling, product safety, and illegal price-fixing. Meeting ethical objectives can reduce profit margins, slow growth, and so on—but the same can be said for *not* meeting them. In the early 1900's stockholders might have objected to an honest statement of ethics. At present they will accept the notion that management is expected to be *more* ethical than an average person—and that it is being forced to discuss its ethics in public. The dynamics of change are fully evident.

Yet, as we have said, the definition of objectives is rarely a simple matter. Take, for example, recent controversies over truth in packaging.[3] There is agreement that it is possible to attract consumers with psychologically attractive imagery; there is disagreement as to the ethical validity of doing so. Some hold that the consumer can protect himself, while, in the opinion of others, illusions in packaging are a means of defrauding the consumer. Advertising images are also a controversial topic. One group contends that the consumer obtains increased enjoyment from such images, and economic benefit as well. The opponents of this position state that the consumer gets no benefit from "image" advertising but must nevertheless pay for it. Who is correct?

As another case, consider the position of the critic who attacks automobile design for the great amount of (useless?) variation presented to the consumer. Is this an instance of consumer exploitation? After all, there is no more positive way of stating the value of a Rembrandt painting or of a Ming Dynasty vase than of determining the value of decorative chrome strips on automobiles. What people are willing to pay cannot be considered a satisfactory measure for pure arts but a worthless one for industrial arts. And we cannot legislate taste without depriving individuals of their basic freedoms. It is clear that a basis for the controversy exists but that no simple approach to its solution has yet been found. It is one of the more complex problems of objective definition with which management must deal.

On the other hand, there should be no question that the safety consideration comes first in the design of an automobile. Ethics and economics are in agreement on this point. Both would rule out, for instance, a design that had aesthetic appeal but inhibited the view of the driver. Unfortunately, we have no way of defining, much less achieving, total safety. Yet safety considerations must be included by management in all their models. The amount of service given to airplanes is a good example. Chiefs of staff and heads of state fly in airplanes that are more thoroughly cared for than those used by ordinary citizens. But how is this greater care measured? Is there a rational relationship between the amount of service done and the value of the lives involved? Such questions plague the area of ethical objectives.

The consideration of ethics with respect to the consumer is critical. Stan-

---

[3] Does the container misinform the consumer as to, say, the purchased quantity? What, for example, does "giant economy size" mean?

dards to protect the consumer must be generated internally, and objectively, by management. As long as the view prevails in a large part of society that management is Machiavellian, there is little hope that management will (or can) take an entirely rational approach to its ethical problems. It is worth asking how ethical management views itself to be in its dealings with the consumer. The answer would seem to be, no more ethical than the mainstream of society seems to be. Today, many individuals contend that this attitude has far too long affected management's actions in such matters as product quality, safety in usage, price protection, and appropriate guarantee periods.

Management-science models can only touch on these matters, and the manager generally must include them subjectively in the implementation phase of his work. The model, for instance, by indicating that price-fixing removes uncertainty, could be used to calculate the benefit of such pricing strategies. The analysis might even account for the fact that at some point, because of legal action, price-fixing must be discontinued subject to an estimated penalty. The model might go further, attempting to indicate how much good will is lost by price-fixing. In theory, the gains and losses yield a measure of resultant profit, but in no sense is this a normative solution with long-term profit maximized. Even if a totally objective model seemed from the company's point of view to justify what appear to be antisocial activities, we must all be aware that the real implications of fundamental social values cannot be represented properly in a model. It is impossible to reflect all the intangible considerations, including how managers feel about their roles.

Similarly, critics of management behavior can present their positions only in a philosophical sense. In its response, management must take into consideration, not only society's present set of values, but the extent to which its actions will affect future values. For this reason, critics of the present establishment, such as Arnold Toynbee and John Galbraith, fashion arguments that lie outside the present abilities of management models. Arguments using economic and mathematical models as part of the evidence should be used with the utmost care.

Ethical Objectives for Labor

Ethical questions in the labor area are as difficult to consider as those in the consumer sector, even though management has less latitude to plan and control than in the consumer area. Perhaps this is because management's relations with labor are closer and more immediate than those with consumers. Unions, which grew up to counter management abuses, have now assumed much of the responsibility for protecting labor's interests. Nevertheless, management's active responsibility to provide proper reimbursement and an adequate environment for its employees cannot ever disappear—even when nearly all the employees are machines.[4] (One solution to labor problems has been to replace workers with machines.)

As a result of social forces that have encouraged working together with unions, management has come to accept the fact that it has an ethical responsibility for the "whole" worker, the person having diverse wants and needs. Adequate pay is only one facet of the total requirement, which includes a reasonable job in terms of work load, time schedule, content, and environment; the ultimate in safety considerations; recognition of achievement; and opportunity for self-improvement.

Safety standards must be under continuous review as new machines and processes are introduced and procedures changed. Machine tools tend to become less safe as workers invent new ways to use them to achieve greater piecework outputs. For example, though a punch-press shield or knock-away can ensure that workers' hands and clothing do not get in the way, such safety devices have often been removed by workers looking for faster production rates and higher take-home pay. For certain jobs, workers' eyes should be protected by goggles, but laziness, forgetfulness, and even the feeling of being "chicken" can prevent the use of goggles and result in serious eye accidents. Management can reduce and prevent accidents by developing the conviction that protective measures are necessary (and, often, by giving rewards for their use). The worker's environment is often enough polluted by noise or unbreathable air, or uncomfortable because of high temperature or crowded spaces, to make us aware of the fact that in some cases management still accepts the ethics of the last century in place of those of the present one.

The setting of performance measures is a direct outgrowth of objectives and expectations. Time standards for performing a repetitive job must include a far less precise judgment concerning what constitutes reasonable rest allowances. Pay scales have to be related to general economic conditions and cost-of-living realities. Reasonable levels of absenteeism should be allowed for. But it is clear from the prevalence of strikes and work stoppages that ethics in the labor area are far more complicated than any generalities such as those we have discussed can portray.

Models can be sensitive to changes in the labor picture, although measures become more difficult to represent when the outcome takes the form of a slowdown or a strike. Morale is exceedingly difficult to express in a model. On the other hand, gradual raises in pay occur in accordance with a recognizable momentum of the system, and it is reasonable to expect that they can be predicted. Generally, unions lead in effecting changes, but union ethics themselves are not easy to model. True, unions are portrayed as considering the long-term effects of automation, of a guaranteed annual wage, and the like,

---

[4] See pp. 510–11 for an explanation of this point.

but this image is based on stereotypes of the union movement. The ethics of competition between union and management are sufficiently complex to make all of us reflect on the impermanence of even the most ingrained stereotypes.

In spite of these uncertainties, union-management ethics have been ritualized to a great extent. Simultaneously, machines have begun to replace the production (blue-collar) workers, not only for the obvious economic reason of efficiency, but because of the economic consequences of ethical problems that do not exist with machines. Furthermore, the production of services has been increasing faster than the production of goods, and, with the growth of services, new ethics have been called into play to define the roles of the clerical (white-collar) workers who supply those services. The whole picture has been enormously complicated, moreover, by the close relationship between computers and white-collar services. The system is so dynamic that present-day ethics concerning how workers, managers, and companies relate to one another through computer hardware and software are still in the formative stages. Leasing, service-center operations, program patentability, and pricing policies are just a few of the areas for which ethics are not yet clear. Another reason for new problems in ethics derives from the fact that management has come to identify more closely than previously with white-collar functions.

This raises the question of the particular ethics appropriate to management and the influence of those ethics on institutional objectives. Management's ethics are complicated by the power and control that management exercises over the system. Unlike the worker, management can vote itself a raise. Its ethics impel it to consider the institution before it considers its own advantage —clearly not an easy task. (In this respect, union management is hardly different from company management.)

Management ethics at the higher administrative levels are most difficult to define. This would not be so if each executive was viewed as an individual. The ethic of the individual, and what is expected of the individual, becomes clearer and more sharply defined as the individual's administrative level decreases. Top management is a group function responsible for and to an entire pyramidal hierarchy. It is far more readily identified with "the company" than any worker is. Around the negotiating table, the conflict within groups may be less direct but more complex than that between different groups. When, to the "in" executive group, a member is no longer understandable in terms of his objectives or useful in terms of his abilities, he can, of course, be fired. But institutions generally prefer a process of "dehiring," which usually includes a new title, a relatively empty office, and few positive assignments. Older executives are fair game for this treatment, and one might well ask whether the reason for this is that their energy is low or that their objectives have become vague because of what the Greeks called "wisdom." Such problems in the hands of the philosopher become the essence of ethical quandary. Management, although unable to include intangible factors in a rational analysis, has methods (such as dehiring) for resolving them that may not satisfy the next generation's ethics.

Ethical Objectives for the Community

The firm is part of the community, but its ethical relations with the community have only recently been receiving serious attention. Its real part in the system would require complex representation in Venn diagram form. To the community, the company is more than its managers and employees; it is a medium of social benefit, a source of cash flow, a taxpayer, a trainer of skills—in total, an integral part of the political and economic well-being of the community. It provides more than employment. Recently, its ability to train workers to new skill levels, permitting them critical social mobility, has been recognized as an obligation within the framework of newly evolving management ethics. The plant is part of the community environment. It changes traffic flows, and it can be either an attractive or detractive element in the visual aesthetics of the community. The facility affects and is affected by zoning regulations; it influences sewage and garbage disposal, community transportation planning, fire and police protection, and so forth.

No discussion of industry-community relations would be complete without due consideration of the pollution problem. There are at least two kinds of pollution to be considered. The first concerns the fabrication process and the way in which it pollutes air and water supply. "We have not run out of water; we have simply run out of new streams to pollute."[5] Organizations now are being forced by public opinion, by legal action, and by the growing social ethic to take steps to reduce such contamination, and this pressure promises to become far stronger in the future.

The second type of pollution, arising from the *use* of products, is also a growing community issue. How responsible are automobile manufacturers or oil companies for the exhaust gases their products produce; how responsible is the detergent manufacturer for foam buildup that blocks sewer systems; who is responsible for contamination that arises from the use of DDT as a pesticide? Pollution is a by-product of technology. It can be significantly reduced, but at very high economic costs in some cases. The ethics in this situation have not been fully worked out as yet, but the future promises severe penalties for some kinds and degrees of pollution. The only questions are how directly responsible industry will be held, and by whom.

Industry must become sensitive to the buildup and decay characteristics of

---

[5] E. Roy Tinney, Director, State of Washington Water Research Center.

toxic substances. It must consider the gradual, long-term effects of pollutants (including noise) on consumers and communities, as well as develop an awareness of *threshold* levels that can be reached without sudden consequences. As technology makes greater and greater advances, more issues of this kind will arise. Protecting the consumer and the community therefore represents a growing challenge. No single company, of course, will be able to resolve such problems, and multi-institutional ethics will surely be involved, where coordination is achieved either through governmental regulation or by some other supraorganizational means.

Ethical Objectives for Stockholders

It is generally agreed that companies must protect the interests of their stockholders. But how should stockholder benefits be defined? The broadly stated ethic cannot be used as a clear guide for action. Dividends and stock value should be combined in such a way as to provide the stockholder with as large a benefit as possible. And, since present as well as potential stockholders are involved, behind-the-scenes manipulation of stocks by management cannot be condoned. SEC regulations provide the stockholder with some minimum protection; full-disclosure requirements at least provide some useful information. Unwarranted management behavior that benefits certain managers out of proportion to the rest of the shareholders is coming under intense scrutiny. But beyond the clear case of willful manipulation, the ethical issues become much more complex. This, too, is a problem of achieving multi-institutional ethics.

One problem management faces is that of conflicting objectives. Many companies, for example, own stocks of other organizations—in pension and profit-sharing plans as well as through partial ownership, mergers, and subsidiaries. Conflicts arise easily. It is often said that a primary responsibility of management is to uphold the value of its stock. However, actions of management that may be beneficial to the corporation's long-term affairs often result in an immediate down-swing in the stock market's evaluation of the company's worth. How is management to choose between these objectives?

To make matters worse, management lacks control over many of the determinants of stock prices. The stock market is a psychologically motivated and economically energized system of such complex characteristics that even the most experienced individuals are frequently taken aback by its performance. It is often difficult to determine how the behavior of a company will affect its stock. What if a company does not pay a dividend? If the company is considered in the market to be a growth company, the passing of a dividend will have little effect on the stock, whereas if it is judged to be a nongrowth company, the same action will probably be taken as a definite sign of regression in that company's value. Brokers' reports on individual companies are responsible for some swings. So is the financial community's assessment of the state of the economy, present and future. The existence of ethics in the financial area tends to provide some sense of stability for large organizations, but the individual investor's vulnerability is so great that the financial community's sense of ethics fosters instability for him. Credit regulations and margin requirements represent additional issues that need to be questioned. They were instrumental in the stock-market crash of 1929 and the ensuing depression, which was not just an economic phenomenon but the cause of a great social catastrophe. The stock market's behavior in 1970 amplified the fact that ethical considerations had not been resolved in the forty intervening years. But other aspects of the situation must be considered.

Changing Attitudes and Regulation

An undercurrent of changing attitudes is present in the issue of ethical objectives. For example, many new stock-trading patterns exist. Many stockholding and trading conventions are now acceptable that might not have been at certain times in the past. The concepts of financial manipulation are undergoing changes, as are the notions of industry responsibility to the community, to the consumer, and to employees. Fundamental assumptions of right and wrong are not likely to be altered, but the interpretations of how to achieve the right way are undergoing constant revision, which is leading to broader responsibilities for managers. Since formidable criticism of the present framework exists, management can anticipate that future developments will be significant, and it should take this into account when preparing its objectives.

Perhaps ethical issues are never entirely clear, but for this generation they seem to have been particularly obscure. As evidence, government has become increasingly a regulatory agent and enforcer of ethics. But the difficulty of establishing ethical norms in this way is no less evident when the government attempts to influence the prices of basic metals than when the government asks for truth in packaging. Deep antagonisms develop if for no other reason than that the profits of industry are affected. Our society has always supported the generation of profit, placing real value on an organization capable of doing this. Yet, at the same time, it has had negative attitudes toward this profitability. And attitudes toward profit seem to be responsible for the deepest complexities in fashioning objectives. Freud related money to the most fundamental psychological problems of individuals. Anthropologists have found one or another configuration of profit similarly important in a variety of cultures (e.g., the Kwakiutls' view of profit, which was previously discussed).

And in the communist world, economic regulation has played a critical role in the conditioning of objectives.

International business investments are similarly involved in highly complex systems of objectives. The ethics of foreign aid are not clear; some see it as exploitation, while others do not. Generally, in these issues, one side argues "personal motivations" and the other "intended accomplishments." The ethic, in any case, is dynamic. It is not easily converted to law or subjected to regulation, and seems far more sensitive to attitudes than one might suspect.

How do the kinds of consideration we have been discussing affect the manager's conclusions of what is optimal? Optimization is a purely transitory phenomenon when viewed in this context. In many of the minor quantitative models that management science has created, these basic issues are generally overlooked. And in some small-scale scheduling problem (where the goals of management are said to be either minimization of costs or maximization of profit), it is difficult to recognize that the accepted pattern of ethics with respect to consumers, labor, the community, stockholders, and the total society is an implicit part of the solution. How consistent and coordinated, for example, are the objectives behind the granting of patents or the antitrust activities of the government? If they are not consistent and homogeneous, how can management embody them as objectives? Even a casual observer will detect major fluctuations in the interpretations placed by the courts on patentability. Whether this is caused by a changing ethic or a high degree of confusion is a matter of opinion. But management itself has helped to fashion this kind of environment within which it must function.

We know that vital ethical issues will significantly swing results, but we do not know how to illuminate and rationalize the problem. We can easily overlook it as an issue of effectiveness because we are accustomed to dealing with it only in terms of efficiency. Models of management's problems must reflect ethical considerations so that their solutions are rational with respect to ethics. Social, legal, and other elements must be included. Is our major task to formulate predictions of tomorrow's behaviors so that we can prepare the resources and configurations today that will be able to cope with them? Or are we asked as well to help create tomorrow?

COMPLEX OBJECTIVES AND PARSIMONIOUS SOLUTIONS

When I first assumed the presidency of the National Bureau of Economic Research last year, I asked many people what they felt the Bureau should emphasize in its research activities through the 1970's. No one answer predominated to the point of being a majority response, but one suggestion was made more than any other: "The Bureau in the 1970's should do for social statistics what it did for economic statistics in the 1930's."[6]

Goals are often antithetical to one another—that is, "You can't have your cake and eat it, too." Managers know this. Maximization of profit is not achieved when costs are minimized. Even maximizing sales volume does not assure maximum profit, and brand share can be maximized by giving away the product. The relationship between various objectives, however, is not always one of clearcut, direct opposition. Objectives are often related by more complex functions. And it is important to have some idea of how much fulfillment is possible along one objective scale as degrees of achievement are measured against other objective scales. Complex models alone do not ensure sufficiently complex results; the solution we obtain must be as complex as the problem demands. A decision model can be rich in structure, using many variables and relationships, and also rich in data, yet provide a solution that is not sufficiently broad. No amount of model richness can guarantee solutions free of superficiality and oversimplification.

Most real decision problems have far greater complexity than the single-objective systems we discussed in Chapter 4. Competitive decision problems of the zero-sum type (which were the primary focus of our analytic models in Chapter 5) are also too simplistic for the manager to accept. What the manager tries to find is models that yield parsimonious solutions. By *parsimonious* we mean the simplest *adequate* form—though it will not necessarily be a simple form. Everyone prefers a simple solution—if it is appropriate. Lacking that, everyone would choose the simplest possible model—again, the simplest that is *adequate*. This we have called parsimonious.

Assume that (as is frequently the case) more than one relevant objective is in a manager's mind. This manager cannot accept a model, no matter how complex its structure, that maximizes the attainment of just one of his objectives. We previously discussed a similar issue (see pp. 53–57), in which the implementation of an optimal subsystem model could produce far worse total systems results than might be obtained from an informal approach to the system as a whole. The parsimonious solution would be just complex enough to relate satisfactorily the relevant multiple objectives.

There is a confusion between complex models and complex solutions. A parsimonious solution is readily accepted because it ensures that the objectives of the manager will be satisfied in the simplest way possible. To achieve this result, a sufficiently complex model is used. For example, consider this inte-

---

[6] John R. Meyer, "The National Bureau: Continuity, Change and Some Future Perspectives," *Toward Improved Social and Economic Measurement,* 48th Annual Report (National Bureau of Economic Research, Inc., June 1968), p. 1.

Figure 7–2

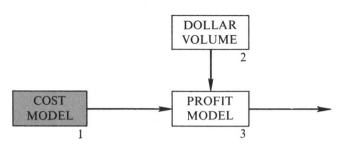

grative problem of the division manager. His production manager's model may be designed to minimize costs; his sales manager's may be based on maximizing the dollar volume of sales. Although both objectives are measured in dollars, it is rare that cost minimization and volume maximization can ever be achieved at the same time. The division manager resolves this problem (at least, in his own mind) by asking for the maximization of profit. As shown in Figure 7–2, cost is the dimension of the first model's output, dollar volume of the second model's. These, in turn, are linked to a third model, which has the output dimension of profit. Ordinarily, the profit model would not be used as input to either the first or second model. Taxonomically, it is a classification of a higher order. Still, once we recognize *feedback effects,* then we can see profit as a determinant of advertising and promotional efforts, as well as of pricing strategies, which clearly interrelate with the dollar-volume model and the cost model. Can we then abide the production manager's objective of minimizing cost? To achieve profit maximization, in many cases, costs have to be raised well above the minimum-cost configuration of the production system. Non-optimal production runs and nonoptimal inventory policies may be essential. The difference in cost and profit dimensionality is further compounded when we consider other possible simultaneous objectives, such as maximum share of market, company growth, stockholders' dividends, minimum profit for the competitor, labor turnover, and probability of antitrust action.

The complex-objective problem, from the manager's point of view, *must* be solved in one way or another. Three approaches suggest themselves:

1. Try to *find a way of transforming the complex of objectives to a single dimension.* We can select one objective, ignoring (discarding) the others. This is done frequently, and it is a reasonable approach whenever the single objective chosen is clearly more significant than any of the others. In some cases, this approach may seem to have been used because a single objective is the model's focus. In fact, however, the manager may have combined the model's output with the host of other nonmodeled subsystems *in his mind* to achieve his decision. Such situations are more likely than those cases where a single outcome provides a satisfactory approximation.

2. *Face the complex-objective problem directly.* We can agree to treat all the objectives by the same method but to differentiate between them according to their rank order of importance or by some other measure that includes distance (see pp. 50–53). By using weighted index methods, with all their attendant difficulties, we can attempt to solve the problem in this fashion. The approach can be considered as formally modeling the manager's subjective attitudes and opinions concerning the complex objectives.

3. Using a programming format, we can *choose one objective as paramount* and treat all the other objectives as subobjectives transformed into restrictions, or constraints, on the main objective. This alters the nature of the problem in a way that is frequently acceptable. Since opposing objectives cannot be realized simultaneously, the programming approach finds a logical way around the dilemma. We shall examine this alternative, demonstrating the importance of linear programming in this connection.

In the balance of this chapter, we shall consider these possibilities.

MATHEMATICAL TRANSFORMATION TO A SINGLE OBJECTIVE

Generally, the first method to try is to see if a single objective can be found that satisfactorily encompasses all relevant objectives. For example, the desire to maximize guidance-system performance, $P,$ while minimizing guidance-system weight, $W,$ might be reformulated as maximizing performance per pound, $\frac{P}{W}$. Of course, such use of a *ratio model* may not provide a sensible objective for the project manager; but often it does, and the approach is widely used. In advertising, the number of exposures achieved per dollar— that is, cost per thousand exposures—is frequently used. The return on investment is another example that brings to mind a host of accounting ratios.

Models that succeed in unifying the dimensions of various objectives do so by making the attainment of individual objectives subordinate to the attainment of the system's objective. Turning to the profit model,

$$TP = SV(p - c)$$
Total Profit = Sales Volume (price per unit − cost per unit)

we can show explicitly how this might occur. Generally, sales volume will drop as price per unit rises. Usually, there will be some pricing point at which dollar volume, $pSV,$ will be maximized. But cost will be affected by sales volume. Up to the point of full capacity utilization (where overtime charges begin to occur), the per unit cost decreases. Furthermore, product quality may improve as the cost per unit increases, and improved product quality helps to boost sales volume.

When such interrelated factors are subsumed within one model, it is not essential that all independent variables be reduced to one scale. We are familiar with the use of the derivative to obtain a maximum value for one dependent variable (the objective) and one independent variable.[7] That is, at point *a* in Figure 7–3,

$$\frac{dTP}{dSV} = 0$$

Figure 7–3

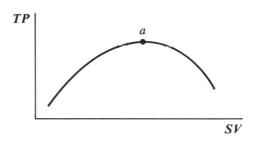

It is also possible, using partial derivatives, to obtain the same kind of result where several independent variables exist. Thus, at point *b* in Figure 7–4, *TP* is maximized with respect to *p* and *SV*:

$$\frac{\delta TP}{\delta SV} = \frac{\delta TP}{\delta p} = 0$$

The greater complexity of the model does not, however, remove the problem of finding one dependent variable to represent "the" objective of the system. It does indicate mathematical facility in treating complex systems where many factors (not reducible to a single scale) affect a unique outcome.

Breakeven Analysis as a Unifying Model

A well-known management concept that has been used for many purposes is breakeven analysis. It was first developed by Walter Rautenstraut in the 1940's, and, later, Joel Dean's work in managerial economics expanded its application to financial planning for the firm.

The breakeven model is a synthesis of the costs of inputs and the revenues of outputs of any process. The volume of output is treated as an independent vari-

---

[7] The slope at all points on the curve is measured by $\frac{dTP}{dSV}$. The only point at which the slope equals zero is *a*.

Figure 7–4

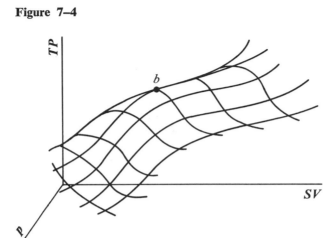

able, which is, in fact, responsive to consumer demand. The breakeven model makes no specific assumption concerning demand, but it permits examination of what would be the result of different demand levels. *Inputs* are defined as those factors that can be represented by *variable costs*. These are costs incurred on a per-unit-of-output basis and contrast with *fixed costs,* which are incurred regardless of the volume of output (i.e., they do not vary as a function of output rates). A *process,* as we define it, consists of those factors that represent fixed costs. Direct labor and direct material costs are typical variable costs; plant and equipment are typical fixed costs.

There are, however, some anomalies in the application of these concepts. For example, depreciation that results from aging is independent of the amount of use that the equipment receives, and is properly classified as a fixed cost. On the other hand, depreciation that results directly from use should be assigned as a variable cost. For the most part, however, fixed costs arising from investments in plant, facilities, and so on, are depreciated as a function of time and not of output volume. Taxes are another example of costs that are part variable (e.g., taxes based on revenue) and part fixed (e.g., real estate taxes) but are nevertheless usually all classified as fixed costs. Similar considerations apply to insurance charges and to power and storage costs. In many instances, the seeming inconsistency is due to difficulties in measurement. Indirect labor charges associated with office work, for example, are difficult to assign on the basis of cost per unit of output. The same is true of salaries paid to supervisory personnel.

Basically, materials, labor, and energy constitute the inputs; plant and equipment make up the fixed costs, or process. The output is supposed to have *greater value* than the combined costs of inputs and amortized investment in the process. Management achieves this objective by controlling the input rates, quality, and so on, and by rearranging the process elements so as to control fixed systemic costs. Most of management's day-to-day control over output is exercised by means of control over inputs. Process alterations are more difficult to achieve because the process elements are usually expensive and are costly to alter or replace.

By now it should be clear that the management problem can be divided conveniently into three parts:

1. Variable-cost systems: a major production management responsibility.
2. Fixed-cost systems: a major responsibility of financial management.
3. Revenue: a major marketing responsibility.

To illustrate the way in which the breakeven model *unifies* these three factors, let us examine Figure 7–5. The chart consists of an ordinate, *y* axis, and an abscissa, *x* axis, so it can be represented by conventional Cartesian coordinates. The ordinate presents a scale of dollars against which fixed costs, variable costs, and dollars of revenue can be measured. The abscissa can be measured in terms of the output volume over a given period of time. It is not difficult to translate this into a percentage of the total capacity that the company has available.

Three lines have been marked on the figure. Line *A* is a fixed-cost function.

Figure 7–5   The Breakeven Chart

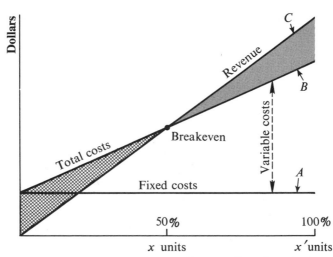

**Output volume in units or
in percentage of total capacity**

We observe that the fixed charges behave in the expected manner—that is, they do not change as a function of increased volume or increased utilization of capacity. Line *B* is a linear, monotonic[8] function that increases with greater volume. In the real world such linearity is neither expected nor usually obtained, but it will simplify matters for us to assume it here. Furthermore, many situations are close enough to being linear that the assumption can be made without jeopardizing the analysis. Line *B* is a *total-cost line,* which results from the summation of fixed and variable costs. The triangular area lying between the fixed-cost and total-cost lines represents the variable costs that are assigned to the system. The total-cost line shows a constant increase because it reflects the variable-cost components, which by definition increase linearly with additional volume. And it does not begin at the zero cost level because it reflects the fixed costs, which would exist even at a zero production level.

Line *C* in Figure 7–5 is the revenue line. It is also a monotonic function that increases with greater output volume. And we are again using the assumption of linearity, although we know that at some point total revenue will not continue to increase at the same rate. When the market for the item becomes saturated, it may be necessary for the company to lower its price in order to further increase its volume. Alternatively, it might begin to spend more to attract additional customers. This would result in a nonlinear total-cost curve. In actual practice, however, a linear relationship is often used to describe revenue. It implies that the firm has a relatively small share of the total market (i.e., small enough that its volume of output does not affect the market price) and reminds us of the economist's description of free competition.

The crosshatched area between the total-cost line and the revenue line represents loss to the company. This is the area to the left of the breakeven point. The shaded area between these same lines represents profit to the company and lies to the right of this point. Therein lies the definition of the breakeven point—no profit, no loss. The breakeven point occurs for a given volume of production or a given utilization of plant capacity. Figure 7–6 shows the relationship of profit to output volume. The ordinate is now measured as amount of profit. Here we observe some of the disabilities of the linear system. Profit begins as negative profit, or loss, and increases linearly throughout the range of values; as a result, if the managerial objective is profit, the indicated solution for how much to produce is to expand output volume as much as possible. For these linear assumptions, that result was known before we started. Moreover, the supposition is made that the manager can expect to sell as much as he can make. The importance of this point, as well as the implications of nonlinear relations, will be examined shortly.

---

[8] Never reversing direction—and, in this case, changing at a constant rate because of the assumption of linearity.

Figure 7–6

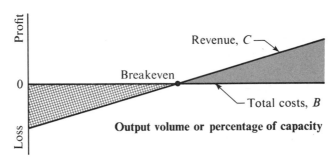

The Decision Matrix as a Unifying Model

We are now ready to observe that the linear breakeven chart succeeds in unifying various objectives by concentrating interest on only one—namely, the position of the breakeven point. As soon as some further questions are raised, however, the multiple-objective problem reappears. Certainly the manager prefers a low breakeven point to a higher one. However, consider Figure 7–7, which illustrates a situation in which the breakeven objective must be considered simultaneously with a profit objective, because each objective can be better met by using a different alternative. In this figure (as was the case

Figure 7–7

NOTE: 1 and 2 are breakeven points; 3 is an indifference point between strategies *A* and *B*.

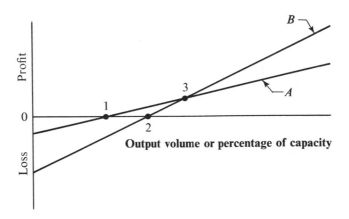

in Figure 7–6), the horizontal line represents zero profit. The other two lines represent the profitabilities of two independent strategies, *A* and *B*, at different levels of output volume. We observe that breakeven point 1 is preferred to breakeven point 2, so *A* would seem the preferred strategy. On the other hand, after point 3, as greater percentages of the capacity are utilized, strategy *B* can produce a greater profit. It should also be noted that, because of the assumption of linearity, the penalties for operating *below* point 3 become proportionately greater for the *B* strategy. So the selection of strategy will depend on the level at which the manager expects to be operating with respect to capacity utilization. Below point *a* strategy *A* is preferred, and above point *a* the choice should be strategy *B*. The table of measures for the two objectives might be

	Breakeven point	Slope[9]	Point of indifference
S_A	25%	4	$a = 54\%$
S_B	50%	5	$a = 54\%$

What to do? In this case, there is still another unifying model that will resolve the problem. We note that breakeven analysis, as it is described here, is a deterministic form of analysis. What is lacking is some estimate of the probability of different capacity-utilization values. With such information we can convert the entire breakeven analysis into a decision matrix, as shown in Table 7–1. The profit and loss values entered in the matrix for each strategy

Table 7–1

Capacity utilization:	0%	20%	40%	60%	80%	100%	
Probability for demand at each capacity level:	.00	.05	.25	.35	.20	.15	Expected-profit values
Strategy *A* profit values	−100	−20	+60	+140	+220	+300	+152
Strategy *B* profit values	−1,500	−900	−300	+300	+900	+1,500	+390

can be read directly off the appropriate lines of the breakeven chart. The data could apply equally well to the capacity utilization of a computer or a production plant or to the load factor of commercial aircraft. Our values are, of

---

[9] The slope measures the increase in profit per additional unit of capacity.

course, hypothetical, but they suffice to illustrate the case.[10] The decision model successfully unifies the previously opposing factors. In this case, it indicates a choice of strategy *B*, but if the probability distribution had been heavily weighted below point *a*, the choice would have been for the *A* strategy.

Another multiple objective problem arises. We are no longer interested solely in the position of the breakeven point. Neither are we single-mindedly concerned about any one particular capacity-utilization figure and the profit that promises to result at that level of operation. Instead, the problem has been transformed so that an expected value totally describes the situation and we can thereby choose between alternative configurations.

Yet is it absolutely certain that the expected-value criterion should override the breakeven-point location and the rate of change of profit with increased capacity utilization? We know that if both the breakeven point and the rate of change of one strategy are superior to those of another, then the expected value of that alternative will also be superior. Of course, in such a case there is no need to use the higher order decision model; the breakeven model would suffice. It is only when conflict occurs between the rate of change and the breakeven point that a problem arises. And it is not entirely clear that the manager should then ignore the breakeven point, for it provides a different kind of information from the expected value, whose use will depend on the degree of belief that the manager has in his estimates for demand and capacity utilization. Perhaps because it has little belief in its ability to forecast demand for seats or mileage, the air-transport industry, for example, has depended on breakeven-point (or load-factor) analysis.

Another multiple-objective problem can now attract management's attention. Let us propose that the expected values of our two strategies turn out to be equivalent and that the probability estimates are believable. We have already explained to the manager that, commensurate with his complex objective, he should choose the maximum expected value. However, two strategies that are not identical have yielded the same expected value. Consider the decision matrix in Table 7–2. The variability of the second strategy is much greater than that of the first, even though they both end up producing the same expected value. By almost any criterion known to them, managers would prefer the strategy with the lower variance. So far, there is no real problem.

What would happen, however, if one strategy had a greater amount of variance but a higher expected profit than the other? How does one treat this situation? Once again we have developed a conflict between objectives. The

---

[10] They have been derived from the linear relations. For strategy *A*, profit = 400 (percentage of capacity) − 100; and for strategy *B*, profit = 3,000 (percentage of capacity) − 1,500.

Table 7–2

Capacity utilization:	0%	20%	40%	60%	80%	100%	
Probability for demand at each capacity level:	.00	.05	.25	.35	.20	.15	Expected-profit values
Strategy 1 profit values	−100	−20	+60	+140	+220	+300	+152
Strategy 2 profit values	−1,738	−1,138	−538	+62	+662	+1,262	+152

variability tells us something about the stability of the system's performance. The expected value presents another measure of the extent to which the manager succeeds in achieving his objectives. The expected-value criterion by itself does not seem to be sufficient. When the problem exists, it can be treated by a number of the methods still to be discussed in this chapter—but see, in particular, the iso-curve model (pp. 272–75).

The nonlinear breakeven chart. It is readily apparent that the anticipated volume of operations is a critical factor in the determination of a system's design. If the market is such that at a certain price *unlimited demand exists,* then for these linear systems we would always operate as far to the right as possible, including the effort to increase capacity above its present level at 100 percent utilization. Of course, in reality, linearity usually ceases at some point to be a reasonable description of the market's responses. Increased volume can be obtained only by a decrease in price or an increase in promotional and selling costs. These two situations are shown in Figures 7–8 and 7–9. The combination of these effects is illustrated in Figure 7–10. Each of these diagrams is accompanied by a graph of the profit that can be obtained by operating at different percentages of capacity.

In each of these cases, there is a "best possible" point—that is, a point at which the total profit is maximized—which is at less than full capacity. To achieve this level of production and sales requires cooperative effort on the part of all the major management divisions. Financial management must provide enough funds to create the facilities necessary for the specified volume. The marketing department must be able to deliver the estimated number of sales at the price that is incorporated in the revenue line. And, of course, production must be able to deliver the goods in the required volume. Management, in other words, must determine a *configuration of elements* that will yield a maximum profit—if that is the company's objective.

Figure 7–8   **Breakeven Chart with Decelerating Revenue**

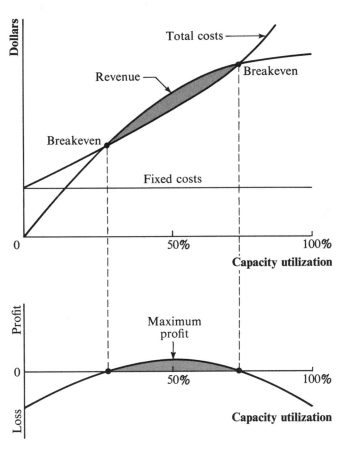

However, the difficulty of doing this is complicated far beyond anything that a breakeven chart can show. And one must be very careful in applying such a unifying or simplifying tool as the breakeven chart. Let us examine this warning. The breakeven chart, even in nonlinear form, represents only one product. For most companies, decisions must be made in light of product mix. The product line consists of a number of different items or services that must share resources, including capital and management time. The breakeven chart is difficult to utilize when such additional complications are encountered. Moreover, a specific period of time is embodied in each breakeven chart. If we assume that the company can sell 5,000,000 units over a five-year period but only 10,000 in the first year, then a five-year breakeven analysis may be quite appealing, whereas the product would be rejected on the basis of a one-year analysis. But cost estimates applied to a five-year period might not be suffi-

Figure 7–9   Breakeven Chart with Accelerating Total Cost

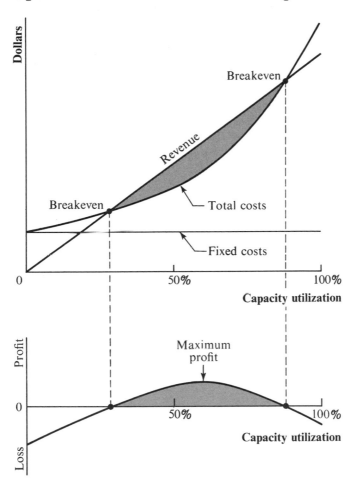

ciently believable for management to act on them. Furthermore, unexpected costs can arise. For example, if the company overproduces, then overstock units could be sold only by reducing the price. If the unsold units are held in inventory, they will create storage, insurance, and carrying costs.

For each situation some maximum-profit (optimal) situation exists. Whether it can be found or not is another matter. *But only with the nonlinear breakeven chart does this fundamental objective of management even appear;* the traditional breakeven approach overlooks this aspect of the problem. The determinate, nonlinear model used to unify the potentially conflicting objectives of a minimum breakeven point and a maximum-per-unit rate of profit produces a *normative* model. It has a clearly designated optimal value for

**Figure 7–10   Breakeven Chart with Both Assumptions—
Decelerating Revenue and Accelerating Costs**

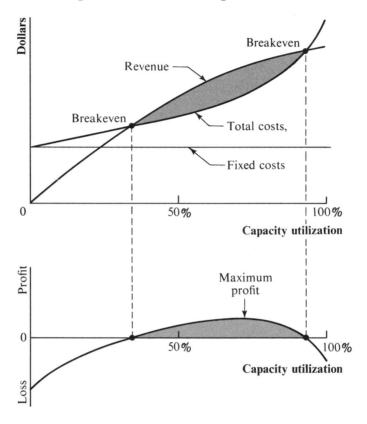

the output level. If the manager cannot control, but must forecast, the operating level, then the expected-value criterion of decision-making under risk can also be applied to this nonlinear case to determine the optimal strategic alternative, in the same sense that this was done in Tables 7–1 and 7–2. The conceptual difference between such a risk optimum and the determinate one of, say, Figure 7–10 deserves the reader's close attention.

The iso-curve example of a unifying model. A distinction may be drawn between *marketing variety* and *production diversity* to illustrate the creation of a model that can be used to resolve a complex-objectives problem. Later we can apply this model to the problem of the conflict between the variability and expected value of the decision matrix of Table 7–2.

Although *variety* and *diversity* are more or less synonymous, it will serve our purpose here to make a distinction between them. We will define the creation of variety as a marketing function and that of diversity as a production function. In this sense, marketing variety, *MV*, emphasizes *characterizational* differences in the attributes of the product class, while production diversity, *PD*, refers to *physical* differences in the attributes of products.

Variety and diversity are measurable *only* in terms of the system, a characteristic that commonly leads to complex-objectives problems. Other qualities, such as the harshness of soap, the sweetness of drink, the horsepower under the hood, or the price of painkillers, are physically measurable properties of a particular brand in isolation from the others. Certainly, ratios comparing brands in these terms *can* be derived, but they do not have to be. Variety and diversity, on the other hand, *cannot* be described except by systems measures. That is, they can be defined only in terms of the range of comparative qualities of existing brands.

It is generally agreed that with increased affluence, the public has increased its desire for both variety and diversity. With increased pressure for variety and diversity, marketing and production are pushed to higher levels of integrated action. Under such conditions, how much *MV* and how much *PD* should a product line have?

Assume that the consumer's level of satisfaction, *K*, is related in the following way to the variety and the diversity he perceives:

$$(MV)(PD) = K$$

This relationship is illustrated in Figure 7–11. The curve seems plausible, and

Figure 7–11   An Iso-satisfaction Curve

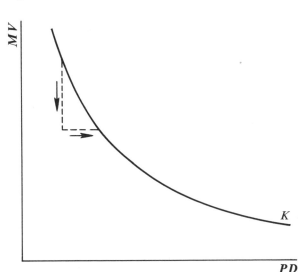

it fits in with concepts derived from utility theory and economics. More important, it satisfies, albeit in a crude way, our requirement for relating several objectives by means of a curve of equal satisfaction or iso-satisfaction[11]—that is, a curve along which all points show the same degree of satisfaction. As the dashed lines in the figure indicate, a decrease in MV requires an increase in PD for the same level of satisfaction to be maintained. The reverse changes would also apply.

But there is a cost for variety and a cost for diversity. These costs are incurred by the company and passed on to consumers. Our assumption will be that the costs can be represented as linear and of the form $aMV + bPD = B$, where a is the cost per unit of market variety, b is the cost per unit of production diversity, and B is the total budget for maintaining MV units of marketing variety and PD units of production diversity. As is familiar in economics, the optimal-cost line will be that one which is tangent to the iso-satisfaction curve $(MV)(PD) = K$. When the marketing-variety cost, a, is much smaller than the production diversity cost, b (i.e., $a << b$), the point of tangency will be high on MV and low on PD (i.e., $\dfrac{B}{a} >> \dfrac{B}{b}$) as shown in Figure 7–12, where the point of tangency is at Q'. But the reverse could be as true if $a > b$. Then the curves would touch at some point below the $MV = PD$ line—say, at S.

The important question to answer, of course, is: Which cost relation applies? This model will not answer that question, but it does succeed in relating the two objectives concerning MV and PD. Point Q in the diagram is eminently sensible *for one particular cost relation* in which $a < b$, whereas other points, showing other combinations of variety and diversity, are not. Critics of marketing variety have called for a point such as S' because they believe that a is significantly greater than b. Others ask only for a decrease of MV such as would be achieved at point S. Whether these suggestions are sensible will not be determined by our present model but must be reserved for an analysis of the actual costs of providing MV and PD.

Our iso-satisfaction curve is called a *rectangular hyperbola*. The same type of curve can be derived to model other situations. For example, the equation: $(VAR)(EV) = K$ might relate the variability, VAR, and the expected value, EV, of the decision-matrix problem that was discussed in connection with Table 7–2. Inherent in all such approaches is the concept of *trade-off* between two variables whose product is a constant value. In this case, the cost of

---

[11] More complex (and perhaps more satisfying) forms of these "iso" equations can be developed—for example, $(MV)^\alpha(PD)^\beta = K$, where α and β, having values other than one, will change the shape of the iso-satisfaction curves. With α and β equal to one, the shape of the curve is called a rectangular hyperbola. With unequal values, the symmetry of the hyperbola is disturbed, and MV and PD no longer contribute equally to satisfaction.

Figure 7–12   Optimal Cost for Satisfaction

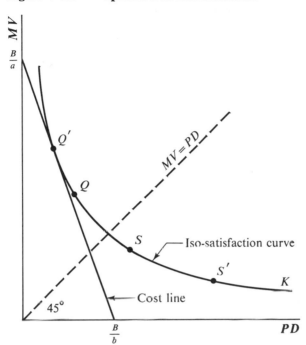

variability and the cost of deviating from the optimal expected value must be estimated before a solution can be found.

The discounting model. An important multiple-objectives problem exists in the relationship between short- and long-term profits. There is no problem when both can be maximized by one strategy. However, as goals they frequently are in conflict. A solution to this problem has been made available by a unifying model that is well known and widely used—namely, the discounting model.

In this model, all future costs and profits are related by present-worth equations, which determine how much interest must be earned or paid on present monies to make them equivalent to future sums. An example of such an equation is

$$\text{present worth} = \sum_{n=1}^{N} R_n \left(\frac{1}{1+i}\right)^n$$

where i is the interest rate, n equals the specific time period, starting with the first ($n = 1$) and ending with the Nth ($n = N$). R_n is the payment made at the end of the nth period, where n equals 1, 2, 3, ... N.

As an example, let us find the present worth of $300 to be paid in three installments of $100 at the end of each of three years, where $i = 6$ percent per year. Without discounting, we would say that the three payments are worth $300. But clearly, since we have to wait for the money, it is worth less than if all $300 were paid to us immediately. Considering the deferred nature of the payments, and using the discounting model, we obtain

$$PW = 100 \left[\left(\frac{1}{1.06} \right)^1 + \left(\frac{1}{1.06} \right)^2 + \left(\frac{1}{1.06} \right)^3 \right] = \$267.30.$$

The difference is easily accounted for. In order to have $300 at the end of three years, we would need today only $267.30 paid immediately and invested at 6 percent. This is another example of a unifying model, where the complexity of the objectives is related to their timing.

Psychological transformations. Frequently, it is impossible to construct mathematical models for transforming complex objectives into simple ones. The reasons include the inability to describe complex relations between variables, the impossibility of observing or measuring the values of the variables, and the intractability of the models to mathematical treatment.

Much attention has been paid to the problem of measuring intangible dimensions. The fact that intuitive management abilities exist implies that such observation is being done all the time in a purely subjective way. And it is reasonable to question whether a means of objectifying such subjective behavior can be found. Utility theorists have made a beginning. In its present form, utility theory is highly technical and has not yet offered managers the kind of empirical evidence that could interest them in this "universal" form of currency. But its underlying ideas are interesting. We first encountered it in this book in our discussion of Paretian optimality (see pp. 11–12), where we recognized that each person manages his own values system and that the comparability of the value systems of different individuals is not apparent or accessible. Therefore, we concluded, a societal or group model can be constructed only if we can obviate the need to differentiate between individuals' value characteristics. Pareto tried to do just that.

For each individual, however, a further problem exists—namely, how he can be consistent in the way he allocates his values. Let us now consider this utility problem and the promise of utility theory to assist in its solution. A consumer could express his preference for each of the specific qualities (shape, weight, label, color, etc.) of package A as against each of the same qualities of package $B;$ or he could express his preference for one or the other package as a whole. The result of the individual preferences would not necessarily be the same as the single estimate. One reason is that while A might be preferred for shape and B preferred for color and label, the influence of shape in the individual's overall judgment might outweigh the influence of both color and label. The obvious question is: What is the relative importance of each characteristic?

The package as a whole has many descriptive dimensions. The multiplicity of dimensions accounts for the fact that in paired comparisons a person could say: *A* is better than *C, C* is better than *B, but B* is better than *A*. This is called a breakdown of *transitivity,*[12] and there is little that can be done about it. Only if we can relate the multiple dimensions to a single objective can we be sure of avoiding such a breakdown. How, for instance, can one rate the following three locations—25°N–15°W; 16°S–4°E; 60°N–1°E—except by measuring resultant distance (or time) from a specific point that is the goal? If the locations are to be related to a preferred set of climatic conditions, then the problem becomes multidimensional again with respect to temperature, rainfall, and so on.

There is no right or wrong to be found in such cases. Selection cannot be dictated until the *basis* for selection is established. That basis is one of personal utilities unless management establishes and articulates a policy for utilities. In some organizations this has been attempted by having the top managers set down a common credo aimed at replacing the exercise of individual ones. Lacking such a framework, managers can raise no argument when differing utilities account for different final decisions.

We are face to face with one of the most fundamental of philosophical positions, which can be expressed succinctly as the inherent right of anyone to value things as he wishes. And we see that differences of opinion arise on this score even though on all other points the managers are in complete agreement. Conflicting values systems within decision groups can be irreconcilable and produce confused behavior in the search for resolution of conflicts. We attempt to objectify the managerial process in an effort to eliminate those divergent opinions that are not traceable to value differences. If we can do this, the value differences may then be recognized for what they are and, perhaps, discussed and compromised.

Utility theory has treated the nature of different scales and has the admirable ultimate aim of being able to reduce all variables to a single dimension—the util. Preference measures, widely used in marketing, are a psychological variant of the utility measure. Dimensions of cost, quality, and good will and the effects of guarantees, advertising, and product-line variety can sometimes be cast in this mold—but not without trepidation. After all, seldom can such preference transformations be checked against reality. The ability to estimate utilities is always to be questioned, perhaps only a little less so when the dimension to be evaluated is measured on a monetary scale. When psychological scaling can reduce complex objectives to a single scale, the problem of

---

[12] As we discussed in Chapter 2, transitivity refers to the internal consistency of all relations within a system—for example, if *A* > *B* and *B* > *C,* then *C* < *A*.

unifying to a common objective is solved. However, it is always understood that preference measured along one dimension is a different kind of preference from that measured along another dimension.

COMPLEX OBJECTIVES RESOLVED BY MEANS OF DIMENSIONAL ANALYSIS

We have tried to emphasize that a manager usually deals with situations in which the problem of complex objectives is not trivial. The manager has many objectives in mind that cannot easily be reduced to a single goal. Moreover, any set of objectives can change, frequently as a result of the prior objectives that were used and the results that were experienced.

Many times, the best that we can do when confronted with a number of alternatives is to measure several factors that relate to our objectives. Some of these measures may be simply degrees of preference for different situations. For example, there are cases in which safety is a primary consideration and must be included in the analysis. But how do we evaluate the trade-off between safety and profit? (How much safety is equivalent to one unit of profit?) Another example of this kind of problem occurs when weapons systems are evaluated. Here, profit—at least in its usual sense—is an almost meaningless concept. Factors such as firepower, accuracy, and maneuverability must be weighed against cost, safety, and expected obsolescence. Still another instance would be the evaluation of alternative designs for surgical instruments, in which case cost would have to be weighed against the remedial properties of the instruments. From the point of view of an airline's management, the traffic it obtains, its revenue, the safety that is assured, its share of the market, its route structure, the type of equipment that is used, and its accommodations at the terminals are all interrelated factors. Some of these must be relinquished as others are obtained. Preference embodies such multiple components. It is in some ways a balancing of *many factors* and an attempt to estimate their contributions to the achievement of the objectives.

The problem that must be solved, however, is how to derive a meaningful measure of preference in such cases.[13] We shall begin in a simple way by using a common method of evaluation, which is to obtain a weighted index by addition. And it is of great interest that often this approach is wrong. Naturally, we are concerned that it be made entirely clear when the additive method is right and when it is wrong. Let us compare choices *A* and *B*. Two objectives are isolated as being the major determinants of preference (and therefore of

---

[13] Where relationships are unknown and guessing is used, estimates of profit are really no more than preference measures, and the dollar dimension lends an air of authenticity that must be viewed with suspicion.

attainment of the objectives). We shall call these objectives 1 and 2. The quality of each choice is rated with respect to the two objectives (thus A_1 is the evaluation of A with respect to the first objective), and there are altogether four considerations—A_1, A_2, B_1, and B_2. By switching from an analysis of the alternative as a whole to a comparison of each characteristic of the two choices, the dimensional difficulties that are inherent in overall evaluation can be avoided.

Next, a set of weighting factors is chosen to objectify the relative importance of the two characteristics. Individual members of the management team may not agree on the assignment of weights. For that matter, there will probably not be complete agreement on the characteristics or on the measurement scales to be employed. At least, all such disagreements can be discussed because they are expressed objectively.

Now let us see how the weighting factors are used and what can be wrong with the method that is commonly employed. Let the weights be w_1 for the first objective and w_2 for the second. When Q stands for "the value of," then the evaluation of alternative A is given as $Q_A = w_1 A_1 + w_2 A_2$, and for alternative B it is $Q_B = w_1 B_1 + w_2 B_2$. By taking a specific example we shall uncover the fundamental error that is being made. Say that we want to compare the qualities of two boxes, each of which contains one apple and one orange. To begin, let us assume that a highly skilled fruit grader determines the following: Box A contains an apple of grade 2 and an orange of grade 5, where 5 is the highest possible grade and 1 is the lowest. Box B contains an apple of grade 4 and an orange of grade 3. One of the designers of the box of fruit states that in his opinion the contributions of the apple and the orange to the overall quality of the combination are equivalent. By this he means that preference for either one of the boxes will be influenced equally by both types of fruit. (The implicit assumption is made that he is not speaking about his own preference but is attempting to mirror the consumer's attitude and make his preference equivalent to the profit potential of each type of box.) Then, at least for this decision-maker, the quality measures would indicate equal quality evaluations for both boxes. Thus

$$Q(\text{Box } A) = (1)(2) + (1)(5) = 7$$

and

$$Q(\text{Box } B) = (1)(4) + (1)(3) = 7$$

We are not going to quarrel with the choice of weights. Market surveys could be conducted to lend support to or contradict the contentions that they represent. Neither shall we disagree with the quality evaluations of the grader, since he is presumably a sensitive measuring instrument.[14] Here, too, market surveys could be employed to lend credence to the grading system. It is the

---

[14] If one doubts this, another grader can be called in and the test procedure replicated.

procedure itself that we find objectionable, and the reason is a flaw in the dimensions or character of the evaluation measures. We have just added the dimension of apples to the dimension of oranges, and our result is expressed in these terms. But what does the dimension "apples plus oranges" mean? Nothing we can understand.

It might be thought that since the importance of apples and oranges in the box was evaluated as being equal, we could drop those dimensions and unify them by calling both units of fruit. *If this can be done,* then the additive model given above would be correct. But we must then expect that the grader's values would change. He would be grading fruit, not apples with apples and oranges with oranges. Such a grading problem might pose impossible difficulties. In that case, the additive model could not be used, since, as we said, the dimension "apples plus oranges" means nothing we can understand.

Let us underscore this conclusion by considering another example. Assume that two designs are to be evaluated in terms of their dimensions of cost, size, and weight. The objective for each of these characteristics is to obtain the minimum value. (The objective for the fruit box was a maximum value.) Assume the following data:

	Cost	Size	Weight
plan C:	$3	12 in.	1 lb.
plan D:	$2	24 in.	2 lbs.
Importance (weights):	5	2	3

Using the incorrect method we obtain

$$Q(\text{plan } C) = 5(3) + 2(12) + 3(1) = 42(\text{dollars} + \text{in.} + \text{lbs.})$$
$$Q(\text{plan } D) = 5(2) + 2(24) + 3(2) = 64(\text{dollars} + \text{in.} + \text{lbs.})$$

Plan C, having a smaller evaluation number, is the indicated choice. But what would happen if we now transformed inches to feet? If the method of evaluation were correct, then plan C would continue to be preferred, since using an inch scale instead of a foot scale does not change the size of either design. The result of the new calculation, however, is

$$Q(\text{plan } C) = 5(3) + 2(1) + 3(1) = 20(\text{dollars} + \text{ft.} + \text{lbs.})$$
$$Q(\text{plan } D) = 5(2) + 2(2) + 3(2) = 20(\text{dollars} + \text{ft.} + \text{lbs.})$$

The plans are now reported to be equivalent. Apparently this method of evaluation is not invariant to the scale of our measuring instruments.

As another example, let us change dollars to cents. Then

$$Q(\text{plan } C) = 5(300) + 2(1) + 3(1) = 1,505(\text{cents} + \text{ft.} + \text{lbs.})$$
$$Q(\text{plan } D) = 5(200) + 2(2) + 3(2) = 1,010(\text{cents} + \text{ft.} + \text{lbs.})$$

The preference has now switched to Plan D. The results are intolerable. This system of evaluation has been discredited by example. It does not fulfill the basic requirement of dimensional consistency but instead produces dimensional abominations.

How, then, should we proceed? We must multiply the quality measures instead of adding them. The weighting factors will be exponents associated with each characteristic. Thus

$$Q_A = A_1^{w_1} A_2^{w_2}$$

and

$$Q_B = B_1^{w_1} B_2^{w_2}$$

The form of this model calls to mind the iso-curve model (and particularly the footnote on p. 274).

For the box of fruit this will give

$$Q(\text{box } A) = (2)^1(5)^1 = 10$$

and

$$Q(\text{box } B) = (4)^1(3)^1 = 12$$

Since the objective is to obtain the highest number—box B is preferred. With respect to our second example we obtain:[15]

$$Q(\text{plan } C) = (3)^5(12)^2(1)^3 = 34{,}992\,(\text{dollars} \times \text{in.} \times \text{lbs.})$$
$$Q(\text{plan } D) = (2)^5(24)^2(2)^3 = 147{,}456\,(\text{dollars} \times \text{in.} \times \text{lbs.})$$

Our objective was the smallest number, so plan C is preferred.

Now let us go through the same set of scale transformations that we used previously.

$$Q(\text{plan } C) = (3)^5(1)^2(1)^3 = 243\,(\text{dollars} \times \text{ft.} \times \text{lbs.})$$
$$Q(\text{plan } D) = (2)^5(2)^2(2)^3 = 1{,}024\,(\text{dollars} \times \text{ft.} \times \text{lbs.})$$

This time, plan C continues to remain the choice. Lastly,

$$Q(\text{plan } C) = (300)^5(1)^2(1)^3 = 243^{10}\,(\text{cents} \times \text{ft.} \times \text{lbs.})$$
$$Q(\text{plan } D) = (200)^5(2)^2(2)^3 = 1{,}024^{10}\,(\text{cents} \times \text{ft.} \times \text{lbs.})$$

which also arrives at a choice of plan C.

To understand the nature of what we have done, let us find the ratios of each paired comparison. These are, for the method of addition:

(1) $\dfrac{42}{64} = .66$ (2) $\dfrac{20}{20} = 1.00$ (3) $\dfrac{1{,}505}{1{,}010} = 1.49$

and for the method of multiplication:

(1) $\dfrac{34{,}992}{147{,}456} = .24$ (2) $\dfrac{243}{1{,}024} = .24$ (3) $\dfrac{243(10)^{10}}{1{,}024(10)^{10}} = .24$

---

[15] For ease of computation, this can also be written as
$$\log Q_C = w_1 \log C_1 + w_2 \log C_2 + w_3 \log C_3$$

In dimensional terms, the ratio of the qualities of the two plans evaluated by addition is of the type:

$$\frac{(\text{dollars})}{(\text{dollars} + \text{in.} + \text{lbs.})} + \frac{(\text{in.})}{(\text{dollars} + \text{in.} + \text{lbs.})} + \frac{(\text{lbs.})}{(\text{dollars} + \text{in.} + \text{lbs.})}$$

This cannot be further reduced. The ratios derived from multiplication yield a pure, or dimensionless, number; for example,

$$\frac{(\text{dollars} \times \text{in.} \times \text{lbs.})}{(\text{dollars} \times \text{in.} \times \text{lbs.})} = \text{pure number}$$

Conclusively, in this case the multiplication method is the correct approach.[16]

Only ratios have significance when we apply this method to obtain preference measures. Our outcomes are therefore only relative, but that is enough for the purpose of choosing one strategy from a set of possibilities. Thus, for the box of fruit the outcome ratio is

$$\frac{\text{Box } A}{\text{Box } B} = \frac{10}{12} = \frac{5}{6}$$

and, since we want as large a number as possible, we choose box B.

The best possible design for the box of fruit would be an apple of grade 5 and an orange of grade 5. Using the weighting system previously specified, our ratios with respect to some standard design (in this case, let us choose the "best possible" as the standard) would be

$$\frac{\text{Box } A}{\text{standard}} = \frac{5}{25}$$

and

$$\frac{\text{Box } B}{\text{standard}} = \frac{6}{25}$$

It is useful also to standardize the weighting system. This is easily accomplished by making the weights sum to one, ten, or one hundred. We used ten for the three-characteristic example. In the case of the box of fruit we could

---

[16] This conclusion assumes that a scale with a natural origin (see pp. 51–52) exists for all the objectives. Such an assumption is often difficult to defend, especially when psychological variables are involved. For a further discussion of the problems of dimensional analysis, see P. W. Bridgman, *Dimensional Analysis* (New Haven: Yale University Press, 1922), pp. 21–22, and C. Radhakrishna Rao, *Advanced Statistical Methods in Biometric Research* (New York: Wiley, 1952), p. 103. See also L. Ivan Epstein, "A Proposed Method for Determining the Value of a Design," *Journal of the Operations Research Society of America,* Vol. 5, No. 2 (April 1957), pp. 297–99; and Walter R. Stahl, "Similarity and Dimensional Methods in Biology," *Science,* Vol. 137 (July 20, 1962), pp. 205–12.

have utilized weighting factors of one-half. Changes of this sort will affect the ratio values, but the order of preference will remain the same.

One additional characteristic of the multiplication method should be noted. If a mix of objectives exists, it is necessary to use negative exponents. For example, if we wish to have a minimum of cost and a maximum of strength, we would select the alternative with the smallest evaluation number from the set of such measures.

$$\frac{Q_j}{Q_*} = \frac{(C_j)^{w1}(S_j)^{-w2}}{(C_*)^{w1}(S_*)^{-w2}} = \frac{(C_j)^{w1}(S_*)^{w2}}{(C_*)^{w1}(S_j)^{w2}}$$

where C_j is the cost of the jth plan, S_j is the strength of the jth plan, and the asterisk represents the standard plan. This standard could be the best possible alternative, or it could be a theoretically ideal plan that is not in fact feasible. The whole point of the standard plan is to have some point against which all other plans can be compared. Such use of standards is well known in other fields, particularly in engineering.

We now have developed a practical means for assigning outcome values for complex objectives when other approaches cannot be used. A noteworthy benefit of using this procedure is that it forces all members of the management team to specify the factors that are playing an important part in their individual thoughts about the problem. First, the critical objectives and their associated characteristics must be listed. Usually a *master sheet* is drawn up that includes every characteristic suggested. If there is disagreement as to what should be included on the list, the dispute can be resolved when the weights are assigned. (A zero weight produces the value of one, since $C_j^0 = 1$, which in effect is equivalent to dropping consideration of the disputed characteristic.) The operation of assigning weights is of great utility. It is the only effective means of achieving the vital understanding of the attitudes and ideas of each manager that is required if their differences of opinion are to be resolved and work is to proceed toward the company's objectives. At the same time, there is nothing conclusive about these value judgments. They will differ from individual to individual and frequently can differ for the same individual over a fifteen-minute period.

There is no question that the measurement problems can be severe, particularly with respect to arbitrary standards for evaluating characteristics. We recognize that when the fruit grader rates the orange in Box A as the best possible grade, he must have his own criteria. But we may not be willing to agree with this fruit grader until we know what rating scheme he is using. He must spell it out in detail. He obviously employed various values of w by deciding that certain qualities of an orange were more important than others. We expect that his basic measurements of quality levels are reproducible, but we cannot find out until we make him break down the decision-evaluation system that he used. He may have had such categories as the shape of the fruit, the color, the firmness, the size, the weight, and so on. Notice that these categories begin to become measurable as they become more detailed, and a standard for such measurement can be set.

What is needed is a measure of the favor or importance that the manager bestows on each objective as compared to the others. From our previous discussions we know that different methods might be used. For example, we could simply rank the objectives in terms of their importance to us. Or we could obtain additional information by placing distance measures between the rankings we have achieved.

One possible assignment of weight would be to make all characteristics equally important. Many problems are solved with either the unconscious or conscious assignment of equal weights. And no matter what weight assignment is used, it is clear that individual preferences will be embodied in the weighting systems. Also it is important to recognize that any selection *imputes* a set of weights to the manager's behavior. A variety of techniques, including averaging and correlation, are available for attempting to combine the preferences of various individuals into a single representative measure. Technique, however, is frequently overridden by the attitudes of stronger executives. In Chapter 15 we shall have more to say about such managerial interrelations.

THE PROGRAMMING OPTION

The problem of complex objectives can be reformulated so that only *one* major objective is considered. All others become subobjectives, or *constraints* on the main objective. The approach has significance for management because the difficulties and the intangible qualities of the multidimensional method can sometimes be by-passed in this way. The key is to maximize the objective function (which expresses the nature of the one main objective) in such a way as to stay within or satisfy the constraints. The constraints can be expressed as a lower or upper bound or as a range within which the final solution must lie.

Consider the following. *Example 1:* Maximize one-year after-tax profits (the objective function) subject to the constraint that three-year gross profit provides a return of at least 10 percent on invested capital. *Example 2:* Minimize the risk involved in a new venture (the objective function) subject to the constraints that annual operating costs be no greater than C and that annual profit be no less than π. *Example 3:* Maximize the firm's one-year profits subject to the constraints that growth in sales volume be no greater than 30 percent and no less than 10 percent.

Typically, the organization wishing to maximize its benefits will have a number of constraints that deal with not exceeding its resources in facilities, manpower, and materials. In general, the programming method for dealing with complex objectives begins by *decomposing* each alternative being considered into activities that relate and contribute to the major objective and the sub-objectives. Thus, a matrix can be set up, as in Table 7–3. A plan is composed

Table 7–3   Matrix of Activity Coefficients

		Activities:					
		A_1	A_2	...	A_j	...	A_n
Constraints:	C_1	a_{11}	a_{12}	...	a_{1j}	...	a_{1n}
	C_2	a_{21}	a_{22}	...	a_{2j}	...	a_{2n}
		.	.		.		.
	C_i	a_{i1}	a_{i2}		a_{ij}	...	a_{in}
		.					
	C_m	a_{m1}	a_{m2}		a_{mj}	...	a_{mn}
Coefficients of the objective function:		p_1	p_2		p_j	...	p_n

of a set of n activities. The size of each activity is represented by the value of its particular A. The measures a_{11}, a_{21}, and so on, describe the activity's contribution to (or use of) the constraints. If the p's are profit coefficients, then total profit $= p_1A_1 + p_2A_2 + p_jA_j + \ldots + p_nA_n$. This is the objective function that the manager intends to maximize. There are m constraints written in either of two general forms—that is, more than or less than (equality may occur with each).

$$a_{i1}A_1 + a_{i2}A_2 + \ldots + a_{ij}A_j + \ldots + a_{in}A_n \leq C_i \text{ (or } \geq C_i)$$

where C_i is the top or bottom of the allowable range.

Linear programming is one of the mathematical methods closely associated with the operations-research developments that grew out of the Second World War.[17] It is a method of decision-making under certainty. The first step in utilizing LP is to name the various basic activities that, like building blocks, can be combined to form the various possible strategies. The method uses a clever

---

[17] Credit for the development of linear programming belongs to a number of people but primarily to George Dantzig of the RAND Corporation. The reader desirous of becoming proficient in linear programming is advised to consult one of the many texts that describe linear programming in its full mathematical context. Several of these are listed in the Bibliography.

gambit to relieve us of the burden of enumerating all conceivable strategic combinations. Briefly, a combination strategy is chosen. This strategy specifies various levels for each activity. Next, a change is made in the first combination strategy. But the only changes that are considered are those that would improve the attainment of the major objective. Furthermore, the change that promises the greatest improvement is the one that is used first. This new combination is then viewed in the same light. What additional improvement can be made? The one alternative is chosen that seems likely to offer the greatest improvement. Proceeding in this way, we do not have to enumerate all possible combinations. In fact, usually only a small subset will be considered.

From the description above we see that we require: (1) the matrix of information concerning the a_{ij}'s, the C_i's, and the A_j's; (2) a means of selecting the initial activity mix; (3) a rule for separating changes that lead to improvement from those that do not; (4) a procedure for making the indicated change; and (5) a rule for determining when to stop making further changes. By repeating the third and fourth steps until the fifth tells us to stop, we can successfully disregard most of the combinations that are possible but not rewarding.

Let us consider an example. Management is attempting to choose the best strategy composed of two independent activities, A_1 and A_2. Without any constraints, there is an infinite number of combinations of A_1 and A_2—for example, $A_1 = 10$, $A_2 = 0$; or $A_1 = 0$, $A_2 = 6$; or $A_1 = 5$, $A_2 = 7$. The major objective is to maximize the total profit: $p_1A_1 + p_2A_2$, where p_1 and p_2 are the profits obtained for each unit of the respective activities that are employed. Two constraints are believed to exist: the first concerns the cost of using a unit of each activity where there is a total-cost constraint; the second reflects the subobjective of not exceeding present capacity. The basic data are assumed to be the following:

	A_1	A_2	Size of constraint
Cost constraint per unit:	$4	$8	$200,000
Capacity required per unit:	.004%	.005%	100 percent
Profit objective per unit:	$2	$3	

We can set this information down with inequations:

The cost constraint: $4A_1 + 8A_2 \leq 200{,}000$ (1)
The capacity constraint: $.004A_1 + .005A_2 \leq 100$ (2)
Neither activity can have negative value:
     $A_1 \geq 0$; $A_2 \geq 0$ (3)
The major objective concerns total profit (π):
     Maximize ($\pi = 2A_1 + 3A_2$)   (4)

Figure 7–13   Geometric Representation of Cost and Capacity Constraints for the Planning of an Optimal Activity Mix

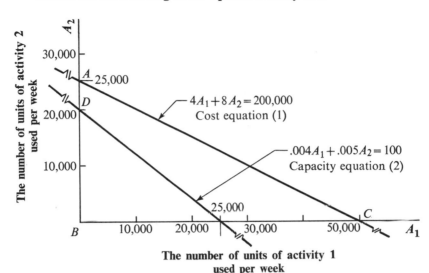

We can now solve this problem if we understand the mathematics of inequations. The most direct way to explain the nature of inequations is to use Figure 7–13. Here we see four lines. Two are the familiar axes of Cartesian coordinates. They are labeled A_1 and A_2. The equation $A_1 = 0$ is a straight line lying directly on the axis marked A_2. The inequation $A_1 \geq 0$ represents, not a line, but all the space lying to the right of the axis A_2. It excludes all negative values for A_1—that is, values to the left of the A_2 axis. Therefore, the two inequations (3) describe the entire area of the upper right-hand quadrant, including the axes themselves. A moment's reflection shows that no matter what the nature of the problem and no matter how many dimensions are involved, negative activity rates must be excluded from the solution. Consequently, $A_j \geq 0$, for all j activities, must be enforced. This is known as the requirement of *feasibility*.

Now let us turn to the other two inequations. The appropriate lines are also found in Figure 7–13. The uppermost line represents the condition of equality for inequation (1). The space within which a possible solution might occur is bounded at the top by this line. Conditions (1) and (3) thus describe the large triangle ABC. These constraints taken together state that the solution to the problem must lie somewhere in that area or on the bounding lines. However, condition (2) must be considered. All points falling on the line DE and lying below it describe a smaller triangle, DBE. Here we find the existence of dominance. Since the smaller triangle lies entirely within the larger one, it is evident that condition (2) dominates condition (1). The solution to the problem must lie within the smaller area (or on its bounding lines). In other words, condition (1) is a superfluous statement. In this example, only the capacity constraint need be considered, since it alone determines the feasible solution space.

So much for the constraints. We know that any point in the area DBE is a possible strategy—for example, $A_1 = 10,000$ and $A_2 = 10,000$. This strategy uses up 90 percent of the total capacity. The point representing the combination strategy falls inside the triangle. When $A_1 = 10,000$ and $A_2 = 12,000$, the point falls on the line, meaning that capacity is fully utilized. In this light, it becomes obvious that the number of feasible strategies to be considered can be very large. Technically there is an infinite number of possible solutions. Sometimes, however, it is absurd to consider using fractional units of an activity. The size of the problem is then reduced, since only integer solutions are allowed.[18]

We have found a way to define the great number of strategic possibilities without having to list each of them individually. In this way we are able to resolve the complicating circumstances of complex objectives. Programming methodology seems far removed from the underlying cognitive approaches of intuition and is consequently an attractive alternative to dimensional analysis for solving problems with complex objectives.

In our present example, we developed a plane surface (since only two activities were considered). Frequently we must work in n-dimensional space (i.e., there are n activities), but this in no way affects the concepts—it simply changes the methods. With three activities we would describe a three-dimensional solution space, which could be built as a solid figure. For more than three we must enter the realm of the abstract. It remains for us to determine a method of search that will locate the best possible strategy. In small problems, this can be accomplished geometrically; in problems that are larger (as most real problems are), we must resort to computing algorithms, such as the Simplex technique.[19]

In Figure 7–14 we observe the same four lines that appeared in the previous

---

[18] For a discussion of the special methods of integer programming, see R. E. Gomery and W. J. Baumol, "Integer Programming and Pricing," *Econometrica,* Vol. 28, No. 3, 1960. Although the requirement for integer solutions reduces the number of strategies that must be considered, it complicates the method of computation. When the answers are of reasonable size, we can merely discard the fraction—for example, treat 2501.3 as 2501, but when they must be sets of zeros and ones, integer programming is essential.

[19] The Simplex algorithm is a mathematical procedure that uses the same kind of reasoning as the geometric approach, but does so in terms of the properties of linear equations and matrix algebra. Simplex is one of several algorithms that can efficiently solve problems having the linear programming structure.

Figure 7–14   Geometric Representation of an LP Problem

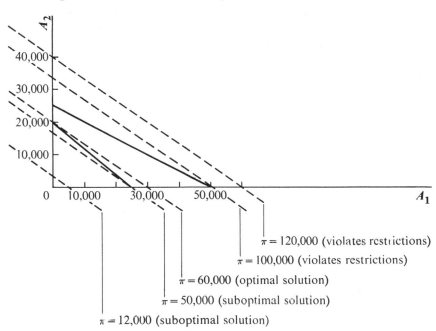

$\pi = 120,000$ (violates restrictions)

$\pi = 100,000$ (violates restrictions)

$\pi = 60,000$ (optimal solution)

$\pi = 50,000$ (suboptimal solution)

$\pi = 12,000$ (suboptimal solution)

figure, but in addition there are several representatives of a family of lines that describe the objective (profit) function. It was our stated intention to maximize this objective function. We observe that three of these dashed lines pass through the interior of the small triangle or touch at least one point of it. Each line represents the total profit that can be obtained by utilizing any one of the strategies that fall on that line. For example, Table 7–4 lists five different strategies that fall on the $\pi = \$50,000$ line.

The greatest profit can be obtained by the topmost line that still touches the solution space and thereby gives us a solution that meets the restriction of

Table 7–4

Feasible strategy	Activity Mix A_1	A_2	Profit
1	25,000	0	$50,000
2	16,000	6,000	50,000
3	10,000	10,000	50,000
4	7,000	12,000	50,000
5	0	16,667	50,000

capacity. This is the $60,000 line. All lines above this (e.g., $\pi = \$100,000$ and $\pi = \$120,000$) would produce a greater profit, but they ignore the fundamental capacity limitations. Since the $60,000 line touches the solution space at 20,000 on the A_2 axis and at 0 on the A_1 axis, the optimal solution that we have found is to use 20,000 units of A_2 and no units of A_1. If both activities had equal per-unit profits, then the slope of the family of profit lines would change. Each line would intersect equal values on the A_1 and A_2 axes. Under these conditions, the last line to leave the solution space would do so at the point $A_1 = 25,000$ and $A_2 = 0$. Thus, only A_1 would be used. Similarly, the only way that some A_1 and some A_2 could be used would be if the ratio of the per-unit profits were 4:5 for activities one and two, respectively. Such a profit line would overlay the capacity-constraint line, so all combinations of A_1 and A_2 falling on that line would be acceptable solutions.

An important rule of LP follows from its *fundamental theorem*: namely, the number of activities that will be part of the solution cannot be *larger* than the number of constraints (excluding the constraints for feasibility).[20] Since we have two such constraints—conditions (1) and (2)—we know that, at most, two activities will be in the solution. Each combination of activities that occurs at a vertex of the solution-space polygon forms what is called a *basic feasible solution*. The idea is to go from one basic feasible solution (or vertex) to another until the optimal solution is found. It is apparent that the last line to leave the solution space must always depart from a vertex.

What is the significance of the fundamental theorem as it applies to managerial objectives? The answer is that as the number of subobjectives, or constraints, increases, the number of activities that could enter into the final solution increases. Therefore, for example, as the number of real (undominated) company constraints increases, the number of different products that the company might produce increases. This is something of a *fundamental rule governing variety,* but it goes even further.

We will no longer assume that the per-unit profit of any one activity remains constant no matter how much is produced. Instead, we will explore what happens when, as is frequently the case, conditions such as those described in treating the nonlinear breakeven chart (see pp. 269–72) create a nonlinear situation such as that shown in Figure 7–15. The curve in the figure is a typical curve of diminishing returns. Because of its *concave* shape

---

[20] One way to explain this is by drawing the geometric representation for two activities where there are two constraints that cross each other in the feasible region. The crosspoint vertex allows a mixture of the two activities. With three activities and two constraints, the crosspoint vertex still allows only two activities for the solution, but with three constraints, a three-activity solution could occur. The same reasoning can be generalized to any number of dimensions.

Figure 7–15   Curve of Diminishing Profitability

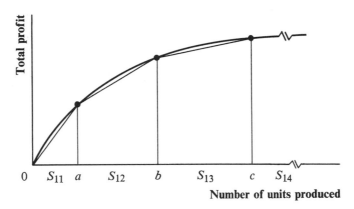

we can break this profit function into linear components, using as many seg-ments as seem needed to get a fairly good fit. The process is known as *partitioning*. According to the number of segments deemed useful, we derive new constraints on the system. Thus, with respect to Figure 7–15, we obtain: $0 \le S_{11} \le a;\ a < S_{12} \le b;\ b < S_{13} \le c;$ and $c < S_{14}$. For LP purposes this will be converted to

$$S_{11} \ge 0;\ S_{11} \le a \tag{1}$$
$$S_{12} \ge 0;\ S_{12} \le b - a \tag{2}$$
$$S_{13} \ge 0;\ S_{13} \le c - b \tag{3}$$
$$S_{14} \ge 0 \tag{4}$$

In this case, as a result of the diminishing returns, or saturation effects, three new constraints have been allowed to enter the picture. They indicate that the mix can contain a greater number of activities. The fourth is simply an-other feasibility requirement.

Management decisions must be rendered in the light of the results we have just examined. The economics of recognizing complex objectives interacts with the character of the system and with managerial values, since objectives are statements of value. The existence of one goal frequently creates the need for others to exist (e.g., *The Monkey's Paw*). And the nature and number of objectives, in turn, will influence all activities of management. Furthermore, if management pursues its activities to levels of diminishing returns, then this behavior produces new values through partitioning. The new constraints tend to force management to enlarge its activity mix rather than to continue to pursue a few activities to ultimate saturation. Such principles and theory are significant managerial developments of recent years.

SUMMARY

This chapter presents a study of how objectives influence the managerial process. To begin, organizational objectives are identified by an *intersection* of many participating individuals' roles and goals. Conflicts occurring at the intersection, for various reasons, can produce rapid changes in the structure of the organization's objectives. (The story of the Kwakiutl Indians is introduced because it provides an excellent illustration of the dynamics of such change.)

Environments are identified as being composed of those objectives of individuals that fall *outside* the intersection. These environments influence, and are influenced by, the organizational objectives. The environments tend to produce a multiplicity of complex organizational objectives. When such complex objectives are not recognized, serious problems can result. *The Monkey's Paw* illustrates this vital point, which is frequently overlooked in organizational as well as individual statements of objectives. Single objectives are liable to be superficial and even spurious with respect to the actual underlying objectives of the organization.

Management ethics are the foundation for all management objectives. But ethical goals are not entirely consistent with one another. Neither are they shared equally by all members of society. As a result, multiple objectives and conflicts between objectives exist. Spurious objectives also exist and often can be attributed to unreasoned ethical positions. Management self-awareness begins with a conscious understanding of existing ethics and of the dynamics of change. Toward this end, the influences of ethics with respect to management objectives for the consumer, labor, the community, and stockholders are examined in some detail.

Complex objectives can seldom be treated by simple models. A satisfactory model must be able to interrelate and synthesize them. It cannot maximize the attainment of a simplistic objective, because this procedure is likely to result in inferior performance of the total system. Therefore, the notion of a parsimonious solution is introduced, by which we mean an approach that is "just complex enough" to satisfy the manager's needs (or, alternatively, "not simpler" than what is needed to do the job).

Three approaches to parsimonious solutions for complex problems are presented: first, reduction of the multiple dimensions to a single dimension (without, however, discarding any of the objectives); second, use of a dimensional analysis; and, third, use of a programming format. Each of these approaches is discussed in some detail. When feasible, the use of mathematical transformations to a single objective is most desirable. An example of such a model is the breakeven chart, which combines a number of objectives in a model of single dimension. Unfortunately, however, this approach cannot be applied in many cases. Its applicability breaks down when certain multiple objectives contained by the model begin to conflict with one another instead of working together. Sometimes a decision model can resolve this problem by means of the expected-value criterion. Yet even the decision model under risk is shown to contain a complex-objective problem. There is always the question of whether or not the manager wishes to recognize the problem. The nonlinear breakeven model is introduced, illustrating the normative property of a best percentage of capacity at which to operate. Since it is an optimizing model, it introduces yet another aspect of unifying models for complex objectives. Then a discounting model is presented to illustrate an important problem of complex objectives for which management has found a reasonable solution. Another approach is to determine psychological utility transformations so that multiple dimensions can all be evaluated on a single scale. Although this resolution of complex-objective problems is widely used (especially by marketing management), it is fraught with difficulties.

Methods of dimensional analysis are described as another major means of treating complex objectives. Generally, a variety of scales exists to describe the qualities, preferences for, and performances of the alternatives. The question of how to combine such a multiplicity of scales is addressed, and one often-used way is shown to be frequently incorrect.

The third approach suggested for treating complex objectives is that of mathematical programming. In this case, one of the objectives is selected as being the most important one, and it alone is to be set at an optimal value. All the other objectives are treated as constraints upon it.

None of the three methods can be guaranteed to fit any situation. In various circumstances, complex objectives cannot be treated by any method. But, among the three that have been described in this chapter, a great number of important variants are covered. Above all, the nature of complex objectives should be evident.

EXERCISES

1. Comment on these assertions:
   a. "One seldom holds to objectives he believes to be unobtainable."
   b. "People have a strong tendency to think that their objectives are far simpler than they really are."
   c. "People generally lack an awareness of how highly interconnected their own objectives are."

d. "An individual frequently chooses objectives for superficial reasons."

e. "Little thought is given to the need to differentiate between the intensities with which individuals wish to satisfy their objectives."

2. In what way does the story *The Monkey's Paw* illustrate the fact that multiple objectives are so frequently intertwined that they are not recognized as being several? Give some instances in which this characteristic of multiple objectives creates unforeseen problems. (Note: O. Henry was a master writer of such situations.)

3. Comment on the importance of management's awareness of ethics. Would you agree with the argument that ethics for management are fundamentally an economic issue? Explain your answer. Is there any difference between societal ethics for management and management's ethics for society? List some ethical considerations that might illuminate this discussion. Try to introduce ethical issues that have not been mentioned in the text.

4. A consumer injured by a pressure cooker that exploded during use collected a substantial amount from the store that sold it to her. Although the accompanying instructions indicated that it must be used correctly to be safe, the sales clerk, when questioned, had stated that it was absolutely safe. Such cases support a requirement of adequate warning against hazards by both the manufacturer and the retailer. What kind of ethical problem is involved? Can you give any examples of how this consideration might affect other products?

5. Certain industries create significant pollution and contamination. For example, the existence of paper production is often recognizable, before any facilities are seen, by the gray-white coating on the landscape for miles around. Sulphur-using factories can be identified by odors, drop-forge operations by noise. Clearly, such industries are essential, providing needed products and employment. What, then, can their managements do about their responsibilities to the community? Relate this to management's responsibilities to labor.

6. Discuss the statement that management is ethically responsible to its stockholders to consistently uphold the value of the company's stock.

7. Why has the air-transport industry used breakeven considerations—specifically, load factors—in making decisions about equipment alternatives? Can the same argument be applied to computer usage?

8. If fixed costs are $100,000, total variable cost at 100 percent of capacity is $50,000, and the revenue at 100 percent of capacity is $200,000, what is the breakeven point? Assume that all relationships are linear over the entire capacity range. What is the relationship of this problem to complex objectives?

9. Assume that an alternative to the strategy of Exercise 8 is the following: fixed costs are $40,000, total variable costs (at 100 percent of capacity) are $125,000, and the revenue is unchanged. Why is this an example of complex objectives reasserting themselves?

10. Let the probability of the percentage of capacity utilized in Exercise 9 be distributed uniformly. Does this take care of the problem of complex objectives? What solution is indicated? Does the answer change if the distribution is more nearly of the normal type? (Hint: Rearrange the probabilities by hand and judge by eye.)

11. What complex-objective problem always exists for DMUR? Give some examples in which conflict between these objectives might have a significant impact.

12. Under what circumstances would the nonlinear form of breakeven analysis apply? How do these differ from those situations in which the linear form is appropriate? Why does nonlinearity change the fundamental character of the problem of objectives?

13. How does the discounting model qualify as a means of unifying complex objectives? Why is this an important model that has been used widely by management?

14. What is the present worth of
   a. $500 paid as a single sum, 5 years hence? (The interest rate is 10 percent per year.)
   b. $500 paid out in equal amounts over a 5-year period? (The interest rate remains at 10 percent per year.)

15. What is the basis for using dimensional analysis as a means of resolving complex-objectives problems? Discuss the concept of dimensional consistency as it applies to the manager's job.

16. Deep-C Divers, Inc., has been expanding its production of snorkels, masks, and scuba equipment in response to increasing demand. The present plant (rented) is far too small. The company has to move, and it has been agreed that a simple but attractive one-story plant will be built. The only question is where.

Jones and Dugin are equal partners in the company. They have always gotten along well together. They are in complete accord that Los Angeles is the right place, but they are at odds concerning the location in Los Angeles where they should build. Being reasonable men, they agree to a procedure suggested by their plant manager.

First, a list of all feasible sites in and around Los Angeles is prepared. Next, Jones and Dugin rank these sites according to their preferences. (The rank assignment of 1 is considered to be best.) The plant manager then proposes that the site that maximizes the combined preferences of the two partners be the one chosen. The relevant data are shown below.

Site	Preferences		Distance from center (miles)
	Jones	Dugin	
1	4	7	7
2	2	3	4
3	1	5	3
4	7	4	12
5	6	2	5
6	5	6	10
7	3	1	6

    a. What location would this approach select? (Note: The definition of "combined preference" is not specified.)

    b. Is there any apparent relation between each man's preferences and the distances of the sites from the center of Los Angeles?

    c. What is your opinion of this approach? It may help you to know that Jones and Dugin discarded the solution that the plant manager obtained. They are still in a quandary—and they have not yet chosen a new site. What would you suggest?

17. How does the concept of linear programming relate to the resolution of problems with complex objectives? Why might it be said to be a compromise solution? Discuss the possibility and significance of two executives choosing different variables to be optimized. They might also elect to use different constraints. What might that mean?

18. A diet problem (say, for cattle feed) requires analysis of the following data:

	Ingredient 1	Ingredient 2	Minimum daily requirements
Vitamin x:	.01 units per lb.	.02 units per lb.	1.6 units
Mineral y:	.10 units per oz.	.15 units per oz.	22.0 units
Cost:	10¢ per lb.	16¢ per lb.	

Solve this problem for minimum cost using the geometric approach to LP.

Part III

PLANNING

The Framework of Managing

MODEL-BUILDING AND MODEL USE

DECISION-MAKING

PART III
PLANNING

The ability to plan conciously may be the most
distinctive feature of man. Every person plans, but
striking differences among people and cultures can be
noted on the basis of three factors: the planning methods
used, the detailed richness of the plans, and the extent
of the period ahead (called the planning horizon) for which
the plans are drawn.

Sometimes major rewards come unexpectedly and without planning —like the inheritance of a stupendous fortune from an unknown great-uncle or the kind of good luck associated with serendipity, whereby, as the result of one activity, a related but unexpected benefit for another activity is obtained. Roentgen discovered X-rays because a photographic plate that had not been exposed to light was mistakenly developed and revealed an image. Scotch tape, originally intended for book-mending, unexpectedly dwarfed that market with its other applications.

Unexpected success is no less destructive of the rational view of corporate activity than is unexpected failure. . . . When the new plastic, designed for a cheaper molding process, turns out to perform well in a completely different application—the corporate manager can only react with a wry smile. In ways he did not understand, and was unable to state before the fact, things have gone well; but what has he learned that will prepare him to cope with the next time?[1]

We like to think that the highest rewards go to those who plan and that attention to the future brings benefits even in the small events of everyday life. In our society, because of its structure and values, planning is a compulsive activity; we take for granted that it is good to plan. But we are not clear as to what good planning is. Does good planning mean that the future is accurately predicted and adequately prepared for? Or does it mean that an intended future state is brought to pass?

According to Edmund Burke, "You can never plan the future by the past." How then *can* you plan the future? How can we reconcile our emphasis on planning with the fact that Edmund Burke, a statesman of considerable knowledge and sophistication, dismissed the ability to plan on the basis of what has happened in the past? Before we can understand the managerial function of planning, we must recognize that there is a great deal of confusion about this function and that a variety of meanings can be associated with the term "planning." We plan an evening out, plan to be at the office early, lay out the plans for a nuclear power plant, plan to achieve a 10 percent increase in sales volume next year.

The term *planning* is a dressing gown (also called an omnibus word)—it fits many wearers. In the next three chapters we shall delve into some of the fundamental meanings associated with planning. We shall try to distinguish between the various levels of planning as they are representative of the many meanings of the term.

---

[1] Reprinted from *Technology and Change* by Donald A. Schon. Copyright © 1967 by Donald A. Schon. A Seymour Lawrence Book/Delacorte Press. Used by permission.

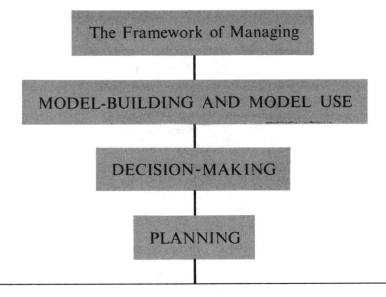

The Framework of Managing

MODEL-BUILDING AND MODEL USE

DECISION-MAKING

PLANNING

Chapter 8
The Framework of Planning

The term "planning" is generally used ambiguously by
managers, but a rational definition of planning can be
obtained by contrasting plans and policies. A key factor
is the degree to which decision environments are repetitive.
Stable, recurrent environments lend themselves to
policy formulation, whereas transient environments (i.e.,
those unlikely to recur) require planning. Three types
of planning are examined: The first type, called fully constrained,
appears when the future environments can be predicted
with a high degree of certainty; partially constrained planning,
the second type, is needed when contingencies can occur
because some future environments cannot be predicted with
certainty; the third type, threshold-constrained planning,
arises when the occurrence of a future environment could
produce catastrophic results.

Chapter 8

THE FRAMEWORK
OF PLANNING

THE STATE OF THE ART

Planning is understood by executives only in the most general terms, and discussion about it produces at best a vague communion. When a group of managers are pressed to be specific, their confusion about the word emerges. This situation invites our speculation. Perhaps the term "planning" is used so often because of its attenuated power to communicate and not despite it. No doubt the vagueness is appreciated by managers who fear that more of their time could be consumed in defining planning than would be spent in doing it. But the vagueness is also a distraction, and the flexibility it preserves might readily be obtained in other, less confusing, ways. Moreover, while the intuitive side of management might be able to live with such vagueness, the scientific approach cannot operate constructively with it.

Any conscientious review of the literature on planning models would indicate that what management needs has little resemblance to what has been delivered by management scientists. Although there are a few notable exceptions, planning belongs to a class of models with which management scientists are least familiar. The difficulty of developing adequate planning models becomes more significant as the urgency of using planning methodology increases in the upper managerial levels. Part of the explanation for this state of affairs rests with management scientists, who have not really become involved in planning for the enterprise. On the other hand, management has added to the problem by resisting the incursion of scientific method into the inner sanctum of the upper-management planning function. Though there is general agreement concerning the importance of the planning function, any change in the respective roles and relationships of the model-builders and model-users must be motivated by increased mutual understanding.[1]

DEFINITION OF THE PLANNING FUNCTION

In common usage, a plan is a scheme or method of action. Planning, then, is selecting a particular set of feasible decisions from among a number of alternative sets. Consequently, decision-making authority is an essential ingredient of the planning function. And, as in decision-making, without alternatives we cannot say that we are planning anything. As a matter of fact, our definition of a plan is similar to that of a *strategy*. When an executive says, "That is my plan," frequently he is referring to a strategy.

Decision-making, however, is not a sufficient description of planning, and managers understand that the planning strategy possesses certain specific characteristics that distinguish it from other decision strategies. We can begin at this point to make the distinction by stating that the planning type of decision is one that takes into account the imperfect stability of the environments and the possibility of changes in their probabilities of occurrence.

When the term "planning" is used to refer to a future that is more than six months ahead, it is very likely that the planners are situated in the upper hierarchical levels of the organization. Longer reaches in planning functions are found in upper managerial regions; at the lower levels, planning is done for relatively restricted time intervals. Yet planning occurs in both the long- and short-term cases, so the period of time is not directly at issue when planning is being defined.

Further, we can observe that a useful definition of planning should define not only that part of decision-making which is planning but also that part which is not. Fortunately, current knowledge about decision environments and their stability can be used in this way to reduce the confusion that surrounds the meaning of planning.

---

[1] See C. West Churchman and A. H. Schainblatt, "The Researcher and the Manager: A Dialectic of Implementation," *Management Science,* Vol. 11, No. 4 (February 1965), pp. 69–87, and the response to this article, a symposium published in *Management Science,* Vol. 12, No. 2 (October 1965), pp. 1–42.

Plans and Policies

Let us first compare planning and policy-making. The planning function is found at all levels of the management ladder, but the planning horizon broadens, and the importance of the plans increases, as we go up that ladder. A pyramid effect occurs, in which plans at each hierarchical level limit the scope of plans at lower levels. Operating policies, which can also be formulated at all managerial levels, are subject to the same kind of pyramidal constraint. Policies become broader in their scope, and management becomes more sensitive to their importance, as their point of origination moves up the hierarchical ladder.

How, then, do plans and policies differ? To begin with, policies are sensed by members of the system to be directives sent down as rules to be followed. Plans, on the other hand, are not easily perceived or communicated. The oldest precedent for this division is biblical—the policies of the Ten Commandments were carried down from the mountain, while the planning function remained on top.

Pursuing this analogy, we might point out that *plans are transformed into policies.* Often, however, the plan may not be known, although numerous policies derived from it are clearly spelled out. The policies may, in fact, force the creation of an objective statement of the plan rather than being derived from it. Nevertheless, management's intent, whether or not it is rational, is to have policies follow plans. Moreover, the manager sees planning models as preceded by forecasts, which are used as the basis for planning. This linear relationship between forecasts, plans, and policies is illustrated in Figure 8–1.

If, however, we draw the feedback links shown in the figure between policies and plans, between policies and forecasts, and between plans and forecasts, a number of complexities become apparent. First, it becomes difficult to identify which come first, plans or policies. Undoubtedly, this ambiguity is closer to reality than the belief that policies simply follow plans. Second, we can see that policies are more closely associated with plans than with forecasts. Third, it is clear that forecasts are affected by plans and somewhat

Figure 8–1

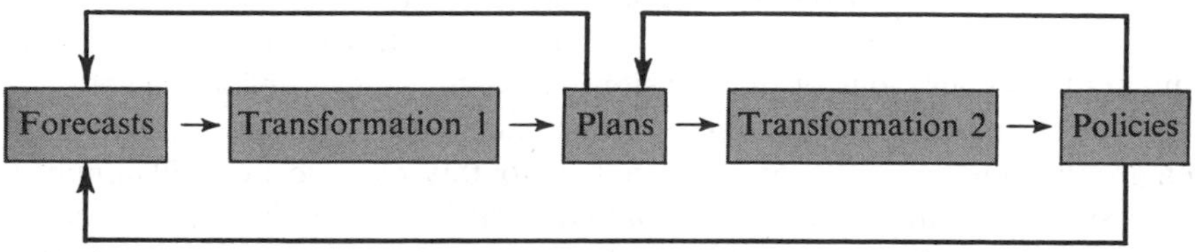

less by policies. These are typical of the interrelations that occur when feed-back is recognized. Unfortunately, in the context of planning, feedback too frequently is overlooked. As a result, a record of the continuing interaction that takes place between the manager and the system is lost.

Ultimately, the utility of the management principles that can be developed depends on a wider range of systems types than we recognize at present. In line with this, we shall now turn our attention to the description of systems properties that affect the manager's decision as to whether he should "plan to plan" or plan to make policy instead.

Basic building blocks—unit decisions. Decision-making activities can be divided into (1) the formulation of policy (for recurrent situations) and (2) the development of plans (for transient situations). Shortly, we shall spell out in some detail the definitions of "recurrent" and "transient." First, however, since the base components of a plan *or* a policy are *simple unit decisions,* let us briefly define these.

1. *At least two* possible strategies, x_i's, exist. Strategy variables are controlled by the decision-maker.
2. There are *one or more* "effective" environments, z_j's. Environmental variables are not under the decision-maker's control.
3. A set of results, or outcomes, can be observed for each combination of a particular strategy and a particular environment: $R_{ij} = f(x_i, z_j)$.
4. The environments are distinctly individual and mutually exclusive. Accordingly, for each environment $(j = 1, \ldots, n)$, we can attempt to estimate the probability of occurrence: Prob p_j. We do so, however, with varying levels of success; a degree of belief is always associated with the estimates.
5. For each unit decision, only one of the strategies can be used at any one time.
6. A particular decision criterion is invoked to select from the total set of available choices the one strategy that will maximize the decision-maker's achievement of his objectives—for example, select that x_i which produces Max $\sum_j$ Prob $p_j R_{ij}$.

Policy controls versus planning investments. The plan or the policy is a set containing one or more unit decisions. By identifying significantly different configurations of the decision elements, we can divide the total class of decision models into planning models and policy models. The degree of environmental repetition provides a key to this classification. *Planning sets are associated with evolving environments, policy sets with repetitive ones.*

Let us be more specific. When the same type of unit decision problem *occurs repeatedly,* the situation can be categorized as a policy situation. The phrase "the same type of unit decision problem" is not meant to imply that the same problem, requiring an identical answer, repeats itself. It is intended to convey the idea that the initial decision elements are stable, remaining relevant and unchanged as the decision problem repeats itself. As a result, the *same decision functions* continue to be applicable over time. Under sufficiently repetitive circumstances—defined in terms of frequency and time span —it becomes economically reasonable to formulate a policy. The economic basis for differentiating between policies and plans is what makes this distinction so relevant to managers.

The issue is one of degree, however, and not one of rigorous definition. The conditions that describe "sufficient repetition" may be sensibly relaxed, in terms of economic effect, without changing the situation from one of policy to one of planning. For example, a stable decision system might be *improved* by obtaining additional information that alters the number and nature of the environments as well as the likelihood estimates. Such modification of a policy-type situation would not be likely to necessitate changing it into a planning problem. Similarly, a decision format may be expanded without changing its status—simply by adding new strategies to the original set. This represents a potential policy shift, but not a change to planning.

Policies, in these terms, are preplanned, deferred decisions waiting to be activated by the occurrence of the specific situations for which they were designed. To render a set of policies operational, it is necessary to design and construct a policy-control unit (mechanical, human, or both) that can perform a required set of functions. The controller is instructed concerning what to observe, how to measure, how to respond to error, when to initiate operation, and how and when to follow up on it. These attributes of policy control mirror the repetitive character of the system to which they are assigned. And the standards for policy control are assumed either to be unchanging or to change in a predetermined pattern. Therefore, when a policy-control unit is installed, the decision stages for implementation are nonrepetitive. So control implementation, by these definitions, requires planning methodology. Prepackaged decision systems have been designed and implemented for such situations as controlling aircraft in flight, maintaining the temperature of chemical reactions, and changing machine settings in accordance with predetermined standards of performance.

It is sensible to use policy control only when the range of situations $z_j(j = 1, \ldots, n)$ can be anticipated with relative certainty. (The number of perceived states included within the range will be determined by the sensitivity of the monitor's perception and should be a function of the precision considered necessary for adequate control, as determined by economic criteria.) Strategies can be prepared and then stored to deal with known situations as they arise. The less likely specific occurrences become, the more speculative and the less economically justified is the application of policy-control models. Therefore, when the situation is not clear-cut, a decision must always be made to go one way or the other. This requires a comparison between the following:

1. Assuming recurrent environments: Develop the cost of preparing *policies,* based on forecasts of recurrent environments; the cost of enforcing policies with appropriate control units; the benefits that can be expected from using this procedure; and the penalty for not assuming that transient events exist.

2. Assuming transient environments: Develop the cost of *planning* for a trajectory of events by means of forecasts for a sequence of transient events; the cost of tracking the trajectory of events with schedule-control units;[2] the benefits that can be expected from using this procedure; and the penalty for not assuming that recurrent events exist.

If the decision is to accept the hypothesis of recurrent environments and to develop a policy-control system, it must still be recognized that there are occasions when the package of predesigned strategies has to be superseded. Often this takes place because a transient element, a new z_j, temporarily enters the system, not because the basic set of environments changes. If a significant new element becomes a permanent part of the system or if new transients appear frequently in it, then a modification will be required in the design of the control system.

With planning models, on the other hand, the transient is the rule and not the exception. Since the environments are expected to evolve over time, any *one* control action can be used only *once* (or a few times at most) and then must be discarded. Generally, it would not be economical to design a control system that could deal repetitively with nonrepetitive situations. Additional strategies have to be introduced into the decision system at appropriate moments to cope successfully with the new environments as they appear. If the appearance of new environments has been correctly anticipated, then the plan should achieve the best possible result under the circumstances that occur. If other than the anticipated set of events should occur, revisions in plans must follow—assuming that sufficient latitude exists to permit such dynamic adaptability.

In the planning situation, sequential sets of unit decisions that are different from one another are expected. Age, measured by $T,$ is by definition a nonrepetitive environmental factor. Under some circumstances, T can be transformed to behave as if it were a repetitive variable—for example, clock time or calendar time.[3] Economic justification is required for either option. The relevance of the temporal stream in planning models contrasts with static decision situations in which environments are not evolving and in which

---

[2] See pp. 329–30 and p. 458.

[3] If one ignores the passage of years, the calendar also repeats itself.

changes in strategy are introduced to maintain control in the face of a well-known range of disturbances. Dynamically evolving environments are the essence of what we mean by a "planning situation." That is why planning models should include procedures for developing, implementing, and modifying plans.

A More Formal Definition of Planning

A more rigorous basis for the distinction between policy and planning can be given by introducing some simple notation commonly associated with the theory of recurrent events.[4]

1. Assume that the jth environment has just occurred and is the state of the system at time T_0.
2. Let $f_j^{(n)}$ be the probability that the *first return* to the state z_j occurs at the nth time period, T_n.
3. Then $f_j = \sum_{n=1}^{n=\infty} f_j^{(n)}$ is the total probability that the system *will ever return* to the environment j.
4. Further, $m_j = \sum_{n=1}^{n=\infty} nf_j^{(n)}$ will be the mean recurrence time of the state z_j. One possible example of this is shown in Figure 8–2.

The figure shows the probability distribution for the first return to the initial state occurring in the nth time period. If the area under the curve for all values of n does not equal one, then there is a probability that the system will never return to the initial state. This situation is discussed below. The average of the distribution is $\bar{n}$, which is described in point 4, above, as m_j, the mean recurrence time.

Recurrent events. Stringent policy models can be defined as those in which a set of environmental states is perfectly known and highly repetitive; thus, $f_j = 1$ and $m_j <<< \infty$ for all environments of the set. This means that the system is closed with respect to environments, and all of them are *certain* to repeat themselves within a reasonable time period. Under these circumstances, it is likely that a deferred-decision control unit can be designed to handle economically the policy affairs of this system. Each environment for

---

[4] For elaboration of this theory see William Feller, *An Introduction to Probability Theory and Its Applications,* 2nd ed., Vol. 1 (New York: Wiley, 1957), Chap. 13.

Figure 8–2

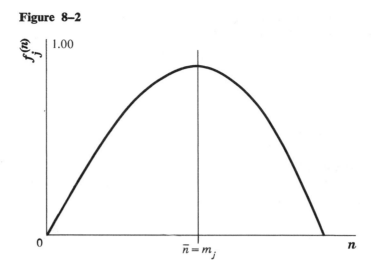

which $f_j = 1$ can be described as a *recurrent state*—one that is certain to occur repeatedly.

Periodic and null events. On the other hand, the pattern of the system returning to its initial state may be recurrent only periodically, or it may be recurrent in the null sense. A *periodic* environment will repeat itself in a cyclical fashion over time. Various policy systems have been designed to deal with regular, periodic fluctuations—for example, the entire theory of business cycles is related to such patterns of regularity. The *null state* exists when the mean recurrence time, m_j, is infinite—in other words, even though the environment promises to repeat itself, the expected elapsed time between repeats is infinitely long. In such situations, it is improbable that an investment in the development of policy and in the construction of a control system would be warranted; a sensible balancing of all relevant costs would militate against the policy-control approach under null circumstances.

Transient events. There is still less likelihood that the cost of a policy to cope with z_j's for which $0 < f_j < 1$ will be justified because of the uncertainty of their recurrence. An event falling within this range of uncertain recurrence is called a *transient event*. The payoff for policies designed to deal with transient environments will be a function of the distribution of f_j values. When the f_j's are distributed over a narrow range, a policy is more likely to be justified if the mean $\bar{f}$ (taken across f_j for all j environments) is close to 1 than if $\bar{f} = .40$. On the other hand, whenever the variance of the distribution is large, policy controls might be warranted for only part of the system—say, for those environments where $f_j \geq .95$. Thus, the part of the system's states that conforms to policy controls would receive relatively automatic or preprogrammed treatment. The remainder, being viewed as an exception, would require the personal attention of the manager—who may or may not have developed his plans in terms of such eventualities.[5]

Issues of this kind, when discussed in economic terms, provide a fertile area for *researching* the policy/planning interface. All else remaining constant, as $\bar{f}$ decreases, approaching zero, it should become increasingly difficult to justify the use of policy. Also, as the variance increases, it becomes easier to consider *partitioning* a system into policy segments and planning domains. There are substantial theoretical reasons why such system partition can be successfully achieved. There are also practical ones, in that the parts of the system that have repeating patterns tend to be noticed quickly by an intuitive manager and isolated by him so he can take advantage of the regularity he has observed.

When $\bar{f}$ is small, the procedures comprised by planning models will generally be economical because of the strongly nonrepetitive character of such evolving systems. Similarly, as $\bar{m}$ increases (considering the distribution of m_j's with respect to all j environments), the use of planning methods is indicated. But, ultimately, these descriptions of the measures are only approximations of the extent to which a system qualifies for planning. Similarly, the decision of what is not to be treated as a planning problem may also be an approximation of the recurrent (non-null) and periodic conditions required for policy control.

Reusable strategies. One more distinction between policy and planning models should be noted. Contrast these strategies:

S_1: Ship part x (reusable as long as x is in stock, after which it must be replenished).

S_2: Change heading two degrees (reusable on command).

S_3: Blow up bridge (nonreusable).

S_4: Maintain sixteen man-hours of repair skill per day (used up automatically with the passage of time but self-replenishing).

It is characteristic of policy models that the same set of strategies will usually suffice for each repetition of the problem. Often, the resources for the strategies do not have to be replenished, as in S_2 above. In other words, the tools, instruments, power, and materials of such strategies may be reusable when they can be stored as inventory of one form or another. But for planning models it is only coincidental when the same strategy can be used more than once. Note

---

[5] Management by exception will be discussed in greater detail in Chapter 11.

strategy S_3 above. It does not come as a surprise that the environmental conditions for planning discourage carrying inventories of the materials used for planning strategies. On the other hand, we note that for certain kinds of policy, the resources for the policy strategies do not have to be replenished (S_2), while in other cases they do require direct action for replenishing (S_1) or are self-replenishing (S_4). Therefore, that a relationship exists between strategic structure and the behavior of the environments in a system does not come as a surprise. We can further differentiate between planning and policy-making by noticing how the manager handles the inventory of resources associated with the various strategy patterns of the policy and planning models involved.

TYPES OF PLANNING MODEL

Now that we have divided management systems into policy models and planning models, we can turn our classification efforts to differentiating between various forms of planning model.

We can classify planning models into three basic types, which are listed below and explained briefly. They will constitute the focus of our attention in Chapters 9 and 10.

1. *Fully constrained planning systems* (epitomized by determinate, plan-scheduling models) are based on preparedness for a unique chain of events, which we can call a *single planning path*. They are more compelling for their power to describe the technological phases of an existing plan than for their methodological assistance in creating a plan.

2. *Partially constrained planning systems* are based on the preparation for various possible chains of events, which we can call *alternative planning paths*. They are significantly closer to the planning reality than are fully constrained systems. Consequently, they are more complex, and, because of this, they are methodologically underdeveloped, requiring investments in research and development. At the present time, much interest is focused on the use of simulation procedures in partially constrained systems, even though such systems are amenable to statistical analysis. These simulations utilize heuristic methods, which, it will be remembered, are rules of thumb developed from experience. The heuristics are employed to help create the plans. Such an approach operates partly in the sense of traditional science and partly in that of such art forms as sculpture and architecture.

3. *Threshold-constrained planning systems* are distinguished by their relatively high level of vulnerability to ruin. These models are a special class of partially constrained planning systems, which, as previously stated, require alternative planning paths. They span what are called corporate planning,

master planning, and long-range planning. The state of this art is even more rudimentary than those we have described before.

At this point, these descriptions convey only a limited sense of the purpose for which they are intended. However, by emphasizing the nature of the planning system's constraint, we shall be in a better position to discuss the planner's attitudes as they relate to strategic structures, environmental configurations, and the motivating forces of goals and payoffs.

Policy Planning Map

At this point, it will be useful to offer a diagrammatic representation of the policy/planning dichotomy and the three classes of planning model (see Figure 8–3). Although it is a simple map, it succeeds in providing a visual recapitulation of materials that must otherwise remain verbal or mathematical. An annotated form of this diagram is shown in Figure 8–4. It utilizes some of the terminology that will be developed at a later point and may be convenient to refer back to while reading Chapters 9 and 10.

WHY THE MANAGER PLANS

In the preceding material we have attempted to show that every system has its own environmental characteristics. On the basis of these properties, we can differentiate between the managerial functions to determine whether planning

Figure 8–3

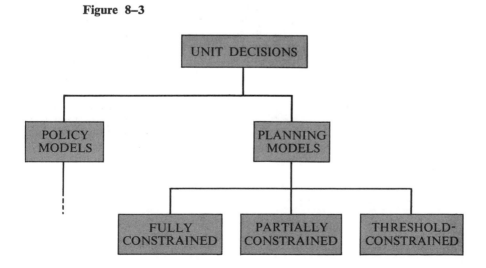

Figure 8–4

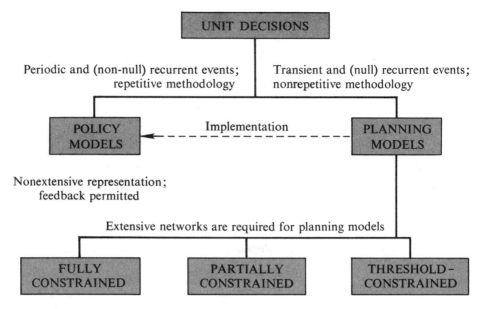

UNIT DECISIONS

Periodic and (non-null) recurrent events; repetitive methodology

Transient and (null) recurrent events; nonrepetitive methodology

POLICY MODELS   ← — — — — — Implementation — — — — — — —   PLANNING MODELS

Nonextensive representation; feedback permitted

Extensive networks are required for planning models

FULLY CONSTRAINED

PARTIALLY CONSTRAINED

THRESHOLD– CONSTRAINED

- The strategic sequence is settled.
- Environmental configurations are considered to be perfectly predictable.
- All network paths are set down with certainty and all must be completed.

- The strategic sequence is tentative.
- Environmental configurations are ascertained as dynamic forecasts or alternative predictions.
- Some network paths are stochastic; from a given junction point either one or another path—but not both—can be followed.

- The strategic sequence is speculative.
- Environmental configurations are ascertained as dynamic forecasts or alternative predictions.
- Some of the potential payoffs are catastrophic.
- Network branches that are associated with probabilities of RUIN that are in excess of some value define a ruin path, which must be discarded.
- Ruin paths are more likely to appear when a large percentage of total assets are involved in the planning decisions.

or policy-making is more appropriate to a given system. At the same time, managerial attitudes play an overriding role in determining whether planning will be used and, if so, to what end. The purposes for which management plans generally can be matched to the manager's view of the system's characteristics, and these may not be apparent from a simple analysis of the recurrence properties of the environments. For example, we can list the following kinds of intention:

1. To prepare for eventualities—to forecast what is inevitable, probable, possible, improbable, and impossible. (According to Sherlock Holmes, "After we have eliminated the impossible, that which remains, however improbable, must be truth.")
   a. To prepare for the inevitable—that is, to accept the riskless part of the future and be ready for its occurrence.
   b. To prepare for the probable— that is, to select those events that appear to have a high likelihood of occurrence, and to do something about them.
   c. To prepare for the possible, where this category is defined as ranging between the probable and the improbable.
   d. To prepare for the improbable. (Management is not usually thought of as participating in such doomsday activities, but there is always room for exception.)
2. Not to accept eventualities and instead to tap potentialities that exist to make the future.
   a. To develop an early warning system in order to be able to take steps to avoid undesirable events and, thereby, to change one's own particular future, though not the actual course of future events.
   b. To gain control over the environments and the forces that are nominally accepted as being uncontrollable. This is achieved by new technology or behavioral knowledge and is therefore based on research and development.
   c. To determine the degree of change in objectives that will be required or desirable to alter the value of future events. By modifying traditions, customs, and expectations, perceptions of what occurs in the future will be changed. At the end of the spectrum, the manager can plan to maintain the status quo (essentially to deal with what is reparable—"the finger in the dike" and other holding strategies). At the other extreme, revolutionary changes in objectives can be sought. In the broad middle ground there are evolutionary changes in objectives.

Figure 8–5

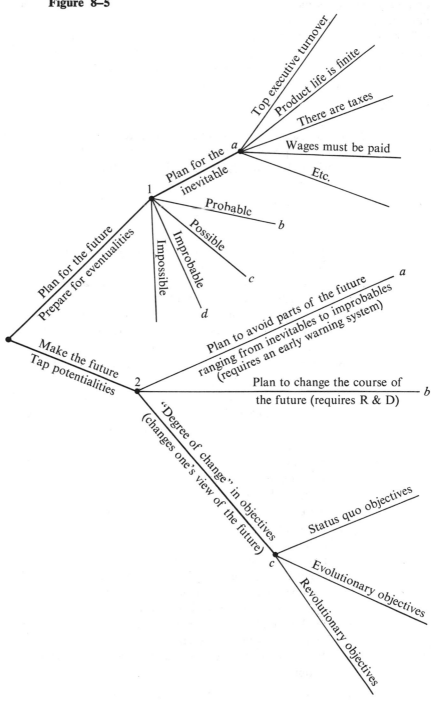

We have constructed a planning tree (Figure 8–5) to portray these planning alternatives. It offers the advantages of a visual construction of the taxonomy we have been discussing, and it encourages the consideration of additional branches, such as those growing out of node 1-*a*.

The Planning Compromise

By the *planning compromise* we mean that managers do not restrict themselves to one or the other of the main branches of the planning tree (Figure 8–5) but mix preparedness for a forecasted future with efforts to make certain futures come to pass. To achieve this goal, they operate on all branches and at all levels of the tree, as seems appropriate.

Removing impossibilities. The forecasting process sorts out, into different groups ranging from the inevitable to the impossible, the relative likelihoods that the different situations will occur. Management's first logical step is to remove from consideration those environments categorized as impossible. The remaining range of potential happenings spans the improbable and the inevitable. Strategies and their required resources can then be assembled to meet the entire set, or some subset, of the remaining eventualities. In most cases, it is impossible to think of preparing for all eventualities. At the upper management levels, it is equally unusual to prepare for just one potential future.

Preparing for the inevitable. An entirely reasonable approach is to determine what is "inevitable" and then to figure out how best to take advantage of that knowledge.[6] Certainly, within the set of future eventualities, that which is inevitable provides some of both the greatest dangers and the greatest potential benefits. Since it is the riskless part of the system, management can assume it as a fixed basis for planning. It can decide to steer either around inevitables or directly toward them, depending on the benefits or penalties involved. At the same time, a cautious question begins to emerge as to how really inevitable some set of events may be. We have good reason to accept inevitables only as a point of view that might be changed by managerial creativity.

---

[6] "I one time heard Russ Ackoff describe good planning as a two step process. First, he said, you figure out what is inevitable. Then you find a way to take advantage of it. That seems to be pretty good advice, and I've used it to great advantage more than once." Quote taken from Kenneth Longman, "Marketing Science," *Management Science,* Vol. 15, No. 2 (October 1968).

Planning for the inevitable should certainly be one of the first phases of all managerial planning. If, in fact, management sees no way to change the course of events, it should be ready to suffer the least damage or take the most advantage of that which will come. It *is* inevitable, for example, that the members of top management will grow old and have to be replaced. It is nearly inevitable that existing products in certain competitive industries will experience a falling-off in sales volume. It is also virtually inevitable that strong competition will exist in certain markets. Here we observe degrees of inevitability. The existence of "competition" may be inevitable, but the manner in which it occurs may not. Training an executive to replace the president can be called planning for the inevitable. Having a number of tested and researched products in the background will make the falling-off of a present part of the line less serious. The possibility of planning for the inevitable is not nearly as limited as one might suppose at first, since the plans can take advantage of new potentialities and their eventualities.

Maintaining a familiar, probable future. Many organizations plan so as to ensure maintenance of the status quo. Part of this effort consists in replacing things that are worn out with new things that are identical or as nearly identical as possible. By maintaining the familiar, management hopes to create a high probability that the organization will continue to experience the same forces in the future with which it has been successful in the past.

The unfamiliar generally projects a less predictable future. It offers new opportunities but presents new dangers as well. Because of these dangers, managers often attempt to reduce or subvert innovation. This may seem startling (especially in view of elaborate statements by the same managers to the contrary), but it occurs nevertheless in many managerial systems. Donald A. Schon has pointed out that corporate society pays lip service to innovation, while often firing, demoting, or isolating innovators, reducing the financial support of innovative projects, or oscillating in its position between support and resistance. He states that "the corporation may encourage the development of new product ideas only to find consistently that none of them meets the stringent criteria laid down in advance (just as a mother may want her son to get married but never approves of the girls he brings home)."[7]

Planning based on possibilities. Planning based on forecasting future developments assumes the ability to use the future to one's advantage. Most forecasting, however, deals not only with probable events but with a broad range of possible events, and management can seldom afford to be prepared for all possibilities. What it can do is construct an early warning sys-

---

[7] Donald A. Schon, *Technology and Change* (New York: Delacorte Press, 1967), pp. 70–72.

tem to tell it what may be expected to transpire. Such a system can operate beneficially as long as it provides sufficient lead time to enable management to do something about the warning it has received. Economically sound decisions are necessary to determine how large a share of potential eventualities should be covered by such warning systems and to what degree they must be backed up with resource abilities.

Any warning system is at least one step removed from the events. It can take the form of creating monitors (such as the DEW line) with special instructions to provide warnings when something is changing. In such cases, the result is either to invoke a policy or, if no policy exists for the specific circumstances, to initiate planning. Every management policy system has a deferred planning capability. But if the system is to make sense, there must always be sufficient time to allow the planner to think about what should be done once the signal of an impending change is given.

It is also reasonable to expect that the existence of early warning systems will change the nature of what will happen if there is cognizance that such a system exists. This effect is characteristic of competitors' intelligence systems. Possibilities can be altered by informing an intelligent opponent of the existence of early warning devices.

Another approach for dealing with possibilities is the Delphi method,[8] which pools expert opinions in order to develop a set of potential futures. Each sequence of possible future events can be assigned a probability indicative of its likelihood. Such measures are derived from the consistency, frequency, and interrelation of the independent predictions. As a result, what might be considered at first glance to be an improbable path into the future may turn out to be highly probable when related to the predictions and forecasts of many other disciplines projecting developments for a variety of fields. Moreover, among the possibilities some futures are more probable than others, and these may not be in accord with the preferences of management. However, the relative probabilities of sequences might be altered by operating on some of the controllable elements in a system.

Belief that the future can be changed in a rational way has led to the creation of a number of new organizations. In the United States, The Committee on the Year 2000, supported by The American Academy of Arts and Sciences, is directed by sociologist Daniel Bell. A similar group exists in Britain, and in Europe an important influence has been exercised by political theorist Bertrand de Jouvenel, whose concern with "futurism" has flourished in France, Switzerland, and the Netherlands. The RAND Corporation, the Hudson Institute, the UN, and the U.S. Department of Health, Education, and

---

[8] For one of the foundation statements in this area see Olaf Helmer and Nicholas Rescher, "On the Epistemology of the Inexact Sciences," *Management Science*, Vol. 6, No. 1 (October 1959), pp. 25–52.

Welfare are some other organizations that have undertaken to study the adaptiveness of the future. Underlying these approaches, which "have to do with new ways to analyze, anticipate, and control the social environment,"[9] is the idea that social technicians can help to arrange the future. Many of these future-oriented organizations are founded on the belief that management and government are more interested in spending time making the future than in having it happen to them. Several large companies have gone along with this notion by investing research funds in studies of how they might affect their futures. We can expect to observe an increasing number of these efforts to "analyze, anticipate, and control" the future course of events rather than to just meet the situation.

Preparing for the improbable. Management is far too rational to place a value on serendipity in its balance sheet, nor does it plan for Armageddon. Often, however, one sees real interest in the improbable. For example, numerous company studies have tried to determine "the effects on our business" of a nuclear holocaust, a severe depression, a revolution, and the like. Particular sets of extreme events are not as improbable in some countries as in others. Nevertheless, the difficulty of planning for extreme situations, and particularly those that involve threshold constraints, raises questions concerning the effectiveness of such procedures.

Another aspect of planning for the improbable seems to have a more positive side. Certain funds of an organization go into *pure* research, which is quite unlikely to yield a return in the foreseeable future. Occasionally, however, the improbable comes through, and as a result the company enjoys the existence of nylon, penicillin, or the transistor. The value of such a discovery to the developer is as difficult to predict as the timing of the discovery itself, which makes planning for it a highly questionable activity. But belief in the improbable is a human trait. Therefore, it is irrational to study management's approach to improbable futures in a strictly statistical way. The logic of the situation includes the irresistible qualities of dealing with the unexpected.

Management knows for certain that some improbable events will occur. Part of the planning function is to *anticipate* the unexpected. Yet it is clearly impossible to prepare for even a few such eventualities. What, then, can management do? It can plan in such a way as to remove as many improbables from the situation as possible. In other words, management, through planning, can develop a relationship between the organization and its environment that alters the organization's vulnerability, making it relatively immune to many of the so-called improbable happenings. For example, by signing a contract, management can ignore many unexpected eventualities. Only the probable

---

[9] From Andrew Kopkind, "The Future-Planners," *New Republic*, February 25, 1967, p. 19.

eventualities of the contract must be prepared for directly. (The possible opportunity costs of not being involved in risk ventures, of being tied to the contract conditions, are, of course, a counterbalancing force.)

Forecasting the nature of future events is always a complex matter when the system is evolving and the pattern of change is only partially understood. One way to avoid the penalties of unexpected fluctuations and the perturbations of unexpected happenings is to design a strong course of action that has sufficient momentum to develop in a predictable way despite the sequence of futures that can occur. The contract mentioned above might be an example. The development of product lines (such as cosmetics) that tend to be immune to swings in economic affairs is another example of the ways management can try to override the risk and uncertainty inherent in an "aimless" future. By "aimless" future we mean one that is considered to be improbable and beyond managerial control.

SUMMARY

The intent of this chapter is to define planning as unambiguously as possible. To begin, the state of the art of planning is discussed: management usage of the term is vague, but much more is known than may at first seem apparent.

The definition of planning is aided by distinguishing between plans and policies. Together, all decisions and decision sequences can be explained in terms of this dichotomy. The basic building blocks of both plans and policies are unit decisions. A rapid review of the fundamental decision model is therefore given at this point. This time, however, emphasis is placed on the degree of repetition of the environments and the extent to which their pattern of occurrence can be called stable.

It is recognized that situations seldom exist in which it is clear whether investments should be made in policy-control procedures or in planning. A discussion of this choice and the underlying economic consequences is presented.

Ultimately, a formal basis for defining the planning function is offered in terms of the degree to which events recur. Specifically, the likelihood of environments persisting in a stable pattern or changing over time are classified into: *recurrent events,* which are repetitive and stable; *periodic events,* which are stable in a cyclical pattern; *null events,* which appear unstable in the short run but have stability over a very long period of time; and *transient events,* which are unstable. It is shown that planning is required for transient-event systems and that policy is available only when conditions are sufficiently periodic or recurrent.

Three major planning situation classes and their models are introduced. These are called *fully constrained planning systems, partially constrained planning systems,* and *threshold-constrained planning systems.* The issues are explained only briefly at this time because they are dealt with extensively in Chapters 9 and 10, but a diagrammatic map of these planning and policy functions is presented.

Then a discussion is developed of the different ways that managers plan. These relate to the manager's view of his abilities to contend with the future. Among other things, the discussion touches on preparing for forecasted futures, making the future, removing impossibilities, preparing for the inevitable, maintaining the status quo, heeding early warnings, and preparing for the probable, the possible, and the improbable. A planning tree is presented that portrays these alternatives.

EXERCISES

1. Differentiate between plans and policies in terms of which comes first—that is, their input-output relations as shown in Figure 8–1. Emphasize the feedback potentials that exist as connectives between planning, policy-making, and forecasting. Would you like to see any additional elements included in the figure?

2. Using the concept of the unit decision as a basic building block for plans and policies, describe critical differences in these unit decisions that account for the distinction between policy formulation and the planning function.

3. Categorize the following situations with respect to how stable their environments are likely to be and the degree of repetition that can be anticipated for the relevant environments:
   a. Plans for the expansion of accommodations for a ski lodge.
   b. The control the Coast Guard maintains over the pattern of dispersion of its ships. For how long ahead should the schedule be set?
   c. The policies of the Post Office, concerning the amounts and types of mail that are delivered, and the price of postage stamps.
   d. Planning changes in the size of the maternity ward of a large metropolitan hospital.
   e. Policies for the amount of variety to be handled by the production line of a major automobile manufacturer.

Add an additional example of your own, and discuss the nature of its environments.

4. What types of environment does the Public Health Service deal with? For example, when there is a so-called epidemic of Asian flu, what approach should be taken (planning or policy)? Would a cholera epidemic receive the same treatment? What about an outbreak of the common cold?

5. It is not always entirely clear whether environments should be categorized as recurrent, transient, periodic, or null. In such cases, a reasonable investment decision cannot be made easily about treating the situation as one of planning or policy formulation. Give some examples of when this decision might be difficult to reach and explain how an economic criterion might be used to help.

6. How should a manager deal with periodic events? Why are these classified as policy situations? Give some examples of periodic systems and describe how they are presently treated. (Hint: Remember such periodic systems as night and day, the tides, etc.)

7. Describe the three fundamental types of planning model that are discussed in the text. Give some examples of situations that might be encompassed within each of these categories. Do you see a need for such a taxonomy? Explain.

8. What is meant by "planning to tap the potentials that exist in a system"? Would potentialities be viewed by all managers in the same way? Why could a semantic problem account for confusion in this case?

9. How pervasive is planning to maintain the status quo? What ramifications could this have for society? What is meant by "planning to prepare for the probable"? Contrast this with planning for the inevitable, especially in economic terms.

10. How does the concept of "planning futures" reflect the fact that planning has recently taken on new dimensions as compared to previous understanding of the planning function? Is this direction simply a fad or is it a new force with which management must prepare to contend?

The Framework of Managing

MODEL-BUILDING AND MODEL USE

DECISION-MAKING

PLANNING

The Framework of Planning

Chapter 9
Project Planning

A fully constrained plan (the most prevalent
form of planning) is like a map that has
one best route between the starting point
and the destination. The advantage of
assuming that a fully constrained system
exists is simplicity of planning, with attendant
lower costs. Planning becomes a matter
of schedule and resource control. But questions
must be raised concerning the validity
of assumptions, in specific cases, that permit
the manager to approximate his real situation
with full-constraint modeling conditions. The
application of three techniques—linear
programming, dynamic programming, and
simulation—to specify a fully constrained
plan is discussed. In general, planning
principles, which tend to be conservative,
are giving way to theory, which
is permissive to opportunity.

Chapter 9

PROJECT PLANNING

I call our world Flatland, not because we call it so, but to make its nature clearer to you, my happy readers, who are privileged to live in Space.

Imagine a vast sheet of paper on which straight Lines, Triangles, Squares, Pentagons, Hexagons, and other figures, instead of remaining fixed in their places, move freely about, on or in the surface, but without the power of rising above or sinking below it, very much like shadows—only hard and with luminous edges—and you will then have a pretty correct notion of my country and countrymen. Alas, a few years ago, I should have said "my universe": but now my mind has been opened to higher views of things.[1]

Edwin Abbott's *Flatland,* from which the above quote was taken, is considered a classic in the literature of logical "what if's." Abbott presented a consistent system of life constrained by existence in two dimensions. We are asking for a consistent view of plans that are not limited to spatial or temporal dimensions but are intrinsically involved with the dimensions of *opportunity.* The conception of *Flatland,* written in 1884, is a lot more sophisticated than anything that can presently be said about the dimensions of alternatives offering different opportunities.

There is a range for the degree of constraint of plans. Most plans of managers are very constrained with respect to alternatives. As

---

[1] Edwin A. Abbott, *Flatland* (New York: Dover, 1952), pp. 3–4.

Flatland imposes constraints on the "what is" of real life, so managerial planning imposes constraints on the "what can be." But organizational needs are gradually forcing the managerial mind to be "opened to higher views of things." In this chapter, we will concentrate on fully constrained planning systems; then, as we move to Chapter 10, we shall be examining systems with increasingly fewer constraints.

EXTENSIVE NETWORKS OF DETERMINATE FORM

We have just said that most management plans are very constrained with respect to alternatives, by which we mean that project planning usually assumes that only determinate systems exist. In other words, every element is treated as though it were completely known and understood. Accordingly, a project network is designed as a sequence of unit decisions that have been made by management. Each actionable step is represented by a single link. When several of these links (including the beginning and completion of the project) are joined together, they form a branch of the total system. In Figure 9–1 (which shows a planning *network*), *ABCGHIJK* is one branch, and *ABCFIJK* is another. There are five in all.

All planning models require extensive network representation because, by definition, planning time never repeats itself. Thus feedback must be represented in the extensive form $A \rightarrow B \rightarrow A \rightarrow B$ rather than in the nonextensive form $A \overset{\frown}{\smile} B$. Feedback networks have a nonextensive form that can be applied only to policy systems (which will be discussed in Chapter 11). The

Figure 9–1

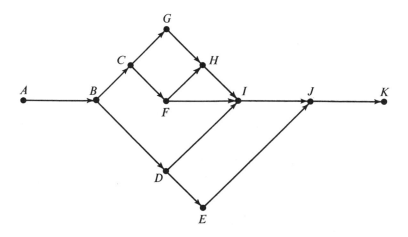

extensive form includes time in the following way: $A(t_0) \rightarrow B(t_0) \rightarrow A(t_1) \rightarrow B(t_1) \rightarrow$ etc. (where t_0 is beginning time, t_1 is the next time, and so forth).

Chance is removed from fully constrained networks by design. Some variability is controlled by technology; the remaining randomness is ignored. The resulting models (which we call *fully constrained*) are considered by managers to be ideal for project planning. (The reasons for this preference will be discussed shortly.) At the same time, every manager knows that the premise of full constraint is false. The question is, "How false?" Approximations to remove ambiguity, risk, and uncertainty are always involved, but they are sometimes warranted and sometimes not.

Fully constrained planning models (FCPM) are representable by *deterministic* networks (such as that shown in Figure 9–1) because no chance elements are *allowed*.[2] For example, assume that an expansion in plant capacity is being planned. Several strategic and tactical alternatives are considered. The possibilities are narrowed down and discarded until, finally, a single plan of action is accepted. That final plan is detailed as though no worthwhile opportunities for deviating from the plan will occur.

Planning Alternatives

Managers prefer the deterministic approach to planning for several reasons. First, it allows them to substitute a simple, formal procedure for what might otherwise have to be accomplished with difficulty through a complex planning scheme requiring much informal coordination. Nondeterminate planning imposes enormous and costly burdens on memory. Second, the deterministic approach allows efficient logistical support. Third, it emphasizes control rather than planning by measuring success and accomplishment *only* along control dimensions. Fourth, it requires no recognition of uncertainty. (Of course, the approximation of certainty may be justified or it may be only self-seduction. Ample evidence exists that ignoring uncertainty sometimes can be a "rational" approximation, while at other times it becomes a destructive assumption.)

Cost may also be a factor in managers' preference for constrained planning. The costs of planning in different ways (e.g., using assumptions of full or partial constraint) will vary greatly. And when the planning cost is balanced against the benefits to be derived from each approach, the result may often favor constrained planning. This is the same net-benefit concept that was used in Chapter 6 to determine optimal predecision investments. However, for a variety of reasons, not the least of which is the increasing instability of sys-

---

[2] Network forms appropriate to other forms of planning model (i.e., partially and threshold-constrained) will be shown at a later point.

tems (see pp. 537–39), the familiar cost/benefit relationships are likely to be changing in favor of less constrained planning.

Despite managers' preferences, there are significant difficulties in the deterministic approach to planning. For example, many managers will say that they are always prepared to change their plans if the opportunity presents itself; but the opportunities must come as *surprises,* and the possibilities to do something about them must arise *fortuitously.* This seems like a fair definition of serendipity. And, in fact, present management planning principles tend to be highly constrained in their openness to opportunities and receptive only to serendipity to bring about change. Even worse, if a plan turns out to be unworkable, the manager can attempt to modify it only by using whatever new strategic alternatives he can avail himself of. From that point on, decisions are last-minute affairs, and actions are taken under the pressure of emergency conditions. This is, of course, because the original sequences of the network were designed to handle only one specific evolving scenario.

When we considered decision models, we recognized that although the best–expected-value strategy was chosen, an environment could occur that would make a different strategy preferable. If the same thing happens to a plan, it is likely to affect the remainder of the plan in ways that have not been taken into consideration. That is, a dynamic modeling concept is called into play. Although fully constrained planning models are dynamic (as all plans must be), they are structured on the static principles of determinism. When technological factors are the dominant determinants of how well a plan works out, the deterministic assumptions are far better than when behavioral forces are at work. This point involves a well-known contrast between men and machines. But even technological determinants will project varying degrees of uncertainty, depending, for example, on how novel the application of the technology is.

The manager can try to measure his *degree of belief* that plans composed of single-step, deterministic considerations will suffice. If his degree of belief is high enough (and he takes into consideration the penalty for being wrong), then planning as though the system is fully constrained is acceptable. If he ignores the assignment of a degree-of-belief measure, the manager is sidestepping one of his most fundamental planning responsibilities.

In fact, the manager knows intuitively that deviations from expectations might *force* the acceptance of a new plan while the project is in midstream. He must be prepared to pay the price for assuming that the outcome of every design step is well known.

The costs of fully constrained planning are several. Since constrained planning networks are composed of single-path sequences, the manager must design with singlemindedness his intentions and expectations. He does this as accurately as his knowledge permits. But he seldom knows the cost of accuracy, and he does not represent the lack of accuracy in his model. Furthermore, the cost and value of improving his estimates are really unknown. We can say only that the manager is well aware that his estimates of time and cost are inexact and that unconsidered and unexpected environmental and behavioral effects will dictate the actual degree of inexactness. Within this framework, it is evident why the manager may at some point lose confidence in the fully constrained approach, although he is most likely to try first to improve his estimation procedures for single-path networks. For such reasons, planning often fails to perform in the intended fashion; it never catches up with what it should be doing.

If planning is to catch up with itself, it is necessary first that administrative abilities keep step with new developments. And perhaps this is happening, for principles are being replaced by theory, which offers significantly greater opportunity for relaxing constraints. Planning principles are fundamentally conservative, while planning theory is permissive. The principles are axiomatic, designed to ward off undue dangers, and they thereby tend to reduce the manager's freedom to behave in entirely new ways. They lead the manager to adopt full constraint. Theory, on the other hand, establishes boundaries intended to maximize the manager's degree of freedom.

DESIGN CONSIDERATIONS

Good design of the plan should be the first consideration in all planning. Within the framework of fully constrained planning, the one plan will be chosen that seems best suited to the needs of the organization. Unfortunately, because of "not seeing the woods for the trees," lack of innovative ability, or pressure to speed up the design of the plan, a better plan may go unnoticed. Certainly those project managers who have a strong tendency to dwell on schedule control are likely to by-pass a plan that promises better performance because they are so centered on cost and time considerations. Such opportunity-cost penalties will go unobserved. All efforts will focus on the achievement of the assigned project, and questions will seldom be raised about alternative configurations—unless the assigned plan turns out to be unworkable.

Criteria for "good" project design exist just as do criteria for "good" art and architecture. The contribution of science to good design is channeled primarily through the indirect influences of planning criteria and design evaluation. The process of *informing* the manager about alternatives is, at best, informal.

The two major phases of project work are *design* and *schedule control*. Design, which is primarily subjective and intuitive, is assisted by objective and scientific approaches for informing the manager about alternatives and evaluating the designs. Schedule control, which is primarily objective and scientific, can accomplish some important design-related functions, such as allocating resources, estimating completion dates, and monitoring progress. In turn, these considerations influence design by leading to a reconfiguration of the network. The original design must be completed before schedule control can be used. The criteria for schedule control influence the project design. At some point, this feedback ceases and the design is accepted.

The total *creative* aspects of network design are crucial and not to be overlooked. Fully constrained planning models are more likely to slight creativity than partially constrained models. Better plans always exist. Eureka strategies await discovery by the innovators. But the costs of being innovative may be too great, and imitative strategies are supported by inertia. Managerial styles affect innovative capability, and organizational attitudes are responsible for managerial styles. In practice, these difficulties often take the form of disputes as to what decision criteria can unambiguously specify the characteristics of a best plan.

The number of links that appears in the network is a function of the planner's point of view, which also is reflected in the span of time that the project plan covers. If the manager sees microscopically, then the number of links will be great, while a macroscopic viewpoint will fuse many branches into a single link. Certain professional attitudes—for example, accounting and engineering— are known for their attentiveness to detail. Corporate planners, on the other hand, tend to avoid detail to "see the whole picture." The level of detail of a plan should not be confused with its inherent degree of certainty. The level of detail used is characteristic of an attitude.

By collapsing links, however, an unintended illusion of certainty will sometimes be created. The plan is shown in terms of strategies, but tactics are not included. Such a plan might be strategically certain but open in tactical considerations to the effects of risky environments. This is like stating that the plant will be in Altoona but the site has not yet been chosen, or that television spots will be used for advertising but not even the story boards have been drawn up yet. In project planning, there can be too much or too little detail. Managerial styles exist that appear to exhibit compulsions for *only one* or the other tendency, but the issue should really be decided on a net-benefit basis.

Searching for the Optimal Project Design

When a network does not include risk elements and has not been designed with significant latitude for corrections at a later point, the planner presumably views the future with considerable certainty. Shipbuilding typifies this situation. Technological factors plus previous experience reduce the search for the optimal project design to a very few possibilities. The likelihood of a strike occurring part way through the project raises the kinds of issue that complicate the search process and so, by definition of full constraint, must be ignored in constructing the formal network. Since environments are (said to be) known with certainty, then even for the strike situation the problem boils down to *searching* for an optimal strategy chain.

There are cases where the "best" network configuration is simply assumed to be known without doubt, and search is not required. Such an assumption can arise in various ways, only some of which are sensible. Mixtures of dogma, imitation, tradition, power, experience, intuition, and logic produce an instantaneous solution and managerial accord on the selection. Generally, however, when a single network is chosen *without creative acts of search,* it is a warning that *dogma* and *imitation* may have been heavily involved in the selection process.

Examination of various real planning situations lends support to this contention. Because of the increasing size of organizations, many project-design steps are accomplished without any active support by the manager. First, he is too far removed to know how many alternatives were seriously explored. Second, scientific methods tend to create an impression of competence and well-being. However, this impression is not necessarily justified; the fact that formal procedures are used to *represent* a network does not by itself indicate that either penetrating intuition or scientific methods of search were used to *construct* that network. In addition, project networks are usually very complex. The confusion caused by complexity can inhibit "architectural" judgment. For example, critical-path models, which will be discussed shortly, are often thought to structure planning. In fact, they are primarily control models, and, although they affect planning and design secondarily, they do not assume responsibility for the design of the network.

The Gantt project-planning chart. Ancestors of critical-path methods were undoubtedly being used eons ago for such projects as the Great Wall of China, the Pyramids of Egypt, and the Colossus of Rhodes to make sure that all the project steps were coordinated and on schedule. But, to present knowledge, the first steps toward *formalizing* the control of fully constrained planning systems were taken by Henry L. Gantt (1861–1919). Gantt created a systematic approach for specifying the work required by the project and the order in which it must be done. With a Gantt chart, the manager can determine what work is lagging, what is on time, and what is ahead.

Preparation for the Gantt project-planning chart begins by *listing* the steps that must be taken to complete the plan. The phrase "must be taken" should be taken with a grain of salt. Design opportunities are too numerous to suppose that one listing is immediately obvious as the best. In any case, there is seldom proof that the chosen arrangement of steps is optimal. With Gantt charts, a feasible "beginning" design is chosen. The basis for selection is experience. (Properly, this reminds us of the first basic feasible solution of LP, in Chapter

7, pp. 286 and 290.) Then, *systematic search* is used to improve the listing. Such a design approach, proceeding systematically but unrigorously to improve the design network, characterizes the use of the Gantt chart. It also describes more recent project efforts such as critical-path methods.[3]

Listing and *sequencing* are the core operations of the design phase of planning. The project is organized so that each activity properly follows whatever other activities must be completed before it can begin. Sequence determination may have less planning importance than listing, but it has as much freedom and is of substantial economic consequence. The determining factors for sequencing decisions are (1) technological constraints and (2) methodological considerations concerning cost-effective resource-allocation patterns. It is with the second that the concept of "total planning" is frequently confused. This is because cost-effectiveness analysis frequently delivers a narrower end result than cost-benefit analysis (see p. 579).

Once the activities are named and sequenced, then time estimates for each activity must be obtained. With this information, a Gantt-type chart (as in Figure 9–2) can be drawn.

Network Methods

This format is easily revised into a directed planning network (see Figure 9–3) such as is used in PERT and other critical-path models. By associating an estimate of time with each activity line (A, B_1, B_2, etc.), we can incorporate in the design the total time that must be spent in the network. The direction of flow through the network is fully indicated. Steps are taken with certainty. No stochastic elements are involved. The cost of completing each activity within the stated period of time is often included. The quality of the project—that is, its delivered performance—can also be explored, but less is known about how to include it. The triumvirate of *time, cost,* and *performance* is more susceptible to probabilistic effects than are time estimates alone. To a great extent this is because performance has so many complex dimensions.

Trade-off functions between time, cost, and performance describe how much of one dimension must be given up in order to achieve an incremental gain in the other. For example, if a week is added to the schedule, the cost is

---

[3] Recently, simulation models have been developed in which alternative project-design configurations can be considered formally (in the sense of descriptive models) as well as systematically. But the use of planning methods that can generate normative network designs remains a matter for the future. Improvement algorithms characterize the present state of the art. Management can gain by learning to use them and by supporting their further development. Recognition of how managers can participate directly and in dialogue with such heuristic models is critical.

Figure 9–2   Gantt-Type Chart

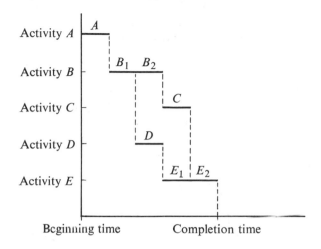

Bcginning time   Completion time

SOURCE: Martin K. Starr, "Planning Models," *Management Science,* Vol. 13, No. 4 (December 1966), p. 124.

reduced by $5,000; by changing the tolerances from ±.005 to ±.004, the cost is increased by $20,000, and an extra three days must be added to the schedule. Trading back and forth in this way allows for improvement in the use of the system's resources according to the manager's objectives and *subject to the network configuration that is used.* Such trade-offs have nothing to do with redesigning the *listing.* Consequently, we say that trade-off is a high-level, control-type operation that can influence design, but only indirectly. Again, it is clear that no systematic procedure exists for optimizing network design.

Weaknesses of the Gantt chart provided one form of stimulus for significant further developments in project planning. A method was required

Figure 9–3   Figure 9–2 Converted into a Directed Network

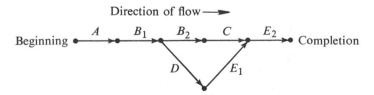

SOURCE: Martin K. Starr, "Planning Models," *Management Science,* Vol. 13, No. 4 (December 1966), p. 124.

that would permit sequencing dependencies (i.e., noting which activities have to be finished before others can be started) to be quite clear. The Gantt chart could deliver neither this advantage nor adequate control for large projects. In the late 1950's, various network methods received a great deal of attention from applied mathematicians and operations researchers, as their mathematical techniques grew more capable of handling such problems. Other network models had already been developed for distribution analyses[4] as well as for a variety of logistics problems. Third, computer facilities were simultaneously developing into a powerful support. Without the computer, the network approach could not have been applied because the use of network models on the large scale of real problems surpasses human calculation capacities. Yet the model requirements are not too big for present computer systems, so a perfect symbiosis occurred. All three elements were part cause and part effect. Change arose that matched and balanced methodology, information technology, and need.

Before network models can be constructed, three steps are required. (1) First, all the elements, jobs, steps, tasks, stages, activities, and other terms associated with bringing the project to fruition must be detailed. (2) Then a sequencing order must be determined, based on technological and administrative dependencies. In other words, all necessary sequential constraints must be made explicit. (3) Finally, the time (and cost) of performing each task or activity must be estimated. (Performance specifications can also be stated.) When all this information has been assembled, a critical-path PERT network can be constructed.[5]

Many applications can be found for project-network methods. An operating enterprise may wish to develop a new process, build a plant, work on a government contract, provide a new service, consolidate and shift its warehouse locations, begin to use air freight, or open up an entirely new area of endeavor. Libraries have used network models to change their operations, and a Broadway play was brought to the stage with the aid of a network model. Government agencies frequently require companies working on government contracts to use the network approach, particularly when an integrated effort on the part of several companies is needed. In effect, the individual company networks are tied together to form a project grid. The network approach

---

[4] The transportation algorithm, for example, was readily applied to the problem of shipping goods from factories to warehouses (see pp. 656–60).

[5] PERT (Program Evaluation and Review Technique) was developed by the U.S. Navy Special Projects Office in conjunction with the management consulting firm of Booz, Allen, and Hamilton. One of the first network methods, it was used for the Polaris project. Critical-path methods (CPM) were developed by E. I. du Pont de Nemours & Co. and Remington Rand at about the same time as PERT and were used to plan the construction of a plant. "Critical path" has come to be used as a descriptive term that is generally applied to PERT as well as to other, similar, network methods.

unifies the totality of activities, problems, decisions, and operations that constitute the project-management field.

When a network is constructed, each of the project activities is shown as an arrow (see Figure 9–1). The completion of an activity is called an *event* and is shown as a circle. In relatively long-term projects, some activities often go through a cycle of steps and then repeat themselves several times at increasing levels of detail (for example, design-test-redesign-test, etc., or mix batter–add spices–taste–add spices, etc.). Cycles of activities are also characteristic of control-system functions, but these are seldom treated in extensive network form. As previously noted, cycles are not permitted in planning networks. The changes shown in Figure 9–4 must be made.

Figure 9–4   PERT Networks Require Extensive Representation

An inspection-rework cycle:

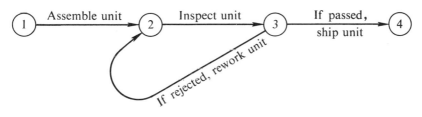

Extensive form for PERT networks:

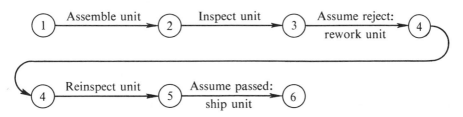

Different configurations of activities and events will occur with different plans. Series arrangements, in which the preceding activity must be finished before the succeeding one can begin, are common. In other cases, where activities can parallel one another, several arrows emanate from a single event-circle. Whenever materials, parts, subassemblies, or particular procedures come together to begin a new activity, the arrows converge at a particular event-circle, signifying that all the previous activities have been completed. If we proceed in this way, it is tedious but not difficult to lay out the relevant network of activities and events.

Time estimation. PERT requires three estimates of completion time for each activity. The planner is asked to supply (1) an optimistic estimate, called *a;* (2) a pessimistic estimate, called *b;* and (3) an estimate of what is considered most likely, called *m*. These three estimates are then combined to give an *expected activity time,* called t_e. The formula often used for achieving the combination is

$$t_e = K_1(a + b) + K_2(m)$$

where K_1 and K_2 are derived weights. Frequently, these weights are assigned as $K_1 = \frac{1}{6}$ and $K_2 = \frac{2}{3}$, values associated with the estimate of the mean of a Beta distribution.[6] A hypothetical distribution for the elapsed-time estimates is shown in Figure 9–5. Some project planners think that the combination of three estimates provides greater accuracy in estimating; others do not agree.

Because estimates can be checked against actual results it may be possible to determine what is best for a particular kind of project. In Figure 9–6, the

Figure 9–5   A Beta Form of Distribution for the Completion Times of an Activity

NOTE: The shape of the curve is determined by the time estimates for *a, b,* and *m*.

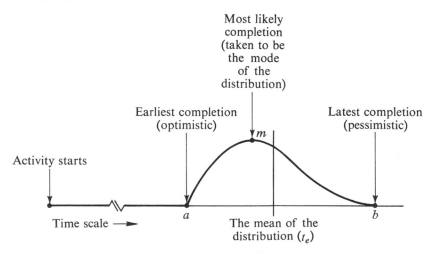

------

[6] Though these are only approximate values they are sufficiently accurate to describe the statistical frequency distribution called Beta. One example of a Beta distribution is shown in Figure 9–5. It is a unimodal (i.e., a single-peak) distribution, which does not have to be symmetrical and has finite end points (i.e., it does not continue on to infinity as does the normal distribution).

Figure 9–6

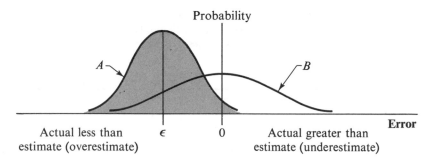

Probability

A

B

Error

Actual less than ϵ 0   Actual greater than
estimate (overestimate)   estimate (underestimate)

error distributions for two estimators (A and B) are illustrated. Underestimates occur when the actual result turns out to be greater than the estimate; overestimates arise when the actual result is less than the estimate. We are assuming that a record is kept of actual project times over a period of time and that these are subtracted from the original estimates to derive characteristic estimating-error distributions for A and B.

We observe that B has a mean error close to zero but a large variance, while the estimates of A show a mean propensity to overestimate of ϵ, with a smaller variance than B has. All other matters being equal, we would prefer A as an estimator. By regularly using the correction $-\epsilon$, A's distribution can be centered over the zero error, making A's and B's mean errors equivalent. Then A's smaller variance is preferred. Not much is known about how to reduce an estimator's variance, although perhaps training can be effective. At the same time, A might not continue to perform in the same way once informed that an ϵ correction is being used regularly to modify his estimates. Our point in this discussion, however, is that managerial understanding of the estimating function goes beyond intuition alone. For project planning there is a need *and an ability* to develop reasonably good estimates for the expected elapsed times required for the completion of activities.

In addition, estimates of the *variances* associated with the expected values of elapsed time are also frequently supplied for PERT. In common notational form, σ_i^2 is the variance for the ith activity. The sum of the variances of a number of consecutive estimates of sequenced, *independent* activities measures the variance of the total sequence. For example, if three estimates, t_{e_1}, t_{e_2}, and t_{e_3} are made, each of them having a particular variance measure σ_1^2, σ_2^2, σ_3^2, then the variance of the sum of these estimates is given by $\sigma_1^2 + \sigma_2^2 + \sigma_3^2$. This relationship is depicted in Figure 9–7. The formula for the variance of an elapsed-time estimate is given by $\sigma^2 = [K_3(b - a)]^2$, where K_3 is a derived weight. Generally, $K_3 = \frac{1}{6}$, which is associated with the estimate of the variance of a Beta distribution.

Figure 9–7

NOTE: The *mean* value of combined activities is the sum of the separate means; the *variance* of combined activities is the sum of the separate variance estimates, assuming the activities are independent.

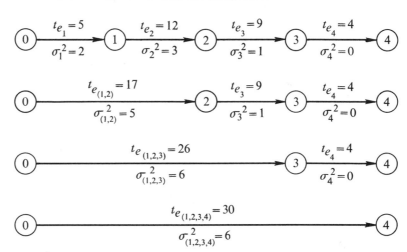

The critical path. Let us examine a hypothetical PERT network (Figure 9–8) that presumably satisfies the manager—that is, one that he believes to be an appropriate design for the project he is managing. The estimates, we assume, are also acceptable. Each link is labeled with an expected elapsed time, and the variance for each activity σ_i^2 is shown as a number in parentheses.

We can obtain a cumulative value for each branch, moving along the particular branch from the beginning of the project to the end. We call this value T_E; it gives the earliest expected *clock time* at which each activity can be finished. The event-circles, or nodes, enclose these numbers. It will be noted, as we sum along different branches until we arrive at a junction node, that the joining branches can carry a different cumulative number to that node. Whenever this condition arises at a junction node, we accept the *largest* value of T_E. All further accumulation proceeds with this largest number. The *last node* in the network, which represents *project completion,* therefore bears a value that is the measure of the *maximum* cumulative time—that is, the time required to perform the longest time sequence of activities in the network. In Figure 9–7, the middle branch dominates the cumulative total that has been carried forward, since that branch requires the longest elapsed time for completion. It is consequently called the *critical path* of the system. However, it is usually awkward to find the critical path by inspection. A means for

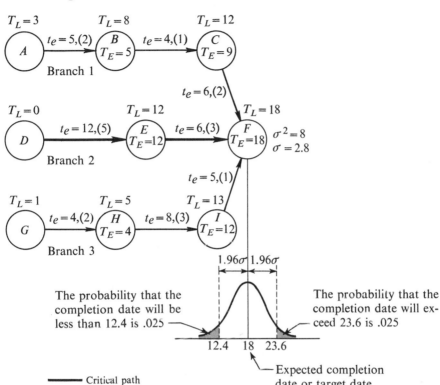

Figure 9–8   An Abstract PERT Network

SOURCE: Martin K. Starr, *Production Management: Systems and Synthesis* © 1964. By permission of Prentice-Hall, Inc., Englewood Cliffs, New Jersey.

working backward in the network from maximum completion time is required, and is available, for measuring project slack.

The concept and measure of slack. Slack is a measure of the leeway available on noncritical paths. It is the amount of time that the estimates along a specific branch can slip without delaying the completion time of the total job.

Starting with the largest cumulative total, $T_E = 18$, which resulted from the middle branch and which is the estimated time for *job completion,* we now move backward through the network. We subtract from 18 the three values of t_e (6, 6, and 5), deriving the three values of T_L (12, 12, and 13), where T_L is the latest possible time at which an activity can be completed without changing the project completion time. We then continue to move

Figure 9–9

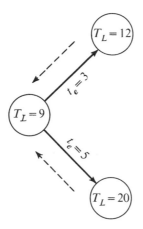

backward, successively subtracting from each T_L the t_e value that immediately precedes it in the network. Eventually, every node has a T_L value assigned to it. When two or more branches converge on a node so that the values of T_L produced by subtraction are not equal, then we accept the smallest value of T_L. For example, see Figure 9–9.

The difference $T_L - T_E$ can now be obtained for each event node. It describes the amount of *slack* that exists at each node. As expected, at every node of the critical path (which, by definition, dominates the system), $T_L - T_E = 0$. A total branch has as much slack as the time required to complete the branch requirements is *less* than the time required to complete the project stages that make up the critical path. In our example, the top branch has more slack than the bottom branch.

Slack offers the manager some degree of freedom. But it also may indicate overstaffing of men and overallocation of materials. Slack is not bad *per se,* but it is always useful to evaluate why it exists, how much of it there is, and whether anything can be done about it. Finding, specifying, and analyzing the reasons for slack are not trivial occupations. The results affect all project operations. In the example, it would appear to be wasteful to expedite on any but the middle branch, which, being the critical path, cannot be allowed to slip. If it does, it will directly affect the project-completion date. Of course, if some paths have very little slack, they can easily become critical paths themselves. Similar observations have been made about paths that parallel the critical path for long stretches and have high variance estimates.[7] These

---

[7] See K. R. MacCrimmon and C. A. Ryavec, "An Analytical Study of the PERT Assumptions," *Operations Research,* Vol. 12, No. 1 (January–February 1964), pp. 16–37.

too can become critical paths. After trade-off potentials have been considered, the major emphasis of project control should be assigned to the critical path, but careful consideration should be given to the other paths as well.

The approach we have been following is often called PERT/time, because time, which is traditionally the fundamental dimension of the planners' objectives, is the only factor under consideration. Variance measures, which can be summed along the critical-path branch, add important schedule information and give the manager additional degrees of freedom. He obtains not only the expected time for project completion but also an estimate of the upper and lower bounds of this completion time. Figure 9–8 shows a distribution with its left and right tails cut off at 1.96 standard deviations. Each tail contains the probability of an event occurring approximately 25 out of 1,000 times.[8] The right tail contains very long completion dates. The left tail contains very short completion dates. As shown in Figure 9–8, by having moved 1.96 standard deviations in either direction from the target date, we obtained a range of times for job completion—and there is a 95 percent probability that the actual completion date will fall within this range of 12.4 to 23.6. Stated another way, utilizing a 1.96σ criterion, we have determined an *earliest* and *latest* reasonable project-completion date.

The computations to determine the critical path, slack, and variance effects do not require that the actual network be drawn up. They can be handled in tabular form, similar to computer formats, as shown in Table 9–1.

Trading Off Resources

The existence of slack can be interpreted to imply that a better arrangement of resource utilization might be found. Any alteration that reduces the length of the critical path would decrease the amount of slack that has been observed in the other branches of the network. A reasonable approach would be to obtain and employ *new* resources toward this end and/or to *shift* resources wherever possible from the branches having the largest amount of slack to the critical path.

---

[8] Assuming that a normal distribution applies, we would have:

Number of standard deviations for the specification of the range	Probability that the actual time falls within the specified range
1σ	68.0%
1.64σ	90.0%
1.96σ	95.0%
2σ	95.4%
3σ	99.7%

Table 9–1   PERT Computations

Event	T_E	T_L	Slack $(T_L - T_E)$	Cumulative variance
F	18	18	0	8
C	9	12	3	3
I	12	13	1	5
E	12	12	0	5
B	5	8	3	2
H	4	5	1	2
G	0	1	1	0
D	0	0	0	0
A	0	3	3	0

Considering the second alternative, let us assume that the time it takes to complete each activity is linearly related to the number of men employed on the job. Assuming also that the skills required are interchangeable among branches, we could bring the entire network into better balance by shifting manpower resources from slack branches to the critical path. This has been done for the previous example, and the results are shown in Figure 9–10.

In this case, a perfectly balanced network is achieved by trading off resources. We let x equal the amount of project time added to the top branch,

Figure 9–10

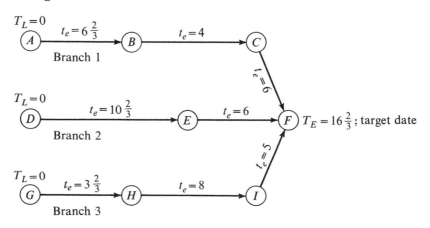

SOURCE: Martin K. Starr, *Production Management: Systems and Synthesis* © 1964. By permission of Prentice-Hall, Inc., Englewood Cliffs, New Jersey.

which had the greatest oversupply of resources. An appropriate quantity of these "extra" resources is now to be shifted to the other branches. (We do not have to state the amount of resources equivalent to a unit of time, but we are assuming that it would be known.) Then we divide x time units into two parts, mx and bx, where m and b represent the percentage of x to be subtracted from the middle and bottom branches, respectively. To balance the top and middle branches, we have $18 - mx = 15 + x$. That is, the time for the top branch is increased from 15 to $15 + x$ because resources have been taken from that branch. The time for completion of the middle branch has been decreased from 18 to $18 - mx$ because resources have been added to that branch. Reasoning similarly for the bottom and middle branches, we obtain $17 - bx = 15 + x$. Since $m + b = 1$, we can solve these three equations for the three unknowns, x, m, and b. The results are $x = 1\frac{2}{3}$ (time units), $m = \frac{4}{5}$, and $b = \frac{1}{5}$. The time units, $x = 1\frac{2}{3}$, $mx = \frac{4}{3}$, and $bx = \frac{1}{3}$, can now be transformed by the manager into their manpower equivalents for project planning. All branches are now critical paths, and *no slack* remains in the system. The target date has been improved by $1\frac{1}{3}$ time units.

A simple linear trade-off function, such as we have used for this example, would seldom be suitable; but the manager generally can estimate the effect of shifting resources, and these estimates can be used in the same way. Moreover, the manager does not hope to achieve perfect network balance. Men, machines, and other resources cannot be fractionated at will; skills and facilities are not readily interchangeable between branches. But, to the extent that changes can be made, the manager will achieve considerable improvement in the time performance of the system. The advantage, for planning flexibility, of *general,* rather than *special-purpose,* resources can be seen clearly.

Management theory can be extended to relate investment flexibility, the design of facilities, and trade-off potentials—which underscores our contention that a basis for planning theory exists above the level of "rules of thumb." The ability to recognize slack paths, to measure slack, and to trade off resources makes critical-path modeling significantly more useful than the older Gantt project methods. Lacking slack measures, managers often expedite activities that seem likely to slip. But such schedule slippage can be readily tolerated on high-slack paths, so the effort is wasted and, worse yet, could have been applied where it counted.

Another aspect of expediting is that preplanning its use by reserving manpower for this function allows the estimates of variance along the critical path to be decreased. While this would not change the target date, it could reduce the risk of deviating from the target date by a substantial amount. Since contracts for projects can have penalty clauses for exceeding the target date by given amounts of time, the improvement in variance can have important economic consequences.

PERT/Cost Networks

The network project-planning method has been extended in a number of ways
to assist the manager in his planning function. Among these are the inclusion
of cost and quality objectives in addition to those of time. Military planning
usually emphasizes time and cost. Construction tends to accentuate time because the opportunity cost of an empty site is of large magnitude as compared
to the difference in project costs of building fast or slowly. Manned space
projects pursue quality. In all cases, managerial values are involved in determining the dimensions for tracking the project.

Let us consider what might be done when the major objective is to minimize
cost. The relationships of cost and time have received considerable attention.
Various cost/time systems have been developed, and others are being developed, to attempt to resolve this problem of *conflicting multiple objectives.*
PERT/cost starts in the same way as does PERT/time—that is, we construct
the representative network of activities and events. (We shall use the hypothetical network shown in Figure 9–11.) In this case, however, we have
developed two different estimates for each branch. These are (1) a *minimum-
time* estimate and its cost and (2) a *minimum-cost* estimate and its time.
Figure 9–12 shows the way these factors might be related for each branch of
our network.

Figure 9–11   A Hypothetical Cost/Time Network

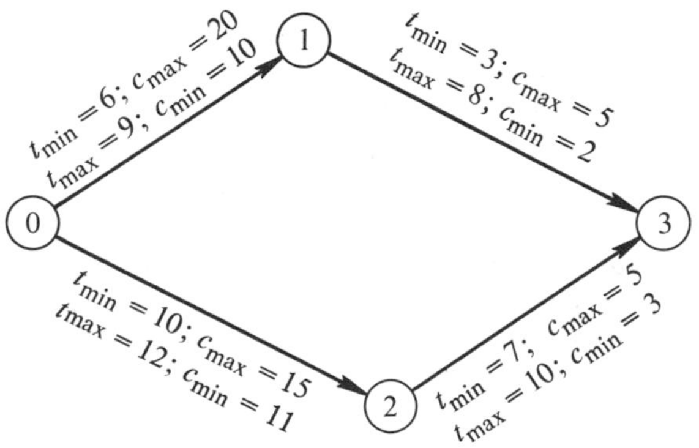

t = time estimate
c = cost estimate

Figure 9–12   Some Representative Cost/Time Relationships

NOTE: The "weak" assumption is made that linearity prevails over the specified range, and the end points are assumed to be limits.

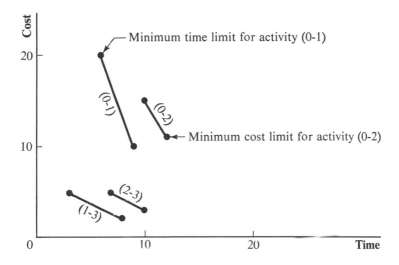

SOURCE: Martin K. Starr, *Production Management: Systems and Synthesis* © 1964. By permission of Prentice-Hall, Inc., Englewood Cliffs, New Jersey.

The *minimum-cost* estimate is used for each activity, and the critical path is determined for those data. The result will then be a completion date based on minimum cost requirements for completing the project. The length of time required to complete the project under minimum-cost conditions may be too great to be tolerated. Accordingly, alternative times, requiring greater costs, can then be substituted for chosen minimum-cost activities along the critical path. In this way, the critical path can be shortened until another branch becomes critical or a satisfactory compromise with the original critical path is achieved. As a rule of thumb, compromises are made for those activities along the critical path where Δcost/Δtime is smallest.[9] Then the next biggest ratio is used, and so on until a satisfactory compromise between time and cost is achieved.

For the example in Figure 9–11, with minimum cost, 0-2-3 is the critical path. It has T_E of 22 and cost of 14. Slack for the path 0-1-3 is $T_L - T_E = 5$. Let us assume, for illustrative purposes, that T_E must not be greater than 20. The *best* cost/time ratio *applying to the critical path* is associated with activity

---

[9] The Greek capital letter Δ (delta), as used here, should be read "change in."

2-3 (see Figure 9–12). Making the required change, we obtain: $t_{23} = 8$; $c_{23} = 4\frac{1}{3}$. This gives us 0-2-3 as the critical path with T_E of 20 and cost of $15\frac{1}{3}$. The slack for 0-1-3 is reduced: $T_L - T_E = 3$.

Neither the manager nor his project staff can be expected to do this kind of work for all links of a large and complex project. A computer program can be used if the estimates are available along with sensible heuristics for determining which links to change. The cost/time estimates demand a great deal of project knowledge, and the heuristics can profoundly affect the final results. Methodology and computer power are available, but the real challenge lies in the manager's ability to formalize his understanding of the project in terms that are compatible with the planning model's capabilities. PERT/cost should not be confused with an optimizing technique. It is a logical attempt to utilize reasonable trade-offs between cost and time to obtain an *approximation* of an optimal result.

Planning Horizons

Another way to represent the project network is by means of a matrix. The Gantt network example shown in Figures 9–2 and 9–3 can be presented in the matrix shown in Table 9–2. All entries of transition (1, not 0) lie above the matrix diagonal.[10] This matrix depicts an evolving system that ends up in

Table 9–2

	→	A	B_1	B_2	C	D	E_1	E_2	U
	To activity:								
From activity:	A	0	1	0	0	0	0	0	0
	B_1	0	0	1	0	1	0	0	0
	B_2	0	0	0	1	0	0	0	0
	C	0	0	0	0	0	0	1	0
	D	0	0	0	0	0	1	0	0
	E_1	0	0	0	0	0	0	1	0
	E_2	0	0	0	0	0	0	0	1

SOURCE: Martin K. Starr, "Planning Models," *Management Science,* Vol. 13, No. 4 (December 1966), p. 125.

---

[10] The matrix is even more descriptive when the actual times for completion are substituted for unit values. Such a matrix represents both the direction and magnitude of the activity vectors. Matrices possess advantages for quantitative manipulation, while graphs, since they convey information in more tangible form, are said to have greater comprehensibility.

the state U. It has the unidirectional flows required of the graph. Reading from the matrix, both C and E_1 go to E_2; E_2 then goes to U, which is meant to represent completion.

But the nature of state U is not specified; it remains an unknown state. Once U is reached, the system may lock into a closed set for which policy can be formulated. For example, once construction is completed, the office building is to be opened for occupancy at 7 A.M. (F), closed at 8 P.M. (G), and cleaned at 10 P.M. (H).

$$U \equiv F \rightarrow G \rightarrow H$$

On the other hand, U may be seen as closing the project, as in the case of a successfully concluded experiment. Most often, however, it will represent the beginning of another planning series, such as $U \rightarrow F \rightarrow G \rightarrow H \rightarrow U'$.

The span of time (and the activities included) between A and U or that between U and U' is a *planning horizon*—that is, the interval between the plan's beginning and end. Successive planning horizons do not have to be of the same length. A five-year plan can be succeeded by a three-year plan.

The project manager whose planning horizon moves from A to U' in eight years is asking questions that are different from those of the manager who plans from A to U in five years and then from U to U' in three years. Who is better off? To begin with, only the manager who recognizes that the ending conditions of one planning horizon constitute the beginning conditions of the next one is in a position to make a choice. Many projects seem to have a natural planning horizon—say, the time it takes to complete a specific project. But in many cases the clear definition of the project can serve to hide the actual planning continuity that exists—the fact that *the* project is embedded in a nest of projects. Polaris is followed by modified Polaris. A new product eventually becomes an established one; and, since most companies want to have both new and established products in their line, planning is viewed as a continuing activity. *Continuous planning* is rapidly gaining interest and endorsement, especially at upper-management levels. It embodies the concept of $U \rightarrow U' \rightarrow U''$ and so forth. Continuous planning must unceasingly reassess such considerations as how many projects to use, which projects to use, and how to schedule them.

METHODS FOR CHOOSING THE NETWORK DESIGN

Search methods are basic to the manager's planning function. Knowledge of *alternative plans* almost always exists; the problem is to find among the contenders at least a near-optimal plan.[11] Given only a few possibilities, the manager might study each plan and choose the best one. However, when the number of possible plans is large, search techniques must be found that do not require the examination of *every* alternative network configuration. This is not like finding one special part in N items where, on the average, $N/2$ tests are required. The discovery of an optimal value requires the full N tests unless a theory of search exists that reduces that number. We shall consider three major search-reduction techniques—namely, LP, dynamic programming, and simulation.

Linear Programming

The linear-programming model provides an efficient search routine, but it is not suitable for many kinds of planning problem. Ignoring certain complex variants, the fundamental operations of LP reflect the assumption of certainty that characterizes fully constrained planning systems. The LP requirement of linearity seldom blocks the search procedure. As was previously shown (pp. 290–91), simple ways to circumvent such difficulties frequently can be found. LP can be used to obtain complex blends of fuels, determine elaborate animal-feed mixes, and schedule work in a job-shop even though the constraints, the activity coefficients, a_{ij}, or the objective function change periodically.[12] When the variations are regular and recurrent, LP constitutes a policy device. If they are not recurrent but are regular (so that the trajectory can be specified with certainty), then LP fits the conditions for a fully constrained planning system.

But under what circumstances can linear programming be used in this role? The question concerns the nature of a planning period. Unless time is included as a relevant variable in the linear program, successive planning periods must be assumed to be independent. Even when time is included, it is difficult to use LP in such a way that the set of decisions for each planning horizon, U, optimizes the results for the total planning period, U'.

An LP solution can identify the network components to be used for a given period but not the *sequence* of activities within that period. The solution to the blending problem, for example, specifies the output blends to be obtained by mixing given inputs, but it does not specify the order in which these mixtures should be made. Consequently, for transient environmental conditions, LP

---

[11] The approach used is related to network-reduction methods for partially constrained planning systems; the difference is that in the present case only one plan is developed. See pp. 382–90.

[12] For the definitions of these terms, see pp. 284–85.

may not be able to provide even a reasonable guide for planning the network.

The fundamental issue concerns the degree of independence of adjacent planning periods. If planning is done in monthly periods (say, for twelve months ahead), then the sum of the best possible monthly results should produce a sensible pattern when reviewed on an annual basis if LP is to be useful. This *relation* will hold if the consecutive monthly periods are independent of one another. In other terms, if environments are independently distributed between planning periods and not affected by prior decisions, then the *relation* will hold. Otherwise, a suboptimal result will occur. So the decision to use LP for planning will be acceptable if the opportunity costs that result from acting as though each planning period is independent are not large.

The optimal size for the LP planning period is another matter. The advantages of a longer planning horizon must be weighed against the increasing unreliability of data for longer time intervals. It is only natural to want to extend the planning horizon when the penalty for using LP with smaller planning periods is large because, in fact, the many successive periods are not independent of one another. But no time interval may be long enough to overcome the liabilities of using LP with interdependent planning periods, and another approach may be warranted.

The manager wrestles intuitively with these issues. Much planning is never identified with a specific interval. This relieves the manager of a difficult burden, but it obscures a balanced view of the problem. It does not assure that there will be a consistency of planning horizons for projects that are constrained by the same budget. It does not balance the project commitments or the cash flows (in and out) at all future points in time.

The factors y = planning horizon and x = updating interval are major variables for consideration (see Figure 9–13). Note that when we have

Figure 9–13

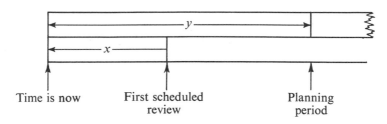

| Time is now | First scheduled review | Planning period |

a long planning horizon that is reviewed very frequently, then $x << y$. The opposite extreme is when $x = y$, which produces a regular periodic planning system; in such a system, at the end of each period a plan for the next period is prepared. In another situation, y might be a long-range planning period and *x* a short-range one. This kind of overlap between plans would be most likely to occur when partially constrained systems are used, permitting alternatives to coexist in the form of multiple paths. LP's temporal abilities are too limited to cope with such matters. When LP cannot be accepted as an adequate planning model, we may turn to other, more elaborate, programming methods.

Dynamic Programming

Dynamic programming is an obvious alternative. It succeeds in improving search procedures, in changing static intervals into dynamic ones, and in overcoming many of the interval-dependency difficulties of linear programming. Bellman's dynamic-programming rules[13] (which we shall discuss shortly) offer strong assistance in the search for optimality. Dynamic programming is not immune to interaction effects or discontinuities—for example, it may not be able to represent the situation in which the estimate for a result in January may have to be changed because of an action that can be taken in February—as an illustration, note the situation that arises when a discount is offered for a given number of advertising inserts, where the discount suddenly applies to the costs for all the ads and is not assigned to only the last one. Still, with clever transformations, dynamic programming has more flexibility than linear programming. The complexities it can handle are illustrated in Figure 9–14. For this example, resources can be allocated only in amounts of zero, 1, or 2. We will assume that payoffs P_0, P_1, and P_2 result. This tree begins at the left, where the different resource-allocation plans (0–2) are shown for the $n =$ first stage (i.e., the beginning).

Proceeding to the next stage, we have additive combinations of the resources as shown in the matrix below. Note that for each diagonal of the matrix every cell has the same resource total. In illustration, only the diagonal for the total resource value of two is shown (see Table 9–3).

Table 9–3   Matrix of Total Resources Allocated Over Two Stages

		Second stage:		
		0	1	2
First stage:	0	0	1	2
	1	1	2	3
	2	2	3	4

(All values on the diagonal are 2)

---

[13] See R. Bellman, *Dynamic Programming* (Princeton, N.J.: Princeton University Press, 1958), p. 83.

Figure 9–14   A Tree Representation of Dynamic Programming

NOTE: Tracing back from the last stage results (in this case the third stage), an optimal path (based on data presented in the text) is shown as a darkened line for each potential total allocation, ranging from zero to 6.

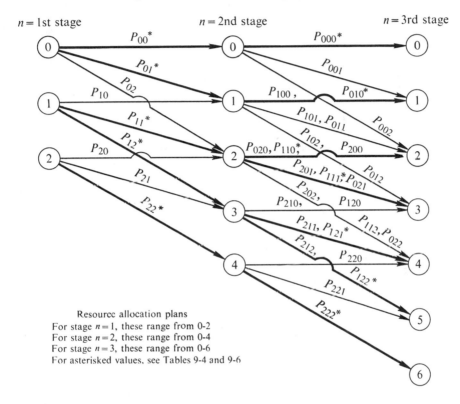

Resource allocation plans
For stage $n = 1$, these range from 0-2
For stage $n = 2$, these range from 0-4
For stage $n = 3$, these range from 0-6
For asterisked values, see Tables 9-4 and 9-6

Each resource pattern has a payoff associated with it. In other words, a matrix of *payoffs* can be constructed, as shown in Table 9–4. At least one value of payoff observed along each diagonal is the largest number on that

Table 9–4   Matrix of Payoffs for the Different Resource-Allocation Plans Based on Two Stages

			Second stage:		
			0	1	2
First-stage payoffs					
P_0	First stage:	0	$P_{00}{}^*$	$P_{01}{}^*$	P_{02}
P_1		1	P_{10}	$P_{11}{}^*$	$P_{12}{}^*$
P_2		2	P_{20}	P_{21}	$P_{22}{}^*$

diagonal and therefore the maximum payoff that can be achieved for that level of total resource allocation. The asterisks in the payoff matrix are intended to represent hypothetical second-stage optimal values. Thus, for 0, the payoff must be P_{00}; for 1, it can either be P_{01} or P_{10}; but, since P_{01} is asterisked, that is the hypothetical optimal in this case. For the diagonal value 2, the indicated value is P_{11}; for the diagonal value 3, P_{12} is asterisked; for the value 4, the optimal payoff must be P_{22}.

The optimal (asterisked) values are the only ones that are brought into the next stage of calculations—here, the third stage. (The optimal values are shown as heavy lines on the tree diagram.) Moving to the third stage, we combine the first and second stage allocations, so that only the optimals for each resource total (through the second stage) are represented. None of the other values need be considered. (See Table 9–5.) Again, all resource totals

Table 9–5   Matrix of Total Resources Allocated Over Three Stages

	Third stage: 0	1	2
First stage and 0	0	1	2
second stage: 1	1	2	3
2	2	3	4
3	3	4	5 (The diagonal value of 5)
4	4	5	6

are the same for all cells of any diagonal of the matrix. The payoff matrix (Table 9–6) is also easily written. The asterisked values in the table are hypothetical third-stage optimums, at least one appearing on each diagonal (total resource level).

The values in parentheses in the table do not need to be calculated, so time and effort are saved. It is clear, for example, in the row of P_{11} only three possible third-stage payoffs can begin with the index 11. These are P_{110}, P_{111}, and P_{112}. Similar reasoning applies to all other matrix values in parentheses. Such savings become considerable when the size of the matrix is large, as will be the case when many planning options exist at every stage or when limited allocations are considered over many stages.[14]

---

[14] Another source of computational saving should be mentioned. If no more than, say, a total of four resources units can be used for the plan, there is no need to calculate the values for diagonals 5 and 6 in the third stage, and no need to calculate entries on the diagonals having values greater than 4 for stages greater than 3.

Table 9–6　　Matrix of Payoffs for the Different Resource-Allocation Plans Based on Three Stages

Optimal second-stage payoff values		Third stage:		
		0	1	2
P_{00}	First stage 0	$P_{000}{}^*$	P_{001}	P_{002}
	and	$\{(P_{100})$	(P_{101})	(P_{102})
P_{01}	second stage: 1	$\{P_{010}{}^*$	P_{011}	P_{012}
		$\{(P_{200})$	(P_{201})	(P_{202})
P_{11}	2	$\{P_{110}{}^*$	$P_{111}{}^*$	P_{112}
		$\{(P_{020})$	(P_{021})	(P_{022})
		$\{(P_{210})$	(P_{211})	(P_{212})
P_{12}	3	$\{P_{120}$	$P_{121}{}^*$	$P_{122}{}^*$
P_{22}	4	P_{220}	P_{221}	$P_{222}{}^*$

In the above matrix, some hypothetical maximum third-stage payoff values have been asterisked and these optimal payoff combinations are shown on the tree figure. In analyzing the system, we read the tree backwards. Here, starting with stage 3, for every given allocation value (0–6), we find the best payoff value. For example, if 4 is the selected diagonal, then P_{121} is indicated as the chosen value. (We should also note that if more than one payoff on a single diagonal is maximum, then the several optimals offer alternative ways of proceeding). The subscripts can be used to help us trace back to the prior planning stages that contributed to the third-stage optimum. We know that P_{121} requires an allocation of one unit in the third stage, preceded by the allocation plan for P_{12}. The payoff P_{12} required the allocation of two units in the second stage and one unit initially. The plan is, therefore, fully determined, fully constrained, and optimal, subject to the resource constraint of four units.

If the total of resources that can be allocated is not a fixed constraint, then it is possible to obtain an unconstrained optimum payoff by selecting the one largest payoff in the matrix of P_{ijk}'s. In another case, only an upper-bound constraint on resources might exist, such as no more than twelve units over ten stages. Tracing back, we find the allocation plan that gave rise to that value. The tree contains all this information; it does not have to carry forward nonoptimal payoffs. When there are several payoffs associated with any branch, only the best one need be remembered. In essence, what dynamic programming does for us is organize a great deal of information by removing the information that can never enter into any optimal planning configuration.

Unlike linear programming, each dynamic-programming model tends to be a unique structure, so it is impossible to generalize about the models in a more concise fashion than we have done. Planning-horizon considerations are not resolved by dynamic programming, but a good deal more insight concerning the effects of changing the planning horizon is generated than with LP. It can be shown that the prescription for an optimal solution will change according to the planning horizon that is used. In theory, all the factors required to decide on an optimal planning horizon could be included in the dynamic-programming model. However, the required estimates usually cannot be obtained by the manager, and even when they can the problem is likely to be too large to handle economically.

Let us consider briefly a numerical illustration of the dynamic-programming algorithm. Assume that a profit can be obtained for each unit allocated and that a cost is incurred for each unit not allocated. Assume also that the per unit profit increases as unit allocations are made in the later planning stages. As in our general example, no more than two units can be allocated at each stage. The profit and cost functions we will use are as follows:

Stage	For units allocated per unit profit	For units not allocated per unit cost
I	n	n
II	$2n$	n
III	$3n$	n

The corresponding first-stage net profits would be obtained from $nx_I - ny_I$, where x_I is the amount that is allocated in the first stage and y_I is the amount that is not allocated. In general, we will use x_i to represent the amount allocated in the ith stage and y_i the amount not allocated in the ith stage.

Allocation	0	1	2
Net Profit	$-2n$	0	$+2n$

Then the second-stage matrix (Table 9–7) is developed, from which the second-stage net profits are easily determined.

$$\text{(Profit) } (x_{II}) \; - \; \text{(Cost) } (y_{II}) \; = \; \text{Net profit}_{II}$$

(Profit)	(x_{II})	(Cost)	(y_{II})	Net profit$_{II}$
$(2n)$	(0)	(n)	(2)	$-2n$
$(2n)$	(1)	(n)	(1)	$+n$
$(2n)$	(2)	(n)	(0)	$+4n$

The matrix entries are simply the sums of the net profits for each stage's allocation plan.

Table 9–7

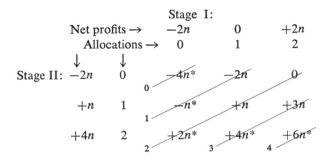

Stage I:

| Net profits → | $-2n$ | 0 | $+2n$ |
| Allocations → | 0 | 1 | 2 |

Stage II: $-2n$ 0 $-4n*$ $-2n$ 0
            0

$+n$ 1 $-n*$ $+n$ $+3n$
      1

$+4n$ 2 $+2n*$ $+4n*$ $+6n*$
      2   3   4

Next, the optimal net profits for each total allocation (as represented by the asterisked values along the diagonals) are carried forward to the third-stage matrix. (See Table 9–8.)

Table 9–8

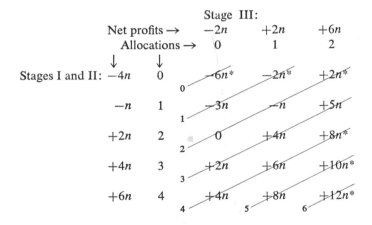

Stage III:

| Net profits → | $-2n$ | $+2n$ | $+6n$ |
| Allocations → | 0 | 1 | 2 |

Stages I and II: $-4n$ 0 $-6n*$ $-2n*$ $+2n*$
            0

$-n$ 1 $-3n$ $-n$ $+5n$
      1

$+2n$ 2 0 $+4n$ $+8n*$
      2

$+4n$ 3 $+2n$ $+6n$ $+10n*$
      3

$+6n$ 4 $+4n$ $+8n$ $+12n*$
      4   5   6

The calculations are now completed for three stages. If the optimal value is constrained only by the fact that no more than six units can be allocated, then $+12n$ is the maximum net profit. It is obtained by allocating two units in each stage. But assume instead that no more than five units can be allocated. The asterisked value along the appropriate diagonal is $+10n$. This is achieved by allocating two units in the third stage and a total of three units in stages I and II. Returning to the second-stage matrix, we find that the asterisked value along diagonal 3 is $+4n$, with an allocation plan of two units in the second stage and one unit in the first stage. Thus, with $x_i =$ units allocated per stage:

$$\text{Allocation constraint} = \sum_{\text{I}}^{\text{III}} x_i = 5$$

Stage	I	II	III	Total
Allocation plan	1	2	2	
Profit	0	$+4n$	$+6n$	$+10n$

The answer is entirely in keeping with what we would expect intuitively. Often, however, the problem is too large to use intuition, and the relations producing the payoffs are almost always far more complex than those in our example. Using dynamic programming to help plan under complex conditions is greatly facilitated by the computer. In some cases, such a planning approach cannot be accomplished without a computer facility. Yet at other times even computer capabilities are surpassed by the amount of information that the model involves.

Simulation

Simulation methods are noteworthy as a means of searching for a *near*-optimal planning configuration. Simulation models are as varied in structure as there are problems to solve and imaginative approaches to solve them. We shall present an example here that will illustrate the generality of the method as much as possible, but we must emphasize that only in the broadest sense is simulation generalizable.

Simulation of fully constrained planning configurations can be useful. For example, a PERT network may be simulated by selecting at random an activity time drawn from the statistical distributions that characterize each activity. The critical path and slack time for each simulation are aggregated to provide a pattern of expected behavior. Simulations can be designed to derive the complex probabilities that we have associated with the various branches of a decision tree. A computer simulation for dynamic programming would constitute a method for obtaining the kinds of calculation that we have just been describing, and, in addition, many further complications (including statistical variation) could be examined to determine how they seem to affect the solutions.

For our example we shall consider a stochastic simulation of the previous dynamic-programming planning problem. Let us recast the profit and cost relations for each of the planning stages. To keep the problem at a workable size, only two stages will be considered, but the reader should have no difficulty visualizing how to extend the simulation to any number of stages.

Assume that the per-unit profit for allocated units is not known with cer-

Table 9–9

Stage	Per-unit profit for units allocated	Probability	Monte Carlo numbers
I	n	.58	00–57
	$2n$	.32	58–89
	$3n$	.10	90–99
II	n	.30	00–29
	$2n$	.50	30–79
	$3n$	.20	80–99

tainty. Instead, the distribution shown in Table 9–9 is said to hold. Because the per-unit profits are variable, the net profits will be distributed statistically. For our example, all other factors will remain as they were before.

Monte Carlo numbers (MCN's). It will be noted that for stage 1 the per-unit profit of n is expected 58 percent of the time. As a result, 58 Monte Carlo numbers have been assigned to that event category (per-unit profit equals n). Similarly, 32 Monte Carlo numbers represent the first-stage event that per-unit profit equals $2n$. The same reasoning applies to all other potential events of both stages.

What, then, are Monte Carlo numbers (hereafter called MCN's)? MCN's are like uniquely numbered chips (say, 100 two-digit numbers, all different) that can be mixed together in a bowl so that when one chip is withdrawn at random, it could equally well be any number from 00 through 99. For our example, the 100 chips, numbered 00–99, would be thoroughly mixed in the bowl. Say that the first chip withdrawn is 95. We are simulating a first-stage event, and so we consult the above table for stage 1. The number 95 falls into the category 90–99. Therefore, the first per-unit profit to apply in our simulation will be equal to $3n$.

The chip numbered 95 must be replaced, otherwise the probabilities for the various events would be changed thereafter, and successive events would not be independent of one another. (For this example, we are assuming independence, but we should note that in some cases a lack of independence would be desired to make the simulation accurately model the situation. For such cases, drawn chips would not be returned to the bowl.)

Proceeding with our example, we now turn to the second stage. Say that the second chip withdrawn is 24. (It is as likely to be drawn as any other.) The appearance of this number would be interpreted (for the second stage) as a per-unit profit of n. It is now possible to calculate the appropriate values for the second-stage matrix, using the net-profit calculations shown in Table

Table 9–10

For stage 1:
(Profit) (x_1) — (Cost) (y_1) = Net profit$_1$
  $(3n)$ (0) (n) (2) $-2n$
  $(3n)$ (1) (n) (1) $+2n$
  $(3n)$ (2) (n) (0) $+6n$

For stage 2:
(Profit) (x_2) — (Cost) (y_2) = Net profit$_2$
  (n) (0) (n) (2) $-2n$
  (n) (1) (n) (1) 0
  (n) (2) (n) (0) $+2n$

Table 9–11

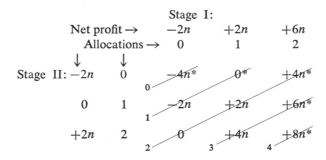

Stage I:

	Net profit →	$-2n$	$+2n$	$+6n$
	Allocations →	0	1	2
Stage II: $-2n$	0	$-4n^*$	0^*	$+4n^*$
0	1	$-2n$	$+2n$	$+6n^*$
$+2n$	2	0	$+4n$	$+8n^*$

NOTE: Asterisks indicate optimal net profit. The diagonals represent equal values of total resource allocations.

9–10. These results are different from those we had before. Table 9–11 shows the second-stage matrix. We note that a marked shift has occurred from the previous second-stage matrix. If a total allocation of 3 were to apply here, then the second-stage allocation would be 1 (whereas previously it was 2), and the first-stage allocation would be 2 (previously 1).

    In other words, the simulation produces a variety of plans, depending on which events occur. For example, if we had worked through the simulation six times, the record for three stages given in Table 9–12 might have appeared, given the total allocation constraint of 5.

    The variety of results that occurs in this simulation (using MCN's) is frequently a typical effect of using stochastic data. One question that often arises is how large a sample should be used. Will five simulations do? We can say "no" to the latter question, but it is far more difficult to answer the former. In fact, we cannot answer it until we know how we will use the

Table 9–12

| | Stage | | |
Simulation number	I	II	III
1	1	2	2
2	2	1	2
3	2	2	1
4	2	1	2
5	1	2	2
6	2	2	1

results. Each three-stage pattern can be identified, and the patterns can be counted by type. The one that occurs most frequently could be used as the plan. But, as can be seen, simulations of this kind actually raise more questions than they answer. The hope of those who prefer fully constrained plans is that one simulation pattern will emerge as clearly dominant. When this does not happen, the manager may be well advised to consider the partially constrained plans explained in the next chapter.

Another way to use the simulation is to determine what would happen to net profit if a particular plan (such as 1, 2, 2) is chosen and the profits vary according to the distributions. Thus, for the MCN's 95 and 24, the net profit would have been $+4n$ for the plan 1, 2 as compared to the optimal, in this case, of $+6n$ for 2, 1. Average profits for following different plans could be compared in this way.

The simulation flow diagram. Let us turn to another example. The Lambda Company produces a product that is known to fail as a function both of age and of the number of times it is used. The present design, D_1, is to be compared with a proposed new design, D_2. The company's plans will be greatly altered if the decision is made to switch to D_2.

The outcome measure—failure rate—must be determined so that a thorough analysis can be made. The failure rate can be identified with the manufacturer's guarantee period, the product's repurchase rate, repair and maintenance costs, and such intangible costs as lost good will. We can assume that experiments have yielded the table of cumulative failure probabilities given in Table 9–13. Every unit of both types has failed by the sixth time period no matter how often the product is used. Nor are there any units that survive the twelfth use, no matter what the age. The data reflect an evident dependence of failure rate on both age and frequency of use.

The key to each design's performance will be a function of the use frequencies over time. If these were fixed at, say, two uses per month, then the

Table 9–13 Cumulative Failure Probabilities as a Function of Number of Uses and Age

Age (months)	Number of uses													Design alternative
	0	1	2	3	4	5	6	7	8	9	10	11	12	
1	0	.05	.10	.15	.20	.25	.30	.35	.40	.50	.60	.80	1.00	D_1
	0	.04	.09	.12	.15	.18	.20	.25	.35	.45	.55	.75	1.00	D_2
2	.20	.25	.30	.35	.40	.45	.50	.55	.60	.65	.85	.95	1.00	D_1
	.15	.20	.25	.45	.55	.65	.75	.80	.85	.86	.87	.88	1.00	D_2
3	.40	.45	.50	.55	.65	.75	.82	.85	.85	.90	.90	1.00	1.00	D_1
	.35	.45	.55	.65	.75	.85	.85	.85	.87	.87	.89	1.00	1.00	D_2
4	.60	.61	.62	.63	.65	.76	.83	.85	.85	.89	.90	1.00	1.00	D_1
	.65	.70	.75	.80	.81	.82	.85	.85	.87	.89	.90	1.00	1.00	D_2
5	.80	.80	.80	.81	.82	.83	.84	.85	.86	.97	.98	1.00	1.00	D_1
	.75	.76	.77	.80	.81	.82	.85	.90	1.00	1.00	1.00	1.00	1.00	D_2
6	1.00	1.00	1.00	1.00	1.00	1.00	1.00	1.00	1.00	1.00	1.00	1.00	1.00	D_1
	1.00	1.00	1.00	1.00	1.00	1.00	1.00	1.00	1.00	1.00	1.00	1.00	1.00	D_2

Table 9–14

Age	Design 1 Probability of failure	Design 2 Probability of failure
1	.10	.09
2	.30	.25
3	.50	.55
4	.62	.75
5	.80	.77
6	1.00	1.00

failure curves could be obtained by inspection. The statistics would be those of Table 9–14.[15] Design 1 has better life characteristics than Design 2 only in the third and fourth months. The failure curves for these two designs—with use frequency equal to two—are depicted in Figure 9–15.

Now let us look at the failure data that would apply if the frequency of use were fixed at one per month and also at three per month. These are given in Table 9–15. With respect to a use frequency of one, Design 1 is superior for only the four-month period. Considering the data derived for three uses per month, Design 2 is preferred for the first and fifth months, but it is decidedly inferior for other times.

We see that the evaluation of these designs is a complex matter. This is especially true when use frequency is not a fixed number per month but is instead a random variable. And, to make matters worse, the frequency of use can be a function of the type of user. Let us assume that three types of user

Table 9–15

Age	Design 1: Probability of failure		Design 2: Probability of failure	
	1 use/month	3 uses/month	1 use/month	3 uses/month
1	.05	.15	.04	.12
2	.25	.35	.20	.45
3	.45	.55	.45	.65
4	.61	.63	.70	.80
5	.80	.81	.76	.80
6	1.00	1.00	1.00	1.00

[15] The material on this and the next 7 pages has been adapted from Martin K. Starr, *Product Design and Decision Theory* (Englewood Cliffs, N.J.: Prentice-Hall, 1963). Copyright © 1963 by Martin K. Starr.

Figure 9–15   Failure Curves for Design 1 and Design 2

NOTE: The use frequency per month is equal to 2.

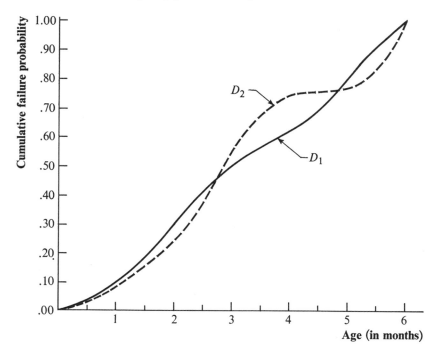

exist, *A, B,* and *C.* To really complicate matters, we will suppose that any combination of users can operate on each unit during its lifetime. (For example, the product is rented on a monthly basis, or different operators are assigned to use the unit during its lifetime.) Specifically, let us take the data in Table 9–16 as the monthly use frequencies of each type of user. In addition,

Table 9–16

| Frequency of use/month | User | | |
	Type *A*	Type *B*	Type *C*
1	.20	.00	.10
2	.50	.10	.20
3	.30	.30	.40
4	.00	.60	.30

the frequency of each type of user must be determined. We will choose these to be

Probability of user type	User type
.25	A
.45	B
.30	C

The problem that we have constructed is a reasonable representation of the kinds of relationship that might ordinarily have to be handled in order to determine outcome values. Analytic methods are too burdensome—if they can be used at all—to resolve such problems. And so we turn to simulation methods.

Let us first construct a flow chart of the system that will be used. Figure 9–16 presents such a chart. It has not been drawn to be totally general, since the failure data shown are peculiar to the first design when it is one month old. But by doing this we can explain the specific steps to be taken in order to run through the simulation. The different paths in the figure are the various things that can happen. For example, one unit of the product might be utilized by an A-type user in the first month. He might make use of it twice in the month and experience no failure. In the second month a B-type user takes it. He operates it four times without having a failure. At the third month a user type is again chosen. It happens to be a repeat of a B-type user. With one use in this third month a failure occurs. Therefore, in our hypothetical example the product has failed in the third month. If this falls within the guarantee period, the unit must be replaced by the Lambda Company.

The important question that remains is: How can we generate historical patterns of user type, frequency of use, age of product, and failure rates that are in keeping with the probabilities that describe the system? Once we can do this we can obtain outcome measures for both designs. What we are trying to do is to simulate the occurrence of the states of nature that interact with the design strategy. The states of nature must appear in the correct statistically determined proportions.

Simulation of this kind can be accomplished by the use of the Monte Carlo method. But the use of a bowl is primitive. In practice we work with a table of random numbers like Table 9–17. The table is read in a systematic way, either left to right or right to left, top to bottom or bottom to top, or along some diagonal. Each pair of digits represents a chip withdrawn and recorded.[16]

---

[16] If the probabilities are specified to three places we would use 1,000 chips, or, equivalently, three-digit sets of random numbers. For example, if $P(A) = .252$; $P(B) = .305$; $P(C) = .443$, then we would use number sets 000–251, 252–556, and 557–999.

Figure 9–16   Decision Flow Chart for Simulation Model (Design 1)

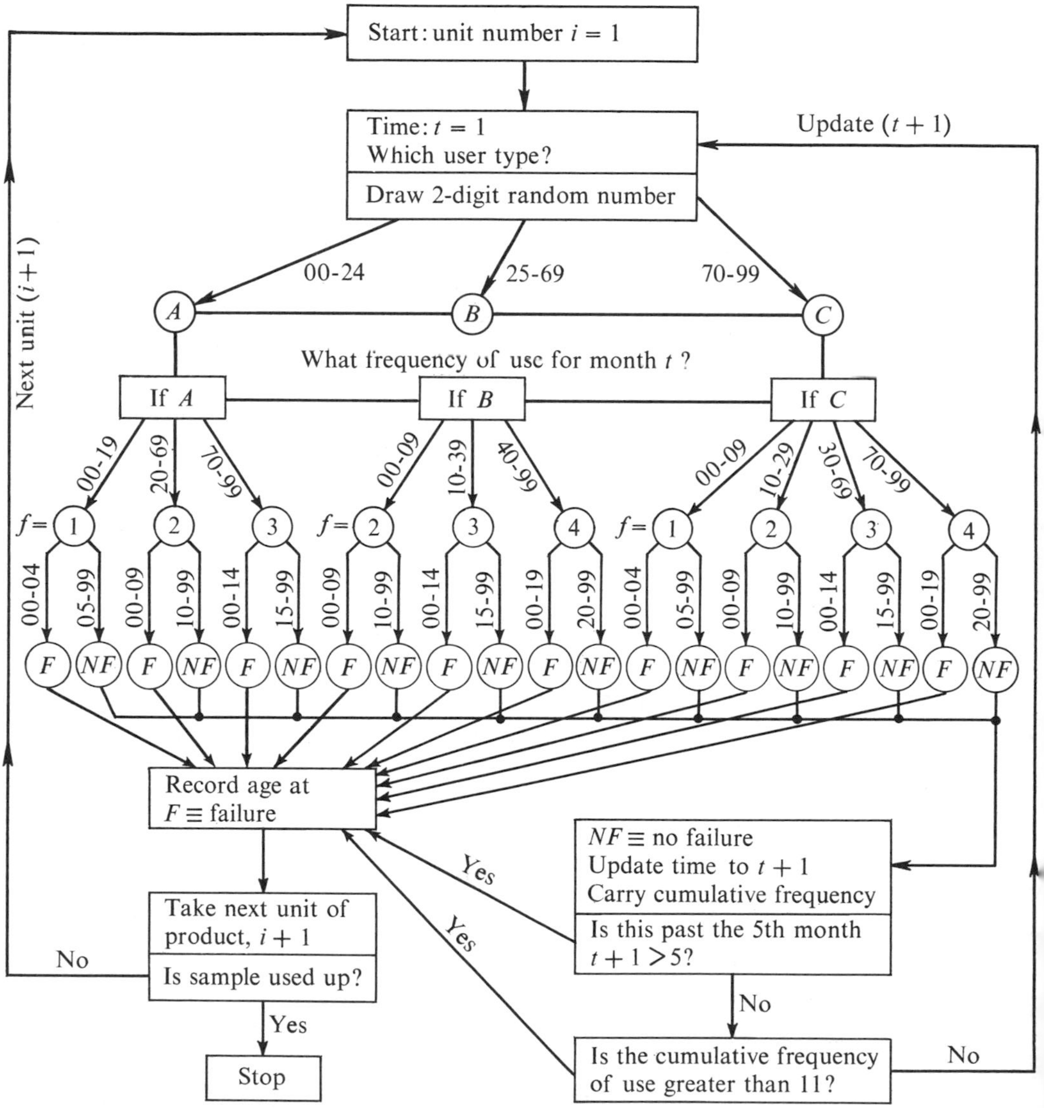

The tabled numbers have no pattern, just as properly drawn chips would have no pattern. That is why they are called random numbers. Every number from 00 through 99 has an equal likelihood of appearing. Therefore, the Monte Carlo number assignments 00–24, 25–69, and 70–99 will yield just the right proportion of A-, B-, and C-type users. These number assignments are shown on the branches of the flow diagram in Figure 9–15.

Table 9–17   A Table of Random Numbers

87879	01629	72184	33853	95144	67943
50702	78555	97442	78809	40575	79714
52971	85974	68067	78814	40103	70759
74220	84157	23241	49332	23646	09390
26526	80335	58090	85871	07205	31749
04359	45538	41435	61103	32428	94042
81699	84904	50163	22625	07845	71308
55960	23149	07370	65065	06580	46285
29459	23032	83242	89938	40510	27252
35675	81645	60479	71035	99380	59759
31258	78156	07871	20369	53947	08534
36674	46255	80541	42903	37366	21164
69344	44260	90570	01632	21002	24413
57797	34660	32510	71558	78228	42304
48805	59480	88092	11441	96016	76091

Let us use the following set of random numbers:

61275   33498   43580   74935   96602   17870   65187

Our first pair is 61, and this indicates a *B*-type user. *B*-type consumers have their own characteristic frequencies of use per month. These are zero for one use, 10 percent for two uses, 30 percent for three uses, and 60 percent for four uses. We assign Monte Carlo numbers 00–09 for two uses, 10–39 for three uses, and 40–99 to represent four uses. As before, the assigned numbers are in the correct proportion to the occurrence probabilities. The next two-digit random number is 27, which indicates three uses by this *B*-type user in the first month of the product's life. We are beginning to build the history of the first product unit. It is being spun out of an imaginary world that we hope models the real world.

We ask, at this point: Did the unit fail in this first month? And to answer the question we must turn to the data of Table 9–13. Design 1 is our subject; the age of the unit is one month; the use frequency in that month was three. Then the number at the appropriate intersection is .15. This means that 15 percent of all units would fail, but did this one? We assign Monte Carlo numbers again. For F (failure) we use 00–14, and for NF (no failure) we use 15–99. The next random number is 53, so no failure occurred. Following the directional arrows in Figure 9–15, we arrive at the box that tells us to begin our computations for the second month.[17] Now we ask whether the month under consideration is greater than five, because each product unit must fail in the

---

[17] If more than one user type can occur in a month, we merely adjust our time units and make weekly or daily runs.

sixth month if it has not previously done so. The answer is "no," and so we follow the "no" arrow to the next question. This is the cumulative frequency-of-use test. Again the answer is "no." Therefore, we move to the next time period and begin a new iteration.[18]

Starting the second month with the first unit of product we draw random numbers 34, 93, and 43. This is translated as follows—the B-type user continues in the second month; the frequency of use in the second month is four (making the cumulative frequency of use equal to seven); the failure probability of 0.55 is specified at the intersection of: D_1, age two months, and $7 = 3 + 4$ uses. The appropriate Monte Carlo assignment is F(00–54), NF(55–99); therefore, *a failure has occurred in the second month.* Obeying the instructions given by Figure 9–15, we record the age at failure. We then take a new unit of product, since the sample of twenty-five units sold in January is not used up. With this new unit we return to the beginning and repeat our procedures with the next set of random numbers.

A comparison of Designs 1 and 2 is presented in Figure 9–17. Only five units have been simulated for each design. (This sample, of course, is much too small to provide a reliable assessment, but it illustrates the procedure.) The two designs have almost identical histories in this limited sample. Let us summarize and tabulate a few of the outcome measures that might be of interest to the Lambda Company (see Table 9–18). Although we pretend that the sample is of sufficient size to warrant the drawing of such conclusions, it is apparent that the results deviate substantially from expectations. A-type users should be represented about 25 percent of the time. In this sample they are too infrequent, as are the C-type users, who should appear about 30 percent of the time.[19] Of course, this means that the percentage of B-type users is overstated.

Table 9–18

Outcomes	Design 1	Design 2
Average life	2.2 months	2.0 months
Average number of uses before failure	6.2 uses	5.6 uses
Average number of uses per month	2.81 uses	2.80 uses
Percentage of A-type users	$\frac{2}{11} = .182$	$\frac{1}{10} = .100$
Percentage of B-type users	$\frac{8}{11} = .727$	$\frac{8}{10} = .800$
Percentage of C-type users	$\frac{1}{11} = .091$	$\frac{1}{10} = .100$

---

[18] By *iteration* we mean the successive passes through the system.

[19] A crude way of judging sample sufficiency is to check probabilities that are known to have been built into the model.

Figure 9–17   Comparison of Failure Rates by Simulation Method for Designs D_1 and D_2

Unit	Month	Random number	User	Fre-quency	Cumulative frequency	Design 1 F	Design 1 NF	Design 2 F	Design 2 NF
1	1	61	B						
		27		3	3				
		53					•		•
	2	34	B						
		93		4	7				
		43				•		•	
2	1	58	B						
		07		2	2				
		49					•		•
	2	35	B						
		96		4	6				
		60					•	•	
	3	21	A						
		78		3	9				
		70				•			
3	1	65	B						
		18		3	3				
		78					•		•
	2	52	B						
		13		3	6				
		39				•		•	
4	1	08	A						
		10		1	1				
		87					•		•
	2	70	C						
		18		2	3				
		16				•		•	
5	1	66	B						
		15		3	3				
		79					•		•
	2	46	B						
		11		3	6				
		26				•		•	

With a sufficient sample, Lambda would be in a position to test different guarantee policies with respect to each design. Knowing the costs of the replacement units would not be sufficient, however, since the guarantee terms may involve a discount policy that varies as a function of the age and the amount of wear experienced by the failed unit, and perhaps total replacement of the unit would not always be necessary if certain components could be replaced or repaired. In this case it would be necessary to keep track of the types of failure. Many other considerations could also affect a real simulation attempt. For example, weather might be an extraneous factor that would change the probabilities of failure. (This would be true of an automobile battery, for example.) Then failure rates would vary seasonally, and users would be subdivided geographically as well as by the type of use[20] to which they subject the units. User distributions might vary as a function of the design being considered. Sequential dependencies of user types can easily be visualized as a serious consideration—in other words, a user who does not experience a failure is likely to employ the unit in the next period, whereas a user who does experience a failure might switch to a different brand. The probabilities of such switching would be a function of the individual's satisfaction with the performance of the Lambda Company's product.

Sensitivity testing. All these considerations and many others can be included in a simulation model with little difficulty, but they require the exercise of a great deal of care. Sufficient relevant data must be available. However, there is leeway. For those data that have been crudely estimated, we can determine whether greater precision is worth the cost and effort. This is done by varying the values that are suspect within whatever range is deemed reasonable. (It is much easier to specify a range within which an estimate may fall than to state an exact value.) If the outcomes are affected noticeably by the set of alterations, then we must conclude that the system being investigated is sensitive to that variable. To obtain meaningful results, additional information must be collected. On the other hand, it is not unusual to find that the system is relatively invariant to the alterations that have been made, from which we can conclude that our estimate is good enough. Thus, for example, we could change the user type distribution and observe the extent to which this modification affects the average unit's lifetime. A degree of control over the user type (through distribution channels or advertising) might be exercised if the outcome results are affected by this variable.

A word of caution about sensitivity testing is in order. Seldom is the estimate of only one variable of a system suspect. And, if the possibility of interaction exists, it is not a sufficient test to hold everything constant and vary only one of these suspicious variables at a time. It is necessary to test each variable at several different levels of the other variables. This requirement imposes considerable computational burdens in addition to the basic simulation, which is itself a demanding clerical operation. Because of this, computers should be tied into serious simulation efforts whenever possible. Small simulations can certainly be done by hand, but this encourages a tendency to oversimplify the

---

[20] In our example, frequency of use was a function of user type. In general, however, the failure rate also would be a function of the type of use. This would modify Table 9–13 by including the additional characteristic of user type.

model and to understate the sample requirements in order to justify manual procedures. As in all similar situations, a balance must be found between the costs of the study and the value of the answers. With the use of a computer, many years of performance can be simulated in a few minutes, but substantial investments of time are required to prepare the computer program.

Figure 9–18

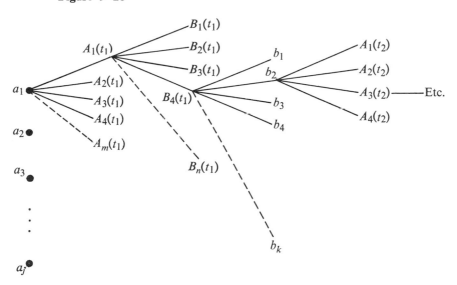

A competitive simulation. Before we leave the subject of simulation, let us consider briefly one more planning problem that further exemplifies the utility of the simulation method. Figure 9–18 shows a competitive situation set up for simulation where states of nature intervene. The states are identified by a_j, b_k, . . . , depending on the time at which they occur. The a's occur first, then the b's, and so on. They might represent mean monthly temperatures or various levels of the economy or different combinations of such factors.

To keep this discussion simple, we will follow only one branch of the network, namely, a_1, $A_1(t_1)$, $B_4(t_1)$, b_2, $A_3(t_2)$. We can describe this particular chain of events as follows: In the first time period, the state of nature is a_1. The alternatives that could have occurred are a_2, a_3, . . . , a_j. The manager uses his strategy A_1 at time t_1; the competitor uses his action B_4 at time t_1. Then the state of nature becomes b_2. The manager responds with A_3 at time t_2. This chain of network events can be continued for as many time periods as it is reasonable to consider. The manager's plan, in this case, is composed of the strategies $A_1(t_1)$, $A_3(t_2)$, and so forth; the competitor's plan begins with $B_4(t_1)$.

Probability values (p_j's) are associated with each a_j (and later with each b_k, etc.), and MCN's can be assigned accordingly. As for strategies, the manager is free to choose those he considers best. Both the manager's and the competitor's strategies are subject to the kind of game-theory considerations that were developed in Chapter 5. Once the simulation tree is drawn up, the manager can propose a specific plan and assume specific counteractions by the competitor. Then, given the simulated environmental conditions, the payoffs can be evaluated by using Monte Carlo analysis.

Determinate competitive planning systems are characteristically composed of a large number of strategy chains. At every stage in the evolution of the system (i.e., after successive moves by the players), there is at least one chain that is optimal for each player. This follows the simple convention that each player will always do what is best for himself. Chess conforms to our requirements for a fully constrained planning system. The board configuration changes in a nonrecurring way except when there is a stalemate. But neither chess nor any other competitive situation is necessarily a fully constrained situation, since competitors may not be completely rational.

A military situation is like a chess game if we assume that all the competitive alternatives can be described (see pp. 167–69). Assuming further that, like chess, the situation has the characteristics of a two-person, zero-sum game and that both sides behave rationally, then the minimax criterion establishes the system as fully constrained. But these assumptions are not valid, for in actual military situations an unknown variety of strategic sequences is possible through invention. The degree of innovation in generating military strategy is not constrained by a rule book. Nevertheless, the minimax criterion is used by the military as the basis for planning, while chess is so rich in extensive alternatives that neither party can really apply the minimax criterion. The contrariness of this situation is apparent—chess, which is really constrained, is played as though it is not, and military strategy, which really cannot be constrained, is treated as though it is. The way to account for this reversal is that far fewer *reasonable* strategies are available in military situations than in chess. In other words, the number of likely strategies seems to be the governing factor here.

Under certain conditions, the *best one* of all possible competitive plans is *known with certainty* to include random elements whose manipulation is guided by a *determinate* decision rule (see pp. 174–76). We have previously called these *mixed strategies*. As we proceed along such paths, the next activity link is not known with certainty beforehand. Rather, the *set* of next possible activities is known, as is the probability that each of these alternatives might be used. For our networks, we can represent a single step of the mixed-strategy case as in Figure 9–19:

Figure 9–19

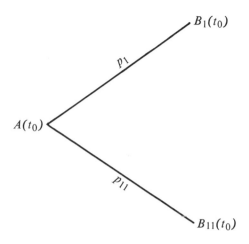

where p_1 and p_{11} are determined under certainty. We should note that with mixed strategies we cannot have a fully constrained planning model. When part of the network includes any form of choice that cannot be determined until the actual prior events occur, then the plan must belong to the class of partially constrained models discussed in the next chapter. We can classify mixed-strategy cases as a special form of partially constrained planning models.

MANAGERIAL CONCLUSIONS

A variety of well-known model forms can assist in planning. But analytic techniques such as linear programming and dynamic programming have many limitations that have to be considered in the ever-present light of their strengths. Simulation is a most attractive alternative. Jay Forrester, for example, has constructed elaborate simulations of industrial transfers of materials and orders in response to sales, advertising, and production-scheduling options.[21] His work, which has been continued also by his students, is called "industrial dynamics." The special name is deserved because industrial dynamics is one of the closest approaches to total systems planning that has ever been made.

The simulation-builder is like an architect. He must envision the total structure, yet contend with details. As in architecture, there are no all-encom-

---

[21] Jay W. Forrester, *Industrial Dynamics* (New York: Wiley, 1961).

passing rules that will work for any situation. Each planning problem is unique, and each fully constrained solution requires a high degree of inventiveness on the part of the model-builders. Moreover, planners participating in the process are exposed to many concepts and facts that ordinarily are routed past them.

The most obvious weakness of the simulation approach is that a great deal of detail is required to produce a result that cannot be shown to be optimal or even near-optimal. Heuristic procedures are used to differentiate between one neighborhood of payoffs and another. The neighborhood notion is a useful one, intended to represent a group of relatively homogeneous payoffs. By inference, simulation can locate the *neighborhood* of the system's optimal plan. That inference is based on the assumption that the neighborhoods are large enough for a "good" simulation sample to pick *all* of them up and represent them so that the "best" one can be chosen. Since even planning systems that will be reduced eventually to full constraint may be excessively rich in combinatorial potential, the simulation method requires great inventions of effective and believable heuristics to locate near-optimal neighborhoods. The alternative is the bulldozer tactic of inordinately large samples.

Simulations have been used with success for many years—for example, in job-shop situations where the recurrent environmental factors of successive periods are distributed in a reasonably independent fashion. Although they fall far short of locating a system's optimal performance, fully constrained planning simulations have also been used for designing aircraft, dams, and missiles and for other situations where the sequence of environmental conditions can be specified with some success and the "sensible" range of strategies *seems* to be limited. Most frequently, this occurs when the limitation can be attributed to technological factors.

Each fully constrained plan is like a map that has only one *best* route between any two points. That is why we exclude competitive situations that demand mixed strategies (where variations of route are first set by design, but then respond to an act of nature such as the toss of a coin). Logic, tradition, and technology are the factors that underlie the choice of an optimal route. If the basic assumptions give the manager pause, he may do well to consider the possibility of using some form of multiple-path planning—that is, planning for a partially constrained system.

The advantages of assuming that fully constrained systems exist are apparent. Perhaps they are so attractive as to cloud the issues or to hide the fact that alternative planning procedures are available. With single-path thinking, the need for risk and uncertainty decision criteria is eliminated. The search problem is simplified, though certainly not removed. Emphasis is shifted from planning to schedule and resource control. The notions of how to plan become entrenched. Deterministic planning is epitomized by such slogans as "form follows function," "never change a horse in midstream," and "the shoemaker should stick to his last." In spite of its popularity, however, it is frequently likely to prove a poor assumption in the long run.

SUMMARY

The chapter begins by emphasizing that the dimensionality of planning involves opportunity. Constraints on plans are created not only by the manager's perception of what the situation is, but also by the manager's judgments of what could be. These perceptions and judgments produce attitudes that affect all plans.

Definition of the planning function is critical for understanding what can be accomplished through planning. Toward this end, the concept of extensive, determinate project networks is introduced. The notions of "extensive" and of "determinate" networks are explained for the purpose of describing fully constrained planning models, which are the most prevalent form presently in use. The reasons that the manager prefers to use fully constrained assumptions for his project planning are developed throughout the chapter, so only a beginning is made at this point. But a question is raised concerning the kinds of assumption that must be made by the manager to approximate conditions of full constraint.

Fully constrained planning models are detailed as though no opportunities to deviate from the plan will occur. Generally, such plans will be altered only when serendipity or its opposite intervenes. The widespread use of fully constrained models may be explained partially by the fact that net-benefit considerations, with emphasis on the high cost of complex planning studies, favor the simple approach. But increasing penalties for missing opportunities plus greater systems instability may be changing this situation. In general, principles of planning, which tend to be conservative, are giving way to theory, which is permissive to opportunity.

The discussion of network-design considerations points up the two major phases of project work, the first dealing with the actual design configuration of the network and the second with schedule control and resource allocation. It is emphasized that few objective models exist to guide the design of the planning configuration but that by feedback, well-developed schedule-control models often affect the manager's design decisions. Gantt charts are introduced, accenting the listing and sequencing functions that are at the core of the design phase of the planning operation. Gantt charting is then contrasted with the far more flexible network methods that are broadly known as critical-path models and include the well-known PERT systems.

Providing time estimates for completing network activities is a major undertaking. The importance of problems of estimation cannot be overlooked. Given the network design and the estimation of time, it becomes possible to determine the critical path and to measure slack on network branches. Slack is the amount of slippage that can be permitted for various activities without affecting the planner's target date for completion of the project.

The notion of trading off resources is developed by example. This capability of network analysis represents a considerable advantage over the older Gantt technique. Then, by the introduction of cost estimation in the network, time and cost trade-offs are explored, allowing the distinction to be drawn between minimum-cost and minimum-time project plans. Various relationships between planning horizons and updating intervals are also explored, and the notion of continuous planning is introduced.

Ultimately, some method must be chosen for selecting one design of the fully constrained network. Three major techniques are described and their pros and cons examined. These are linear programming, dynamic programming, and simulation. In general, the complexity of the approach increases as we move from LP to dynamic programming to simulation. Consequently, net-benefit considerations are clearly warranted to justify the level of search that is used in deciding which plan to employ for the fully constrained system.

EXERCISES

1. The chapter begins with a quote from *Flatland,* where two-dimensional beings live in a two-dimensional world. Would the nature of planning differ in such a world? What is meant by "the dimensions of planning"?

2. In what sense does planning with fewer constraints represent "a higher view of things" for management?

3. Identify all five branches of the project-planning system in Figure 9–1. How do they constitute a determinate project network?

4. What are fully constrained planning models? When the conditions for full constraint do not exist, what liberties can the manager feel free to take in order to approximate such conditions? What difficulties might be encountered as a result of approximations of full constraint?

5. Discuss the assumption of full constraint in connection with
   a. constructing an office building
   b. selecting a plant location
   c. shifting production from an old plant to a new one
   d. maintaining a stock portfolio for a pension fund
   e. transferring the leadership of a company to a new president

6. Differentiate between the design of a network (in the sense of the architecture of its configuration) and the use of network models to control project schedules. Is it true that the design of the network must be completed before schedule control can be considered? Would it be reasonable to say that design modifies schedule and schedule modifies design? If so, how does a plan ever get specified?

7. Develop a Gantt chart designed to treat the writing of a report as a project. Explain your steps and present time estimates for the accomplishment of each activity. Then convert your Gantt chart into an appropriate PERT-type network model.

8. The following problem is to be solved by a three-man group: The first twenty prime numbers[22] are to be added together and the sum is to be divided by the square of the first three-digit prime number.
   a. Develop a PERT chart that will use these three individuals in as efficient a pattern as possible. Make use of the Beta function to estimate times for accomplishment of each individual's tasks. Find the critical path of the network, and then, utilizing the concept of slack, suggest manpower trade-offs that might improve your network's target date.
   b. Next, provide some hypothetical cost estimates for working the tasks at different rates wherever such alternatives are feasible in your network. Then determine the minimum-cost target date and compare it with the minimum-time target date.

9. How does expediting affect the use of PERT networks?

10. Describe the planning horizon and updating interval for
   a. the construction of a new dam
   b. redesigning an airport so that it can accept larger aircraft
   c. converting a manual filing system to a computerized one
   d. revamping the postal system

11. Describe how stimulation might be used to help plan the Post Office revamping mentioned in Exercise 10d. What are the advantages and disadvantages of tackling this problem through simulation?

---

[22] A positive integer, x, that is greater than one is called prime when its only integer factors are 1 and x. Thus, the first five prime numbers are 2, 3, 5, 7, and 11.

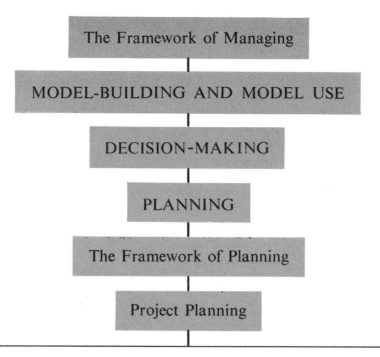

The Framework of Managing

MODEL-BUILDING AND MODEL USE

DECISION-MAKING

PLANNING

The Framework of Planning

Project Planning

Chapter 10
Planning for High-Risk Systems

The pace of social and technological changes has
made fully constrained planning more difficult
to accept. Acknowledging risk elements by
means of contingency planning has become a competitive
necessity. Using contingency planning, management
maintains alternative strategies to take
advantage of opportunities that might arise and
to avoid serious future threats. When several
plans are proposed to meet various contingencies,
the resources required by these alternatives
must be inventoried. Prediction is needed to
reduce planning networks to a reasonable
number of multiple paths. And new concepts
are needed to deal with multiple-path
properties. When particular contingencies can
result in ruin, action limits may be specified
as thresholds to ensure the system's survival.

Chapter 10

PLANNING FOR HIGH-RISK SYSTEMS

"The Clairvoyant Society of Bristol regrets that due to unforeseen events the meeting for tomorrow evening must be cancelled."—From an actual newspaper announcement

MANAGEMENT RESPONSE TO HIGH RISK

If there is choice, a plan with high risk of large losses would never be accepted unless, at the same time, it has an offsetting potential for large gains. Even so, a plan with lower risks might well be chosen. Figure 10–1 illustrates two significantly different types of

Figure 10–1

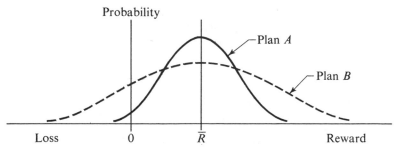

risk-reward system, plans *A* and *B*. Both plans have the same expected value of reward, $\overline{R}$.[1] But plan *B* has a much higher risk of both large losses and large gains than does plan *A*. Which plan should be chosen?

Unusually good opportunities and high risk of severe penalties often go hand in hand. Users of ouija boards and tarot cards, astrologers, and clairvoyants work their mysteries at the extremes of such systems. What replaces the superstition, the mystique, or the long-shot hunch when management wishes to be rational about plans involving high risks? The choice between plans *A* and *B* can always be made if there is available a perfect prediction of exactly what will occur if either plan is used. Then the "one best way" is obvious. But such perfect predictions are rarely available, and even very good predictions, when possible, are extremely expensive. Lacking clairvoyance, management can achieve a feeling of security by ignoring high-risk complications. That is, by forgetting plan *B,* management can feel some sense of assurance—but only at the opportunity cost of missing the potential of plan *B* rewards.

The assumption of "one best way," no matter how it is achieved, is the basis for fully constrained planning models. But risk continually infiltrates systems, like weeds in a garden, and risk reduction requires ceaseless and often brilliant effort. In recent years, social and technological changes have affected our enterprises at such a high rate that experience with most systems cannot be developed to a point where risk can be reduced or eliminated. Consequently, the "one best way" concept cannot operate effectively.

Another approach is to speed up management's response rate and to plan for periods that are short enough to be relatively stable. Short planning periods have all the dangers of suboptimizations (see pp. 412–14), but, if consecutive periods are relatively independent, then a good deal can be gained from faster decision-making, more rapid action, and so on. Speed is accomplished partially through increased experience, but more completely by means of model-building and coordinated use of information technology. Formal approaches have been developed that treat larger portions of the total system, and this helps, too, in fully constrained planning. Ultimately, however, the inclusion of risk elements in planning becomes a competitive necessity. And the recognition of risk requires planning for *contingencies.* (Contingencies, of course, can be good as well as bad.) With contingency planning (if *x* occurs we use *A,* but if *z* occurs we use *B*), management maintains preplanned alternatives to take advantage of the possibilities.

---

[1] $\overline{R}$ is also called the (arithmetic) mean and, most commonly, the average value.

PARTIALLY CONSTRAINED PLANNING MODELS

Planning for "bad" contingencies becomes increasingly crucial as a greater percentage of the company's assets are at risk. And it is apparent that the percentage of assets committed to any single plan tends to increase rapidly as the management level moves up.[2] Planning for "good" contingencies, on the other hand, is related largely to how likely they are to occur. Contingency planning models (which are equivalent to what we will call partially constrained models) exist in various forms. Informal approaches to partial planning constraints are being used regularly in a small number of advanced management systems, while formal methodology is being developed continuously both in industry and at the universities.

The amount of constraint incorporated in a plan is related to the degree of variability that is perceived to exist in the system. Planning can range, in theory, from no constraint at all to full constraint. Full constraint, which we examined in the preceding chapter, concedes no variability; it is not always a very realistic basis for planning, although it is widely used. The notion of totally unconstrained systems, on the other hand, is particularly elusive. It would mean complete ignorance concerning the environments that might occur as the plan evolves, a situation as theoretical and unrealistic as decision-making under ambiguity (see pp. 140–44). In most cultures, even "life after death" plans are not unconstrained. Plans dealing with explorations of the planetary system of Pleione (if there is one) would not be highly constrained, since, for safety, the astronauts would be given as many options as possible. But even here constraints would exist, and this situation epitomizes contingency planning with partially constrained models. Systems strictly dominated by technology are highly constrained, whereas planning for the creation of advertising copy, while hardly unconstrained, is at least noticeably less restricted by procedure.

Partially constrained systems require basically different treatment from fully constrained ones. This is because they do not provide "one best way" to proceed, and the planner therefore is not searching for such a procedure. Instead, he purposely makes his plan open to the risk nature of environmental conditions. In other words (in cases that are not trivial),[3] partially constrained systems do not have an unambiguous optimal strategy. Each planning alter-

---

[2] A log-normal type of distribution (see p. 572) would probably describe the small percentage of top managers responsible for plans concerning the largest portion of the company's assets.

[3] I.e., in cases in which a single plan does not dominate the other alternatives under *all* environmental circumstances.

native is open to chance, and every commitment is to some degree susceptible to regret. Managers are likely to feel that partially constrained planning models (PCPM's) are more realistic than FCPM's, but the latter are so much easier to conceive and use that managers tend to prefer them.

When several plans are proposed to meet various contingencies, the resources required for all the proposed plans must be maintained. It is not possible to say at the beginning which strategy will be followed ultimately, because that depends on what happens. The manager is prepared to cope with a variety of eventualities. For example, sales of the product far exceed expectations, so the plan for the larger plant is used. The new airplane does not get off the ground, so the plan for phasing it in by spring is replaced by the summer plan, which is not a last-minute thought born of necessity. Just as the stock issue is about to be made, the market drops severely, so the alternative plan for marketing bonds is thrown into gear. Clearly, contingencies can be taken into consideration by preplanning such PCPM's. In network terms, these kinds of system literally have *multiple paths*.

A planning network may consist of many branches that intertwine and share common activities. A specific activity (say, six months in the future) might be usable no matter which plan is being followed. In other words, the activity requirements at certain future points can turn out to be the same no matter which prior route was followed. In general, however, we assume that the best possible results for each unique set of environmental conditions will come from a unique network route. The outcomes from such basically different planning systems will not be alike. The manager's expectations are tentative, whereas with full constraint they are settled.

Figure 10–2

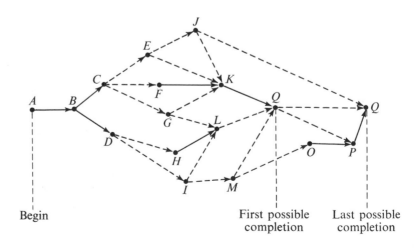

An example of a partially constrained network is shown in Figure 10–2. Dashed lines are used to represent the multiple paths of the system; solid lines represent paths that must be followed (including those that must be followed simultaneously, e.g., *BC* and *BD*) once the preceding node has been reached. The completion node, *Q,* can occur at different points in time, depending on which set of activities is used. In the figure, two possible completion points are shown.

Performance Variability of Plans

The design of a multipath planning network, even the question of how many alternatives to represent, is affected by the manager's view of the situation. In line with this, Hasan Ozbekhan has made an important distinction between types of plans by characterizing the levels of plans as normative, strategic, and operational.[4] For our purposes, we can simplify and say that his *normative plan* specifies what "ought" to be done. This step requires *value definition.* It is sensitive to the various ways that managerial objectives might be satisfied. Alternative network configurations can arise because the manager is not yet sure what ought to be done. He keeps options open by employing multiple-path networks. Figure 10–2 would have to be changed in such a case to have more than one type of end point in the network—that is, *Q, Q', Q'',* and so on. (Under some circumstances, *Q, Q',* and *Q''* might be considered to represent performance differentiation.) The present figure allows only that the end point *Q* can follow different schedules.

Strategic plans detail what "can" be done (and what "might happen"). Structural feasibility of alternative plans would be the crucial consideration at this step. For example, several different copy approaches might be tested on prime television time, various packages brought to the test market, or several air-traffic control systems built in prototype form and tested along different air routes. At this stage, most of the partial-constraint characteristics can be expected to occur. The end point, *Q,* is not affected as far as performance (i.e., as far as satisfying the planning objectives), but the time of completion is changed because at many of the nodes there is a choice among next steps, each of which requires a different amount of time.

Operational plans are concerned with what actually *will* be done. In other words, they are related to the implementation phase of the plan. Accordingly, for partially constrained systems there must be a mechanism at each node of an operational plan for deciding which of the alternatives to follow in order to arrive finally at point *Q.*

---

4 "The Triumph of Technology: 'Can' Implies 'Ought,' " Systems Development Corporation publication, SP–2830, June 6, 1967.

Forecasting in Planning

In fully constrained plans, both the normative and the strategic planning questions are assumed to have been resolved. As a result, such plans are particularly vulnerable to the effects of unexpected occurrences, since no allowance has been made for such events. Operational needs will alter the plan in unforeseen ways, and the manager may wish that he had allowed for some alternatives. Because of the obviously greater latitude of multiple paths, partially constrained planning models have superior flexibility. However, with respect to costs, both of planning itself and of maintaining resource adaptability, partially constrained systems are more expensive.

The level of flexibility that can be achieved is related directly to the forecasting strengths that can be brought to bear. Forecasting is the key to partially constrained planning. But, since forecasting for planning must deal with nonrecurrent states (by our planning definitions in Chapter 8), the key does not easily fit too many doors. Forecasting ingenuity is essential.[5] And forecasting difficulties are amplified many times when one is dealing with unstable systems. There are forecasters who say that under such circumstances forecasting cannot be done at all. This is apparent with respect to the use of classical statistical methods of forecasting. More subjective and Bayesian methods are not as readily dismissed because the statistical definition of stability is far more attenuated than an intuitive one. So we can accept the existence of some ability to derive a believable forecast in partially constrained networks.

Assume that at each and every node of the planning network all possible future activities and events could be described with their associated likelihoods. If all such paths were then fully extended from start to completion, total forecasting information would be built into the system. Under some circumstances it might be reasonable to trace out the single path that promises to maximize the expected value of the planner's objective. This reduces the plan to full constraint. Such homomorphic transformations are possible and can be decided on at any point in the network. The advantages are obvious: Only one set of resources is required. But there is always the countervailing disadvantage of being unable to cope with possible, even very likely, deviations from the expected-value path.

Expected values, which *require* a forecast, can also be used to reduce *selected parts* of a network. Great caution is required, however. To illustrate, we have chosen the branch in Figure 10–3 containing S_1 because the S_1 link has the highest expected value, as shown in the accompanying table. But S_1

---

[5] This is the analysis of any economic performance measure that is observed over time, made with the hope of improving on forecasts and predictions.

Figure 10–3

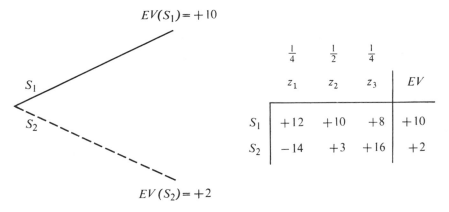

$$EV(S_1) = +10$$

	z_1	z_2	z_3	EV
	$\frac{1}{4}$	$\frac{1}{2}$	$\frac{1}{4}$	
S_1	$+12$	$+10$	$+8$	$+10$
S_2	-14	$+3$	$+16$	$+2$

$$EV(S_2) = +2$$

and S_2 are embodied in a larger planning network. It is conceivable that if the next stage had been included in the system studied, S_2 would have been chosen in conjunction with S_5. (See Figure 10–4.)

If contingency planning had been used, the main reason for the forecast would have been by-passed. The occurrence of event z_1 would dictate the use of S_1 (obtaining $+12$ instead of -14), and the event z_3 clearly favors S_2 (with $+16$ instead of $+8$). This analysis assumes the ability to react rapidly to whichever state of nature occurs. Slower reaction rates demand modified analyses but do not alter the nature of the reactions. More important, consideration of a larger planning system (with a more distant planning horizon) might well have tempered such advice. For example, if the combination S_1z_1

Figure 10–4

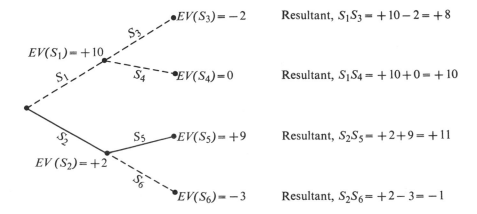

$EV(S_1) = +10$

S_3 $EV(S_3) = -2$ Resultant, $S_1S_3 = +10 - 2 = +8$

S_4 $EV(S_4) = 0$ Resultant, $S_1S_4 = +10 + 0 = +10$

S_5 $EV(S_5) = +9$ Resultant, $S_2S_5 = +2 + 9 = +11$

$EV(S_2) = +2$

S_6 $EV(S_6) = -3$ Resultant, $S_2S_6 = +2 - 3 = -1$

(yielding + 12) could thereafter lead only to losses, the single-stage suboptimization would not be used.

Although planning potentials, flexibility, and information are lost when network reduction is used, some way of simplifying complex forecasts for multiple-path plans is essential. Simulation provides another possible approach to choosing one path for larger systems by generating expected values. Various management options for parts of the plan can be examined in different combinations and the overall plan, which combines these parts, can be evaluated. Characteristically, there is no normative implication to be drawn from such simulations. All possible expected values cannot be obtained. It is folly to entertain the notion of finding "one best path" through simulation unless the system is very close to being fully constrained to begin with. Yet the distinct liability of analyzing and selecting isolated links of the plan is overcome by simulation. As we have shown above, when expected values of subsystems are used as the criteria of choice, the performance of the combination of best–expected-value links is unlikely to be the best possible plan. So simulation is appealing where the networks are really far too complex, cumbersome, and unwieldy to be reduced in any other way.

Fine measurement increases complexity. Another way to control the unwieldiness of forecast information is to measure the class size of events in as gross terms as possible, thereby restricting the number of alternatives to a tractable few. Extreme grossness can reduce a partially constrained system to a fully constrained one. The loss of information that results is the opposing cost, which urges the use of finer classification.

Network Reductions Based on Feasible Activity Structure

Under some circumstances (usually when no general agreement can be reached regarding the set of plans that should be considered initially), it may be desirable to start by setting forth as many plans as possible. This approach magnifies the problem. Still, if the situation warrants complication at an early stage, a method can be offered that has practical as well as conceptual benefits. The method is based on straight multiplication and an orderly arrangement of the planning stages. Its use requires no sophisticated mathematical knowledge, but for a situation of any real scope the assistance of a computer is necessary.

Let us consider the simple planning tree shown in Figure 10–5. There are 5,184 unique planning configurations (unique paths, or branches) that start at α and end at Ω. We have $(4 \times 2 \times 3 \times 4 \times 3 \times 2 \times 3 \times 1 \times 3) = 5,184$. One of these might be a–2–4–7–11–k–f–13–16. Spending only five minutes on each of the 5,184 possibilities in order to evaluate them would require almost eleven weeks of one man's time. Problems of realistic size would require many complete lifetimes. So this approach is out of the question. If,

Figure 10–5   A Planning Tree with Three Phases, Each Having Three Stages, Giving Rise to 5,184 Unique Branches

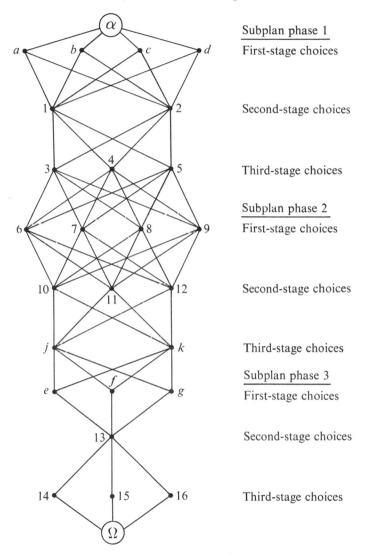

Subplan phase 1
First-stage choices

Second-stage choices

Third-stage choices

Subplan phase 2
First-stage choices

Second-stage choices

Third-stage choices

Subplan phase 3
First-stage choices

Second-stage choices

Third-stage choices

however, the individual subplan phases are treated as though they were independent of one another, then there are twenty-four alternatives for phase 1, twenty-four alternatives for phase 2, and nine alternatives for phase 3. Assuming no interaction between the subplans, a choice of plan for a single phase must be made twice from twenty-four alternatives, and a choice from nine alternatives must be made once. The total number of alternatives considered in this case would be $24 + 24 + 9$, which equals only fifty-seven evaluations—a matter of less than five hours' work if five minutes is needed for each choice. For obvious reasons, this method of fragmentation of partially constrained plans is closer to present-day technique than is the consideration of extensive planning trees where phase plans are interlinked.

But we have learned a great deal from systems analysis, and the need for the systems approach becomes all too evident when the plans that are being considered are complex. Even in the case of project planning, the failure to recognize component interaction has led to malfunctioning units. We cannot simply pick the best rocket-engine design from the set of feasible rocket engines and then ignore that choice and proceed to pick the best control system. This procedure is doomed to failure when dependence exists among the components. We repeat a previous definition: A system is a group of activities, subplans, or components that can be bounded. The bounding rule is that *all relevant interdependencies and interactions must be enclosed.*

Utilizing the systems approach will increase substantially the number of alternative plans that must be considered. The upper limit in our previous example would be 5,184 alternatives. Figure 10–6 depicts only a portion of these branches. Unlike Figure 10–5, which is compact since the branches or paths intertwine, Figure 10–6 is an extensive tree, in which all the branches have been separated so they can be analyzed as individual possibilities. We have assumed that interaction exists between the first stage of phase 1, the first stage of phase 3, and the third stage of phase 2. We can now proceed in several ways to evaluate the various combinations of these three interacting stages. A value can be placed on each of the twenty-four unique configurations. Branches with low values can be *discarded* from consideration. In fact, if these three related stages can truly be considered a system (see the bounding rule above), then the one best branch can be selected and incorporated into the final integrated plan. All that our method does is make explicit the relationships of the stages and the combinations that must be considered together in order to select among alternative plans. Such combinatorial evaluation is not always required. *A plan may well be composed of several different subplans that are clearly independent of one another.*

If the network is large—say, the 5,184 unique branches illustrated in Figure 10–5, then an evaluation procedure must be found that will not require the eleven man-weeks previously derived. Many times it is helpful *just to construct* an extensive planning tree, since by studying this diagram it is often possible to eliminate certain branches that are obviously inferior or unfeasible. If, for example, the link 10–*j* is an impossibility, then the size of the tree is reduced from 5,184 alternatives to 4,320, a reduction of more than 16 percent. Proceeding in this manner, one can greatly reduce the number of possibilities actually to be considered. Relationships and dependencies between phases and

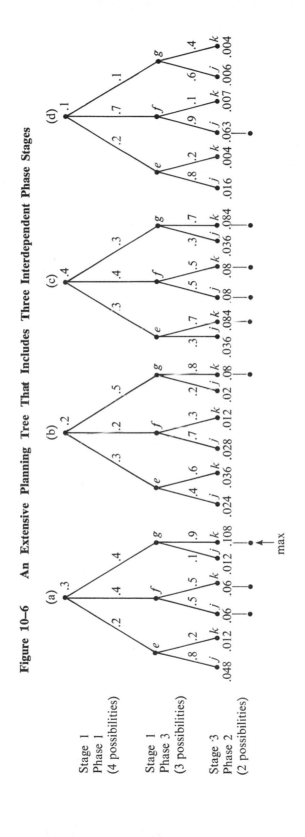

Figure 10-6   An Extensive Planning Tree That Includes Three Interdependent Phase Stages

stages can be recognized more easily. And, because of the concrete nature of the method, communication among participants in the planning process is facilitated.

Under some circumstances it is possible to utilize a quasi-quantitative method for reducing the number of alternatives that eventually will be submitted to the planner for evaluation. Returning to Figure 10–6, we note first that the stages are ordered in their expected (or required) sequence of precedence. Thus, stage 1 of phase 3 precedes stage 3 of phase 2, because the latter is dependent on the former. Stage 1 of phase 1 precedes both.

Next, we will observe that the numbers assigned to a, b, c, and d sum to 1, as do the numbers for each set of e, f, and g and for every j and k set as well. All these numbers are assigned by the manager to express his *preference* for the strategies of the particular subplan with which they are associated. Let us illustrate how this is done. We assume that a method of ranking is employed. Each manager participating in the planning process can assign his own rankings (for example, to e, f, and g for the d tree, and then to j and k for, say, the d–f tree). This kind of analysis can be carried through so that everyone derives his own set of weights for the alternatives, or average ranks can be used and a single analysis conducted. The former method is most appropriate when significant discrepancies exist among the preferences of the participants. (Discussion of preference measures and ranking will be found on pp. 276–84.) If the assigned ranks are 3, 2, 4, and 1, respectively, then their sum is 10. Dividing each rank by 10 we obtain the numbers shown in the first row of Figure 10–6; the division step has made them sum to 1, providing a significant numerical convenience, since they can be treated in much the same fashion as probabilities. However, these ranks might have been 1, 2, 3, and 2. Here the sum would be 8 and we would divide by 8, obtaining .125, .250, .375, and .250. These values would then replace those shown in the first row of Figure 10–6.

Next we proceed to the branch link that connects the stage 1 choice for phase 1 with the stage 1 choice for phase 3. As we have noted, each triad of possible connections sums to 1. In this case, the question by which the ranking is to be achieved would be something like: "If a is used, how do we evaluate the combinations ae, af, and ag?" These are the only possible combinations. We have used a conditional statement, since we required the assumption of a in order to proceed. As before, we rank the possibilities and then apportion them so that they sum to 1. The same is done for alternatives b, c, and d.

Next we proceed to the terminus of link ae and another conditional statement: If the plan incorporates the link ae, what preference do we have for alternatives j and k of phase 2? We may note that if we are indifferent about which option will be used with the combination ae, then equal ranks will be accorded to links ej and ek. The result will be that each link will be assigned a preference factor of .5. If one of the links is totally preferred, it will receive a value of 1. The other link receives zero, with the consequence that further elaboration of that plan is pointless since a final value of zero will be accorded to all plans that incorporate the zero link. This is precisely what we assumed for the link 10–*j* considered before.

It is simple to illustrate the fallibility of our approach when it is improperly applied. If 10–*j* were technologically an impossibility then no danger would exist. If, however, based on the prior parts of the tree, we greatly preferred 11–*j* and 12–*j* to 10–*j* and accordingly assigned a zero value to 10–*j*, then the possibility of an interaction would have to be considered. An interaction would occur, for example, if the coexistence of 10–*j* and *f*–13 created a special kind of preference for 10–*j*. It might be worthwhile to go back and look at the discussion of dynamic programming (pp. 350–56) in this regard. As a concrete example, let us assume that the combination 10–*j* is easily attacked by anti-trust laws, so easily in fact that we eliminate its consideration by assigning a zero value to the link. However, continuing our hypothetical case, when 6–10–*j* is used in association with *g*–13–16, a totally different situation prevails, wherein government approval is assured. Many other examples of these kinds of dependency can be given, so we must be conscious of the possibilities at all times.

After having assigned all link values to the network, we proceed to multiply these numbers successively along each branch. In this way we succeed in using these conditional statements to properly apportion the initial preference weights for *a*, *b*, *c*, and *d* to all the end points of the tree. The final row of Figure 10–6 presents the results. The maximum value of .108 belongs to the branch *a*–*g*–*k*. This was obtained by multiplying .3 × .4 × .9. Dots have been placed under all those evaluations that exceed .05. There are nine such branches. If our plan existed at just these three levels the manager could begin his analysis with nine alternatives.

It should be noted that this method of choosing alternatives is like a first filter of the planning system. It is intended to reduce the planning problem to a manageable size by filtering out the obviously unsuitable combinations. Clearly, there is nothing sacred about the cut-off point of .05; it was chosen so that a sufficient number of contending plans would remain. At the same time, a basic use of this approach emerges. As we move sequentially through a network, low-valued branches begin to appear. When they fall below a specified threshold, further computation along that branch is discontinued. Thus, using the numbers in Figure 10–6, the cumulative branch multiplications are shown in Figure 10–7. We see that six links have been eliminated since their estimated values fell below the threshold at a stage preceding the last one. It is impossible for any value to increase—at best it can remain unchanged—unless interactions occur. If, every now and then, such an approach assists the manager in discovering potential interactions (either good or bad) by structuring the problem in such a way that his vision is improved, then the cost of the filter would

Figure 10–7   Cumulative Branch Values

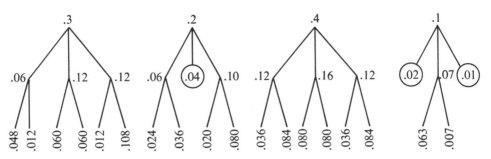

be paid for many times over. At the same time, it is entirely rational to let the filter reduce the number of combinations that will be considered as early in the game as possible.

A few additional comments are necessary. It is of great importance that the crude filter just described not block the passage of plans we later intend to use as part of our multiple-path model. We observe that if a stage is independent of its preceding network elements, then all its link values will be repeated throughout the level. For example, if our preference for the third-stage alternative of phase 2 is independent of *all* other stages of the plan, then the value $ej = fj = gj$ and all twelve of these branches will be equivalued. A symmetrical statement can be made for the k alternative. If, on the other hand, the third-stage alternative of phase 2 is independent only of the first stage of phase 1, then $ej \neq fj \neq gj$. There will be four equivalued ej branches, four equivalued fj branches, and four equivalued gj branches.

Many interesting characteristics of the planning process can be discovered by using the tree approach, but our emphasis must now shift to predictive methods and how they are used to deal with the states of nature that give rise to partially constrained planning models.

Managerial Predictions in Planning

To make a workable multipath system, *a few high-probability events* can be selected for each node from the total forecast spectrum. In fully constrained systems, only one choice is made. When multiple paths are used, the resulting partially constrained plan is assumed to include *preparedness* for the important contingencies that have been determined. Planning flexibility will be increased by the manager as the penalty for lack of it grows.

The reason the manager uses predictions for planning is clear. One of the basic causes of multiple-path planning is that while opportunities exist, we are able to describe only in risk terms what is likely to happen. Predictions about what *will* happen serve to reduce the number of multiple paths that should be considered, moving PCPM's closer to FCPM's. Forecasting has the opposite effect by introducing likelihood measures for all relevant environments.

The means by which the manager makes predictions to reduce the number of planning paths raises some interesting questions. Although much scientific effort has been spent on forecasting problems, comparable attention has not been paid to prediction. Recent emphasis on the predictive aspects of Bayesian analysis, however, may signal a shift. The melding of systematic procedures with subjective information partly opens some of the doors that otherwise would remain tightly closed. In brief, without a forecast (and by-passing the use of astrology[6]), predictions can be derived subjectively by hunch and intuition.

Use of the mean, the median, or the mode as the basis for making a prediction is worth examination. Although in Table 10–1 use of the mean, the

Table 10–1

Frequency of occurrence	Value of event	(Frequency × Value) for computation of average	Cumulative frequency
1	4	4	1
2	5	10	3
3	6	18	6
4	7	28	10
5	8	40	15
4	9	36	19
2	10	20	21
3	11	33	24
1	12	12	25
25		201	

median, and the mode all produce essentially the same result, the processes by which that result is reached are noticeably different. The highest frequency shown in the table is 5, so 8 is the *mode* event. The median number is 13, since there are twenty-five observations. The thirteenth number is found in the event class 8, so 8 is the *median* event; that is, 4556667777888 . . . . The *mean* value is $\frac{201}{25} = 8.04$, which is very close to both the mode and the median.

Among the various ways managers can make predictions, some managers

---

[6] See, for example, Neil Ulman, "Some Investors Turn to Stars for Answers to Market's Riddles," *The Wall Street Journal,* April 16, 1963, p. 1.

behave essentially as "mode predictors." That is, they *remember* frequencies of occurrence and react to that stimulus to which they have received the maximum number of exposures. Learning of sorts is indicated, and forgetting may also exist in tallying the counts. The mode appears to require less memory for detail than the median and more than the mean. On the other hand, the mode seems to use a more developed integrating (gestalt) circuit than the median and a less developed one than the mean. Mode memory seems to be *cumulative*. It requires the recall, not of individual events, but only of the latest *sum* of the number of each type of event. Many, if not most, people have a strong propensity to behave in this way, and there is no reason to think that managers are different.

A "median predictor," on the other hand, would have an accounting orientation and a strong memory for *individual* and *isolated* events. Cumulative, resultant, and gestalt-forming abilities are not evident. The memory requirements are greater than for the other methods of prediction, while the gestalt or integrating ability is least significant. The use of the median measure is further removed from intuition than any other predictive approach. Derivation of the median requires the greatest cataloging ability.

At first glance, it might seem that the "mean predictor" requires more memory and computing effort than any of the others. The mean as a basis for prediction requires the computation of frequency $\times$ value for each event, and the resulting sum of these products must then be divided by the total frequency. Certainly this requires greater computing ability than the other measures. But the mean can be obtained in a far simpler fashion. Assume that the latest value of the mean is $\overline{X}$ based on N events. Then another event occurs, say X. The new mean is computed by adding the value of X to $N\overline{X}$ and dividing that number by $N + 1$. Thus, the new mean $\overline{X}' = (N\overline{X} + X)/(N + 1)$. Little memory is required to maintain an updated mean value.

In Chapter 9 (see pp. 336–37) the Beta distribution was introduced as still another form of predictor. It is used presumably because the mean, median, and mode provide poor predictive measures in certain cases. The Beta distribution has appeared in behavioral literature so often that we can suggest that when human factors are important determinants of the system's performance, the mean, median, and mode are poor descriptors of that performance. Yet Zipf, as we shall see (p. 617), prescribed the mean as a fundamental basis for prediction of people's behavior.

Predictions can be derived by extrapolating a curve that represents past performance. Many statistical methods have been developed to facilitate such speculations. Extrapolation and interpolation are typical of predictive techniques that rely on the assumption that a reasonable degree of inertia exists in the system. The simplest illustration of this effect is embodied in the statement that the best prediction for tomorrow's weather is that it will be like today's. Often statistical correlation methods can be applied, pinpointing one or more events to serve as predictors. Sometimes the logic of a system (or a sense of its *inherent causality*) seems sufficiently apparent to permit believable predictions to be made based on an explicit model. But, often as not, this view of predictability is misleading. For example, in the first quarter of the twentieth century some extravagant hopes were expressed for the logistics curve (see p. 105) as a means of predicting the future of industrial systems. The model still seems reasonable, but the lack of situations for which it applied destroyed the notion of it as a universal predictive panacea. Experiments, tests, and surveys have been widely used to aid prediction for reducing multiple-path systems to fully constrained ones. These approaches have been geared to an economic criterion concerning the value and cost of information—that is, net benefit. The same approach can be extended to multiple predictions.

Multiple predictions. To use the mean, median, or mode we require *exposure* to all the information contained in a forecast. But we do not have to store all this information or have access to it, and we do not need perfect isomorphic recall. We observed previously that two numbers will always suffice to update the mean value.

The same reasoning applies to multiple predictions, where the plan is developed on a contingency basis—that is, use A if X happens, use B if Z happens. Here, X and Z are the possible predictions of happenings that might occur. There could be others as well. The net-benefit concept and the degree to which X, Z, and so on approach 100 percent of all likelihoods would be the determinants of how extensive the prediction multiplicity should be. The selection of one key event for a single prediction makes sense if the probability of that event is close to 1 and the outcomes of other events are not extremes. Since the average, median, or mode can be used to lead to a single prediction, would it be logical to use the closest neighbors of the mode, the median, and the mean for deriving multiple predictions? Or would it be better to represent a broader range of potential happenings? Only after the outcomes and the event probabilities are combined in an economic analysis can the manager obtain a reasoned answer. A ranked ordering of the ordinate values of the probability distribution (which is equivalent to ranking by frequency) would have some appeal when the distribution has several modes. Bayesian procedures (as described in Chapter 6) might also be used, and one could hardly discourage intuitive determinations.

Since planning involves nonrecurrent events, for which forecasts are not too believable, multiple predictions based on some combination of formal method, logic, and intuition are especially appealing. Furthermore, the manager would seldom wish to provide resources to cover all eventualities spanned by the forecast. The other extreme, of compressing a forecast to a single prediction (e.g., by means of a sequence of maximum expected-value strategies), also seems highly restrictive.

A simple model for comparing FCPM's with PCPM's. What is the reasoning that underlies the selection of a particular degree of partial network constraint? To what extent should multiple prediction be used? Each situation demands its own analysis to answer these questions, but certain fundamental elements tend to occur in all cases. The list below treats a number of these elements and offers some hypothetical magnitudes by means of which to contrast them.

	FCPM	PCPM
Cost of plan	C	$3C$
Probability that plan will succeed	.8	.9
Benefit derived if plan succeeds	V	V
Probability that plan will fail	.2	.1
Penalty if plan fails	$5C$	$3C$

To find out under what cost/benefit conditions PCPM's would be preferred, we write two equations and set the benefit of the FCPM less than that of the PCPM. Thus

$$.8V - [C + (.2)5C] < .9V - [3C + (.1)3C]$$

Solving, we obtain $V/C > 13$. In other words, when the benefit, V, is more than thirteen times the cost of the plan, C, the use of partially constrained planning models is indicated. Similar constructions could be used to compare the fully constrained and partially constrained approaches with respect to the probabilities of success, the relative costs of the plans, and the like. It is worth noting that in this case the benefits, V, of both approaches were chosen as being equal, although in many contingency situations this would not be so. The main advantage of PCPM's here is the improvement in the probability of planning success.

Other PCPM's having greater or lesser degrees of constraint, and their own particular costs and benefits, could be compared as well. (In other words, in the previous analysis substitute $PCPM_1$ for FCPM.) Such models will help the manager determine the extent to which he should make use of multiple predictions, if at all.

MULTIPLE-PATH NETWORKS

Multiple-path systems can be represented in both network and matrix forms. The relative likelihoods assigned to paths emanating from each node of the network are *determinate* estimates. They can be used in the matrix as well. The manager has placed odds on his predictions. This is equivalent to a forecast, but the number of states included in the forecast may be considerably fewer than if forecasting methods had been used. The probability assignments express the potential diversity of the situation as the manager *wishes* to see it, not necessarily as it is. An overall pattern of the situation, as the manager perceives it, is reflected in the extent to which his network has multiple paths. The extent and nature of the multiple paths reveal planning flexibility, which is directly related to investment costs.

The matrix in Table 10–2 describes a PCPM. As was the case with FCPM's,

Table 10–2

$\rightarrow$	A	B	C	D
A	x	$\frac{1}{3}$	$\frac{2}{3}$	0
B		x	1	0
C			x	1
D				1

all entries must be on or above the diagonal. This is a requirement of *extensive* networks, where backward movement is not allowed.

The same flow of planning activities and events is represented in network form in Figure 10–8. In this diagram, the activities are shown as nodes,

Figure 10–8

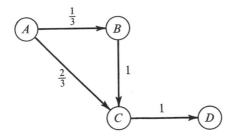

whereas previously they were drawn as the links of the network. We observe that path ACD has twice $ABCD$'s likelihood of occurring. Perhaps A is a testing activity. Then, with odds of 2:3, the project is expected to pass the test and by-pass activity B, which remedies defects discovered by the test, A. It is evident that these estimates are determinate statements of the relevant proportions, even though they apply to probabilities. If they were not treated as being 100 percent believable, a probability distribution would be required—for example:

Probability	0	$\frac{1}{4}$	$\frac{1}{2}$	$\frac{1}{4}$	0
Estimate for path AC	$\frac{1}{3}$	$\frac{1}{2}$	$\frac{2}{3}$	$\frac{5}{6}$	1

The expected value of the AC estimate is $\frac{2}{3}$. Compensating changes would be required for the AB estimates. The recognition of variability in the estimates might be important. Sensitivity testing could be used (see pp. 129–32 and 368–69) in conjunction with Monte Carlo procedures (see pp. 357ff.) to determine how important the variability is.

Sequencing Control

Frequently a plan can be accomplished with a given set of activities but a variety of degrees of freedom for the order of accomplishment and for the assignment of time and facilities. Many sequencing problems can be treated without risk methods. The relevant environments are assumed to be known by the planner.

For example, a well-known sequencing algorithm was developed by S. M. Johnson.[7] To illustrate its use, let us assume that a plan calls for six different activities to be completed but that they can be accomplished in any order. Each activity is begun at facility A and completed at facility B. This algorithm requires that *no passing* be allowed, which means that the activities must be processed in the same order by B as by A. Time estimates are developed for the accomplishment of each activity at each facility. A hypothetical set of numbers is given below.

	Activity:					
	a	b	c	d	e	f
Facility: A	6	8	3	7	4	8
B	5	2	9	5	1	7

This is read for activity d, for example, that seven hours are required at facility A and five hours at facility B. The method for ordering these activities in the best possible way can be stated in simple terms. The algorithm is based on network principles that do not have to be understood to use the method.

First, select the *smallest* time in either row. If the smallest number is in the

---

[7] S. M. Johnson, "Optimal Two- and Three-Stage Production Schedules with Setup Times Included," *Naval Research Logistics Quarterly,* Vol. 1, No. 1 (March 1954), pp. 61–68.

top row (facility *A*), place that activity first in line. If the smallest number is in the bottom row, place that activity last in line. For our example, activity *e* goes last.

Second, from the *remaining* matrix, select the *smallest* number. If it is in the top row, place that activity first in line (or second if the first place has already been assigned). If it is in the bottom row, assign the activity to the last place (or next-to-last if the last place has already been assigned). For our example, activity *b* goes into fifth place.

Third, with the *remaining* matrix, continue in the same fashion until all assignments have been made. Thus, activity *c* goes to first place. Activities *a* and *d* are tied (with the value of 5 in the bottom row). All ties can be resolved by choosing either option, so we could put activity *a* into fourth place and activity *d* into third place, or vice versa. If a tie number appears in top and bottom rows, either one can be assigned first. It doesn't matter which of the tied activities is given first consideration. Activity *f* is assigned to second place, the only available opening.

Two optimal sequences have resulted, either *cfdabe* or *cfadbe*. This allows the manager two additional options in his planning. It is worth noting that in this case partial constraint arises in the selection of strategy and the controllable variables, whereas in all previous discussion the variety was occasioned by environments.

Using a Gantt chart (Figure 10–9) let us compare these two scheduling variants with each other and with a nonoptimal ordering, *abcdef* (purely a

Figure 10–9

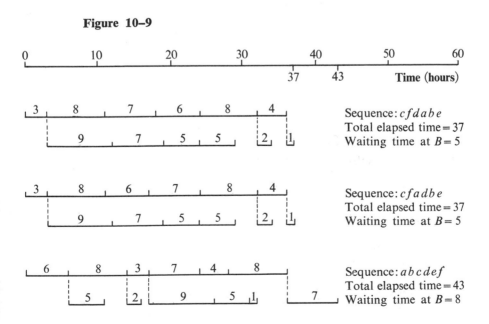

random choice). The results that we had anticipated are evident. Sequence control has been obtained.

Other formal methods have also been developed. In fact, there is a growing body of literature on this subject. We have simply given an example of the kinds of analytic model that exist to assist management planning. Neighborhoods of good strategies can be determined, so that strategy alternatives can be introduced into the multiple-path network based on the knowledge that they are all close to being optimal.

While analytic approaches such as these are always applicable for scheduling fully constrained planning models, they may not be adaptive enough when multiple-path planning is intended. Simulation techniques become attractive because they make it convenient to deal with probabilities and longer chains of activities and events. Using simulation, the manager can examine a variety of schedule sequences and choose the one or more that seem most desirable. As actual events occur, following along specific paths of the multiple alternatives, schedules can be revised and updated by running new simulations.

Meeting Targets and Encountering Contingencies

A partially constrained planning system can have several possible real evolutions—that is, it can finish at alternative target dates and end points, or results, in the network. An end-point state is characterized by a unit diagonal value of the matrix. It is a recurrent state that exists only to signify the plan's conclusion based on the practical necessities for an imposed finite planning horizon. It stops all further forward planning. In fully constrained planning systems there is only one target point, but in PCPM's there can be several such acceptable end points. Some will be considered by the manager to be more desirable than others. In general, the number of undesirable diagonal unit values constitutes a measure of the system's potential for unwanted contingencies. But it is also useful to consider the relative likelihoods that each of these end-point states will occur.

Consider the matrix of transition probabilities shown in Table 10–3. Three

Table 10–3

→	A	B	C	D	E
A	0	$\frac{1}{4}$	$\frac{1}{2}$	$\frac{1}{4}$	0
B	0	1	0	0	0
C	0	0	0	$\frac{1}{2}$	$\frac{1}{2}$
D	0	0	0	1	0
E	0	0	0	0	1

Figure 10–10

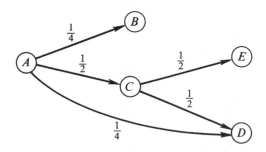

end points, *B, D,* and *E,* appear. Which end point is most likely to occur? The most direct way to find out is to trace out the network and determine the end-point probabilities (see Figure 10–10). The probability that *B* will occur is $\frac{1}{4}$. To arrive at *E,* we must go *AC, CE,* with a probability of $(\frac{1}{2} \times \frac{1}{2}) = \frac{1}{4}$. End point *D* can be reached by two routes. There is direct transit from *A* to *D,* with a probability of $\frac{1}{4}$, which is added to the probability of moving from *A* to *C* and then from *C* to *E,* which is $(\frac{1}{2} \times \frac{1}{2}) = \frac{1}{4}$. The sum of these probabilities is $(\frac{1}{4} + \frac{1}{4}) = \frac{1}{2}$.

In more complex multiple-path planning systems, other methods for determining the likelihood of the various end points can be used. Where many matrices interact with one another and where they can change in value over time, simulation methods may be preferred.[8] Of particular relevance are those end points that represent ruin (the subject treated in sections that follow).

Clearly one of the main purposes of discovering end-point likelihoods is the question of what the manager should do when high probabilities exist for unwanted results. Two possibilities appear that warrant attention. *First,* the manager can accept the network as it is but attempt to alter the probabilities, increasing those that move toward desired results and decreasing those that do not. He may try to do this by spending more in time and cost at the proper points in the network. Through research, he might be able to exercise greater control over contingencies. Early warning systems can help him learn whether the plan is moving in the direction of unwanted results. If it is, then he can muster his resources to meet specific challenges rather than attempting to remove all trouble spots at once, which would be a costly and wasteful procedure. Not all potential trouble spots will be encountered in the normal course of the plan's evolution. So the manager need spend only against impending contingencies. *Second,* the manager can try to change the network— for example, to add new links by undertaking additional activities such as

---

[8] Richard M. Van Slyke, "Monte Carlo Methods and the PERT Problem," *Operations Research,* Vol. 11, No. 5 (September–October 1963), pp. 839–60.

agreement by contract or insurance protection. These new activities shift the probabilities and can lead to the formation of new end points that are far more favorable.

These notions lead to questions concerning *how to change the state* of partially constrained planning systems over time.[9] How often should progress along the path be monitored? With what frequency should the network's remaining multiple paths be updated? As the plan evolves, under what circumstances should the design be changed and the resources allocated in a different way? Should a test point for a project component be skipped to save time and money? If the test is skipped and at a later stage (say, following assembly) it is discovered that the unit fails to perform properly, then all activities that followed the skipped test point were wasted. To resolve this design question the cost of testing must be *balanced* against the penalties of failing to obtain early diagnosis of unsatisfactory performance. The balancing equations will include probability statements that can change over time. Also, the penalties of failing to detect defectives will vary according to the position of the test point in the network.

Even in carrying out such a simple plan as one to prepare perfect soft-boiled eggs, the multiple-path planning approach reveals some real complications. Figure 10–11 is intended to catch some of the nuances of this plan. The multiple path is used, instead of fully constrained treatment, on the assumption that different eggs demand different treatment—and also because the lack of control over some of the plan's stages (e.g., the sizes and weights of eggs, the temperatures of water) may be equivalent to converting strategic variables into states of nature. Reference to a number of cookbooks will usually reveal as many different recipes. Once we recognize that designing a good egg tree is difficult, we may begin to have proper respect for managerial planning problems.

Changing Network Status

Sometimes the manager begins to suspect that his FCPM is masking the existence of catastrophic end points, and he then wishes to convert to a PCPM. By so doing he can uncover dangerous contingencies, and he can find out whether his plan is heading into trouble.

But the change from full to partial constraint can occur for other reasons, some of which are related to social and technical forces—for example, rejection of tradition, change in the planning premises, or technological innovations.

---

[9] See, for example, Howard Eisner, "A Generalized Network Approach to the Planning and Scheduling of a Research Project," *Operations Research*, Vol. 10, No. 1 (January–February 1962), pp. 115–25.

Figure 10–11   An Egg Planning Tree

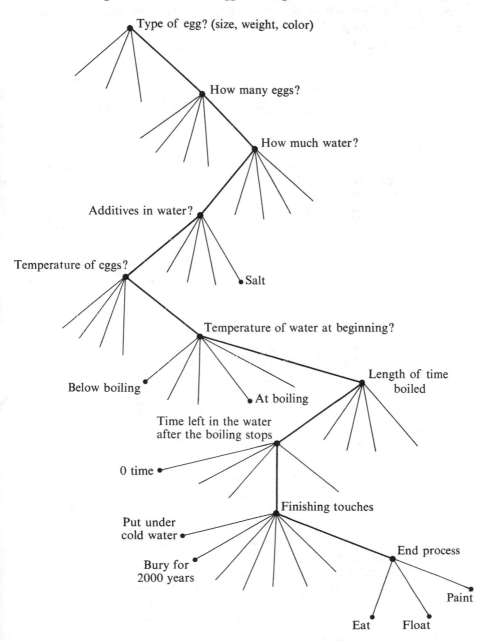

1. Axioms, proverbs, and rules of thumb have been handed down for generations, forming and reinforcing a body of tradition that is accepted without thought as to the validity of its premises. We all accept without reason many conditions as being fixed and unalterable, and management is no different. We accept the ability to question as a form of "creativity" because it encourages us to overcome blocked sight and insight (which blockages produce unnecessary constraints on the planning function).

Much remains to be learned about this ability, which Harold Rugg describes as follows:

> There is first a long, *conscious* preparatory period of baffled struggle; second, an interlude in which the scientist or artist apparently gives up, pushes the problem back or down or "out of mind," leaving it for the nonconscious to work upon. Then, third, comes the blinding and unexpected "flash of insight," and it comes with such certitude that a logical statement of it can be immediately prepared. These stages are present whether in art, science, technology, or philosophy.[10]

While creativity, after a "period of baffled struggle," may break out of the region of overaccepted ideas, it behooves us to recognize that tradition may nevertheless reflect "truth" and represent an adjustment to reality synthesized from generations of experience. But awareness of the specific influences of tradition is a minimum requirement. Partial constraint occurs when the new idea options are maintained in conjunction with the traditional ones.

2. In regard to changes in the planning premises, we can distinguish between premises that are not recognized because they are part of a traditional fabric and those that are consciously accepted and even formally stated. To illustrate the latter, if we presume that each subplan of a sequence of subplans is independent of the others, we can test this assumption of independence. We may not, because the need may never occur to us. Similarly, the condition of environmental certainty is an assumption that can be verified, if one remembers to question the assumption's validity. The determinate notion that there is only one best plan to accomplish some set of objectives can always be examined. The logic of a planning model proceeds from premises that can be stated explicitly and clearly. As premises are questioned, revised, and enlarged, we can expect to develop new models that are more apt to be partially constrained than fully constrained.

3. Technological (and methodological) innovations can be delayed by traditional biases as well as by false premises. We see that tradition, premise, and innovation are interrelated in a variety of ways. Given a technological change, prior fully constrained planning sequences can yield to new ones that incorporate partial-constraint potentials. In other words, as a result of

---

[10] Harold Rugg, *Imagination* (New York: Harper & Row, 1963), p. 289.

innovation, the number of alternative paths that should be considered will increase, up to a point. At first, choice will multiply because the ideas are new and untested. As test results are obtained, generalizations emerge that help the manager discard various alternatives. Ultimately, experience with the new technology allows the manager to select the one best way of using it.

Figure 10–12 relates experience with the system to the number of paths that might be included in a planning model. The curve depicts an increase from full constraint to some maximum number of planning paths. Thereafter, the degree of partial constraint will decrease until full constraint is achieved once again. However, just when things seem to be stabilizing at point *S,* new innovations are likely to come along, and once again understanding of the system must be achieved through experimentation.

The above discussion presupposes that risk conditions do not persist after the new technology is understood. If this is not the case, the same general curve form will exist, but the minimum number of multiple paths will not be one (i.e., FCPM).

Figure 10–12   Learning Increases and Then Reduces the Degree of Partial Constraint

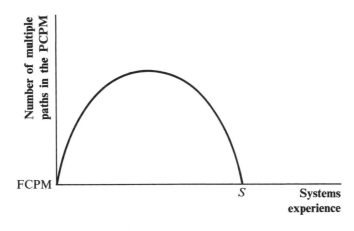

THRESHOLD-CONSTRAINED PLANNING MODELS

Threshold-constrained planning models apply when severe (ruin-type) penalties threaten the system. Here, thanks to Russian and French interest in gambling theory, a tentative basis for model-building exists. But even for casino gambling, the theory of ruin is revealing but incomplete.

What constitutes threat to one company may not be threat to another. The differentiating factors are the size of penalties, their probabilities of occurrence, and the effects of (or vulnerabilities to) such penalties. Even in the same company, two executives may disagree in a specific situation. Their difference of opinion can be traced to psychological, value-based considerations. At the root of this issue are lifetime attitudes concerning fundamental utilities (see pp. 171 and 277). Given two companies with different circumstances, the problem becomes easier to visualize. Companies can be differentiated with respect to many relevant factors, including their total assets and the percentage of total assets that a plan puts at stake.

Threshold-constrained planning systems are *a special subclass* of partially constrained system. The same extensive type of network can be drawn for both but with the notable difference that some of the end-point states represent ruin for the threshold-constrained system. There is a strong resemblance between what are loosely called *long-range* planning models and the threshold models that have been discussed here. The threshold concept is preferable because it relates directly to the manager's concern, whereas time span is related to performance only to the extent that uncertainty increases as time span lengthens. In fact, as will be seen subsequently, the term "long-range planning" substitutes a misleading temporal context for the real managerial issues.

Action Limits

The distinguishing characteristic of threshold-constrained planning models is the existence of a criterion for discarding plans that contain *ruin-prone nodes.* Thus, a dynamic action limit is set on the results of evolving plans to indicate those that will not be tolerated. The objective function of the manager may be changed from maximization of profit to minimization of penalties, or even avoidance of ruin. Otherwise, profit might be maximized subject to a severe ruin-probability constraint.[11] Figure 10–13 illustrates this at one point in time. Plan A has a higher expected value than plan B but entails a probability of ruin in excess of .0001 and is therefore discarded. The threshold value of 10^{-4} is purely arbitrary. Émile Borel has suggested 10^{-6} as a reasonable level for safety where life is concerned.[12] The question has endless potential for fascinating discussion.

Action limits (or thresholds) are designed to act as cut-off points and are

---

[11] This is another multiple objective problem. Unlike the situation in Figure 10–1, in this case the $EV(A)$ is greater than the $EV(B)$.

[12] See Émile Borel, *Probabilities and Life,* trans. by Maurice Baudin (New York: Dover, 1962).

Figure 10–13

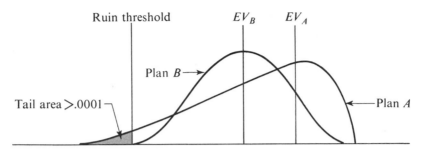

the triggers for taking preventive measures against the possibility of wandering too close to ruin precipices. Sometimes the limits are formalized; more generally, they are vaguely held. Conventional breakeven (or load-factor) analysis is an example of a commonly used but vaguely held limit (see pp. 262–72). Threshold-constrained systems are intimately involved with *extreme-value analysis,* an area of study that will require intense research if management is to move ahead in the planning field.[13] It can be applied to events such as floods, earthquakes, and contests. But it is quite as relevant to exceptional executive decisions, which characterize threshold-type systems. *Because of a conservative ruin criterion or overprotective action limits, many organizations forego unusually promising opportunities.* Extreme-value analysis can help to shed some light on the optimal settings for action limits.

A ruin threshold might be set so that probability of ruin $< k$. This could apply to gamblers' wagers, self-insurance, liquid reserves, or breakeven points. The pertinent constraint is usually derived for only one tail of the distribution. But often ruin can occur when either the extreme upper or lower limit is breached. For example, an excess or an insufficiency of air pressure can cause death. And it is possible that too much sales volume could prove as catastrophic as too little.

Several threshold levels may also be designated, as is sometimes done in statistical quality control. Figure 10–14 illustrates such a system. Measures (e.g., *A, B,* and *C*) are taken over time, with the expectation that deviations from $\overline{X}$ will occur. In this case, three limits are set in both directions that indicate various degrees of threat to the system. It is increasingly unlikely that the results will fall outside the limits as those limits move farther out. Penetrating a less severe limit (closer to the mean, such as the first limit) would not spell ruin but provide a signal of threat to the system. Passing the second limit might call for preliminary steps to be taken, while reaching the

---

[13] A pioneering work in this field is E. J. Gumbel, *Statistics of Extremes* (New York: Columbia University Press, 1965).

Figure 10–14   A Two-Tailed Control Chart

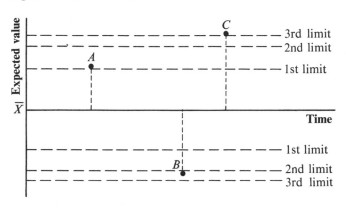

third would entail a full-scale remedial effort. Following this approach allows the elimination of dangerous plans—that is, plans that might violate the ultimate ruin threshold—while permitting the use (with caution) of high-profit and less threatening ones.

Whenever a ruinous end point remains in the system there is a possibility, no matter how small, that the system will come to a catastrophic halt. As a result of ruin potential, even relatively secure paths must be viewed as being in jeopardy. The stories of Ford's Edsel, General Dynamics' jet airplane, and the many seemingly secure millionaires whose business empires have fallen are evidence of the fact that ruin potentials can be overlooked and thereby bring ruin to a previously profitable system. This knowledge produces self-protective ruin-avoidance procedures. Taking out insurance against loss is one example. Another is provided by the commodity-user, who, since he cannot avoid the large-scale speculative operations involved in the purchase of that commodity, instead looks for protective alternatives. For example, there are *hedging procedures* that can be used when commodity-trading markets exist. By subscribing to this approach and, if need be, helping to create such a market, an organization can be *relatively* immune to substantial fluctuations in the market valuation of the commodity.

Liquidity measures. Threshold planning is frequently dependent on the assessment of the organization's liquidity, which acts as its protection against ruin. Liquidity is the cash position of the company. Other assets that can be converted rapidly into cash are also considered part of the company's liquid position. If the company has so much of its money tied up that it cannot meet its obligations, it is flirting with bankruptcy and ruin. Therefore, sufficient liquidity is one major consideration of threshold planning.

Although most assets have some present value (see p. 275), in many cases the conversion to cash can be obtained only with a severe penalty. But these same assets may have long-term convertibility to cash that is financially acceptable. Only sunk costs, which can never be reclaimed, do not provide liquidity at some point in the future. Cash-flow analysis is a strong planning technique used to track the assets of a company *as* they become liquid. Matching and synchronization of needs with convertibility to cash is recognized as a critical managerial necessity. Since intangibles contribute to cash in ways that are difficult to explain, they are frequently ignored in ordinary planning situations. However, in threshold planning it may be a serious mistake to overlook intangible values.

A cash-flow curve of the sort shown in Figure 10–15 is an important model for planning. It is a particularly significant form of analysis when threshold constraints are involved. Cash-flow analysis tracks the movement of funds in and out of the system over time. Credits and debits are portrayed as increases and decreases in the company's liquid position. Discounting of future funds to their present value (see pp. 275–76) is usually applied to bring these future funds into closer alignment with their *immediate* cash value to management.

The curve shown in Figure 10–15 is intended to represent a company's liquidity (*related to a given plan*) at any moment in time. When $t = 0$, point a is the cash value assigned or budgeted for the plan's investment. The decision to stop at this stage would permit the return of a dollars—intact—to the company's cash reserves. Long-term investments and sunk costs of various sorts made over time will cause this curve to decrease monotonically (see

Figure 10–15   Curve of Cash Flow

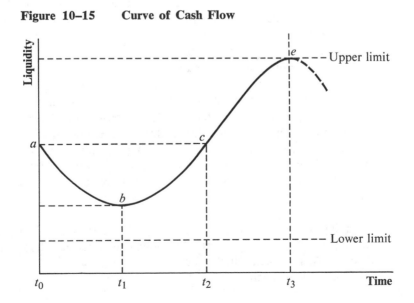

footnote 8 on p. 265) until point b is reached at time t_1. Point b represents the salvage value for the plan at time t_1, while $a - b$ represents sunk costs as of that particular time. To determine a point on the curve we obtain the cumulative sum of the outflows of capital, subtracting the cumulative inflows of revenue. Usually, continual cash outflows will be made starting at $t = 0$, but gradually the investments will taper off and revenues will begin to counteract the outflows. The liquidity curve begins to rise when the plan achieves a return rate that exceeds the project's rate of outflow. Up to that point, liquidity is a decreasing function; some return is realized on the investment but not enough to reverse net outflow. In real systems, the inflows and the outflows do not always match smoothly. Fluctuations will occur in the trajectory of the liquidity curve. But a lack of smoothness in the curve is not a problem unless the downside of an oscillation violates a liquidity threshold.

To use threshold planning we must develop models that properly represent time. Our intention is to evaluate an entire planning trajectory for which limits are designed to protect the plan from the inherent variability of its multiple paths. The limits are designed specifically to call attention to undesirable contingencies. Action can be taken if the liquidity (or any other critical performance measure) reaches threshold conditions. Appropriate models are characterized by the fact that all strategic moves are time-tagged so that closeness to thresholds can be monitored and evaluated continually over the entire interval.

There will be two thresholds: a minimum threshold (the lower limit), which is concerned with ruin, and a maximum threshold (the upper limit), which is concerned with making new investments, since the company's liquid position is becoming excessively high. Point e in Figure 10–15 might serve as an example of an upper limit for liquidity. However, in many (if not most) cases, it would be desirable to stop the process before a point as high as e is reached. In the first place, the rate of adding to liquidity has slowed, and an alternative plan may promise a greater return rate. Second, the cost of excessive liquid assets is the foregone opportunity of having invested them in other ways. At the minimum, the savings-bank return is lost; but, more realistically, other projects, or perhaps an expansion of the scope of the present plan, should be growing out of the benefits of this plan. If the lower-limit threshold is violated, the liquidity level is nearing the danger point. The resource configuration should be rearranged, and the use of alternative paths in the network is indicated. Because a reasonable comparison of alternative paths is so dependent on the timing of the cash flows, discounting procedures are generally essential.

A planning system containing multiple paths can receive many different warning signals. The manager must know how to interpret these signals. A few likely ones can be mentioned:

1. A threshold is breached.

2. A run occurs—that is, the fluctuations of actual liquidity are observed to fall continually above or below the plan's expectations. Such a run of values could occur through chance fluctuation, but if it persists there is a reasonable probability that a trend toward a limit may exist. Action might be warranted if extrapolation of the trend indicates that some small interval of time, Δt, remains before the upper or lower limit is likely to be breached.

3. A point of inflection is reached or not reached (or an interval, Δt, remains before it will be reached), by which we mean that the rate of flow changes from acceleration to deceleration or vice versa. For example, a signal occurs if the point of inflection for expenditures minus revenues is not reached by some expected time. After the first point of inflection is reached, the occurrence of another point of inflection probably signals trouble.

4. If excessive risk of ruin (determined in ways yet to be explained) threatens the system's survival, then a criterion is provided for shifting the plan, stopping the project, or taking other remedial action.

Precisely what constitutes a basis for setting limits and thereby defining "excessive" value is a criterion (formal or intuitive) supplied by management.[14] Such judgments can be expected to vary by industry, by company, and as a result of personal prejudices, preferences, and perspectives. Limit-setting is controlled more often by tradition than by logic. Some sensible statements can be made by way of comparison, however. We would not expect, for example, that similar action limits would be chosen for situations that do and do not have ruin potentials.[15]

Sequential Planning

A necessity for threshold-constrained models (and a matter of urgency for partially constrained systems) is the development of sequential planning procedures.[16] By this we mean the procedures necessary for modifying the plans, which include continuous review of the choice of a planning horizon as well as the selection of the updating interval (see the discussion and figure on p. 349).

---

[14] This is similar to the selection of a cut-off value for testing purposes. Above some level, k, the instruction is "reject." The same also applies in the selection of control limits.

[15] We can hypothesize that in social welfare systems (e.g., city planning and hospital administration), national planning systems (e.g., military preparedness and economic planning), and personal needs systems (e.g., safety measures and police protection), the allowable ruin thresholds might be kept as low as one in a million. This is in line with the thinking of Émile Borel, previously footnoted (see footnote 12 in this chapter).

[16] For an example of sequential planning methods, see Philip Carlson, "A Staged Sequential Action Procedure," unpublished Eng.Sc.D. dissertation, Columbia University, 1962.

In 42 B.C. Publius Syrus wrote, "It is a bad plan that admits of no modification." The importance of being able to adjust a plan is evident for updating and trade-offs in fully constrained planning, as previously discussed. In partially constrained systems, sequential procedures are essential if use is to be made of the investment in multiple paths—that is, if adjustments are to be possible. But sequential planning is especially important when ruin is imminent. The use of sequential procedures can change, over time, both the nature of the plan and the action limits that are designed to detect the occurrence of contingencies.

The planning horizon can also be modified by sequential procedures. The advantages and disadvantages of enlarging the planning horizon have been discussed previously, but the reentry of this issue affords us the opportunity to consider a simple but convenient analogy, the beam of a flashlight. When the instrument is far from the target, coverage is extensive but intensity is low. Nearness brings gain in detail and loss in scope. Similarly, plans can be made to reach far ahead if there is willingness to accept the accompanying uncertainties. This is a difficult position to take when ruin possibilities exist. Many false action-limit signals can be anticipated. Conversely, plans can be formulated that reduce uncertainty by dividing a long planning horizon into a number of smaller ones, but the penalty is suboptimization, which *can be particularly serious for ruin-prone systems*. The signals are not allowed to operate with sufficient notice to be operationally useful. The development of a planning process that can provide a sequence of dependent decisions may help to bridge the gap between these planning-horizon alternatives.

Scale of Available Resources

Management would not consider it threshold planning to commit a small percentage of its total resources to a new activity. So if a plan involves a minor investment of M dollars and the enterprise has available large (liquid) assets of R dollars, then M/R would constitute a small percentage.

For any investment of a fixed amount, the M/R ratio reflects the company size—it is a larger number for smaller companies and vice versa. Ruin thresholds are sensitive to this ratio. Accordingly, *for any given level of investment a small company may require thresholds where a large one would not*. This conclusion can be amplified by a ruin model such as the following.[17]

---

[17] Further discussion of ruin models will be found in David W. Miller and Martin K. Starr, *Executive Decisions and Operations Research,* 2nd ed. (Englewood Cliffs, N.J.: Prentice-Hall, 1969), pp. 507–17. Some different points are covered by the same authors in *Inventory Control: Theory and Practice* (Englewood Cliffs, N.J.: Prentice-Hall, 1962), pp. 201–04.

$$\text{Probability (ruin)} = \frac{B^C(1 - B^W)}{1 - B^{C+W}} \qquad \text{(for } p \neq q)$$

where $C = R/M$ = the ratio of available capital to the size of planning investments; $C \geq 1$.

let S = net profit or gain to be acquired at the end of a given planning horizon (i.e., If the original investments are to be reclaimed but without additional profit, then $S = 0$ . . . which is equivalent to not investing).

let $W = S/M$ = the ratio of required net profit to the size of planning investments.

p = the probability of a plan's success. (In this case, $2M$ is achieved for a successful plan.)

q = the probability of a plan's failure. (M is wasted when the plan is unsuccessful.)

$B = q/p$ (generally $B < 1$).[18]

Also, for ($p = q$)

$$\text{probability (ruin)} = 1 - \frac{C}{(C + W)}$$

Using these equations, we can show that a large organization with a great deal of available capital will operate at lower ruin probabilities than will an organization with a smaller asset base. Also, a company that insists on high-return projects must have a commensurately high asset base in order to keep ruin probabilities at a reasonable level. Critically important guidance for management is available from such theoretical considerations. And often what we can learn from these models cannot be determined through intuition and in some cases even seems to run counter to it.

Some additional points merit attention. First, a plan may appear (perhaps for accounting reasons) to absorb a small percentage of total available assets, when the plan is in fact a subplan of a larger plan that strongly affects it. The illusion of a plan's simplicity can cause extensive damage when dependencies and interactions that actually exist are obscured. For this reason, we have advocated the *systems procedure* for defining the "real" boundaries of a planning problem. Second, a company's utility for resources (that is, how much a given resource is worth *to that company*) will vary according to the size of the company's total assets and their relative liquidity. Asset liquidity affects the value of R. Companies may have great fixed assets that are not, in large part, convertible into cash. This condition will increase the necessity for threshold planning. Third, the inventory of a company's resources cannot exclude intangible assets such as good will and the talents and morale of its

---

[18] From Martin K. Starr, "Planning Models," *Management Science*, Vol. 13, No. 4 (December 1966), pp. B136–37.

employees. Many companies require such resources in formidable quantities for the success of their plans. We must assume that if intangible resources represent a significant proportion of the total available resources, then the utilization of ruin thresholds is justified.

The ruin model we have used above is not a particularly good description of all the real-world elements and relations. It assumes that repeated investments will be made until all the capital is used up or the plan achieves the "required" gain. Meaningful modifications of the model can be developed, however, to fit specific cases. In the planning field, the importance of the ruin considerations that we have been discussing will relate to the managerial level. The ruin concepts are critical to top management even though the model is not.

Planning horizons for threshold systems. So far we have avoided the span-of-time factor in threshold-constrained planning models because it contains a trap. When one speaks of long-range plans, he defines nothing but intimates a great deal. The concept of "long range" will differ according to whether it is applied to a butterfly, a man, a company, an industry, or a nation. If the nature of a problem is such that a long planning period is defined as about one-tenth of a man's expected life span, then this should be understood to be a product of the situation, its speed of evolution, the reaction rates of managers, the intervals between cause and effect, and the ability to discern future states of the environment.

Many real situations are assigned planning horizons of three, five, or ten years. Hopefully, the assignments are justified; perhaps, in fact, executive judgment on such matters is not likely to err by a great deal. On the other hand, it would be interesting to know if the Russian five-year plans would have been less effective had they been treated originally as four- or six-year plans; or whether the French four-year plans should really span five years; or whether companies with three-year plans would not be well advised to choose a four-and-a-half-year span.

Specific answers to such questions are not presently available, but the framework for considering them in a reasonable way can be constructed. Simply stated, there is an optimal planning horizon, which balances the spurious identification of ruin (caused by attempting to forecast too far into the future) against the nonidentification of ruin (caused by shortsightedness).

Variable planning horizons. The concept of action limits can be translated into planning-horizon terms. To illustrate this, let us take an example of capacity planning. Assume that:

1. Forecasts are available giving the expected demand for capacity in a particular system over time.

2. As the forecasts span a longer time interval, their believability decreases.
3. There are penalties (known and estimated) for having excess capacity (C_c in dollars/unit/unit time) and for not having sufficient capacity (C_u in dollars/unit/unit time).
4. There is a set-up cost, applicable each time a project to expand capacity is undertaken and independent of how much capacity is added (C_o in dollars/project).
5. There is a limit to the total penalties that can be withstood—that is, a total cost beyond which ruin situations develop.

One way of looking at the limit mentioned in point 5 is in terms of too much or too little capacity. When capacity passes either limit, threshold reasoning prevails. It will be noted that the cost of the added capacity need not be considered, since at some point in time capacity will have to be provided in any case. The penalties occur for providing it too soon or too late. But it is also necessary to add capacity in reasonable amounts at one time in order to avoid excessive occurrence of the cost C_o. Adding any amount of capacity in, say, n separate increments will cost nC_o. Since C_o can be presumed to be large, it tends to decrease the number of new project starts. A second way of viewing the limit on total penalties is therefore in terms of how often capacity is added and how much is added at one time. This is a typical inventory-type situation (see pp. 61–62) for which a minimum-cost balance can be achieved.

A third approach exists. We can treat the cost limit as it arises from choosing too near or too distant a planning horizon. When we do so, some interesting conclusions can be drawn about the effects of multiple-path planning. If we assume that the forecasts that are used can be perfect for long periods, then the best result will always be obtained with the longest possible planning period. Shorter periods can provide solutions that are only *as* good, never better. So, if perfect forecasts for five periods are available, then the solution based on planning five periods ahead (1–5) will be as good as or better than that derived from any other planning horizon, such as (1–3) + (4–5), for example. With perfect forecasting, the amount of capacity provided over time would be just right; the schedule of adding capacity would be optimal.

But what if the forecasts are not perfect? The quality of the forecasts is assumed to improve as the planning horizon decreases. But contingencies arising from the often questionable assumption of independent planning intervals also appear more frequently. Forecast errors and contingency suboptimization both have costs that include some probability of the inherent ruin potentials.

The temptation to pursue longer planning periods to avoid suboptimization increases as the managerial level rises. To override forecast deficiencies, which increase rapidly, the manager moves to the use of partially constrained planning models (which can relate to a range of planning horizons) and, in particular, to the threshold variants. Thus, pressure for multiple-path planning and for the setting of action limits grows as we move up the hierarchical management tree.

To illustrate this point, Figure 10–16 represents the factors that determine planning-horizon limits, as well as an optimal planning horizon. If we assume

Figure 10–16

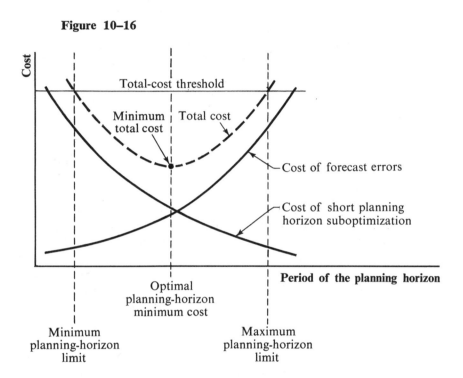

that, with ruin potentials in the planning system and with multiple-path planning, the entire cost curve of contingency suboptimization falls more slowly than the cost of forecast errors rises, we observe that the optimal planning horizon gets longer. The action limits on the planning horizons also move (unequally) to longer intervals—that is, the interval between the two limits decreases because the lower limit moves to the right more rapidly than the upper limit. These contentions seem appropriate for upper managerial systems and high-risk planning. Planning-horizon determination is not merely incidental to the planning situation.

SUMMARY

High risk and unusual opportunities often go hand in hand. Special planning approaches are required to treat situations having such potential benefits and threats. The importance of such approaches is evident now, when risk levels are increasing because of social and technological forces. Several alternatives are possible. Management can, of course, simply ignore "risky" plans, but by so doing it also eliminates the opportunity for extremely good results. Or, management might speed up its response rate and decrease the planning period. Ultimately, however, a situation will probably arise in which management will have to use risk elements in the plan. We can call this "planning for contingencies," for which partially constrained planning models are required.

Contingency planning becomes increasingly desirable the greater the percentage of company assets tied up in the plan. Clearly, then, at higher managerial levels, contingency planning comes closer than other types to satisfying managerial requirements. The extremes of partial constraint are no constraint and full constraint, but the former is seldom encountered. Partial-constraint models do not have an unambiguous optimal; instead, they are designed to react in the best possible way to what has already occurred, considering what is still likely to occur. To do this, they are constructed of multiple strategies producing multiple potential planning paths.

Greater resources are required for multiple-path networks than for single-path ones. The cost is related directly to the extent to which uncontrolled variability can affect the plan's performance. Performance, on the other hand, can be measured in different ways. To explain this, we have used Ozbekhan's distinction between types of plan—normative, strategic, and operational. We have interpreted these variants in our own terms as follows: Normative plans can be partially constrained because the manager is not yet sure what should be done. In other words, his objectives are not entirely clear, so different end results might be sought. Strategic plans can have multiple paths because of the variability of events that are likely to alter performance. In this case, the objective remains the same, but the various paths have different actions, times, and costs associated with them. Operational plans exist as the combination of single choices that must actually be made in the multiple-path network.

Forecasting abilities affect the normative, strategic, and operational characteristics of plans. In general, forecasting is essential to planning design, but as part of the planning process, classical forecasting is especially difficult to achieve. Fortunately, subjective, Bayesian approaches and simulation methods have increased the range of what can be accomplished. Partially constrained plans are particularly dependent on the existence of predictive abilities. The idea is to reduce the complex network to a few paths that can provide the greatest planning flexibility. Expected values based on reasonable forecasts can be used to reduce selected parts of a network. Great care must be exercised, however, because of suboptimizations caused by dependencies—that is, the combination of best-expected-value links is unlikely to produce the best plan. Monte Carlo simulations based on forecast data can be used to test out larger sets of network links. As before, simulation results have no normative implications, but they can assist greatly in the construction of reasonable alternatives for multiple-path planning networks.

Networks can also be reduced by recognizing independence of activities and by eliminating steps and sequences that are not feasible. An example is given of a system that initially has 5,184 unique planning configurations. By means of subjective evaluations on the part of the manager, the network is reduced to twenty-four and then eighteen branches that have to be evaluated.

The use of managerial predictions to reduce networks to a reasonable number of multiple paths raises questions concerning how the manager can make several predictions about what might happen, so that he can be prepared for contingencies. While much attention has been paid to forecasting, the same cannot be said for predictions, and little thought has been given to multiple predictions. A discussion of mean, median, mode, and Beta-distribution predictors lays the groundwork for recognizing that there are special requirements for deriving multiple predictions. Then a simple model is offered as a basis for deciding how much multiple-path elaboration to use.

Given the utility of partially constrained planning systems, new concepts and techniques are required to deal with its multiple-path properties. It is necessary to decide on the relative likelihoods that one or another path will occur. This question can be treated in a determinate way by stating odds or by using statistical or simulation methods. A sequencing-control algorithm is described, which recognizes that partial constraint may exist in the order of accomplishing a set of activities rather than in the choice of which activities to use. When alternative sequential arrangements are equally good, another dimension of partial constraint in planning emerges. Through the use of alternative optimal (or near-optimal) strategies, additional degrees of freedom are obtained.

Several planning targets may exist in PCPM's, but analysis can also reveal undesirable end points that might occur. To be able to spot such contingencies is part of the reason for using multiple paths. Of particular relevance are those end points that represent large loss or ruin. There is discussion of what the manager can do under such circumstances—that is, attempt to change network probabilities or add new activities to the network.

Such actions also describe concrete steps that could be used to convert FCPM's to PCPM's. If the manager suspects that the fully constrained model is hiding the presence of potential large losses, he may wish to convert to partial constraint in order to uncover dangerous contingencies. Moreover, generally forces today are operating to change FCPM's to PCPM's. At the same time, increasing experience with a system's general characteristics will at first increase the number of multiple paths that seems desirable and then decrease that number.

Threshold-constrained planning models are required when ruin situations can occur with the use of a particular plan. The threat of ruin has an economic base, but when it is viewed in terms of utility theory (as it should be), then psychological factors also play a part. Long-range planning is usually closely related to this special subclass of partially constrained planning systems. The utility concept is a more pertinent basis for describing what is meant by long-term planning than is the apparent length of the time period.

Action limits are part of threshold-constrained planning models. Plans that entail potentials for ruin greater than some set amount are discarded, and the criterion is applied in a dynamic sense over time. The action limits can be designed to detect different levels of ruin potential. Since cash liquidity is frequently used by management as the measure by which ruin propensities can be determined, a graphic example of this reasoning is presented and explained. The factors that control the interpretation of action limits are directly related to planning-horizon considerations. All these issues are connected to the scale of available resources. This is shown in terms of ruin models. Long- and short-term planning are redefined so that ruin considerations interact with planning horizons, and action limits that monitor the planning horizon are developed.

EXERCISES

1. The existence of high risk in planning situations leads to the use of partially constrained planning models. Explain what distinguishes these models and give some examples of situations that would be best treated in this fashion.

2. Since contingency planning concerns both good and bad results, the avoidance of trouble also means missing the possibility of some highly desirable effects. Explain the implications of this statement for management and give an example of each type of result.

3. Give an example of the least constrained planning situation that you can think of. Is the planning for the landing of men on Mars more or less constrained than your proposal?

4. How much multiplicity of planning paths would you suggest for:
   a. formulating a gambling strategy at Monte Carlo Casino
   b. establishing a desalinization plant for Los Angeles
   c. developing a television tape unit to sell for under $100 that can be attached to any set for home recording
   d. selling an insurance policy to the president of a large corporation
   e. housebreaking a duck

5. Develop an example of a planning tree that can be reduced by determining dependencies and feasible strategies. (See, for example, the reduction of 5,184 to eighteen possibilities, pp. 384–90). How does this approach relate to what is actually done? Why has the method been referred to as "filtering"?

6. What approach should be used to provide multiple predictions for:
   a. betting on a horse race
   b. marketing a new product
   c. planning a vacation

7. Compare alternative PCPM's where:

	$PCPM_1$	$PCPM_2$
Cost of the plan	$2C$	$3C$
Probability of success	.90	.85
Benefit of success	V	$1.5V$
Probability of failure	.10	.15
Penalty of failure	$3C$	$2C$

8. Use the Monte Carlo simulation approach as described in the text to analyze the network properties of the matrix below. Explain your analysis.

$\rightarrow$	A	B	C	D
A	x	$\frac{1}{3}$	$\frac{2}{3}$	0
B		x	1	0
C			x	1
D				1

where:					
Probability	0	$\frac{1}{4}$	$\frac{1}{2}$	$\frac{1}{4}$	0
AC estimate	$\frac{1}{3}$	$\frac{1}{2}$	$\frac{2}{3}$	$\frac{5}{6}$	1

9. Employ the Johnson sequencing algorithm for the following problem:

	Planning stage:							
	a	b	c	d	e	f	g	h
Phase: A	10	9	17	3	2	3	14	11
B	18	5	1	9	7	2	9	12

What kind of situation might this represent? Use a Gantt chart to illustrate your solution.

10. The text states that a two-tail action limit for ruin potential would exist if too much or too little sales volume could prove catastrophic. Explain this statement.

11. In what sense is liquidity an adequate or preferred measure for high-risk, ruin-type contingency planning systems? Explain Figure 10–15 in this regard.

12. Using the ruin model presented on pp. 410–11, analyze the following situations and comment on your results.

Situation	R	M	p	S
1	20	5	.8	.20
2	25	5	.6	.20
3	15	5	.5	.25
4	15	5	.5	.10
5	10	5	.2	.20

Part IV

CONTROLLING

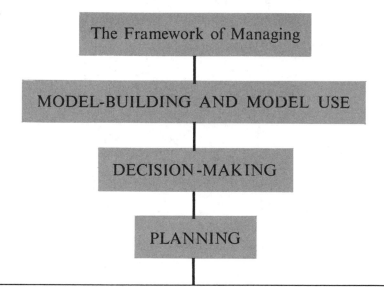

The Framework of Managing

MODEL-BUILDING AND MODEL USE

DECISION-MAKING

PLANNING

PART IV
CONTROLLING

Control ability is based on clear perception,
intelligent reactions, and the means to correct deviations
in line with objectives. Information is the common
denominator of the control function. While planning
determines what should be controlled, even a
good plan loses its effectiveness when no
adequate control system exists to implement it.
As a result, the current thinking is that since
large-system control is poor, emphasis must be
placed on control theory before stress on
improving the planning function can make
sense to managers.

The two major components of control theory are perception and reaction. Perception requires knowing *where* to look, *how often* to look there, and, of critical importance, *what to expect* to perceive. If what is sensed deviates from expectations, then it is necessary to know *what to do about the deviations*. This is the reactive component of control. Being able to take the right kind and amount of remedial action at the correct points in time is essential to the control function.

Information, which flows into and through all of the control system elements, provides the connections that make it possible to perceive situations and to react to them. Clearly, expectations are one form of information, and they can be explicit enough, in fact, to be written down. "Explicit expectations" is another name for "standards," which are an integral part of any *policy* statement. What is done about performance that deviates from standards is a strategy choice, and that choice is dictated by policy. So policy can be viewed as laws that underwrite the control function. And authority must back up policy to encourage implementation. The effective controller uses his authority selectively in conjunction with an appropriate choice of corrective actions.

The essence of controlling is described above, and it is clear from this description why in Chapter 11 we dwell at length on the nature of management policies that include programmed reactions to errors and the use of management by exception to allow policies to operate without managerial intervention. The information flows that unite the operations of the control system are treated at first in a relatively mechanical way, but then, in Chapter 12, the broad philosophical and behavioral aspects of information flows are examined as they relate to communication.

Managerial developments in the last fifty years have been directed toward policy-forming and controlling rather than planning. When uncertainty is recognized, managers *talk about planning and go about controlling*. They do this by first isolating the system from unwanted environmental effects and then imposing their own environments. The isolation approach, which can be likened to a "greenhouse strategy," attempts to achieve closed systems, which are decidedly easier to control than open ones. The closed-system effect can be achieved in many ways: by entering into contracts, by buying insurance, by hedging, and, above all, by initiating others so that well-known inertial effects can be shared. The pioneering of new frontiers in management has not been an obvious attraction for many years. As a result, control and the policies of control have played the dominant role in managerial systems. But the need for new forms of control to cope with open systems has led to much study and theory development. Management has become increasingly interested in these far broader aspects of its control function.

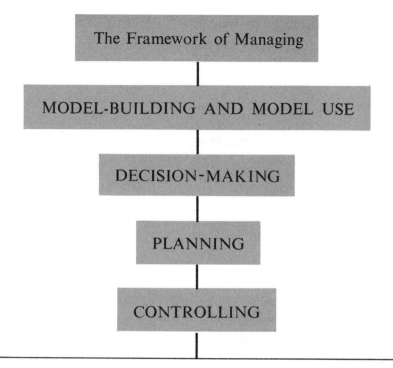

The Framework of Managing

MODEL-BUILDING AND MODEL USE

DECISION-MAKING

PLANNING

CONTROLLING

Chapter 11
Policy Formulation and Management by Exception

Some types of policy are based on scientific reasoning;
others reflect social values. One difficulty of
a scientific approach to policy is that the method
is not suited to the intangible characteristics
that often apply to human systems. On the other
hand, social-value policy tends to seek stability
of systems rather than optimization of benefit.
In policy evaluation, many different positions
can be defended. Once there is consensus
on the fundamental values, rational procedures
offer advantages. The structure of control
systems can be related to the judicial, legislative,
and executive functions of management. The role
of the computer and the nature of management by
exception are highly relevant in policy considerations.

Chapter 11

POLICY FORMULATION
AND MANAGEMENT
BY EXCEPTION

"Thou shalt" and "thou shalt not" are related to, but not at all the same as, "you should" and "you should not."

SOCIAL POLICY AND SCIENCE-BASED POLICY

Much of man's heritage is social policy, which has been handed down over the centuries in "thou shalt" forms of commandments. It is always difficult to argue about such policy because social values are its foundation.[1] It is primarily the growth in scientific knowledge that has led to discussion and change. Policy derived from this scientific knowledge is supported by the authority of the rationalism that lies behind it and by the supposedly concrete, observable, and predictable nature of its reality. Science-based policy, therefore, should be more susceptible to reasoned argument than social-based policy, but this is not always clearly so.

Scientists have quarreled among themselves about the reality of their observations and about the utility of a science that reasons in closed systems from chosen premises. Logical positivism and operationalism are two related schools of scientific and philosophic

---

[1] By *social values* we intend all political, religious, organizational, and institutional values.

425

thought that have criticized science for improper observation and reasoning. Percy Bridgman, the world-famous physicist and Nobel Prize winner, severely chastised scientists for being nonoperational—that is, for using intangible dimensions and unmeasurable variables in their models of the physical world. And the scientific community has criticized itself for proposing normative solutions to problems based on models that cannot be supplied with sufficient operational data.

At issue are the important decision variables that are assigned numerical values based on the manager's memory, attitudes, and feelings. It must be recognized that such data are likely to be biased and that they are postulated only because of the need to describe the system under study. As in Bayesian estimation (see pp. 225–30), the use of personal information may be helpful, but not when it is fed into models for direct normative interpretation and not when it is accepted as evidence having the underlying rigor of scientific law. The managerial community tends to regard policies derived by scientific techniques as the products of accepted theories. And it is not the theories that are in question. The problem concerns those observations on which the interpretation of theory is based. Facts deduced from theoretical models should always be tested with this point in mind.

Since science can have such difficulties with its own policies, it is not surprising that society gets entangled with policies that are structured on social and personal values.

Policy Potentials for Equilibrium and Optimization

Developing and maintaining effective policy is an end in itself. An objective of all individuals is to belong to groups that have such policies. By *effective policies* we mean those that are supported by the group over a long enough period to become accepted practice. Policies that effectively dictate human behavior allow the group that accepts those policies to be distinguished from the rest of society, which neither accepts nor rejects the policies. In other words, the participants view themselves as part of a cohesive group with specific objectives that are consistent and separable from the objectives of the larger systems that surround the group. Such subsystems are usually distinguished from larger systems by values rather than by measurable performance and operating characteristics. Therefore, there is a tendency for social-value policies to prevail over scientific-rational policies. There is also little impetus to develop scientific policies that deliver superior performance, because they are often rejected as threatening traditional values.

Cultural or social values lend themselves to many types of policy, whereas systems performance measures do not. An important reason is that the social-value objectives of obtaining and maintaining *equilibrium* in society have many solutions, whereas the scientific-rational objective of *maximizing benefits* does not. The total social-value system can be brought to equilibrium far more readily by segmenting it into subsystems than by treating it as wholes. Thus, we get groups and clubs; departments and divisions; counties, states, and countries. And each such subsystem adheres to a body of policy that it calls its own. Many other kinds of division also would have produced equilibrium conditions. Obviously, there are great overlaps in the policies of the subsets. Nevertheless, each subsystem's equilibrium tends to be independent of that of the others. As a result, there is a tendency for politicians, statesmen, administrators, and managers to develop subgroups having segmented value systems that can prevail over the large system of many interacting values that they must manage. There is ample empirical evidence in many spheres to justify this statement. On the other hand, there has been increasing (and unwanted) pressure to be responsive to the larger system and to provide *maximum* benefits rather than social equilibriums. The need arises for many reasons, including increasing population and new technology, which seem to support larger, independent subgroup formations. Social attitudes, affected by these factors, have become forces in their own right, producing powerful new groupings.

When *maximization* (rather than equilibrium) is the primary goal, it often becomes impossible to isolate subsystems that can be considered independent of all other subgroups. Maximization requires knowledge of how all the systems interact. Subsystem policies cannot even be tested in isolation for their contribution to maximization so that faulty policies can be rejected. It is hardly surprising, therefore, that in general, equilibrium policies, which merely keep things going, are simpler to design and easier to manage than optimization policies. And, since it is an observed tendency of segmented value systems to achieve their own equilibrium, the evident conclusion of this line of reasoning is that the effort to achieve policy that seeks the optimal performance of large systems is rare. What *is* usual is policy to maintain the equilibrium of small value systems.

Policy formulation requires a master hand. The elements and principles can be studied and, to the extent that they are understood, made into rules. Three such rules for formulating commonly used policies might be: (1) Strive for equilibrium, not optimization; (2) use ethics and social values as a basis and stay away from consideration of larger systems; (3) call on accepted tradition and avoid innovations. As some examples of the policies resulting from such rules, we can suggest: keep the inventory investment low, invoke the teamwork concept, insist on the punctuality of workers. These policies provide the manager with a stable system that avoids situations with unassessed potentials for ruin. On the other hand, the potential benefits of maximization policies that also maintain equilibrium are equal to or greater than those of value-based equilibrium policies. Little is known about maximization policies that maintain equilibrium, and they are generally looked upon with great suspicion. Much more must be understood about maximization policies if management is to choose policies that are as effective as possible. But this much is certain: Using a far broader base than tradition, we can establish policy that strives for optimization and permits social and behavioral values to interact with all other characteristics of the system.

Policy Mystiques

In Chapter 8 we discussed an important distinction between planning and policy—that is, that planning deals with unique environments, while policy deals with repetitive ones. The repetition can be wholly imagined or physically real and observable. A fundamental policy mystique is the belief that repetitive environments exist. The effect of this belief is to create the conditions for making the belief into reality. If the performance of the system is judged largely in terms of value intangibles, then the use of policy tends to make the values themselves behave like repetitive environments. Disagreement with such policies is usually interpreted as an attack on the system's environment, because the two have become synonymous. The obvious effect of this mystique is the utilization of suboptimal policies in situations that might have benefited from careful and imaginative planning. On the other hand, in scientifically rationalized systems, the tendency to imagine that repetitive environments exist when in fact they do not is negligible. As previously mentioned, the operationalist school might not concur, stating instead that imagination was obscured by scientific jargon. Even so, scientific policy formulation is less susceptible to this mystique than policy-making based on values.

Another fundamental policy mystique, related to the first, is that a unique equilibrium is a natural property of systems and must be found and used. An obvious problem exists if in fact there are many different policy equilibriums that are not equally good. The mystique prevents the search for "better" equilibriums, let alone optimal ones. Again, potential benefits from planning are by-passed.

If we examine such policy notions, the conditions that account for many management policies become readily apparent. For example, since repetitive states can be induced as an aid to achieving equilibrium more easily for social-value systems than for rational ones, management often chooses to emphasize the so-called human problem. For example, with the promulgation of such value policies as "thou shalt be on time," systems become self-adaptive,[2] and management gains control—but not optimal results. The suboptimal value policies become repetitive environments (i.e., everyone who stays is on time),

---

[2] By *self-adaptive* we mean that the system's fundamental properties embody and reflect the policy to which the system has adapted.

and the subsystem achieves its own individual and independent equilibrium. At present, more of management's policy know-how is focused on these kinds of small-system relations than on the rational kind that large systems demand.

In this regard, we should note that *policy* is often interpreted as a set of rules, and *principles* are considered to be specific, well-thought-out rules. *Theory,* however, is not constructed along similar lines. Theory implies that rational reasons exist for the policies and principles. Theory is a structure from which policy can be defined, but it does not follow that all policy must be obtained in this way or that when it is, such policy will be implemented. Even where theory exists, policy mystiques can persist, because the theory cannot span the gap to reality.

To be effective, policy must be communicated—properly disseminated *and* understood. That is why so many textbooks are written about those principles of management that tend to induce self-adaptive equilibriums. Where such principles are at work, it is easy to confuse them with the fundamentals of theory. Value statements provide unconscious subterfuge, and the system may even seem to be optimizing effectiveness and maximizing achievement. How many of management's policies are clearly known for what they are—equilibrium-motivated ruin-avoidance mechanisms? We know that normative models are most common at lower managerial levels. We can surmise, therefore, that top managements' policies are involved with value-system mystiques relying to a great extent on the fact that other top managers subscribe to the same (self-adaptive) mystiques. Top management's policies, therefore, may be even more dependent on the equilibrium mystiques than policies formulated at lower levels in the organizational hierarchy.

Are there better approaches to policy-making than the ones currently in use? Are alternative policies available based on objective maximizations? As we will show in this chapter, a great deal can be done to improve the policy-making situation by the use of *operational* scientific reasoning.

Evaluation and Interpretation

We know that the body of law is social policy and that all levels of courts participate continually in the interpretation of law. Lawyers and judges are employed full time in policy *interpretation* and only incidentally in policy *evaluation,* which is a legislative and executive function. But in the business organization, these functions are entrusted in combination to the manager, who tends to avoid evaluation. Managers know that the more detailed a policy is, the more readily it is evaluated. Consequently, by keeping policy as vague as possible, they increase the likelihood of interpretation rather than evaluation.

It is evident too that existing policy not only slows down the development of evolving policy but also inhibits the discovery of new ideas. For example, shortly we will consider management by exception, in which the manager does not receive information unless an exception not covered by the policy occurs. There is little potential for planning, for inventing new ideas that apply to areas already treated by an exception principle. Only when the exception occurs is attention drawn to these areas. And from what we have previously pointed out, exceptions are less likely in equilibrium-motivated systems than in optimizing ones. Thus, policies, as they are intended to do, provide risk avoidance and regularity. Rightly, no manager who could achieve them would be without such policy capabilities. Lacking policy, managers would have to devote as much time to trivia as to crucial considerations. But there are dangers inherent in the misuse of policies and, above all, in the use of the wrong ones.

CHOOSING AMONG ALTERNATIVE POLICIES

> The "interests" of people and organizations are multiple and complex, and policy problems are sufficiently complex that for the vast majority of individuals or organizations it is conceivable—given the objective features of the situation—to imagine them ending up on *any* side of the issue.[3]

This statement highlights an important aspect of policies—namely, that many different positions can be defended rationally.[4] Bauer's remark stems less from basically different kinds of behavior (say, the scientific and the intuitional approaches in the manager's case) than from the unresolvability of many issues—until a value position has been taken. Once such a position is taken, however, the possibility of other value orientations tends to get lost, even though there is nothing that might disqualify them. There is, in fact, a psychological basis for defending whatever one has committed himself to, no matter how that commitment was taken—a situation called congitive dissonance (see p. 595).

We have explored previously our inability to prescribe what values individuals should hold. In those cases where the consistency of all premises with the basic values is important, science may be of help. Scientifically

---

[3] Raymond A. Bauer, "Social Psychology and the Study of Policy Formation," *American Psychologist,* Vol. 21, No. 10 (October 1966), p. 36.

[4] It can be argued that the complexity of issues is often so great that the individual cannot determine where he stands on the issues. But, as in competitive situations, rationality can lead to different strategies, and the individual's problem is to determine which side he is on.

derived policy (such as an inventory policy) frequently has the additional advantage of being able to be framed in the context of a normative model. But if scientists insist that the manager wait until all premises have been checked out before he uses normative reasoning, they will be by-passed more often than not.

The manager has no vested interest in using scientifically constructed policies. For highly complex problems, he can call more easily on value mystiques. Science can be applied to organized complexity only in special, restrictive ways, and even then its application is difficult. On the other hand, for problems of limited scope and relative simplicity, scientifically derived policies are often economically advantageous. For entirely logical reasons, managers accept whatever help in deriving policies is likely to produce the greatest immediate benefit. In a very crucial sense, policy needs are immediate, while planning is concerned with the future. And equilibrium-type policies may be the best immediate course of action. However, the inertia of such policies, once they are instituted, makes them difficult to remove. The acceptance of a set of policies makes it difficult to see that other possibilities exist, especially if the accepted policies work well in the short run. As a result, the best immediate solution may have deleterious effects in the long run. To further develop this important notion of alternative policies, let us now discuss two interrelated options that affect all policy formulation.

Type I and Type II Policy Errors

Bauer's remark is provocative. It suggests that a person could reasonably offer either to support some policies or not to support them. To illustrate, we can examine an important policy situation (which also has great generality) where there is a sensible basis for either a pro or a con position. As we proceed, we will see that ambiguity as to what to do exists because of a lack of information and that the information vacuum is filled with value judgments. In many situations, this one included, the necessary information cannot be obtained. Consequently, the manager resolves the situation in the only way that remains—namely, he expresses his values for different kinds of outcome. The policies that reward his high-value options and avoid his low-value ones are chosen. The use of such judgments, when it is feasible, represents typical managerial strategy.

For example, the manager states that he intends to follow a tough pilot-plant policy.[5] What he means is that if a pilot-plant operation does not perform as well as he expected (say, with respect to productivity rate or cost per unit),

---

[5] A pilot plant is a less than full-scale production system. It is used in an experimental capacity to infer how the full-scale system would function.

Figure 11–1   Hypothetical Distribution of Pilot-Plant Results Based on Known Technological Factors Assuming That the Actual Full-Scale Plant Operates at the Mean Value *M*.

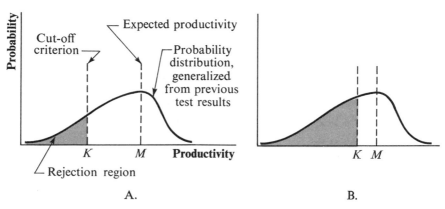

A.   B.

then he will reject the process. The policy is tough if his expectations are high. In Figure 11–1A, a distribution is suggested for what might be the productivity of a pilot plant created to represent a full-scale system.[6] It is a hypothetical distribution based on the knowledge of how pilot-plant operations might deviate from the true reading that would be observed if the full-scale plant were built. Since a pilot plant is a test model of less than full scale, there are good reasons for believing that it will not perform in exactly the same way as the full-scale system. It is possible that the specific pilot plant's productivity will be relatively larger or smaller than that of the actual full-scale system. If the test results of this particular study indicate that the full-scale system would yield higher productivity than had been expected (i.e., the value *M*), the manager usually does not worry. But his intuition is misleading him, and we will show why shortly. If the test results are less than *K*, the manager rejects the process that the pilot plant modeled. When *K* is close to *M*, as in Figure 11–1B, nearly 50 percent of all pilot-plant results will lead to process rejection.

This is a tough policy in one respect but not tough in another. It commits many Type I errors and few Type II errors. That is, the manager wants to avoid accepting a "bad" process (a Type II error), so he has set his cut-off criterion in a position where he can often make the mistake of rejecting an acceptable process (a Type I error). This is not unusual managerial behavior. The organization is always aware of Type II errors. For example, the

---

[6] The distribution arises because the pilot plant is an imperfect representation of the full-scale system.

full-scale plant is built and turns out to have poor productivity; or an aircraft design is accepted for manufacture, based on the performance of the prototype models, but the plane is later found to have higher operating costs than expected. Type I errors, on the other hand, are rarely discovered by the organization, since the future of that which is rejected is seldom traceable. We do not know what would have occurred if we had gone to work with the company we turned down, chosen the other school, or married a different person. Even if a friend who made a different choice moves rapidly to success, we cannot be sure that we would have done the same.

While it is apparent that the manager, at any level, might prefer to avoid Type II errors, it should also be clear that the organization's welfare is not necessarily enhanced by such policies. Some economic balance of the costs of these two types of error is indicated. But many of the essential ingredients of these costs cannot be measured. Managerial intuition can be put to work if the manager understands the concept of these errors and particularly the fact that as the likelihood of either kind of error increases, the likelihood of the other decreases. Let us examine this interrelationship.

A Type I error occurs when what is actually true is rejected as being false. An important and obvious example is of a new product that would be successful if distributed nationally. The test-market result, however, can indicate incorrectly that the brand is a failure. The statistical problem of a false negative was known at the time that the test-market design was approved, since some probability of a false negative cannot be avoided. Perhaps the test was designed so that five out of a hundred mistakes of this kind could occur. The allowable percentage of mistakes is as much a part of the specification of management policy as it is of the test-market design.

A Type II error occurs when what is actually false is accepted as being true. The test market has a certain predetermined probability of indicating a successful product when in fact the brand would fail if distributed nationally. There is also a prespecified probability of going wrong in this way.

The distinction between Type I and Type II errors can be made in a simple table (see Table 11–1); to explain the relationship between them requires an additional notion—that is, how false is false? Consider Figure 11–2. The

Table 11–1

		Actual situation The assumptions are:	
		True	False
Test result indicates that	True	No error	Type II error
the assumptions are:	False	Type I error	No error

Figure 11–2

NOTE: The distance d can be very small, for example, less than 1 percent. The cut-off criterion may be set at the value that the manager decrees is minimal for success. It may also be set by specifying the assumed mean, the shape of the X distribution, and the allowable size of the α error.

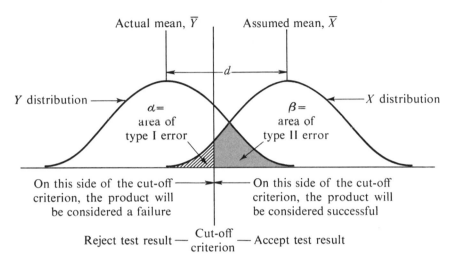

assumption is made that the test-market observations will be distributed around the mean value $\overline{X}$, as shown.

If the *test-market result* (such as brand share) falls to the *left* of the cut-off criterion, then the new brand is rejected as probably not coming from a successful product, such as X. We must bear in mind that the reason an X distribution exists is that a sample is being used to reflect what the real situation for the total population would be. Imagine that the *real* value is Y. The sample distribution of Y is the actual source of the test-market observations. The value of Y is too low a measure (of brand share or dollar volume), and the brand would be rejected if the manager knew that this was the case. Now, let the Y distribution move farther to the right by improving the value of Y. In fact, move Y far enough to coincide exactly with $\overline{X}$. Observations to the left of the cut-off will still be rejected in error. α is fixed by the manager who does not want to falsely reject too many acceptable products. On the other hand, if the Y distribution is widely separated from the X distribution (as shown in the Figure), then the cut-off criterion will reject most of the values that could have come from Y.

Now let us consider the area to the right of the cut-off criterion, which measures the probability of committing a Type II error—that is, accepting a false conclusion. Looking at Figure 11–2 as shown, most of the Y distribution falls to the left of the assumed distribution, yet a significant percentage of its tail area crosses the cut-off criterion and lies in the acceptance region. All such test results would be falsely accepted as having been derived from the X distribution. The area of the Y distribution that lies to the right of the cut-off criterion is therefore falsely in the acceptance region. It is called the β error and will vary in size according to the distance, d, that separates the means of the two distributions. β measures the area of possible Type II error for any given distance, d. Of course, d is unknown, but for any hypothesized d, the size of the error can be determined. In other words, for a given α region, the size of the β error changes according to how far the actual Y distribution falls from the assumed X distribution. The β error is small when the two distributions are widely separated—that is, when the difference (X mean $-$ Y mean) is large. But the significance of whatever β error exists can be severe, since when the means are widely separated, the incorrect acceptance of an assumed X value will carry the large penalty of a distant Y-valued mean. As the difference, d, decreases, the β error increases in a not at all linear way. Figure 11–3 illustrates a typical relationship where the α region is set at .05.

Figure 11–3

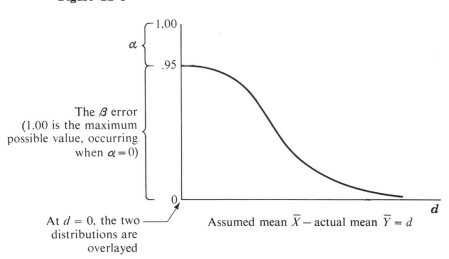

We note that under the assumption of an exact overlay of the two distributions, the β area (the Type II error) equals $1 - \alpha$. While this is a large β error, its consequences are zero, since there is no penalty for $\overline{X} = \overline{Y}$ values. As the distance, d, increases, the penalty for $\overline{X} \neq \overline{Y}$ rises, while the β error diminishes.

When the manager moves the position of the cut-off criterion to the left, the Type I error decreases. But this raises the β error across the entire range of Figure 11–3. If the cut-off criterion is moved to the right, the likelihood of making a false reject of X increases; while that of accepting a false X conclusion derived from Y decreases.

This discussion gives additional insight as to why management tends to worry more about making a Type II error than a Type I error. As we have stated, the β error is largest in the immediate neighborhood of where the assumptions that X exists are correct. The consequences of the error are zero when the actual and assumed distributions are identical. Then, as the penalty for distance increases, the probability of the error decreases. The relationship is far too complicated for intuition to work. As a result, a "safe" policy is chosen. The cut-off criterion is moved as far to the right as possible. Since when good results are rejected the opportunity-cost penalty is rarely measured, an equilibrium of mediocrity is achieved. Usually it is not even known that any error has been made. On the other hand, our culture supports a dislike for visible mistakes, even when economic benefit accrues from a sensible policy that allows just "enough" such mistakes to be made. A policy that allows "enough" visible mistakes permits more than compensating advantages. But in a competitive society one tries to *look* as little bad as possible. Is it worse to buy a stock that drops than not to buy a stock that rises in value? The investor might answer, too quickly, in the affirmative, and his investment policies tend to support that position. Management is not much more sophisticated than the small investor in this regard, so management policies have the effect of stabilizing performance to make it neither very good nor very bad.

An information policy. An additional point should be made. Both types of error can be decreased by diminishing the variance, or spread, of each of the distributions. Increased information usually decreases assumed variance. The imputed variance level is increased rapidly as a protection in the face of insufficient information (see pp. 511–12). So, with more relevant information, such as a larger sample, a larger pilot plant, a longer and more detailed testing procedure, the tails of the distribution are pulled in. As shown in Figure 11–4 below, the effect is to decrease both the Type I and the Type II errors.

What is not shown in the diagram is the fact that the cost of information rises as the variance decreases. An optimal policy exists, which minimizes the total cost (of information and the Type I and Type II penalties).

The notion of minimizing the total costs to determine an optimal policy is important for management theory. Through new information, the policy problem changes its character. Furthermore, methods exist for achieving a balanced solution—balanced in the sense that the α and β errors are conflicting multiple objectives. Rational policies can be obtained by applying models appropriate

Figure 11–4

NOTE: By means of additional information the distribution's variance is decreased, thereby diminishing both types of error.

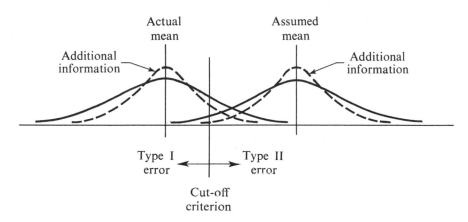

for treating multiple objectives (see pp. 273–84). Yet the ability to identify the relevant costs and to understand their relations with management options is far more fundamental to policy formulation than any other factors. Thus, our example clearly differentiates between social and scientific policy and illustrates how management can exercise a great deal of control over the nature of the policies it employs.

Algorithmic and heuristic policies. If we had a set of rules that could be used, *without any intervention by the manager,* to determine how much information to obtain and how to set the α cut-off criterion, we would have a policy algorithm. This can be contrasted with the value-judgment basis for policy. For example, lacking any objective information about the shape of the sampling distribution, we heuristically set a tough rejection policy based on the notion that any brand-share test result less than some given value cannot be tolerated. This is equivalent to choosing the cut-off criterion so that it provides a large α area. We do this because we do not want to be visibly wrong.

In the same sense, many algorithms for problem-solving are triggered by arbitrary standards that do not apply to the specific situation but are assumed to be generally applicable. For such cases, if the problem-solving procedures cannot be interrupted by the intuition of the manager, then a strictly algorithmic approach to policy is being used. Algorithms are familiarly associated with science, but they are not necessarily scientifically valid. Astrological "policy" is an example of this. It is a form of policy that has the trappings of science because a system is involved. But we err if we assume that the underlying system is therefore scientifically justified. In general, algorithms, whether or not they are based on scientific method, are complete policy procedures that produce normative conclusions concerning what "ought" to be done.

As we can see from the prior discussion of Type I and II policy errors, it is rare that an algorithm will completely satisfy the manager's needs. Instead, he will feel a need to combine algorithms with subjective judgments, which we have called heuristics. Heuristics are smaller than policies. They can bridge the gaps left by steps missing in the algorithm (for example, at what level to set the α criterion). Frequently called "rules of thumb," they are like sensible thoughts or common-sense descriptions of an approach to a particular *part* of a problem. They are expected to have some empirical justification. Managers are considered to be the great library of heuristics. Their experiences are replete with evidence of knowledge that, at best, can be cogently verbalized. But this knowledge must be sorted and understood. The real value of heuristics is yet to be determined. There is much about them that is not yet recognized. Meanwhile, an increasing number of scientific algorithms that include heuristics are being developed and released by management-science groups. In general, by formulating algorithmic policies that embody effective heuristics, management science has to date made its most significant contributions to management practice.

Executive, Legislative, and Judicial Functions

The computer is almost always required for the successful application of algorithms because of the quantities of data to be processed. As a result, management tends to view management science and computer use as inseparable. But this is an unrealistic and exaggerated view that blurs the critical differences in their respective roles.

The computer plays an important part in policy *enforcement*. Its role is far more *judicial* than might at first be recognized, and it carries many of the same liabilities as judges, courts, and enforcement agencies. These include abstraction of the issues, reduction of individuality, and single-minded obedience to the law. Also, the fact that special interests can gain access to the system cannot be overlooked. Bribing a computer is not too different from bribing its human counterpart. Generally, the amount of detail will be so great that minor aberrations caused by neglect, fraud, or overdedication cannot be traced. (This discussion, being of great importance, is developed further in Chapter 12, which deals with information management.)

As the computer is the judiciary, the models of management science come closest to being the legislative arm of the system. And, using the policy formulations of models, algorithms, and heuristics, managers assume the role of the executive. To the extent that science cannot provide policy, the manager must also contribute to the legislative function. But he is being called on with decreasing frequency to provide judicial components. Would it be ideal if these divisions could be neat and clean? That depends on how little is known about many pertinent areas. If enough were known, the division could provide a highly effective management system.

One critical executive function is *evaluation*. Recommendations for new legislation and alterations of the judiciary are sensible executive functions. As we have stated previously, the details of scientific policies are susceptible to evaluation, whereas policies based on values are not readily altered. On the other hand, as the level of detail grows and the complexity of computer languages increases, it once again becomes simpler to interpret and directly implement policy than to evaluate it—and this is a judicial rather than an executive function. In other words, what is happening in policy development has many components. Some policies are freeing the manager so that he can be more of an executive, while others are depriving him of critical executive functions. As the basis of policy formulation becomes more scientific, a new kind of stability is developed. Treating larger systems and performance maximization rather than the equilibrium of independent subsystems encourages executive evaluation. These evaluations appear to lead to greater integration of functions and to the belief that independent subsystems are disappearing.

Automatic Policy Decisions

Many decisions derived from policy legislation are relatively automatic. They are interpreted as direct translations of rules, and we will subsequently discuss them as forms of *management by exception*. Other descriptive terms would be "decisions in absentia" or "decisions from semiautomatic procedures." These are prepackaged decision systems, which have been designed and constructed in anticipation of the fact that certain known situations can or must arise. It is precisely because certain kinds of situation follow a pattern (which has been recognized and categorized) that it is possible to prepare activities in advance for dealing with the anticipated circumstances. The prepackaged decision systems do not have to be elaborate to qualify as policy, but they can be, sometimes requiring an entire manual of rules or even a library of books[7] to spell out the policy guidelines.

Sometimes the guiding rules are directed to men who interpret them and then take action. Directions can be to exact specifications or to the intended "spirit of the law." At other times, the policy package is independent of human

---

[7] For example, the library of law books.

intervention. It is communicated to mechanical and electronic components. Reading can be done from punched cards, magnetic tape, or other forms of information storage. The judicial interpretations are carried through by computer programs. Intentions are communicated by transducers,[8] and actions are taken by means of gears, levers, valves, and other physical components. Many projections for the future raise the specter of the prime judicial interpretations being relegated entirely to nonhuman components. The prospect is simultaneously both attractive and frightening, but it is nonetheless real.

Most common systems exhibit varying degrees of automatic behavior. Usually, whether the rules are mechanically programmed and actuated by a physical control unit or verbally interpreted by a human being, an alarm device has been included with which to signal *on-line* management that an emergency (or exception) has occurred. "On-line" means that immediate access to management is available, and management's response is similarly direct. To understand these interrelationships, it will be useful to describe the fundamental components of the control system.

THE CONTROL FORMAT

Policies are *deferred decisions* that are triggered by the occurrence of specific situations. At the heart of the triggering mechanism is a control system. The design of the control system is based on full and unambiguous managerial specification of appropriate instructions for the questions that follow.

What must be observed? What variables should be studied? How should their condition be measured? These questions involve perception of both dimension and scale. And there is always the question of whether environments or outcomes should be observed. The values of the relevant dimensions are keyed to the deferred-decision triggers. When certain critical combinations of dimensional values occur, then a particular deferred decision is *activated*. The relevant process dimensions must be kept under observation, but this does not usually mean constant surveillance. Sampling intervals are more commonly used by management (e.g., monthly statements, daily or hourly reports, annual profit and loss statements). How often to monitor the system, including the possibility of continuous monitoring, must be determined by weighing costs against benefits. Figure 11–5 is representative of the situation and indicates how an optimal monitoring interval might be determined. The figure can be interpreted easily by reference to standard breakeven analysis (see pp. 262–65).

---

8 *Transducers* are devices that *translate* various input forms into appropriate outputs so that they can be read by the action devices.

**Figure 11–5   Derivation of Two Breakeven Points (BEP's) and
Optimal Monitoring Interval**

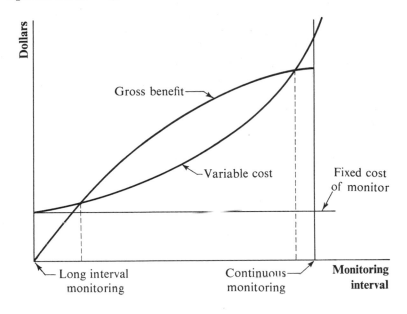

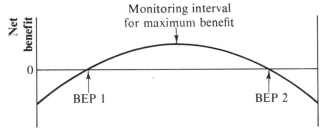

The scale of measurement affects the amount of descriptive information that
will be developed about environments and outcomes. Scale should be thought
of in terms of the degree of magnification or reduction of the system under
study. A large interval between successive samples is a form of information
reduction. Proper scaling and system size are at issue. At the two ends of the
spectrum are a large system simplified and a small system in great detail.

Perception of the system's variables is the monitor's function. The *monitor*
is a perceiving unit capable of observing one or more dimensions and comparing the observations with a previously determined standard. Deviations can be
stored or transmitted. The transmissions always involve some delay. The
monitor is the system's *sensor.*

The monitor's level of perceptive sensitivity and the frequency and fineness of its observations are not merely technical issues; they are basic descriptors of the management function. Recognizing that the first question is which variables to observe, and that the next is how often to observe them and in how much detail, we obtain greater clarity about management's role than if we simply philosophize about management's responsibility to formulate adequate policy. Every policy implies a control system, and every control system requires a monitor. When the policy is a product of legislative-type functions, it is treated as a *rule*. Increasingly, management has interpreted and administered rules and has not evaluated them or created new ones that might provide more satisfaction. When we divide the policy function into its essential components, many detailed questions arise. Scale, for example, is a critical policy determinant. Inches represent greater magnification of scale and potentially greater policy control than do feet. The importance of scale effects is humorously underscored by the following story.

POOR MAN: Lord, is it true that to you a thousand years is like a minute?
THE LORD: Yes, that's true.
POOR MAN: And is it also true that to you a thousand dollars is like a cent?
THE LORD: Yes, that's so.
POOR MAN: Then, Lord, could you give me a thousand dollars?
THE LORD: Yes, in a minute.

The irony of the story is related directly to the question of whose utilities are involved and to the fact that different scales are appropriate. There is the Lord's scale and the poor man's scale, and there is the Lord's scale for the poor man and the poor man's scale for the Lord. The monitor must be designed and constructed to be capable of perceiving the system in a fashion commensurate with the manager's abilities and requirements. In this case, there is the system and the manager, and there is the manager's perception of the system and the system's responses to the manager's perceptions. The monitor is constrained by technology, but it is limited even more by the interaction between technology and human values and perception.

What should be the response? A control unit is designed specifically to react to the monitor's messages. It receives information concerning deviations from the monitor and takes corrective actions according to a set of rules or a policy book with which it is invested. The controller (either human or mechanical) is the system's *mind*. It intercepts, translates, and responds to the signals that are sent by the monitor. For example, the monitor could be an accountant who prepares quarterly statements for the controller of the division. The basic structure of this situation is essentially the same as that of a mechanical monitor that reads the thickness of a sheet of plastic and transmits this information to a control unit, which then automatically adjusts the speed and separation of the rollers. The only difference is that the latter is a technological policy, while the former is related to policies of budgetary control, cash-flow policies, inventory-control policies, or machine-replacement policies. We usually associate technological policies with physical control systems, value policies with behavioral control, and procedures and methods policies with information-systems control. The actual character of the control system, however, tends to be a trivial matter. The concepts of policy are transferable.

For most types of man-machine control system, the critical design factors concern the arrangements that are made so that the controller knows *what to observe* and *when and how to react*. The use of a standard against which to measure performance is based on the standard's intimate connection, and at times equivalence, to the management objectives. Each check of the system's condition requires a comparison of the observed state with the standard. Deviation from the standard is used to generate an error signal. The *strength* of this signal will depend on the *degree of divergence* between the situation actually observed by the monitor and the preset standard designed for the system. When the standard is met, a zero error signal is produced. The fundamental structure of the control model is shown in Figure 11–6. Deviations can be measured for many different dimensions. The monitor can have any number of channels—for example, reports on deviations of sales volume, direct labor costs, quality of output, shipments—and these can be simultaneous or sequenced. Reporting times are part of the predesigned control instructions.

Figure 11–6   The System Required for Operational Policies

NOTE: All components can be man or machine or combinations.

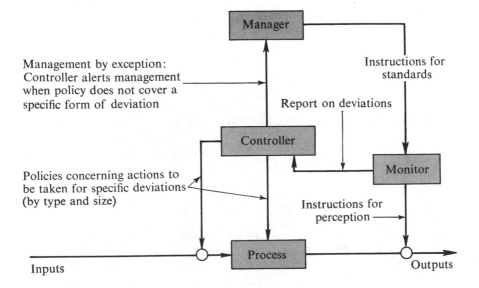

The language of policy and control that we have developed here may not sound like management talking about its policies, but it is fast becoming so, for greater communication precision is attainable through use of these terms and this model, and nothing is lost from the capabilities of the older management language of vague generalities. We must stress that this policy model is not mechanical. To believe so is to confuse vagueness with richness of communication and ambiguity with concepts that are too complex to penetrate. Rational is not equivalent to mechanical, unless it causes attenuation of concept formation, which this policy model does not do. On the contrary, it enhances management's power to discuss policy formulation.

Policy Response Systems

Policy systems designed to cope with conditions of certainty will be far less complex than those constructed to handle conditions of either risk or uncertainty, since the latter policies must succeed in reducing or eliminating the effects of risk or uncertainty. However, while it may not be immediately apparent, it is nevertheless easy to show that one does not need to know the forecast or probability distributions for environments to design a successful control device.[9] What is necessary is the *technology* to design and build a monitor and a controller that can call up the appropriate strategy and effect it with sufficient dispatch.[10] For example, in terms of Table 11–1, if the monitor

Table 11–1

	N_1	N_2	N_3	N_4
S_1	3	5	1	6
S_2	2	4	8	6
S_3	1	9	2	6

signals that N_3 will occur, or is occurring, then the controller must be able to call forth strategy S_2 in time to produce the maximum profit of 8 in the N_3 column. Assume that the monitor next reads N_1. Then the policy instruction (which includes the matrix) is the algorithm: Search the N_1 column; select

---

[9] Reference to pp. 230–33 in Chapter 6 will serve to reinforce this point.

[10] In order for the selected strategy to be effected, the instructions of the controller must be carried out. The real system must be touched, moved, manipulated, for an effect to be realized. This is accomplished by the *effector*, which is, in other words, the system's *toucher*.

that strategy which is associated with the largest value in the N_1 column; effect the selected strategy. This is S_1, with a value of 3. And if N_4 is next, what should the controller do? The best answer probably is to stay with the prior choice of strategy, since there is likely to be a cost for changing strategies. In other words, the monitor sequence N_2–N_3–N_2–N_4–N_1 would produce S_3–S_2–S_3–S_3–S_1. More complicated relations can be developed for situations in which the choice of strategy affects the next state of nature.

In the example that we have just used, the monitor was tuned to the state of nature, but the monitor could just as well read the latest output of the system. In either case, there is a standard system performance to be maintained. The principle is the same as that of an automatic pilot modifying the course of an aircraft exposed to *uncertain* wind conditions. The forecast is not necessary because the monitor provides the necessary information. However, without a forecast, all strategies must be maintained in inventory. The one advantage of the forecast, therefore, is that it allows economic design. If one particular state of nature has a very small probability of occurring and a very high-cost optimizing strategy, the forecast allows a decision to be made to forego this opportunity. That is, the best possible strategy for that particular state of nature will not be kept on hand.

The flows of information according to instructions are part of what is meant by *management of information systems,* sometimes called MIS. Designed information systems may take the form of automated organization, but these designs lend themselves as readily to people-based systems. Men may report to one another or to machines (computer inputs, for example); machines can communicate with other machines or with people (e.g., computer outputs). Policy instructions can be contained by gears and cams, capacitors and potentiometers, or by manuals and books of rules that the manager reads when each specific occasion arises. Types of deviation have to be catalogued for easy access. A good index is assumed, and, as with case law, the Dewey decimal library system, or naval regulations, familiarity with the policies greatly assists the search procedures.

The operation of the controller's policy is dependent on its programmed response to the error signal. Serious delays can occur when the search for the relevant policy takes a significant amount of time. Such delays, if they are unexpected, can profoundly affect the exercising of the control function. A portion of the design considerations relates to the measurement sensitivity of the monitor. Each component's behavior determines the operating characteristics of the total system. Economically, the controller's response configurations (as represented by the variety of its stored decisions) should be matched to the monitor's information capabilities. Consider the manager and his accounting system. The manager will discard excessively fine accounting information, while too-crude measurement scales will inhibit or destroy his discernment and control ability. The policy model accents the requirement of designing an operational accounting system, one that spots critical deviations and alerts the controller in time.

For complex situations, a variety of error functions (i.e., different kinds of deviation from standards) must be available to provide sufficient clarification concerning which policies to use. It may be feasible to have unique control responses for each of the many different signals that can be generated by the monitor. This can be called a *one-one* response system.[11] Because of their detail, one-one systems are likely to be efficient only when mechanized.

Ambiguous signals from the monitor, or insufficient information to track down the exact policy prescribed, or a poor indexing system for policy re- trieval can lead to uncertainty about which policy response the system will give. That is, *several* different responses become possible for a single signal. We can call this kind of response pattern a *one-many* policy system. Although such variability usually arises as a result of the individual's inability to in- terpret the monitor's signal precisely, a system may be designed intentionally as a one-many system. Cost may be the cause. Even with an exact perception, ambiguity can occur in translating the policy statement, and it may not be worthwhile, or possible, to remove such ambiguity. What is more, even grant- ing perfect perception and translation, variability can enter also because of an inability to perform a particular action. By treating such attributes, we recog- nize why behavioral components can and often must be included in policy models.

Some situations do not require that a unique control-response capability exist for each unique signal capability of the monitor. Instead, a single control response will suffice for a range of monitor signals. This can be called a *many- one* policy system. In such a system, an efficient *classification* of monitor responses is required. Thus, certain traffic violations are lumped together, or several medical symptoms are interpreted and treated in the same way.

It is not difficult, in view of the above, to believe that most real policy sys- tems are of the *many-many* kind. The less studied and delineated the situation, the more "many-many" the policies will be. Ideally, the degree (and kinds) of "many-manyness" will have been determined by an economic analysis and not by managerial reluctance to tamper with vagueness. However, the decision to have really effective guideline policies calls for a many-one policy at the least, and a one-one policy for critical situations.

Nevertheless, there is a place for each mode of behavior that we have de- scribed. The controller can "read" the inputs and can "write" outputs in these various ways, according to the net-benefit determinants of the specific situation. There is no point in moralizing and no need for compulsive taxonomies. Net- benefit considerations are crucial to the design of policy systems. Where a

---

[11] For more explicit discussion of this and the following types of response pattern, see pp. 543–45.

rational approach to net-benefit determination is lacking, human-behavior patterns emerge to take control. The most ambiguous forms of many-many policies are likely to occur where no policy studies have been conducted. Highly rigid forms of many-one policies are apt to prevail where limited studies have been undertaken and (or because) the design of policy for the sake of policy has been accepted.

The manager needs to know, not only *how* to react to the monitor's signal, but *when* to react. This includes consideration of the period of time that will be required to implement the programmed action. Must the monitor be on-line with the controller? Even if it is, a delay can occur if the controller is busy or if the controller is a slow thinker and reactor. After policy selection is made, the interval that elapses before the chosen action can be taken might be significant, and the speed with which the action can be completed is also an important part of the measure of *implementation* time. In general, the design of the control system requires awareness of how long a period can be permitted to elapse between the occurrence of the disturbance to the system and its correction. This determines a set of critical response times to be associated with each and every policy of the complete catalogue of available policies. Managerial self-awareness is essential when the manager plays a part in the control system, since the managerial role is less easily programmed than electromechanical units, and being intuitive, is subject to greater variability.[12]

Diagnosis and prescription. It is reasonable that the policy catalogue be changed from time to time. The situation is analogous to the medical provision of both diagnosis and prescription. Diagnostic techniques change and situations alter, so new dimensions should be brought into the analysis. Previously unsuspected correlations between dimensions are discovered, and this constitutes new knowledge. The scale of measurement may be magnified because a new type of monitor is invented. Rates of information flow can shift. The policy model should be updated when diagnostic elements are modified.

On the prescription side, when an improvement in medical technology occurs and the doctor finds that he has available new tools or drugs, he rapidly puts them to work. Similarly, in the industrial world, we find that technology is continually providing new materials, process techniques, power sources, and so forth, that can be incorporated into the catalogue of policies. Management may not accept a new finding easily, but once it does, it responds rapidly—at least with respect to modifying its *plans*. It modifies its *policies* less swiftly. Inertia may account for this fact—the inertia built in by the deferred-decision

---

[12] It should be emphasized, first, that the manager is a less reliable component of a relatively automatic control system than a machine equivalent and, second, that this situation is not the same as management by exception where policy controls have failed.

nature of policies. In other words, altering policy is changing what *is,* which may be far more demanding than altering plans, which is changing what *will be.* In consequence, it is important that specific provision be made to keep policies updated.

Our discussion concerning the various types of monitor-control system has dealt with varieties of diagnostic-prescriptive relations. In the *one-one* system there is exact diagnosis and exact prescription—that is, if x_1 occurs, then utilize y_1. For competitive systems, we can have exact diagnosis followed by exact but random prescriptions (a particular one-many relation)—thus, if x_1 occurs, then use y_1, with the probability of $1/6$, and y_2, with the probability of $5/6$ (the specific action to be determined by a process of random selection).[13] We can have exact diagnosis with inexact prescription. For example, if x_1 occurs, then use y_1, y_2, or y_3 according to best judgment. It is worth considering whether this last situation is appropriate for a control system or whether it might be handled better by management by exception. On the other hand, it does seem efficient to say that if x_1, x_2, or x_3 occurs, use y_1—if y_1 is really an adequate treatment for all these kinds of occurrence.

Judgment

In general, the liberal exercise of managerial judgment is not in accord with our notions of policy decisions. If it is limited to judgments about only a few alternatives, the manager might feel more secure. "One of our greatest barriers to understanding how policy is formed . . . has been our tendency to judge before understanding."[14] This tendency is an aspect of human behavior that accounts for a great deal of existing policy. The use of judgment should be reserved for situations where satisfactory policy cannot be developed. The impediments may be either a lack of time and funds to develop the policies or situational characteristics that resist or defeat policy formulation. Perhaps it would be too costly to discover the relevant factors or to relate them to one another and to the system's objectives.

In such cases, the penalties for errors generated by the intuitional approach to policy may be constrained by meta-policies. For example, a minimax policy (of least worsts) might be established by a department that is forced to operate under tight budget controls and a small budget. As another example, only actions that have been used previously might be allowed. The dangers of such generalization are apparent enough; they are restrictions concerning how far the manager can go. This recalls our discussion of managerial anxiety con-

---

[13] This situation was described in Chapter 5 in terms of mixed-strategy games with competitors (pp. 174–76).

[14] Bauer, *op. cit.,* p. 934.

cerning Type II errors. Such anxiety helps to account for the moralizing to which Bauer refers when he says that "moralizing and generalizing are not the same thing as policy making. Worse, moralizing and generalizing are often done to avoid the responsibility of thinking concretely in policy terms."[15]

How to follow up on policy results. To evaluate the effectiveness of policies over time, it is necessary to program for regular checkups on the results of actions. To have designed a monitor and a controller, the policy designer must have understood the organizational objectives—at least at the time of the design. We can assume also that the designer believed in the relative stability of the system within which the policy would operate. But did he arrange for some procedure that would detect a change in conditions?

One of the best ways of following up on a system's stability is an indirect one. It operates on the assumption that a change in the underlying conditions of the system can be detected more readily by studying the policy results than by watching for causes. Even if there is suspicion that the policy itself is deficient, this method of evaluation is still useful. For example, rather than trying to determine whether the demand has shifted for a specific inventory-ordering policy, we review regularly the measure of effectiveness, such as stock outages or carrying costs. It may be that the vendor's lead time has changed or that some other new element has entered the system, but we would undertake a search for the source of the trouble only when the policy's performance deteriorates. This is like a control system on a policy system (which is equivalent to controls on control or policies about policy). Figure 11–7 depicts this kind

Figure 11–7   Process Policies are Evaluated by Observing the System's Outputs

NOTE: *M* is the system's monitor.

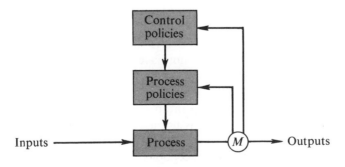

---

[15] *Ibid,* p. 933. Although, in the original context, Bauer means "national" and "political" policy, his observation nevertheless remains relevant here.

Figure 11–8   Process Policies are Evaluated by Observing the Policy Decisions

NOTE: *M* is the system's monitor.

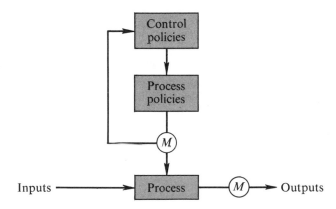

of relationship. The alternative would be to monitor the output of the process policies, as shown in Figure 11–8.

Both forms of evaluation have their place. The need to alter a process-policy model would be indicated more rapidly by one or the other approach depending on the situation. For controlling the introduction and implementation of new policies, the second system possesses the advantage of giving a check on whether the expected policy responses occur.

One of the most interesting points to observe is how controls beget their own controls and how policies about policies become reality. The line of checkers who check on checkers can be extended indefinitely with increasing costs and time delays. Systems that have been carefully studied for policy formulation are far less susceptible to such hierarchical redundancies. Policies based solely on value systems are the most vulnerable—a thought that reflects on many managerial and public administration systems.

The advantage of preplanned policies is that the manager's *know-how* to determine and implement them does not have to be maintained in ready form at all times. In fact, the manager can forget about these issues until there is a signal that the policy does not apply to a specific event that has occurred *or* that the policy is no longer working in an acceptable fashion. The ability to spot the second of these conditions is not assured even when the first kind of signal occurs—which is why it is necessary to consider policy-evaluation methods as separate from policy exceptions, even though both may lead to a change in the design of the controller, the monitor, or the objectives of the system.

Policy changes. Decisions to change the design of policy mechanisms are usually rendered at a high management level—often at a higher level than that at which the original policy designs were developed. This may be because additional, unanticipated conditions have become involved. On the other hand, it may be that the change will be decided on and instituted at *very low* managerial levels because no mechanism exists to reestablish communication with top management about this policy. Once having accepted the initial design, top management often withdraws from the particular policy area. The situation is worse yet when management leaves the feeling (even unintentionally) that problems with the policy will be interpreted as operating mistakes. Then policy redesign may be viewed by lower echelons of management as a patching process and used to hide ineptitude.

Enough such "patches" can leave upper management totally unaware of what policy is actually being followed. There is particular danger with "computer patches" in this regard. Computer-programmed policy usually runs into program "bugs" at the outset, and these, being purely technical, do not interest management. But their correction can alter the intentions and performance of the policy system, which is why formal consideration should be given, at the time of inception and introduction, to rules concerning how to change policies. When inconsistencies in results begin to appear, their source may be hard (if not impossible) to trace unless a perfect record of all changes has been maintained. Computer-based policies are particularly vulnerable to this loss of traceability because great attention to detail in a highly specialized language is required. Tracing is, if nothing else, too time-consuming.

The concept of *a theory of the firm,* which goes back to the early 1900's, was rooted in the notion that eventually the total enterprise (including the planning function) could be reduced to a system of policies. This fits with the belief of the same era in the ultimate attainment of total control through the perfection of scientific knowledge. We now know this to be a naive position. The belief has been growing that policy changes may play a larger part in the theory of the firm than does an established body of policy. As a result, the promise of future developments and of major advances in the theory of management has increased.

MANAGEMENT BY EXCEPTION (MBE)

If there is programmed policy to cover *every eventuality,* and the policies are stored in machine memories and executed by machine controls, then we have *full automation.* If there is programmed policy to cover *every eventuality,* and those policies are stored in books and in myths and tradition and executed by *man*-machine controls, then we have highly organized systems that are suggestive of ancient kingdoms and science fiction rather than modern societies. In most industrial situations, the policy framework covers *only some of all possible eventualities,* even though the states of nature are assumed to be repetitive. But the net benefit of supplying full policy coverage is not the optimal net-benefit value. Perhaps the level of repetition is not high enough to warrant the expenditures. In any case, the cost of programming adequate policy is too great for the benefit that can be derived.

A sensible alternative exists: to assume that the manager will be called on when a policy problem that has not been studied occurs. In other words, when the policy program is working, the manager is not. When exceptions arise, the manager is called in and must exercise his judgment. This procedure seems properly named "management by exception" (or MBE, to save time and space). Specifically, MBE applies to those situations where deferred decisions are not being used, whether or not they could work. The criterion for the use of MBE must be based on the computation of net benefit for programmed policy as compared to executive judgment. Managerial action can always be used as a substitute for predesigned policy systems. But the reverse will not hold. There are many policy-type situations that policy-control models cannot treat and for which only the manager has a chance of recognizing what needs to be done or of doing it.

Clerical employees can be fully *programmed* for policy—that is, given complete instructions about how to behave. Clerks may thus be substitutable for machines, but they are not equivalent. Some jobs can be done only by machines (punch presses for heavy metal work, computers for rapid data processing, etc.). Other jobs can be done only by people (e.g., writing advertising copy). Even when people and machines are able to do the same job, they do not do it in the same way. People have slower response rates, higher variability in performance, inaccuracies in memory, and greater error proneness in performing calculations. On the other hand, people possess far greater associative memories, significant learning abilities, a capacity for independent judgments, and a will to exercise them.

When the policy functions are performed entirely by executives, on an MBE basis, no cost of policy formulation is incurred. If programmed policies are handled by clerks, then one form of operating-policy investment has been made. In addition to this investment is the cost incurred because clerk-programmed policy is always less reliable than machine-programmed policy. The countervailing assets enumerated above account for the "human use of human beings"[16] and efforts to understand, predict, and control man in these circumstances are going forward on many fronts. Contributions from the behavioral

---

[16] The title of a book about cybernetics by Norbert Wiener, in which he raises questions about the implications of controlling man.

sciences are welcomed and rewarded, and pressure has been building to get such contributions. If the decision is to use machines to monitor and control policy, then the major investments (excluding the model-building phrase) are in technology.

Which is the most beneficial course to follow—clerk-effected policy, machine policy, or executive substitution for policy? In this area, many kinds of critical question arise. For example, if policy models are employed, should they be of the same legislative structure regardless of whether clerks or machines are used? While a "no" answer can be given quickly, the specifications of how these models should differ are not easily drawn. There are different sizes and types of memory to be used effectively. Access times and transmission rates for information processing are markedly unalike. Problems of delay must be handled in different ways. Error-checking through verification procedures will not be at all similar. Verification requires investment in additional manpower or in error-detection facilities and duplicate equipment. Error-proneness varies according to the system used. The verification procedure can be justified only by establishing that the cost of removing errors is less than the benefit of doing so. Furthermore, the performance of the executive, the mistakes that he can make, and their costs are all typically different from those of machines and even from those of other men effecting programmed policy—and they are more difficult to assign.

How Much MBE to Use

As a beginning, we can consider the transmission characteristics of different forms of control system, the effects of alternative verification procedures (including the employment of duplicate systems), and some general considerations of managerial performance under varying levels of MBE. The analysis of how much MBE to use must take into account the expenditure required to formulate programmed policy, as well as the cost of enforcing control. Control-enforcement costs include:

1. The cost of a monitor to observe deviations from standards and to report deviations to a controller unit.
2. The cost of channels for communication between the monitor and the process and between the monitor and the controller.
3. The cost of the controller, including its policy data bank and the facilities (including amplifiers)[17] that enable it to modify the system.

---

[17] The *amplifier* is the means by which the signals of the monitor and of the controller can be changed in strength so that a greater or lesser effect can be achieved by the effector. The amplifier is the system's *multiplier*.

4. The cost of matching the capacities and rates of the monitor *and* the controller to process transactions with minimum delays resulting from the design specifications.[18]

5. The cost of verification based on the penalties for Type I and Type II errors—namely, a false signal for management intervention and a missed signal or an unidentified situation that requires managerial attention. (Verification will be considered in some detail in Chapter 12.)

Within this list of costs for essential policy-control activities there are the almost hidden investments in policy design and formulation, as well as the critical operating costs for policy control and enforcement. All these notions, 1 through 5, are compatible with the language, needs, understanding, and abilities of management. The term "policy," when referred to a cost basis, has sufficient rigor to permit unambiguous identification of its vital elements.

We have been able to define the nature of management by exception in terms that are unambiguous and useful to managers. Now, we would like to develop a model that can provide an *economic criterion* suitable for answering the question: What is the optimal amount (or percentage) of management by exception that should be used in any particular case? We shall consider two approaches.

MBE model 1 (the breakeven approach). Since policies are based on repetitive environments, sufficient repetition makes it easier to justify the investment in programmed policies, predesigned monitors, and prepackaged controllers. We shall call the variable for the amount of repetition R. On the other hand, the executive is not as specialized as the monitor-controller. Let the manager be priced as having fixed costs, FC_1, and variable costs, VC_1, when he is operating on a given policy problem. The assignment of costs is an accounting problem, but we are interested in the relative sizes of the costs rather than in exact figures. The hardware control unit is specialized; it has lesser delays but also less adaptability to modify a procedure. It is, in fact, single-minded to the point of moronic behavior. We shall assign its fixed costs as FC_2 and its variable costs as VC_2.

In general, it seems fair to say that $FC_1 < FC_2$ and also that $VC_1 > VC_2$. The manager has already been hired, and his fixed costs should be allocated across a great *many* different activities. But, precisely because he is not specialized, when an exception arises it takes the manager a lot more time to apprise himself of the situation, consider alternatives, make a decision, and take action. He is not programmed to move efficiently under these circumstances. Alternatively, a study group is required to build the policy-control

---

[18] Matching relates to queuing-type decisions about delays (see pp. 565–71).

system. The project undertakes to study and formalize many different situations. The control unit is generally specialized to include hardware; the policy models become the software that is to be programmed.

We use simple breakeven analysis to obtain the trade-off point, as shown in Figure 11–9. The indifference point is R^*. As the level of repetition increases

Figure 11–9 A Breakeven Analysis to Determine the Threshold for Replacing the Manager with a Policy-Control Unit

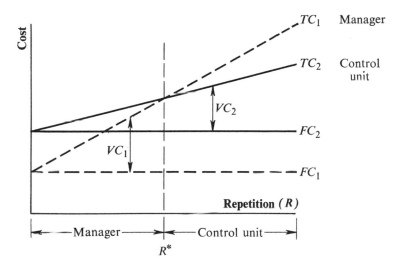

above R^*, we would decide to employ the control unit, unless other factors that are not included in our analysis would indicate otherwise. This is because the total cost of using the manager is greater than that of the control unit after the threshold value R^* is passed. In the figure, we have shown the total costs (which are the sums of the fixed and variable costs) as TC_1 and TC_2.

The repetition should be measured for a set of policy decisions—for example, all ordering policies for a certain class of item. Say that the (fixed) cost of an inventory study for these items might be $25,000 and that the (variable) cost for each repetition of the ordering decision using the policy model would be $.50. (We will assume that the breakeven analysis is based on a two-year period against which the $25,000 is charged.) Assume also that our inventory manager is paid $300 per week and that each repeat of the ordering decision for this particular item takes thirty-six minutes of his time. If the manager works a sixty-hour week, as most do, then thirty-six minutes is one percent of the work week and equivalent to $3.00. For this example, we will ignore assigning any fixed costs to the manager's participation. It follows, then, that the total cost of the control unit is $25,000 + .5R$, and the total cost of the manager is $3R$. Setting them equal and solving will yield the cross point at R^*: $25,000 + .5R^* = 3R^*$, we find that when $R^* \geq 10,000$ repetitions, it would be reasonable to consider developing a programmed policy unit.[19] Of course, these numbers are purely hypothetical, but they serve to illustrate the nature of the alternatives that exist in the policy area.

MBE model 2 (the optimization approach). Our second model is designed to determine the optimal percentage for management by exception. Figure 11–10 pictures the relationship between the costs (scaled on the y axis) and the percentage, P, of all situations handled by the programmed policy system (scaled on the x axis). At what level should P be set? When

Figure 11–10   What Percentage of Policy Situations Should be Handled by the Programmed Policy Unit?

NOTE: The remaining policy situations are exceptions.

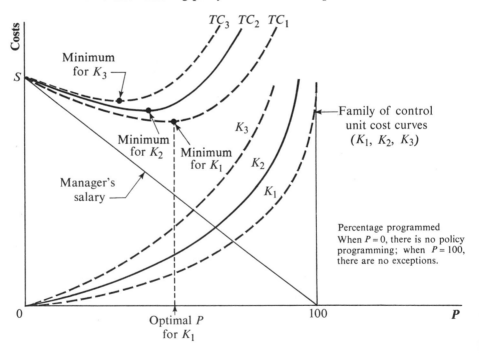

[19] It will be seen that the manager working full time can barely handle a repetition rate of 10,000 per two years, unless he learns ho\. to reduce the required time.

$P = 0$, everything is managed by exception. When $P = 100$, the manager will never be called; nothing is managed by exception. A family of control-unit cost curves is shown. For a specific set of policies, only one of these curves would apply. Depending on which curve fits the situation, a different value of P will qualify as the optimal point. For example, assume that the costs of providing the various levels of P are described by the K_3 curve. These costs are *everywhere* greater than if K_2 applies. Similarly, K_2 is more expensive for *all* percentages of P than is K_1. The shapes of these curves are realistic. The situation resembles that of improving one's golf score, where each subtracted point of improvement becomes increasingly harder to obtain. In this case, "improvement" becomes geometrically more costly as we inch our way along toward the (unattainable) goal of bringing 100 percent of all policy decisions under programmed control.

The other investment-cost line decreases linearly from S to zero. It reflects the *part* of the manager's salary that can be allocated to this policy area. When $P = 0$, the full portion of the manager's salary S, is used.[20] He manages these policies completely. If $P = 100$, then no part of this salary component is required; the manager is never called on. The potential for cost trade-offs is apparent. At any level of P there is a managerial-salary cost and a control-unit cost. By moving toward higher or lower P values, incremental increases and decreases occur in these two kinds of cost. The optimal value of P is that for which the sum of these two kinds of investment cost is minimized.

The family of curves TC_1, TC_2, and TC_3 are the total-cost curves combining the managerial-salary component with the control-unit cost curves K_1, K_2, and K_3, respectively. Each total-cost curve has a minimum point associated with some particular value of P. The optimal P for each K system is shown as a minimum value in the figure. The minimum total cost improves and simultaneously moves toward higher values of P (i.e., a greater percentage of all policies are programmed) as the control unit's costs decrease. The result is as anticipated, but the selection of the optimizing P value falls outside the grasp of intuition.

An analytic result for curves of these shapes can also be obtained. A typical result could be P (for minimum total cost) $= (S - .4K_i)/S$. As K_i increases in value, the control-unit cost curve rises (so in the figure $K_3 > K_2 > K_1$). Suppose, as an example, that $S = \$8,000$. This is the portion of the manager's salary that will be apportioned to treat the particular policy area if no programmed policy investments are made. Let $K = \$12,000$. (For our type of curves, this cost would represent the achievement of 90-percent programming of all policies.) Then the optimizing value of P would be $(8,000 - 4,800)/8,000$, which equals 40 percent. In other words, 40 percent of the policy de-

---

[20] The full portion may well be only some part of the manager's total salary, of course, if he can manage the policies fully in only part of his working time.

cisions would be controlled and treated as routine matters that can be handled without any managerial intervention.

It may be helpful to recognize the (obvious) relationship that exists between MBE and automation. If $K<<<S$, then P approaches 100. The system moves with justification toward full automation.

Planning Control and MBE

Policy models have been clearly distinguished from planning models. Nevertheless, it will be useful to discuss both planning and policy in terms of control. First, consider the use of *policy* to manage an established inventory. The policy rules are rigidly prescribed, even though they are designed to cope with many different demand situations and inventory configurations. The inventory policy can be programmed at a relatively low cost. Much experience has been gained in this regard, and such control systems are rather easily maintained by on-line capabilities of third-generation computer systems. An appropriate value of P might be 95 percent or better. On the other hand, we must *plan* for the inventory requirements of a *new product*. We cannot invent policy to manage the inventory of a newly introduced product, for it has a growing share of the market, and these dynamics entail uncertainties. This is so evidently a planning problem that it is highly unlikely to be economical to develop any policy rules that might apply.

On the other hand, certain kinds of planning can also lend themselves to MBE—most often, for example, in relation to the control of project schedules. After the stages and phases of the plan have been specified and the schedule for implementation is derived, planning-control models can be developed to monitor and adjust deviations from expected costs, qualities, and the schedule. For example, if stage X is one day behind, do nothing; two days behind, expedite; three days behind, increase manpower; and so forth.

Quality of performance can also be included. Careful attention must be paid to the nature and number of demensions used to categorize the plan's performance as well as to the refinement or crudity of the scales of measurement employed. Speed in schedule control can be critical because delays in transmitting information about what has been accomplished can produce a distribution of ages of information in the system. Being on schedule assumes a simultaneity of all participants' reports. Accuracy in reporting and precision are also important, and the two should be distinguished. Precision reflects selection of the appropriate dimensions to evaluate planning performance (i.e., validity), whereas accuracy refers to the closeness of the observations to the existing state of affairs (i.e., reliability).

Although a somewhat different economic basis is required to justify planning control as compared with policy control, the general lines are similar. Economic criteria should determine the design characteristics as well as the extent of the planning-control system—just as was the case for policy control. The greater the possibility of significant deviations from schedules occurring, and the larger the penalty for the deviations, the greater the investment that is warranted in the planning-control system. The investment in control will determine how well the project fares as to both time and cost. In terms of design, combinations of man and machine can be used so as to secure the best capabilities of both; but the resolution of man/machine interface problems is critical. For example, monitor action can be continuous or discrete depending on the nature of the plan and the systems' penalties for aged information. Verification is used when penalties for error are high, but it can also delay the reporting process. If data delay is potentially costly, then special verification procedures must be used. If people are involved, the output rate must be carefully matched at the man/machine interface. In short, planning control is very similar to policy control.

TRENDS IN MANAGEMENT CONTROL

We have observed that it *is* possible to develop integrated models of the policy function. The optimal level for the mixture of managerial judgment and programmed policy *can* be obtained—albeit in the broadest terms. Because of trends that can be expected to continue, the degree of programmed policy that industry will employ should continue to increase. The costs of technology for control systems has been decreasing, which moves P up. And S has been increasing, with the same effect. In many cases, this kind of change will occur at an accelerating rate.

Over time, in the development of the management function, we have observed:

1. Increased stress, time, attention, and investment in the policy area; simultaneously, a growth in control-unit design abilities.
2. Development of a corps of middle managers who can deal with policy that is computer-based.
3. Increased interest in planning by top managers and their gradual removal from the policy area. Even plans, as they are handed down, are interpreted and translated into policy by the computer and management-science-oriented middle managers. To some, the fact that these new middle managers do not appear in traditional places on traditional organization charts has obscured the fact that they are nevertheless managing, but using new patterns and different lines of communication.
4. Susceptibility of the policy area to management science.

5. Less direct applicability of management science to the planning area, except for planning control.
6. Shifting of policy controls, at an increasing rate, to the computer.

The trends described above show no signs of abating and in fact can be expected to accelerate. To underscore the dynamics of change, Table 11–2 traces the changes in top management, middle management, and management scientists from yesterday, through today, to tomorrow.

SUMMARY

The basis for distinguishing between planning and policy formulation was made previously, and planning was studied with care. Now we proceed to examine in some detail the nature of policies. One of the striking distinctions between types of policy is that some are based on scientific reasoning, while others reflect social values. Both have been, and continue to be, subject to criticism.

The objections to scientific policy are based on the use of intangible dimensions and variables that cannot be observed. This runs counter to the demands of scientific operationalism. The objections to social-value policy are several. For example, it can be argued convincingly that social-value policy strives for equilibrium conditions rather than for optimization, and that the invention of social-value policy itself creates the repetitive conditions essential for policy, rather than the reverse. By so doing, policy substitutes itself for planning. Furthermore, suboptimal equilibriums are obtained, and these force the existence of subgroups instead of responding to demands for larger-systems considerations. Related aspects of these points are discussed, and it is noted that in spite of the objections, such effects may be desirable at times. This is especially evident when maximization goals are untenable.

Equilibrium policies have various fundamental structural attributes in common. A discussion of policy mystiques, which underlie some of these attributes, highlights various weaknesses of equilibrium policies. These include retarding change and achieving ruin avoidance at the cost of mediocre performance. It is held that by using *operational* scientific reasoning a great deal can be done to improve the policy-making situation. Vagueness can be dispelled, increasing the manager's ability to evaluate what is going on and improve on it, rather than limiting him to interpretations of policy.

Even so, it is critical to establish the fact that in all kinds of policy, many different positions can be defended rationally. Many of the determinants of

Table 11–2   **Management Trends**

Yesterday	Today	Tomorrow
Top management plans and *controls* the evolution of its plans. It participates in policy formulation and often oversees the implementation and application of its policies.	Top management plans but turns over much of the control of plans to middle management. Policy formulation is also relegated to middle management and control over the policies is seldom considered.	Top management interacts with management science in the planning function. Control of plans is entirely in the hands of computer-oriented middle management. Policy and its control is totally delegated.
Middle management seldom handles policy formulation. It enforces policy, however, subject to the intended constraints of top management.	Middle management exercises judicial control over plans (e.g., PERT) and interacts with management science in the legislative policy-formulation area. Middle management begins to accept the computer as a pervasive force in exercising policy control.	Middle management and management science are merged in the pursuit of planning control, policy formulation, and policy control. Quantitative methods and the computer become overriding features. MBE is the rule —introducing it and supervising it are the new middle-management functions.
Management science has a relatively narrow view of policy formulation and almost no insight or intuition concerning the top-management planning function.	Management science assumes significant responsibility for policy controls, interacts with middle management in policy formulation, and begins to gain a sense of what management means by top-management planning.	

policies are strictly in the eyes of the beholder. But once there is consensus on the fundamental values, rational procedures offer considerable advantages. To illustrate this point, the conflicting nature of two kinds of error (called Type I and Type II errors) is related to a most fundamental policy problem that is scientifically resolvable. The already broad applicability of this situation is further expanded by including the costs and benefits of investing in additional information as part of the total systems policy. Algorithms and heuristics are examined as policy components, using the sense of the policy-error problem previously described.

It is noted that the computer takes on a judicial role and plays an important part in policy enforcement. Models (or algorithms and heuristics) are the legislative arm behind much of rational policy. The managerial function, as the executive branch, is often weakened in its evaluation abilities because of the intractable characteristics of model-building and computer use.

The automation of policy through control-system operations follows the same line of reasoning. The various critical components of the generalized control system are explained. Questions concerning what the control system should observe, when it should observe, and how it should respond are examined. Various response systems are discussed, as is the framework for considering policy changes.

With this background, various models of the management-by-exception principle are introduced. Management by exception (MBE) means that the treatment and exercise of policies is automatic except for special situations not covered by the preprogrammed policies. The manager does not receive any information unless such an exception occurs. Two models are directed to different ways of answering the question: "How much MBE should be used?"

Control systems embodying MBE capabilities can be used for plans as well as policies. Schedule, cost, and project performance can be monitored and controlled in much the same fashion as policy. With this in mind, trends in management control are examined.

EXERCISES

1. We have contrasted social policy and science-based policy, indicating that they are different in many ways.
    a. Describe and discuss the relevant differences between these two types of policy.
    b. In these terms, state how you would characterize the following policies, and explain why.
        1. All employees through middle management will punch the time clock.
        2. Cigarettes are not to be advertised on television.
        3. The Justice Department will prosecute monopolies.

    4. Production should be regulated according to economic laws of supply and demand.

    5. The product-line make-up will be determined by the use of the linear-programming algorithm.

2. Does it seem legitimate to criticize scientists for being nonoperational? What arguments, both pro and con, can be used with respect to this issue? Does the fact that man has walked on the moon affect this discussion?

3. Contrast policies based on equilibrium objectives with those that strive for optimization. Give some examples of both types of policy.

4. It has been said that jokes and social-value policies have a great deal in common. Suggest a taxonomy for jokes and then try to relate this to an equivalent structure for policies. Does the comparison stand up under scrutiny?

5. First define the term "mystique"; then give some examples of policy mystiques. Can the existence of such mystiques be supported or defended?

6. Type I and Type II policy errors are encountered in almost every managerial-choice situation. For what type of decision situation are they not found? Give some examples of Type I–Type II conflicts and explain how the manager should go about resolving them.

7. Under what circumstances might a manager prefer to avoid Type I errors rather than Type II errors? Why is it that an investment in information can relieve the pressure on the manager to resolve the Type I–Type II policy problem? Does this mean that an overriding policy can be found that incorporates the costs of both types of error and that of information as well?

8. It has been said by some marketing managers that the managerial policy to reduce advertising expenditures in regions where sales fall off is based on an insupportable heuristic. Do you agree? Discuss the nature of heuristics in explaining your answer.

9. Explain the statement made in the text that "the computer plays an important part in policy *enforcement*. Its role is far more *judicial* than might at first be recognized." What are the ramifications of this remark, assuming that it is true? Do you think it is correct?

10. Management by exception is an absolutely critical aspect of all policy considerations. In explaining why this is so, fully discuss the nature of MBE. Give some examples of MBE at work. Is it likely that managers are consciously aware of their use of MBE?

11. Describe the general characteristics of a control-system model and discuss how it applies both to policy *and* to planning. List all the components of the control model and treat the issues that must be resolved before any form of control can be exercised.

12. Differentiate between one-one policy systems and those characterized by one-many, many-one, and many-many patterns. Explain the significance of these differences for management.

13. What is meant by "There is particular danger with 'computer patches' "? (See p. 451.) Expand on the concepts inherent in this statement.

14. Two models were introduced in the text to aid in determining how much MBE to use. Propose a reasonable example of a managerial situation where MBE exists. Estimate sensible values for the costs and other parameters of these two models. Determine the solutions for each case and compare your results.

15. Expand on the trends in the use of policy that are described in the closing pages of this chapter. Explain those positions with which you agree as well as those with which you disagree. What implications do these lines of reasoning have for management in the next twenty-five years?

16. Examine the probable consequences of the following factors on the evolving policy roles of management. (Try to maintain differentiation between the various management levels.)
   a. Decreasing working hours and increasing leisure time (augmented by the growth of automation)
   b. A broadening base of social welfare support for all members of society

   c. Greater emphasis on individuality and uniqueness of attitudes and possessions

   d. Growing prosperity and broadly dispersed affluence

   e. A substantial increase in the number of years of compulsory education

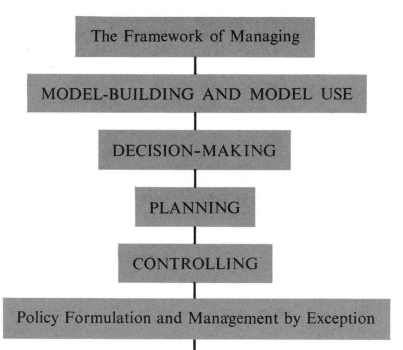

The Framework of Managing

MODEL-BUILDING AND MODEL USE

DECISION-MAKING

PLANNING

CONTROLLING

Policy Formulation and Management by Exception

Chapter 12
Communication and Information Control

Information flow, the bloodstream of the organization,
must have *directed relevancy* . This means that specific kinds
of information should be transmitted, at the proper rate
and in the right amounts, to those individuals who need it
and know how to use it. Such information can be viewed
as currency. Other relevant concepts are:
the value of having information privileges,
verification procedures and the information audit,
the utility of information surprisal, the disutility of noise,
and the relationship of information and knowledge as they
differentiate between specialists and generalists. The design
configuration of information networks can be examined
by information-theory measures of entropy and redundancy.
The relevance of information theory is supported
by the nature of semiotics and the Law of Requisite Variety,
and it is reflected by the character of pseudo-events
and futures-events.

Chapter 12

COMMUNICATION AND INFORMATION CONTROL

When Linus asks his mother why he cannot "slug" Lucy, who has taken his book of stories, his mother answers, "That's just one of those things I can't explain." But Lucy has an explanation: "Listen dope!" she tells Linus, with her fist in his face, "If you slug me, I'll slug you right back!!" "Never mind, Mom," says Linus after silently watching Lucy turn and walk away with his book; "It's just been explained to me in language I can understand." [1]

INFORMATION AS A FORM OF CURRENCY

Information ties together all physical components of the enterprise (man, machine, money, material). Without information there can be no decision-making, policy, or control, and there is no point in planning. Information is the internal currency of an organization. In addition, it has recently become increasingly convertible into external monetary terms. Information is bought and sold as a product in its own right; it is treated as both a good and a service. The possibility of buying and banking by telephone is the subject of much current research, and there is sure promise that it

---

[1] Robert L. Short, *The Gospel According to [Charles M. Schulz's] Peanuts* (Richmond, Va.: John Knox Press, 1965), p. 13.

will be tomorrow's reality. The consumer will not touch his cash. He will call in his order. Automatically, his bank account will be verified and the appropriate sum entered as a withdrawal transaction; the same sum will then be written as a deposit into the vendor's account. No cash will be handled. Input and output transactions by teletypewriter will link various organizations' computers to one another, so even most of the communication process will take place without any human intervention. These developments are practical necessities because the number of informational transactions that organizations need in order to operate exceeds human data-handling abilities. For such reasons, and others as well,[2] information can be viewed as having concrete economic value.

Already today, information viewed as currency can be shifted among a large number of accounts in a network without the need for cash to change hands. As goods are shifted physically in the network, information about these shipments parallels the materials' flows and has a definite equivalence to the related set of currency transfers. As a result of better information systems, closer and more detailed tracking of what is happening in the process is possible. And because this is economically feasible, a not-so-subtle shift is occurring in the handling of information. Information is taking on fundamental *value* aspects of money. Information is purchased and sold, stored, exchanged, traded, and consumed in economic terms. It is allowed to substitute for currency because it can do the same job (and it is cheaper and far faster to handle). Also like currency, it must be managed. In the future, it will become commonplace to view information as currency. Gross national product figures will increasingly reflect information values, or some other measure of those values will be found necessary. The economic growth rates of developing countries can be strongly correlated with the level of their ability to communicate. The same can be said for industrial enterprises and other organizations. It is not that some absolute amount of information produces prosperity; what is of value is information capability.

The analogies of information as a cash flow of currency and of information capability as a capital investment are at least as complex as their equivalents in the money value system. The value of both informational and monetary investments is determined by their productivity—that is, by the resulting benefits of using them. Many other similar comparisons can be made. For example, unused capacity of information systems is as wasteful as unused capital. Information ages and suffers other losses that are not unlike those of committed funds, sunk costs, and tied-up capital. There can be too much information, which may, at first, seem untrue of money. But money is often incorrectly valued for its own sake rather than for what it can do, and information collec-

---

[2] Chapter 6 established a parallel set of reasons for determining the (currency) value of information.

tion suffers from this same mixup of utilities. Moreover, advertising budgets, research funds, and plant investments can be too great when the objectives of the larger system are brought into focus. From the larger system's view, small systems can indeed have too much money. The problems of too little money and too little information do not require any exercises in managerial conjecture to be understood. Information delays have striking similarities to the nonliquidity of funds and insufficient cash flow. Many other congruences can also be noted.

Nevertheless, the analogy we have developed between information and currency should not be taken too literally (i.e., as an isomorphic model) because monetary and informational views of currency are not totally alike. Each has many problems unique to itself. The point we wish to make is that a shift is occurring from money to information, which creates new problems and poses many challenges for management at all levels and in all systems. As communication improves, the inherent value of the process increases (which is similar to the result of a speedup of cash flow). Furthermore, added information links produce pressure for even more. Information is fed forward and backward, up and down. Chardin's vision of a totally interlinked world network of shared information comes closer to reality all the time.[3]

The Value of Information Privileges

The individual works toward maximizing not only his salary or wages but also his *information* (currency) *privileges*. The concept of job enlargement is readily related to expansion of information sources, increased information-transfer functions (both sending and receiving), and responsibility for information management. Hierarchies of information access exist, and one's prestige is increased by working with larger generalizations that encompass more subclasses. Delegation of information-handling tasks to subclasses is considered a major information privilege. It enlarges the information base of the higher jobs in the hierarchy. More and more, the computer is assigned to information-handling tasks, but, as was previously mentioned (p. 105), computers also exhibit job-enlargement tendencies. In terms of information privileges, the reason computers tend to seek job enlargement is their programmed drive for relating all interdependent data sources and control points. As the computer is delegated an increasing number of subclasses of information, it ties them together, moves up in the hierarchy, and indicates need for additional subclasses of data.

Many forms of information privilege can be shared by a group. Last month's

---

[3] See Pierre Teilhard de Chardin, *The Future of Man* (New York: Harper & Row, 1964), Chapter 10, "The Formation of the Noosphere."

sales, the size of the payroll, the amount of the boss's salary, the outside temperature, are examples of information that may have utility for a number of individuals within the group. But some information is not, or cannot be, shared. And, in general, the less widely shared information is, the greater its value becomes.

At present there are in society strong group pressures to share information in its broadest sense and at the same time strong individual pressures to maximize information value by not sharing. That is why to "spread the wealth" and yet to maintain organizational morale are not readily compatible goals. Far more complex objectives than can be modeled by Paretian optimality principles are at work in this context. Yet it is clear that organizations are reacting to social pressures for greater disclosure.[4]

INFORMATION SURPRISAL VALUE

The individual's utility for information is dependent on what he already knows. Sometimes people want to be surprised by new information. That is what makes baseball and football so popular. Surprisal can be derived only from high potential variety. Management, on the other hand, usually does not want to be surprised. It takes steps to decrease the likelihood of being surprised even at the cost of eliminating research and development potentials or exceptional new-product strategies.[5] Receiving essentially the same information every day adds increasingly smaller amounts of utility to the message, until, like a ticking clock, the message becomes background noise and is blanked out of one's consciousness. Only when the clock stops is new information generated. Management reacts remedially; the person looks up, aware of a change, and is as often as not grateful for the surprise.

For the individual, repeated information leads to boredom and fatigue.[6] Other things being equal, both management and the individual place lower value on repeated messages than on unique ones. For example, in Figure 12–1, events B and D carry high surprisal when they occur, whereas the others constitute the "normal course of events." If a run of D events occurs, the

---

[4] One way to do this is to find and conceal information keystones without which all the revealed information becomes merely noise. For example, a manager friend instructed his staff to find "the carburetor" and remove it before he would disclose certain "privileged information" he had been instructed to release. The effect of this was to maintain the appearance, but not the reality, of the privilege.

[5] See Donald A. Schon, *Technology and Change* (New York: Delacorte Press, 1967).

[6] When the person ceases to listen for the information but instead perceives only the lack of it, then the repetition of information has led to a sense of security.

Figure 12–1

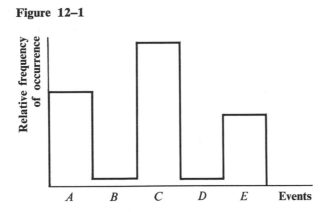

effect will be to lower the relative frequencies of *A, B, C,* and *E,* while raising that of *D.* Depending on the total number of events that gave rise to the original distribution, *D*'s relative frequency will move slowly or rapidly toward equality with the other high-frequency events. *B,* meanwhile, will gain in its surprisal potential.

For management, high repetition leads to a desired state of stability and predictability, which is beneficial for control and a sense of security. The emphasis management places on stable growth (repeated increments of equal change) is readily understandable, for stable growth avoids the evils of a continuing status quo, while culling the benefits of a minimum of information surprisal. The individual, the group, and the organization place different values on the opposing costs and benefits of surprisal and stability. And, since information dynamics are such that repeated surprises of the same kind become expectations, management strategy to avoid the effects of surprise can be either to steer away from the sources of surprise or to head directly into them. Through the latter course, surprise becomes expectation, and policy can be devised.

The frequency distributions of the occurrence of events are continuously evolving. Because people, groups, and organizations can seek out the messages they receive, they have a good deal of control over the shape of their informational event distribution. It is possible to hide from or block certain messages or, conversely, to search for and expose oneself to certain kinds of information.[7] Both personal and management philosophies are intrinsic to the decisions that are taken about which kinds of information to seek and which to avoid.

---

[7] The game of "hide and seek" provides basic training in our formative years for just such a dualism of roles. Ideally, both capabilities should be found in each person, but it seems apparent that some turn out to be better hiders and others better seekers.

Management of information plays a great part in determining the relative frequencies of the information environment that are experienced. As much as possible, individuals choose the parts of the network they prefer. For example, some people gravitate toward new products, which tend to have more surprisal value than established ones. Conversely, managers of stable product systems may reject new-product opportunities as being inadequate when they are in fact judging their own interest in and ability to cope with low-frequency situations. A highly routinized pattern of life and work has more security than that of a soldier of fortune, and each way of life has its adherents. For some, "variety is the spice of life," while others would not think of "changing horses in midstream." The disparity is so general as to indicate how fundamental a conflict exists between the opposing patterns of collecting and avoiding new experiences.

High surprisal will have great value in some situations and low value in others. Anyone looking for opportunities to achieve change will seek out surprisal systems. An apparent way to increase surprisal is to alter the number of perceived events that can occur. Thus, if perception of what constitutes an event is refined (e.g., C is recognized as being three different states, C_1, C_2, and C_3), then the frequency of event C must be shared by three events and greater potential for being surprised exists. This process of introducing a greater number of refined categories is essential to specialization. We can observe that the costs and benefits of being surprised will depend on how specialized the individual is for a specific kind of circumstance. Rare books, a Flying Eagle Cent of 1856, the unexpected effect of long-stemmed roses, all have different values for various individuals under different conditions. The subclasses, C_1, C_2, and C_3, have more surprisal than the event, C, that subsumes them, but their effects may be the same. Nevertheless, when the event system is expanded to many states, the system generally becomes more vulnerable to surprise; conversely, a simplistic view that decreases the perceptions of difference makes the information system less prone to surprise. We must be careful, however, not to confuse this situation with that of the generalist, who although he perceives with less refinement, sees a larger canvas and thus achieves the potential for increases in surprisal.

The Rate of Information Generation

The rate of information generation is also extremely important in determining information surprisal values. This rate has increased greatly in recent years. New technology is responsible, and new methodology is required if the increase in information is to be handled. With high rates of information throughput, the nature of surprisal events can change quickly, and the occurrence of surprises becomes more frequent. Forgotten events are experienced as surprises, and old surprises become expectations. The importance of information rate is related to the reaction and forgetting rates of individuals, groups, and organizations and to the prevailing sense of available time.

Groups, when properly organized, can handle high throughput rates, which is one of the fundamental purposes for which they exist. Information is funneled to members with specialized functions. But group assignments do not always succeed. For example, it is generally agreed that the British invention of radar played a key role in the development of operations research because radar was too information-rich (both in amount and rate) to be coped with in any of the traditional organizational modes. OR provided methodology that increased the system's ability to respond to and use such augmented information. As a result, the informational utility of radar increased the overall value of the military system. By an extension of this reasoning to economic values (such as a trade-off between so much radar and so much heavy military equipment), we could develop another example of the currency interpretation of information. Similarly, computers with high information-rate capabilities are assets that increase organizational net worth. The eventual effect of communication satellites on the world system of organizations is, at present, a highly speculative matter, but they are certain to increase surprisal rates and to readjust the costs and benefits presently associated with specific events.

Information Crises

Let us examine an extreme form of surprisal and, at the same time, return to the notion that being over- or underinformed can be related to the currency-investment concept. The value of electric power systems has been increased by the development of interconnected communicating grids. In these systems, power is shared and shifted through the network to meet demands as they arise. As a result of this "informational" coordination, smaller investments in local power plants are required. The total investment in the grid system is less than that which would be required to supply the same demands with equal efficiency on a purely local basis. But the system has been known to fail. A power (information) crisis caused a total blackout for many hours in large sectors of the northeastern United States and parts of Canada as well. Similar blackouts of less spectacular dimensions have occurred elsewhere.

The management of such information crises poses special problems. Being so new to large-system information management, we are just now becoming aware of such problems and learning how to cope with them. In the blackout example, information is so interrelated that a *domino effect* is experienced. The first failure creates conditions for a second, and so on. In other terms, the first information surprisal generates conditions and responses that support a string of surprisal events. (This situation has been described as the crisis of crises.) Other information-management overloads raise other questions. Consider in informational terms the decision to reduce the working hours of the stock market in order to reduce one such overload. Does a shorter work period mean that demands on an overloaded system become less in absolute number or simply more dense in the time allotted for transactions to take place? Perhaps some information systems should be designed to handle peak periods, leaving unused capacity at all other times. If so, which systems and under what circumstances? And what is the alternative for other systems?

The questions we are raising are becoming more general all the time. Information design problems, similar to those of power systems and the stock market, exist for libraries, hospitals, and automotive traffic. Parking can be construed to be as much of an informational problem as radar utilization, warehouse withdrawals systems, the informational value of Zip Codes for the U.S. mail, or education as an information-transfer process. Air-traffic control can be treated as an information investment to increase air-transport throughput under delay-cost and value-of-life constraints. The notion of information currency expands with each such exploration.

INFORMATION AND KNOWLEDGE

An important distinction should be drawn between information and knowledge. There is the contention that information can exist in records, books, and computers, whereas knowledge is a behavioral attribute. As Kenneth Boulding has put it:

> Knowledge is something that exists in human nervous systems or in their equivalents, whatever they may be, and nowhere else. It does not exist in libraries. If the people who could read books were to disappear the books themselves would not generate any new knowledge. Knowledge as a growing organic system requires apparatus of the complexity of human life to sustain it.
>
> . . . Knowledge is a kind of capital structure of information. Knowledge, that is, is the segregation of entropy[8] and the building up of more and more improbable arrangements of something or other. Knowledge, therefore, to steal a famous phrase from UNESCO, is something that exists only in the minds of men. It may be assisted by

---

8 *Entropy* is a direct measure of the degree to which any system is disordered and therefore unpredictable. The entropy measure increases as the level of variety in the information system rises. In other words, entropy exists in proportion to the degree of uncertainty about what will happen. With high uncertainty, one is not likely to be surprised. It is the unexpected event that creates surprise, and, accordingly, low entropy measures describe surprisal events. [M. K. S.]

> computers as it is by libraries, but until we have a self-organizing, self-generating computer, computers must be regarded as strictly auxiliary to the processes which go on in human minds.[9]

Present-day computers are far from this high state of development. Yet their auxiliary nature is becoming increasingly important. It is clear that the human/computer symbiosis results in greater knowledge than the parts alone possess. And some of the self-organizing features of which Kenneth Boulding speaks are being predicted as eventualities.

Consider a human playing chess against a well-programmed computer. At this level of engagement (chess being a deterministic game), the computer does surprisingly well. Of course, chess-playing, difficult as it may be, is an example of a special form of knowledge. But there is a type of learning that takes place as a result of the computer program. It might be called incipient knowledge, relating to self-modifying heuristics. ("We believe that an information-processing system—human, computer, or any other—that plays chess successfully will use heuristics generically similar to those used by humans.")[10]

The game of chess has a history of attracting those who would build knowledge into machines. Undoubtedly, chess is a fair first approximation of real world problems because it has so many potential alternative selections that it does not matter whether it is thought that stochastic or deterministic behavior prevails. There is a fine story dating back to the close of the eighteenth century.

> During the late 18th and early 19th centuries a Hungarian inventor named Wolfgang von Kempelen astounded Europe with a device known as the Maelzel Chess Automaton, which toured the Continent exhibiting before large audiences. A number of papers purporting to explain its operation, including an analytical essay by Edgar Allan Poe, soon appeared. Most of the analysts concluded, quite correctly, that the automaton was operated by a human chess master concealed inside. Some years later the exact manner of operation was exposed.[11]

While this story exemplifies human reluctance to believe in machine knowledgeability, there are technological changes and an impressive and growing body of individuals who think things are changing.

---

[9] Kenneth Boulding, "The Specialist with a Universal Mind," *Management Science,* Vol. 14, No. 12 (August 1968), p. B647.

[10] Allen Newell, J. C. Shaw, and H. A. Simon, "Chess-Playing Programs and the Problem of Complexity." From *Computers and Thought,* by E. A. Feigenbaum and Julius Feldman, eds. Copyright 1963 by McGraw-Hill Book Company. Used with permission of McGraw-Hill Book Company. The authors have given much thought to this question, since they are the creators of one of the few comprehensive computer chess-playing systems that have been devised.

[11] From "A Chess-Playing Machine" by Claude E. Shannon. Copyright © 1950 by Scientific American, Inc. All rights reserved.

SPECIALIZATION AND GENERALIZATION

Boulding's Specialist with a Universal Mind

In the same article we quoted earlier, Boulding also suggests that an important view of information is embodied in the distinction between specialized and generalized knowledge, a distinction he feels is very important for the continued growth of knowledge. He argues:

> Our own society is so accustomed to constant increase in knowledge that we forget that over most of the centuries of human existence the rate of increase of knowledge has been extremely slow or even zero, with the children reproducing the society of the parents almost exactly. It is only in the last two or three hundred years that we have had a parametric shift in the equations of the knowledge system . . . with much intensified production of knowledge . . . and therefore a much more rapid increase in knowledge with no equilibrium at the moment in sight.
>
> The law of diminishing returns however is practically an article of faith for the economist and I have a good deal of confidence that even science, which is of course the process that has produced this parametric shift, will eventually reach an equilibrium and come to an end. This, however, seems a long way off at the moment and it is shocking to a scientific audience even to contemplate the possibility that science might reach an equilibrium. This position of equilibrium may be closer than we think, however, with science growing at the rate that it does. With knowledge in many fields doubling every ten or fifteen years it may not take very long to get to the point where the sheer quantity of scientific knowledge is so great that it takes the whole intellectual resource of the scientific profession to transmit what it knows to the next generation. Research then becomes completely gobbled up in teaching in a desperate attempt to transmit what one generation knows to the next, before the hand of death removes it. We are accustomed to think of science as growing exponentially, but every scientist ought to know that exponential growth never goes on for very long, for if it did, there would be only one thing left in the universe. There is, therefore, a non-existence theorem about exponential growth, as all growth processes must eventually reach an equilibrium. Not even science is exempt from this fundamental scientific principle. . . .
>
> We have to be very careful, however, in projecting any kind of system with constant parameters, for one of the things that seems clear about evolutionary systems is that they are always subject to parametric change. Even as they begin to approach equilibrium states in fact there seems to develop what might be called pressure on the parameters

and the equilibrium boundaries are broken through in some new shift of the system.

One of the breakthroughs which already has taken place is the development of specialization. The day is long past when any one person could know everything there was to know, yet knowledge still manages to retain an organic and developing structure. The process of specialization itself, however, may exhibit diminishing returns, and one can perhaps look forward to a world of a hundred billion people with a hundred million scientists, each of them containing a single specialty in his head and none of them able to talk to anybody else. At some point in the development of specialization it could well be that the organic structure of knowledge would be so fragmented that it would cease to be a self-perpetuating and self-generating organization. The metaphor implied in the expression "body of knowledge" may be dangerous like all metaphors but it conveys an important truth. A body consists of specialized organs but these organs are bound together by a network of communication through the nervous system, the blood, and the lymph. Similarly in the body of knowledge, unless the output of most specialists becomes the input of others, knowledge breaks up into a mere aggregation of isolated entities and ceases to be a single body.

There is a similar situation in regard to economic development in the familiar economic principle that specialization implies trade and that neither without the other creates an ongoing process of economic development. . . . It is one of Adam Smith's astonishingly acute perceptions that "the division of labor depends on the extent of the market." The division of labor, however, itself increases the extent of the market simply because we get specialization in traders and in trade itself, which facilitates further specialization in production, which facilitates further trade and so on in a magnificent process of disequilibrating feedback.

There are striking parallels to this process in the intellectual field for it is only as we produce intellectual traders, that is, popularizers, organizers, go-betweens, and so on that specialization really pays off. . . . This specialization of the trader . . . is absolutely essential to the development of large and complex organizations and we need to think very carefully in the world of science about how this kind of specialist may be continued and propagated. In an age of information overload we have to develop new roles, for instance, active rather than passive librarians who will actively condense and filter information and push it out to the people that they know need it. Filtered information under pressure may become one of the principal outputs of a new profession. The role of the computer in all this may turn out to be critical although its main virtue to date seems to be storage and manipulation rather than in information condensation and exchange.

What then can be done in the educational process and by the great institutions of the educational world to improve the trading functions in the knowledge system? This indeed should be one of the major interests for research. There seem to be two major tasks here, neither of which is now being very well performed. The first is the development of educational processes and experiences which will create motivation to receive unfamiliar input and to achieve an optimum degree of flexibility in existing images. In the famous words of Will Rogers, "The trouble with most people isn't what they don't know, but what they do know that isn't so," and it is precisely this development of what might be called "negative knowledge" which is the principal source of trouble with social systems of all kinds.

It is the peculiar property of the scientific subculture that it has led to a reduction in negative knowledge and an increase in positive knowledge largely because it developed a very unusual system of both values and payoffs. It developed a value system which in the first place put a high value on curiosity, a human trait that we may have inherited from the apes but which is severely discouraged in most folk cultures. Curiosity is supposed to have killed the cat—I don't believe I ever found out how—and children in most rural or working class cultures around the world are admonished sharply against it. The second value of the scientific subculture is the high value which is put on veracity, that is, not telling lies. Not telling lies is not quite the same thing as knowing the truth, but it is the prerequisite of the development of a culture devoted to the production of truth. If curiosity has traditionally been discouraged in lower class cultures, veracity has been discouraged in upperclass cultures, where telling lies and getting away with it has been almost the essence of social intercourse. We see this particularly in the international system which is highly representative of upperclass culture in which successful lying is very highly regarded. How in the northwestern peninsula of the old world a small subculture developed, which put such high value on both curiosity and veracity and as a result developed the knowledge explosion, is still one of the real puzzles of history.

The second great task which lies ahead of us in the education process is the development of better methods for learning the languages of the specialists. I suspect, indeed, that the major task of formal education is likely to become that of learning the languages of specialists so that communication among them may take place. This is perhaps only another way of saying that the major task of formal education in the future is to teach people how to learn, not to stuff their mind with particular content. The learning of content will have to go on during the whole life and the period of formal education will be much too short to permit the transmission of the total knowledge stock. This principle sounds innocent but could involve a profound revolution in the whole system of education.[12]

---

[12] Boulding, *op. cit.*, pp. B649–52.

In urging that methods and abilities for communicating specialized information be developed, Boulding focuses on our educational system. But in a real sense, this is also one of management's most important jobs.

Special abilities are required to generalize. And the method is of greater importance than the details of given situations. The method often takes the form of analogy, which is essentially a means of transferring what is known about one thing to another thing about which less is known. Three factors that can help differentiate specialization from generalization should be mentioned. These are *feedback, sensitivity analysis,* and *imputation.* They are all related to analogy, which can be viewed as a model of information transfers. While the specialist also uses them, he does so less than the generalist. (After all, the distinction between the specialist and the generalist is one of degree more than kind; yet that is enough to account for many significant differences between them.)

Feedback and "feedforward" between two situations are required to discover common principles that bring the two situations into a common focus. They provide corrective information, allowing the manager to improve on his system's performance. Such feedback can be called disequilibrating; it is essential if a system is to change and grow. There is also, however, equilibrating (or self-reinforcing) feedback, which is also called homeostasis. This word is derived from the field of biology, and for its definition we shall quote from L. L. Langley:

> Cannon's word, *homeostasis* embraces the fixed, or constant, internal environment, but then goes on to suggest dynamic, self-regulating processes that serve to maintain that constancy or to return the internal environment to normal should it get out of whack. This is the concept now referred to as *negative* feedback, that is, if there is a deviation in one direction, there is a reaction in the opposite direction.[13]

The flow of information also highlights discrepancies and deviations, however. Sensitivity analysis is vital to determine how important divergencies really are; to find out whether they are destructive of an assumed generalization or will lead to a larger one. The criteria for what is too sensitive and the analysis itself are implicit parts of the methods of generalization.

Imputations are essential to provide structure and measure for the areas that cannot be observed and cannot be covered by analogies. Imputation is a complex feedback notion, involving induction and inference in special ways. To impute is to ascribe vicariously, not by direct measure but by inferring from some indirect measure. For example, some set of observed behaviors is

---

[13] Reproduced from *Homeostasis,* by L. L. Langley by permission of Van Nostrand Reinhold Company, a division of Litton Educational Publishing, Inc., Litton Industries, New York, 1965.

judged as being composed of good or bad actions. But the judgment is not rendered on the basis of the actions; rather, it is made on the basis of sincerity, intelligence, and like characteristics of the people involved. (This is typical of how a reference or letter of recommendation is used.) Another example is when an employee is considered a good worker because he seldom leaves before 6 P.M. Quantitative imputations based on the assumption that the manager has the capacity and interest to use optimal actions are frequently used. The manager's actions are inferred to be optimal so that the conditions that would have led to such actions can be imputed. To illustrate this point, assume that the manager is known to buy in lots of 100 units. The costs of ordering and carrying units are then imputed on the assumption that the manager is performing optimally. When the manager is confronted with these imputations, which tell him that he is acting "as if such and such conditions hold," he is led to reexamine what he is doing. He can move back and forth between such generalizations until he is satisfied. Indeed, imputation is a special form of generalized information.

There are many ways of achieving generalization, and there is greater potential for surprise in all of them than in actions associated with specialization. The generalist is far more likely to discover the unexpected because he is coping with what was previously unrelated. His is innovative work. The specialist, on the other hand, is simply refining his categories as he improves his performance. He should not be surprised too often, or he will be doing a poor job for one as expert as himself. Furthermore, the generalist's categories are fewer and broader than the specialist's. In the management context, we observe that (logically, at least) upper managerial levels require more generalization than do lower levels. Top management can use its advantages of greater potential information surprisal or can take action to avoid what it interprets as the disadvantages of that greater variety. At lower management levels it is harder to generalize because the situation does not provide the essential ingredients for breadth.

The Analysis of Consequences

Let us return to chess as a means of further describing the different qualities of specialized and generalized knowledge. Three choices must be made for an information investment in a chess-playing program. First, the program can call for inspecting a great or small number of alternatives from any given position on the board. Second, for whatever number of alternatives is chosen, the consequences of these moves can be examined for a few or many subsequent moves. Third, for whatever number of alternatives is chosen, and for whatever number of moves ahead, the analysis of the consequences of the moves can be handled in great detail or based on only a few observations. The three alternatives can be summarized as: (1) *breadth of view*—the number of alternatives considered; (2) *depth of view*—how far ahead in steps or time one looks; and (3) *degree of analysis*—how carefully each evaluation is made. Quite different performances can be expected, depending on the information investment that is decided on.

In 1956, a group at Los Alamos programmed their computer to explore *all* alternatives to a depth of two moves (for each player) with a relatively weak analytic function for evaluation.[14] Even so, the Los Alamos system required approximately twelve minutes to make a move. But the program could beat a beginner in chess. In 1958, Alex Bernstein developed a chess-playing program that considered at most seven of *all* possible alternatives. A set of heuristics was used to determine which initial moves were to be considered. As was the case with the Los Alamos program, a depth of two moves for each player was used. However, the evaluation function for those alternatives chosen was relatively stronger than that of the Los Alamos program. If a move leading to a losing position was made, then a change in the evaluation function would be made that would prevent this fault from recurring. It was observed that this program took about the same computing time per move as that of Los Alamos. It had never played a weak player and had lost to a good one, so it was difficult to evaluate.

Nevertheless, the conclusion is drawn by Newell, Shaw, and Simon that in extension (i.e., with an increase in depth) the Los Alamos program would require increasingly greater amounts of time than the Bernstein program to make a move. The analytic selectivity of the Bernstein program would rapidly overcome any breadth advantage of the Los Alamos program with respect to both speed and performance. In other words, an investment in information specialization is a good one as long as the heuristic basis for selectivity is broadly applicable. That is what Boulding meant by "The Specialist with a Universal Mind." The manager who touches lightly on all information possibilities is apt to work harder and to less avail than the manager who concentrates on principles and theory that allow him to choose and evaluate selectively a limited number of chosen alternatives.

THE STRUCTURE OF INFORMATION NETWORKS

The Size of Information Networks

The amount of time that the manager spends communicating both externally and internally could rapidly get out of hand as the size of the organization

---

14 Described in Newell, Shaw, and Simon, *op. cit.*, pp. 46–50.

increases. The total volume of relevant information coming from outside the organization's system (so-called exogenous information) is likely to grow at a decreasing rate, as shown in Figure 12–2A, but internal discussions and data transfer (endogenous information) increase at an accelerating rate, as in Figure 12–2B. One reason for this difference is that increased external

Figure 12–2

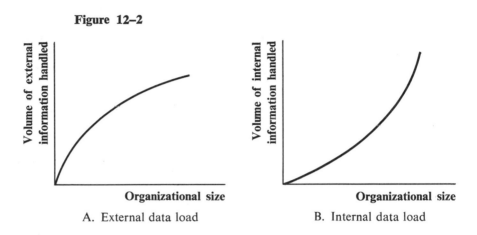

A. External data load   B. Internal data load

activity tends to produce *larger* numbers (for order sizes, sales volume, etc.) rather than *more* numbers. An increase in number of transactions is more likely to occur with the growth of internal specialization of function. Yet the variety of dimensions for reporting in generality what is going on in the company to those outside (such as profit and loss statement, balance sheet, etc., to stockholders and tax bureaus) does not increase greatly, even though the number of business transactions grows rapidly. Averages and summary figures that are normally employed simply span a larger set of figures.

This is not to say that external informational dimensions do not increase at all, but their rate of increase is lower than that of internal transactions. For example, the number of salesmen should increase less rapidly than the number of customers and sales for a growing company. It is only when a new line is established that the reverse occurs. This is like starting out, and it will be noted in our diagrams that the *initial* portion of the external information curve has greater acceleration than that of the internal data load. On the other hand, inside the company, jobs multiply to meet the new demand levels. The number of potential communication links increases as a function of the square of the number of individuals, n, that is, $n(n-1)/2$. (We say "potential" links because not all are used.) Between three employees, three different communication channels can exist. Between six employees there are fifteen possible channels. (See Figure 12–3.) The number of communication channels increases exponentially with the number of employees. Twenty persons have

Figure 12–3   Potential Communication Links

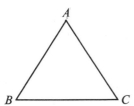 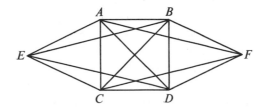

$20(19)/2 = 190$ different channels for discussion. (We are ignoring the fact that a difference exists between an *A* to *B* communication and one from *B* to *A*, although discussions in Chapter 15 will capitalize on this difference.)

The Manager's Position in the Network

The amount of time that the manager spends communicating also has a tendency to increase rapidly as he rises in the organizational hierarchy. To offset the obvious effect of being at the apex of an organizational tree, the manager must alter the amount or kind of detail that he is willing to receive and the message dimensionality (related to the number of different topics) he is able to send. He achieves this through information policies that are for the most part unwritten and informal descriptions of informational behaviors in an administrative culture. Organization of the information system can also help to reduce the number of potential paths that are actually used for communication.

Without some set of reduction principles, the internal information network loses coherence. One example of a self-organizing principle is the following. Assume that in communicating upward, the lower organizational echelons report to their immediate supervisor in such detail that the volume of input information to him is at his threshold.[15] Because they are competing for a relatively fixed amount of time, the subordinates begin to merge reports, remove duplications, and abbreviate their results in summary statistics. They do this in order to get some of their supervisor's time and, especially, to give him the opportunity to reach conclusions and make decisions concerning their inputs. As much as he can, the boss deals with his subordinates in terms of their requisite levels of input detail, but he knows that he cannot pass along information at this level of detail to *his* boss, who is receiving other reports as well. So he also merges his data into larger classes of information. The

---

[15] See the discussion of the Peter Principle, p. 680.

progress is continuous and self-adaptive because there is no other way for the system to respond when transaction limits are passed.

As information moves up in the managerial hierarchy, the nature of the classes becomes increasingly generalized. The differences in knowledge that result affect the behavior of the organization. At the same time, exceptions exist; there are cases where information is communicated from the lower ranks of the organization to the top with no loss of detail. However, the usual information network is based on the rule that data compression is essential if the top of the organization, with its broad range of responsibilities, is to be able to communicate with the managers responsible for the specialized functions of which the organization is composed.

Centralized and Decentralized Information-Network Patterns

An additional approach to handling the exponential growth of the internal information load is to decentralize, or at least to separate from the central organization, certain functions, giving their respective managers autonomy over their own information systems. Decentralization reduces the breadth of the generalist's function and increases the degree to which specialization can be used. Separation is equivalent to removing many communication links and substituting just a few. It enhances selectivity by allowing each decentralized management to tailor heuristics to its own needs. On the other hand, given the specialization of decentralized units, we can readily question how a "Specialist with a Universal Mind" can be developed. The answer lies in designing an appropriate information system that enables the decentralized system to communicate effectively with a central administrative core.

The advantages of centralized or decentralized information systems will differ depending on the specific organizational situations and on the means that are found for integrating the components of the system. For example, centralized information permits volume discounts to be obtained. It allows smaller stock levels at local warehouses because a central warehouse exists to meet unusually great demands. It avoids duplication of records that are in common demand by providing a centralized memory bank. Centralized information permits top management's judgment to aid in planning for each branch instead of relying on branch management's judgment alone. It offers the asset base of the aggregate system for information investments and for credit and risk ventures that smaller assets could not underwrite. The use of the currency concept of information can be helpful in evaluating the pros and cons of centralization.

The appropriate configuration of centralized and decentralized information must be approached through careful design analysis, which recognizes that computer networks have revolutionized the cost and efficiency of interrelated systems. By removing the prohibitively costly delays that previous information technology entailed, computer technology has radically altered the nature of the centralization/decentralization debate. In fact, there is no longer any debate because the question is now one of finding the optimal mixture. (See also the discussion on pp. 487–88.)

INFORMATION SYSTEMS DESIGN AND CONTROL

The mere passage of information through the network is of little value unless that information is first perceived by a monitor and then responded to by a controller. This entails talking *and* hearing, writing *and* reading. But neither listening nor hearing corresponds to understanding, and reading is not equivalent to perceiving. Much organizational information is neither heard nor read. Some of the unused information can be eliminated and steps taken to ensure that the remainder is actually perceived. By formalizing information systems, we can, if nothing else, change management's awareness of such problems. The second difficulty is converting perception to understanding. The information that is actually being used can be characterized by its distance from the existing base of management knowledge. When understanding is not immediate, decreasing that distance might be extremely difficult. It would necessitate altering management's accustomed information culture. The achievement of both perception and understanding involves high levels of detailed work and complex problems of cognition, and both are therefore crucial in the design of adequate information systems.

The most difficult information flows to handle are indirect or intangible— for example, projections of personality, such as leadership, especially "charismatic" leadership. "Coordination" is a term that describes the interrelationships of information flows, but the critical essential properties of coordination are intangible. It is interesting to note that there are many good measures of direct systems flows but only poor ones for intangible information. The circulation of blood in the body can be evaluated, as can the traffic patterns of road systems through urban complexes. But these standards of performance do not specify how good the system could be. Just as we cannot define good bodily and mental health but can identify poor health, it is similarly difficult to judge the good health of any information system, and this gets more difficult as the amount of indirect information that is transferred increases. In general, that amount is a sizable one, increasing in volume at the higher organizational levels.

Still, some evaluation and regulation are possible. *Audits* are as vital to the information system as physical checkups are to the individual. The structure of the information system, in conjunction with its flow dynamics, is the system's equivalent of what we mean by organization. By relating organization with information, we move far closer to a comprehensive theory of organizations than if we deal with terms such as "authority" and "responsibility" in a quasi-psychiatric context. The analysis of information flow and information-systems structure is related to concepts of connectivity, flux rates, and degree of change, as well as to momentum and inertia. These flow analogies are stronger for the purposes of measurement than are the more elusive psychological descriptors. Even though they may not be sufficient for decision-making, planning, and policy-making, they do provide useful analogies.

For example, informational flow patterns tend to become established quickly because of their high frequency of occurrence and throughput. The costs of purposefully redirecting these flows are too high to accept. A friend, who has been highly successful in managing many large project groups, has described his attempts to counteract these inertial effects in information systems as his "make waves" theory. In other words, he introduces selective perturbations, which lower the inertial levels of the system. In effect, this is accomplished by introducing surprises. Inertia is, after all, the antithesis of surprisal. The new equilibrium situations that occur have the advantage of being somewhat different from the previously established ways. Such shifts have two benefits. First, although the morale of the project people is adversely affected by the artificial disturbances of the system, the effect of shifting the status quo eventually produces a morale lift that overcomes the adverse effects. Second, the change in established states offers management its only opportunity to introduce rapidly some positive control over the system's evolution.

The "make waves" theory has been practiced formally by a number of companies (and informally by many executives). A famous research laboratory followed the procedure of regularly reassigning a small percentage of project leaders. The changes, which could never be predicted, affected so small a number of individuals that a great deal of continuity existed, and yet everyone was left wondering if he might be affected next. Many highly respected students of industrial relations would fault this approach as causing debilitating insecurity, and no one has yet been able to prove whether they are right or wrong.

Informed and Informing Systems

We can characterize systems, following Greniewski,[16] as *informed* systems, *informing* systems, and *information* systems. He defines an informed system as having at least one information input for which receptors are required. But

---

[16] H. Greniewski, *Cybernetics Without Mathematics,* trans. by D. Wojtasiewicz (New York: Pergamon Press, 1960).

the system has no output. An informing system is just the reverse, having at least one information output and no inputs. The environment (or external information system) is frequently treated as an informing system. An information system is defined as both an informed and an informing system. Different diagnostic and prescriptive procedures are available for each type of system. Monitor design is critical for informed systems. Questions to be answered are: the number of channels (or dimensions) observed; the observation interval, moving from continuous to periodic or sample-data procedures; and the number of classes to be seen (as a result of the fineness of perception).

Probabilistic analysis is often called for in designing the appropriate informed system to deal with the informing one. Consider a fighter plane and an antiaircraft unit that is programmed to track the fighter and shoot it down. The fighter plane is the informing system in this case. Is all possible information being obtained from the informing system at the proper rate for operational use? The tracking device could simply extrapolate from the plane's present trajectory to calculate a point ahead where the plane and the missile could meet. But, when intangible information, such as the behavior of pilots (their training, background, and reactions with the type of plane being used), is also taken into account, then the informing quality of the output system increases, and the efficiency of the antiaircraft unit rises. In addition, the probabilistic analysis of prior encounters would provide tangible information that might be invaluable. Most systems in which management is interested have both informing and informed qualities. And, as indicated above, when the rates and types of input and output information are matched viable systems performance is achieved.

Internal and External Systems

We can apply the distinction between informed, informing, and information systems to centralized and decentralized organizational configurations. Under centralization, an overall information system exists, consisting of many information subsystems. Under decentralization, the number of subsystems decreases markedly, and the specific roles of informing and informed subsystems emerge as relevant differentiations. For the total system, the amount of internal communication decreases under decentralization, and the amount of external communication increases.

To illustrate the internal communication effect, we let $n = n_1 + n_2$, where n_1 and n_2 are the number of communicants in the first and second decentralized subsystems, respectively, and n is, as before, the number of individuals in the entire system.[17] Under centralization we have $n(n - 1)/2$ potential

---

17 See p. 482.

communication links. With decentralization, we would reckon on $n_1(n_1 - 1)/2$ $+ n_2(n_2 - 1)/2$ potential communication links. It can readily be shown that the number of potential links under centralization is greater than under decentralization by an amount $n_2(n - n_2)$ or $n_1(n - n_1)$. Thus, if $n = 100$, $n_1 = 60$, and $n_2 = 40$, we would have 4,950 potential links under centralization and $1,770 + 780 = 2,550$ potential links under decentralization. The former has an excess of 2,400 over the latter. Although a greater percentage of the decentralized potential would probably be utilized, the difference would continue to be significant.

At the same time, the number of external communications increases almost linearly with the number of decentralized units, since each one must establish its own vendor relations, salesmen's territories, and insurance, tax, and other relations. For the example above, of a two-unit decentralization, let N represent the number of external relations per decentralized unit. Then $2N - N$ represents the increase in the external information load. So when $2N - N <$ $n_2(n - n_2)$, the total information load of the decentralized unit is less than that of the centralized system.

This analysis barely scratches the surface of the decentralization question. Nevertheless, it furnishes some simple numerical guidance, so that analysis of this question can rise quickly above such issues to the less tangible factors.

THE NATURE OF INFORMATION

Pseudo-Events

Much information that is transferred in an organization does not refer to an event that has occurred but instead aims to *create* the circumstances for an event *to* occur. Supposition and speculative prediction are typical of this class of information. To state that riots will get worse next year, that more women will become criminals, or that theater and literature will become increasingly pornographic are conjectures that are reported as though they were fact. As Daniel J. Boorstin has written in his stimulating book on pseudo-events,

> The making of the illusions which flood our experience has become the business of America, some of its most honest and most necessary and most respectable business. I am thinking not only of advertising and public relations and political rhetoric, but of all the activities which purport to inform and comfort and improve and *educate* and elevate us: the work of our best journalists, our most enterprising book publishers, our most energetic manufacturers and merchandisers, our most successful entertainers, our best guides to world travel, and our most influential leaders in foreign relations. Our every effort to satisfy our

> extravagant expectations simply makes them more extravagant and makes our illusions more attractive. The story of the making of our illusions—"the news behind the news"—has become the most appealing news of the world.[18]

Literacy is widely sought after as the central requirement for freedom of the mind. It is supposed to be the basis for intelligent choice. Yet it appears to carry with it intensified production of pseudo-events and increased societal susceptibility to them. The present-day informational climate has increased the vulnerability to pseudo-events, not only of society, but also of the organization and the individual. Companies put forth unrealistic images of themselves in their advertising. Many in-house magazines conjecture on the company's product line, degree of automation, and the like in terms that previously were expected only of Sunday supplements. Illusory stories about managers and their projects are transferred rapidly by business media for reasons that are often difficult to fathom, and these alter the belief structures of the project groups and the communication patterns that might otherwise have existed. Reputations are created and then nourished by the belief in the constructed mythology. Reality eventually bends to myth.

Ultimately, however, it may be hoped that a supraliteracy will emerge that can evaluate pseudo-events for what they are. Meanwhile, the power of information transfer to create either unreality or, as might be desired, a comprehensive picture of reality should not be underrated. Our purpose is not to render moral judgments of pseudo-events, although there surely are both acceptable and questionable uses of them. But we should try to differentiate here between accidental and purposeful uses of pseudo-events, for when the publication of pseudo-information is intentional, it becomes a special form of planning for the future. Moreover, management must recognize that it is both a user and a consumer of pseudo-materials and that neither configuration is rare.

Futures-Events

More powerful in concept than the pseudo-event is the set of future events. Each future event is one of many events that *can* occur in the future, given the present state of affairs. The set of all such future events is what is meant by futures-events. For each future, a *scenario,* or detailed description, of what the future might be like is constructed. The environments for each potential future are examined. Controllable variables likely to influence specific futures

---

[18] Daniel J. Boorstin, *The Image: A Guide to Pseudo-Events in America* (New York: Harper & Row, 1964), p. 5.

are included in the analysis.[19] Unlike creation of the pseudo-event, futures control does not stem solely from the use of journalism. Rather, more direct interference with the system is implicit. Consequently, we need to distinguish between pseudo-events, which are ends in themselves, and futures-events, which are used as means to other ends. Unlike the concept of planning, futures control is envisioned on a much broader systems scale. Since the system is so large, ordinary planning controls are not capable of coping with the character of eventual states and so futures control is used to alter the probabilities of what can take place.

A voting model. To illustrate some of these points, let us examine the use that could be made of election polls as pseudo-information to provide some degree of futures control. We will use a two-candidate election for our model, but the model can be extended to situations where there are more than two candidates and where only a few people constitute the electorate. Assume that the election is to be held in about a month. Some people will deliberately tell the pollsters one thing and do another; some are undecided; some will change their minds before the elections. When the poll results are released, at least two effects are possible. Some voters will switch their vote to get on the bandwagon, while others will sympathize with the underdog and, for a variety of reasons that might be thought up (but which are not necessarily the correct ones), will switch their vote to him. Both the bandwagon and underdog effects have been observed to occur. We will illustrate the bandwagon effect first.

Look at Figure 12–4. On the vertical axis is recorded the *actual* vote that exists for a certain candidate (*A*) in a two-man election *before* the results of a preelection poll are published. We have indicated that *A*'s actual vote at the time that the poll is taken is 54 percent. The *published* poll results are recorded along the horizontal axis. The diagram shows a published result of 50 percent. This is not necessarily the same result that the pollster discovers from his survey. A problem exists for the pollster. Note the curve marked "Bandwagon effect." Its shape is related to the behavioral characteristics of the voters and to the fact that the actual vote is 54. A different curve may well exist for other values of the actual vote. The bandwagon-effect curve passes through point *c* (actual vote = 54, published vote = 50). In other words, only

---

[19] The Delphi Technique of Olaf Helmer and T. J. Gordon, developed under the sponsorship of the RAND Corporation, has been discussed widely in this regard. It examines the conditional probabilities of various futures. See Olaf Helmer, *Social Technology* (New York: Basic Books, 1966). Many organizations, such as Bertrand de Jouvenel's Institute for Futuribles and H. Kahn's Hudson Institute, are involved in similar activities concerning the future. For information on the Hudson Institute, see Herman Kahn and Anthony J. Wiener, *The Year 2000* (New York: Macmillan, 1967).

Figure 12–4   A Voting Model for Candidate *A*, with Bandwagon Effect

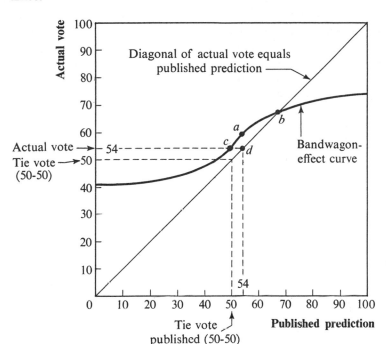

when the published prediction states that a tie exists will there be no bandwagon effect. But the poll has revealed that the actual vote is 54. (We will assume, for simplicity, that no polling error exists.) Now, if the pollster's published prediction is 50-50, there will be no bandwagon effect—but he will be wrong. On the other hand, if he predicts and announces the result he has actually measured—namely, 54—he will also be wrong. The bandwagon effect, operating at point *d*, increases the actual vote to 58, at point *a*.

What should the pollster do? Note the line called "Diagonal of actual vote equals published prediction." The bandwagon-effect curve must cross this line.[20] At the point of crossing, in this instance *b*, the actual vote must equal the published prediction. Thus, to be correct, and enhance rather than hurt

---

[20] For a more detailed statement of this point, see Herbert A. Simon's book, *Models of Man*, (New York: Wiley, 1957), Chapter 5, "Bandwagon and Underdog Effects of Election Predictions," pp. 79–87. Simon credits Émile Granberg and Franco Modigliani for their paper in the *Journal of Political Economy* (December 1954) and others as well for their work on this subject. Simon's description of the voting model has been used as a basis for this discussion.

his professional image, the pollster is forced to convert the true result of 54 to a false result of 68, which will then turn out to be correct at point *b*.

Is this manipulation of the future acceptable? Some might say that it is, since *A* was going to win the election anyway and alteration of the poll does not change that result. But the question is surely debatable. By altering information, *A* moves close to an election sweep, whereas without manipulation he does not get too clear a mandate. *B*'s political career is likely to be ruined after manipulation, whereas without it he might be portrayed as a near winner, who should be given another chance. We call attention to the fact that the bandwagon-effect curve does not have to be symmetrical on either side of point *c*. To the left of *c,* candidate *B* is the winner, and a published announcement of the percentages might create a larger (or a smaller) bandwagon effect than a similar announcement for *A*. The images that the candidates project to the electorate will affect the sympathy that would be generated by predictions of winners and losers.[21]

The bandwagon effect can produce far more serious kinds of manipulation. The basis of such a situation is shown in Figure 12–5. If either point *e* or point *f* is used (predicting candidate *B* winning with 60 or 80 percent of the vote), the actual situation (which is *A* winning with 54 percent of the vote) is reversed. The manipulating pollster would not report the result of 54 percent for *A,* which he has actually measured. Nevertheless, he will be shown to have correctly predicted the election if he chooses either point *e* or point *f*.

Such manipulation of the future is certainly a use of pseudo-events that has great potential danger. Information transmission (or publication) is used to alter public opinion and actually reverse the course of events. This is a remarkable example of a means-end chain modification that could encompass a long planning horizon. It should be noticed also that the public is unaware that any manipulation of futures has occurred. Awareness of manipulation alters eventualities, and these interactions would have to be included in the futures analysis.

The fact that other pollsters probably will not agree with the manipulator of the future certainly helps to ameliorate these effects, but collusion becomes a special danger. Of course, we may question whether it is actually possible to obtain such a significant bandwagon response. An understanding of political fads is obviously essential; candidate *B* would have to understand bandwagon psychology and play to it. But such large swings cannot be considered an impossibility. With great quantities of money and an understanding of pseudo-events, the achievement of large swings might not be too great a task for political scientists.

---

[21] We should not overlook the way in which the poll is announced, the candidates' personalities, and the interaction of these two factors. Conflict between the results of different polls further complicates the picture.

Figure 12–5   A Voting Model for Candidate *A*, with a Bandwagon Effect That Permits Manipulation of the Election Results

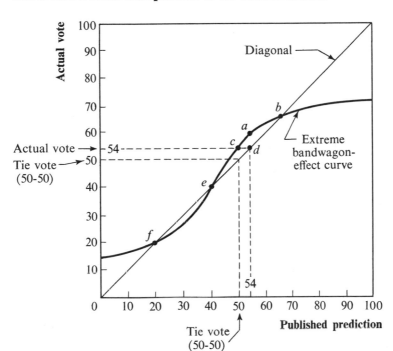

Let us now consider the underdog effect. Perhaps the population could be divided into two segments, bandwagon types and underdog types. Separate analyses of information effects and futures control might then be conducted for each population segment, to be combined at a later point when the larger (total) system is analyzed.

An example of the underdog effect is shown in Figure 12–6. The actual vote at point *d* will lead again to an incorrect published prediction. The pollster can, however, be correct by changing the prediction to the one represented by point *a*. It is not possible, in the two-candidate underdog case, to manipulate a switch of the election results.

Analogous situations exist in the management context—for example, a rumored prediction of who will be the next president of the company or which one of two product variants will be chosen by the executive committee. These are internal situations. External relations (for example, consumer choice of brands) can also be affected by the use to which information systems are put. Dissident stockholders engaged in a proxy fight with management present a different kind of external situation to which our model could apply. Even the

Figure 12–6   A Voting Model for Candidate *A*, with Underdog Effect

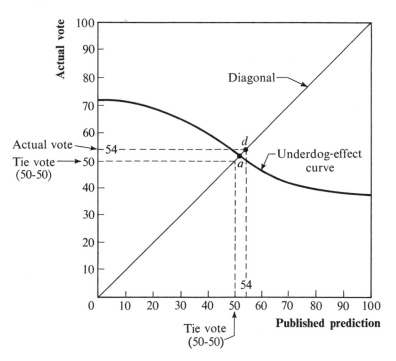

choice of a vendor could be affected. The operation of futures-events systems could well be a crucial aspect of management information systems.

Blind Spots

In information systems many signals of *real* events arise that are properly transmitted to the individuals responsible for handling them but are not "perceived" by these individuals. The situation is the reverse of the pseudo-event problem, where unreal events are projected into reality; here, real events either are not seen or are *treated like* phantom events. As we noted before, both perception and understanding are required before information becomes communication. And communication is essential before knowledge transforms of information (in the Boulding sense) can take place. Because of the inertial characteristics that exist in all systems (and are actually a part of the *definition of a system*), there is strong resistance to spotting perturbations in the information flow.

Everyone knows that humans are great pattern-recognizers. But in the process of seeking an established pattern to which the unknown conforms, humans add an inertial resistance to change which Arthur Porter, '39, Head of the Department of Industrial Engineering at the University of Toronto, calls "the time-constant of man."

The professional in a field tends to operate in an "environmental" manner in that field—his background and experience render him insusceptible to change. But the amateur is uninhibited by outmoded patterns and imprints, and his new approach to the problem provides the "anti-environment." "Science councils, for instance, are made up of scientists; and arts councils of artists and humanists," Professor Porter notes. "The anti-environmental approach would be to include a small minority of arts men on science councils and of scientists on arts councils."

In some fields, the computer is still "anti-environmental," says Professor Porter. But if present progress continues it will soon become part of the environment, a factor serving not change but the *status quo*.[22]

Perturbations are a particular form of information. The fact that they disturb the status quo does not mean that they are necessarily undesirable. Perturbing information may hold great opportunity, serious threat, or simply some minor degree of change in performance. The key is to *perceive* such information. Then appropriate action (e.g., the decision-making discussed in Chapter 4) can be taken.

Lateral thinking, as described by Edward de Bono, may be relevant. "Lateral thinking is based on biological information processing principles which differ from the physical information processing principles of mathematics, logic and computers. For instance, with biological information processing there may be a need to be wrong, which is unthinkable with physical information processing."[23] Lateral thinking can be contrasted with linear thinking. The linear processing of information requires that each arrival be treated before the next in line can be acknowledged, while lateral processing permits items to be taken out of line. But, since the simple rule of "next" does not apply, one has to know how to proceed. We can extend the linear role to *any* rule; in one sense or another, any rule can be considered to be linear. But when no pattern exists, lateral thinking applies. Let us consider some comparisons. Say a flock of sheep are blocking the way along a mountain road. The linear thinker sits in his car waiting for the flock to move away. The lateral thinker

---

[22] As quoted in *Technology Review,* December 1967, p. 53. Published at the Massachusetts Institute of Technology, copyright 1967 by the Alumni Association of the M.I.T.

[23] From *New Think* by Edward de Bono, Basic Books, Inc., Publishers, New York, 1968. De Bono indicates that biological processing is "dictated by the functional organization of the brain which determines the pattern of thinking."

gets out of the car and finds ways to help move the sheep along. The nine dots shown below are to be connected by four straight-line segments. In connecting all dots, the pencil cannot be lifted (i.e., the line is to be continuous), and *no* retracing of lines is permitted. The lateral thinker will have no trouble solving this problem.

Perhaps an even better example can be found in the Aesop fable of the thirsty crow whose beak was too short to get into a pitcher that had just a little water in it. This lateral-thinking crow dropped pebbles into the pitcher, raising the water level until he could reach it.

It would be misleading to suggest that all complex management problems can be solved by lateral information processing, but its usefulness can hardly be overlooked. The essence of lateral thinking lies in perceiving information *out of order,* for in the "ordinary" order, much information is blocked because it falls outside the accepted pattern of perception.

Serendipity. The term "blind spots" tends to emphasize the act of perception, but once the seeing is accomplished there remains the difficulty of understanding. Clearly, those who recognize blind spots for what they are will be in an excellent position to use this knowledge for futures control. But futures control is not essential; serendipity too can produce benefits that can be lost because blind spots are not recognized, as the following example shows.

> A problem of both theoretical importance to psychology and of pragmatic importance to the military, concerned the nature of team or crew behaviour. A small group of psychologists at RAND, as well as a few professionals of other disciplines, became interested in this problem. Since RAND was an Air Force research organization, the RAND scientists "naturally" focused upon military crews; [and] . . . a decision was taken to study an Air Defence site crew.
>
> It was impossible to study an Air Defence crew *in vivo* so the decision was taken to set up a special laboratory, called the Systems Research Laboratory—"system" being a very popular and "scientific" word—where a model of an Air Defence site could be set up; this was called, correctly, simulating an Air Defence site—"simulation" being another very popular and "scientific" word. As a crew for this simulated Air Defence site the standard subjects for psychological experiments were chosen—undergraduate students. . . .

The first step was to visit the site to be simulated in order to know what to simulate. The researchers came back from their visit with all the necessary information concerning the site environment, the nature of the air traffic picture that appeared on the radarscopes, as well as who did what with that input. Information which later was to become crucial was the size of the air load which the crews could "hack" efficiently, under what conditions, on the average, the crews became overloaded and ceased to function efficiently, etc. Input scripts for the simulated sites contained loads which in real life would lead to crew overloading or system breakdown.

The second step, after setting up the simulated site and checking it through, was to train subjects. Since training the subjects was not the focus of research interest it was given little theoretical thought. The researchers intuitively set up a training programme which they felt would be efficient, the purpose being to bring the subject crew as fast as possible up to a skill level comparable to the skill level of the military crews. . . .

The unexpected occurred with the second step. Not only did the student crews all too soon hack the loads normally hacked well in real life, but they also soon, with the greatest of ease, hacked loads that would overwhelm real crews. The original research purpose had to be abandoned because the prepared scripts which were intended to stress the crews proved to be too easy, there was not enough team behaviour worth recording. (But inadvertently a team training programme was born.) Military crews were brought in, subjected to the training procedures and given heavier and heavier loads, loads which could not conceivably be hacked in real life. Yet they managed to hack them effectively and efficiently. The military were alerted and, properly, requested that the training programme be implemented in the field. This was accomplished by setting up a special corporation to administer, and direct the implementation of, what by now came to be called, the "System Training Programme."

What occurred until then is not too rare in science; a group of scientists set out to study one area and find something which is very valuable in another area. But what followed is more or less unique to contemporary American academic social science in general, and to academic psychology in particular—no attempt was made to think through why the training programme was so effective. Four experimental crews were run through the Systems Research Laboratory. Almost everything the crews did and said during the runs was recorded accurately and systematically. A mass of originally invaluable data were accumulated. Yet nothing was done with all this.* They are probably still to be found, untouched, in filing cabinets.

---

* Data tend to deteriorate with disuse, hence what was originally invaluable generally *becomes valueless* with disuse over time. [N. J.]

Later, as the training was implemented in the field and involved hundreds of professional social scientists, primarily psychologists, very valuable lessons were learned concerning problems intrinsic to the training effort, and extrinsic to it, but relating to practical problems of implementing a training programme in an "alien society." Yet all these hundreds of man-years of experience have gone to waste. There are no publications sponsored by the scientists involved in this gigantic effort that attempt to reduce this rich experience to conceptual coherence.[24]

Serendipity always produces an awakening to opportunity for benefit. The existence of negative serendipity is an obvious reality as well. When a situation is perceived and understood to have negative consequences, there is a tendency to believe that the situation is newer than it really is. The fault or threat in the system is usually measured from the point of perception rather than from its unnoticed inception. As a result of this incorrect diagnosis, improper treatment is accorded to the unwanted intruder. A "wait and see" attitude is adopted in the hope that this "new" element will simply go away (if it is a step-type perturbation) or not return again (if it is an impulse-type disturbance).

Figure 12–7 portrays three types of information perturbance in systems in which x was expected to continue unchanged over time. The impulse perturbation hits the system and then disappears. At unexpected times it reappears. Depending on the long-term systems effects of the disturbances, the manager may be unaware for a substantial period of time that anything is happening. His control devices (monitors, etc.) will determine what he will see as

Figure 12–7   Three Types of Information Perturbance, Where x Is the Desired Performance

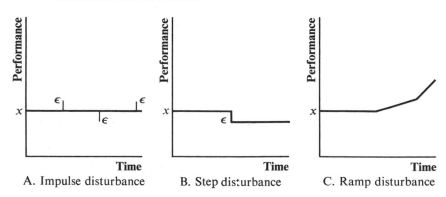

A. Impulse disturbance   B. Step disturbance   C. Ramp disturbance

---

[24] Nehemiah Jordan, *Themes in Speculative Psychology* (London: Tavistock Publications, Ltd., 1968), pp. 172–74.

well as what he is not likely to see. Blind spots are built into the system by MBE and by the nature of the information that is monitored regularly. Step disturbances are more likely to be picked up quickly, but their effects are usually more serious. Consequently, the manager has less time to take remedial action. In other words, the manager will pay a greater penalty for lack of dispatch in reacting to the situation, so any delay resulting from blind spots can be costly. The extreme situation is depicted by the ramp-type disturbance. While it is most likely to be discovered quickly, it allows the least time to make suitable corrections. The information concept permits us to diagnose change more rapidly than would otherwise be possible, providing a theoretical basis for determining the causes of disturbances at particular points in time. Diagnostic techniques can help to distinguish between these three classes of disturbance, no matter what the specific nature of the information involved. For example, without a good memory in the system, the impulse disturbance may always be interpreted as "too new to bother about." (Chapter 13 deals with memory as a powerful organizing force in the system; see pp. 548–55.)

SEMIOTICS: THE FUNDAMENTAL FRAMEWORK OF COMMUNICATION

The real difference between information and *communicated* information begins to emerge when we consider the three-level classification system of semiotics, shown in Figure 12–8. *Semiotics* is the name that is generally given to the science and theory of signs, which would seem a narrow field indeed. But its applications are extremely broad, and it is an important conceptual aid in understanding how we really communicate.[25]

Roughly, we comprehend the meaning of the diagrammed levels as *grammar* for structure, *meaning* for semantics, and *rapport* between the sender and the receiver for pragmatics. While the three levels appear to be independent (because the drawing emphasizes sequence), they are in fact highly interrelated. The diagram shows precedence—that is, there must be structure before there can be meaning, and meaning must exist for pragmatics to operate. But the character of each level is affected by the others. For example, a strictly structural analysis will reveal semantic and pragmatic influences. So a Venn dia-

---

[25] Charles Morris, who defined the three categories in the figure above, described semiotics as being the broadest study of language. John Locke had used the term "semeiotic" in a reasonably similar way. But it was Charles S. Peirce who, before Morris, had been a major contributor to the triadic classification of language. An excellent development of these notions will be found in Colin Cherry, *On Human Communication* (New York: Science Editions, 1961).

Figure 12–8   The Three-Level, Semiotic Structure of Communication

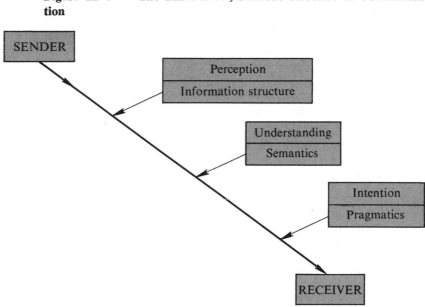

gram (see, for example, p. 83) with massive overlapping of areas would really characterize this situation best. Bearing in mind that these dependencies exist, let us now be more precise about each level.

1. *Structural information* is composed of symbols (such as phonemes, numbers, or letters) and syntax describing how the symbols should be used to form words and sentences. There are word-frequency counts, word-length counts, letter frequencies, rates of transmission, and many other measures to describe the structural properties of a message. Because of typical "common" usage, language has characteristic frequencies of letters, words, and phrases, and any one message can be compared with general usage in these terms. (For example, analysis of Bible passages has indicated that certain sections could not have appeared in an original version.)

A physical medium is used to transmit the message. According to Marshall McLuhan, "The medium is the message."[26] By this he means that the characteristics of the medium used—of television, radio, newspapers, books, Morse code, and so on—change the purely structural character of the message by altering the perception of the receiver. McLuhan goes on to characterize the various media in different ways. He concentrates on television, which he de-

---

[26] This is the title of Chapter 1 in Marshall McLuhan, *Understanding Media, The Extensions of Man* (New York: McGraw-Hill, 1964).

scribes as nonlinear, especially in comparison with printing, which is highly linear. It is his thesis that the changeover from linear to nonlinear media has profound implications for the fabric of society. We have no wish to engage in a controversy about such points. Whether the medium has a strong or a weak effect on the message, it has *some effect* and is part of the structural level of semiotics.

2. *Semantics* is a rather recently coined word. Michel Bréal, in 1897, is credited with having named this field of investigation, which deals with the meaning intended by symbol structure. Even the best dictionary presents but a crude approximation to the word meanings shared by individuals who communicate with each other about "things." The semantic rules are intended to connect unambiguously the signs and the "things" through relations of action, quality, and so on. In this way, information about things is shared by the sender and receiver, and meaning is thereby conveyed.

The field of general semantics[27] has attacked the effectiveness of language to convey "meaningful" meaning (and has, in turn, been attacked for its ideas for as many years as it has been in existence). A primary belief of the general semanticist is that words do not reflect the changes in meaning that are continually taking place over time but instead create static images that mislead. Be that argument as it may, none of us has not at some time been told, "We really agree; it's just a semantic problem." In other words, the meaning of words is sufficiently imprecise that management may successfully transmit structural information only to discover that its intended meaning is not understood. And communication cannot take place until meaning is successfully transmitted.

The ambiguity of language is, of course, well known, but we can highlight some of the inherent difficulty in the following simple way. A teacher addresses a class and asks the students to perform the simple computation: "three times five minus two times two."[28] Four basically different results are obtained:

$$[(3 \times 5) - 2]2 = 26$$
$$(3 \times 5) - (2 \times 2) = 11$$
$$3(5 - 2)2 = 18$$
$$3[5 - (2 \times 2)] = 3$$

Clearly, language is weak in describing these number concepts. This is not the same as crossing a seven (7) to avoid having it read as 1 or slashing a zero (∅)

---

27 This field was developed by A. Korzybski; see his *Science and Sanity* (Lakeville, Conn.: Institute of General Semantics, 1958) or any of the many publications of the Institute of General Semantics.

28 This example is based on material from Leonard Bloomfield, "Linguistic Aspects of Science," *International Encyclopedia of Unified Science*, Vol. 1, Part 1 (Chicago: University of Chicago Press, 1955), p. 248.

to eliminate the possibility that it is the letter *o*. These are structural problems of information transmission, whereas the example above is simply vague with respect to the semantics (meaning) of the arithmetic operators. Similar problems not based on number relations (which are particularly vulnerable) arise frequently.

3. *Pragmatics* is the way we describe the relations between the *users* of the signs and the signs themselves. Value systems and personal behavior, including psychological response patterns to certain types of symbol, reopen the door to individual behavior at a level that is lower intellectually but more complex behaviorally than that of semantics. Basically, the pragmatic concept in information transfer operates at two levels above the receipt of a structurally perfect message transmission and at one level above the existence of a perfect semantic (meaning) accord between the sender and the receiver. Yet we still do not have communication if the intended effect of the message is not what the sender had expected. In other words, the operational nature of communication becomes apparent at this third level of pragmatics. If the receiver is able to know just what the sender means but does not intend to do what the sender wants him to do, then the underlying purpose of the sender's use of information is thwarted, and his communication is faulty. Consider, for example, the desperate message of the sinking Titanic, which was received but thought to be a joke (because the Titanic was supposed to be unsinkable). This example is hardly what we would call communication, even though the first and second levels of information transfer were accomplished.[29]

Information Transfer

Without an understanding of semiotics, it is pointless to study the communication systems of managers (which is why a theory of management is just now emerging). Based on the knowledge of the semiotic classification we will now carefully examine the first level, that of structure. Information theory, which deals with the probabilistic structure of the medium and the message, is of recent origin. (Note, for example, from the previous footnote, that Shannon published his work in 1949. Several years before that, his work had been a

---

[29] We should note that Warren Weaver, in his discussion of Claude Shannon's landmark work in information theory (Claude Shannon and Warren Weaver, *The Mathematical Theory of Communication* [Urbana: University of Illinois Press, 1949]), treats three levels in terms other than semiotic ones: (1) technical issues, (2) semantic issues, and (3) effectiveness issues. Perhaps, using this more externalized view of an information system, it is possible to note that the subjective probability (see pp. 225–30) is deeply involved with the pragmatic level of information transfer. We also call the reader's attention to the related aspects of the value of information as discussed in Chapter 6. Such information value decisions are at the core of the pragmatic level.

Figure 12–9

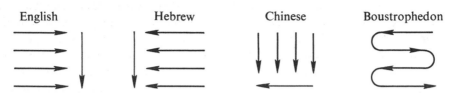

strictly internal publication of the Bell System.) Information theory deals with the relative frequencies of letters, symbols, or words and the way in which these frequencies interact with one another to produce information potentials. When a transmitted symbol is received, it can be classified as to how unexpected its receipt was. This concept is the foundation of information theory.

The order in which information is presented can vary greatly. Even in written transmissions many styles have grown up. Figure 12–9 illustrates some fundamental differences of scanning patterns for various cultures. It shows that English is read along descending rows from left to right, Hebrew along descending rows from right to left, and Chinese along descending columns from right to left, while the Coptic language Boustrophedon (in a most interesting pattern) reverses the reading direction with each row.[30] The direction of reading must be specified for the information system and, like all the system's symbols, syntax, and grammar, forms a critical part of the structural rules shared by the sender and the receiver. Radio has less ambiguity than television because the listener has only to hear one word after another, whereas television message direction has a considerable amount of ambiguity. The pictures are blurry; each person can look at what he wants to. The sound is not relied on to transmit all necessary information, as those who read their newspaper while "watching" television can attest. McLuhan's remarks, previously mentioned on p. 500, are based on his observations of such characteristics.

The significance of fixed direction (such as that which characterizes radio) is that the probabilities of symbol appearance are highly constrained. Where direction is ambiguous, the individual as a receiver controls some part of the experienced frequencies and calculated probabilities. Many management information functions belong to the latter class. Only on-line information, which must be treated in FIFO (first in, first out) order, is really constrained. Many

---

[30] Boustrophedon is clearly efficient, since the eyes can be engaged continuously in reading rather than returning "empty" for half of the scanning motions. However, dehgiewtuo evah ot smees snoitcerid htob ni daer ot gnivah fo ytluciffid eht the other advantages.

managers choose to shuffle their letters and memos and thereby gain some control over the informational character of their system. The telephone, on the other hand, is an on-line interrupter unless a secretary acts as a buffer for the manager. The on-line nature of the telephone wrests a significant amount of information control from the manager who usually receives his communications in this fashion. The telephone also ensures a FIFO system, with the near certainty that the most demanding information is not always being treated first.

The variety of structural information characteristics involves more than the direction of information flow. For example, the size of the data classes affects the number of such classes (much as the number of letters in its alphabet is one of the fundamental characteristics of a language). But, for *any* information structure, the system for transmission can be generalized by much the same format. The elements and operations are:

1	2	3	4	5	6
Sender's purpose	Sender's message	Encode	Transmit	Receive	Decode

7	8	9	10	11
Received message	Perceived intention	Receiver's reaction	Receiver's actions	Evaluation and feedback (return to 1)

All these steps will not necessarily appear in every communication attempt. There may be no provision for, say, step 11, the evaluation and feedback. In that case, the sender will not learn what effect his message had, or whether, in fact, it was a successful communication at all. For example, there is the request, "please think about it," which is not easy to check. Frequently, however, evaluation is built into the message. For example, the sender's request for a *list* of items is self-evaluating. Tangible requests for return actions (or receipts) are automatically evaluated by the sender. The evaluation link is costly, so each case must be decided by comparing the benefits of providing evaluation, delaying it, or ignoring it.

Steps 8 and 9 are related at the pragmatic level. If the receiver's *attitude* (reaction) is congruent with his perception of the sender's purpose, then one of the most important conditions for communication has been satisfied. Of course, the perceived intention (8) must match the sender's purpose (1). This raises questions of structural efficiency in steps 3 through 7. Semantics enters into the relationship between steps 1 and 2 and between steps 7 and 8. The relationship between steps 9 and 10 is relevant to implementation, and the receiver may not always be able to achieve the results that he has agreed (and wishes) to furnish.

Modeling study has centered on steps 4 and 5, where a channel for information transfer must exist between the sender and the receiver. Note that what McLuhan calls the medium is what we have called a channel. McLuhan's thesis that the medium (channel) becomes part of the message is not hard for anyone to believe. What is surprising is the extent to which the channel and the message interact. The channel must be suited to the language structure, and vice versa. Benjamin Whorf's studies led him to conclude that the total structure of an information system significantly affects the pragmatic level of communication. In describing Whorf's work, Edward T. Hall says:

> We dissect nature along lines laid down by our native languages. The categories and types that we isolate from the world of phenomena we do not find there because they stare every observer in the face; on the contrary, the world is presented in a kaleidoscopic flux of impression which has to be organized by our minds—and this means largely by the linguistic systems in our minds. We cut nature up, organize it into concepts, and ascribe significances as we do, largely because we are parties to an agreement to organize it in this way—an agreement that holds throughout our speech community and is codified in the patterns of our language. The agreement is, of course, an implicit and unstated one, *but its terms are absolutely obligatory;* we cannot talk at all except by subscribing to the organization and classification of data which the agreement decrees.
>
> This fact is very significant for modern science, for it means that no individual *is free to describe nature with absolute impartiality* but is constrained to certain modes of interpretation even while he thinks himself most free.[31]

Information transfer through the encode-decode phases of the information system tends to be structural but not necessarily uncomplicated. Television cameras convert light and color to directed, linear electrical impulses, which the television receiver then reconverts; the viewer is unaware of the encode-decode operations. Military coding studies aim at encoding in a way that prohibits decoding except by selected receivers; this accounts for emphasis at steps 3 and 6.[32] Tape recorders encode and decode from magnetic tape. Computers use special languages that convert information into 0, 1 (binary) form.

When the television signal is interfered with (by planes, diathermy machines, etc.), we say that *noise* has entered the channel. This noise combines with the

---

[31] From *The Silent Language* by Edward T. Hall. Copyright © 1959 by Edward T. Hall. Reprinted by permission of Doubleday & Company, Inc. See also Benjamin Whorf, "Science and Linguistics," *Technology Review*, Vol. XLII, No. 6 (April 1940).

[32] An interesting study of coding can be found in D. Kahn, *The Codebreakers: The Story of Secret Writing* (New York: Macmillan, 1967).

encoded information and is present at the decoding stage. Somehow it must be recognized and removed if the original message is to be recaptured. Noise is responsible for distorting the encoded message so that it is not isomorphic to the decoded message at receipt. Somehow, the isomorph must be found if real communication is to occur. *Structural noise* can enter at the transmitter, in the channel, or at the receiver. *Semantic noise* can occur at steps 1, 2, 3, 7, and 8. Management is responsible for both types of noise and can design the system to control the situation.

First, steps can be taken to prevent noise from entering the system. For example, the variability of statistical data is usually referred to as noise. While it cannot be entirely removed, a larger sample can help to decrease it. (See pp. 225–28; it should be noted that we can now treat the imperfection of a test as noise and use sample size to control the absolute levels of noise.) For physical systems, shielding can be used to prevent radio jamming; coaxial cables are designed to prevent crosstalk between circuits; a good hi-fi set has circuits constructed to ensure the fidelity of the received signal. Examples are legion in business as well, where continual efforts are being made to purify accounting data, market-research reports, financial evaluations, and wage-rate structures. On the other hand, management is not averse to introducing its own noise into a competitor's information system—for example, by lowering prices during a competitor's market test.

The second possible approach to handling noise is to design the information system so that a certain amount of noise in the informing system will not adversely affect the informed system. *Redundancy* is the key concept in this case, by which we mean that specific patterns that are known to the sender and receiver alike are built into the language. Thus, for example, in English, a message that had the word *q een* could be completed immediately since the letter *q* must always be followed by the letter *u*. Take any paragraph and delete some of the letters. It is surprising how much information can be distorted or destroyed before the message is impaired—surprising, that is, until one realizes how high a level of redundancy all languages have.

Information Theory

Information theory provides a useful basis for evaluating the structural characteristics of an information system. Two measures are most important: the first, *entropy,*[33] is frequently designated by *H;* the second, *redundancy,* is usually represented by the symbol *R.*

---

[33] "Entropy" is a term borrowed from thermodynamics. The information equivalent is similar in some respects to the second law of thermodynamics.

To the information theorist, entropy measures the ordering of information. The entropy of an information system is an important property that only recently has been brought to management's attention. By its studies and surveys, management looks for a reduction of uncertainty. The entropy of the system is driven down as random variety is structured and classified, increasing the possibility of making forecasts based on patterns. And, in effect, this increases the potential for surprisal.

Specifically, the entropy measure, *H*, is based on *averaging* the logarithms of the probabilities for all of the different elements, letters, or symbols in the language pattern. Thus

$$H = -\sum_{j=1}^{n} p_j \log_2 p_j$$

An example here might save innumerable words. Say that eight different orders can be transmitted from the bridge of a ship to the engine room. If those orders are equally likely, than all p_j's equal $\frac{1}{8}$. Entropy, *H*, equals

$$-8(\tfrac{1}{8} \log_2 [\tfrac{1}{8}]) = \log_2 8 = 3 \text{ bits},$$

which is the amount of *information* that can be transmitted by each one of the eight possible messages. The logarithm to the base 2 is used because in this way all information can be expressed in *binary digits* (bits) of 0 and 1. For the above example, we note that $2^3 = 8$, or, in general, $2^H = N$, where *N* represents the number of different information classes and *H* stands for the number of binary digits, or amount of information, that must be transmitted to specify a particular message.

Another way of looking at this measure is to consider the eight different orders as coded into binary form, as shown in Table 12–1.

Table 12–1

Order number	Binary form
0	000
1	001
2	010
3	011
4	100
5	101
6	110
7	111

Three binary digits is just the right number to take on eight different message forms. Now, consider a catalog item that has *M* different sizes and *N* different colors. The physical variety level is $M \times N$. Using $X_M = \log_2 M$ and $X_N = \log_2 N$, we can write this as $\log_2 MN = \log_2 M + \log_2 N = X_M + X_N$. X_M and X_N are the information levels of M and N, respectively. $X_M + X_N$ equals the number of binary digits that can be used to represent this combined amount of informational variety.[34] If $M = 8$ and $N = 16$, then seven binary digits (or seven two-position switches, or relays), are needed to be able to transmit 128 unique configurations.

The entropy of English, French, Russian, or German can be determined in the same way—or can it? Consider English and assume that we have twenty-six letters plus a space, for a total of twenty-seven unique informational states. (We won't concern ourselves with punctuation, lower- and upper-case letters, numerals, and so forth). The $\log_2 27 = 4.755$ bits. See Figure 12–10. According to this measure, each letter that is transmitted carries 4.755 bits of information. It would be necessary to display sets of numbers composed of five binary digits to do the job.

But language, as it is used, is not properly represented in this way. We can quickly agree that the letters in English do not appear with equal frequency.

Figure 12–10   The Relationship of H to N

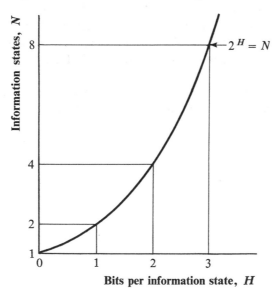

N	H
10	3.322
12	3.585
15	3.907
16	4.000
20	4.322
25	4.644
27	4.755
32	5.000

[34] Assuming that each catalog item is equally likely to appear in whatever context the analysis has.

Table 12–2

Consonants	Probability	Morse code	Vowels	Probability	Morse code
t	.09	–	a	.07	. –
n	.07	– .	e	.13	.
r	.07	. – .	i	.07	. .
s	.06	. . .	o	.08	– – –
h	.06	. . . .	u	.03	. . –
Total	.35		Total	.38	

Table 12–2 lists some approximations of the probabilities of the most-used letters in English.[35] The (international) Morse code form of these letters has been listed in the table to show how well the concept of *coding for efficient channel use* was understood by Samuel F. B. Morse. The highest probabilities arc assigned the shortest symbol set. (It should be noted that Morse code is a binary language, where dot and dash are equivalent to 0 and 1). *H* is the only four-digit letter present in this table, where twelve out of twenty-seven Morse-equivalent letters have four characters. At the same time, with just these ten letters (or 37 percent of all symbols), 73 percent of the language's use is accounted for. (See the reference to the log-normal distribution in Chapter 13, pp. 572–73). The redundancy is high, but it is actually even higher when letter sequences (such as *qu* and *th* are taken into consideration). The designers of secretarial shorthand languages recognized the unequal use of certain letters and the high probability of particular letter pairs.

The entropy measure for unequal probabilities of symbol use is an average value. If, for example, four information states, *A, B, C,* and *D,* appear with probabilities of $\frac{1}{8}$, $\frac{1}{4}$, $\frac{1}{2}$, and $\frac{1}{8}$, respectively, we have

$$H = -\tfrac{1}{8}\log_2 \tfrac{1}{8} - \tfrac{1}{4}\log_2 \tfrac{1}{4} - \tfrac{1}{2}\log_2 \tfrac{1}{2} - \tfrac{1}{8}\log_2 \tfrac{1}{8}$$

$$= -(.125)(3) - (.250)(2) - (.500)(1) - (.125)(3) = 1.75 \text{ bits}$$

In other words, on the average (noting that $\Sigma p_j = 1$), each symbol transmitted carries 1.75 bits of information. If these four symbols were equally likely, the entropy measure would have been $H = \log_2 4 = 2$ bits. *The equally likely condition always produces maximum entropy.* It is the condition of greatest uncertainty, maximum information variety, and least organization for the system. At the opposite extreme, when any one state has a probability of one, the system's entropy measure is zero. Thus, if $A = 0, B = 0, C = 1,$ and

---

[35] In German, *e* has a probability of over 18 percent; in French it is almost 16 percent. Of course, variations in all frequency figures will occur, no matter what the language, depending on the source that is sampled.

$D = 0$, then $H = \log_2 1 = 0$. This is the *minimum* entropy value that can be obtained. *Maximum* entropy can increase indefinitely as more states are included in the information system.[36] The implications for management can be summed up as follows: The larger the H value, the more complex is the situation with which management must deal. H can be cut down by considering a smaller system or by establishing policies that increase the system's redundancy. Thus, H will vary depending on the fineness of classification that management uses, the size of the system with which it deals, the amount and kinds of policy and MBE it employs (see pp. 451–59). Control over the relative frequencies of the information can be used to increase redundancy and reduce H. Such factors apply to the design and operation of an adequate information system.

Redundancy is defined in terms of the actual entropy and the maximum potential entropy of the information system; thus $R = 1 - H_{actual}/H_{max}$. With twenty-seven symbol states, all equally likely, $H_{max} = 4.755$. But because of approximately 75 percent redundancy in English, we find that $H_{actual} = H_{max}(1 - R) = 4.755(1 - .75) = 1.189$ bits. This is a striking result. It tells us that between two and three equally likely letters could supplant the entire English alphabet and convey the same amount of information.[37] But *any* noise in the system would be catastrophic. So language has evolved with many more informational states to balance off the cost of an error.

From our equation for redundancy we see that when H_{max} is large and H_{actual} is almost as large, the redundancy is low. Thus, in our previous four-state example, the redundancy would be $R = 1 - 1.75/2.00 = .125$. By emphasizing tradition, building habits, ignoring the unusual, and so on, management could operate on H_{actual} to reduce it. This would increase R and thereby improve managerial control, but the penalty is a decrease in the efficiency with which information can be transmitted and used.

R can range from 0 to 1. Therefore, it is a relative measure for any system. We can think of entropy as being a measure of the *absolute* complexity of a management information system, while R measures the *relative* safeguards and controls built into the system. When $R = 1$, there is no information potential in the system—that is, no variety. $H = 0$ and everything is deterministic as clockwork. Only when the clock stops is there some surprise. Such systems are not self-adaptive and are usually highly vulnerable when surprise perturbations arise.

The above discussion stressed structural properties of the system, yet both the semantic and pragmatic levels get involved with structure in the McLuhan and in the Whorfian senses. Machines (including computers) are more easily

---

[36] Surprisal potential will depend on the number of information states that have to share the possibility of occurring. Thus, there would be little surprise with two equally likely states and a great deal of surprise with a thousand.

[37] $\log_2 2 = 1$; $\log_2 3 = 1.585$

viewed in structural terms than are people, but entire complexes of man-machine systems can be studied structurally. Especially significant descriptions relate to man-machine communications. Man has channel capacity and processing limits with respect to the entropic properties of both the input and output *rates*. Machines are constrained, but in a different way. Technology can expand the channel capacities of machines as well as their sensory input abilities and their output rates. With respect to aptitudes for the structural level of information, the machine has it all over the man, but at the semantic level and especially at the pragmatic level, the man side of the system emerges as clearly superior in dealing with high surprisal and great variety.

MANAGERIAL INFERENCES CONCERNING INSTABILITY

The manager's estimate of a situation depends on the completeness of his information about the scenario. If the system has no recorded history, or if the manager is inexperienced in the information characteristics of the system, he reacts cautiously. Caution takes a specific form: When there is little knowledge about the system's states, the manager tends to overestimate the entropy with which he must deal. The reverse tendency exists when there is almost (but not quite) total information. Over some middle range of knowledge about the system, the increase in entropy accelerates as less is known about the system. It then slows down as maximum entropy is approached. (See Figure 12–11.) A new product is a good example of a system without much history. The situation is not a total mystery, but the manager's degree of belief in the estimates of the situation cannot be high. The resultant managerial attitude is to assume that the potential entropy is large rather than small.[38] As knowledge of the system grows, the reverse position is taken; the manager tends to assume that potential entropy is small rather than large. In this way, he approximates certainty when it does not exist. He uses deterministic linear programs when he knows very well that some surprisal and variety exist in the system and that his model does not include them.

---

[38] We must emphasize the difference between the concept of entropy and that of variance, or standard deviation, which is normally associated with probability distributions. Entropy is a measure of the shape of a probability distribution. It does not embody the values of the characteristic that the distribution describes. The states $A, B, C, D, \ldots$ may have large or small numerical values and can apply to lengths, sales volumes, or temperatures. The entropy measure will describe them all in the same way if the measures $p_A, p_B, p_C, p_D, \ldots$ are the same. We might say that the entropy measure does not carry the *semantic* information about the state. It is a straightforward structural measure of the variety and surprisal of the system of states with which the manager must deal.

Figure 12–11   How Management Estimates Its Entropic Situation at Different Information-Completeness Levels

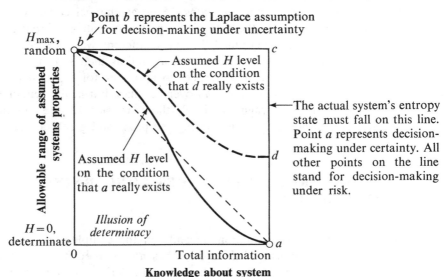

Point *b* represents the Laplace assumption for decision-making under uncertainty

H_{max}, random

Allowable range of assumed systems properties

Assumed *H* level on the condition that *d* really exists

The actual system's entropy state must fall on this line. Point *a* represents decision-making under certainty. All other points on the line stand for decision-making under risk.

Assumed *H* level on the condition that *a* really exists

Illusion of determinacy

$H = 0$, determinate

0   Total information

Knowledge about system

We say, not that the tendency we have just described is good or bad, merely that it appears to characterize managerial behavior. And we can comment on what it seems to mean—namely, that the manager prefers to operate at the lowest possible entropy level. Therefore, he is reluctant to acknowledge entropy —at least initially. But once his confidence in the assumption of low entropy is shaken, he inflates his estimates of the system's variety at an accelerating rate until he nearly reaches the maximum. Being near the maximum forces him to slow down the rate at which he imputes additional variety. The consequences of this tendency are for the manager consistently to overestimate the difficulties of dealing with new systems. In a new system, the manager starts his thinking in the "neighborhood" of the point *b*. Therefore, he projects very high *H* values (by extrapolation) onto the line *adc*.

Requisite Variety

Intuitively, the manager knows that the *Law of Requisite Variety* exists: "Only variety can destroy variety."[39] This law, formulated by Ashby, states that the manager, in order to *control* or regulate a system, must have as much variety

---

[39] W. Ross Ashby, *An Introduction to Cybernetics,* (New York: Wiley, 1956), pp. 206–13.

available for his use as the system possesses. The relationship is not difficult to demonstrate. Assume that B's strategies are α, β, and δ; A's strategies are 1, 2, and 3; and three different outcomes, a, b, and c, arise.

| | B's strategies: | | |
	α	β	δ
A's strategies: 1	a	b	c
2	b	c	a
3	c	a	b

A wants to maintain the system in condition a. He can do this, because no matter whether B uses his α, β, or δ strategy, A has a countermove available to return the system to a (thus $\alpha 1$, $\beta 3$, $\delta 2$). Now, strip A of any one of his strategies and B finds that he always has one strategy that can override A's attempt to maintain the system in a. We should note that if A had a new strategy, such as 4 in the matrix below, it would dominate A's strategies 1 and 3 (with respect to the objective a)

| | B: | | |
	α	β	δ
A: 1	a	b	c
2	b	c	a
3	c	a	b
4	a	a	c

and replace them. This would mean that the requisite variety would be reduced. This occurs because α and β merge and become as one state with respect to the attainment of a. Thus

| | B: | |
	$\alpha\beta$	δ
A: 2	b,c	a
4	a	c

So the requisite variety now consists of only two strategies for A and, effectively, two for B. Whenever we speak about the "Law of Requisite Variety," we always assume that all dominated strategies have been removed and that such transformations have been made so that we are working with the *essential* matrix of variety.

To management theory, the concept of requisite variety adds a critical dimension. If a manager overestimates H, then he bases his planning and decision-making on overestimates for the cost of controlling the situation, which leads him to prefer situations where he starts out with most of the relevant information—that is, close to line adc in Figure 12–11. As a result, the planning alternatives he uses are skewed away from high entropy systems (larger and longer-term systems) and an opportunity cost is thus incurred. Concurrently, because he underestimates the entropy in the vicinity of line *adc,* the manager incurs another penalty for providing insufficient control variety.

Another interesting corollary relates to the inexperienced manager. To him, systems are unstable until such time as their underlying patterns can be discovered. He always faces the equivalent of an unstable system to begin with, although he learns the system's pattern quickly if it is apparent. He can also learn from his predecessor if his training and the information transfer are sufficient. But his tendency will be to accept tradition rather than to question it because in this way he avoids having to deal with high-entropy systems.

The Entropy of Planning Horizons

Information management adds a new perspective to management theory. The terms and relations with which we have been working shed specific light on many previously vague areas. For example, extending the planning horizon increases the information potentials of the system. In entropy terms, it raises the estimated H levels, as shown in Figure 12–12. But, for the manager having close to zero information, the difference between six-month, one-year, and two-year planning horizons is slight with respect to entropy estimates. We can see how the manager's preference to work with low-entropy systems leads him to operate on shorter planning horizons, meaning that he does not consider the impact of any but relatively immediate events, about which he knows a great deal.

Figure 12–12

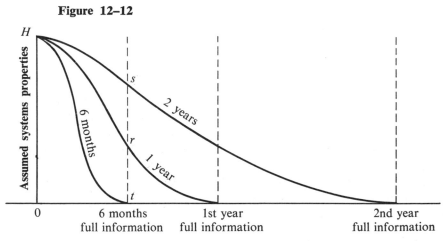

Knowledge about system for three planning horizons

Recalling the planning horizon concept introduced previously, the manager has a planning horizon, y, and an updating interval, x (see Figure 9–13, p. 349). If $x = y =$ six months, then the estimated entropy (at point t in Figure 12–12) averages out at close to zero. If $x =$ six months and $y =$ one year, then the estimated entropy would average about point r in Figure 12–12. (This situation is depicted by the middle curve in the figure.) The control investments for requisite variety for this planning procedure are substantially higher than in the previous case. The situation $x =$ six months and $y =$ two years would produce an even higher level of entropy (averaging around point s in Figure 12–12). The cost in this third case far exceeds that in the previous ones, and the control investment could be expected to be commensurate. If we think in terms of partially constrained planning networks, the way in which these added costs arise becomes evident. So there is an understandable tendency for management to choose short planning horizons. The counterpoint, which it is easy to lose sight of, is the fact that higher entropy levels and greater opportunity for benefits are positively related. There are opportunity costs lurking in every shortened planning horizon for the overavoidance of Type II errors.

INFORMATION VERIFICATION

The simplest concept of the information system includes the sender, the receiver, and the channel. Noise entering the *channel* causes poor communication, so redundancy is designed into the language. But different forms of noise can also enter the system at either the sender's or the receiver's side. A mistake can be made at encoding or decoding. An error can arise at the transmitter or receiver. For an example of an error made at the input side, consider the job of a punch-card operator who is supposed to punch the number of hours worked by each of several hundred employees in the previous week. Within rather broad limits, an error made in punching this kind of information cannot be spotted easily by an external logic check. It is perfectly possible that employee x worked five hours last week, just as it is possible that he worked fifty hours. (Of course, the EDP—electronic data-processing—system could be programmed to pick up such obvious absurdities as a credit of 5,000 hours in one week.) [40] In any case, whether man and man, machine and man, or machine and machine communication is involved, a *verification procedure* can be used to remove informational errors. For example,

---

[40] There are cases on record of government checks being issued for, say, five million dollars instead of five dollars. A verification step in the computer programming could have detected this occurrence. It is not believed that too many of these checks have been cashed successfully.

Verification consists of passing a card through a device known as a verifier, and depressing keys which sense the holes already punched. The machine gives a warning when the user of the verifier strikes a key to which no hole corresponds, or omits to strike in the cases in which a hole is available to be sensed. When the warning is given, either the verification puncher or the original operative has made a mistake. Recourse may then be had to the original data, so as to choose between them.[41]

The nature of the verification model we shall describe[42] is strikingly similar to that of the Bayesian test matrix previously discussed on p. 226. We begin with a set of states to be communicated. These are the inputs in Figure 12–13.

Figure 12–13

Inputs ——————▶ Operator ——————▶ Outputs

Let us choose for this example five input states and call them *a, b, c, d,* and *e.* The probability of occurrences of each state is

p_a	p_b	p_c	p_d	p_e
.10	.25	.30	.25	.10

Presumably, these data would be available from the historical records of the company; if not, other sources, including simple experiments, could be used. Next, Table 12–3 gives the *conditional* probabilities for what is likely to be

Table 12–3   Matrix of Operator's Characteristics

		On the condition that the *input* is 1,				
		a_1	b_1	c_1	d_1	e_1
then the	a_2	.95	.05	.03	.00	.00
probability that	b_2	.03	.90	.05	.02	.00
the output will	c_2	.02	.03	.85	.08	.10
be 2 is given by	d_2	.00	.02	.05	.80	.15
the matrix entries	e_2	.00	.00	.02	.10	.75

---

[41] J. L. Jolley, *Data Study* (New York: McGraw-Hill, 1968), p. 178.

[42] See also Robert H. Roy, "The Development and Future of Operations Research and Systems Engineering," in Charles D. Flagle, William H. Huggins, and Robert H. Roy, eds., *Operations Research and Systems Engineering* (Baltimore: The Johns Hopkins Press, 1960), pp. 8–27.

Table 12–4

Information states	(1) Operator's errors	(2) Probabilities of states	(3) Product (1)×(2)	(4) Verifier's errors	(5) Product (1)×(4)	(6) Product (2)×(5)
a	.05	.10	.005	.25	.0125	.00125
b	.10	.25	.025	.20	.0200	.00500
c	.15	.30	.045	.15	.0225	.00675
d	.20	.25	.050	.10	.0200	.00500
e	.25	.10	.025	.05	.0125	.00125
			.150			.01925

punched, given what should have been punched. We can call these the operator's characteristics.

In Table 12–4, we note that the total errors made by the operator when punching each state are the sum of that state's column values excluding the entry on the matrix diagonal (see column 1). The probabilities of each state occurring at the input are given in column 2. Column 3 represents the product of columns 1 and 2. The sum of these products is .150. It can be interpreted as the average percentage of errors. That is, of each 100 inputs that are processed by the operator, ten are *a* states, twenty-five are *b* states, thirty are *c* states, and so on. Of the *a* states, 5 percent are incorrectly punched; of the *b* states, 10 percent are incorrectly punched, and so forth. Therefore, the sum of .150 means that out of every 100 inputs, fifteen, on the average, are incorrectly punched.

This measure of average performance can be improved by altering the system's configuration to include a verification procedure. For example, assume that another operator (human or machine) is introduced in a serial configuration, as shown in Figure 12–14. Column 4 of Table 12–4 has the verifier's error characteristics, which are not identical with those of the operator; they are, in fact, just opposite. Column 5 gives us the joint error distribution of the operator and the verifier, assuming that their behaviors are entirely independent—by which we mean that the verifier is not in any sense affected by the mistakes of the operator or prone to make a mistake because a prior mistake has been made. Then, in column 6 of the table, we obtain the product of the joint error distribution with that of the information-state probabilities, column 2. Column 6, which gives the average percentage of errors

Figure 12–14

for the system with the verifier (.01925), can be compared with column 3, which gave the average for the operator alone (.150). By adding the verifier, we have reduced the number of structural information errors that will be passed through the system from 150 in a thousand to slightly more than nineteen in a thousand. Whether or not such a verifier should be used depends on the costs of errors and the opposing costs of the verifier. Thus, if each error passed by the system is estimated to cost $.20, and if the verifier costs $100 per week (assuming that the throughput of the system is 5,000 operations per week), then

> Cost without verifier
> (5,000)(.15)($.20) = $150 per week, and
> Cost with verifier
> (5,000)(.01925)($.20) + $100.00 = $119.25

Therefore, other things being equal, the verifier should be used.

Many additional points could be developed. What, for example, is the ideal form for a verifier, given a specific set of operator's characteristics? In general, the verifier should be designed or selected so as not to commit the same kinds of error as the operator. At the minimum, we would hope that the operator and its verifier are not positively correlated on making the same kind of errors. At best, they should be strongly negatively correlated, as in the example used above. Self-verification is frequently used, especially in an informal way, but it violates the independence principle and is also likely to produce a strong positive correlation of errors.

Additionally, we should note that a parallel configuration (such as that shown in Figure 12–15) could be used instead of a serial arrangement, especially since serial arrangements tend to create delays. The acceptable size of verification delays is determined by the properties of the specific system. Simulation can be applied readily to observe the performance (in terms of rates, throughputs, errors passed, delays, and costs) of different systems.

Verification by information sampling is frequently used instead of the complete verification that we have just modeled. Sampling verification can be used in various ways, one of which might be to check up only on *deviations*

Figure 12–15   A Parallel Verification Configuration

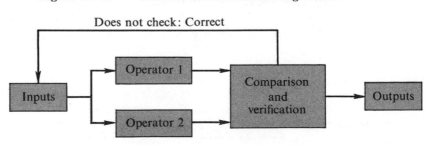

from expectations, thereby controlling Type I errors. (For example, any deviation from the standard number of hours worked by an employee might be considered something to check.) Sampling rules could also be designed to check various output values that *accord with expectations* in the hope of controlling some Type II errors. (A sample representing average paychecks could be verified.)

The verification of information can be used for many different functions. Because of the greater error-proneness in all man systems, it is particularly characteristic of input or output situations in which people participate and less usual in machine-to-machine relations. In the control system, it is often used for the monitor's operations as well as for those of the controller. For management of information, it is a critical consideration whenever MBE is used.

Contributions to Information and Communication Theory

At this point, it will be useful to try to tie together the many facets of the enormous system of effectors that relate to communication.

Figure 12–16 is hardly complete in any sense. But it has been included here to give some feeling for the comprehensiveness and complexity of communication theory, and of the richness of the demands that must be met before a theory of communication can exist.

Information Audit

Because the concept of information has been extended to every aspect of organizational thinking, the idea of the information audit becomes inescapable. Information throughput rates are continually rising. As information becomes more like currency, its objective reality grows and the utility of auditing information demands attention.

The audit is equivalent to a systems analysis aimed at finding out who gets what information; how much of it is duplicated; where decisions are really being made; where information is being stored and if the memory is of the right kind and large enough; what errors are being committed and how verification is being used to control errors; whether coding procedures are making efficient use of channel capacities; whether protection against espionage is necessary and, if so, whether it is being given; how much delay occurs in data transfers; what are the cost and value of information, and so on. Clearly, many measures of performance can be used. The extent of differentiated interests in the system is considerable, and the needs of both generalists and specialists must be met.

Standards must be set in order to detect the condition of being over- or underinformed. Standards must also be created to deal with redundancy to

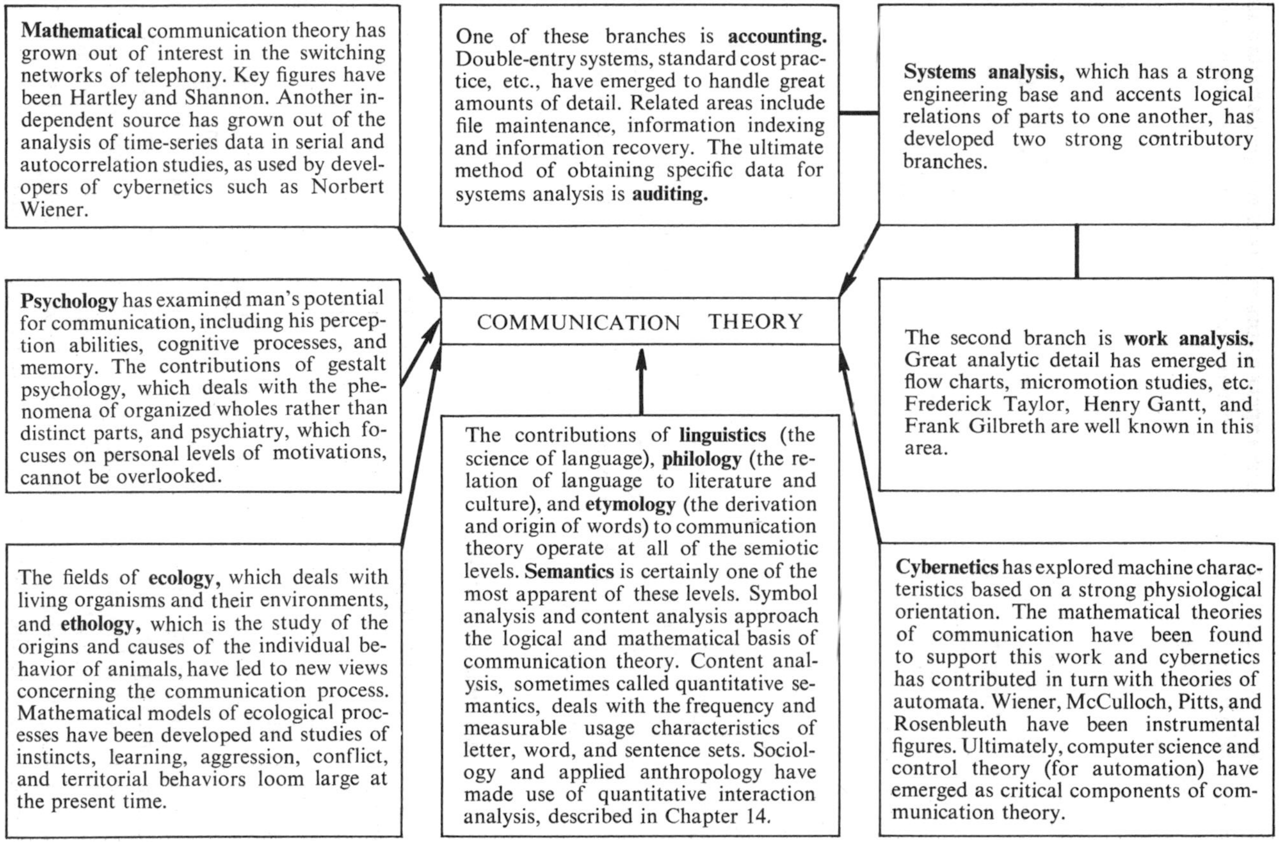

Systems analysis, which has a strong engineering base and accents logical relations of parts to one another, has developed two strong contributory branches.

Mathematical communication theory has grown out of interest in the switching networks of telephony. Key figures have been Hartley and Shannon. Another independent source has grown out of the analysis of time-series data in serial and autocorrelation studies, as used by developers of cybernetics such as Norbert Wiener.

One of these branches is **accounting.** Double-entry systems, standard cost practice, etc., have emerged to handle great amounts of detail. Related areas include file maintenance, information indexing and information recovery. The ultimate method of obtaining specific data for systems analysis is **auditing.**

The second branch is **work analysis.** Great analytic detail has emerged in flow charts, micromotion studies, etc. Frederick Taylor, Henry Gantt, and Frank Gilbreth are well known in this area.

COMMUNICATION THEORY

The contributions of **linguistics** (the science of language), **philology** (the relation of language to literature and culture), and **etymology** (the derivation and origin of words) to communication theory operate at all of the semiotic levels. **Semantics** is certainly one of the most apparent of these levels. Symbol analysis and content analysis approach the logical and mathematical basis of communication theory. Content analysis, sometimes called quantitative semantics, deals with the frequency and measurable usage characteristics of letter, word, and sentence sets. Sociology and applied anthropology have made use of quantitative interaction analysis, described in Chapter 14.

Cybernetics has explored machine characteristics based on a strong physiological orientation. The mathematical theories of communication have been found to support this work and cybernetics has contributed in turn with theories of automata. Wiener, McCulloch, Pitts, and Rosenbleuth have been instrumental figures. Ultimately, computer science and control theory (for automation) have emerged as critical components of communication theory.

Psychology has examined man's potential for communication, including his perception abilities, cognitive processes, and memory. The contributions of gestalt psychology, which deals with the phenomena of organized wholes rather than distinct parts, and psychiatry, which focuses on personal levels of motivations, cannot be overlooked.

The fields of **ecology,** which deals with living organisms and their environments, and **ethology,** which is the study of the behavior of animals, have led to new views concerning the communication process. Mathematical models of ecological processes have been developed and studies of instincts, learning, aggression, conflict, and territorial behaviors loom large at the present time.

Figure 12–16   A Small Guide to the Contributors to Communication Theory

overcome noise and verification to reduce errors to an acceptable level. Machines are somewhat less prone to big mistakes than to small ones. This is because much effort will go into checking the machine program for big mistakes, while small errors cannot be given the same attention, and some may slip through. Moreover, the big errors, being far more obvious than the small ones, are likely to be spotted quickly and corrected. The small errors may never be noticed without auditing procedures. However, the machines will continue to repeat the small errors, and they can accumulate into sizable penalties.

The major issue to be faced by the audit is that of *directed relevancy*. Are information needs being matched by appropriate information flows? Does the information system aid the organization in meeting its *accountability* to citizens, stockholders, consumers, employees, managers, and society at large? It has been said that technicians often determine what computers will do once they are installed. Information throughput is so high, computer and machine languages so specialized, and information flows so uncharted, that management can easily lose track of the means by which decisions are reached and plans carried forward. Small programming changes made with the intention of increasing data-handling efficiency can turn out to affect the decision process in unsuspected and undiscernible ways. Management's goal to remove "irrelevant" and "marginally useful" information from the throughput opens up opportunities for technicians unwittingly to shift decision-making bases. Conversely, management's acquisitive instincts to bring more "relevant" information to bear in order to "feed" the system's potential for handling information and to improve the decision-making process can result in contrary evaluations, inconsistencies, delays, and an ultimate inability to find out what is going on. One of the major functions of the audit operation is to detect such problems so that they can be remedied. Therefore, it should not be staffed by information technicians or directed to their needs. It must be an independent function that reports to management.

Critical informational objectives. Management's confidence in its information system is essential. We have suggested that management cannot have such confidence without adequate information auditing. But *purity* of information works two ways, for management is a purveyor as well as a user of information.

Management creates and uses information, both internally and externally, in an enormous variety of ways—through memoranda, press releases, financial statements, and so on. Usually, such statements are truthful and factually accurate. But there are difficulties, and there are exceptions. The need to interpret and condense, particularly in journalistic reporting, remains a possible source of misinformation. And there are clear cases where information has been altered to suit a purpose. In the short run, this may benefit management, but in the longer run, significant penalties can be expected.

Even an honest reporting job by management cannot avoid the evident fact that some people will be privileged to have *advance* information. For example, press releases give advance notice to a special few. Moreover, press information has astounding value. We have shown how published polls might affect election results and how this principle might apply to a variety of management notices concerning stock splits, dividends, new products, and so on. There is also the question of the way in which enormous information capabilities in the hands of management infringe on the abilities of others. For example, consider the following quotation from *The Wall Street Journal.*

> And as Dana L. Thomas noted in a recent article in *Barron's* on the effect of computerization on the market, the stock market's volatility has been increasing.
>   That is due, in part, to the professionals' use of computers to detect "buy" and "sell" levels purely on the basis of statistical grounds with little or no reference to earnings. "In Wall Street," says Mr. Thomas, "what is sauce for the goose is definitely not sauce for the gander." While the professionals, armed with computers, are riding higher than ever, the Street, always a perilous place for the amateur investor, has become even more dangerous than before. Now that electronic brains have come to the Street, the pitfalls for the unsophisticated stock market dabbler are deeper than ever.[43]

Great circumspection and control over information are required on the part of management to protect its credibility over the coming decades.

SUMMARY

Information is at the heart of the concept of control. Much thought has been given in recent years to the nature of information and its fundamental purpose, communication. To begin with, information is rapidly becoming equivalent to monetary currency. In many ways, the need for actual currency is disappearing; it is being replaced by the efficient transmission of information.

The new functions of information are explored in various ways. The currency concept is extended to the notion of information privileges, which reflect the fact that persons in an organization who are responsible for the collection, use, and storage of various forms of information treat their position as a real advantage. Systems hierarchies play a large part in defining information privileges. The privileges of top management are greatest but, at the same time, it is shown that the computer is beginning to provide a new channel for obtaining and sharing these privileges.

---

[43] From "Frisbees on Wall Street," *The Wall Street Journal,* September 5, 1967. Reprinted with permission of *The Wall Street Journal.*

The surprisal value of information is an important aspect of its utility. Management generally does not like to be surprised; but this is not a fixed rule, and the notion is developed that managers can steer themselves toward or away from surprise, each direction having advantages and disadvantages. The rate at which information is generated has been changing, and this affects the frequency with which surprise can occur. Properly organized groups (with varying combinations of specialized and generalized information functions) can handle high throughput rates, but group organization cannot always cope with the rate at which surprises occur in a system. Consequently, information crises are examined, and the "domino" effect, which can be very destructive, is explored.

Knowledge is a term frequently associated with information. The difference between the two terms is fully developed in an article written by Kenneth Boulding. Boulding shows that the rate at which knowledge is being produced is so great that society will not be able to continue to cope with it unless it learns how to develop specialists' languages that can be intercommunicated through generalists.

The text continues by examining the role of feedback, sensitivity analysis, and imputation. These functions are particularly characteristic of the generalist, and high surprisal is more common in such functions than in those the specialist normally uses. An important analogy is developed in terms of two chess-playing programs that operate in fundamentally different ways. One approach stresses the breadth of view, or the number of alternatives considered. The second system emphasizes the depth of view, or how far ahead in steps or time one looks. The latter system employs a more intensive degree of analysis; in other words, evaluations are more carefully made at each step. Based on the chess-playing analogy it is shown that an in-depth approach with strong evaluation heuristics provides advantages over a broadly based one. This conclusion amplifies the important distinction that is being made in information terms between specialist and generalist.

The arrangement of information networks is examined, focusing on the size of the system and the difference in the external and internal data loads that results. The hierarchical position of the communicator in the network also is examined. It becomes apparent that data must be merged into larger information classes as the communications level moves upward. Then the effect of centralization and decentralization on the information network patterns is discussed. The computer affects the amount of centralization or decentralization that will provide an optimal configuration.

The design of information systems and their controls must focus on the difference between physical information transfer and behavioral communication. An even more important distinction exists between perception and understanding. Inertial effects in information systems delay perception and block understanding. However, since inertia is vulnerable to selective perturbations, managers can encourage understanding by "rocking the boat."

In the same vein, but in greater depth, a distinction is made between informed, informing, and information systems. This classification is useful because it highlights the fact that in different systems different kinds of questions should be asked to promote understanding. Similarly, an examination of internal and external systems, and the effects of varying communication loads, indicates that it is possible to determine, in a quantitative fashion, when it is advantageous to decentralize a system. Of course, only a few, tangible factors are considered in this relationship; so it is simply a way to begin such analysis.

Information often exists in the form of pseudo-events. These are fictitious information events aimed at creating the circumstances for the actual events to occur. The importance of pseudo-events in the managerial system is not to be overlooked, because they are widely used—although, significantly, no one likes to admit their existence. The concept of pseudo-events is then developed into a futures-events framework. By this term we mean that a plan is developed to bring about particular futures rather than simply to forecast them. A voting model is used to illustrate how pseudo-events can be utilized to control futures. For the voting model, two behavioral functions—called the bandwagon and underdog effects—are treated. But many other behavioral responses to pseudo-events can be shown to exist. Blind spots are considered as inertial factors that prohibit breaking through traditional modes of thinking. They are especially serious when perturbations that threaten the system are not perceived by the manager because he assumes that they represent the "normal" course of events.

Blind spots can be circumvented through lateral thinking or its equivalents. There follows a brief discussion of this nonlinear fashion of reasoning. In spite of even a serendipity effect, it is not unusual for a blind spot to exist that obfuscates the critical issues. The example of training for an air defense system emphasizes this fact. In a more general sense, disturbances of the impulse, step, and ramp types are introduced to facilitate our understanding of perturbations.

The topic of semiotics is introduced because it is essential to an understanding of communication. The underpinnings of the semiotic viewpoint include the structural form of information, its semantic form, and, finally, its pragmatic level. Using the notions of semiotics, we explore the most fundamental concepts of information transfer. An eleven-step information-transmission model is developed, and the variety of ways in which the model operates are treated. Noise is explained as erratic information that gets into the communication channel and disturbs transmissions. Structural and semantic noise usually develop, and steps must be taken if the manager hopes to clear his channels. In line with this reasoning, information theory is presented. Here, critical new terms—*entropy* and *redundancy*—are fully defined and examples of their use explained. The entropy concept provides management with a new way of considering the flows of information in its organization.

Once we understand the way managers utilize their information for communication, it becomes apparent that managers think about the stability of their systems in terms that parallel the entropy notion. The manager imputes greater entropy to large systems and those with greater planning horizons, and he acts accordingly. The Law of Requisite Variety explains the manager's plans, policies, and decisions as a function of the amount of entropy that he perceives in the system. This law states that in order to control a situation, the manager must be able to utilize as much entropy (or variety) as exists in the system to be controlled. Various examples of how this law operates are developed. The entropy of planning horizons is treated in much the same way. It is shown that as the planning horizon is lengthened, the amount of entropy imputed to the system will increase; as a result, the manager must have available increasing amounts for investment in more elaborate control systems.

With such increases in complexity it becomes useful to explore the notion of information verification. Verification is a means of controlling noise that enters an information system. A verification model is fully developed. Characteristics of verifiers and an economic analysis of when verification seems feasible are presented.

Similarly important is the information audit, which is suggested as an essential part of organizational practice in the future. The notion of the directed relevancy of information—whereby information is fed to those who need it in the proper amounts at the right times—becomes a matter of accountability on the part of management. The information area is specifically entrusted to management, and management should recognize it as a domain in which the special purposes of selected individuals can be served only at the organization's expense, severely damaging management's credibility.

EXERCISES

1. What special characteristics must information have for it to be a reasonable substitute for monetary currency? How can information (as a form of currency) be designed so that its theft can be prevented? Is it possible to expedite the transfer of funds by viewing information as a form of currency? How does a dollar sent through the mail in check form compare with a dollar transmitted by teletype between computer systems?

2. Comment on the fact that the value of information increases as it is less able to be shared among members of a group. Explain how an organizational advantage accrues to individuals who are able to find so-called information keystones without which all the remaining published information can be interpreted only as noise.

3. What is meant by the statement that management can either try to avoid surprisal situations or steer directly into them? Discuss the effects of each approach and the managerial attitudes that are likely to be involved. Why may a manager who dislikes situations that occur with low frequency not be able to evaluate new product opportunities? Is it advisable for an organization to have executives who enjoy surprisal situations?

4. How does the increased rate of information generation and throughput affect the occurrence of surprisal events? Does the rate of forgetting have anything to do with these effects? In what sense are groups more able than individuals to handle high rates of information throughput? In what ways are communication satellites likely to affect information surprisal rates? Discuss the costs and benefits of the new surprisal levels that the satellite system will create.

5. The surprisal quality of an information crisis has been related to a "domino" effect. What relationships does this "domino" model suggest? Can an information system designed to handle peak periods be justified for its ability to avoid crises since it leaves substantial amounts of unused capacity at other times? Why is it that a relationship such as $VT = K$—the period for transactions (T) times the velocity of transactions (V) is equal to a constant (K) —might mitigate the advantages of reducing the hours for conducting transactions on the stock market? Does this kind of model have any further application?

6. With respect to the various hierarchical levels of management, comment on the importance of information investments that provide (a) breadth of view, (b) depth of view, and (c) a higher degree of analysis for evaluation. Be sure to relate these to management performance.

7. Discuss the significance and applicability of each of these generalized principles:

  a. For new systems, the external data load increases at a faster rate than the internal data load.
  b. For established systems, the external data load grows at a slower rate than the internal data load.
  c. The time that the manager spends communicating increases more rapidly as he rises in the organizational hierarchy, so

he adopts information policies that can bring his information load under control.
d. Without reduction principles, the internal information network of a growing organization loses coherence.
e. As information is transferred upward in the managerial hierarchy, the character of the information becomes increasingly generalized.
f. The exponential growth of the organization's internal information load can be brought under control by decentralizing the total information system into autonomous subunits.

8. Discuss the advantages of following a policy whereby a small percentage of employees are regularly reassigned to new projects before the original project assignment is completed. Note that the probability of anyone being affected by such a policy has to be very small in order to maintain surprisal at each change. This situation should be clearly distinguished from that in which there is high expectation for changes that are well known and about equally likely to occur.

9. A system consists of 220 individuals and a plan has been developed to decentralize this group by splitting it into two equal parts. How would the number of potential information links under centralization compare to the number under the decentralized plan? Relate this analysis to the difference between the external and internal information loads that are likely to arise under both configurations.

10. In discussing blind spots (which are, in effect, circumstances and events that resist the perceptive mechanisms of managers), we singled out perturbations as being particularly difficult to spot. Using the terminology of Arthur Porter, we recognize that an anti-environment is desirable as a means of breaking down inertial barriers to perception. Explain this point. Professor Porter states that the computer is still "anti-environmental" but that it is becoming part of the environment. Explain what Professor Porter means and give some examples of other potential anti-environments that exist. How does lateral thinking, as developed by De Bono, influence the use of anti-environments?

11. What is meant by the linear processing of information? Is such linear thinking always undesirable? Explain your answer. How would a lateral thinker solve the following nine-point problem?

Problem: To cover all nine dots without lifting your pencil; no more than four connecting line segments are permitted.

• • •

• • •

• • •

12. Negative serendipity is defined as an unexpected occurrence that produces awareness of a difficulty in the system's performance that would not otherwise have been known. It is stated that incorrect remedial action may be taken if an attempt is not made to locate the time at which the difficulty originated. Toward this end three types of disturbance are discussed—impulse, step, and ramp changes in the information pattern. Discuss these statements, giving some examples of how such disturbances might occur and what should be done about them.

13. Big and Little sat on a fence. Little was the son of Big, but Big was not the father of Little. How can this be explained? This situation is often used to illustrate a problem in information transfer. Why do you think it is used? Relate your answer to the semiotic classification. Give examples of communications that are faulty at the structural level, at the semantic level, and at the pragmatic level.

14. When noise enters a channel between the encode and decode operations, the resulting message is not isomorphic to the sender's intentions. What steps can be taken to remove or override the noise problem? How do such problems of noise affect the communications of managers? Can noise enter the system at any other place in the eleven-step model that is used in the text to describe the transmission of information from sender's purpose to the evaluation and feedback function? Why is it that the isomorphic transformation from sender to receiver must be found if communication is to occur?

15. The following sequence of orders for three different items has been recorded by management:

		Months:					
		1,2	3,4	5,6	7,8	9,10	11,12
Item:	A54	650	402	355	531	654	327
	A38	215	183	165	104	98	213
	C12	117	208	365	495	572	613

Using information-theory measures, describe some of the characteristics of these demand patterns that might be relevant for the objectives of management. Are there any other forms of analysis that you might use to provide additional insight? (Note: Treat demand classes, such as 600–699, as if they were a transmission symbol, and note the sequential order of such symbols.)

16. Discuss the inferences managers are likely to make about the systems with which they must deal based on their knowledge of the entropy properties of the following situations:

    a. A technologically new product is to be marketed nationally.
    b. A plant is to be constructed overseas to manufacture a product that was formerly imported to that country.
    c. The common-stock portfolio of a company is to be doubled.

17. Explain the Law of Requisite Variety and illustrate how it applies to some specific managerial considerations of control. In particular, discuss the situation of the inexperienced manager who, because he is part of a system, imputes less stability to it than it probably has. Would it be advisable for an inexperienced manager to impute more stability than the system probably has? Consider, in these terms, the effect of extending the planning horizon.

18. Discuss the kinds of noise that can affect an information system and describe the use of verification procedures to help alleviate the difficulties that might arise. What is meant by an independent verifier? Is this the best form of verification available? What are the advantages and disadvantages of having the operator self-verify— that is, check on his own work? (Note: Since self-verification violates the independence principle for verifiers, it is likely to produce a strong positive correlation of errors.) What arrangement might yield a strong negative correlation of errors? Would the manager prefer this negative correlation?

19. Why is it said that the use of information audits is becoming inescapable? In the process of answering this question explain how such audits might be conducted and what they have to do with the notion of the directed relevancy of information.

Part V

ORGANIZING

The Framework of Managing

MODEL-BUILDING AND MODEL USE

DECISION-MAKING

PLANNING

CONTROLLING

PART V
ORGANIZING

Organizing the structure of information flows for the
management process includes consideration of
decision-making, planning, policy-making, and
controlling. Organization determines the extent
to which groups of individuals can perform
such functions successfully. Aggregation of individuals
and machines into groups and the interaction of many
subsystems of groups do not lend themselves to a
static concept of organization. On the contrary,
they emphasize the fact that the character
and quality of an organization exist in its
ability to change and evolve rather than
remain in a prescribed form.

Organizing can be done formally, with charts and with job descriptions explored down to the smallest detail. Or organizing can be done informally, with an unspecified flux of relations, unstructured communications, and an unspoken multiplicity of purposes. In either case, organizing effort begins by interlinking components, by hooking parts up to one another with the purpose of realizing a *new* beneficial effect. Organization is living proof of a whole that is greater than the sum of its parts. We call this *synergy,* and it can be contrasted with *antagony* (which is derived from the word "antagonism," the opposite of synergism). We could also call the organization a *gestalt.* In any case, it is made up of components (man, machine, energy, materials, time, and so on) that enter into a voluntary constellation.

We usually think of organizations as being composed of people only, but this may be too small a view. We usually think of organizations as *being* and *existing,* much like a snapshot, but we should think of them instead as evolving, much like a movie. The quality of an organization may well reside in its changes rather than in what it is at any one time.

Management process is composed of decision-making, planning, policy-making, and controlling. Organization underlies the ability to perform such functions. The figure below shows the general lines of what must be done—but it does not show the principles for organizing effectively. Yet such principles and some theory do exist.

The basic ingredients of organization theory require consideration of the problems of aggregating components into subsystems and

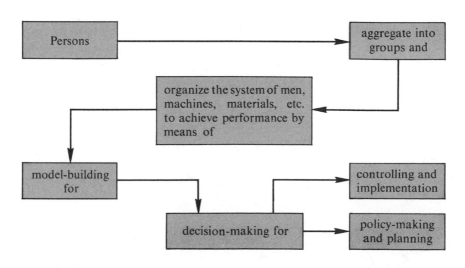

subsystems into larger systems. Such aggregation is treated in Chapter 13, where we deal with the inherent and dynamic structure of organizations. We have already spent considerable time with the circulatory system of organizations—that is, the information system. Now we must consider the components that get aggregated. Machines are supposed to be understood under the rubric of technology. But this is not entirely true, and so we shall address the question of organizing machines. Our main concern, however, will be with the human behavior that is the dynamic flux of organizational structure.

Our attention to human behavior will reflect some quantitative methods, but they will be few in comparison to those assorted principles of wisdom concerning human behavior that represent the present state of the art. We cannot quantify what is only barely understood. The essence of the problem is human behavior; it is the one most important behavior in any management system. Fortunately, by the time we are adults, each of us knows something about dealing with other people, to engage their friendship, obtain their trust, and to secure their cooperation in an undertaking of mutual interest. So we do not "start from scratch" in our discussion, but we must be equally careful to take nothing for granted. What may seem to be the case, because it is accepted and it is done, could turn out to be an erroneous position. For example, we could say that all people like to be treated well and point out that if this principle is followed, a big forward step will have been taken in providing suitable organization. But we must ask ourselves whether this principle stands up as a theory. Does the point exist as an inherent part of human make-up, or does it characterize a culture that is here and now, or even a culture that used to be? Accordingly, in Chapter 14 we shall discuss the individual, then individuals aggregating into the group, and then, as best we can, the aggregation of groups into the organization.

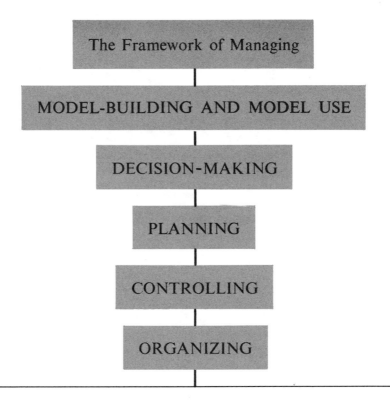

The Framework of Managing

MODEL-BUILDING AND MODEL USE

DECISION-MAKING

PLANNING

CONTROLLING

ORGANIZING

Chapter 13
The Organization of Simple Systems and Aggregations

The consideration of larger systems, composed of increasing numbers of aggregated units, is becoming essential. The organization of aggregated subsystems holds the key to understanding management's need to control greater amounts of entropy. Aggregations develop from the association of the most elemental input-output units, each of which has its own trajectory, repertory, and calendar. High-order aggregation systems exhibit queuing-model attributes. Trajectory analysis of units that interrelate at different levels provides information essential for management to understand the organizational properties of its budget-control and profit centers, as well as its approach to cost-effectiveness and cost-benefit analyses.

Chapter 13

THE ORGANIZATION
OF SIMPLE SYSTEMS
AND AGGREGATIONS

"To understand a complex thing you must take it apart systematically."[1]

THE FORCES FOR LARGER SYSTEMS

The mid-1800's through the early 1900's were years that emphasized the analysis, design, and control of *little* (low entropy) systems. It was a time of great invention. New technology was harnessed at an incredible rate. The telephone (patented 1876), the saftey pin (patented 1849), the radio (patented by many people, about 1895–1905), the vacuum tube (patented 1907), and nylon (publicly announced in 1938) are all examples of the work of individuals. But increasingly great expenditures were required to underwrite inventors (nylon, for example, required over a million dollars of investment), and corporate support became essential.

The system required to induce technological change and support the growth of markets was expanding rapidly. Small systems became less and less tenable. Marketing, distribution, and production were found to provide superior economic results as their scale was enlarged. There was increasing use of mass communication, mass

---

[1] Hans Selye, *The Stress of Life* (New York: McGraw-Hill, 1967), p. 48.

production, and national distribution. These trends accelerated during the middle part of this century and will unquestionably continue to do so. Logistical problems during World War II, population growth, greater prosperity, the advent of the computer, faster media and more messages, all created a population whose information age (that is, the number of issues perceived and understood) was substantially greater than before. Figure 13–1 depicts this concept, not precisely, but in a generally descriptive way. If we define the size of the system in terms of its H measure, each individual, as a result of his increased information level at any given age, is equivalent to a larger system. The larger system has a higher H level, based on a larger number of states, N (i.e., $H_{max} = \log_2 N$), and on *less* pattern and ritual. The trend of society's values has been toward H_{max} and away from $H = \log_2 1 = 0$. Product life is shorter, fads occur more often and dissipate more rapidly, styles change abruptly and continually.

Figure 13–1   **Increase in the Information Age of an Average Individual**

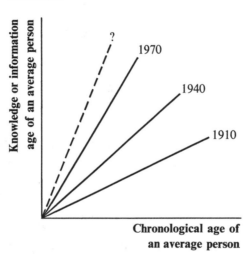

The Entropy of Planning Horizons, Supply and Demand

At the same time, and perhaps in compensation, the social planning horizon of the individual seems to have become shorter, tending to lower the H level. For example, high-entropy cathedrals like Notre Dame and Chartres cannot be built any more, not only because of the economic issues of cost and substitute technologies, but because they require too long a planning horizon. But the shorter planning horizon of the individual tends, in its turn, to produce a further decrease in ritual and thereby a countervailing increase in H. The result of these forces is, in fact, a larger systems H. The increasing population produces a growth in total entropy for the system. The effect of a shorter planning horizon appears to be more than compensated for by the instability that arises when individuals do not plan far ahead.

Because of greater affluence, the individual can display his own personal increase in entropy by purchasing many things. In economic terms, the increased demand functions of many individuals become the *aggregate demand that is experienced as pressure on the suppliers' ability* to match that entropy level. Population growth, increased affluence, less social stability, more information, all interact to increase markedly the entropy of the aggregate choice or demand system. An effective consumer organization would decrease the entropy of the total demand system, but none has arisen.

Now let us consider the entropy or variety of supply. The number of producing organizations might have expanded to match the consumers' total demand for variety, each organization maintaining about the same level of production. Newly formed organizations would enter the marketplace and introduce new products just as fast as demand for them grew. Other new companies might share in the growth of existing product markets in line with population changes. We know that this is *not* what is happening. Instead, existing organizations are growing larger, increasing the size of their productive output and the variety of their product lines. In fact, there are evident pressures to have *fewer* organizations that increase their output capacity to match the circumstances. As a result, the entropy per company is that of a large system, and there is continual economic and behavioral pressure for it to grow even larger.

INPUT-OUTPUT MODULES OF DECISION

The larger the organization, the more severely it must control its internal entropy. If many small organizations had evolved to meet the consumers' demands, the extent of this control problem would not have been excessive. As we have seen, an information system experiences transactions according to $N(N-1)$. The large system must take organizational measures to keep this effect in check.[2] Policy is one of the most effective means for reducing entropy. But organizational structure imposes fundamental constraints on

---

[2] See Z. S. Zannetos, "On the Theory of Divisional Structures: Some Aspects of Centralization and Decentralization of Control and Decision Making," *Management Science,* Vol. 12, No. 4 (December 1965), pp. B49–68. Zannetos shows that the growth of communication channels is at least proportional to the square of the organization's size. Also, in this text, see pp. 481–83.

policy design. The use of centralized, large-system policy as compared to decentralized, smaller-system policies is as much an outgrowth of organizational design as a cause of it. To understand fundamental organizational relations, it is reasonable to begin with small-systems components, exploring their behavior before we begin to aggregate them into larger systems.

Decision models were developed in Part II to provide a basic structure for analysis that could be used throughout this text. Now, however, we are dealing with *aggregation,* starting with the smallest systems and moving to the largest. So the question arises: Does the decision model carry segmentation of the management function to the smallest useful size? And the answer is no. There is a smaller basic organizational unit.

A *microview* of any decision model requires specification of the *transformation function* required to convert strategic and environmental inputs into outcomes or results—that is, an input-output model of the type shown in Figure 13–2. There are as many such input-output models as there arc cells in the

Figure 13–2   Representation of an I/T/O

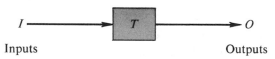

$I \longrightarrow T \longrightarrow O$

Inputs   Outputs

decision matrix. The T inside the box represents the system's *transformation process,* which represents a physical or mental change of inputs into outputs. The outcome can result, for example, from a chemical transformation, a mechanical deformation process, or a behavior or attitude change. Previously, we have written such transformation relations in mathematical form, as $O = f(I)$. The symbol for function, f, is equivalent to that of the transformation, T. The former tends to accent the abstract qualities of mathematical relations, while the latter focuses our attention on process and its attendant causality. Figure 13–3 is a better representation of the individual outcome cells of the decision matrix, because it differentiates between controllable and uncontrollable variable inputs. We can also include the competitors in our input-output diagram of the cell construction of the decision process, as shown in Figure 13–4.

The input-output model stresses the most basic elements of the process, emphasizing the transformation, T. Each individual or machine can be represented as a dynamic input-output system where every element, including T, can change over time. Groups of individuals and machines can also be aggregated and organized within the transformation box. Larger aggregations to department and division size raise questions about the extent to which indi-

Figure 13–3   **I/O Representation of the *ij* Cell of a Decision Matrix**

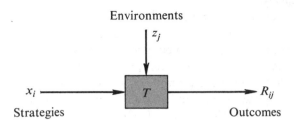

viduals and groups should communicate with each other and rely on each other for interrelated decisions and actions. Such questions about the degree of centralization, management must answer, even if by default. Further, the results of varying inputs, changing the transformations, and obtaining differing outputs can be predicted and analyzed with this model of *process* in mind. It is important to note, however, that input-output models do *not* have the *normative* properties of the decision matrix. They are strictly *descriptive* models, the building blocks of the decision matrix.

If the inputs, the process, or both are unknown, often much can still be said about the outputs. Different kinds of conjecture are involved. Sometimes outcomes can be predicted from parallel experiences with the process and/or the inputs. Often an exact and logical mathematical representation (such as mass × gravitational acceleration = weight) is available. Other approaches for predicting outcomes include guesses, reasoned estimations, and laboratory-type experiments. And there are cases where the outputs can be observed although nothing else is known, so conjecture can be used to describe what the inputs and the process must be. Since the dynamic view of organization is based on the recognition that organization is composed of interacting input-

Figure 13–4   **I/O Representation of the *ijk* Cell of a Decision Matrix**

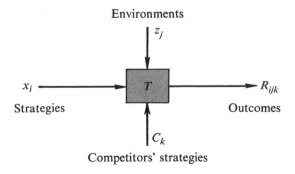

output systems, it can be seen that organizational study is possible through logical, abstract means.

When we aggregate I/O's to form decision matrices, it is not unusual for different T's to apply to different parts of a matrix. For cells of a given T, each outcome entry stands for a particular configuration of the inputs to the model. If there are i strategies and j states of nature, then the decision matrix requires $(i \times j)$ input-output calculations, estimates, or experiments. The amount of work required to complete the matrix increases as the number of relevant T's grows. Often, once the model for a given T is built, the values of cells can be determined rapidly simply by solving the model for the specific ij circumstances. Extrapolation and interpolation are also speedily accomplished. Clearly, the input-output model is a smaller unit to consider than the decision matrix and can provide management with a great deal of additional insight.

The Nature of Transformations

Process models are basic to all manufacturing industry and to many other activities as well. Transportation represents spatial transformations. Communication is an information-transformation process. Implementation is a theory-to-practice transformation, part of model-building, which (as explained in Chapter 3) is a multistep transformation process. Mining is a transformation process, and so are learning, forgetting, and reacting. Many other personal, group, and organizational behaviors qualify as transformations.

The impact of advertising on the consumer's mind is a legitimate example of an input-output transformation in which the consumer's mind is said to be a *black box*. Some transformation processes are fully transparent, others partly opaque. The term "black box" is used here to describe a transformation process that cannot be observed or understood.[3] Since individual behavior is regarded (with good reason) as the transformations of a black box, the importance of this kind of system for managerial understanding of the organizing function can hardly be overestimated, so let us consider the effects of a black box in the input-output system.

Assume that plugs for various inputs can be attached to the box and that outputs can be measured on dials and other performance-measuring instru-

---

[3] "Black box" is a term used by electrical engineers to indicate that the circuitry within the box (system) is unknown. Exactly how this term was coined is also unknown. According to Ross Ashby, ". . . the original Black Box was that said by the Duke of Monmouth (who rebelled against James II) to contain the proofs of his legitimacy, which was suspect. The box, although always on the point of appearing, was always somewhere else, so it became legendary for that whose contents are quite unknown and unknowable." (Van Court Hare, Jr., *Systems Analysis: A Diagnostic Approach* [New York: Harcourt Brace Jovanovich, 1967], p. 30 *n*.)

ments. Based on the settings of the inputs and the readings of the outputs (following a period of probing experimentation), prediction of expected outputs for untried inputs can presumably begin to be made. Sometimes the nature of the internal circuitry might be guessed at or transformation characteristics within the box inferred and thereby rendered no longer totally unknown. Usually, a high degree of ingenuity is required to study the black box systematically in this way. The job of the scientist is readily seen as just such probing of the unknown. The design of experiments in both the technical and statistical sense is crucial to what can be learned, and Type I and Type II errors play a central role. A fundamental approach exists: namely, the study of stimulus-response patterns by means of *trajectory analysis*. We will examine this shortly.

Many different forms of transformation can be described. The complexity of transformation gets richer as the extent of included history in the trajectory increases. But we shall list three fundamental types of Markovian (prior-state dependent) transformations,[4] and, for convenience, depict them in Figure 13–5. There is, first, the one-one transformation, which is an isomorphic, deterministic transform. Second, there is the transformation of the one-many type, which, although it is isomorphic, can produce the appearance of stochastic properties. Third, there is the many-one transform, which is homomorphic and deterministic. The reason that the many-one transform is homomorphic, we can recall, is that the initial classifications (*a* and *c*) are subsumed by a

Figure 13–5   Three Basic Markovian Transformations

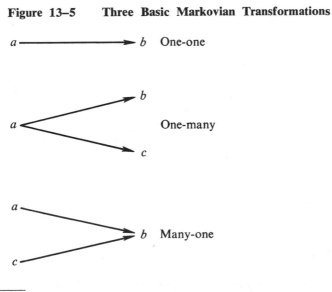

---

[4] Previously described on pp. 446–48.

single class (called *b*) after transformation. In just that way, many individuals agree to give up to the group, *b*, part of their identity (which the one-one transform, *a* to *a*, preserves). Consider an individual at *a*. If he is reporting upward to his superior, then the one-many configuration creates the problem of having two bosses, *b* and *c*. But the many-one arrangement makes complete sense to him. The organizational hierarchy is made up of many-one transforms going from the bottom up, and one-many transforms going from the top down. The sense of direction for transforms is critical in interpreting their organizational function.

Matrix form lends itself to presenting these organizational transformation relations, which we have previously shown (pp. 40–41), and network diagrams such as K_I and K_{II} in Figure 13–6 can add further clarity. Another way

Figure 13–6   Matrix and Network Representation of System Flows

		a	b	c
	a	0	1	0
M_I:	b	0	0	1
	c	1	0	0

		a	b	c
	a	0	1	1
M_{II}:	b	1	0	1
	c	0	1	0

K_I: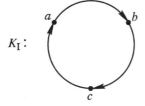

K_{II}: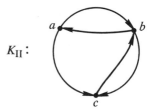

of depicting these same relations is in terms of operands and their transforms, given that a particular operator (such as T_a) is the effective process. Thus, we have the *closed* transform systems T_I and T_{II}.

Operator: T_I $\left| \begin{array}{ccc} a & b & c \\ b & c & a \end{array} \right.$ $\begin{array}{l} a \ldots \text{Operand} \\ b \ldots \text{Transform} \end{array}$

and

Operator: T_{II} $\left| \begin{array}{cccc} a & a & b & b \\ b & c & a & c \end{array} \right.$ $\begin{array}{l} c \ldots \text{Operand} \\ b \ldots \text{Transform} \end{array}$

Closed means that all states are *reachable* by some path after a given number of steps. Most organizations are designed to be *closed;* but the number of steps required may be very great indeed, and the effort required to reach all states can be so great as to render the organization *open* for all intents and purposes.

The lack of one-one relations is apparent in different ways in the representational forms of M_{II}, K_{II}, and T_{II}. The matrix M_{II} has more than a single one in the two rows a and b (these are one-manys), and more than a single one in the two columns b and c (these are many-ones). The network K_{II} is not one-one; the visual evidence requires no explanation. As for T_{II}, the same operand has several different transforms, which are one-many transformations. So, clearly, the closure of a system is not dependent on all transforms being one-one. It is dependent on there being a pattern of transformation that permits all states to be reached from any other state in the organization. When a sequence is *open*, we expect to be blocked from ultimate access to certain former states. Thus, we may never be able to get back to a. The similarity to our definition of *planning* (p. 309) is not coincidental. *Open* transformations can proceed in their development of states either according to some pattern, such as in T_{III}, or to unknown states, as in T_{IV}.

$$T_{III} \downarrow \begin{array}{ccccccccc} 1 & 3 & 5 & 7 & 9 & 11 & 13 & 15 & 17\ldots \\ 3 & 5 & 7 & 9 & 11 & 13 & 15 & 17 & 19\ldots \end{array}$$

and

$$T_{IV} \downarrow \begin{array}{ccccccc} 3 & 7 & 8 & 2 & 8 & 2 & 0\ldots \\ 7 & 4 & 6 & 6 & 7 & 4 & 7\ldots \end{array}$$

Being able to "read" patterns is the key to understanding the organization of any system.

The discovery of patterns is a complex matter requiring creative insights and unblocked perceptive abilities—perhaps "lateral thinking," referred to in Chapter 12 (pp. 495–96). Type II errors can be made in abundance, since spurious patterns are *bound to exist*. Even with sufficient data, erroneous identifications are easy enough to come by. For example, anyone finding a pattern in T_{IV} should be advised that the numbers were chosen from a table of random numbers. Of course, randomness has a distinctive quality, and one is led to conjecture that certain random art works might have achieved distinction because of their "true" randomness, which is not easily achieved. The almost classic joke about the man who gave up water to avoid getting drunk can be told in a transform table; it demonstrates beautifully the *illusory pattern*.[5]

$$T_V \downarrow \begin{array}{cccc} \text{Gin} + H_2O & \text{Rye} + H_2O & \text{Vodka} + H_2O & \text{Scotch} + H_2O \\ \text{Drunk} & \text{Drunk} & \text{Drunk} & \text{Drunk} \end{array}$$

So the man gave up water.

---

[5] See Mill's Canons, pp. 45–46.

The kinds of transformation (such as who reports to whom, seasonal sales volumes, memoranda flow patterns in the research and development lab, etc.) will determine what *can* be learned about an organization from the patterns found in its transformations. Clearly, however, there is a lot of such information available for each organization, and much that can be learned by thinking in these terms. On the other hand, if the transformed operand states are measures of who follows whom on the bowling team, this information probably will be so far removed from immediate interpretation as to render it worthless for everyone except perhaps the company psychiatrist.

The Nature of Trajectories

The dynamics of organizational relations for each type of information can be represented as a trajectory. Various trajectories can then be related to each other. The models we have developed can be used for trajectory analysis in many *different ways*:

1. Operands and transforms can be used to describe *input* information alone. For example, let the *input* change following the pattern of T_1: *a* to *b*, *b* to *c*, *c* to *a*. The *trajectory* for this change is shown in Figure 13–7.

Figure 13–7

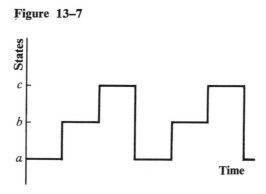

2. A trajectory composed of operands and transforms can also be used to represent only the *outputs*. For example, assume that the output is observed to change as in T_1. The same figure as above applies for this trajectory, but in this second case it is based on observation of the output instead of measurement of the performance of the input.

3. An input-output system can be described in this same way. Let the states of the operand row be inputs and the states of the transform row be outputs. Then we can derive two trajectories, that of the input and that of the output,

Figure 13–8

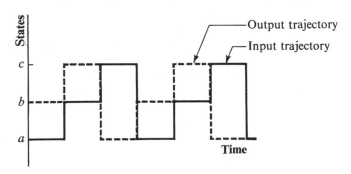

which can be related to each other. The operand (input) trajectory would be tracked as *abca* . . . , and the transform (output) trajectory would be "read" in the same way, but offset by one step, as shown in Figure 13–8.

4. If the condition of the process, *T*, is known, a trajectory can be developed to describe its behavior in terms of its own states.

Sometimes, only the operand row can be observed. At other times, only the transform row can be tracked. Many combinations of inputs, outputs, and process trajectories can exist and be used for analysis of organizational behavior. All temporal measures have a trajectory.

The organization is perceived and understood in these terms. But another factor of importance must be noted. Evolution, morphology, change—call it what you will—can be timed either by *clock* or by *sequence*. A clock gives us temporal *distance* between events, whereas sequence is simply an ordinal precedence relation. Much information about the organization comes to the manager with a sequence trajectory rather than a true sense of time. A dynamic view of organizational change is available through sequence, but clock measures convey more information. Of course, either is an improvement over the static view, which has neither sequence nor time and which presently dominates much organizational thinking. The use of trajectory analysis for each individual[6] and machine in an organized system represents a positive diagnostic step, much as electrocardiograms and electroencephalograms greatly aid medical diagnostics. And, in addition to diagnosis, the trajectory is a powerful designer's tool; it is the essence of simulation's appeal. The manager who thinks in terms of trajectories is capturing much more of the organizational realities than the manager who thinks in terms of static organization charts and related policies.

---

[6] No single trajectory dimension perfectly describes an individual, but many dimensions can be interrelated.

TRAJECTORY ANALYSIS

A *scenario* is a trajectory of possible, logically connected future events. It deals with the evolution of environments or uncontrollable variables. Controllable variables, when placed in a time order, have their own trajectories, which we have called policies and plans. The controllable-variable trajectories, inter-acting with the uncontrollable-variable trajectories (including the competitors' trajectories), produce the output trajectories of performance and results. The balance sheet reflects limited trajectory information, but when used in conjunction with the profit and loss statement, yields a trajectory that does a reasonable job of informing the manager. The typical organization chart has no trajectory properties whatever. It is surprising to find that so many basic management techniques for presenting information are trajectoryless and therefore static. By thinking in terms of trajectories, we can alter static decision models so that they take on dynamic characteristics, cell by cell. Then, aggregating across all cells of a dynamic decision model, we can begin to perceive the real complexity of the problems that the organization faces.

Interest in trajectories is recent. To a large extent, the new field of cybernetics has been responsible for the emphasis on trajectory analysis. In cybernetics, change is central.[7] The trajectory is composed of the system's *repertory* and a clock or sequence counter. The repertory consists of the various states to which the system can shift over time. We have already pointed to scenario analysis as a trajectory method; we can now extend that concept to *dialectic* argument.[8] Different organizational scenarios can be proposed and examined

---

[7] "The most fundamental concept in cybernetics is that of 'difference,' either that two things are recognisably different or that one thing has changed with time." (W. Ross Ashby, *An Introduction to Cybernetics* [New York: Wiley, 1956], p. 9.) The field of cybernetics has been defined in a variety of ways. Norbert Wiener used the word cybernetics to describe a theory of control. He derived it from the Greek word for "steersman" (κυβερνήτης). Control and feedback are so intimately related that many use the term cybernetics in the sense of a theory of feedback systems. Information theory plays such an important role in control analysis that the word cybernetics is often taken as being synonymous with it. André Ampère in 1834 used the word *cybernétique* to talk about the science of government control. And in recent years Soviet managers have been using the term cybernetics to stand for the control of economic planning. (See, for example, Ivan M. Siroyezhin, "Man-Machine Systems in the U.S.S.R.," *Management Science*, Vol. 15, No. 2 [October 1968], pp. B1–10.) We believe, as do Ashby and others (see his Chapter 1), that the word applies to control of large systems and is, therefore, one of the fundamentals of organization theory (but not the only fundamental, since human behavior is not readily translated into cybernetic terms).

[8] See Richard O. Mason, "A Dialectical Approach to Strategic Planning," *Management Science,* Vol. 15, No. 8 (April 1969), pp. B403–14. In this article, Mason describes the use of the dialectic approach and its advantages in an actual company situation.

in the dialectic framework. Dialectic procedure depends on the construction of an argument between two opposing positions (or scenarios). In other words, the system is organized to develop a challenger to any policy or any plan for testing that policy's acceptability. The notion of studying "difference" is used, and comparison is the basis for choice. Either different inputs are tested, or T is varied, or both are altered. The output trajectories of the contenders are contrasted. Complex aggregations can be examined in this way.

Let us turn, therefore, to the methods of trajectory analysis. Consider an output trajectory of the form *aaccbdbacb*. . . . Using a *cross-sectional data* approach, we lose the sequence information and conclude that based on our information, *a, b,* and *c* each appear 30 percent of the time, on the average, and that *d* appears about 10 percent of the time. Such judgment is based on the assumption of relative *stability* for the input-output system. That assumption would have to be carefully checked out, or our further analysis of the trajectory would provide meaningless results. Assuming stability, we can obtain the H measure $(H = -(3) \frac{3}{10} \log_2 \frac{3}{10} - \frac{1}{10} \log_2 \frac{1}{10} = 1.896)$ and the R measure $(R = 1 - 1.896/\log_2 4 = .052)$, as we previously did. Our results indicate very little organization in this system. Using the cross-sectional approach offers no insights into patterns in this situation. But trajectories lend themselves to *time-series* analysis, and we may be able to do better by raising the information level of the analysis in this way.

The trajectory information is recorded by a digram matrix (i.e., a two-step format—thus, *a* starts the trajectory, *a* follows *a*, *c* follows *a*, *c* follows *c*, etc.).[9] This is shown in Table 13–1. (Note: we have assumed that the cycle repeats

Table 13–1

	→	Output or second: a	b	c	d
Input	a	1	0	2	0
or	b	2	0	0	1
first:	c	0	2	1	0
	d	0	1	0	0

and have therefore used *b* goes to *a* for the last transition.) It is easy to change this matrix of frequencies into a transition-probability matrix, where each row sums to one (See Table 13–2). The rows are now equivalent to conditional probability statements. In other words, on the condition that the first state is *a*,

---

[9] A *digram* is any pair of adjacent states of a trajectory; the digram transition matrix presents the probabilities, given a specific initial state, of all possible succeeding states.

Table 13–2

	Output or second:				
→	a	b	c	d	Row sum
Input a	$\frac{1}{3}$	0	$\frac{2}{3}$	0	1.00
or b	$\frac{2}{3}$	0	0	$\frac{1}{3}$	1.00
first: c	0	$\frac{2}{3}$	$\frac{1}{3}$	0	1.00
d	0	1	0	0	1.00

the probability that the next state will be d is 0, c is $\frac{2}{3}$, and so on. We should observe the strong similarity to the Bayesian test matrix in Chapter 6 (p. 226). The relationship is an important one because it ties together so many different factors that underlie the concepts of the organization of information, including Bayesian estimation, the value of information, Type I and Type II errors, information verification, and so forth. These dynamic elements of organization are operational ways of talking about authority, responsibility, coordination, and so forth.

To analyze the entropy of the matrix we obtain the average entropy per state—that is, for each row.

$$H(\text{row } a) = -\tfrac{1}{3}\log_2\tfrac{1}{3} - \tfrac{2}{3}\log_2\tfrac{2}{3} = .918$$

$$H(\text{row } a) = H(\text{row } b) = H(\text{row } c) = .918$$

$$H(\text{row } d) = -1\log_2 1 = 0$$

This information cannot be used until we obtain a weighting for each row's contribution to the total system's entropy. We obtain this information in the section below.

Steady State Analysis

Measures of the expected probabilities of being in states a, b, c, or d are derived. This can be done in several ways, one of which is to multiply the rows and columns of the matrix in the following way. The new matrix entry O_{ij}' for the ith row and the jth column is obtained from the old matrix entries:

$$O_{ij}' = O_{i1} \cdot O_{1j} + O_{i2} \cdot O_{2j} + \ldots .$$

This multiplication is performed for all cells of the matrix. It is repeated until the *steady state* condition becomes evident by dint of the fact that the matrix hardly changes its values with multiplication thereafter.[10] The steady state represents an *average* for each of the system's states.

Another, more convenient, approach is strictly algebraic. We write the following set of equations.

$$a' = \tfrac{1}{3}a + \tfrac{2}{3}b + (0)c + (0)d \tag{1}$$
$$b' = (0)a + (0)b + \tfrac{2}{3}c + (1)d \tag{2}$$
$$c' = \tfrac{2}{3}a + (0)b + \tfrac{1}{3}c + (0)d \tag{3}$$
$$d' = (0)d + \tfrac{1}{3}b + (0)c + (0)d \tag{4}$$

Each equation states that the inputs from a, b, c, and d of the rows flow into the columns (called a', b', c', and d') in the proportions shown. Consequently, when $a = a'$, $b = b'$, $c = c'$, and $d = d'$, the flows will exactly balance, leaving the probabilities of the system's states unchanged—that is, steady state is reached. We also note that

$$a + b + c + d = 1 \tag{5}$$

Then, replacing a' with a, b' with b, and so on, in equations (1), (2), (3), and (4), we obtain

$$0 = -\tfrac{2}{3}a + \tfrac{2}{3}b \tag{6}$$
$$0 = \quad - (1)b + \tfrac{2}{3}c + (1)d \tag{7}$$
$$0 = +\tfrac{2}{3}a \quad - \tfrac{2}{3}c \tag{8}$$
$$0 = \quad + \tfrac{1}{3}b \quad - (1)d \tag{9}$$
$$1 = \quad a + \quad b + \quad c + \quad d \tag{10}$$

We have five equations, but with four unknowns only four equations are required. Equation (10) must be used so that the probabilities of a, b, c, and d sum to one. As a result we can use any three of the first four equations—(6), (7), (8), and (9)—with equation (10). We find that $a = b = c$ (equations (6) and (8)) and that $d = \tfrac{1}{3}b$ (equation (9)). Substituting these values into equation (10), we obtain

$$1 = b + b + b + \tfrac{1}{3}b = 3\tfrac{1}{3}b$$

So, $b = \tfrac{3}{10}$, $d = \tfrac{1}{10}$, and $a = \tfrac{3}{10}$, $c = \tfrac{3}{10}$. These are the same results that were obtained by the cross-sectional analysis *because* the actual complete cycle, *aaccbdbacb* . . . , was used to obtain the digram matrix of transition probabilities. Often the trajectory is not available but the transition probabilities can be estimated, in which case the method we have just described becomes

---

[10] Not all matrices will approach a steady state. For example, a matrix that will run through a cycle of values is called *periodic*. Knowledge of the types of matrix that exist can provide a great deal of insight concerning the organizational character of the system. The subject is, however, mathematically demanding and will not be treated here.

particularly useful. Had we used multiplication, the steady state matrix would eventually have taken on this form:

→	a	b	c	d
a	.3	.3	.3	.1
b	.3	.3	.3	.1
c	.3	.3	.3	.1
d	.3	.3	.3	.1

The number of iterations required for it to converge and what happens to the matrix during that process (oscillations of values, etc.) add to the analyst's information about the organizational properties of the system and the inter-relations of a, b, c, and d.

Entropy of the Trajectory

The expected probabilities of being in states a, b, c, and d, based on either a cross-sectional, frequency-count analysis or a matrix study of the steady state were .3, .3, .3, and .1, respectively. We can use the entropies of the rows and obtain an overall system average as follows:

$$\overline{H} = .3H_a + .3H_b + .3H_c + .1H_d = .3(.918)3 + .1(0) = .826$$

This represents a considerable decrease from the value previously derived through cross-sectional analysis only ($H = 1.896$). The maximum entropy value that the system could take on remains $-4(\frac{1}{4}\log_2\frac{1}{4}) = \log_24 = 2$. No row could exceed that value, and the average of the largest possible row values could not, therefore, be larger than 2. We observe that transition, time-series information has considerably increased the apparent organization of the system. The reason is that a sequence pattern was found, which helped to explain the system's behavior. It is not that the system itself is any more or less organized for our having discerned a relevant pattern. But our ability to cope with the organization has been considerably enhanced by our knowing about its pattern.

The redundancy measure becomes $R = 1 - \dfrac{.826}{2.000} = .587$, showing again that an important pattern has been found. Yet not all of the system's behavior is understood. That would be the case only if redundancy was equal to 1. Such a system would have no mystery; it would be perfectly predictable. A pattern that might yield superior H and R measures remains to be found. The decision to continue the search is a managerial function, and art and science blend in the quest. Perhaps a two-prior-state dependency would reveal greater organization (i.e., aa is followed by c, ac is followed by c, etc.). Strong patterns could emerge that reflect dependencies on, say, the sixth prior state. It is also possible that the definitions of the states could be changed to improve the understanding of the organizational behavior. For example, a', b', c', d', and e' might provide organization flow patterns that reflect more one-one transformations than a, b, c, and d.

Interrelated Trajectories

Psychology has developed and refined the concept of stimulus-response models. The test subject is brought, as much as possible, into a range of controlled circumstances and conditions. The idea is to isolate the subject as a black box system in a controlled environment in order to exclude the possibility of extraneous factors operating. Then a given set of inputs is administered, and the subject's outputs are observed.

Stimulus-response models are a special form of input-output analysis in which the transformation process is that of an organism rather than a machine. The distinction is an important one because it implies that the black box of a machine is fundamentally dissimilar to that of a living organism. Clearly, mechanistic and human behavior are different, and, for obvious reasons, more is known about the former than the latter. Therefore, a study of each begins with different expectations concerning the laws of transformation that apply. The T's of groups and organizations can also be set apart. Thus, in none of these cases is the black box really a total mystery. The fact is that a true black box does not exist because we can always begin to classify group and individual behavior of the organisms as against that of systems of machines. This becomes all the more apparent when we are dealing at the man/machine interface.

We observe that machine input-output analyses differ markedly from those of stimulus-response. The latter recognize the existence of motivation, association, conditioning, and the like, whereas present machine technology has not (yet) left the firmer ground of mechanical, chemical, and electrical cause and effect. It is, therefore, relatively easier to study machines even when the inputs to it and the outputs from it are man-related. Furthermore, machines are not really black boxes except for analytic convenience. With much further machine development, the lines of these distinctions might begin to blur. For the time being, however, it is only when men and machines are *aggregated* within a black box that a mixture of input-output and stimulus-response conditions results and raises the complexity of input-output analysis to that of the larger system.

If we relate the output that follows an input to that input, or the response that follows a stimulus to that stimulus, then we have the basis for an input-output or stimulus-response Markovian analysis. These are systems so organized that each output is solely dependent on the preceding input's state. If the output were affected by what the input had been, say, three or four periods before, then the Markovian condition would not exist, unless we could represent it through a transformation of terms. Often, non-Markovian systems can be transformed into Markovian ones by redefining variables (especially the use of cumulative variables, such as a continuous sum, which carry all prior history in the system with them) and by using ingenious transformations of system states. The reason we care, of course, is that our abilities for analyzing Markovian-type systems are particularly strong.

Previously, we studied a Markovian-type transition matrix and measured its entropy properties and its redundancy (pp. 549–52). In that situation, only one trajectory was involved. The prior state was simply the previous output of the trajectory. Many variants of Markovian organized systems exist. We shall list four basic types, recognizing that there are many non-Markovian forms that might be suitably transformed. Each model emphasizes the dynamic characteristics of a system's operations in terms that are highly generalizable. The fourth variant succeeds in *aggregating two systems' components* into the higher-order of a group organization.

Variant 1: Input-output or stimulus-response analysis, Figure 13–9A.

Order:

	1st	2nd	3rd	
T ↓	a	b	c	... Input or stimulus
	5	2	6	... Output or response

The transformation process is assumed to be a black box, *BB*.

Variant 2: Feedback analysis, Figure 13–9B.

Sequence:

	t_0	t_1	t_2	
T ↓	1	2	3	... Input
	2	3	4	... Output

Only the first input is assumed to be known—in this case 1 at t_0. Thereafter, each output is fed back and becomes at least part of the next input. In this example, the feedback alone is the next input.

Variant 3: Trajectory analysis where only the output of the system is observed and the remainder of the system is unknown, Figure 13–9C.

Pairs of adjacent outputs:

	1st	2nd	3rd	
T ↓	O_1	O_2	O_3	... Prior state (first)
	O_2	O_3	O_4	... Succeeding state (second)

The transformation process and the input trajectory are assumed to be unknown. We have previously analyzed such a system of digram transitions for a single trajectory, which could be production output, monitor input, and so on.

Figure 13–9

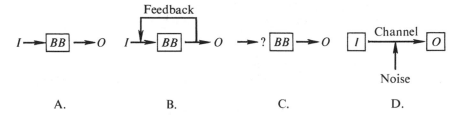

A.   B.   C.   D.

Variant 4: Transmitter to receiver, Figure 13–D.

	Symbol order:			
	1st	2nd	3rd	4th
T	1	2	3	4 . . . Symbol sent
	1	2	2	4 . . . Symbol received

In this example, because of channel noise, the third symbol sent, 3, is incorrectly received as 2. There is no apparent black box. The transformation process is the medium (channel), and it is understood. However, noise is an additional input to the system, and, characteristically, it is not perfectly predictable. It can be treated as the black box of a single input-output system.

With a minor alteration in our perspective of variant 4, we can consider the input, *I*, to be a component that is communicating with a second component, *O*. Both components could be either man or machine. We can now observe *O*'s output, *Q*, which is the resultant output of a two-component system's behavior (see Figure 13–10A). *O*'s behavior becomes the process, *T*, or the black box. In this way, we have begun to aggregate a number of individuals into an organization. Figure 13–10B attempts to show this by depicting a many-component aggregation.

Figure 13–10   Diagrams of Aggregation

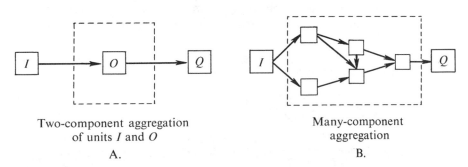

Two-component aggregation
of units *I* and *O*
A.

Many-component
aggregation
B.

SHARED INFORMATION IN A
TWO-COMPONENT AGGREGATION

One of the simplest ways to evaluate the structural relationship of two components is to find out what symbols they transfer (in the sense of variant 4 but usually based on two-way, or feedforward-feedback, communication), then how effective the transmission process is and how free of noise. Table 13–3 represents the kind of data that might be assembled, where A "talks" to B. Their language consists of the four symbols a, b, c, and d. The matrix records the number of each kind of communication sent by A to B over some given period of time and the way in which B received the message.

Table 13–3

		A (sends):				The number of symbols of each kind that B receives:
$\downarrow$		a	b	c	d	
B (receives):	a	20	5	5	0	30
	b	5	15	5	0	25
	c	0	5	10	0	15
	d	0	0	5	25	30
The number of symbols of each kind that A sends:		25	25	25	25	100

We observe that A sent 100 symbol messages, twenty-five of each kind. *Perfect* communication would have produced the number 25 in each diagonal cell. But, because of noise, B received, for example, only twenty of the a's without error. Five a's were misread as b's. The reader will note that the model we are discussing is framed in a way that has great relevance for verification procedures (see pp. 515–18) and also for Bayesian matrix analysis (see p. 227).

First, let us calculate the average entropy of each symbol that A sends (this is a measure derived from the bottom row of the matrix).

$$H(A) = -4\left(\frac{25}{100}\right) \log_2\left(\frac{25}{100}\right) = \log_2 4 = 2 \text{ bits}$$

Next, we can calculate the average entropy of each symbol that B receives (this measure is derived from the right-hand column of the matrix).

$$H(B) = -2\left(\frac{30}{100}\right)\log_2\left(\frac{30}{100}\right) - \left(\frac{25}{100}\right)\log_2\left(\frac{25}{100}\right) - \left(\frac{15}{100}\right)\log_2\left(\frac{15}{100}\right)$$
$$= 2(.3)(\log_2 100 - \log_2 30) + .25\log_2 4 + .15(\log_2 100 - \log_2 15)$$
$$= .6(6.644 - 4.907) + .25(2) + .15(6.644 - 3.907) = 1.953 \text{ bits}$$

Finally, we determine the average entropy of each symbol pair (sent and received) within the matrix.

$$H(A, B) = -\left(\frac{20}{100}\right)\log_2\left(\frac{20}{100}\right) - 6\left(\frac{5}{100}\right)\log_2\left(\frac{5}{100}\right) - \left(\frac{15}{100}\right)\log_2\left(\frac{15}{100}\right)$$
$$-\left(\frac{10}{100}\right)\log_2\left(\frac{10}{100}\right) - \left(\frac{25}{100}\right)\log_2\left(\frac{25}{100}\right) = 3.004 \text{ bits}$$

Figure 13–11 represents these quantities in a convenient way.

Figure 13–11

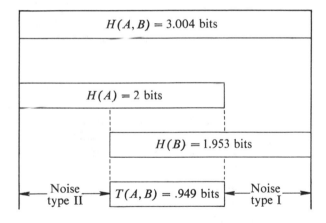

NOTE: Shared information is measured by $T(A,B)$; the remainder is noise of two types.

Since the average information transmitted per symbol state ($H(A) = 2$ bits) and the average information received ($H(B) = 1.953$ bits) are very close, it would seem at first glance that the performance of the two coupled components should be entirely satisfactory. Noise, it would be concluded, is not a problem. But this conclusion would not be supported by a study of the matrix. Our analytic model reveals that the average joint entropy, $H(A,B)$, of the total matrix is considerably larger than that of either the sender or receiver in the aggregate system. By adding the sender's average entropy to the receiver's entropy and subtracting the joint matrix entropy, we derive the size of $T(A,B)$, which is the average *shared* information (degree of association or shared variety) of this coupled system. Thus

$$H(A) + H(B) - H(A,B) = T(A,B)$$
$$2 + 1.953 - 3.004 \quad = .949 \text{ bits}$$

The average amount of information shared by the sender and receiver per symbol transmitted is less than half of the sender's quantity. The coupling is poor. Noise (also an average) accounts for the difference between $H(A,B)$ and $T(A,B)$. The value is $3.004 - .949 = 2.055$ bits. This two-component aggregation has serious structural difficulties.

Improvements can be suggested by studying the two types of noise indicated in Figure 13–11. Type I noise is related to the receiver's inability to read the sender's message. To him, the message is ambiguous, and Type I noise is often called *ambiguity*. We may also account for this situation in nonstructural terms—that is, there could be a semantic or a pragmatic problem, whereby the receiver simply uses any response on a random basis because he does not have any clear idea about what to do. The appropriate remedy will depend on the level of the problem. If the difficulty is structural, the receiver must be given the means to positively identify symbols; if it is semantic, he must be able to be certain of their meaning; and if it is pragmatic, clarification is needed as to what actions should be taken for each of the given instructions.

Type II noise is often called *equivocation*. It is typified by "jamming" of radio signals. All messages are read as identical by the receiver, even though the sender's variety is ample. In organizations, jamming is often practiced to prevent clarification of an issue, to reduce personal vulnerability as information flows upward, and to keep someone else from being recognized as a competitor for one's own job. In competitive practice, companies frequently try to introduce as much equivocation as possible into a competitor's test market. Remedies for equivocation are often dependent on the most fundamental kinds of behavioral analysis. For example, in group meetings, hyperactive individuals are always jamming or blanking out potential contributions from others who must wait for an opportunity to speak and do not have facility at interrupting.[11] These are but a few of the many instances of Type II noise.

The methodology of this shared-information model can be applied to stimulus-response or input-output analysis (variant 1), feedback analysis (variant 2), or trajectory analysis (variant 3), with minor modifications. Let us consider briefly the stimulus-response case. There are n kinds of stimuli, called $s_1, s_2, s_3, \ldots, s_n$; and there are m kinds of responses, $r_1, r_2, r_3, \ldots, r_m$. Do the responses adequately describe the reactions to the stimuli—or, in other

---

[11] Perhaps T-group methods, discussed in Chapter 14, would have some relevance here.

terms, is the shared information between s_i and r_j sufficiently high? If not, what accounts for the discrepancies? What kinds of noise are at work, and what, if anything, can be done about them? Aggregations greater than two (and, in theory, up to any size) can also be studied using this form of model.[12] Moreover, larger systems, such as the one shown in Figure 13–10B, can be segmented so that many different combinations of individuals can be related as two-component aggregations. It is a question of the way that the boundaries are drawn. And this is a function of the purposes to be served, not the least of which may be to determine whether *requisite variety* exists for control to be exercised by the sender or receiver. That is, does the sender's variety match the receiver's? We see that it is *not enough* for $H(A)$ to equal $H(B)$. Requisite variety must exist in terms of the *shared* information, and this point significantly extends our concept of control and coordination in the organization.

The measures themselves have certain similarities to statistical descriptors. Just as H and R are related to variability, T is a correlation-type measure, which possesses both advantages and disadvantages when compared with more classical statistical methods. However, one of the great benefits of the information-theory approach is the dimension of bits, which carries fundamental significance for communication analyses and organization theory.

SIMPLE DETERMINISTIC AGGREGATIONS

The operations of an input-output model can be studied over time. Surprising complexity can appear even when the system is strictly deterministic, as would be the case for most all-machine aggregations. Figure 13–12 illustrates a system whose inputs can take on different α-states and an input unit that responds to the input states in different ways, depending on what state it is in when the input changes.

Figure 13–12

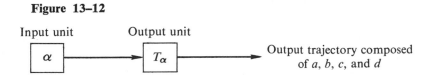

Input unit
Output unit

α → T_α → Output trajectory composed of a, b, c, and d

T_α is the transformation process, whose outputs *change* according to its α-setting. So, by controlling α, management is able to exercise control over

---

[12] See Fred Attneave, *Applications of Information Theory to Psychology* (New York: Holt, Rinehart and Winston, 1959), pp. 51–61.

the output process. On the other hand, α may be the value of an environmental input over which no control is exercised, in which case we would want to know whether the process operates satisfactorily under the existing conditions.

For example, assume that α is produced by a monitor (input unit) that reads the effects of wind conditions as the deflection of an airplane from its intended course. This α value (measured as deviations from some standard) is input to the control (output) unit. The control unit (acting on the rudder, ailerons, etc.) corrects the flight path of the plane through its own output trajectory of states *a, b, c,* and *d*. In this case, α is not determinate, although T_α is. With cross-sectional knowledge of the α probability distribution, or with Markovian transition information (if the next state of α is dependent on the preceding one), we can simulate the behavior of T_α.

Let us illustrate a fully deterministic simulation first. Say that the α-trajectory has been preset as the *repeating* cycle 1, 1, 2, 2, 3, 4, 3 and that the *initial state* of T_α is *a*. Illustrating the rules of the transition matrix (given in Table 13–4), the state *a* changes to *b* under the influence of $\alpha = 1$. Further, *b* changes to *c* when $\alpha = 1$; *c* becomes *b* when $\alpha = 2$; it stays *c* when $\alpha = 4$.

Table 13–4

$\downarrow$	*a*	*b*	*c*	*d*
T_α: T_1	*b*	*c*	*d*	*a*
T_2	*c*	*d*	*b*	*a*
T_3	*d*	*a*	*b*	*c*
T_4	*a*	*b*	*c*	*d*

The output trajectory of this causal system is *simulated* as shown below, for the *given* input trajectory.

T_α's output trajectory: a b c b d c c b c d a c b b a . . .
α's trajectory: 1 1 2 2 3 4 3 1 1 2 2 3 4 3 1 . . .

We observe that in this case, α's trajectory must repeat fully *two* cycles before T_α completes *one* cycle. In other words, here a small input cycle is *magnified* by T_α's properties into a larger output one. Management's policy is embodied in the rules designed for the matrix T_α. Even in this simple deterministic example, we observe an unexpected complication arising out of the matrix rules for transformations. The implications for higher-order aggregations are that strictly deterministic rules can produce complex effects whose patterns often cannot be anticipated and resist detection.

We have not discussed the *length of time* involved in accomplishing each transition. Equal intervals do *not* have to be assumed, and this applies both to the time for changes to occur in α and to the time required for changes of state (such as *a* to *b*) to take place. This further complicates what might ordinarily be considered a straightforward situation, although a variety of impressive methods is available for including time in the model.

Several other questions can be asked. What would the effect be if the *initial state* of T_α is changed? What might be the effects of altering α's trajectory? For example, starting at *a,* how should α be set to provide the closed and repeating cycle *abcd?* Two possibilities exist—namely, $\alpha = 1, 1, 1, 1$ or $\alpha = 1, 1, 1, 2$. But, if more than one path can be used to accomplish the same result, is the "policy machine" unnecessarily redundant? Are *unused* paths wasteful or unimportant in view of the methodology and technology involved? Is it possible to conceive of a purely human organizational component operating as T_α does? Models of the sort just described raise more questions than they answer, which seems both reasonable and beneficial given the present state of organization theory.

Let us continue now with a deterministic T_α, but an uncontrollable α. We will assume that α-transitions are independent of prior-state values and that the α probabilities are as below, with their respective Monte Carlo numbers (MCN's).

$$\alpha = \quad 1 \qquad 2 \qquad 3 \qquad 4$$

$$p(\alpha) = \quad .30 \qquad .20 \qquad .10 \qquad .40$$
$$\text{MCN} = 00\text{--}29 \quad 30\text{--}49 \quad 50\text{--}59 \quad 60\text{--}99$$

We will select random numbers and generate a trajectory for α (see Table 13–5).

Table 13–5

Trial	Random numbers	α-value	Trial	Random numbers	α-value
1	62	4	6	54	3
2	19	1	7	09	1
3	43	2	8	33	2
4	75	4	9	57	3
5	80	4	10	21	1

Following the same procedures as before, with *a* as the initial state, we find:

T_α's trajectory   *a a b d d d c d a d a* ...
α's trajectory   4 1 2 4 4 3 1 2 3 1 ...

The T_α trajectory now has to be evaluated. Everything depends on what the states *a, b, c,* and *d* signify. Let us assume that the transition *a* to *d* is *prohibited*. It did not appear in the previous T_α trajectory, but it does appear here. The simulation procedure helps to reveal faults of this kind and enables the evaluator to determine how probable such occurrences are. It is certainly impossible to examine *all* possible two-component aggregates[13] in this way, but, led by its intuition, management can develop a variety of significant probes. And, of course, complex simulations can be developed for more than two components, but the computational burdens rapidly become enormous.

DETERMINISTIC FEEDBACK AGGREGATIONS

The *simple system,* just described, produced only one-way communication. In most organizations, however, components relate to each other in *two-way* communications. Let us examine a feedback aggregation such as the one illustrated in Figure 13–13. We require the rules of transformation that relate

Figure 13–13   A Feedback Relationship Between T_α and R_β

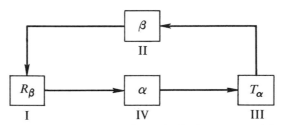

these two components. Thus, a hypothetical system might be that shown in Table 13–6.

Table 13–6

I.		↓	*k*	*l*	*m*	III.		↓	*a*	*b*	*c*
R_β:	R_1		*l*	*k*	*k*	T_α:	T_1		*b*	*a*	*b*
	R_2		*m*	*l*	*l*		T_2		*c*	*b*	*a*
II.		↓	*a*	*b*	*c*	IV.		↓	*k*	*l*	*m*
	β:		1	2	2		α:		2	2	1

---

[13] Bearing in mind that large systems can be subdivided into two-component systems in a great many ways.

These matrices are an extension of the one previously described. The difference is that while α is input to T_α, as before, now the output of T_α affects β, which is input to R_β; and the output of R_β affects the input, α. Thus, the α and β transforms are *interface* communications between R and T. For example, the state of T_α (a, b, or c) at III will be translated at the β surface II into instructions for the component, R_β, at I. Similarly, the state of R_β (k, l or m) at I will be translated at the α surface IV into instructions for the component, T_α, at III. This will become clear in the simulation below.

Assume that the initial conditions of the components are the states a and k, respectively. The transforms that produce the T and R trajectories shown in Table 13–7 are totally deterministic.

Table 13–7

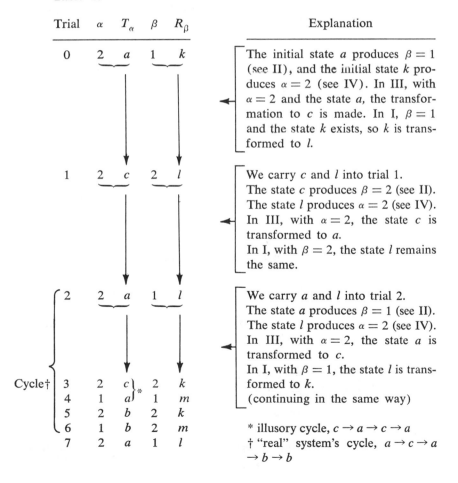

Trial	α	T_α	β	R_β	Explanation
0	2	a	1	k	The initial state a produces $\beta = 1$ (see II), and the initial state k produces $\alpha = 2$ (see IV). In III, with $\alpha = 2$ and the state a, the transformation to c is made. In I, $\beta = 1$ and the state k exists, so k is transformed to l.
1	2	c	2	l	We carry c and l into trial 1. The state c produces $\beta = 2$ (see II). The state l produces $\alpha = 2$ (see IV). In III, with $\alpha = 2$, the state c is transformed to a. In I, with $\beta = 2$, the state l remains the same.
2	2	a	1	l	We carry a and l into trial 2. The state a produces $\beta = 1$ (see II). The state l produces $\alpha = 2$ (see IV). In III, with $\alpha = 2$, the state a is transformed to c. In I, with $\beta = 1$, the state l is transformed to k. (continuing in the same way)
3	2	c	2	k	
4	1	a	1	m	
5	2	b	2	k	
6	1	b	2	m	
7	2	a	1	l	

Cycle† encloses trials 3–6.

* illusory cycle, $c \rightarrow a \rightarrow c \rightarrow a$
† "real" system's cycle, $a \rightarrow c \rightarrow a \rightarrow b \rightarrow b$

The real cycle will be found to exist between trials 2 and 6. The seventh trial repeats the beginning of this cycle. (All conditions at the seventh trial replicate those of the second trial.) However, if the observer happens to be watching only the T_α trajectory, he will find an illusory cycle, ca (trials 1 and 2; then trials 3 and 4). If the time lapse for each trial is one year, management might easily come to believe in this illusory cycle and to plan on the basis of it.

The message is a critical one. It tells us that management can be misled seriously by observing parts of a system. In this case, only by monitoring both T_α and R_β can the nature of the "true" pattern be discerned. This example is so simple that it may be all the more convincing with respect to the problem we are attempting to illuminate: namely, the parts of an organization cannot be treated in isolation unless they are truly independent of one another.

There is still another illusion to contend with. That is the imputation of stochastic properties to what are really fully determinate systems. Note the trajectory of R—namely, $kllkmkm$. . . . Perhaps these states have been observed over as much as a seven-year period. It is easy to believe that such information must have been produced by a system with stochastic properties. As a result, the manager might turn to Markovian analysis to determine the extent to which an "organized" pattern exists. But first let us examine the results of a cross-sectional study.

State	Frequency	
l	3	$H = -(2)(\tfrac{3}{8})\log_2 \tfrac{3}{8} - (\tfrac{2}{8})\log_2 \tfrac{2}{8} = 1.561$
k	3	
m	2	$R = 1 - 1.561/1.585 = .01$
	8	

Then, the time-series Markovian analysis is performed in the same fashion as in our previous examples. (Again, we have created one additional state for computational facility—namely, $l \to k$.) The matrix and computations are:

→	k	l	m	
k	0	1	2	$H(k) = -\tfrac{1}{3}\log_2\tfrac{1}{3} - \tfrac{2}{3}\log_2\tfrac{2}{3} = .918$ bits
l	2	1	0	$H(l) = -\tfrac{2}{3}\log_2\tfrac{2}{3} - \tfrac{1}{3}\log_2\tfrac{1}{3} = .918$ bits
m	1	1	0	$H(m) = -\tfrac{1}{2}\log_2\tfrac{1}{2} - \tfrac{1}{2}\log_2\tfrac{1}{2} = 1.000$ bits

Using the coss-sectional frequencies,[14] $p(k) = \tfrac{3}{8}$, $p(l) = \tfrac{3}{8}$, $p(m) = \tfrac{1}{4}$, we obtain the overall average entropy for the system:

$$\overline{H} = (\tfrac{3}{8})(.918)2 + (\tfrac{1}{4})(1.000) = .939$$

---

[14] Which would be unchanged by the derivation of the steady-state results (see pp. 550–52).

The redundancy has increased markedly:

$$R = 1 - .939/1.585 = .41$$

These results reconfirm how the time-series approach uncovers organizational patterns that the cross-sectional approach misses. At the same time, it is indicated that stochastic properties exist in this organization (but we know that our observations were derived from a determinate system). Had the principles of organization been understood, then the cycle *lkmkm* would furnish the basis for a fully deterministic view of the system. We leave it to the reader to prove this point to his own satisfaction in the exercise section of this chapter.

COUPLED STOCHASTIC SYSTEMS

Many kinds of input-output system exhibit stochastic properties in aggregation. In these cases, even if an underlying deterministic pattern really exists in the organization, it cannot be identified. One form of such aggregations that has created a great deal of interest and has, therefore, been studied in depth is the queuing model (see Figure 13–14).

Figure 13–14   The Basic Characteristics of a Single-Channel Queuing System

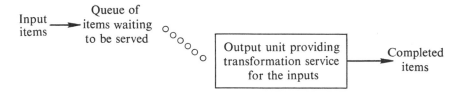

The word "queue," derived from the French word for "tail," is used here in the sense of a waiting line. Queuing models are concerned with the properties of systems in which waiting lines can develop and the delays can have important consequences for the system's performance. For physical systems, the queue can be composed of trucks waiting to unload, planes "stacked up" waiting to land at an airport, ships standing by for berths, materials waiting to be machined or shipped. The line at the bank, the people in the doctor's waiting room, those waiting for elevator service, the line at the supermarket or in the cafeteria, are other examples of the ubiquitous queue. Consider the decisions waiting to be made, reports to be written, studies to be conducted, even the contents of the in-box and the out-box to be attended to. There are letters waiting to be opened and calls held at the switchboard.[15] And in every two-component, man-man interaction, queues of compliments, greetings, data, and gossip are developed (see Eric Berne's model in Chapter 15, p. 643).

In man-machine systems, because of the different processing rates of the components, the machine component usually can produce an enormous waiting line of information that can never be serviced (read or treated) by the manager, so it must be reduced by means of statistical and numerical measures such as averages, sums, modal values, and so forth. On the other hand, the man component of such aggregations often must wait while the computer processes the information that he has fed to it. Managers expect such a waiting line.

Managers are accustomed also to a second kind of queue. Assume that the manager receives the results as soon as the machine finishes the job. He determines quickly what he wants to ask the computer to do next, but he cannot communicate immediately with the machine because other managers are before him on the computer's waiting line. Even with on-line terminals that appear to permit instantaneous access to the computer, a waiting line develops, although it cannot be seen in any physical sense because it exists within the computer. Certain terminals are on "hold," while others are working with only parts of the computer's processing units assigned. Since the terminals are scattered geographically, the user seldom has any idea of the demand that exists on the system at the time he wishes to use it. The relation of the computer center to its users is an excellent example of a stochastic organizational problem of component aggregation.

Bottlenecks and Idle Time

Waiting-line problems of a man-man nature frequently precede man-machine relations. For example, the manager must work through programmers who are so often overloaded that a queue is usually expected. Nevertheless, the queue is viewed as the consequence of a *bottleneck,* a term that is reserved for queue-forming situations that carry significant penalties because they slow or stop production. But what should be done by the computer center, under such circumstances, is not readily apparent to each individual manager. The manager reasons that the bottleneck situation could be avoided by balancing the supply and demand for programmers' time and scheduling tasks in line with

---

[15] Queuing theory was first developed in application to the telephone. It has continued to be widely used in the communications field. But its breadth is amazing; it has found, for example, important application to problems of epidemiology and ecology.

machine availability.[16] Since, say, three out of five of his requests to the computer center are put on a waiting line, he concludes that there are too few programmers. This may well be true, but only the computer center knows how much of the time the programming staff is actually idle waiting for machine time.

An aggregate organization model of the computer center is required to determine how much queuing is optimal and how much idle time for the facilities this entails. This organization study may well differentiate between users, establishing priorities for some managers' requests over those of others. The computer situation is close to the classic queuing problem of machine repairmen. How many repairmen is the optimal number? The machines have specified breakdown characteristics (i.e., a probabilistic demand for repairmen's time), given repair-time distributions, costs of repairmen's time, and costs of machine idle time. The machines can be differentiated, some being more important than others, and appropriate priorities can be developed.

Variable rates of input and output. In view of the generality of the queuing problem, we must determine the fundamental reasons why queues can develop in systems where *average* supply and *average* demand are balanced. Since arrivals are variable, it is possible that no arrivals will come for service in some periods and that the service unit will be idle, "wasting" time that cannot subsequently be saved. On the other hand, a large number of arrivals can suddenly show up, which will result in their waiting at the bottleneck, wasting their time. Similar effects occur because of variable servicing rates. The combined variability of arrival and service can create extreme situations in which the effective output rate is significantly less than the system's specified average. For example, in a system where the averages of arrival and service are well balanced but large variability exists, the inputs can occur at excessive rates at the same time that the output rate slows down. There may be extreme imbalance from which a very large queue can form. Management, acting on an exception, will then employ special expediting and processing routines.

Usually, when machine is input to machine, the input-output situation is (essentially) deterministic, and arithmetic (not statistical) line-balancing is called for.[17] Say that the input is ten units per hour and that the transforma-

---

[16] In addition to requests for writing programs, frequent calls are made for "debugging" (correcting program errors) and for "compiling" programs (where a shift is being made from one language system to another). Compiling and debugging are man-machine operations often delayed by overloads on both man and machine.

[17] This ignores the probability of machine downtime for repairs, which is commonly ignored when equipment is reliable. Another probabilistic element that is often by-passed is worker absenteeism.

tion process is provided by a machine capable of servicing five units per hour. For deterministic line-balancing, two such transformation units are required (i.e., $5 + 5 = 10$). Machines usually operate in this fashion—but not always. For example, information retrieval from the computer's memory may have variable times associated with it. When random access is used[18] or sequential access is used (because a magnetic tape must be read from the beginning), the recovery times will vary greatly. Though such recovery times are exceedingly small, when a great deal of information must be recovered and the throughput volume of the system is large, the total delays encountered become significant.

Generally, we think of machines as having almost zero performance-time variability and the man-component as having significantly large performance-time variability. The variability introduced by man into the system will vary with individuals and also will change for one person over time. Attitudes, fatigue, practice, and incentives are some of the factors that affect man's variability as both an input and an output unit. One reason for substituting machines for men in an organization is the reduction of variability that can be achieved. This applies to both blue- and white-collar jobs and increasingly to middle-management executive jobs as well.[19] Machine replacements are significantly affecting the organization chart, and this trend will continue, because with reduced variability, queue sizes are significantly diminished and arithmetic line-balancing can be used to provide better utilization of capacity. For example, as we will show shortly, if constant service time is achieved, the average waiting line and the average waiting time can be cut in half (as an upper limit of improvement for a certain class of very common input-output situations).

What kinds of input and output variability are usually assumed? For most intermachine systems, we have already stated that the input rates (called λ's) and the output rates (called μ's) are close enough to being consistently regular to be treated as constant. For human behavior, an exponential distribution is often assumed. It has a form similar to that shown in Figure 13–15 below— in this case, however, for a processing unit having an average output rate of μ. The same exponential form often can be used to describe satisfactorily the probability distribution of intervals between input arrivals.[20]

---

[18] For example, the starting point for an information search is based on a random entry into the file.

[19] Especially for routine decision-making tasks such as are frequently encountered in handling scheduling and inventory problems.

[20] Equivalently, we frequently say that the input is Poisson distributed, i.e., $P(n) = (\lambda T)^n e^{-\mu T}/n!$, where n is the number of arrivals in the interval T; then the interval between arrivals is exponentially distributed.

Figure 13–15   An Exponential Distribution Describing the Probability That the Interval Between Successive Outputs Is *t*

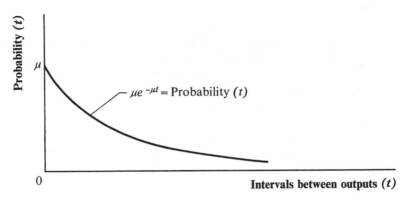

NOTE: We observe that the probability that long intervals will occur is small and gets smaller as the size of the intervals increases.

Models of queuing aggregations can be characterized in many different ways. Among the most important differentiating characteristics are the following:

1. The input and output distributional forms (which can take on many shapes other than the constant and exponential shapes already discussed).

2. Single-channel (two-component) aggregations or multiple-channel ones. See Figure 13–16. In this multiple-channel case, a single waiting line is formed. Whichever output unit is the first to complete service and become available is given the next input.

Figure 13–16   Single-Channel and Multiple-Channel Queuing Systems

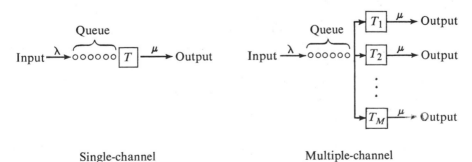

3. Accommodations for the queue can be considered to be infinite, or they can be of limited size (say, N berths), which means that after the limit is reached, arrivals are turned away.

4. The source for arrivals can be considered to be infinite, or it can be of limited size (say, S machines that can break down or S projects that will require programming). The input rate is also affected when arrivals are *discouraged* and do not join the queue, because it is too long.

5. The order in which units are taken (called *queue discipline*) can vary. Many models assume that FIFO (first in, first out) applies, but variants such as LIFO (last in, first out) and special priorities are used. It is even possible that an arrival will displace a unit that is already being serviced, the latter having to return to the queue until it can be taken again. *Defection* from the queue is another consideration, as is *switching* from one queue to another (e.g., when an adjacent bank line becomes smaller than the one you are on).

6. Entry rules can include batch-processing capabilities as well as one-by-one treatment. An elevator is an example of a batch-processing system. Many production and computer functions are designed so that a batch of units will be treated together. Sometimes, the system operates on a minimum batch size; in other cases, it is designed to be periodic, accepting whatever has accumulated by the end of a given period.

We observe that many organizational arrangements are determined by service considerations. How many workers should report to a foreman? Or, conversely, the foreman viewed as a single-channel service system can adequately serve how many workers? Similar reasoning applies to every organizational level. The queuing-model approach to aggregations of communicating individuals, groups, departments, and so on, highlights many features of organizations that otherwise can remain unspecified and be overlooked. For example, how many priority items are queued up before the president? Would decentralization decrease queue time but increase idle time of organizational components? The dynamic approach we are talking about not only identifies the components in the system (characteristically expected of organization study) but also observes the flows between them and the rates and character of such flows. These are powerful descriptions of organizational arrangements. The queuing models are *descriptive* and not in any way normative; they are also mathematically *analytic,* and a large number of different numerical *measures of performance* can usually be derived to describe the behavior of the system.[21] For example, the *average* number of units in the queue; the *average* number of units in the system (which is the number in the queue plus those in service); the *average* waiting time spent by a unit in the queue before

---

[21] The literature is replete with models; there are thousands of variants, and their derivation is usually mathematically demanding. See, for example, T. L. Saaty, *Elements of Queueing Theory,* (New York: McGraw-Hill, 1961).

service begins (in other words, average delay); the *average* time spent by a unit in the system (which includes the delay while waiting and the time to complete processing in the service unit); the probability that any delay will occur; the probability that the *average* time spent by a unit in the system will be greater than some chosen value of time; the probability that *n* units will be in the system (which includes both those being serviced *and* those waiting on line); the probability that no units will be in the system, which is the probability that all *M* service units will be *idle;* the *average* number of idle service units; and the probability that turn-aways will occur because of insufficient queue accommodations.

Another interesting aspect of queuing relations is the fact that entropy measures can be derived for the system. Thus, $H = -\Sigma_n P_n log_2 P_n$ measures the entropy of the organization's queuing configuration (whose $P_n = $ the probability that *n* units will be in the system, which includes both those being serviced and those waiting on line). Alternative organizational configurations can be compared with respect to their entropy measures as well as their waiting lines and waiting times. As before, a low *H* measure indicates less fluctuation and variety than a high *H* measure. The redundancy measure can be used as well, and *H* and *R* values can be obtained for the input and output distributions.

By choosing appropriate dimensions, we can analyze many relevant aspects of organizational performance. But when the aggregation is too complex, simulation methods can be substituted.[22] Issues such as specialization (single-channel systems) versus generalization (multiple-channel systems) of organizational functions can be approached in this way. Similarly, centralization versus decentralization can be modeled. In relatively straightforward terms, the variable loads on the organization can be matched or balanced with appropriate capacities. From queuing considerations it is clear that this matching includes both the average size of the output capacity and the variability from that average output level. Thus, we can begin to answer questions such as: How large should an organization be? What jobs should be specialized? Where should machines be used? What control over delays exists?[23] How can bottlenecks be removed? What types of monitor and controller[24] should be used? Above all, human behavior can be contrasted with machine attributes by means of these stochastic aggregation models.

---

[22] There are well-known computer programs for simulating complex queues. Computer systems for simulation of queuing configurations have received considerable attention because the realities of such organizational problems are more complex than analytic models can handle.

[23] This is equivalent to control over the queue—for example, with respect to delivery dates.

[24] Control system analysis (see pp. 440–47) lends itself perfectly to the model formulation we have been discussing.

ORGANIZATIONAL CLUSTERS

The notion that so many owe so much to so few illustrates a basic truth about organizations. The underlying principle can be represented by the so-called log-normal distribution, which is a normal distribution of the logarithms of numbers. Many other distributions, such as Pareto's and Gibrat's, portray the same skewed effect whereby a small percentage of units contribute most of the action.[25]

Figure 13–17 gives a general idea of the clustering effect about which we are talking. The participants are arranged along the horizontal axis in rank order of their contribution, the highest one being the first listed. In

Figure 13–17   Log-Normal Distribution of Unequal Contributions of Participants

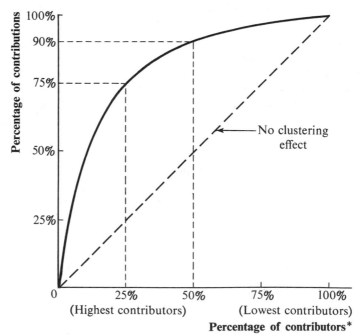

*All participants in rank order of their contributions

---

[25] Pareto's distribution described the skewed distribution of income. (Previously, we made reference to Pareto's concept of an optimum allocation of wealth—see pp. 11–12.)

this case, 25 percent of all individuals contribute 75 percent of the total performance. These figures are not unusual. For example, the contribution to total sales volume of a small set of items is enormous; businessmen, a small percentage of all air passengers, contribute disproportionately to passenger miles flown; a few individuals in a company meeting do most of the talking.

The diagonal line in Figure 13–17 applies when no clustering exists—in other words, when each individual pulls his own weight, contributing equally to the total score. This is so rare that, for example, it is customary in planning inventory to use an *ABC* plan. The *A*-type items are, say, the first 25 percent of all items, which contribute (according to the figure) 75 percent of sales volume. Class *B* items might be the next 25 percent, contributing 15 percent to sales volume. The *C* items are 50 percent of all items, but they contribute only 10 percent to sales volume. Clearly, the *A*, *B*, and *C* items should be studied differently. The greatest inventory savings will be made from the *A* class and, accordingly, the largest part of the inventory study budget will go in that direction.[26] This is not to say that the *C*-type items should be ignored; but broad policies can be framed to handle them.

The same reasoning applies to man-machine aggregations in the organization. As we move to consider and treat larger systems, the *ABC* effect will become *more* pronounced. Some questions occur immediately. Is it desirable that a few men should dominate a group, a department, or an entire organization? The answer clearly is that hierarchical structure, which is essential for management communication, will always produce such clustering in terms of power, authority, responsibility, and so forth. It would be distinctly disadvantageous to move toward the diagonal unless this was accomplished by means of decentralization. We have already shown that the appropriate degree of decentralization is intimately related to particular problems of information management faced by the organization. Appropriate decentralization is also a function of *who* belongs to the hierarchical *A* class. What is their combined knowledge of process and people? What kind of leadership qualities do they have? What sort of abilities to coordinate the variety of functions in the total system? And such analysis must be approached with great care. If we measure the wrong contribution, we might find that an individual who is really a critical contributor to management's success appears to be a *C*-type participant.

The entropy of a highly skewed *ABC* system approaches zero, whereas that of a system represented by the diagonal in Figure 13–17 is maximum entropy. Man systems so typically move toward zero entropy that we cannot be surprised to find that the *ABC* effect occurs repeatedly under greatly diverse

---

[26] There is another log-normal viewpoint, based on how critical it is to have the item on hand when it is required. Thus, an inexpensive part may be essential to maintain operation of a plane, ship, or plant.

circumstances, even though the causes for it are seldom obvious. Noting the drive of companies toward merger and acquisition, we observe that this pattern increases the entropy of the system with which the organization must deal. Then the expanding, centralized organization can reduce its entropy only by means of hierarchy and policy. In other words, the clustering of managerial performance to parallel that of the environment can result in requisite variety.

Information Clusters

Clusters of various kinds occur, such as those of a few individuals with much responsibility, several control points with major impact, and so on. One of the most important clusters has always been that of information (and accounting) centers, where a few measures of performance eventually reach top management. But the computer's propensity for aggregating information has begun to reverse the clustering process for information. Anyone with a computer terminal at his disposal can gain access to almost any kind of information. The cost of such terminals has been decreasing, and units will become accessible, in one form or another, to all individuals in the near future. As a result, information availability has broadened rather than continuing to cluster. Today, many grade-school children are learning to use the new information technology; tomorrow, all will be entirely familiar with it.

As time passes and computer capabilities grow, the likelihood increases of a national "databank"—a supercensus, with up-to-date demographic, historical, tax, medical, and other socioeconomic information about individuals; and with financial, tax, production, marketing, and employment information about companies, institutions, and associations. Through cathode-ray tube terminals (called CRT), which are much like television screens, all such census information as well as the *entire* list of books and documents in libraries could become generally available to any requester. Centralized medical systems will be able to maintain individual health records, and "on-line" diagnosis is expected to become a reality. Schoolchildren can call for computer programs that reduce the subject to be learned to its basic logic. The availability of such programs may change what is considered important to be learned to anything that cannot be so programmed.[27] And, as we have said previously, banking and shopping will be affected considerably.

One result of these possibilities is that the potential for invasion of *privacy* has become a great issue. It becomes increasingly difficult to figure out how to segment information availability in the computer memory system. Special call

---

[27] We should note that this is in line with Kenneth Boulding's belief that "the major task of formal education in the future is to teach people how to learn." The new technology is breaking down the old clusters of information and replacing them with the broadest access to information.

numbers and identification procedures can be used, but these are far from being foolproof.

The overall trend is clearly toward centralized information systems, but because of terminal access, the isolated clustering of (say, departmental) information is decreasing, and the entropy of such systems is moving up rapidly. From a social point of view, the trend must be considered a good one, even though privacy issues will have to be resolved. This democratization of information access will have outstanding effects on organization. Each individual in the company is gaining greater opportunity to obtain equal access to all information. For society, the democratization of information may turn out to signal the greatest change in man's interrelations in thousands of years.

Profit Centers and Budget Control Centers

The clustering of responsibility for profit has been increasing. Thus, a few managers are put in charge of those parts of the organization that account for the greatest percentage of total company profits. A major issue of organizational design is where to establish managerial control points for the organization's profits. The profit-center concept assigns boundaries of jurisdiction and accounting to individual managers. These subsystems can be departments, portions of the product line, or other aggregations that contribute to the organization's total profit picture. Each center can be reviewed by a centralized management for its contribution to profit and evaluated as to its performance. The profit center is, therefore, a subsystem segmented from the whole. As such, it runs counter to prevailing drives for consideration of the total system; on the other hand, it is a form of decentralization,[28] which we have observed as an informational necessity.

The design of profit centers is obviously critical to their performance as useful control subsystems. Lacking specific information, we cannot lay down inflexible rules concerning the optimal segmentation of a system into control aggregations. However, we can raise some important questions. Should profit centers follow the log-normal type of clustering (i.e., should a few profit centers contribute the greatest share of total profit to the company)? More generally, we can change the word profit to benefit, and then, referring to benefit centers, ask whether, say, in a hospital the control centers contributing to benefit should be unequally divided with respect to their contributions. Alternatively, should profit control be spread out in accordance with the diagonal of Figure 13–17? In other words, should the many profit centers relate to approximately equal profit sectors? To achieve this, more profit centers would

---

[28] The profit-center concept is not restricted to physical decentralization, such as by plants in various geographic regions. It can cut across many plants, aggregating on a particular activity.

be set up for the *A* portion of profit contribution than for the *B*, and more for the *B* than for the *C*. To the extent that trends are observable, this does not seem to be representative of what is happening. Highly skewed profit centers emerge, and only occasionally are they removed through decentralization and given the opportunity to start their own system.

Another view of the situation is to consider the aggregation of risk. We refer to risk in terms of the variability of the estimates of return on investment around the expected value. Variability applies to both penalties and rewards. Generally, a small percentage of the company's budgeted activities involves large risk. By design, the greatest percentage of the company's efforts entails little risk and is based solidly on predictable, low variance, highly stable systems. To visualize what this means, assume that each of the profit centers is rated by an estimate of profit variance. Such measures as *H* and *R* could be used, where high *H* and low *R* would characterize a risky profit center.

Figure 13–18 depicts two different allocations of a company's budget across its centers' risk spectrum. Which arrangement is preferable? Expected-value analysis can be used to help derive an answer. Utility theory and multiple-outcome analysis (see pp. 278–84) can also play a part. But how would the design of the profit centers or of the budgetary controls be affected by the choice of curve? Should risk be divided as equally as possible among the profit centers? Or, alternatively, should high-risk centers be isolated? To help frame an answer to this question, let us examine the alternative budget allocations as they are represented in the log-normal, cluster diagram of Figure 13–19. If equal risk levels were assigned to each profit center, then some centers would have enormous budgets to work with and others very small ones.

Figure 13–18   **Contrasting a Risky Budget Allocation, *A*, with a Safer One, *B*.**

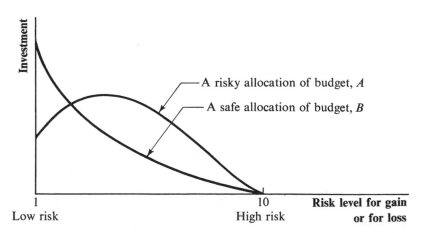

Figure 13–19   Contrasting the Clustering Effects of Two Budget-Allocation Plans, *A* and *B*.

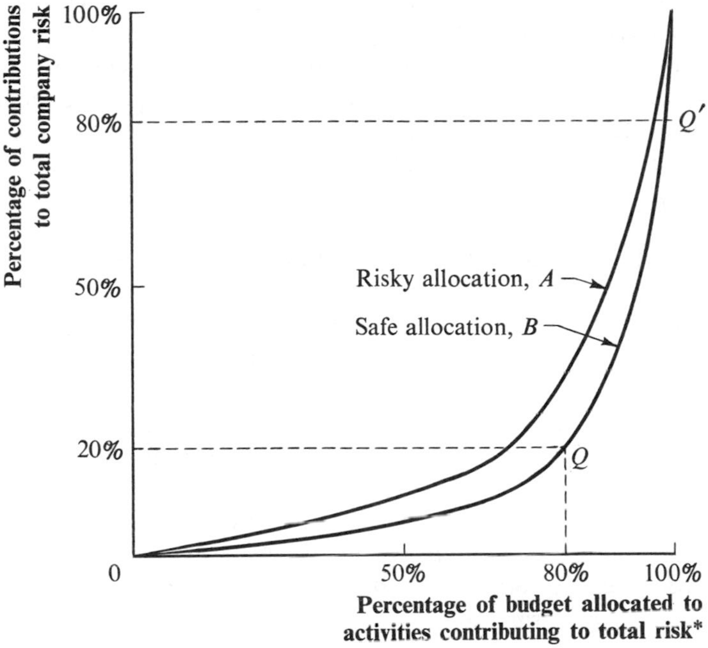

*Arranged in inverse ranked order of contributions

Let us use *B* as an example. With five control centers, the first one would have only 20 percent of the risk, although it would be assigned 80 percent of the budget. This division is shown as point *Q* on the curve. The *last* 20 percent of the risk, shown as point *Q'*, has almost no budget to work with.

The equal division of risk makes no sense. The isolation of risk, however, is appealing to the extent that organizational realities permit it to be accomplished. But which plan should be used? *First:* A number of profit centers could be set up to care for the first 80 percent of the budget allocation, and a very few profit centers could be assigned to control the remaining 20 percent of the budget. This division of profit centers would be based on size-of-budget considerations. *Second:* A number of budgetary control centers could be set up to cope with the *high entropy of the riskier areas.* A proportionately fewer number of budget-control centers would be assigned to the lower-entropy, safer systems.

We observe that coexisting budget-control centers and profit-control centers represent a conflict of objectives, and some balance must be found between them, depending on the extent to which high-entropy risk factors can be isolated in specific sectors of the system. Organizational control aggregations must be designed with such potential conflicts of objectives in mind. And, in making the decision as to whether the riskier or the safer allocation is preferred, we should remember that the entropy of the riskier plan is higher. More controls are required for high-risk systems. Therefore, to manage this higher H level, a company will require tighter budgetary control, more budget-control centers covering the high-risk areas, faster reporting methods, more continuous data flows, and on-line monitoring systems for almost continuously produced profit and loss statements.

Programming, Planning, and Budgeting Systems

When operating centers of the organization are coordinated by procedures so that the subsystems aggregate to become members of a total *unified* network, the large system is expected to operate with great effectiveness. The key is to develop a coordinating core that does not make any attempt to do all of the components' jobs or reach all of their decisions. Instead, it programs a part of their relations with one another, sets up constraints (such as budgets) under which they must operate, schedules the flows of inputs and outputs that are critical for the operation of the entire system, calls for missing information, tracks promised performance, and alerts the separate centers to deviations from promised performance.

The design criteria for such a coordinating unit depend on the characteristics of the system, but some useful generalizations can be made. The unit is in part a master control system, in part a master planning unit. It can make mistakes and therefore is always subject to improvement. Master coordinating units can be identified with autocratic behavior, because the distinction between coordination and coercion is often in the beholder's eye. To provide general assurance, safeguards must be installed. Another element critical to the operation of this "hub" is a memory for what has gone on (in the large system) and an awareness of what is expected to happen. A "large-system scenario" must exist, *meshing* with all the individual smaller scenarios of the profit centers and budget-control centers. Procedures in the form of (large-system) policy must be accepted by all subsystems. Judgment as to what is good and bad for the large system must ultimately reside with the central coordinator. The subsystems may experience some discomfort as a result, but their awareness—and acceptance—of the larger system's values must be expected to override any smaller system's considerations. Information flows through the system and is evaluated by the coordinating unit. The monitored outputs are derived from the policies of each subsystem. Judgments about the failure of some subsystems to add to the success of the large system require an overall systems analysis, which is generally provided by the central coordinating unit with the cooperation of the subsystem units.

The United States government introduced such programmed control over many of its activities. Sufficient time has elapsed since the inception of this program to convince everyone that the idea is sound and can produce substantial benefits. The larger the system, the more appealing is this form of structuring. But programmed evaluation of performance and the programmed allocation of budget are not independent of the way in which the profit and budget-control centers have been set up. For example, a single report for the entire system will not pinpoint those areas that are contributing and those that are detracting from the system's performance. Further, some functions must spend more and produce less profit so that others can function to the benefit of the total organization. Previously, we have discussed some of the problems, which have also been considered by the government program in terms of cost-effectiveness and cost-benefit analyses.[29]

Cost-benefit evaluation deals with profit-type functions. It is always the preferred form of analysis, since it reflects the larger system—that is, input trajectories of cost factors must be compared with output trajectories of benefits in terms of efficiency measures such as return on investment. Unfortunately, under many circumstances, benefits cannot be measured. Then cost-effectiveness analysis must be used, which in essence questions whether the lowest-cost strategy is being used to achieve a specific objective. We can see why cost-effectiveness analysis appears to be used far more often than cost-benefit analysis in problems of the public-service sector, where benefits are reckoned as lives saved, children educated, crimes reduced, and the like. But, even for industry, dollars of profit are no longer regarded as an adequate sole measure of benefit. So, even though cost-benefit analysis is preferred, it may not be used because the beneficial outputs are abstract, multidimensional, intangible, or of *high risk*. In high risk situations, profit is expected to fluctuate widely, so no real fix on it can be obtained, even though an expected value can be derived mathematically. Thus, even dollar benefit is sometimes hard to measure. When cost-benefit analysis is difficult to apply, cost-effectiveness methods are used instead. When the benefit measure is specific and its variance is low, cost-benefit analysis normally prevails.

---

[29] Cost-benefit analysis of a public investment should resemble the analysis of a profit-maximizing business firm; the important differences between the two are in the identification of the costs to be included and excluded in the problem of measuring benefits.

. . . Cost-effectiveness analysis is specifically directed to problems in which the output cannot be evaluated in market prices, but where the inputs can, and where the inputs are substitutable at exchange relationships developed in the market.

From Thomas A. Goldman, ed., *Cost-Effectiveness Analysis: New Approaches in Decision-Making,* Praeger Special Studies in U.S. Economic and Social Development (New York: Praeger, 1967), p. 18.

We should note that the profit-center concept is related directly to cost-benefit analysis, whereas the use of budget-control centers is related to cost-effectiveness programs. Realistic programmed control and planning systems use a *mixture* of cost-benefit and cost-effectiveness criteria. In other words, a mixture of profit and budget centers is required to exercise large-system control. Information is the coordinating flux of the system, which adjusts to the types of information that are available and to the levels of flow. When information is delayed, the program calls for expediting its retrieval. When information is missing, estimates are prepared to fulfill the requirements. The coordinating system of the organization is as complete as possible with respect to the information that is essential for the large system. Many new techniques have been developed to fill in missing data. Data-generators and data-breeders[30] are designed to close open loops and to permit the total interconnection of the system. With adequate information and proper procedures, the separate subsystems can be integrated into a totally functioning larger system.

LEVELS OF THE DECISION PROBLEM

We have discussed clustering of information, profit centers, risk systems, and budgetary controls. Finally, we come to the clustering of executive responsibilities, which can be classified according to their systems level. In many ways, this level is reflected by the organizational hierarchy as indicated by a conventional organization chart. We will use classes of responsibility such that the superior class encloses all the lesser classes.

Accordingly, let us identify, somewhat arbitrarily, five domains of responsibility: (1) the universal level, (2) the global level, (3) the strategic level, (4) the tactical level, and (5) the instrument (or tool) level. By these designations we mean the following:

1. The universal level comprehends *all* phenomena that in any way relate to the coordination of the subsystem centers. It is the highest form of programmed coordination. It may operate at the departmental level, but it works more usually at the industrial or national level. Increasingly, international influences appear (such as EEC, EFTA, NATO, or LAFTA).[31] The most significant characteristic of the universal level is that nothing is outside that system. For example, an investment fund competes with a manufacturing

---

[30] The term "data-breeders" was coined at the advertising agency of Young & Rubicam, Inc., to describe a model that could use incomplete information about the marketplace to induce the remaining information needed to reach a decision.

[31] European Economic Community, European Free Trade Area, North Atlantic Treaty Organization, Latin America Free Trade Area.

enterprise for available capital. For a fixed amount of budget, one product mix competes with another. Merchandising vies with manufacturing, mining, transportation, entertainment, and other services. At this level we are dealing with the way available resources will be committed—in situations in which that choice is totally open. Diversification, expansion, and changeover to a new industry exemplify this level. Actually, it is extremely rare that a universal view is entertained rationally. Precedents and procedures for such study are almost totally nonexistent. Yet the penalties (in the form of opportunity costs) can be catastrophic if in some sense a rational position at the universal level is not taken into account. The ultimate in generalization is required because *all* information about these largest systems is included in the study, even though there is no way to use it without homomorphic transformations of substantial proportion.

2. The global level represents a bounded system. It assumes that major objectives (such as investing in mining or manufacture) have already been determined. Everything else remains open. The exact product line is to be chosen at this level of responsibility. In other words, the organization's resources are specified; the problems at this level concern what is the *best pattern* of utilization for these resources.

3. The strategic domain brings us much closer to the level of operative decision models. It is concerned with questions of how to fulfill the global alternatives that have been selected. In effect, one looks for the best possible "global-strategic" combination that can be found. Consequently, if the global alternatives include the possibilities of manufacturing bicycles or lawn mowers and the decision is made to manufacture bicycles, then the manager at the strategic level must select from the various types, sizes, colors, and qualities of bicycle. The choice between bicycles and lawn mowers may not be clear-cut except by including strategic considerations—for example, where $B_2 > LM_1 > B_1 > LM_2$ shows a set of preferences for different bicycle and lawn mower designs. The strategic alternative plays a critical role in determining fundamental design considerations for the outputs of a system. Strategic alternatives are likely to be involved with the major design features of the process as well, including where the best process location might be and what facilities, in what configuration, will be optimal. As facilities become less special-purpose (usable for only one output) and more general-purpose (adaptable for several different outputs), an increasing number of tactical problems arises.

4. At this level we are concerned with how much product to make, how much material to order, when to start a production run and when to finish it, how to schedule maintenance or the trips of an airline. It is interesting to note that many of the quantitative methods reported in the literature operate at this distinctly low level of responsibility. The expected degree of repetition for essentially the same decision (for example, how much stock to order) is high enough at the tactical level to warrant an investment in collecting and analyzing

historical data. Responsibility is based on the quality of the data and the integrity of repetitive decision-making models. There must be reasonable confidence that the same conditions continue to exist in a stable form and are, therefore, currently applicable. Assurance of stability is a major responsibility of this level. To monitor the stability of the system requires some form of control analysis. Statistical quality control plays a critical role. At the tactical level, penalties for mistakes are not high. A mistake will not jeopardize the organization or threaten ruin. It is relatively easy to correct mistakes that have been made, since the decision situations tend to be repetitive. But when such mistakes are not recognized and corrections are not made, the penalties can accumulate rapidly and assume catastrophic proportions.

5. The tool, or instrument, level is that stratum of decision responsibility that is most frequently ignored by academic studies and most stressed by organizational ones. It concerns the use of instruments, equipment, and mechanical components of the system. At this level the degree of repetition for the decision process is *exceedingly high*. The historical record tends to be unambiguous and complete. Data are entirely visible; their collection is relatively inexpensive and is accomplished in a straightforward manner. Mistakes can occur with high frequency, but the penalties for them tend to be minimal. It is not costly to correct mistakes; they can be spotted rapidly and adjusted quickly. The primary question of responsibility that appears at this level is the ability of the man-machine system to deliver according to specifications. Blueprints, tolerance specifications, machine settings, and material qualities reign supreme at this level.

Dependencies and Interactions

The executive is aware that the different levels of managerial decisions interact strongly. He is producing bicycles because that was decided at the global level. It is not his responsibility that some other product might have produced a greater profit. But it is his responsibility to buy materials at the right price and to inventory them correctly. Why did the global decision-makers not know about the complex problem for this plant layout of sequencing the assembly of each bicycle? Did they consider that it raises the cost prohibitively or that competitive advantage existed in the variety of the line or in the scale of the operation? Perhaps the global decision-makers did know all this, but there is more than a gnawing doubt.

In every organization, one must ask: When is it allowable to reach global decisions without having carefully thought through all tactical and instrument levels of decision-making responsibility? The answer is that in practice, global awareness and responsibility reach down to the lower levels sporadically. The global decision is reached with knowledge of specific details only occasionally. At the present time, any pattern that consistently required including the details of all levels would provoke insurmountable informational problems. Yet really crucial facts for global decision-making can exist at any level, all the way down through the tool and instrument level. Such dependencies are particularly likely to occur when technological factors make big differences in the costs and benefits of alternative plans. Under such circumstances, global responsibilities are as much servants of the tool-area responsibilities as they are masters of them. Everything becomes a part of everything else, responsible to and for it.

With these descriptions in mind, we can see that clusters of responsibility exist that cut across the hierarchical organizational levels for decision-making. Clusters of organizational responsibility tend to aggregate in the log-normal fashion previously described, following the patterns of interrelated decisions. The clusters that emerge account for complex managerial attitudes that exist within organized systems. A *very* few individuals are responsible for the universal decisions in this world. Their entropy is almost too large to comprehend (see point *a* in Figure 13–20). The potential entropy of any point in the figure

Figure 13–20   A Pyramid of Decision Levels for Mapping Dependencies and Interactions

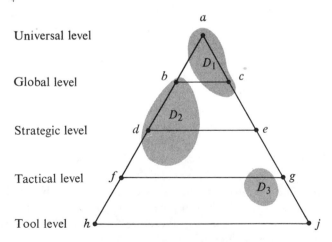

should be construed as the sum of the entropies of all points below it. But clustering reduces the actual entropy with which the individual must deal. At the level of global responsibility, some of the alternatives are removed. For example, area D_1 is specified as a mixture of universal and global considerations so that a bounded set of conclusions can be reached. The mappings of D_2 and D_3 indicate that they are constrained by factors other than those developed at the universal level. In none of the cases shown do the decisions reached above seem to affect the tool level of responsibility (*hj*). The universal level of responsibility is the essence of what the large system is all about, but it is really quite isolated from the managerial system as we presently know it. All to the good, there are definite signs that the strategic and global levels are in greater communication with lower levels than ever before. While such changes are much to be hoped for, they cannot be achieved until the system of communicating with aggregates and interrelating them is improved by substantially increased managerial ability to work with large systems.

SUMMARY

Many forces are pushing us to view systems as ever larger aggregates. For example, special importance can be attached to the increased information age of individuals, which reduces the use of ritual, thereby supporting greater personal entropy. There would be greater total entropy even with a constant population, but with an expanding population, the effect is a marked growth in the total entropy with which management must deal. In this context, the entropies of supply and demand are examined. The number of organizations is not increasing in proportion to the growth in demand, so companies must be able to deal with systems having substantially larger amounts of entropy than any previous systems. Although effective consumer organizations might decrease the general level entropy, there is no evidence that the future holds in store such external regulation of entropy.

To understand the nature of aggregations, we introduce the input-output model and show it to be a component structure of decision models. Each decision model results from the aggregation of at least two (and usually many) input-output units. The key to understanding the input-output model is the transformation function, which takes specific inputs and converts them into sets of outputs. The outputs can then be evaluated as to their fulfillment of managerial objectives. Each cell of a decision matrix is shown to be a unique input-output configuration. Clearly, therefore, input-output models do not have normative properties; they are descriptive of process.

As we aggregate individuals and machines into groups and organizations, we obtain many-component input-output systems that are dynamic—that is, in which every element, and the transformation process itself, can change over time. The obvious next step is to explore the various ways in which what is unknown about the process can be determined from what is known about it. Variants of input-output processes are developed, emphasizing the different kinds of transformation that are available. The use of the black-box concept to describe unknown transformation properties of a system is developed. The importance of trajectory analysis for black-box systems is illustrated, but at the same time the general utility and methodology of trajectory analysis is recognized. Matrix and kinematic diagram representation are contrasted with the use of a two-row transform table. Examples of such transform tables are presented in the text. Throughout, the discussion focuses on the nature of trajectories and the various ways in which trajectory analysis can provide essential information for the manager.

Trajectory analysis is sensitive to the difference between continuous clock time and sequence for recording events that are drawn from a specific repertory. Such factors as the size and stability of the repertory affect the information-theory measures of entropy and redundancy that can be obtained. The concept of Markovian trajectories is broken into four different variants, each of which can be analyzed for patterns. A steady-state analysis, which determines long-run average properties of a system is presented. One of the trajectory variants represents a two-component aggregation that is sharing information. The analysis indicates that two types of error or noise exist in such a system. One of these is called equivocation and the other ambiguity. The method of analysis that follows is a powerful tool for understanding the organization of simple aggregations. Coupled, deterministic aggregations are introduced. Here, the causes and effects are entirely specified in a deterministic fashion, yet complex behaviors can result. When a random generator is introduced to operate on the input, even higher-order complexities are obtained. The next logical step is the study of feedback deterministic aggregations as a higher level of systems aggregation. For example, it is shown that although the interrelated trajectories of the two units operate on deterministic rules, illusory stochastic properties nevertheless confuse the analysis of such simple two-component aggregations. The use of information analysis again sheds considerable light.

Coupled, stochastic systems (best known as queuing models) are introduced. Bottlenecks are considered, and the nature of idle time that arises in such stochastic systems is explained. The effect of variable input and output rates in creating queues is demonstrated. A number of simple queuing models are introduced to exemplify the importance of understanding this kind of aggregation. A great deal of special terminology is required to understand stochastic aggregations. Such language is offered in the process of explaining the behavior of queuing models, their inputs and transformation properties, as well as various measures of output performance. Several numerical examples of the use of queuing models are developed.

A well-known phenomenon of organizational aggregations is the (log-normal) way they cluster with respect to performance. That is, in general, a few high performers contribute most of the output. The aggregation of unequal contributors is more often the case than not, and we develop various examples to illustrate its generality. For instance, the concept of clustering is carried to information systems where profit centers and budget-control centers, each having different forms of unequal contributions, exist. Depending on the measure of assets, profits, or risks, quite different managerial views of the organization emerge. Similarly, programming, planning, and budgeting systems aggregate contributions in different ways, depending on whether cost-effectiveness analysis or cost-benefit analysis is used. We recognize that the choice is a function of managerial level. Responsibility clusters in hierarchical systems must be mapped against responsibility for specific problems. Such aggregates account for managerial attitudes that emerge from organized systems.

EXERCISES

1. Why has the increasing information age of the average person produced greater entropy in the total system? Discuss the effect of increasing knowledge on society's entropy, bearing in mind the fact that information interacts with ceremony and ritual. Explain the application of entropy measures to the facts that product life is getting shorter, that fads occur more often and dissipate more rapidly, and that styles change abruptly and continually.

2. Why is Notre Dame a high-entropy cathedral? Why can such high-entropy cathedrals no longer be built? In the same vein, discuss the possibility that the reduction in social entropy brought about by the decrease of personal planning horizons is more than compensated for by other effects produced. Why would an effective consumer organization decrease the marketplace entropy of total demand? To what extent has this occurred?

3. Discuss the term "black box" and its use. What appeal does this phrase have for the scientist? for the manager? Is this simply a new term for an old concept? When is a black box a satisfactory representation of human behavior? (Bear in mind the character of black-box analysis.)

4. What is a trajectory and what is meant by trajectory analysis? Explain the use of the transform terms one-one, one-many, and many-one as they apply to trajectory analysis. Show that any trajectory can be represented diagrammatically as well as in matrix form. If the properties of the trajectory can be classified, certain advantages accrue to the manager. What are these? Why do we distinguish between closed systems and open systems, and how do these appear in diagrammatic and matrix form?

5. Provide an interpretation for each of the following transform systems. (That is, describe some states to which the operand and transform symbols might reasonably apply.) Also comment on the operators, A through E.

$$T_A \downarrow \begin{array}{ccccc} 1 & 2 & \ldots & 12 \\ 2 & 3 & \ldots & 1 \end{array}$$

$$T_B \downarrow \begin{array}{cccccccc} R_H & R_1 & R_{46} & R_{17} & R_V & R_{17} & R_{46} & R_1 \\ R_1 & R_{46} & R_{17} & R_V & R_{17} & R_{46} & R_1 & R_H \end{array}$$

$$T_C \downarrow \begin{array}{cccccc} 14 & 23 & 34 & 42 & 50 & 59 \\ 23 & 34 & 42 & 50 & 59 & 72 \end{array}$$

$$T_D \downarrow \begin{array}{cccc} O & M & C & P \\ M & C & P & O \end{array}$$

$$T_E \downarrow \begin{array}{cc} 1 & 2 \\ 2 & 1 \end{array}$$

6. Develop suitable scenarios (constructed of operands, transforms, and operators) to describe the following situations:

a. Computer instructions to obtain an arithmetic average.
b. An inspection routine in a spaghetti factory.
c. Assembly instructions for a radio with printed circuits.

Noting the difference between a trajectory based on clock time and that based on sequence, do you favor one or the other for your scenarios? What relevance do the size and stability of the repertory have for the trajectory analysis?

7. Develop the steady state analysis for the matrix shown below.

→	A	B	C
A	.1	.1	.8
B	.2	.2	.6
C	.4	.3	.3

Why is it that the steady state analysis is required in this case, whereas for the example in the text it was not? (Use this matrix to simulate a chain of events and then determine the entropy of the trajectory you have generated.)

8. Assign some simple task to a two-man group composed of friends or fellow students and then observe their pattern of interaction as they go about resolving this problem. You will have developed a communication matrix similar to the one shown in the section on shared information in a two-component aggregation. Analyze the entropic properties of this matrix, as was done in the text, treating the equivocation and ambiguity errors that are inherent in the transmissions. Describe your results. (We have suggested that a real behavioral experiment be developed between sender and receiver because in this way the relevance of theory in application is more readily apparent.) Assume that a receiver-sender system is plagued by extreme ambiguity. Develop a matrix indicating that such a condition exists. Suggest real-world conditions that might give rise to this kind of situation.

9. Using the methods developed in the section on simple, deterministic aggregations and turning to the examples that are presented in that section (p. 560), determine what would occur if T_α's trajectory had started with the initial state d. Now, change α's trajectory to the following: 33322431122. Utilize this α trajectory to compare what would happen if the initial state of T_α is either a or d. Starting with the initial state of d for T_α, explain how the α trajectory should be arranged to provide for the following T_α sequence: *acdb,* regularly repeating in this way. Then, making any changes you deem useful, illustrate the existence of an illusory cycle in T_α's trajectory. Further, show that the entropy of a deterministic system that produces the trajectory cycle (*lkmkm*) regularly and repeatedly must be zero.

10. Explain the reason that stochastic, simple systems develop waiting lines. Are there any situations in which this would not happen? Give some examples of waiting-line situations that would have practical applicability for management. What kinds of cost are involved in the operation of such systems? Why are such models critical to the organization of the enterprise?

11. Explain the nature of clustering, giving some examples of how skewed distributional effects will be encountered in complex organizations. Obtain data of a real situation that allows the exercise of human choice such as "who speaks to whom, and how often." Plot its log-normal curve. How would a log-normal arrangement reflect the fact that generally only a few parts are really critical in a maintenance inventory?

12. Programming, planning, and budgeting systems have been widely used in government. Do they have equal applicability for industry? Explain your answer. Also, treat the question of cost-effectiveness versus cost-benefit analysis in terms that reflect the variety of levels at which decision problems occur in an organization (i.e., from the tool level through the universal decision level). With respect to both cost-effectiveness analysis and cost-benefit analysis, how do their interactions with decision problems map across the various hierarchical levels of managerial responsibility? Why is this mapping viewpoint important in understanding the aggregation of behaviors in an organization?

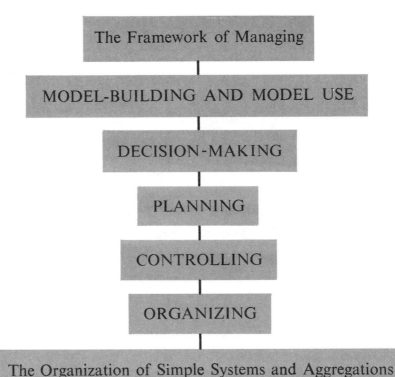

The Framework of Managing

MODEL-BUILDING AND MODEL USE

DECISION-MAKING

PLANNING

CONTROLLING

ORGANIZING

The Organization of Simple Systems and Aggregations

Chapter 14
The Person in the Organization

Explanations of individual behavior can be mechanistic
or cybernetic. These structural viewpoints encompass
tropisms, conditioned responses, operant conditioning, physical
differences, and perception characteristics. Alternatively,
human motivation can provide a behavioral explanation. Much
can be learned from both approaches. A third approach to
understanding the role of the individual in the organization
centers on patterns of behavior. Thus, for example, territoriality
might explain managerial behavior. Learning, intelligence,
skills, and stress are also to be considered, as are Zipf's
principle of least effort and Moran's hypothesis
for maximum entropic change.

Chapter 14

THE PERSON IN
THE ORGANIZATION

"It is better to understand a little than to misunderstand a lot."[1]

THE SUM OF THE PARTS

Management can develop an organization of individuals *only* if it recognizes why individuals are capable of and interested in becoming part of organizations. The identification that any individual has with a specific organization is more or less transient. The degree of permanence is an individual matter. This has always been true, but it is becoming increasingly evident that coordinated individualism is the very essence of organization, and management is well aware of this fact. If they have no alternatives, individuals may seem to give up their identities and become cooperative "bricks" in a complex structure. Now, however, they do have alternatives, so they must be treated as individuals. Organization begins with this recognition. The lack of it may be the end of an organization.

Everything is organized to some extent. Philosophically, interrelatedness is all part of a grand design whether teleology[2] is used as an argument or not. But the sense of organization that we are

---

[1] Anatole France, *Revolt of the Angels*.
[2] The belief that design is *apparent* in nature.

talking about specifically requires human intent and its follow-through in design. Moreover, although nature and man-made mechanisms participate within the organizational framework, organization, as management uses the term, is a human construct for people's purposes.

In this chapter, we start by attempting to understand the person's behavior. The person is the smallest nonmechanical subsystem that management can consider and with which it can deal independently. Then, in Chapter 15, we will examine the aggregation of individuals into small groups and the range of integrated behaviors in these groups. The group has organization, but it is not what we mean by *an organization,* so Chapter 15 concludes by moving on from the group to the largest of human relations, the organization.

A classic definition of organization is "a system of consciously coordinated personal activities or forces."[3] The definition is useful to the extent that all people share word meanings and to the extent that the word meanings are clear. Here, for example, what is "conscious coordination"?

Another definition of organization might be: an arrangement of human entropy designed to provide the maximum possible control over a system's output. Hopefully, with good organization, the outputs will be in accord with the system's total set of objectives. However, the set of objectives is not necessarily either simple or internally consistent. And there can be contradictions between the organizational objectives of various groups within the organization and the personal objectives of the participating individuals. Management, in these terms, is the organization's agent for designing, regulating, planning, and, in general, manipulating the entropic potentials of the system. If it does this effectively, it is said to be coordinating well. Conscious coordination implies rational observation, inference, and evaluation (through feedback).

The *detail* with which the manager can view a small system is extensive, but as the system grows in size, the view must become less detailed, since it is subject to some *human limits* on the *amount of entropy* that can be understood and handled by an individual. (We will have more to say about these human informational limits shortly.) Clearly, we can consider the needs and behaviors of persons in more detail than we can those of groups. The same can be said for small groups as compared to large organizations. But the systems of persons, groups, and organizations are totally interrelated, and we must weave back and forth among them in our quest for real understanding.

Many interesting and critical questions arise at the organizational level of systems behavior. People control organizations and participate in their activities, yet an organization continues when some of its people leave it to join another. Why is this so? When a dissident group takes over an organization, the question arises of how individual equities are to be maintained. Is that

---

[3] Chester Barnard, *The Functions of the Executive* (Cambridge, Mass.: Harvard University Press, 1938), p. 72.

question usually asked? Is leadership a personal quality, independent of situation and therefore completely transferable between jobs and companies? Does stock ownership constitute a measure of organizational equity? How is equity distributed in an organization that does not have a stock base to establish voting rights? Issues such as these cannot always be resolved, but, as our awareness grows concerning the nature of organizations, we may at least begin to ask the right questions. Let us begin here by seeing how others have tried to view the individual in the system.

MECHANISTIC AND CYBERNETIC VIEWS

One of the accusations often leveled at students of individual behavior is that their simplistic analogies are too simple and that their complex models are too broadly stated. In particular, the mechanistic theory has been attacked for being too simplistic. Nevertheless, if human behavior is considered in machinelike terms, some interesting insights can be obtained.

Almost every approach to understanding people as individuals has some mechanistic components, even when the theorist disclaims and attacks mechanism. The reason is clear—we have an affinity with the machines we build. We are capable of understanding them as extenders of human abilities (e.g., a drop hammer for extending muscle power, a microscope and a telescope for extending vision, a computer for extending arithmetic speed and memory). These are all forms of mechanical transformation of input-output models, so the parallel is drawn almost unconsciously. The fact that the machine may be stochastic and not determinate can lead to the illusion that a nonmechanistic approach has been taken. (Typically, the coupled or feedback system discussed on pp. 562–64 is an adequate pattern of a deterministic machine. Queuing behaviors are described on pp. 565–68 to represent the stochastic class.)

In recent years, increasing numbers of analysts trained in the quantitative and cybernetic fields have played a growing part in the study of individual behavior. Their contributions are real but clearly limited, given the present state of psychology, neurology, physiology, and so forth. Two schools of thought exist. One believes that something is *missing* and then when *it* is found a satisfactory theory will emerge. This point of view encompasses the possibility that what is missing is a framework and that when some totally new integration or association of the variety of information that is presently available occurs, a new understanding will be generated. The second viewpoint is that we will *gradually* improve our understanding of human behavior, never arriving at an entirely satisfactory theory but continually closing the gap between what we know and what we want to know.

The machine point of view could belong to either school of thought, but it is predisposed to the first. The study of systems of machines and their relations, which we call cybernetics, gets sufficiently complex to seem to approach a humanistic threshold, but if cybernetic machine systems act with recognizable human traits, they are not expected to feel human emotions. On the contrary, cybernetic systems do not subscribe to nonoperational terms concerning emotions and attitudes because they refer to things that cannot be measured. It is misleading at best to say that A is 2.5 times more emotional than $B,$ and similar measurement difficulties exist for specific emotions.[4]

Perhaps it is the nature of language that conditions our thinking and blocks the completion of a model of human behavior. Language may simply reflect a personal, entirely relative mental state, which is a rationalization for the things we do, not an explanation of why we do them. By avoiding these problems, cybernetics cuts out a part of the system that may be unmeasurable but seems essential. Whatever the reasons, the fact is that viewing man as "a special kind of machine" fails to capture in the model whatever it is that is special. Later, as we undertake to examine groups formed of individuals, we will observe that the behavior of the group is also incompletely projected as an aggregation of machines. It is generally conceded that the human view of human beings is essential if we are to understand our behavior. But this statement is paradoxical, since we are unable to account for the human view of the characteristics that produce the human being. So we come back to cybernetics and machine-type hypotheses.

Having made these disclaimers, we can now approach several of the more mechanistic hypotheses that have been suggested by serious students of human behavior.

Deterministic Tropisms and Behavior

In the early 1900's, a school of behavior developed that predicated the existence of highly mechanical human responses. From the work of J. Loeb on *tropisms* in insects and animals,[5] stemmed analogous explanations of a variety

---

[4] An important school of psychology, following the early work of Charles Spearman, had taken the position stated by E. L. Thorndike that "whatever exists, exists in some quantity, and can in principle be measured." While the same point of view persists in many areas of human studies, it is noticeably tempered by the distinction between principle and practice.

[5] See Jacques Loeb, *Forced Movements, Tropisms, and Animal Conduct,* Monographs on Experimental Biology (Philadelphia: Lippincott, 1918).

of human actions. For example, the moth is phototropic—drawn to light. In fact, it is responding to a chemical reaction caused by the light falling on one of its sides. The chemical change that the moth undergoes is not systematically symmetric and produces a muscular constriction on only one side. This turns the moth toward the light and directs it to the light source.[6] It was supposed that far more complex stimuli (acting on multidimensional physical and instinctual mechanisms) could ultimately be found to explain a great part of human behavior.

Although the school of tropism never gathered great momentum or numerous adherents because it was entirely too physical, the concept of programmed reflexes continued to pervade an important part of managerial thinking. Frederick W. Taylor reflected the prevalent tropistic thinking in his belief that workers could be trained and motivated in essentially mechanistic ways. Many other managerial philosophies were (and still are) rooted in the notion that an optimal (instinctual) behavior pattern can be found to motivate the individual and thereby markedly improve industrial performance. Formulas representing monetary inducements and/or psychological need-fulfillment continue to be propounded in the effort to affect human behavior. The major difference today is that the concept of tropisms is related far less to physical phenomena and far more to the psyche, especially in relation to the mass persuasion of groups of people.

As some examples of management tropisms, we can suggest the following:

1. There is a tendency to measure what is *easiest* to measure.
2. There is a tendency to measure only one thing (or one thing at a time).
3. The manager tends to avoid change until the threat to the system's status quo becomes excessive.
4. Management reluctantly accepts conditions of risk and turns away from uncertainty.
5. Managers are biased in favor of Type I errors (rejecting what is true) in order to avoid Type II errors (accepting what is false).

The era of tropisms has not ended. The concept continues to affect man's social and cultural expectations. And it may, in fact, provide a basis for social progress.

---

[6] Other types of tropism include sitotropism (the response of living cells to the attractive or repulsive influence of food), heliotropism (the tendency of an organism to turn to or grow toward sunlight), and chemotropism (a growth response in plants to chemical stimuli).

Conditioned Responses

The conditioned responses elicited by Pavlov from animals operate at a higher level of (deterministic) behavior than do tropisms, because a form of *learning* is involved.[7] Pavlov relied not on specific tropistic instincts, but on the fact that a generalized learning instinct exists to associate all simultaneous input stimuli with an effect caused by any one of them. Accordingly, Pavlov showed that physical and cognitive behavior could be modified (such as conditioning a dog to salivate when a bell rings by associating the bell with the appearance of food). A large and vocal school of psychological thought emerged in line with the Pavlovian concept. Sometimes called "operant conditioning," it reflects the individual's desire to obtain rewards and to avoid penalties. In other words, the conditioning associations that are used are quite specific. Experiments (which are still being conducted) emphasize stimulus-response situations tied in with the "law of effect," which holds that rewarded behaviors tend to be remembered. The effects of conditioning might be exemplified by the following behaviors:

1. The individual gradually adjusts his expectations to make them closer to actual achievements.
2. Advertising and promotional expenses are allocated in direct proportion to the prior period's sales (i.e., as a reward for sales).
3. New items in the product line are imitations of the most successful, stable items in the present line.
4. Managers seeking promotion strive to emulate their superiors and continue to do so after promotion.

We can find many other examples of associative and reward conditioning, all of which are only partial truths, but truths nevertheless. Much additional work is progressing and would be documented if such were the main purpose of our presentation. F. M. Berger develops the theme that anxiety serves as a major conditioning *catalyst*.[8] Berger's thesis is that people cannot be controlled through drugs and simple conditioning methods unless first perturbed into a state of deep anxiety. He points out that given such a condition the individual becomes vulnerable and capable of being brought under control. Organization is essential to achieve such results. In political situations, for

---

[7] See, for example, I. P. Pavlov, *Conditioned Reflexes,* trans. and ed. by G. V. Anrep (New York: Dover, 1927). Ivan Pavlov (1849–1936) shared in the development of the classic hypotheses of conditioning with such well-known psychologists as G. Stanley Hall, Edward C. Tolman, and John B. Watson.

[8] See F. M. Berger, "Control of the Mind," *American Journal of Pharmacy,* March–April 1966.

example, organizations tend to single out individuals of the opposition rather than to allocate their activities to undifferentiated groups.

Physiological Characteristics

Pavlov noted that dogs of different constitutions reacted in various ways to conditioning. Later, studies were conducted to find deterministic, constitutional explanations for human behavior. At one time, for example, phrenology attempted (unsuccessfully) to relate mental ability to the formation of the skull. We do not wish to discredit these studies. They have had their effect, although they operate at approximately the same level as tropistic theories. Part of their impact is traceable to culture-bound intuitions about the size and shape of people (i.e., somatotype or body build). Whether or not Caesar distrusted lean men, Shakespeare thought the point sufficiently valid to make it.[9]

Raymond Cattell reports[10] that national characteristics show special affinities in some cases for introversion, in others for extroversion. Myriad studies have been aimed at determining constitutional factors in criminality. For management, there comes to mind the question: Are leaders born, not trained? (We will address the issue of leadership shortly—see pp. 644–47.) Sheldon hypothesized that different constitutional forms (classified as somatotypes) reflect specific kinds of individual behavior. His system is frequently identified with three fundamental body types—endomorphic (heavy-set), mesomorphic (muscular), and ectomorphic (lean and fragile)—although he proposes many additional somatotypes in his book.[11] Each type, according to Sheldon, exhibits significantly different personality traits. Modeling schools have used Sheldon's distinctions in helping to train and place the various young ladies who appear in our magazines and on television. Some organizations have attempted to apply Sheldon's schema in the training and positioning of their management-level employees. But the number of disclaimers would be far more vocal than those supportive of Sheldon's work if we could but ask for and get a vote.

Contemporary emphasis has shifted from physiological to psychological classification. For example, we previously discussed (p. 109) the distinction

---

9 "Let me have men about me that are fat,
  Sleek-headed men, and such as sleep o' nights.
  Yond Cassius has a lean and hungry look.
  He thinks too much, such men are dangerous."
              —*Julius Caesar*, Act I, sc. ii.
10 In his book *The Scientific Analysis of Personality* (Baltimore: Penguin Books, 1965), p. 46.
11 W. H. Sheldon and S. S. Stevens, *The Varieties of Temperament* (New York: Harper & Row, 1942).

between "heuristic" and "analytic" managerial temperaments. Additional evidence of interest in classification by psychological variables exists in the marketing field, where there has been a gradual shift from physically measurable demographic characteristics (such as income, age, education) to psychological variables (such as timidity, anxiety, venturesomeness), which are far more difficult to measure.

Perception

A critical area for the study of personal behavior is that of the characteristics of human perception. We have on several occasions mentioned the limitations on the amount of detailed information that an individual can simultaneously perceive and interrelate. The effect was discussed in terms of managerial specialization and generalization, organizational centralization and decentralization, as well as the overall management of the information flows in a system. As George Miller has eloquently documented,[12] the number 7 (plus or minus 2) appears as an empirical limit on detailed information processing with far greater frequency than would ordinarily be expected. "There seems to be some limitation built into us either by learning or by the design of our nervous systems, a limit that keeps our channel capacities in this general range."[13] Miller lists many tests that indicate a human limit of about 7 for unidimensional judgments. For example, in the identification of different tones, absolute judgments of loudness, recognition of taste intensities, and reading a visual control panel, measures between 5 and 9 appear repeatedly.

> My problem is that I have been persecuted by an integer. For seven years this number has followed me around, has intruded in my most private data, and has assaulted me from the pages of our most public journals. This number assumes a variety of disguises, being sometimes a little larger and sometimes a little smaller than usual, but never changing so much as to be unrecognizable. The persistence with which this number plagues me is far more than a random accident. There is, to quote a famous senator, a design behind it, some pattern governing its appearances.[14]

Of the greatest importance is the fact that when several dimensions are involved simultaneously in the judgment, the *total* limit rises—that is, as more

---

[12] George A. Miller, "The Magical Number Seven, Plus or Minus Two: Some Limits on Our Capacity for Processing Information," *Psychological Review,* Vol. 63 (March 1956), pp. 81–97.

[13] *Ibid.,* p. 86.

[14] *Ibid.,* p. 81.

dimensions are added, total discrimination increases (although at a rapidly decreasing rate). But there is a loss in *sensitivity* for detail, a loss of accuracy along each of the scales. It appears that the slightly increased total discrimination must be shared by a greater number of dimensions. The judgments on each scale are not rendered independently. Management seems to need more dimensions and less detail to reach its decisions and to plan for the future. But this is a hierarchical matter. At the top of the organization, greater total discrimination would seem to be desirable; at lower echelons, awareness of detail on fewer scales appears necessary. Organization theory must include design considerations for assigning to managers, in these terms, responsibility for dimensions of performance. The information-perception concept is a fundamental basis for organization theories in general, treating, for example, the hierarchical properties of systems, managerial span of control, and so forth.

We should not feel impelled to accept the perception range of 5–9, but the recognition that some narrow range does exist presents another mechanistic attribute of human behavior. Learning is known to modify this limit. For example, a trained musician can distinguish many more notes played simultaneously than an untrained one. However, a limit (say, ten notes) still holds. And for output, limits (such as that of the fastest typist) also prevail. The flexibility of the rules for grouping details into new sets may be far more significant to the manager than his ability to enlarge this perception limitation. A real distinction between managerial abilities could lie in the ability to define sets rather than in the number of such sets that can be simultaneously considered. *Models* have enlarged the *number* of sets of detailed information that can be interrelated, and the *computer* has increased dramatically the amount of *detail* that can be handled within each set. It remains to be seen how the manager adjusts to these new conditions. Management is presently searching for a new *perception equilibrium*. The dimensionality required to treat the average organizational problem has increased manyfold. The computer is ideal for detail, replacing many middle-management functions that are concerned with few dimensions in detail.

The significance of the mechanistic approach to perception is evident as soon as we consider the increasingly important role played by mechanical systems monitors. If machines are to be substituted for persons, then their perceptive abilities must be equal to the task. Technology has advanced rapidly in many *sensing* areas, and frequently jobs that could not be performed by men can be done by machines. An obvious illustration would be the monitoring of ultraviolet light, but even in the visual spectrum, for speed, reliability, and freedom from error and fatigue, the machine monitor surpasses the human in many instances. When faced with multidimensional scales, machine monitors do not suffer the losses of *accuracy* that men do. But machines cannot *generalize* to many dimensions without enormous and costly studies being made, and, even then, failure is quite possible. Machines also lose out when self-perception is important. Self-perception allows the person to learn what is happening in the system and to observe his own role in the system. As a result of this observation his behavior is modified both consciously and unconsciously. The machine can modify only its choice of role, not the mechanism that chooses roles. Self-adaptive abilities may someday be embodied in machines (there is discussion of this possibility in the cybernetics literature), but the time is hardly imminent.

The most important point about perception in man is that "the facts of raw sensory data are insufficient to produce or to explain the coherent picture of the world as experienced by the normal adult. . . . Indeed, the study of perception is largely the study of what must be added to and subtracted from raw sensory input to produce our picture of the world."[15]

Such a great variety of findings exists with respect to perception that it is inconceivable to present a sufficient catalogue in just a few pages. We are interested in different perception characteristics of consumers, managers, stockholders, and so on. The manager's experience, if he is an aware manager, tells him many things about how he perceives and how others perceive. That is why, at the beginning of this book, we emphasized managerial awareness and self-awareness, for which there are no substitutes. There is reason to believe that the sensitivity of a manager's perception diminishes as he becomes *overloaded* with inputs. Berelson and Steiner report that "man attains his maximum sensitivity under conditions of minimal stimulation."[16] Accordingly, a manager might well profit by "wasting" some of his time, if wasted time cuts down on the inputs he must process. He may wish to control his "differential threshold," which affects his ability to distinguish between stimuli (called "jnd" for "just noticeable difference"). In such ways, as (merely) suggested by the above, the work of the various schools of perception, cognition, and human behavior can back up the manager's experience, and one must surely recommend that the manager consider himself a continuing student of human behavior.

MOTIVATION AND HUMAN BEHAVIOR

Of the many ways human behavior can be examined, the study of motivation may well be the most important. Following Berelson and Steiner, motivation is

---

[15] B. Berelson and G. A. Steiner, *Human Behavior, An Inventory of Scientific Findings* (New York: Harcourt Brace Jovanovich, 1964), p. 87.

[16] *Ibid.,* pp. 91–92.

all those inner striving conditions variously described as wishes, desires, needs, drives and the like. . . . Formally, then, a motive is an inner state that energizes, activates or moves (hence "motivation"), and that directs or channels behavior toward goals. In short, a motive results in and hence can be inferred from purposive, means-end behavior. . . . One note of caution needs to be stressed. . . . Since motives are both inferred from and taken to account for purposive behavior, there is always the danger of accepting circular reasoning—of taking a motive as an explanation of the very behavior from which it was inferred.[17]

Motivation analysis comes closest to providing a nonmechanistic view of the person. The word "motivation" simply does not fit the reasons for a machine's behavior.[18] This fact has the obvious advantage of allowing whatever qualities distinguish people from mechanisms to emerge. The major disadvantage is the difficulty of distinguishing a motivation from a description of behavior. Intuition plays a large part. Being "one of them" ourselves makes it easier for most of us to communicate with people than with machines. However, the rapport can be misleading. Management usually sees machines for what they are but all too readily can read things into other men's behavior that just are not there.

The scientific study of animal behavior is called *ethology*. It applies to all animals and asks the same question: Why does the animal behave as it does? Does it have motives? We may learn something about the nature of human motivation by studying other animals, by attempting to differentiate between their *innate* and their *acquired* behaviors—but in the final analysis, management cannot make much use of such information until the experimental results are generalized to man.[19] The part of ethology that *management* is most concerned with deals with man, the thinking animal, and some part of people's motives can be attributed to instincts that seem to be as primitive as those of any other animal.

---

[17] *Ibid.*, pp. 239–40.

[18] W. Grey Walter, in his book *The Living Brain* (New York: Norton, 1953), describes a simple machine that he built to respond to light by means of a photocell. Walter calls the mechanism (or automaton) a turtle—Machina Speculatrix. The turtle's actions appear to follow from many motivations ascribed to people (e.g., it is gregarious; it has a strong survival instinct, "taking pains" to recharge itself before it runs out; it avoids work; and it "likes" to look at itself in a mirror). Walter points out what Berelson and Steiner caution against—namely, mistakenly attributing motives to what are simply descriptions of actions.

[19] From Berelson and Steiner: ". . . it is worth recalling an observation of the late Edward Tolman, a distinguished psychologist. He once noted how much of American psychology was based on two sets of subjects, rats and college sophomores, and enjoined his colleagues to remember that the former certainly are not people and the latter may not be!" (See their footnote, *op. cit.*, p. 23).

Machines, of course, do not have instincts, but the fact is that their *programmed* behavior resembles instinctual behavior in many ways. In general, machines have begun to exhibit an ever greater share of humanlike qualities. Their programs are becoming more richly endowed. Machines have *memories* that in certain ways surpass those of men; in a limited sense they appear to *think,* and there is no doubt that they can *learn.* Still, for many years to come, human behavior will remain *pragmatically* different from that of machines. This may be because men are entirely more complex in their sensing, thinking, and acting mechanisms, or it may be for other reasons. Operationally, they are different, and it is with those special human characteristics that we now wish to deal.

Personal Needs

Some needs are physically measurable, but above this basic level, it is hard to know whether we are simply describing what we observe. For example, does ambition produce hard work or does the desire to work hard derive from other sources? With circular reasoning it is often said that individual needs underlie specific behaviors and the specific behaviors are defined as the needs. The only way to break out of the circle is by attempting to define specific needs. Many different systems have been proposed to do this. For example, Maslow has defined a hierarchy of needs that range from the root physiological needs at the base to self-actualization at the apex.[20] Specifically, these needs are:

1. *Self-actualization*—the need to realize one's own potential.
2. *Esteem*—the need for recognition accorded to an individual by his associates. Authority and responsibility are organizational descriptions of the distribution of esteem. The reality of the organization chart (as it is perceived) overrides specifications.
3. *Social need*—the desire to belong to certain groups and to be loved by its members.
4. *Safety*—the desire for security and survival.
5. *Physiological needs*—the fundamental motivators such as sex, hunger, and so forth.

Perhaps these categories are helpful. But there is no way to measure how much of a need an action will fulfill; nor can we describe what a person's state is at any time in terms of these needs. Yet management can design a program that is aimed at satisfying some of these needs. A reasonable environ-

---

[20] Abraham Maslow, *Motivation and Personality* (New York: Harper & Row, 1954). The main description of his terms will be found in Chapter 5.

ment in which to work as well as a sense of stability in position and of belonging to a group satisfy the third, fourth, and fifth Maslow categories. The first and second categories are far more difficult to achieve. For example, it is necessary to find a way to give organizational esteem to some without taking it away from others, and to allow conditions for self-actualization by individuals without altering their sense of group identification.

Erich Fromm has suggested that the needs of an individual are centered around two problems: "One, the need for a frame of orientation, and the other the need for a frame of devotion." Fromm goes on:

> What are the answers to the need for a frame of orientation? The one overriding answer which man has found so far is one which can also be observed among animals—to submit to a strong leader who is supposed to know what is best for the group . . . to give the individual enough faith to believe in the leader, the leader is assumed to have qualities transcending those of any of his subjects.[21]

Fromm represents the psychoanalytic school, which Cattell, for example, attacks as "fanciful and presumptuous theorizing of pre-metric, pre-experimental theory, based, moreover, almost exclusively on abnormal cases, as in the writings of Adler, Freud, Fromm, Jung, and countless others who have claimed authority to instruct the public, on clinical therapy in particular and psychological laws in general."[22] But one does not have to take sides, because the mystery of what are human needs remains unanswered. Thus, Herzberg points to yet another consideration: "Man needs mystery as much as he needs to know."[23]

Freudian interpretations of need are based on the human's inherited instincts as well as his conditioning within the family in the early years of development. The Freudian need system is divided into three fundamental parts. The collected drives of the individual (essentially sexual in nature) are represented by the *id*. The *ego* operates to find "socially acceptable" manifestations for the drives of the id. Meanwhile, the *superego* acts to control moral behavior in an authoritarian, parental fashion.

> According to Freud's formulation the child brings into the world an unorganized chaotic mentality called the Id, the sole aim of which is the gratification of all needs, the alleviation of hunger, self-preservation, and love, the preservation of the species. However, as the child grows older, that part of the id which comes in contact with the environment through the senses learns to know the inexorable reality of the outer

[21] Erich Fromm, *The Revolution of Hope—Toward a Humanized Technology* (New York: Bantam Books, 1968), p. 65.

[22] Cattell, *op. cit.*, pp. 333–34.

[23] Frederick Herzberg, *Work and the Nature of Man* (Cleveland: World, 1966), p. 55.

world and becomes modified into what Freud calls the ego. This ego, possessing awareness of the environment, henceforth strives to curb the lawless id tendencies whenever they attempt to assert themselves incompatibly. . . .

In a psychosis, illness results from *a conflict between the ego and the outer world,* and in the narcissistic neurosis from *a conflict between the ego and the super-ego.* For just as the ego is a modified portion of the id as a result of contact with the outer world, the super-ego represents a modified part of the ego, formed through experiences absorbed from the parents, especially from the father. The super-ego is the highest mental evolution attainable by man, and consists of a precipitate of all prohibitions and inhibitions, all the rules of conduct which are impressed on the child by his parents and by parental substitutes. The feeling of *conscience* depends altogether on the development of the super-ego.[24]

But, says Cattell, "Psychoanalysis oversimplified, for it talked largely in terms of three primary factors—ego, super-ego, and id—whereas, the multivariate experimental approach shows sixteen to twenty-five."[25]

Yet another point of view, more in line with Maslow's five categories of need, is developed by Herzberg:

The human animal has two categories of needs. One set stems from his animal disposition, that side of him . . . referred to as the Adam view of man; it is centered on the avoidance of loss of life, hunger, pain, sexual deprivation, and on other primary drives, in addition to the infinite varieties of learned fears that become attached to these basic drives. The other segment of man's nature, according to the Abraham concept of the human being, is man's compelling urge to realize his own potentiality by continuous psychological growth.[26]

PATTERNS OF BEHAVIOR

If a set of needs is postulated to explain *all* behavior, then the requirement exists that this unified theory be able to explain all human phenomena. As we have indicated, many have tried their hand at this, but the results are not in accord with expectations. Another approach is based, not on tackling the whole, but on trying to explain only some part of human behavior.

---

[24] A. A. Brill, Introduction to *The Basic Writings of Sigmund Freud* (New York: Random House, 1938), pp. 12–13.

[25] Cattell, *op. cit.,* p. 102.

[26] Herzberg, *op. cit.,* p. 54.

Aggression and Territoriality

Studies of animals, for example, have been conducted by ethologists in order to discern the extent to which instinctual behavior might account for man's actions. Instincts and tropisms are related, the mechanisms of tropisms helping to explain how the instincts work. For many years the argument of instinct-led man versus man of free will continued, and there still is disagreement concerning this matter.

Konrad Lorenz[27] proposed an instinctual basis for *aggression* in the human animal, that is, aggression as an essential element of life. Many contest Lorenz on this point. Even those who do not (and Lorenz himself), believe that man's destiny does not have to be to fight wars. It is reasoned that if he is aware of his instincts for aggression, and is aware that he is caught in this way, then he can learn how to control such instincts.

Aggression results from infringement of or demand for someone else's space. The concept of *territoriality* seems, therefore, to be intimately related to aggression. Edward Hall states:

> Territoriality, a basic concept in the study of animal behavior, is usually defined as behavior by which an organism characteristically lays claim to an area and defends it against members of its own species. It is a recent concept, first described by the English ornithologist H. E. Howard in his *Territory in Bird Life*, written in 1920. . . . Territoriality studies are already revising many of our basic ideas of animal life and human life as well. . . . It is doubtful if Freud, had he known what is known today about the relation of animals to space, could have attributed man's advances to trapped energy redirected by culturally imposed inhibitions.[28]

If we find this a satisfactory explanation of aggressive patterns of behavior in animals, we can recognize that in applying it to man the definition of territory should be expanded. The organization chart might be an example of an attempt to clearly delineate boundaries for management territories.[29] Other abstract forms of territory could include authority relations, freedom to speak out, and, less abstractly, possessions and wealth. One researcher has identified specialization as a form of territoriality. To us, this might mean the boundaries of professions and the description of jobs. Job enlargement, in these terms, would be aggression for more job "territory."

---

[27] Konrad Z. Lorenz, *On Aggression* (New York: Harcourt Brace Jovanovich, 1966).
[28] Edward T. Hall, *The Hidden Dimension* (New York: Doubleday, 1966), pp. 7–8. See also Robert Ardrey, *The Territorial Imperative* (New York: Atheneum, 1966).
[29] See the discussion of pecking order in Chapter 15, pp. 638–40.

In broader scope, we may consider that there is a conflict between territorial consensus and aggression.

> The ideology of contradictions stands in stark contrast to the ideology of consensus which currently seems to govern American politics. The statesman who believes in consensus seeks to move men by appealing to what unites them. The statesman who subscribes to the principle of contradictions, on the other hand, seeks to move men by utilizing the differences among them.[30]

The same dichotomy will be found in many business organizations where the choice of behaviors is dictated by the topmost managers.

Internal Conflict

Conflict resolution must also occur *within each person.* By definition, when conflict occurs at an instinctual level it cannot be resolved rationally. Jean Buridan, who became the rector of the University of Paris in 1327, proposed a model that raised a fundamental question about the resolution of conflicts within the individual. Like present-day ethologists he paralleled the human issue by substituting the consideration of an animal. The question he asked was, "What would happen to a hungry ass that was positioned exactly between two bales of hay?" Because of his hunger, the ass would try to eat. Presumably, it is "driven" to go to the nearest food supply. Since it is exactly halfway between two food supplies, what would it do? Figure 14–1 and the matrix below might be used to describe the problem of Buridan's ass.

	First step		
→	O	a	b
O	0	$\frac{1}{2}$	$\frac{1}{2}$
a	0	1	0
b	0	0	1

This matrix will be the same for two steps, three steps, and so on to the steady state. The reason is that there is a probability of one-half that the ass will go to the right and the same probability that it will go to the left. From either a or b, it will go on to the nearest bale of hay. And, because of the way our matrix is set up, it must leave the center point (O). There really is no problem.

---

[30] Michel Oksenberg, review of Franz Schurmann, *Ideology and Organization in Communist China* (Berkeley: University of California Press, 1966), *New York Times Book Review,* July 17, 1966, p. 1.

Figure 14–1   The Problem of Buridan's Ass

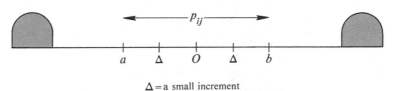

$$\Delta = \text{a small increment}$$

However, the work of ethologists, students of instinct and conflict, and others raises some doubts about the correctness of our matrix. The matrix shown below (marked "First") presents a different pattern based on the fact that as soon as the ass moves toward one of the bales of hay, the farther one becomes more attractive (because he will be forced to give it up). As a result, the ass returns to the center point.

First			Second			Third			Fourth		
0	½	½	1	0	0	0	½	½	1	0	0
1	0	0	0	½	½	1	0	0	0	½	½
1	0	0	0	½	½	1	0	0	0	½	½ ... etc.

In this way, he vacillates, never getting anywhere. Totally frustrated, he is unable to make up his mind and so starves to death. Our matrices illustrate this periodic characteristic.

If a machine were faced with a conflict of instructions (assuming it was not programmed for an override with some additional principle), it would be expected to exhibit aberrant behavior. N. Tinbergen and other ethologists have found that animals actually exhibit "ambivalent behavior" in such circumstances. Tinbergen describes the herring gull, for example, which in the breeding season tries to remove every red object from its nest and sits down on eggs in the nest to incubate them. When faced with

> a bright red dummy of egg shape, it will alternately show the two different reactions in incipient form: first it may peck at the egg and try to get it out of the nest, in the next instant it may raise its ventral feathers and settle down on the egg. The two sign stimuli "something red in the nest" and "egg-shaped object in the nest," respectively, were, as it were, struggling for priority, each activating a different action.[31]

Conflicts at fundamental (if not instinctual) levels may, for the individual, look like indecision. Actions taken may be periodic with ambivalent behavior,

---

[31] N. Tinbergen, *The Study of Instinct* (London: Oxford University Press, 1951), p. 50.

or no action may be taken at all. Quite often we observe the manager to be uncertain and to make an unmotivated decision that then forces him to go along with something halfheartedly. An unfortunate chain of (halfhearted) reactions may result. Perhaps the manager could have been assisted by an additional information expenditure; if not, he might have tried to steer clear of the entire issue. The organization should be comprised so as to avoid as many indecision situations as possible. Reorganization would continually strive to minimize the occurrence of these happenings in the face of changing circumstances.

Stress

We can talk of the need to have territory. But what if the need is not fulfilled? What occurs when any of the needs that provide motivation are frustrated? Stress sets in, changing one's ability to cope with the situation. Sometimes the stress is serious (i.e., pathological). Freud developed a systematic study of the resulting pathologies.

According to Maslow, needs can be destroyed.

> The instinctoid impulses can disappear altogether, as apparently animal instincts cannot. For example, in the psychopathic personality the needs for being loved and loving have disappeared, and so far as we know today, this is a permanent loss, i.e., the psychopathic personality is incurable by any known psychotherapeutic technique. We also have older examples from studies on unemployment in an Austrian village and on unemployment in Scotland, etc., to indicate that long unemployment may crush morale so badly as to destroy certain needs. Such destroyed needs may not return in some even when environmental conditions improve. Similar material has been obtained from the Nazi concentration camps. Bateson's and Mead's observations on the Balinese may also be pertinent. The adult Balinese is not a loving person in our western sense and need not be. Since the motion pictures from Bali show that the infants and children cry and bitterly resent the lack of affection, we can only conclude that this loss of affectionate impulse is an acquired loss.[32]

We hear regularly about the manager under stress. Many studies have been conducted to determine whether the stressful occupation of managers results in shorter life expectancy. The basic thesis in these studies is that stress is harmful to health. But quite generally the results indicate that the manager

---

[32] Maslow, *op. cit.*, p. 131.

lives as long as (or longer than) those whose life patterns avoid employment stress. Hans Selye has brought some useful insight to this area of study. He has examined stress in the medical sense, applying his hypotheses to both psyche and soma. Selye states, "the tweezers of stress have three prongs . . ."[33] He identifies these three factors as, first, the *stressor,* which is the external agent or stimulus that causes antagonism; second, the *defense mechanism,* which is capable of encouraging defense against the stressor; and third, acting at the same time but in conflict, the *mechanism for surrender,* which discourages the system from taking defensive action.

> Only by dissecting our troubles can we clearly distinguish the part played by the stressor from that of our adaptive measures of defense and surrender. . . . Stress is usually the outcome of a struggle for the self-preservation (the homeostatis) of parts within a whole. This is true of individual cells within man, of man within society, and of individual species within the whole animate world.[34]

In dealing with stress, Selye goes on to state, "Fight always for the highest attainable aim but never put up resistance in vain."[35] Lastly, Selye offers a model.

> In analyzing our stress-status, we must always think, not only of the total amount of stress in the body, but also of its proportionate distribution between various parts. To put this into the simplest terms, we might say that the stress-quotient to be watched is:
>
> $$\frac{\text{local stress in any one part}}{\text{total stress in the body}}$$
>
> If there is proportionately too much stress in any one part, you need diversion. If there is too much stress in the body as a whole, you must rest.[36]

Simplifications of this kind, if taken in proper context, are attractive. They do, and undoubtedly should, play a part in our understanding of the behavior of others and in our self-awareness. Clearly, they should not be extended to provide robotlike[37] explanations for patterns of behavior that are far more complex.

---

[33] Hans Selye, *The Stress of Life* (New York: McGraw-Hill, 1967), p. 261.

[34] *Ibid.,* p. 253.

[35] *Ibid.*

[36] *Ibid.,* p. 267.

[37] It is interesting that the word "robot" came into use as a result of a play called *RUR* (Rossum's Universal Robots) written by Karel Çapek in 1926. Çapek chose the word robot from the Slavic word *robotnick,* meaning "worker."

Intelligence and Skills

"Although the only fully precise definition of intelligence is 'what the intelligence tests measure,' the theory underlying the construction of such tests closely matches the ordinary concept of intelligence as general mental ability."[38] According to the dictionary, intelligence is "the power or act of understanding; the power of meeting any situation, especially a novel situation, successfully by proper behavior adjustments; also, the ability to apprehend the interrelationships of presented facts in such a way as to guide action toward a desired goal."[39]

We can be persuaded, without becoming entirely convinced, that an individual's intelligence (as it is defined by the dictionary) can be measured. Persons appear to be more intelligent about some matters than about others. This may indicate that there is motivation for an individual to be intelligent.[40] The fundamental (and deterministic) notion is that intelligence is a human attribute and cannot be learned. Management should take a very broad view of intelligence, requiring that evaluation of it be more multidimensional than an I.Q. test. This applies to hiring, training, and promotion, where a stereotype of what is desired is self-reinforcing and the notion that "like begets like" can operate to the ultimate disadvantage of the organization. By removing difference, the possibility of improvement is limited. At the same time, the advantages of variety for creative management are lost.

Lewis Mumford points out the inevitable evolution of man from the slave of primitive instincts (à la Lorenz) to scientifically intelligent man, the supreme rationalist (in the style of Seidenberg).

> The epithet, "post-historic man," was first coined by Mr. Roderick Seidenberg, in his perspicuous book published under that title. His thesis, reduced to its barest outline, is that the instinctual life of man, dominant all through man's long animal past, has been losing its grip in the course of history, as his conscious intelligence has gained firmer control over one activity after another. In achieving that control, man has transferred authority from the organism itself to the process that intelligence analyzes and serves, that is, the causal process, in which human actors are given the same status as nonhuman agents. By detachment from the instinctual, the purposeful, and the organic and by attachment to the causal and the mechanical, the intelligence has gained

---

[38] Berelson and Steiner, *op. cit.,* p. 209.

[39] *Webster's Collegiate Dictionary,* 5th ed.

[40] Maslow suggests that it may be the other way around: "The needs to know and to understand seem to be *obviously* potent only in intelligent individuals." (Maslow, *op. cit.,* p. 131.)

firmer control over one activity after another: it now steadily pushes from the realm of the "physical" activities to those that are biological and social; and that part of man's nature which does not willingly submit to intelligence will in time be subverted or extirpated.

During the present era, on this assumption, man's nature has begun to undergo a decisive final change. With the invention of the scientific method and the depersonalized procedures of modern technics, cold intelligence, which has succeeded as never before in commanding the energies of nature, already largely dominates every human activity. To survive in this world, man himself must adapt himself completely to the machine. Nonadaptable types, like the artist and the poet, the saint and the peasant, will either be made over or be eliminated, by social selection. All the creativities associated with Old World religion and culture will disappear. To become more human, to explore further into the depth of man's nature, to pursue the divine, are no longer proper goals for machine-made man.

Let us follow this hypothesis through. With intelligence uppermost, thanks to the methods of science, man would apply to all living organisms, above all to himself, the same canons he has applied to the physical world. In the pursuit of economy and power, he would create a society that would have no other attributes than those which could be incorporated in a machine. The machine in fact is precisely that part of the organism which can be projected and controlled by intelligence alone. In establishing its fixed organization and predictable behavior, intelligence will produce a society similar to that of certain insect societies, which have remained stable for sixty million years: for once intelligence has reached a final form, it does not permit any deviation from its perfected solution.

At this point, it is not possible to distinguish between the automatism of instinct and that of intelligence: neither is open to change, and in the end intelligence, too, will become unconscious for lack of opposition and alternatives. If intelligence dictates that there is only one right response to a given situation, only one correct answer to a question, any departure, indeed, any hesitation or uncertainty, must be regarded as a failure of the mechanism or a perversity of the agent. "The party line" must be obeyed; and once scientific intelligence is supreme, even the party line will not change. In the end life, with its almost infinite potentialities, will be frozen into a single mold cast by intelligence alone.[41]

We cannot give a machine an I.Q. test; yet, by the dictionary definition, it seems that in certain *limited* ways, machines (especially computers) possess intelligence. The subject of artificial intelligence will be discussed and written

---

[41] Lewis Mumford, *The Transformations of Man* (New York: Collier Books, 1962), pp. 117–19.

about with increasing frequency in the coming years.[42] Intelligence is one of the prime requisites of organization. It is a resource that is, at least presently, unique to man, which explains why we tend not to describe an association of machines as an organization.

Unlike intelligence, skills are, in many instances, *learned*. Still, there is much evidence and some logic to indicate that the possession of skills is partly constitutional and inherited. Women, for example, have greater manual dexterity than men, whereas men have greater manual strength than women. Here, too, a variety of tests define what skill means. If such measures of performance are properly correlated with the objectives of the organization, then skill testing, at least, becomes operational. Thus, testing is a means of making comparisons between the probable performances of individuals in the context of the positions that are to be filled. Skill resources are not unique to man; in fact, the administrators of organization often prefer to manage mechanical facilities. The intelligent *use of skills* is a fundamental organizational challenge.

Flexibility and adaptability. In some situations *flexibility,* or *adaptability,* is highly desirable. For example, if job enlargement is to be encouraged, the necessity for flexibility is obvious. However, the measurement of flexibility is far from being operational. A humorous (and true) story of the adaptive qualities of individuals illustrates the fact that people often fail to perceive incremental changes, which, over a long period of time, accumulate into substantial differences. Each day, the department manager, who was well

---

[42] This is not to say that artificial intelligence has not been "intelligently" discussed in the past. Isaac Asimov, a great science and science fiction writer, set down a number of years ago the universal laws to govern robots whose intelligence could match (or surpass) that of man. He forecast for his story that the appearance of these laws would occur in the year 2058 A.D.

> A robot may not injure a human being, or, through inaction, allow a human being to come to harm.
> A robot must obey the orders given it by human beings except where such orders would conflict with the First Law.
> A robot must protect its own existence as long as such protection does not conflict with the First or Second Law.
> —*Handbook of Robotics,* 56th Edition, 2058 A.D.
> (From Isaac Asimov, *I, Robot* [New York: New American Library, 1950], p. 6.)

A more useful proposal might be that all robots should be designed so that their recurrence properties would be equivalent to those where $f_j = 1$. It will be recalled from pp. 313–14 in the chapter on planning models that only those systems having states possessing this value could be fully controlled. It is easy to see that creative intelligence would not exist if $f_j = 1$.

known for his handsome walking stick, would enter his office, hanging his cane on the outside coat tree. As a practical joke, members of this firm agreed to remove the cane each day (while the manager was dictating letters) and cut a very thin slice from the bottom. The manager did not recognize the change from one day to the next, but at the end of several months had taken on a noticeable stoop as he walked with his cane. Certainly, at some point, the manager recognized the change in absolute terms, which he was unable to sense in incremental units of day-to-day change. *Habits* are built up in this same fashion. Often they result from various forms of conditioning in which the response is rewarded or penalized through feedback channels. Many management behaviors are strictly habitual. Much of what is commonly called organization is related to ingrained and habitual responses. Eventually, these habits become ritual, and many habits are then reinforced by ritual. Such self-reinforcing systems are hard to escape and are the antithesis of creative management, which is adaptive to change and open to opportunity. On the face of it, flexibility and adaptability should be available without threatening the stability of an organization, but in practice these factors often appear to be inversely related.

Learning

Most of us are persuaded that each individual is unique and not motivated or compelled to behave in a predictable fashion. Because people do not interpret scenarios and dialogues in exactly the same fashion, they learn different things from the same set of circumstances. In fact, much of the indeterminate performance of people is due to learning.

> Learning itself makes for a sort of indeterminacy in the behavior of living organisms, i.e., it makes them, fortunately, *changeable*. We assume, of course, that there is a certain lawfulness about this changeability, this capacity for being modified by experience. But no matter how completely we know *how* learning takes place, it does not enable us at all accurately to predict *what* will be learned—much less *what ought* to be learned.[43]

People don't behave like robots in physical exercise and work any more than in intellectual performance. *Training for skills* that emphasize muscle functions and coordination involves only small degrees of cognition or the attributing of meanings and properties to the system. Nevertheless, large variances will be found between and within individual performances.

---

[43] O. Hobart Mowrer, *Learning Theory and Behavior* (New York: Wiley, 1960), p. 10.

Despite all this, there is a tendency to treat learning deterministically, as the learning model that we will present shortly indicates. As the abstraction of the system that is being learned increases, the indeterminacy that Mowrer speaks of grows. *Training for managerial positions* provides a good example. To begin with, the hiring process cannot adequately discriminate between individuals and performance levels. Consequently, on any attribute (including intelligence) it cannot provide a deterministic dossier on the individual such that a controlled training process will produce a specified set of learned behaviors. At the same time, the more controlled the hiring and training policies used, the less variable the resultant performance is likely to be.

Conditioning and *operant conditioning* are both forms of learning, the latter being adaptive to channeling and direction by management. Clark Hull distinguishes between *discrimination* learning and *trial-and-error* learning: "Simple discrimination learning involves primarily stimulus selection, whereas simple trial-and-error learning involves primarily response selection."[44] If we think in terms of an input-output model, discrimination has to do with the recognition of inputs, and trial-and-error learning concerns the ability to use the transformation (T) in appropriate ways.

Memory plays an important role in learning, since associations are required that integrate the old memories in new ways and the new with the old. Figure 14–2 shows a simple queuing model to provide a representation of the

Figure 14–2   A Simple Model of Memorization

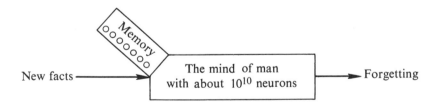

New facts ⟶ Memory ⟶ The mind of man with about 10^{10} neurons ⟶ Forgetting

memorization process. The queue in this case represents the human memory, which shares somehow the 10^{10} neurons that are said to be available in the brain. No one knows how memory really operates or how it should be modeled, and there are disagreements among specialists. For example, Selye says that evidence exists that newly learned facts replace older, stored ones and that stress arises when an individual attempts to remember too much.[45] Another point of view is that human memory is virtually unlimited and that the in-

---

[44] Clark L. Hull, *A Behavior System* (New York: Wiley, 1952), p. 60.

[45] Selye, *op. cit.,* p. 269.

dividual under hypnosis can recall everything that has ever been registered by his sensory system.

There are many forms of learning, and we cannot do justice to this subject in just a few pages. Nevertheless, it will be useful to present another example of a learning model that characterizes the kinds of model being used for estimating the time to accomplish physical jobs, such as those involved in manufacturing operations. More complex forms of the same basic model type are the subject of considerable research. The simple learning model is

$$R(x,n) = rx^{-n}, x \geq 1.$$

Here, x is the learning coefficient—that is, a relative measure of how fast an individual learns. It is an attribute of both the individual and the job, which interact with each other. When $x = 1$, no learning occurs; as learning increases, x grows larger.

$R(x,n)$ is equal to the *average time* required (by a particular worker) to perform a specific operation *after n* experiments; r is the amount of time that was required to perform this operation the *first* time that it was done. We observe that when $x = 1$, no learning occurs. But when $x > 1$, the *average time* required decreases as the number of trials or experiments increases. The learning rate improves as the coefficient x grows larger. Figure 14–3 below represents a family of such curves.

Figure 14–3   A Family of Learning Curves

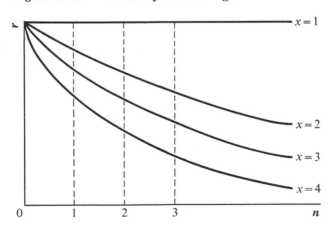

Improvement of the time taken to do a job is a limited interpretation of what we mean by learning. It is hardly a sufficient measure of human learning abilities. The dimensionality with which we view the world is complex, and the ability to associate a number of relevant elements into a coherent whole is what we think of as the root of education. How long it takes to do a task is important, but how the task is done and what is understood—these are the critical evaluators of learning.

Boulding has stated that education can act as a shield against learning. He is referring, of course, to our present system of education, in which imitation is highly vaunted, the basis for grades and success in school. But this is not the basis for success in the business world. The ability to discern the consumers' patterns, for example, requires a form of learning not experienced in school. Getting along with members of a project group involves social learning. The burden might seem trivial in a textbook description but confounding in the organization. Only a small part of a manager's learning function in an organization is related to his ability to perform operations more rapidly. As we move up the managerial ladder the associative abilities that we have discussed become increasingly important. It is essential to understand the term "heuristic" in this regard. Part of what we mean by heuristic ability lies in the manager's knowing how to synthesize a problem in such a way that he develops *actionable* rules of thumb that are adequate to deal with a situation. But, using De Bono's concept of lateral thinking (see p. 495), we observe that creative rules for action are likely to be far more rewarding for the organization than rules accepted for reasons of tradition. Lateral thinking epitomizes the nondeterminate explanation of behavior because it is unlikely to be imitative.

Learning and decision theory are clearly related. The development of the decision matrix for specific circumstances is an exercise in learning about what actually applies in the given situation. The payoff-matrix entries are learned solutions to particular problems. Buridan's hungry ass, whose propensity to move toward one or the other bale of hay is equally likely, is doomed unless he can learn what his problem is. He must discover that although there is no apparent reason to go toward one bale of hay rather than the other, there is an obvious reason to choose one and to go toward it. In decision theory, we often call this kind of situation a *quandary*. Decision models should reflect different organizational values for situations in which the quandary is that of choosing between fully acceptable alternatives and for situations in which *none* of the alternatives is considered desirable. We often describe the latter quandary as being "caught on the horns of a dilemma."

In our treatment of the structure of decision models, we were well aware that human behavior would override our purely formal terms. Language is replete with words that describe behavioral responses to particular decision constructions. Confusion, puzzlement, and determination are but a few examples. Hobson's choice[46] presents a decision where only one alternative appears to be feasible. One *learns* to avoid Hobsonian choices. Seidenberg's

---

[46] So named for Thomas Hobson, who rented horses in Oxford, England, in the 1700's. He did so on the condition that one took the horse he assigned or no horse at all.

thesis that rational men will always reach the same decision in a given fact situation disregards the learning differentials of people and the belief that it is only when all men share the same value system that post-historic man can appear. However, as the computer becomes a more dominant part of the organization, both learning and value differentials tend to disappear, presenting challenge, opportunity, and threat to the organization, as we know it.

Zipf's Principle of Least Effort

George Zipf developed a descriptive model of personal behavior that cuts across the variety of need systems that we have discussed previously.[47] He stated that a person behaves so as to *minimize* the *average* of his expected work load over some period of time that might be called the *personal planning horizon*.[48] (While these are not entirely Zipf's terms, they fit well with the definitions and terminology that we have been developing in this text.) Zipf did not attempt to account for *all* reasons that explain *all* behavior; he proposed what might be called a fundamental (but not sufficient) motivational hypothesis to explain human behavior. The level at which this complex motivational system operates (i.e., the need level) is unspecified; it is easily assumed that it operates at all levels. The Zipfian formulation is fully supported by our previous discussions of the log-normal type of distribution (see p. 572).

Zipf's concept raises many interesting issues, such as: What is a personal planning horizon, and why does it differ from person to person? How does one estimate his expected work load? We do not have good answers for such questions, but we recognize that the questions are bringing us closer to useful concepts than a listing of needs. In other words, whether Zipf is right, wrong, or partially right, his model raises critical questions.

John Galbraith, in a published interview, agreed with the Zipfian principle, though with less apparent sophistication. He stated, "I think that the desire to escape sustained manual effort can be put down as one of the fundamental human qualities."[49] We must note Galbraith's use of the word "sustained." It leads naturally to the question, "Sustained for how long?" and this raises the planning-horizon issue to which we previously referred.

As a simple, but concrete example, consider the two work patterns shown

---

[47] Moran's delta-H principle, which is described in the next section, does the same kind of thing.

[48] George Kingsley Zipf, *Human Behavior and the Principle of Least Effort* (New York: Hafner, 1949).

[49] From Anthony Lewis, "The World Through Galbraith's Eyes," *New York Times Magazine,* December 18, 1966, p. 88.

Table 14–1

	Time period:						
	1	2	3	4	5	6	
Work pattern A	50	40	30	40	50	60	Units of work
Work pattern B	20	20	80	60	80	20	Units of work
	Running averages:						
Work pattern A	50	45	40	40	42	45	Average work units
Work pattern B	20	20	40	45	52	47	Average work units

in Table 14–1. Matrix entries represent units of work in each time period. Pattern A requires harder work than B at first, but by the third period it has posed *average* demands equal to those of pattern B. An individual with a short planning horizon (say one or two time periods) would choose B. A person with a longer view would surely select pattern A, if Zipf's rule is right. The switch occurs after the third time period. Averaging and the planning horizon are both important. Little is known about either mechanism in human behavior. It might be pointed out, however, that the sense of time is relative, being conditioned by many factors. The planning horizon is probably a function of age (and, strangely enough, it is more likely to increase with age). The stability of societal events probably plays a significant role as well. (In this sense, the twentieth century has experienced a decrease in the average planning horizon.) The security and the sensitivity of an individual might be expected to affect his personal planning horizons. The instability of individuals, leading to shifting planning horizons, could account for what might otherwise appear to be inconsistent and irrational behavior.[50]

Earlier we raised the question: "How does one estimate his expected work load?" Again, Zipf offered something of an answer, not complete, but intriguing. Let us turn to the Zipfian model, which can be presented in a number of ways. Essentially, it is a curve of the exponential form ke^{-r_i}, where k is a constant and r_i represents a rank order number for the difficulty of the ith task. The least difficult task is r_1.

According to Zipf, the individual will act in such a way as to perform the least onerous tasks most often and the most difficult ones least often. If we ranked tasks by difficulty (where $r_1 = 0$ for the least difficult, $r_2 = 1$ for the next least difficult, etc.), then the frequency of usage of these tasks would decrease as r_i increases. Zipf offered proof of this principle in many ways. He was an astounding scholar and provided evidence of his principle by studying

---

[50] These notions of planning-horizon effects and effectors are our own, but the Zipfian construct implies some such set of relations.

Figure 14–4   A Characteristic Zipfian Relationship

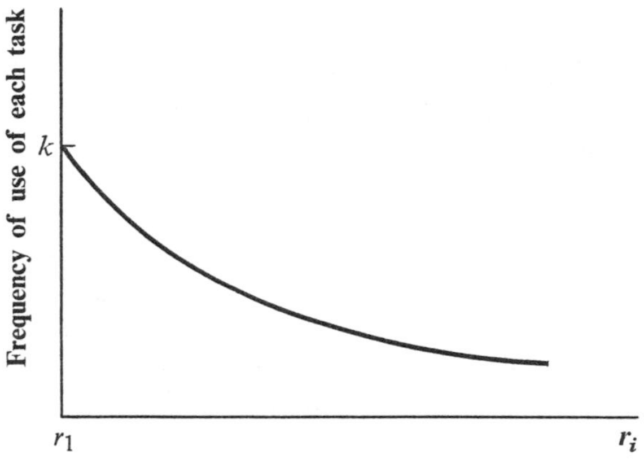

NOTE: As the rank, r_i, increases, the task becomes more difficult.

word lengths and frequency of usage for many languages. He analyzed rank-ordered sizes of city populations and found that the Zipfian relation existed.[51] Mail-order catalogues, the use of tools by workers, the character of speech, the length of items in newspapers, the rationale for procreation, and the roles of cooperation and conflict in international affairs are some of the studies that Zipf undertook to prove his point, which was that opposing forces existed— namely, to increase the number of tasks and to make them all of about equal difficulty and, at the same time, to decrease the energy and costs required to complete all of the tasks. The closeness of the Zipf curve to the log-normal distribution of human behavior is not easily missed.

Moran's Entropy Hypothesis

The hypotheses about human behavior developed by William T. Moran[52] are related directly to information theory. Unlike Zipf, Moran hypothesized that each individual *attempts* to maximize his perceived *absolute* changes of entropy (or variety). This is a highly sophisticated notion and requires comparison

---

[51] As an alternative formulation, Zipf used the hyperbola $F \times r = k$ where F is the frequency of usage, r is the ranked order of difficulty, and k is a constant. It will be observed that this plots as a straight line on log-log paper and is equivalent to a curve that we have previously discussed (see pp. 272–75).

[52] Research on these notions was undertaken at Young & Rubicam, Inc., in the 1960's. Several simulation models were developed that operated on the principles described here, and, in addition, a learning capability was included in the later stages of this research. It was recognized that differences in the ability to learn could account for significant differences in the trajectories of future human behavior.

with statements proposing that each person attempts to maximize his personal entropy (i.e., max H). To review briefly, $H = - \sum_{j=1}^{j=n} p_j log\, p_j$; where $H = 0$ no variety exists, and when $H = $ max, the greatest possible variety exists. (See pp. 506–10.) Claims have also been made that people try to minimize their personal entropy (i.e., min H). The fact that counterclaims of this sort exist, for both individuals and groups, is sufficient to signal that opposing tendencies may exist.

At the Menninger Clinic it has been suggested that there are two different types of people—namely, sharpeners and levelers. Sharpeners increase the level of detail with which they view things; levelers, on the other hand, tend to remove detail and to base their perceptions on generalizations. According to the Moran hypothesis, people could be sometimes sharpeners and sometimes levelers. For example, consider children at the beach building up piles of sand, smoothing and shaping them, and then promptly destroying them. We might also propose two additional behavior patterns, those of enlargers and shrinkers.[53] The enlarger would emphasize big systems; the shrinker would reduce his world to the smallest possible feasible system. And in business we are familiar with the comparison between generalists and specialists. A strong similarity can be seen to exist between all these opposites. An important point to note, however, is that a distinction may have to be made among the various roles of an individual. A sharpener in business may be a leveler at home. There need be no contradiction in this if the individual's behaviors are consistent with his perceptions of the opportunities he has. Thus, an individual may be consistent in each role and still maximize his absolute ΔH, which is his perception of total change in entropy, over some planning horizon.

For a simple example, intended only to illustrate the relationship, consider the following situation. There is a universe of events consisting of A and B. Thus far, A has occurred once and B has been experienced three times. Building on this base, with a two-step planning horizon, we can draw the tree shown in Figure 14–5, which pictures all possible cumulative totals of A and B events. We have calculated the entropy[54] for all the combinations of A and B events (see Table 14–2). According to the maximum ΔH hypothesis, the individual will select that path which maximizes $\{|(H_2 - H_1)| + |H_3 - H_2|\}$.

---

[53] Sharpeners would tend to decrease the variance of a probability distribution, thereby decreasing the H measure; the reverse would be true of levelers. Enlargers would seek larger systems, which would increase the potential for high H measures; shrinkers would decrease the size of systems with which they are willing to deal, and smaller H measures would thereby result. Further insight on this type of classification can be obtained by observing that Erich Fromm (in *Man for Himself* [New York: Holt, Rinehart and Winston, 1947]) has classified individuals according to the following typologies: receptive, hoarding, exploitative, marketing, and productive.

[54] $$H = -\Sigma_{j=1}^{j=n} p_j log_2 p_j$$

Figure 14–5

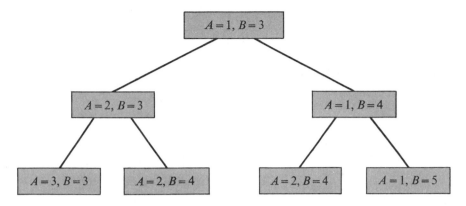

Table 14–2

Entropy (H)	Frequencies of Occurrence		
	Event A	Event B	Total events
.811	1	3	4
.971	2	3	5
.722	1	4	5
1.000	3	3	6
.918	2	4	6
.650	1	5	6

Using straightforward arithmetic procedures, we can see that with a one-step planning horizon, the person will try to experience an A event. (In this way, the absolute entropic change will be .160, whereas for a B event it would be .089.) With a two-step planning horizon, the decision to seek out an A experience will be reversed. Maximum absolute entropy change is achieved by a B event, followed by an A event. (This is determined $|\,(.722 - .811)\,| + |\,(.918 - .722)\,| = .285$.) All possible two-step absolute entropy changes are calculated as follows:

$$A, A = |\ \ .160| + |\ \ .029| = .189$$
$$A, B = |\ \ .160| + |-.053| = .213$$
$$B, A = |-.089| + |\ \ .196| = .285 \longleftarrow \max \Delta H.$$
$$B, B = |-.089| + |-.072| = .161$$

Once again, the planning horizon is a critical issue.

In reality, individuals seldom start with systems that have low total event sums. As a result, individual events do not provide as large increments to ΔH

as in our model. Furthermore, when learning is included in the model, conditioning, span of attention, and other time-dependent elements can affect the behavior of the system. Thus, advertising is believed to alter the value of A or B events, quite apart from their relative frequencies. Nevertheless, the Moran model succeeds in raising more questions than it answers, and this alone makes it worthwhile.

In Conclusion

Much important work has been done in studying the individual; more is being done even as this chapter is being written. Undoubtedly, some of the most exciting ideas are yet to be generated. It has not been our purpose to include all studies and their results. Nor have we tried to present a history of investigation into human behavior. Our intent has been to flesh out the dimensionality of the person in the organization. Only in this way can we truly come to grips with the nature of organization.

We could have expanded upon our lists of needs, but we propose that such lists are far too simplistic to provide any real understanding of the personal properties of human behavior. A greater contribution, in our view, comes from the nonuniversal models that deal with stimulating hypotheses of human behavior. The opportunities for creative endeavor are countless.

Recognizing that such a simple motive as *keeping busy* may have influenced Frederick Taylor's model of organization provides useful insight about what course management has been following. In a period of post-Taylor influence, have the concepts that "work is good because it is work" and "keeping busy is good because one stays out of mischief" been more important than profit? It is useful to remember that being creative and contributory or being indifferent or destructive all fit within the Zipfian concept of the individual and within Moran's hypothesis of maximizing the change of personal entropy. Such conceptual exercises provide management with new ways of thinking about itself and what it is trying to achieve by means of organization.

Present urges for job enlargement, currently explained as the individual's need to avoid repetitive work, can be aligned with Zipf's thesis of least effort. The contributions to management by schools of psychiatry (see the discussion of Eric Berne's *Games People Play* in the next chapter), and more recently reality therapy,[55] emphasize the importance of self-awareness. Not frivolously,

---

[55] See, for example, William Glasser, *Reality Therapy, A New Approach to Psychiatry* (New York: Harper & Row, 1965). The idea behind this therapy is that the individual, rather than seeking to fix the blame for his problems in his past, should attempt to come to grips with himself in the context of the present and the future. See also the discussion concerning T-groups, pp. 668–70.

there seems to be as much need to waste time as to preserve it, to confront as well as to agree, to rebel as well as to cooperate. If one proposes the need to change things, including himself, then perhaps one of the more fundamental needs is to have the minimum number of static needs—that is, to continuously change the need structure. This dynamic view, which in essence is the avoidance of being predictable, would indicate that any attempt to build a framework for organization (above the most fundamental need structure) is open to serious question.

SUMMARY

Chapter 14 divides the role of the individual in the organization into three basic parts. First, the behavior of a person is analyzed in mechanistic and cybernetic terms. Second, the concept of human motivation is developed. Motivation cannot be attributed to machines. It has no significance for a mechanical analysis of human behavior. The third section discusses patterns of personal behavior on a less universal level than the motivational approach.

With these distinctions in mind, we can review briefly the material included in each section. A discussion of cybernetics and deterministic forms of behavior begins with a view of tropisms (such as moths being drawn to light). Then, conditioned responses and operant conditioning are explained. The classification of people by their physical and constitutional make-up is introduced next, followed by treatment of human perception with strong emphasis on perceptive limitations.

In the second section, various approaches to listing the (supposedly) universal needs of people are presented. These needs are shown to be (often) nonoperational explanations of human actions.

The third section discusses patterns of behavior. These are acknowledged to be incomplete explanations of why people behave as they do. Characteristics of aggression are examined with specific reference to territoriality, an important concept quite applicable to the manager. Inner conflicts are studied in terms of the findings of ethologists that ambivalent behavior can result when instinctual and conditioned behaviors conflict. The nature of stress is examined, followed by a discussion of intelligence and the learning of skills. A simple learning model is shown, dealing solely with improving the time for performance, but other characteristics of learning are discussed as well. Then, interactions between behavior and decision-making are related. In closing this section, two hypotheses for patterns of behavior are offered. These include Zipf's principle of least effort and Moran's notion that an individual attempts to maximize the total absolute change in his personal entropy. The chapter provides some thoughts about the individual that should help us to recognize how the individual enters into groups. It is through group behavior that the organizational system emerges.

EXERCISES

1. In what sense is an organization an arrangement of human entropy? Does the entropic concept provide any real insight with respect to the behavior of an individual?

2. Why is it that a company continues to exist in spite of the fact that some of its key people move to another company?

3. Concerning the personal equity of all individuals engaged in achieving an organization's objectives, how should each individual's stake be determined? Apply your thinking to each of the following:
  a. A stockholders' group.
  b. The role of a student in a university.
  c. The position of the faculty of a university.
  d. The position of the administration of a university.
  e. Employees operating on a piece-rate basis.
  f. The advertising manager.

4. Discuss the advantages and disadvantages of using a mechanistic approach to explain the behavior of an individual. Attempt to apply some of the notions obtained from cybernetics, such as the behavior of simple or feedback deterministic systems, to understand the behavior of aggregations of individuals.

5. Which of the following do you subscribe to? First, that we will never have a complete theory of human behavior; second, that we will gradually move to greater understanding of human behavior; third, that a discovery will be made and thereby a new sense of structure will be found, providing important theoretical developments for explaining human behavior.

6. Why is the scaling problem for attributes such as "emotion" so difficult? What other dimensions have similar measurement problems?

7. Describe some behavioral tropisms that affect the role of the manager in the organization. Do you prefer to call these instincts? How would you differentiate between tropistic behavior and that of instinctual responses?

8. George Miller has stated that the number 7 appears far too often to be simply a matter of chance. How do you feel about the validity of the number 7 as the perceptual limit? Try to supply some examples of situations where perceptive limits exist. What have such limits to do with the structure of organizations?

9. Discuss the nature of aggression and conflict in human behavior. In particular, describe how the territorial concept might be applied to the manager's view of his job. What relation does such reasoning have to organizing a system?

10. Use the learning model (p. 615) to predict the amount of time that it will take an individual to learn to type a letter. Notice the problem of interruptions between learning trials, forgetting, and the question of how to define when something is learned. For this question, assume that the end state (subject learned) levels off at about fifty words per minute. Why is learning an important organizational factor?

11. Describe Zipf's principle of least effort. Give some possible instances or applications of the Zipfian relation. Can it be said that Zipf had a theory of organization?

12. Construct an example of an individual's choice system. Use numbers that can then be examined in terms of the maximization of the absolute change in personal entropy according to which choice is made. Try to simulate an individual's behavior using this hypothesis, with different planning horizons. How do entropy and planning horizons relate to organization theory?

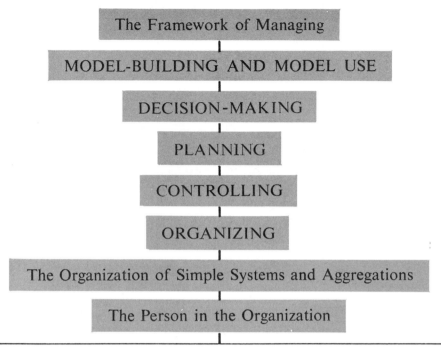

The Framework of Managing

MODEL-BUILDING AND MODEL USE

DECISION-MAKING

PLANNING

CONTROLLING

ORGANIZING

The Organization of Simple Systems and Aggregations

The Person in the Organization

Chapter 15
Groups and Organizational Behavior

Membership in a group is not likely to change personal motivations, but it is apt to affect individual actions. Therefore, the group cannot be treated as a sum of its members, nor can the organization be regarded as the sum of its groups. Men and machines interrelate in organizations, and, as the machine roles grow in power and importance, organizations are being significantly altered. Leadership, which is dependent on environmental (as well as many other) factors, can be studied by analyzing communication flows. A mechanistic view of interactions helps to discern the status structure of the organization. Role-playing considerations further enrich our understanding of the organization. Notions of authority and responsibility are relevant—e.g., Erich Fromm's warning against bureaucracy or the contrast of McGregor's Theory X (the beliefs of authoritarian management) and Theory Y (the views of participative management). We now need Theory Z, the goal of which would be to help individuals relate to one another as people as well as in terms of their organizational roles. While many forms of analysis are helpful to managers, organizational excellence is unobtainable without knowledge of how to achieve synthesis.

Chapter 15

GROUPS AND ORGANIZATIONAL BEHAVIOR

In an era that delights in analogies between the human organism and its possible electrical or mechanical counterparts—where the expression "giant brains" long has been a popular descriptor for high-speed computing equipment—we must tread a path narrow enough to proceed around a conceptual obstacle course whose hazards range from system engineering and psychological conditioning to adolescent fantasies and science fiction.[1]

GROUP BEHAVIOR

The basic unit of the group is the person, whose behavior was the subject of Chapter 14. The group's existence probably does not modify the individual's motivations or change his needs. But group relations do affect the *actions* taken by individuals—in an organizational setting, the behavior of the individual does change. It is therefore unreasonable to approach group and organizational behavior as being some logical composite of individuals' behavior. Similar observations can be made about group motivation. If motivation is an internal force causing an individual to act in certain

---

[1] Robert Boguslaw, *The New Utopians* (Englewood Cliffs, N.J.: Prentice-Hall, 1965), p. 99.

ways, then group motivation is a combination of these internal forces. But it is not their sum or product; it is an inordinately complex notion, probably impossible to measure.

Definition

The group is an aggregation of individuals. When two or more people interact, the ingredients for the formation of a group exist, but in a group the individuals associate for *common purposes*. Usually the purposes persist over a sufficient period of time so that a number of face-to-face encounters develop. The face-to-face consideration may not be essential, but it is characteristic of personal needs that must be met before deep interpersonal relations can develop.

We can distinguish between a group and an organization in many different ways. For example, we can use the cluster and set propensity concepts that were developed in Chapter 3 (pp. 86–95). (The reader is urged to review this material.) Our primary interest in Chapter 3 was to define a system. Now we want to make the transformation to a special system—namely, the organization and the groups (departments, divisions, etc.) that form it. Group membership, for that model, was recognized on the basis of *strong affiliations,* as measured on one or another relevant dimension. The system was bounded to enclose all strong affiliations. On the other hand, in the organization, both strong *and weak* groupings (clusters and nonclusters) interact with one another. The large organizational system is composed of sets of the smaller, highly interrelated, denser subsystems. Therefore, by one standard or another (frequency of face-to-face encounters for communication will do as a start), the group emerges as a dense set of personal relations. The size of the group and the kinds of relation it has with other groups will affect and be affected by its objectives and resources.

Machines are seldom included in the group, which makes sense since it is an aggregate of strong affiliation. But the organization is another matter. Machines are presently excluded from the typical organization chart. Figure 15–1 would be considered highly eccentric, if it would be considered at all, in today's business world. The only real groups, in terms of personal motivations for involvement, could be formed by associations of the president, his vice president, the marketing and financial managers, the (human) OR group members, and so on. But organization charts in the future, if they are to depict responsibility and authority relations, will begin to include particular computer functions that relate to decision-making, planning, policy enforcement, coordination, and so on. More and more, we will find involvement with machines at all levels, and we will have to learn how to deal with them. The old ways

Figure 15–1

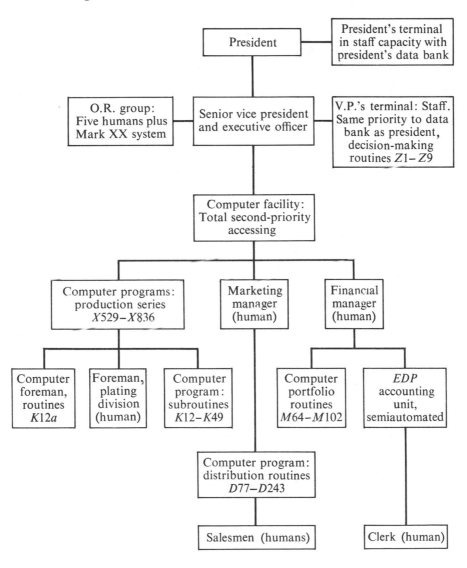

cannot suffice because conditions have changed. Even at the individual level, as Halacy points out, cyborgs (short for cybernetic organisms) exist.[2]

> What are some of the devices necessary for creating self-regulating man-machine systems? This self-regulation needs to function without the benefit of consciousness, in order to cooperate with the body's own autonomous homeostatic controls. For the artificially extended homeostatic control system functioning unconsciously, one of us (Manfred Clynes) has coined the term Cyborg.[3]

Hearing aids, eyeglasses, artificial limbs, heart pacers, scuba equipment, and the like, are typical of close man-machine relations at the personal level. Communication networks of telephones and radios are less extensions than a part of the group. The computer is rapidly becoming a cyborg-member of the organization, and it promises rapid further advances in this direction. Frank Rosenblatt's work on the perceptron (a general model for the investigation of cognitive processes) is a forerunner of IVth generation computing equipment, which is likely to have some unsophisticated learning capabilities.

> Perceptrons are of interest because their study appears to throw light upon the biophysics of cognitive systems: they illustrate, in rudimentary form, some of the processes by which organisms, or other suitably organized entities, may come to possess "knowledge" of the physical world in which they exist, and by which the knowledge that they possess can be represented or reported when occasion demands. The theory of the perceptron shows how such knowledge depends upon the organization of the environment, as well as on the perceiving system.[4]

There is no point in speculating on what the XIVth generation of computing equipment will be like.

Some Primary Characteristics of Groups

Groups can be characterized by their *size* and by the *changes in their size* that take place over time. *Stability* of size is a characteristic that can have a variety of meanings, including (1) the inability to grow, (2) the decision not to grow,

---

[2] See D. S. Halacy, Jr., *Cyborg: Evolution of the Superman* (New York: Harper & Row, 1967).

[3] Manfred Clynes and Nathan S. Kline, "Cyborgs and Space," *Astronautics and Aeronautics,* Vol. 7, No. 9 (September 1960), p. 27.

[4] Frank Rosenblatt, *Principle of Neurodynamics: Perceptrons and the Theory of Brain Mechanisms* (Washington, D.C.: Spartan Books, 1962), p. 3.

or (3) the ability to withstand regression. Decrease in size could mean several different things. It could occur because of defection, but it could also mean increased efficiency. Group-size measures, in other words, are replete with potential significance, but they must be considered in context.

The intended *life span* of a group will relate to its purpose. *Purpose* can be classified in many ways including the desires to participate in profit, to provide public services, to obtain entertainment, or to participate in sports. There is a close affinity between group purpose and individual motivation. However, the types of contribution made by members of the group reflect group purpose more clearly than they are evidence of motivation. Some individuals may participate in a learning role, while others operate in a teaching role. Some may work with their hands but would prefer to be applying their minds, as others in the group do. Other jobs involve information discovery, transmission, memorization, or recording. People often do not know why they are doing a specific job, except that the group assigned it, and they want to remain in the group.

Each person belongs to many groups. This fact was emphasized by the set-propensity analysis in Chapter 3. Therefore, another group characteristic is the measure of its members' *degree of membership* in other groups. We could count the total number of memberships found in any one group, or we could count some special class of memberships, such as the number of workers who participate in community affairs and how broad their affiliations are in this regard. Other classifications might also be meaningful. For example, each person belongs to groups that have different numbers of members. Measures of this number might characterize individual preferences for belonging to large groups, small groups, or a balanced mixture. There is also the *degree of overlap* between several groups, which could be expressed in terms of the number of common members in the set. A large number of overlaps might be interpreted to mean that the group's members like to associate with the *same* individuals in a large variety of group functions.

A further characteristic of membership can be obtained by observing the stability of the membership of a group. Even though the purposeful life span of this group may be long and the size of the group maintained at a constant level, members may come in and go out frequently. Such high turnover could be a significant characteristic of a group. Trends in membership changes might have great meaning. For example, new members might always come from small, public-service groups and leave for large, profit-making enterprises. Thus, the pattern of group movements in real estate have been a growing source of concern, contributing to the urban crisis. A change in political administration or control of the company also produces patterns of group movements that are worthy of study.

The point is that groups have many special characteristics *because they are aggregates*. Personal behavior can help to explain why one or another individual belongs or does not belong to a group, participates fully or poorly, and so forth. The study of groups cannot be unconcerned about such matters, but it must also consider many additional dimensions. The behavior of persons in groups and their desire to stay with a particular group and to identify with its purposes are related positively to the other members of the group and their structure of interactions. Forms of communication in the group, leadership qualities, the character of fellow members, the changes of purpose caused by new environments, the stability of the group's character, and many other group factors make it essential to view the group as a gestalt before perceiving it individual by individual.

A Mechanistic Model of the Group

We can represent the group as a set of individual input-output units, as shown in Figure 15–2. Many of the relations of the individual components within the group (box) are observable in the form of conversations, documents, and actions. Since strong affiliation exists, it is clear that there also exist commen-

Figure 15–2   The Group Input-Output System, Composed of the Visible Individual Input-Output Systems

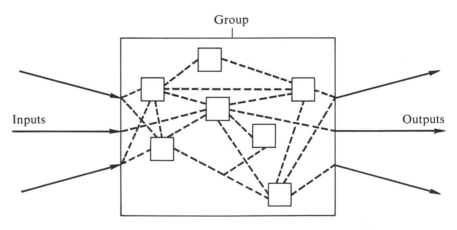

surate feelings, attitudes, emotions (and any other words that describe the intangible character of members' conditions), but these are not readily observed. So the mechanistic view neglects intangibles or else converts them to a mechanical analogue such as pulse rate, respiration, sweating (for example, galvanic measures used for lie detection), and so on.

The performance of the group can be observed in a number of ways. For example, the score of the bowling team or the productivity or output of the die-casting department. We should note that the input-output format lets us distinguish immediately between the simple performance aggregation of the bowling team (where each member contributes to the overall score) and the die-casting department (where performance is dependent on functional interactions between the workers). The latter group has greater dependency of job components and greater complexity of member interrelatedness.

Warren Weaver pointed out that related complexity presents the most difficult problems.[5] It seems apparent that the greater the complexity and the higher the degree of relations between the parts, the more difficult the system is to understand. Disorganized (or unrelated) complexity is usually treated by statistical analysis, which actually decreases our expectations about what we can know about such systems. And simple systems we treat with simple controls.

There is more excuse to use mechanistic descriptions for groups than for individuals. Two reasons can be offered. First, aggregates introduce greater interrelatedness, and the individuals in aggregates tend to have canceling and controlling behaviors. As a result, the aggregate appears to be more stable, its behavior more predictable. The law of averages brings wholly different people to toll booths and ball parks, yet demand and attendance level out with predictable regularity. We do not know who the next mail-order customer will be, but we can predict total daily sales fairly well. Second, there is more observable behavior in the group—that is, people communicating with one another. Therefore, the use of mechanistic models for groups can be understood and can add to what is known about such systems.

In the organization, however, because weak affiliations exist, and because the relatedness and complexity are high, the use of mechanistic explanations usually seems downright silly. Even when studying the group, a combination of relatively sophisticated mechanistic interpretations is enhanced by annotating it with nonmechanistic, human-relations views. *Small-group theory* and *group-dynamics studies* have proceeded in this reasonable fashion. Let us look at a fundamental model of interrelations that (whether or not it is formally used) underlies many descriptions of group behavior.

Interaction analysis. Who-to-whom matrix representation provides a particularly useful structure for studying relational information about the group. For example, between two people (which is the smallest group), interactions flow in two directions—from A to B and from B to A. The situation is shown in Table 15–1. Entries along the diagonal represent the individual communicating with himself (which we have called soliloquies). Some of the most

---

[5] Weaver uses the terms "organized" complexity and "disorganized" complexity, but in our context "relatedness" is a more descriptive term than "organized."

Table 15–1   A Two-Person, Who-to-Whom Matrix

	To: A	B	Total communications initiated:
From: A	Soliloquy	x_{AB}	by A (equals x_{AB})
B	x_{BA}	Soliloquy	by B (equals x_{BA})
Total communications received:	by A (equals x_{BA})	by B (equals x_{AB})	Total interactions $= x_{AB} + x_{BA}$

important conversations (in the thinking or cognitive mode)[6] occur along this diagonal. For example, with respect to the behavior of a research group, the diagonal measure (say, of time spent alone by the person) might be a useful determinant of pure research success or applied research failure. (Pure research tends strongly to result from one person's work, whereas applied-research results improve with cross-fertilization from various disciplines.) The diagonal entries remind us that the individual is the basic unit of the group. At the same time, it should be noted, the motivations and patterns of behavior of the individual create many of the conditions that encourage interactions as expressed by x_{AB} and x_{BA}.

In the two-person case, x_{AB} might equal x_{BA}. This would tend to indicate a leaderless pair and might be called a "balanced-friend" model. But if one interaction rate is much greater than the other, a different interpretation is needed. Two distinctly contradictory hypotheses can be proposed. First, the imbalance is created by the existence of a leader who initiates infrequently, but cogently and succinctly. The leader expects lengthy reports from his subordinate. Alternatively, the leader (by dint of his authority) sends down his requests in lengthy, detailed form and accepts from his subordinate only "yes, sir" and "mission accomplished" or "mission not accomplished."

This simple, two-person analysis clearly shows that the style of the group must be understood before a straightforward, mechanistic, numerical analysis can shed any light on what is going on. Once the group style and purpose are ascertained, however, the matrix entries can reveal a great deal about the workings of the group.

---

[6] The cognitive processes—the means whereby organisms achieve, retain and transform information. . . . The old image of the "stimulus-response bond" began to dissolve, its place being taken by a mediation model. As Edward Tolman so felicitously put it some years ago, in place of a telephone switchboard connecting stimuli and responses it might be more profitable to think of a map room where stimuli were sorted out and arranged before every response occurred, and one might do well to have a closer look at these intervening "cognitive maps." From J. S. Bruner, J. J. Goodnow, and G. A. Austin, *A Study of Thinking* (New York: Wiley, 1956), p. vii.

When we move to larger groups, the same considerations apply, but the problems of interpretation become more difficult. To illustrate, let us assume that the interactions in a five-person group have been observed, with the results shown in Table 15–2. What can be said about this group, just by studying its recorded interactions? Let us refer to the diagrams shown below in Figure 15–3. We cannot be certain about any interpretation we make, but credibility improves as more specific "real" information about the members of the group

Table 15–2

		To:					Totals:
→	A	B	C	D	E	
From: A	x	3	10	2	6	21
B	7	x	13	2	1	23
C	8	1	x	6	5	20
D	4	3	1	x	6	14
E	1	3	11	7	x	22
Totals:	20	10	35	17	18	100

Figure 15–3   To and From Interactions of This Specific Five-Person Group Observed at Some Particular Time

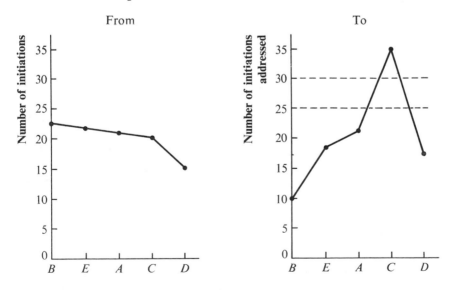

NOTE: Group members are arranged in the ranked order of their level of *initiation*—the largest initiator is placed at the left of both diagrams, the smallest at the right.

and its purposes becomes available. With this warning clearly expressed, we may begin.

First, an unusual equality exists for the initiations ("from"). Perhaps the group's leader has requested that each member take about equal time to present his case. This interpretation would hold for interaction measures obtained at a single meeting, or, if it is always the group leader's policy to have his men take about equal time, it would be applicable to a longer period. It has been observed empirically that in a relatively unstructured meeting, the interaction pattern often follows the Zipfian curve, $I \times r = k$.[7] For example, (letting $k = 30$) the pattern might be that shown in Table 15–3. Since a result

Table 15–3

Interactions	Rank	k
30.0	1	30
15.0	2	30
10.0	3	30
7.5	4	30
6.0	5	30

of this kind has not been observed in our example, we can guess that a particular kind of interaction structure is involved.

But why, then, has D fallen below the average interaction rate of the group? He may be a junior member, or have a less important part (at this phase) in the project than the others. The latter interpretation will differ according to whether the observations were taken at a single meeting or over a long period of time. Member C receives the most interactions. We might guess, therefore, that he is the leader. There is a strong tendency for people to look at and address the *real* group leader (who is not necessarily the same person as the titular group leader). It might have been easy to explain D's difference from the rest of the group, if only D had received the most interaction addresses. We might have speculated that D was the leader.[8] Yet D received a good deal of attention, and therefore it is unlikely that he is a junior member of the group. More likely, he is a specialist in some technical area of the group's interest. The members of the group look more for his approval than for his advice.

We shall not continue with this kind of analysis because our intentions

---

[7] See pp. 617–19. A variety of interaction studies conducted by the author and colleagues (in industry, research laboratories, and artificial problem-solving situations) has revealed that the Zipfian curve seems to occur when the group is functioning smoothly.

[8] The concept of interaction patterns helps us to visualize the many forms of "leader style" that might occur.

should be entirely evident at this point. Remarkable hypothetical insights can be gained simply by studying the matrix of interaction relations—yet they remain hypothetical until they are tested against behavioral realities (see the section on group dynamics, pp. 664–65). Many contributions have been made to interaction analysis, but it tends in use to be so mechanistic that it has never become a firm part of the field of group and organizational study.[9] What seems to be missing is a way to integrate the quantitative analyses with the behavioral factors that account for the overriding human qualities of the group.

In attempting to see the broader view that is possible, we should turn to the increasing knowledge in the systems field and in information management. Matrix entries can be measures of "how much" the "who" likes the "whom." Data can be obtained from interviews or questionnaires. Here too, our knowledge has expanded in recent years. Measures of the frequency of communication might also be interesting, in the information theory sense of Moran's hypothesis (see p. 620). It could be that the frequency with which the speaker uses the imperative or the pronoun "I" would be revealing. Each measure, or set of measures, is designed to test some issue. However, if the interpretations are ambiguous, the use of interaction analysis is less than reassuring. But the weakness is hardly that of interaction analysis; it is that of a reluctance to work with theories of group behavior and systems of measurement to test these theories.[10]

As an example of one application of these measures of interaction frequency some interesting conclusions concerning group size emerge. In problem-solving groups, smooth interaction patterns are generally obtained with five to seven group members. In larger groups, however, there is an increasing tendency to split into subgroups. Entropy analysis, based on the $H(x,y)$ model (see pp. 556–59), could be used to point up information that is shared by the group during its meeting—that is, $T(x,y)$—and analysis of the types of nonshared information—that is, the errors of ambiguity and equivocation—could be obtained. The steady state $\bar{H}$ value might also be used (see p. 552).[11] We get better information from $H(x,y)$, as was previously pointed out, because it is more isomorphic to the group than the $\bar{H}$ model. $H(x,y)$ can always be converted to $\bar{H}$.

---

[9] Some well-known contributors to this field are Arensberg, Chappel, Gold and Horsefall. Chappel built an interaction machine that could be used to record speaker, length of speech, interruptions, simultaneous conversations, pauses, etc. Galvanic skin-response recorders have been used, and various other machine systems for interaction analysis have been designed.

[10] Presumably, because of the acknowledged complexity of group behavior, it is considered "arrogant" to propound simple theories. Humility in this regard should be used with caution, since in the rejection of theory we can often learn a great deal that cannot be learned in any other way.

[11] If necessary, the matrix can be constructed to have subgroup columns (the "to" interaction) as well as person columns, e.g., *AB*, *AC*, *ABC*, etc.

Pecking order relations. Who speaks to whom, who prefers whom, who picks on whom, and, ultimately, who pecks whom are obtainable characteristics of the group. We can learn a good deal by considering such relations as they appear in the animal world. Under the chapter title "Who Pecks Whom," Robert Ardrey gives us an eloquent description of the *status hierarchy* of animals.

Every organized animal society has its system of dominance. Whether it be a school of fish or a flock of birds or a herd of grazing wildebeest, there exists within that society some kind of status order in which individuals are ranked. It is an order founded on fear. Each individual knows all those whom he must fear and defer to, and all those who must defer to him. Self-awareness in the limited sense of consciousness of rank seems to have appeared at some very early moment in the evolution of living things.

Whether or not in such societies as the antelope herd every individual has a separate rank, we cannot yet say. Too little study has been done. In some societies there may be classes themselves ranked which an individual achieves or to which he is relegated. But determination of rank by birth is a characteristic of the insect world alone. Among the vertebrates, from fish to apes, status is competitively determined fairly early in the individual's lifetime. That rank is rarely lost, and rarely improved upon.

Dominance occurs when two or more animals pursue the same activity. It is a type of behaviour long-observed, since all animals— wild, captive, or domesticated—pursue it. But not until zoology turned its attention to the natural state did we begin to comprehend the unyielding fabric of dominance in the texture of animal societies. The social animal does not merely seek to dominate his fellows; he succeeds. And succeeding, he achieves a status in the eyes of the other. That status will be permanent; and oddly enough satisfying as a rule to all parties.

In the halls of science there are many doors, and the one with the sign that reads *Animal Dominance* is one that we have scarcely opened. We have learned much: that it is a force at least as old and as deep as territory; that like territory it benefits sex but stands independent of it; that among social animals it is universal, and among our primate family the source of society's most mysterious subtleties; and that among all animal sources of human behaviour, the instinct for status may in the end prove the most important. But while we may observe it, we still do not truly understand it. And that is why any new study of status in animal societies is apt to leave the most informed reader in a renewed state of stupefaction.

The jackdaw is an extremely intelligent bird who reaps the benefit . . . of a highly organized social life. It is logical, I suppose, that any animal who gains so much from the deathless wisdom of society will see to it that his society operates with the least possible friction. Natural selection would so decree. But I still find my credulity strained by the subtleties of the jackdaw social order. And were Konrad Lorenz a less experienced observer, I should probably wind up in stolid disbelief.

Every male jackdaw has his number, as it were. From Number One to Number Last there is not the least vagueness in the hierarchical position of the individual male bird within a flock. That position is settled upon at an early date in life. Even in chickhood a shuffling about for status begins. Food may be abundant, but quarrels flourish. Somebody pecks somebody, and gets pecked back; somebody retreats. Gradually the timid, the weak, the irresolute fall; gradually the strong and the determined rise. Before too long rivalry of body and character has determined the exact social position of every male bird in the flock. And he will keep that position, most probably, for life. Lorenz never saw a case of change in status caused by discontent from below.

Every barnyard has its pecking order, as every farmer knows. Chickens like jackdaws establish a hierarchy. And the position of the individual chicken determines all pecking rights. Who may peck whom? No chicken may peck another ranking higher in the order. This is known in zoology as a straight-line hierarchy. The high-ranking chicken may peck left and right at the feeding pan; but there is always that lowly chicken who is pecked by all, and can peck no one in return.[12]

Intuitively, we recognize that the human animal has its own forms of establishing a pecking order. The subtleties of these forms should not mislead us into believing that they do not exist.

It is useful for us to now extend the concept of pecking order to the organization chart. Simply, the chart is a map of the organization's pecking order. In this regard, the map is relatively unambiguous, but it reveals little else about relations than the formal statement of status in the organization. That is probably the reason it is so widely used even though its faults are well known and much discussed. In a growing, progressive, and permissive company (with which the author has consulted), the chief executive, being disenchanted with the standard form, drew up his own organization chart. It was based on a circle so that coordination could be emphasized between jobs that were assigned to different parts of the circle. This organizational design was poorly received and dropped out of sight after a short time. Despite any good points it may have had, the chart failed to show the pecking order and was therefore inadequate.

In another company known to the author, the organization chart is of a fully specified standard type. However, no copies are available, and no one is permitted to copy the master chart. The chart has been shown, but only briefly, to middle management. Many companies similarly manage, in one way or another, to keep their organization charts unpublished. While it is hard to

---

[12] From *African Genesis* by Robert Ardrey. Copyright © 1961 by Literat S.A. Reprinted by permission of Atheneum Publishers.

obtain a specific explanation of why this policy is followed, we may guess at the reasons. The chart is known to exist, so the company formally recognizes that a pecking order exists. But by refusing to publish the chart, the company frees the relationships that can exist and reduces the sense of organizational rigidity.

Pecking order, when formalized, becomes "the establishment." At the present time, such rigidity is on the wane, and permissiveness is replacing it. If one takes a step back and tries to view such changes in an historical sense, he can ask whether this is an evolutionary change of a nonreversible sort or whether shifting back-and-forth occurs over time. We cannot step back far enough to give a definite answer, but there seems to be more evidence for the oscillation concept than for that of an ever growing, self-improving system. If this is true, then new behavioral understanding to match our growth in technological abilities will recognize cycles and release us from them.

Group roles. People act differently in different groups. Such behavior differences result partly from the interaction with the personalities of group members, partly from the job assignment, partly from the group's purposes, and partly from other mechanisms that we do not know much about. Yet, despite our limited understanding, we can obtain some insight by considering the specific *roles* of people in groups. In particular, we can examine the interpersonal relations between the roles played by people.

The word "role" immediately leads to the concept of acting and playing a part. This irritates many people who believe they are sincere and honest. And no doubt they are; role-playing is usually performed with earnestness and sincerity. It is nevertheless a kind of acting, in which the payoff is not the entertainment of others or the salary for acting, but the ability to get along in the group, to be welcomed as a member, and to accomplish one's objectives in that group. The desire to be welcomed into the group is not an aimless value that we suddenly throw into the discussion. It is an entirely logical one, since the person has associated with the group for some purpose and therefore does not wish to be thrown out of the group. And, for normal psyches, a desire to be liked does appear to exist. But how these goals are to be achieved by the individual is not apparent and can take many different forms, including aggressive behavior or withdrawal and sulking. It is also to be noted that in any organization, many small informal groups exist that are likely to be in conflict with other small groups and hostile to many organizational purposes. The minimum size of a group to which any individual can belong is two—that is, oneself and one friend. An individual who remains in an organization without any group affiliation is likely not to possess a normal psyche, unless he is constrained to remain there by force or by the need for money and the inability to seek other sources.

How should the manager, bearing in mind the role-playing concept, go about hiring, promoting, and so forth? Can a useful prediction be made about how a person will convert a job into a role or set of roles? How can the manager set straight roles that have gone awry, that are becoming destructive of the group's purposes? Not much is known about such problems. A good intuition about people should be brought to bear—this is still the best advice that can be given in answer to such questions. But this intuition need not be unsupported. Principles, derived from observation, have been formulated about group roles. For example, Robert Bales noted that a specific sequence of stages will generally occur when a group undertakes to solve a problem.[13] One of Bales's most important group stages is that of tension release. Repeated observations of groups attempting to solve different problems indicate that in successful groups, various parties will assume roles that provide comic relief and that thereafter the group can return to the task at hand. Provision or opportunity for such a role (or some alternative) is therefore an organizational responsibility. Selye's notions of personal stress seem entirely applicable to the group in the context of Bales's terms. Group practice at role-playing was stressed by J. L. Moreno.[14] For example, Moreno would have a foreman and a controller reverse their roles in a play-acting situation. As a result, each would learn something about his own roles, those of the other, and the fact that their roles are interdependent.

Chain relations. We have always been able to ask what *seem* to be significant questions about group behavior, but they may in fact be misleading us. On the other hand, perhaps the questions are the right ones and we simply do not know how to answer them. Previously, for the individual, we examined the question of what reactions occur when balanced but conflicting motivations exist. For the group, the analysis of action and reaction sequences (or chains) might also lead to useful results in understanding group behavior.

The Hawthorne studies[15] underscore the difficulties of group-motivation studies. The sequence or chain of reactions began when management experimentally increased the amount of light at the workplace. The observed reaction was greater productivity. Management reacted by increasing the light again; worker response was further increased productivity. When the experiment was *considered* concluded and management removed the new lights, the surprise was that the workers reacted by further increasing productivity.

> There is a significant body of literature investigating the motivations of organization members and groups within organizations. A pioneering study of this subject is the now-famous Hawthorne Research, a

---

[13] Robert Bales, *Interaction Process Analysis: A Method for the Study of Small Groups* (Reading, Mass.: Addison-Wesley, 1950).

[14] J. L. Moreno, *Sociometry, Experimental Method and the Science of Society* (New York: Beacon House, 1951).

[15] See F. J. Roethlisberger and W. J. Dickson, *Management and the Worker* (Cambridge, Mass.: Harvard University Press, 1939).

series of experiments conducted at the Hawthorne Works of the Western Electric Company in the 1920's and 1930's. These experiments were originally designed to determine the effects of illumination, rest periods, length of the work day, wage incentives, fatigue, and monotony on employee satisfaction and productivity. Controversy clouds the contributions of the studies. One important observation that survives, however, is that the staging of such a massive schedule of experiments alters the "laboratory" so that one is no longer measuring the results of a typical work situation but is instead observing in an environment of the researcher's creation. The Hawthorne studies were valuable if they accomplished nothing more than illustrating the complexities of performing empirical research on organizational behavior.[16]

The Hawthorne experience emphasized that group response to a sequence of events is significantly affected by the group's involvement in an experiment. The real basis for interactions between groups of the organization similarly are, in general, far from obvious. Even with the simplest group of two individuals, the basis for interacting patterns requires careful and lengthy analysis. In this vein, it is interesting to note that ethologist N. Tinbergen had to spend many years of research to discover and confirm the interacting chain behavior of the three-spined stickle-back.[17] Here, events are called *releasers* that trigger behaviors leading to other events, which are in turn dependent on what has happened before. Quoting from Tinbergen, "Each reaction of either male or female is released by the preceding reaction of the partner. Each arrow [see Figure 15–4] represents a causal relation that by means of dummy tests has actually been proved to exist."

Such chains are well described by Markovian matrices (see pp. 549–50) where prior-state dependencies exist and the entries in the matrix leading from one state to the next are almost equal to 1. Observe that the above diagram appears strikingly similar to the means-end chain shown on p. 3. In this case, however, a two-person system (the smallest possible group) is involved. Larger groups have multiple chains of this kind that are constantly at work but are far more difficult to disentangle. Interaction analysis holds out some hope.

Eric Berne isolated two-person systems and small groups for a psychiatrically oriented study of chain-type reactions.[18] He showed that people, interacting in groups of two or more, will trade transactions with each other in

---

[16] Marcus Alexis and Charles Z. Wilson, *Organizational Decision Making* (Englewood Cliffs, N.J.: Prentice-Hall, 1967), p. 7.

[17] N. Tinbergen, *The Study of Instinct* (Oxford: The Clarendon Press, 1951), pp. 48–49.

[18] See Eric Berne, *Games People Play* (New York: Grove Press, 1964); see also, by the same author, *Transactional Analysis in Psychotherapy* (New York: Grove Press, 1961).

Figure 15–4   The Chain Behavior of Interrelations for a Male and Female Three-Spined Stickle-Back

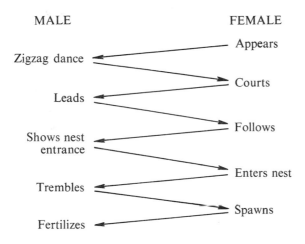

SOURCE: From N. Tinbergen, *The Study of Instinct* (Oxford: The Clarendon Press, 1951).

highly patterned and predictable ways. Each person's behaviors trigger or release behaviors in the others. The concept of "the stroke" as the unit of relation is central to Berne's approach.

> The unit of ritualistic transactions is called a stroke. The following is an example of a typical 8-stroke American greeting ritual:
>
> A. "Hi!"
> B. "Hi!"
> A. "Warm enough for you?"
> B. "Sure is. How's it going?"
> A. "Fine. And you?"
> B. "Fine."
> A. "Well, so long."
> B. "I'll be seeing you. So long."
>
> Here there is an approximately equal exchange comprising a greeting stroke, an impersonal stroke, a personal stroke, and a terminal stroke. Such rituals are part of the group etiquette.[19]

We note that Berne emphasized the content of interaction analysis. Thereby, using a psychoanalytic approach, he began to classify games by the types and

---

[19] Eric Berne, *The Structure and Dynamics of Organizations and Groups* (Philadelphia: Lippincott, 1963), p. 147.

patterns of strokes that are interchanged. Berne called attention to the special stroking rituals of managers and employees, which maintain the appropriate authority relationships.

Berne explained the basis for his game theory by identifying three major components of each individual's personality. He called these the *parent,* the *adult,* and the *child.* (The Freudian categories of superego, ego, and id may shed additional light on this choice, since they appear to come close to Berne's triclassification.) The figure below represents an interaction by A's parent to B's child and a response by B's adult to A's adult. Since B sees himself as an adult in this situation while A views himself as a parent, a game of some kind will begin. The game is pictured in quite the same fashion as the chain reaction of the stickle-backs.

Perhaps an analogous form, which might be more appropriate for management, would trace the interactional patterns between the conservative, status-quo seeker (parent); the progressive manager, seeking balanced, rational change (adult); and the radical perturber (child). Certainly, other categories come to mind as well, including those of sharpeners and levelers (see p. 620). The Berne approach is appealing for studying the *dynamics* of the content of interaction patterns, given that appropriate categories for managerial purposes have been found. We all know of cases where another person's actions seem inexplicable. Perhaps this is because the categories attributed to the other person's actions may not be applicable. In any case, they have not been recognized by him, and in turn, we may not be understood by him. This fact is borne out by the various games that Berne described. His games, however, tend to be oriented to the interaction patterns of social behavior rather than those of formal organizations. We cannot resist suggesting that some interesting discussions would emerge from an attempt to set up conditions for games such as "Empire-Building," "Paternalism for Stability," "The Union-Management Strike Game," and "Perfectionism Keeps Inventions from the Marketplace" (an R & D game).

Characteristics of Leadership

A particular aspect of chain-reaction systems is the appearance of a leader as a special member of the group. His role is to provide direction, coordination, and consistency. Some say that leadership involves acting in such a way as to produce a consistent pattern of group interactions that are congruent with the objectives of the group. Another point of view is that the leader is the epitome of the group's norms and that he understands and represents its values best.

There has been no shortage of students of leadership. Different personal characteristics, such as an individual's persuasive ability, or his ability to increase interaction rates simply by virtue of his presence in the group, or even his own ability to interact at a high level, have been suggested as qualities for leadership. It has been stated that a leader brings about change. There is no doubt that leadership affects the attitudes and morale of a group as well as the group's productivity and output. If anything has been learned in recent years it is that the quality of leadership is not a simple matter to describe and that more seems to be involved than just the personality of an individual.

Consider the following, written by Viscount Haldane in 1913:

> The so-called heaven-born leader has a genius so strong that he will come to the front by sheer force of that genius almost wherever his lot be cast, for he is heaven-born in the sense that he is not like other men. But in these days of specialized function a nation requires many leaders of a type less rare—subordinates who obediently accept the higher command and carry it out, but who still are, relatively speaking, leaders. Such men cannot, for by far the greater part, be men of genius; and yet the part they play is necessary, and because it is necessary the State must provide for their production and their nurture.[20]

An even older statement concerning the qualities of a good leader is given in the following quotation:

> If you are a boss who feels he must take the credit from his subordinates, or if you are callously doing it as a routine course, you would do well to heed the advice of an Oriental philosopher of long ago, Lao-Tze, who wrote:
>
> A Good Leader
>
> A leader is best
> When people barely know that he exists,
> Not so good when people obey and acclaim him.
> Worst when they despise him.
> "Fail to honor people
> They fail to honor you;"
> But of a good leader, who talks little,
> When his work is done, his aim fulfilled,
> They will all say, "We did this ourselves."[21]

---

[20] Richard B. Haldane, "Leaders and Specialists," from *Selected Addresses and Essays* (London: John Murray, 1928).

[21] Charles F. Austin, *Management's Self-Inflicted Wounds, A Formula for Executive Self-Analysis* (New York: Holt, Rinehart and Winston, 1966), p. 112.

Observers of leadership have begun to hypothesize that the leader's personality does not operate alone in determining his success. Styles of interacting with the group have a determining role, and the group's purposes and composition play a part. Pfiffner and Sherwood observed in 1960 that leaders are not independent of the situation in which they find themselves.[22] Figure 15–5 sums up the situation as it is presently visualized. The diagram is helpful because it provides a structure for recognizing that the leader is part of an interactive group. At the same time, the diagram makes apparent the complexity of analyzing and evaluating the leadership role.

Figure 15–5   Leadership—An Interrelated Feedback System

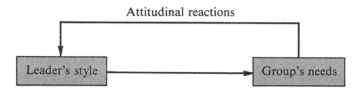

Important research, which takes into account the leadership system, has been carried out by Fred Fiedler. Fiedler introduces his book, which develops a theory of leadership, with the following statement concerning the state of the art in leadership research.

> We take it for granted that groups and organizations will succeed and thrive under good leadership and that they will fail under poor leadership. We look at successful business organizations and ascribe their success to the managerial abilities of their top men. . . . There is little doubt that we hold the leader responsible for success or failure. We admire and respect him, we pay him ten, twenty and even thirty times the salary of the nonsupervisory employee, and we spend millions of dollars on the recruitment, selection and training of executives. And yet, even though we believe that the health of our economy, the success of organizations, and the survival of our institutions depend to a considerable extent on the type of leadership we are able to get, we know next to nothing about the factors that make the leader effective or ineffective.[23]

Fiedler's theory indicates an interdependency between the characteristics of the leader and those of the other members of the group. He builds a con-

---

[22] John M. Pfiffner and Frank P. Sherwood, *Administrative Organization* (Englewood Cliffs, N.J.: Prentice-Hall, 1960).

[23] Fred E. Fiedler, *A Theory of Leadership Effectiveness* (New York: McGraw-Hill, 1967), p. 3.

tingency model that reflects the differing conditions that can exist in different groups. An important point is made that interaction is not the only relation that can be found in a group. What Fiedler calls *coacting* (relatively independent operations within the group) and *counteracting* (opposing forces that exist within the group) exist side by side. In the use of the term "coacting," we recognize what has been previously called a weak affiliation, and we have identified that with organizational relations. Consequently, it may be seen that Fiedler's analysis relates to leadership in the organization as well as in the group.

With all this in mind, how does one get to be a leader? There is no doubt that intelligence, personality, knowledge of specific situations, and even physical size all play a part. But, ultimately, there is a synthesis of factors that determines who will be *allowed by the group* to be their leader and what his leadership style will be. An individual's high level of energy is recognized as a characteristic of a dynamic leader that is attractive to group members. Often, such an energetic style is converted by the situation into what is known as *charisma.* An individual who has such energy and charisma may indeed search for opportunities to lead; but the notion of a "born leader" should not be construed to mean that any group can accept his leadership.

The relationship of aspirations to achievements also plays a part in determining who is to lead. Even in the most democratic systems, there are one or more leadership cliques that play a role in determining who is given a chance to become a leader. How do such "nominators" reach their decisions? Certainly, they consider past performance in meeting the system's objectives. The leader who is not at the top of the organizational hierarchy and who is hoping to achieve further "nominations" and appointments must certainly bear in mind these expectations of his superiors.

The style by which the hierarchy of leadership renews itself and its power to do so creates further complications. In many organizations, it is entirely clear who reports to whom. The power to assign leadership also is unambiguous. Under such circumstances, new leaders are not likely to differ much from old leaders; all leaders will probably talk and act alike. In these situations leadership as we usually understand the word may well have disappeared and been replaced by controllership.

Networks of group relations. We can recognize a distinction between a tactical and a strategic leader—the former is closer to his smaller group. It is particularly at the tactical level of leadership, in the very small group, that a series of interesting studies has been conducted. For the most part such groups are involved in a simple production activity or in a problem-solving operation. It is only with the small group that the laboratory-type operation can be conducted. In them it is possible to examine the nature of leadership, the delegation of tasks, the attitudes of the group, and the effectiveness of the group in terms of some measures of performance.

Figure 15–6   Some Typical Network Configurations of Communication Patterns for Small (Laboratory) Groups

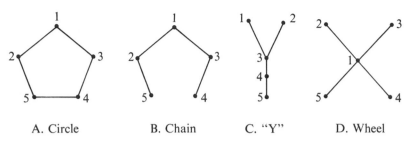

A. Circle   B. Chain   C. "Y"   D. Wheel

Figure 15–6 presents several different configurations of five-man groups. The individuals in each configuration can communicate wherever network links occur. In the circle, for example, 1 can ask a question of 5 either by going through 2 or by turning to 3 and having the request transmitted through 4 to 5. The artificiality of these models is apparent, but, while they are Tinkertoys, they provide some useful insights. For example, strictly with respect to the speed of accomplishing a task, and assuming that 1 is a skilled leader, the chain or wheel-type arrangement allows 1 to expedite the operations of the group. But 1 can also be a stumbling block, if he is not suited to the job. The circle, on the other hand, may take longer to get started, but it is likely to produce more innovative solutions, and incompetence is likely to be by-passed. It has been found that differences in communication patterns will affect the accuracy of a group, its total level of activity, the sense of satisfaction experienced by its members, the type and stability of leadership that emerges, the way in which the group sees its organization, the speed with which tasks are completed, the durability of the group, and the rapport among its members.

Work on this subject, which was begun by Bavelas, has been carried on by Leavitt and Marshall. In a more mathematical vein, using graph theory, Harary, Norman, and Cartwright have made further contributions.[24] The essence of the mathematical approach lies in the word "structure." A comparison can be made with information theory, which, it will be remembered,

    [24] See Alex Bavelas, "A Mathematical Model for Group Structures," *Applied Anthropology,* Vol. VII (1948), pp. 16–30. See also Harold Leavitt, "Collective Problem-Solving in Small Groups," *Journal of Abnormal and Social Psychology,* Vol. XLVI (1951). (This article is also published in Alexis and Wilson, *op. cit.,* pp. 40–55.) In addition, see Wayne Marshall, "Subject Performance in Two Six-Man Communication References," *Management Science,* Vol. 13, No. 2 (October 1966), pp. B93–101, and "Simulating Communication Network Experiments," *Management Science,* Vol. 13, No. 10 (June 1967), pp. B656–65; Frank Harary, Robert Norman, and Dorwin Cartwright, *Structural Models, An Introduction to the Theory of Directed Graphs* (New York: Wiley, 1965).

is the structural level of semiotics. Unfortunately, all too little is known about structure.

> The word "structure" is found extensively in the literature of the social sciences. "Social structure" and such related concepts as "kinship structure," "authority structure," "communication structure," and "sociometric structure" are commonplace. Psychologists speak of such matters as "personality structure," "cognitive structure," and "attitude structure." Linguists are interested in the "structure of a language" or "syntactical structure." And many other examples could be cited. But despite the widespread use of structural concepts in the social sciences, it is fair to say that the formal analysis of structure has been relatively underdeveloped in these fields. The technological terminology employed in describing structures is meager; few concepts are defined rigorously. As a consequence, the social scientific description of structural properties tends to be couched in ambiguous terminology, and detailed studies of structure, as such, are rather rare.[25]

When competition exists in small groups, such as four individuals playing bridge, the communication pattern is established by the nature of the game. For games involving more than two people, a variety of coalitions can form, each of which is represented by a specific pattern of communication. A variety of committees with different purposes exists within the organization. The groups and subgroups with their strong and weak affiliations are far too complicated for any substantial progress to be made by analyzing communication networks of the wheel, circle, or chain types. But some "structural" ideas can be useful. The fact that the speed of accomplishment of a task improves with increasing centrality does not come as a surprise, but the confirmation is useful. The examination of democratic forms of communication networks as opposed to more autocratic ones, the roles of various personality types as placed in different positions in the network to reveal the managerial style, and the placing of the computer in such networks for man/machine interface patterns can be revealing if not determining.

ORGANIZATIONAL BEHAVIOR

"Alice laughed. 'There's no use trying,' she said: 'one *can't* believe impossible things.' 'I daresay you haven't had much practice,' said the Queen. 'When I was your age, I always did it for half-an-hour a day.' "[26] If the reality of the group is hard to conceive of, then that of the organization

---

[25] Harary *et. al., op. cit.,* p. 1.
[26] Lewis Carroll, *Through the Looking Glass.*

is nigh on to impossible.[27] But the lines of an organization chart will do for a start. Of course, we mean more than the lines—namely, what flows and relations the lines stand for.

Defining "An Organization"

Let us define any organization as an aggregation of persons (and/or machines) that communicate with one another as individuals who are affiliated with both formal and informal groups. These persons interact with some common purpose. Their outputs (at least *potentially*) have synergistic value. The organization (of a department, company, country) is not *the complete system,* but it is as close to a complete system as is practical for planning and *control* purposes. Control must be evident, including feedback controls, for an organization to be founded. What cannot be controlled in any way is not inside the organization's boundaries. Classically, the organization is defined as some form of structured interpersonal relations, where structuring implies control. It has also been said that organizations are systems designed to maintain the status quo. Organizations are healthy and sick,[28] incorporated, limited, partnerships, governmental, military, and so on.

We have already discussed the transformations of simple input-output systems. Now we are talking about the most complex kinds of relation between organizational components that are capable of planning, making decisions, controlling, and reorganizing. The appropriate input-output model might be

---

[27] There has been a lot of talk in the last decade or two about organization theory as the up-and-coming thing. Yet the trouble with organization theory to date is its continued non-existence. This is true despite the fact that numerous sporadic efforts in this general area have succeeded in providing a variety of insights into the mechanism of all kinds of organizations.

When I state that there is no organization theory at the moment, I mean that the two basic requirements for a theory are as yet absent. One is the existence of an adequate and unified conceptual framework, within which meaningful statements about the subject matter at hand can be formulated without danger of misunderstanding. The other is a systematic method of proceeding from premises to conclusions and, thereby, of achieving the goal of any scientific theory, which is both to explain and to predict the phenomena observable in its realm of concern.

Olaf Helmer, "The Prospects of a Unified Theory of Organizations," *Management Science,* Vol. 4, No. 2 (January 1958), pp. 172–76.

[28] William Horvath of the Mental Health Research Institute of the University of Michigan has characterized a sick organization as one that has become dysfunctional by losing its learning ability and adaptability. For the present, our best definition of a healthy organization is one that is not sick.

Figure 15–7   The Input-Output Model of an Organization

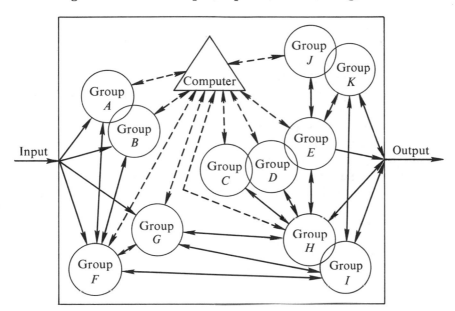

drawn as in Figure 15–7. This figure shows that the input-output model of the organization tends to lose the detail of what is in which group. (Groups are shown as circles). Interactions within the groups are more or less obscured, but between groups the relations become relatively visible. There are so many relationships, however, that it is hard to keep track of what is going on— except, perhaps, for communication both within and between groups that are processed by the computer, which is drawn as a triangle. The memory of the computer for who talks to whom, and about what, may turn out to have an important effect in the years ahead on the nature of organization.

Ecology is the study of animals in relation to their environment. The ecology of the organization is twofold—internal and external. The internal environment is responsive to the external one, which can be characterized by the kinds and degrees of threat that it poses. The self-adaptive abilities of the organization must be sufficient to match the degree of environmental stability. Technological changes, new patterns of competition, price-cutting, advertising campaigns, government taxation, and judicial regulation are some of the elements of the external environment. The internal environment reacts according to its morale, policy systems, size, and wealth, for example. The ecological view has many adherents, those who like to deal with big systems that are not fully specified and probably can never be.

Mechanistic Views of the Organization

If we consider an organization to be composed of a group of machines, we can apply some of the knowledge that has been developed in the field of cybernetics. This specialized view of the organization has utility because it forces us to recognize how little is known and understood about cooperation and coordination in planning and formulating policy. When human behavior is isolated from the system (except in terms of human objectives), a purely rationalistic approach can prevail. Information flows in a cascade, as do decisions: B's decisions follow from A's decisions; B's information is transformed by A; and A and B have a rational, mechanistic relationship.

The cybernetic definition of an organization is a system of machines (including human ones) interacting with some *common purpose*. At a most basic level, the designer of the machine group (say, an automated production system) attempts to assure the system's stability and to protect its survival—for example, not allowing the entire system to be shut down by any one unit's breakdown. At the higher level of self-adaptive systems, some interesting observations can be made. Machine systems, responding to changes in their environment, such as breakdowns and fluctuations in demand, have a tendency to adapt by calling for increased machine investments. According to Parkinson, human systems create work to use up existing capacity—and, because of the new work, additional capacity is required. On the other hand, machines compete with one another in terms of measurable efficiency, forcing the reduction in their numbers by improving designs and work methods. Both effects are observable in machine-system designs. More functions are being done by machines all the time. Fewer machines can do more kinds of jobs. The technological capabilities of machines have produced evident economic forces for "job enlargement." Man, the designer and user, has merely responded to the capabilities of machine systems. Do these machines improve their profit configuration simply to obtain support for continuity and even growth? Ultimately, would communicating machines continue to compete with one another—between firms—or reach an accord based on the rational reduction of overlapping functions?

Simply by shifting our view from men to machines, we find a basis for providing answers to questions that seem unanswerable in human behavior terms. Is it any less realistic to conjecture about human behavior based on analogies with machine systems than on analogies with rats and guinea pigs? While neither may be entirely satisfying, the cybernetic approach has strong appeal in a situation bereft of strong alternatives. Figure 15–8 shows the simplest possible cybernetic organization. It is a two-module system, where each module can produce either a 0 or 1, and four different output combinations result. With the feedback link shown, A and B can begin to modify one another's behaviors.

Figure 15–8   A Two-Machine Cybernetic Organization

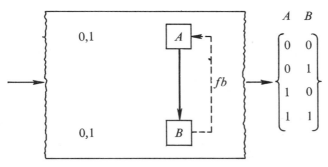

NOTE: Each machine, in this example, can make only a 0 or a 1 decision. With active feedback, greater complexity will result.

The purpose in showing this simple example is to exemplify the conversion to mathematical terms of two binary (0, 1) components. This organization has four unique *A, B* states, and, with some simple feedback rules, quite elaborate organizational behaviors might be observed. Then, with the addition of more components, complex mathematical descriptions of the organization would appear. The cybernetic organization may oversimplify, but it is not simple. The larger view of the cybernetic system is given in Figure 15–9.

Authority and Responsibility Relations

Hierarchy is a *supposed* property of a group of persons or things. The property is assumed to be a *natural* one (as in nature), and the "natural" arrangement that follows from this concept results in *some* rank order of relations. The rule for arrangement is not a mystery, but it is *arbitrary* and, in most cases, *changeable* or *reversible*. Still, the word "hierarchy" is widely used, and most users do not feel that it needs more careful definition. In fact, the concept of ranked-order assignments of responsibility for objectives that underlies organizational hierarchies may be one of the most complex (and misleading) notions ever invented by man. It is, at best, a formal, mechanistic attribute of organizations. Previously, we discussed hierarchical relations in connection with taxonomy (see pp. 39–40), and there are significant similarities between those relations and organizational hierarchies. The taxonomical models are first-stage models rather than powerful models for organizing and directing large systems. Pecking order hierarchies miss a wealth of information concerning individual attitudes, morale, and loyalties.

Figure 15–9   A Generalized Model of the Cybernetic Organization

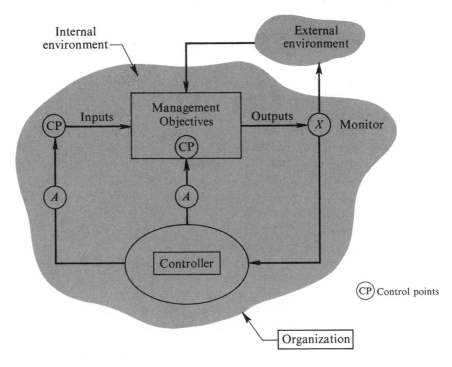

A sensible approach to organizational study, called comparative management, aims to discover what is the same and what is different about various organizations. Too often, however, the comparisons are drawn in hierarchical terms, with emphasis on the categories of authority and responsibility, which remain terms that are almost impossible to define. At the same time, they have produced increased awareness of the problems involved in studying organizations in this way, which are succinctly stated by Tom Burns.

> For a sociologist the use of the adjective "comparative" to qualify the "study of organizations" is something of a pleonasm. Comparative study is the fundamental sociological method and has been since Montesquieu. This is true even for research which has a single community, tribe, or organization as its object. In such studies the social anthropologist (as against the ethnographer) or the sociologist (as against the historian or the reporter) is faced from the outset with the need to eliminate or reduce the uniqueness of the actual people, actions, relationships, and settings he observes.[29]

---

[29] Tom Burns, "The Comparative Study of Organizations," in Victor H. Vroom, ed., *Methods of Organizational Research* (Pittsburgh: University of Pittsburgh Press, 1967), p. 113.

The comparative method when properly applied is a way of generating questions, the answers to which are then discussed in two ways: first, with respect to their own internal logic and, second, against a standard of behavior or expectation. One of the keys to the approach is therefore to have an appropriate taxonomy or classification system to which organizations can be compared. For example, there can be economic dimensions, such as the number of employees, the size of the organization's capitalization, the number of clients, the number of items in the product line, and so forth. There is also, according to Burns, the administrative dimension, which includes the proportion of managers and supervisors to total personnel, the line-staff ratio, the extent of geographical concentration, the span of control; and there is the institutional dimension, which treats job specifications, training requirements, interaction potentials, and so forth. The taxonomy should also include the ecological relations of the organization—group behaviors in the face of changing internal and external environments.

There is no doubt that the comparative approach can teach us a great deal. But there is reason to question the appropriateness and insightfulness of taxonomies that are presently in use. We have already had occasion to analyze the problems of systems of taxonomy, and it is, therefore, to those pages that we refer the reader.

Enormous efforts (comparative management being just one of these) have been poured into the study of organizations in the attempt to find some general patterns that would lend themselves to the construction of a unified theory of organization, and some things have been learned. Nevertheless, a unified theory has not been developed. So management continues to operate on an intuitive understanding of people, backed up (or confused) by the strict relations of the organization chart.

The essence of these strict relations is embodied in the notions of *authority* and *responsibility,* which are impossible to define in such a way that they can be measured as to degree. Nevertheless, since we need some basis for agreement, we define *authority* as the granted (or legal) *right* to act in certain ways —that is, power—whereas *responsibility* is an accepted burden for the accountability of achieving specific objectives. The assignment to individuals of authority and responsibility within the enterprise, and their acceptance, constitute *critical relationships.* But it is seldom clear what commissions have been specified. We should recall Eric Berne's notion of stroking when we consider authority and responsibility. There is (in the cybernetic sense) a trajectory of exercised authority that occurs over time. The organization chart may be a poor projection of these relations, but until we have something better, it will continue to be used (with managerial ingenuity). Any practicing manager knows well that the organization chart does not fully succeed in conveying much of the information that he requires in dealing with his subordinates. Many times individuals who are located on the same level in the hierarchy possess different qualities and amounts of power. Moreover, the chart rarely takes cognizance of the computer, even though numerous programs are now vested with decision-making authority. But the organization chart does succeed in *decreasing* the entropy of the system with which the manager must deal—so he does not attack it, even though he does not like it.

Our reasoning is somewhat clarified when we recognize that the organization chart is but a nominal form of taxonomy. It possesses only weak ordinal characteristics through arrangements of boxes on the page. Although we associate this configuration with ranking, it certainly does not reflect distance measures. If the organization chart does succeed in conveying certain kinds of valuable information, it is largely because all the individuals who appear on the chart recognize the assignment that has been made to them and have a common body of experiences against which to interpret the generalized meaning that is intended. It is in the context of the *actual* organization that the individuals who participate are able to develop an understanding of where they stand with respect to the flows of authority. The members of the organization looking at a static organization chart can then interpret it in dynamic terms. It would be a great benefit if a dynamic form of organization chart were developed. However, attempts that have been made to do so possess none of the necessary vitality.

Management may never be able to specify the actual rankings and arrangements of authority. It is the individual's role and personality that determines the true effects that will be felt within the organization. Consequently, if one individual replaces another in a job, the organization chart remains the same, but the actual interplay of individuals will be significantly restructured. Consider the normative concept of the who-to-whom matrix described in the next section.

Normative who-to-whom model. To examine the degree to which an organization's performance can be mechanistically structured, we can develop a *normative* form of the who-to-whom (pecking order) model. It is based on the well-known transportation model, which is a network algorithm, but it is also amenable to solution by linear programming. In this case, the precise specification of who reports to whom is not given, but the total amounts of each individual's interactions (both to and from) are fully stated.

In an authority-responsibility context, this is an attempt to equate the authority granted each individual with his rights to authorize requests and, in turn, the individual's responsibility with how many authorizations by others each individual is subject to. Or the model may be viewed in terms of the transmission and receipt of information. Here, the number of interactions each person can originate and the number he can receive are both specified. With respect to Eric Berne's concepts, this model could be used to describe stroking patterns to and from all members of the organization. As we begin to apply this model, with its limited kinds of information flows and organizational arrangements, we recognize a new level of mechanistic complexity. We are entering the domain of automated managerial systems, made possible by the existence of a *normative* mathematical model, which we shall describe shortly. But, even to approach a real evaluation of the situation in this way, it would be essential to specify all of the relevant decisions that must be made to run the organization and who is to be invested with every detail of power in the situation. Of course, appropriate measures of authority and responsibility would have to be developed. Hundreds and perhaps thousands of charts would have to be drawn up to take care of all possible situations. As we go on, the homomorphic qualities of the organization chart are emphasized. This is true even if there is some substantial degree of log-normal effect. In other words, by properly grouping decision types it might be possible to develop a few decision matrices to cover, say, 60 percent of all decision-making activities. The fact that no such formats presently exist means, not that the ideas that we are discussing are irrelevant, but simply that we are not ready to be rational and explicit about them.

The transportation model is so called because it can be used to achieve a minimization of total transportation costs for moving a particular number of items from given origins to specific destinations. For example, say that three factories, F_1, F_2, and F_3, produce, respectively, fifty, seventy, and eighty units per day and that three warehouses, W_1, W_2, and W_3, require forty, one hundred, and sixty units, respectively, per day.[30] In the matrix of Table 15–4, the c_{ij}'s are the costs of shipping units from a specific factory to a particular warehouse, and the X_{ij}'s are the amounts shipped. Such problems are easily solved by network methods, such as the stepping-stone method, (which we will explain below) or by the mathematical formulation of linear programming.

Table 15–4

	W_1	W_2	W_3	Totals produced:
F_1	X_{11} c_{11}	X_{12} c_{12}	X_{13} c_{13}	50
F_2	X_{21} c_{21}	X_{22} c_{22}	X_{23} c_{23}	70
F_3	X_{31} c_{31}	X_{32} c_{32}	X_{33} c_{33}	80
Totals required:	40	100	60	200

---

[30] If the supply does not equal the demand, methods exist for resolving the problem. We shall not consider them here but refer the reader to David W. Miller and Martin K. Starr, *Executive Decisions and Operations Research,* 2nd ed. (Englewood Cliffs, N.J.: Prentice-Hall, 1969).

The easiest way to explain the network procedure is to use and solve a numerical example. (See Table 15–5.) Let 1, 2, and 3 constitute a three-person group; F_i's are the interactions originated by the ith person (i.e., from); T_j's are the interactions received by the jth person (i.e., to). We will assume that the costs in the matrix are the hierarchical distances separating these people on their organization chart and that interactions with oneself are blocked by an arbitrarily large cost, called B. Further, let all interactions that go from below to above carry an additional cost of one unit. The hierarchy that we have in mind is a simple line with 1 on top, 2 in the middle, and 3 on the bottom.

Table 15–5

	T_1	T_2	T_3	
	B	1	2	
F_1	X_{11}	X_{12}	X_{13}	50
	2	B	1	
F_2	X_{21}	X_{22}	X_{23}	70
	3	2	B	
F_3	X_{31}	X_{32}	X_{33}	80
	40	100	60	200

We require an initial interaction pattern (to specify a set of values for the X_{ij}'s). It is known that the initial pattern is not necessarily the best one, but it provides a beginning point. This pattern can easily be obtained by what is called the northwest corner method of the transportation algorithm. We start in the upper left-hand corner of the matrix and put as many interaction units into the cell F_1, T_1 as possible. This is forty (the maximum for column T_1), leaving ten units that must be filled to satisfy the first row total of 50. So ten interaction units are placed in F_1, T_2. This leaves ninety units unsatisfied for column T_2. Seventy units can be supplied by F_2, which uses up its total supply. Twenty more units supplied by F_3 complete the requirements of the second column. Sixty interaction units entered at F_3, T_3 completes the matrix allocation, giving us Matrix 1 of Table 15–6.

Our next step is to shift all allocations that have been made to the diagonal cells (which are blocked by B). We can move forty units from F_1, T_1 to F_2, T_1 without causing any negative numbers to appear. (Negative values in the matrix would have no meaning and must be avoided.) To satisfy the totals, forty units must be removed from F_2, T_2 and put into F_1, T_2. The remaining thirty units at F_2, T_2 are then shifted to F_2, T_3. To maintain the totals, thirty units are added to F_2, T_3, subtracted from F_3, T_3, and added to F_3, T_2. This

Table 15–6

Matrix 1

	T_1	T_2	T_3	
F_1	40	10		50
F_2		70		70
F_3		20	60	80
	40	100	60	200

Matrix 2

	T_1	T_2	T_3	
F_1	•	50		50
F_2	40	•	30	70
F_3		50	30	80
	40	100	60	200

Matrix 3

	T_1	T_2	T_3	
F_1	•	50		50
F_2	10	•	60	70
F_3	30	50	•	80
	40	100	60	200

yields Matrix 2 of Table 15–6. Last, to shift thirty units from F_3, T_3, we add thirty to F_3, T_1, remove thirty from F_2, T_1, and add thirty to F_2, T_3. Thus, we arrive at Matrix 3 of the Table.

Now we can look at the other costs to see if a superior arrangement is possible. We have used common sense to obtain the present configuration. First, we obtained a starting point allocation by employing the northwest corner method, which gave us enough positive entries so that shifts could always be made in our allocation pattern. If there are M rows and N columns, then the starting point allocation must always have $M + N - 1$ positive assignments. Then, since diagonal entries are not allowed, we made closed cycles, shifting the interaction units between rows and columns so that the specified row and column totals would continue to be satisfied.

Now, however, we are asking: Is there a better allocation—better in the sense that it will minimize the total hierarchical distance of communication? The question of whether this is the optimal allocation pattern for interactions can be answered by testing alternative arrangements.[31] Because our example is very small, the only cell in the matrix that we can consider is F_1, T_3. We have nine cells, three are diagonal cells, leaving six, and $M + N - 1 = 5$, so only one free cell exists. But, if the matrix was 10×10, we would have seventy-one free cells to consider—$100 - 10 - 19$. Let us see, then, whether an improvement in the total hierarchical cost would occur if one interaction unit is shifted to F_1, T_3. This change can be obtained only in the manner shown in Table 15–7. Read directly from the matrix, the cost change is $+1(2) - 1(1) + 1(2) - 1(3) + 1(2) - 1(1) = +1$, so the change should not be made, since it would increase the hierarchical distance. The optimal allocation (Matrix 3) has 1 speaking only to 2, person 2 receiving equal amounts of interaction (fifty units) from both 1 and 3, and so forth.

Table 15–7

	T_1		T_2		T_3	
F_1	•		−1	1	+1	2
F_2	+1	2	•		−1	1
F_3	−1	3	+1	2	•	

Certainly this example is small, but it does exemplify the lack of behavioral awareness that can result from purely mechanistic approaches to organization. Probably, it is undesirable that person 1 never speaks to person 3 yet is frequently addressed by 3. The difficulty lies less in the model we have used than in the measures to be optimized. Minimum distance between communicators may be a useful goal, but the scale does not reflect the variety of other factors that successful communication entails. We may conclude that organizations are in general far too complex to permit normative modeling. Yet the same approach might work splendidly if 1, 2, and 3 had been machines instead of people because (at least at the present time) measures of machine performance exist that can capture a large percentage of what counts in evaluating the system.

If our model raises more questions than it answers, this is good. It does point out that measures of authority and responsibility would be extremely useful, if they could be found. It makes us wonder whether we know what we are talking about when we use the terms "authority" and "responsibility" in a

---

[31] For a complete explanation of the transportation algorithm see Miller and Starr, *op. cit.*

management discussion. Also, a sense of the difference between man-man and man-machine communication emerges, but it is only a sense and not a scientific understanding. Above all, our normative modeling did not take into account the social environment of the system, which surely affects group decisions.

We are reluctant to admit that many organizational activities are accomplished without careful rational analysis. Often enough, however, a pile of papers will sit on an executive's desk. He intends to study the documents before reaching a decision on a particular problem. But, when the decision must be reached, the executive reaches a decision without even flipping through the pages and with no sense of guilt. It is unlikely that authority will ever be totally programmed (even in military situations, interpretation is legitimate behavior). In fact, too much mechanistic thinking, too many strictures and rigorous rules, can paralyze the decision-making capabilities of the organization. An adaptable manager can hardly accept rigid and unalterable rules concerning who has what authority. Flexible rules for the assignment of authority are essential because the most apparent expectation is that the unexpected will occur. If a manager is involved in a particular problem situation, then, by default, another executive will pick up the decision-making requirements of a new situation. This ability to transfer jobs within the team is one of the synergistic characteristics of organizations that should be encouraged.

Span measures that describe how many levels of authority exist between various members of the organization are implicit in a normative model of the kind we have been discussing. Span measures based on communication patterns and hierarchical ordering have captured management's fancy for many years, although no one has tried to put them to use in an operational way. One of the oldest formal statements of span relations was proposed by V. A. Graicunas in the 1930's. He contended that three types of relation between a supervisor and his subordinates should be considered. The first of these was two-man cross-relations (which we discussed on pp. 479–81), where n subordinates could communicate with one another in $n(n-1)$ different ways (the relation AB being treated as different from BA). The supervisor would have to deal with each of these $n(n-1)$ patterns. Second, the supervisor has a direct line of communication with n subordinates, which produces an additional n relations. Third, Graicunas felt that communication in the presence of others deserved special treatment. He determined that there were $n(2^{n-1}-1)$ such relations. For example, the supervisor speaks to A in the presence of $B;$ he speaks to A in the presence of B and $C;$ and so on. Putting all these together, the Graicunas measure of span is

$$G = n(n-1) + n + n(2^{n-1}-1) = n[2^{n-1} + (n-1)].$$

When $n = 2$ subordinates, the supervisor must contend with 6 relational modes; when $n = 5$ subordinates, $G = 100$; and when $n = 10$, $G = 5{,}210$.

This span measure may be overly sensitive, rapidly growing out of conceivable bounds. Certainly, it is more refined than our use of $n(n-1)$ for the discussion about entropy and centralization (pp. 539–40). Apparently, the measure led Graicunas to generalize about hierarchical limits.

> Graicunas, a Lithuanian management consultant, has appended the more definite principle of the "span of control," that is, that no one person should supervise the activities of more than five, or at most six, other individuals whose work is interrelated. It has also been largely accepted that a "short chain of command," or as few layers of supervision between the top man and the rank and file as possible, are desirable.[32]

The mystique of span numbers must clearly be tempered by the knowledge that they measure only hierarchical structure and, in fact, only a part of that structure. In the earliest days of theorizing about organizations, mechanistic structure pervaded all conjecture. Max Weber had long ago conceived of the organization as a bureaucratic structure.

> Early in the twentieth century the great German sociologist Max Weber, noting common elements in business organizations, government bureaus, and the Prussian military structure, called the new organizational form "bureaucracy." In a bureaucratic system, public or private business was carried out "according to *calculable rules* and 'without regard for persons.'" Functionaries with specialized training learn their tasks better by practice. "Precision, speed, unambiguity . . . unity, strict subordination, reduction of friction—these are raised to the optimum point in the strictly bureaucratic administration, and especially in its monocratic form." Weber said the new form was succeeding because the "bureaucratic mechanism compares with other organizations exactly as does the machine with the non-mechanical modes of production." Around the same time, Frederick W. Taylor in the U.S. promulgated "scientific management" in which workers were regarded as parts of a corporate machine, the excellence of which was to be measured, of course, by its "efficiency."[33]

There has been a surprising permanence of this mechanistic view of "ideal" organizations. As Erich Fromm has stated, "bureaucratic management exists today in practically all large organizations, whether they are industry, government, education, health, religion." Fromm defines bureaucracy as "a method of managing in which people are dealt with as if they were things." He criticizes the destructive effects of bureaucracy on all individuals who participate in

---

[32] Ernest Dale, *The Great Organizers* (New York: McGraw-Hill, 1960), pp. 5–6.

[33] Max Ways, "Tomorrow's Management: A More Adventurous Life in a Free-Form Corporation," *Fortune*, July 1, 1966, p. 85.

such a system and raises the hope that nonbureaucratic, humanistic organization is possible.[34] Cybernetic control theory perceives the supervisor as a monitor and allows us to treat span problems in terms of delay and error. These are advances as long as we understand that human behavior requires additional dimensionality, which may or may not be reduced (someday) to measurable, relatable factors. In any case, we do not want our models to reinforce bureaucracy; actually, they can ameliorate bureaucratic tendencies by provoking recognition of how many factors are not represented.

Human Behavior in the Organization

Organizational behavior cannot be satisfactorily observed until human variables and relations are included. This fact was recognized by many early organization theorists, but they did not quite know what to do about it. As Erich Fromm pointed out, not much has been done about it in actual practice. But a great deal of academic attention has been paid to the point. For example, the reaction to treating the worker as a machine led to studies that accented human behavior. It was recognized that the individual takes on particular role behaviors in groups, so small-group studies followed. Historically, studious concentration in these areas moved from the mechanistic to the ethological and the ecological, then to the anthropological and the psychological, and finally to the sociological. The behavioral view of the organization, while sensitive to the individual, recognizes that to satisfy *all* personal needs would be antithetical to the organization's purposes, because it is the worker's attempts to satisfy his own needs that make him a productive member of the system. Furthermore, to strive with fair and reasonable expectations of success may in itself be a fundamental human need.

The concepts of the authority to direct and the rules for direction are no longer mechanical versions of the control unit, the steering engine, or the aircraft guidance system. What is required is an approach to influencing. Reasoning and persuasion are primary ingredients of the ability to direct. We do not use the term "authority" when we speak of one machine controlling and directing another. The word is reserved for the behavioral aspects of direction. Authority is a far less direct coupling than we achieve in machine systems. Yet, it is not a weak coupling when leadership qualities produce a positive response on the part of those who look for direction. Group dynamics, which has had an important impact on organizational thinking, grew out of the group need to extend the view of the organization to nonmechanistic models.

---

[34] Erich Fromm, "Thoughts on Bureaucracy," *Management Science,* Vol. 16, No. 12, (August 1970), pp. B699–705. Quotations are from p. B700 and p. B701.

Group dynamics. Structural analyses provide a particular view of groups operating together within an organization, but they always over-simplify the situation. When we focus on behavioral factors, the mechanistic view of an organization is almost too readily dismissed as trivial. A new set of terms appears that stresses psychoanalytic interpretations of individual behavior. The approach can be inordinately complex.

> How should we think of the relation between individuals and groups? Few questions have stirred up so many issues of metaphysics, epistemology, and ethics. Do groups have the same reality as individuals? If so, what are the properties of groups? Can groups learn, have goals, be frustrated, develop, regress, begin and end? Or are these character-istics strictly attributable only to individuals?[35]

Mechanistic analyses (such as interaction analysis) can help to locate and describe *informal groups* operating within the formal, specified structure of the organization. These informal groups arise because of conditions that have not been designed by management and that seldom can be anticipated by organizational designers.

> Most of us have an intuitive grasp of what an informal group within a formal organization is like. We tend, however, to be less well oriented regarding the connections between the formal and informal organiza-tions. . . . The most commonly held view is that informal groups are subversive of the purposes of the formal organization. Such informal groups oppose demands coming from higher authority and work counter to the purposes set by management. . . . Management attention has turned to the Group Dynamics movement for techniques by which cooperation of informal groups is secured and sustained.[36]

Group dynamics emphasizes participation by individuals in group decision-making and encourages management to permit subordinates to interact with them as much as possible—a process known as privilege pay. The key point that group dynamics has made is that behavioral realities occur along many intangible dimensions and that unless these are recognized, the model one has in mind of the organization is, not simply incomplete, but poor.

At the same time, theories, principles, hypotheses (or whatever they are called) have developed that are normative in nature. That is, they tell us how to extend privilege pay to the worker—in the extreme, how and when to smile. These normative conclusions may apply at this point in time, but it is not

---

[35] Dorwin Cartwright and Ronald Lippitt, "Group Dynamics and the Individual," *International Journal of Group Psychotherapy* (January 1957), pp. 86–102.

[36] Robert Dubin, ed., *Human Relations in Administration,* 3rd ed. (Englewood Cliffs, N.J.: Prentice-Hall, 1968), pp. 104–05.

necessary that they should continue to work effectively throughout all time and across all cultures.

This characteristic ability to change, this dynamism of apparent needs (even if the primary ones, whatever they are, remain fixed for all time),[37] is probably one of the most fundamental factors lacking in current writings about organizations. Consider the following example. A stereotype criticism of management is that it has given the worker insufficient control over his environment, delegated him to passive roles, and expected him to behave as a subordinate. It has allowed him little opportunity to do any planning or, for that matter, any significant decision-making. All of this, it is said, destroys (or prevents the creation of) worker motivation. Locating this description in its proper place in time and in its appropriate cultural milieu, we can agree that this situation has existed and continues to exist. We can also agree that we do not like this picture of a worker, whether we are playing the role of the worker or the manager. But that does not mean that we have suddenly discovered something new about the primary motivations of man. It does mean that we recognize a common value that presently exists in our culture. We can therefore accept present-day prescriptions without forgetting that they may lose their effectiveness as the morphology of organizations evolves. Someday, the prescriptions may have to change. In another era, the worker may wish to have less responsibility. He may not want to be involved in decision-making and planning. He may wish to play a passive role. But the need for awareness of his wishes will not change. Our point is that the primary discovery of group dynamics is unchanging—namely, that people have complex motivations that should be taken into account. It does not follow that the organizational rules for management are inflexible principles.

Theory X and Theory Y. One of the most important sets of rules that is presently influencing organizational thinking relates to the work of Douglas McGregor, who contrasted authoritarian patterns of management (Theory X) with the interrelations of management and workers cooperating as members of a team (Theory Y). McGregor described the views of Theory X-type management, which stressed the fundamental inabilities of individuals to identify with organizational objectives.

1 The average human being has an inherent dislike of work and will avoid it if he can.
2 Because of this human characteristic of dislike of work, most people must be coerced, controlled, directed, threatened with punishment to get them to put forth adequate effort toward the achievement of organizational objectives.

---

[37] Remember the suggested need for "change for the sake of change" and Moran's hypothesis.

3 The average human being prefers to be directed, wishes to avoid responsibility, has relatively little ambition, wants security above all.[38]

In contrast, Theory Y–type management views of human behavior in organizations emphasize the fundamental desire of individuals to cooperate.

1 *The expenditure of physical and mental effort in work is as natural as play or rest.* The average human being does not inherently dislike work. Depending upon controllable conditions, work may be a source of satisfaction (and will be voluntarily performed) or a source of punishment (and will be avoided if possible).

2 *External control and the threat of punishment are not the only means for bringing about effort toward organizational objectives. Man will exercise self-direction and self-control in the service of objectives to which he is committed.*

3 *Commitment to objectives is a function of the rewards associated with their achievement.* The most significant of such rewards, e.g. the satisfaction of their ego and self-actualization needs, can be direct products of efforts directed toward organizational objectives.

4 *The average human being learns under proper conditions, not only to accept but to seek responsibility.* Avoidance of responsibility, lack of ambition, and emphasis on security are generally consequences of experience, not inherent human characteristics.

5 *The capacity to exercise a relatively high degree of imagination, ingenuity, and creativity in the solution of organizational problems is widely, not narrowly, distributed in the population.*

6 *Under conditions of modern industrial life, the intellectual potentialities of the average human being are only partly utilized.*[39]

Max Ways states that management has begun to respond to the distinction between Theory X and Theory Y and that it is pursuing the latter, with recognition that Theory Y poses greater challenges to managerial abilities.

The fluid business environment of the future will demand not only a different kind of manager but a different organizational structure. Management's need to keep redefining "the nature of the business" applies not only to the product mix but also to the internal arrangements of the organization. One reason why men and their organizations may fail to adapt is that they cling to erroneous ideas about themselves

---

[38] Douglas McGregor, *The Human Side of Enterprise* (New York: McGraw-Hill, 1960), pp. 33–34. An earlier paper of the same title is reprinted in Paul Pigors, Charles A. Myers, and F. T. Malm, *Management of Human Resources: Readings in Personnel Administration,* 2nd ed. (New York: McGraw-Hill, 1969), selection 1. Later ideas developed by McGregor are found in a posthumous book, Caroline McGregor and Warren G. Bennis, eds., *The Professional Manager,* (New York: McGraw-Hill, 1967).

[39] McGregor, *op. cit.,* p. 34.

and/or their situation. The late Douglas M. McGregor, of the Sloan School of Management of M.I.T., believed that the evolution of organizations was being retarded by a set of erroneous beliefs about man and his work which he called Theory X. . . .

Today men respond to certain stimuli that McGregor wrapped in a proposition called Theory Y.

. . .

The business scene . . . shows substantial evidence to support this view. Some of the evidence lies in what business leaders are saying, and some in what they are doing. One significant change is the increasing sense that management is the chief asset of the corporation rather than an overhead expense. "Investment for modernizing plant and equipment is often wasted unless there is a corresponding investment in the managerial and technical talent to run it," says M. J. Rathbone, former board chairman of Standard Oil (New Jersey). He notes that the valuation of a corporation's securities is based more upon appraisals of the quality of its management than upon the corporation's inanimate assets.[40]

It seems fair to note that while Theories X and Y may not be mechanistic, they are simplistic. Undoubtedly, far more complex statements of organizational relationships will be required before organizations can be understood. Also, there are those who continue to say that, in part or fully, McGregor's Theory X is correct—that people dislike work and that passivity in accepting authority is an important aspect of human behavior, even though it is not well understood. There are others who say that neither X nor Y is any good. Military organizations find it hard to conceive of ways of applying Theory Y. Church organizations have not readily embraced it. Universities, on the other hand, seem to be moving in its direction. Clearly, however, for our time and level of accomplishment in understanding organizations, Theory Y has received the acceptance of enlightened management.

It should be pointed out that a manager can accept Theory Y and yet fail to pursue it without even recognizing his failure. Theory X coercion can take many forms, some of which are well hidden from the coercer. Konrad Lorenz indicated a fundamental aggressiveness in all humanity, and the concept of territoriality remains undefined in all these behavioral treatments (see pp. 605–06). We know that coalitions spring up easily and that conflict is not a pathology of many situations but an indisputable property. We recognize that Theory Y assumes one set of objectives (for simplicity, let us call it *participation*) for workers and another one (*profitability*) for managers. Are the territorial instincts of managers not disturbed by the greater worker participation,

---

[40] Ways, *op. cit.*, pp. 87, 148.

or are they disturbed but then repressed by the need to make the organization a profit-generating system in the present cultural climate?

It is not our purpose to malign Theory Y or to do away with it. But it is necessary to note the existence of myriad ways of pursuing cooperative objectives and to note their flaws as well as their strengths.

Sensitivity training. There is a certain delicacy of manners that the use of Theory Y assumes in the relations of all members of the organization. There exist, however, numerous unspoken hostilities that are based on many factors other than the X treatment. Such hostilities often exist, in fact, where no authority relations are required. It is also evident that the worker can achieve his Y needs and yet never really get to understand the people with whom he works as well as he knows his boss. Such understanding is not a requirement of Theory $Y,$ but present trends indicate that a sense of relationship with the group is essential for personal satisfaction. Theory Z (so named by us) may be the obvious next step. (Did McGregor consider that the alphabet would be exhausted after one addition?)

Direct confrontation between people and issues that range from personal feelings to company policies and the boss's style has emerged as a new behavioral force in recent years. Many organizations, large and small, private and public, have employed the *T-group* as a vehicle for confrontation for all of their personnel. T-groups are assembled for *laboratory education*. The education process is also called *sensitivity training*. The core of its purpose is modification of individuals' behaviors, which is achieved by means of self-realizations that improve interpersonal effectiveness.

Chris Argyris has provided an excellent description of the characteristics and functioning of T-groups.

> The core of most laboratories is the T (for training) group. . . . Basically it is a group experience designed to provide maximum possible opportunity for the individuals to expose their behavior, give and receive feedback, experiment with new behavior, and develop everlasting awareness and acceptance of self and others. The T-group, when effective, also provides individuals with the opportunity to learn the nature of effective group functioning. They are able to learn how to develop a group that achieves specific goals with minimum possible human cost.
>
> The T-group becomes a learning experience that most closely approximates the values of the laboratory regarding the use of leadership, rewards, penalties, and information in the development of effective groups. It is in the T-group that one learns how to diagnose his own behavior, to develop effective leadership behavior and norms for decision making that truly protect the "wild duck."

Role of Educator

In these groups, some of the learning comes from the educator, but most of it from the members interacting with each other. The "ground rules" the group establishes for feedback are important. With the help of the educator, the group usually comes to see the difference between providing help and attempting to control or punish a member; between analyzing and interpreting a member's adjustment (which is not helpful) and informing him of the impact it has on others. Typically, certain features of everyday group activity are blurred or removed. The educator, for example, does not provide the leadership which a group of "students" would normally expect. This produces a kind of "power vacuum" and a great deal of behavior which, in time, becomes the basis of learning.

There is no agenda, except as the group provides it. There are no norms of group operation (such as *Robert's Rules of Order*) except as the group decides to adopt them. For some time the experience is confusing, tension-laden, frustrating for most participants. But these conditions have been found to be conducive to learning. Naturally, some individuals learn a great deal, while others resist the whole process. It is rare, however, for an individual to end a two-week experience feeling that he has learned nothing.

Usually the T-group begins with the educator making explicit that it is designed to help human beings to—

. . . explore their values and their impact on others,

. . . determine if they wish to modify their old values and develop new ones,

. . . develop awareness of how groups can inhibit as well as facilitate human growth and decision making.

Thus a T-group does not begin without an objective, as far as the educator is concerned.

. . .

At the outset the educator tends to provide that assistance which is designed to help the members to—

. . . become aware of their present (usually) low potential for establishing authentic relationships,

. . . become more skillful in providing and receiving nonevaluative descriptive feedback,

. . . minimize their own and others' defensiveness,

. . . become increasingly able to experience and own up to their feelings.

Although interpersonal assistance is crucial, it is also important that the T-group not be limited to such interventions. After the members receive adequate feedback from one another as to their inability to create authentic relationships, they will tend to want to become more effective in their interpersonal relationships. It is at this point that they will need to learn that group structure and dynamics deeply influence the probability of increasing the authenticity of their interpersonal relations. For example:

> As soon as the members realize that they must become more open with those feelings that typically they have learned to hide, they will need to establish group norms to sanction the expression of these feelings. Also, if members find it difficult in the group to express their important feelings, this difficulty will tend to be compounded if they feel they must "rush" their contribution and "say something quick," lest someone else take over the communication channels. Ways must be developed by which members are able to use their share of the communication channels. Also, group norms are required that sanction silence and thought, so that members do not feel coerced to say something, before they have thought it through, out of fear that they will not have an opportunity to say anything later.[41]

Sensitivity training is of recent origin, and it is difficult to say where it fits or whether it will last on the organizational scene. The most significant contribution of the T-group approach is that it changes the focus from management versus employees to that of people engaged in interdependent activities and having different roles that require mutual understanding. The T-group approach may be evanescent in its particulars, but in the general sense that it emphasizes self-awareness and awareness of relations between persons, it seems destined to affect the future of all organizational thinking. To the extent that it proposes prescriptions of what should (or must) be, sensitivity training is not sensitizing but quite the reverse. Aggression concepts, hostilities and conflicts, territorial instincts, and the myriad other potential, partial explanations of organizational behavior begin to find the light of day, not in static theories, but in dynamic interactions among the people who have associated for some common purpose.

ORGANIZATIONAL SYNTHESIS

"Urged by the values of past generations, our culture seems obsessed with breakdown, splintering, disintegration, and destruction. Ours is an age not of synthesis but of analysis, not of constructive hopes but of awful destructive potentials, not of commitment but of alienation."[42]

This is a remarkable statement. We can hope that it is wrong; we must worry that it may be correct. But an alternative hypothesis explains all of the

---

[41] Chris Argyris, "T-Groups for Organizational Effectiveness," *Harvard Business Review,* Vol. 42, No. 2 (March–April 1964), pp. 63–66.

[42] Kenneth Keniston, *The Uncommitted: Alienated Youth in American Society* (New York: Harcourt Brace Jovanovich, 1965), p. 4.

evidence quite as well—namely, that this is an age learning to deal with new systems substantially larger than any that have been ever before experienced at a rate of change that is faster than ever before. The challenge originates with society, and it is put to anyone who is willing to manage organizations of any kind. A theory of organizations might help such managers, but none is available as yet.

Any organization can be segmented along the lines of its formal groups and its hierarchical structure. But these divisions may be of little relevance in solving a problem that cuts across the traditional lines of the organization. The concerns of an informal group will be even more difficult to associate with any specific problem. By the very nature of informal groups, traditional partitioning principles for classic organizational functions fail, and substitute arrangements are not at all obvious. Yet customary principles for partitioning systems are derived from present concepts of organization based on formal views of small systems. They reflect ritualistic notions of authority and responsibility, which, by definition, are ideas expressing individual power in overly simple ways (e.g., "he's a vice president") to achieve an image so widely held that it is supposedly entirely clear. Authority is really multidimensional, but it is treated otherwise because individuals tend to look for one dimension by which to govern or be governed. Traditional studies of organization ignore dependencies or relegate them to the realm of mystical phenomena. Systems are becoming increasingly interdependent, so, more and more, standard approaches to organizing a system are failing both the manager and the managed. We are not alone in recognizing that it is time to break away from nineteenth-century stereotypes that govern our organizational actions.

> Science stands today on something of a divide. For two centuries it has been exploring systems that are either intrinsically simple or that are capable of being analysed into simple components. The fact that such a dogma as "vary the factors one at a time" could be accepted for a century, shows that scientists were largely concerned in investigating such systems as *allowed* this method; for this method is often fundamentally impossible in complex systems. . . . Until recently, science tended to evade the study of such systems, focusing its attention on those that were simple and, especially, reducible.[43]

What is the new approach that will change all this? First, it is an integrated approach, which begins analysis with synthesis in mind. Second, it is an approach supported by powerful information techniques and facilities. Third, it is an approach that does not assume that "the problem resides where its symptoms are first noticed."[44] Fourth, it is an approach that does not con-

---

[43] W. Ross Ashby, *Introduction to Cybernetics* (New York: Wiley, 1956), p. 7.
[44] As stated by Stafford Beer in *Decision and Control* (New York: Wiley, 1967).

centrate on what everyone sees but instead observes what everyone takes for granted. Fifth, it is an approach that does not measure one thing at a time and does not prefer to measure what is easiest to measure. These are not all of the differences, but they are representative.

Organizational Parameters

Large systems must be approached differently from small ones. There are many reasons, but perhaps the most important ones reflect complex psycho-physiological manifestations of (1) the capacity of the human mind to process information; (2) the *size of the human body* as it relates to the real world, and (3) the *sense of time* that relates to life span (and in particular to that part spent in preparation for adulthood). In the last decade, the importance of *time* as a critical variable of behavior has received increasing attention. It is too soon to be able to report on results, but at least the focusing process is real. For the present, although we know that a retiring manager is not at all the same in his behaviors as a newly promoted manager, there is a noticeable reluctance to draw distinctions, let alone to include "age" in general theories of organization.

From aesthetic history we learn about collectors of miniatures. At the same time, we observe the use of larger-than-life-size systems (monumentally proportioned statues and buildings) to represent power and strength. Generally, the miniature has great detail and complexity. Its achievement is to bring together much information about the large system in a very small physical volume. The monumental view deals with the same large system but loses detail and accents the proportions of a few variables. On the other hand, there is a third view, the microscopic, which concentrates on enlarging the small system many times to colossal proportions. Analysis is the method by which monumental proportioning of small systems is accomplished. When reentering or reembodying this part in the system, a reduction of scale is required.[45] Different talents would seem to be required for each type of system sculpturing. At the same time, the style of management in carrying out segmentation has changed, especially with respect to how small the subsystems to be analyzed should be. They were smallest in the era of Frederick W. Taylor, who divided systems of work such as metal-cutting and bricklaying into many small components. And this approach was carried to an ultimate of sorts by Frank Gilbreth, who developed the Therblig (almost the smallest

---

[45] It should be remembered that time also affects the size of a system. When a long planning horizon is used, even for an individual, the size of the system changes, and many of the large system concepts have to be considered.

perceptible unit of physical motion) as the most basic unit of the employee's motions.

There is a natural compulsiveness to push analysis toward segmentation on the finest possible scale if a deterministic philosophy prevails. But organizational parameters lose their meaning at fine scale. Only *systems methods* can dictate how fine the analysis should be and this decision must be based on hypotheses for synthesis that *precede* analysis.

By the mid-twentieth century, large systems began to preempt the analyst's interest. This trend appears in the analysis of production systems, financial analysis, market studies, and industrial relations. Yet the precedents, apparatus, and background for detail had been previously set, and management's use of computer systems emphasized what "had been" rather than what was "likely to be." Accounting detail was one major focus. Use of many *independent* measures in great detail and refinement continues to be in style. The issues that are raised by the concept of independence are not unlike those of analytic electrocardiograph methods, which have been monitoring an increasing number of control points as medical technology has improved. But synthesis is required to relate these measures. A synergistic result usually occurs when such synthesis is achieved. In general, the interrelatedness of information monitored at adjacent control points requires a theory of related combinations. When such theory exists, we can begin to study what is happening at each of several control points, not in isolation from one another, but with an awareness of the simultaneity of systems measures.

Management has been properly concerned with little systems because these process *I/O*'s are fundamental units of organization. But the most important issue is how to assemble and assess larger systems configurations composed of these simple units. Analysis of basic process modules is used by the manager to *explain* what is going on in terms that are *organically* and *organizationally* separable. He is readily able to think about a particular job, a specific machine, or a given function. The manager expects that the detailed analysis will be followed by suggestions for improvement *in the little subsystem.* For example, he increases the servicing capacity of a unit, changes the load on the subsystem or the rate of demand for specific transformations. When the *improved* subsystems are reassembled into the body of the *total* system, the expectation is that *overall* improvement will result.

But, as we have had occasion to indicate before, integration does not follow so easily. The subsystem improvements may actually backfire and (in the short or long run) result in a real decrease of the total system's performance. Some systems are more characteristically prone to this effect than others. As a rule, *the higher the management area involved, the less likely it is that subsystem analysis can provide overall systems improvement.* We can readily appreciate why Eero Saarinen said, in 1960, "We should stop thinking of our

individual buildings—always look at the next larger thing." Or, on a behavioral
level, we have a statement by Mary Parker Follett:

> Thus we see that . . . unintegrated difference is pathological, difference
> itself is not pathological. . . . what I think we should do in business
> organization is to try to find the machinery best suited for the normal
> appearing and uniting of diversity so that the difference does not stay
> too long crystalized, so that the pathological stage shall not be reached.[46]

Motivations for smaller systems. Architecture is an obvious area
where many small systems studies have been used, even though everyone
acknowledges that because they are separate they do not provide excellence
for the total system. Some of the reasons should be examined, since the
parallels between management problems and those of architecture are surprisingly strong.

A major force for subsystem planning is the *unwillingness to let others
interfere* when planning for one's own domain. Also, by enlarging the system,
many new and dominant restrictions arise that can severely alter what would
have been done without such constraints. Consequently, by ignoring the additional restrictions of large systems, the *degrees of freedom* for planning are
substantially greater.

Generally in the initial stages of project development many excellent configurations are possible. Ten great architects (or managers) can propose ten
highly different project variations, each of which is (by some acknowledged
standards) worthwhile. The variations are attributable to individual values
and experiences. Because there is much latitude to exercise value preferences
for style, materials, and so forth, in the design of a building, architects responsible for designing isolated properties will produce a chaos of clashing styles,
uncoordinated traffic flows, and unreasonable school districting, park availability, shopping facilities, and the like. This occurs because the architects do
not communicate with one another. They do not have a systems theory that
will permit them to accept the larger system's constraints. Yet, judged as
separate subsystems, the work of each may deserve praise. How then should
we evaluate an architect? Can we hold the architect responsible for not taking
into account the higher order variables of schools, parks, shopping, and traffic?

The same notions apply to business. How should we evaluate a manager
who does a fine job within his own territory but lacks coordination with
others? It is the responsibility of top management to coordinate related functions, and to achieve this it must fix the size of the system. As the size of the
system is increased, many excellent solutions to isolated problems must be

---

46 Mary Parker Follett, "Constructive Conflict from Dynamic Administration," from
H. C. Metcalf and L. Urwick, eds., *The Collected Papers of Mary Parker Follett* (New
York: Harper & Row, 1941), p. 4.

discarded. The variety level has to be reduced so that the larger system's performance can be improved.

One large systems approach is for management to require communication between subsystem managers to facilitate coordination. A second approach is to specify a policy broad enough to cover all the segmented systems. Zoning is an example of such a policy for coordination of architectural efforts. Management policies might be formulated in terms of inventory restrictions, capital expenditures, and operating budget constraints. All such policies can play a major role in the attempt to coordinate activities without establishing the communication required for large systems planning. Invoking tradition is another way to achieve coordination. It may be a suspect policy, but it is not necessarily a bad one, for, while it is short of a rational policy, it can help to unify and homogenize the system. The notion of coordination achieved through policy controls can be expanded to include constraints with respect to cash liquidity, payback periods, types of personnel, vendors, and product line. All tend to produce a controllable uniformity, but this only approximates the gains of coordinated activities.

The fact that the policy approach is less desirable than active coordination does not mean that coordination can always be used. Frequently, the big system is so big that the cost of attempting to actively treat it would be prohibitive. Often, there is insufficient information about the interactions that bind the big system together. In one sense or another, the parts of the system may speak different languages. Many times, top management alone has sufficient *authority* to spread across all of the components, but its information is so poor that it is not even aware of the existence of small, informal groups. Both law and social dictum often prohibit the communication that is essential to large systems planning. These physical and economic realities of the situation must be considered, no matter what the preference for coordination achieved through consensus.

Moving to the larger system. As a rule, *one should deal with the biggest system that is physically feasible and that maximizes net benefit.* Perhaps the net benefit changes with the system size, as illustrated in Figure 15–10. The reason that, in general, there is a falling off of net benefit after some system's size is achieved is that the costs of communication rise and the ability to set beneficial overall policies falls. On the other hand, there are gains in net benefit to be made by increasing the size of the system because the sum of a number of individually optimized subsystems $\leq$ the overall optimum of the sum of these subsystems. In other words,

$$\text{Best } 1 + \text{Best } 2 + \ldots + \text{Best } n \leq \text{Best } (1 + 2 + \ldots n)$$

At some point, these forces balance to produce an optimal value. Various systems exist in which the equality would hold in the equation above. In such

Figure 15–10   Relation of Net Benefit to System Size

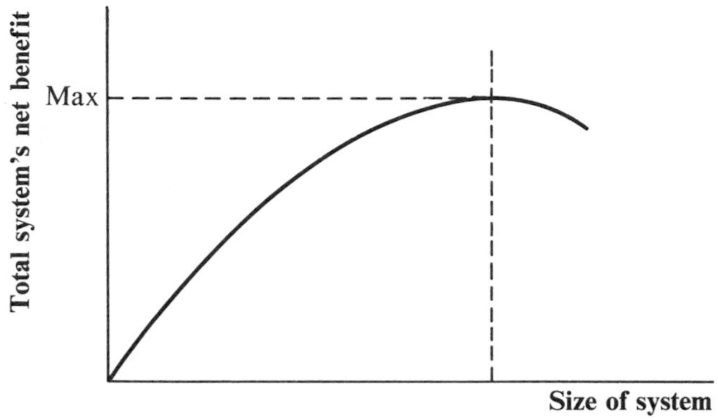

cases, the subsystems are sufficiently independent of one another to be studied and improved without consideration for the other subsystems. But, for the most part, such sufficiently independent systems occur only at low levels in the management hierarchy.

Returning to our analogy of business and architecture, we observe that special interests will be self-serving and conflicting. One building may block another's light, disrupt patterns of ingress and egress, change land values, spoil the scale of the overall conception, and so on. *Natural* and nonintentional conflict will result from following, with honesty and singleminded purpose, one design in ignorance of the others. So a strong coordinator with sufficient authority is needed if the big system is to be treated optimally. Directing, judging, and coordinating are all vital aspects of managing a large system. Everything we have been talking about comes together here. Leadership runs like a thread throughout the aggregation. To achieve large system *synthesis* we must first bring together intuition, knowledge of the behavioral sciences, and quantitative methods. Second, we must relate planning and policy to the objectives of the organization and to managerial ability to control. And, third, we must tie together the lines that cross functional area boundaries. Responsible managers cannot tolerate arbitrary compartmentalization, which creates the illusion that separate marketing, finance, and production decisions can combine to enhance the achievement of organizational objectives. Unequivocally, they cannot.

Managerial styles. What is the style of the manager as planner and controller? What kinds of model does he prefer? Some managers seem to be able to work more easily with prescriptive than with descriptive models. Some seem able to reason heuristically, others move toward the arithmetical precision of the controller, and still others seem to prefer mathematical tools.

In many systems today a polarization of managerial types appears to be occurring. The form that this polarization takes is to isolate a group of managers who work well with computers but not so well with people. These managers then reinforce the split, communicating poorly with others and feeling secure only with their own kind of people. This situation threatens to create a new breed of technocratic managers who are devoted to computer orientation. Such individuals do not find their way easily into top management, but they tend to receive rapid promotion at the lower managerial levels. At one time, management was concerned about functional polarizations—to marketing, production, and so forth. Now, along different lines, another source of psychological separation has appeared. It is a manageable effect if it is recognized, and, in fact, many companies have taken organizational steps to assure positive communication between computer managers and users.

We are, however, also on the verge of producing a new behavioral-rational manager, who is trained in systems diagnostics and treatments and has computer capabilities and an understanding of quantitative methods. Such individuals may, for the first time, become managers with a fundamental ability and inclination to achieve synthesis.

Achieving Synthesis

As we have had occasion to say, it has always been easier to take things apart than to put them back together again. In the production field we know that the use of explosion diagrams for assembly has provided much help in seeing interrelationship and sequencing of parts. In other words, sequential decomposition into subsystems is carefully tracked so that the reverse procedure of synthesis is also achievable. The same reasoning can be applied to nonphysical systems, in which case it means tracing all lines of information that connect the subsystems as they are separated from the larger one. All inputs and outputs between systems must be properly classified and related.

Because of the complexity of large systems, there may be too much information to cope with. Then the organizational system must be reduced in size until an adequate synthesis can be achieved. At the same time, information can be lost inadvertently because *records* are not maintained. Another difficulty is encountered when improvements generated at the subsystem level create the requirement for new information to achieve reassembly. Often, the order in which the organization is examined will affect the sense in which it is understood and the ability to coordinate its activities.

The process is somewhat similar to putting together a jigsaw puzzle. Shape and color provide cues for the jigsaw puzzler.[47] As he searches randomly over

---

[47] Some puzzle aficionados contend that rapid solution occurs if all the pieces of the puzzle are turned over so that no color is seen and only shape operates as the cueing system.

the many pieces, he discovers congruences based on the cues, which enable him to pick up a particular piece and set it directly in place. This notion of being led by cues can be extended to other situations. For example, the optimal inventory policy for any item can be determined entirely apart from total company inventories. Yet that part could be studied not only in terms of its own demand and cost characteristics, but also in terms of its interrelation with all other part inventories and with additional factors, such as manufacturing schedules, the motivation of marketing to push items that are thought to be overstocked, and the projected cost of capital. The decisions for each part are based on insufficient information concerning the total system unless an informal system of cues is used, derived largely from within the organization, but from without as well. The cues are mostly decisions and commitments, made by others, that supply relevant information. The fact that the president is going to take a fishing trip might be interpreted as a relaxed attitude toward the cost of capital; a vendor might supply information about what his other customers are doing. Clearly, each hierarchical level has quite different forms and values of cues.

The problem of viewing parts of the system as unconnected to the whole system must be clearly recognized. An out-of-stock on one item may affect a customer's attitude about buying the total line of the company. The way the organization is described will affect the manager's ability to find the critical common linkages that exist. If a brand is taken off the market what happens to all the other brand shares? What occurs when a new item is added to the product line? In the marketplace, what is the effect of changing price? In a who-to-whom matrix, filled with interaction relations, what happens if you take Jones out of the system? And what occurs if you replace Jones with Smith?

It may help to bear in mind the rule used in baseball and golf: "Keep your eye on the ball." It is a meaningful heuristic for achieving coordination. We cannot explain, nor do even know, how each muscle is directed to achieve the final smooth swing that gets that little white ball up in the air. What is apparent, however, is that if one does not look at the right ball, he is not going to be able to pull the necessary parts together. Finding the right core concepts to keep your eye on is not as easy as it may seem. But keeping your eye on them may be even harder. Reaction rates of the organization can be measured, just as a person's reflexes can be tested. A healthy organization will not over- or underreact, and its timing will be right. Organizational delays arising in the communication system are responsible for decreased coordination. The organization is as likely to suffer as the human organism. The manager may contend that his prime objective is to keep competition from developing or to cut down severely on a certain competitor's profit. This idea of striving to win by spoiling the other fellow's game may seem to be entering through the back door, but it is used, and it is an important competitive aspect of synthesis.

Synthesis through committees is another aspect of managerial coordination. If the right group of individuals interact, various ideas become focused. Certain information is obtained and shared. No actions may result, yet a synthesis of managerial minds is achieved. The president of a well-known organization made all his divisional managers meet regularly once a week at 8 A.M., and he never had any agenda for discussion. When he was questioned about the importance of these meetings, he replied that they were intended to achieve a *general* meeting of the minds. Specific problems that would be discussed at other times by this group reflected selective coordination.

Staffing for synthesis. The ability to obtain a meeting of the minds is strongly affected by the *staffing* of the organization. On the one hand, there is little doubt that "like begets like," but there is some question as to whether organizational performance is improved by having many managers whose strongest tendency is to *honestly agree* with the people who hired them. Some call this inbreeding and say that it lowers creative ability. But there is little doubt that synthesis abilities are raised because coordination is easier among people holding similar values and objectives.

Staffing is a typical organizational problem. When we view the organization as a communication network, it becomes clear that staffing is a major factor in the coordination and synthesis issue. Hiring, promoting, training, job descriptions, and job assignments are related to the building of a team. That coordination of the organization is involved becomes obvious when we compare the organization to a baseball team. At first the analogy may seem less applicable to public and private institutions, but, when it is recognized that coordination refers to an interhuman transfer function, the equivalence is seen.

Organizational maintenance is often overlooked or by-passed, because the staffing function seems complete once the person is hired, trained, and assigned. Coordination, however, is a dynamic force and requires care and nourishing of the coordinating elements. It seems strange that although maintenance is such an overpowering concept in technology, it has received little attention in the sense of specific modeling for the human components of an organization. The promise of satisfaction for group and individual needs is transformed into motivating power, but this synergistic power plant must be carefully maintained (stroked, in Eric Berne's sense).

The essence of coordination and synthesis is embodied in a total simulation attempt. Jay Forrester's work in "industrial dynamics" typifies such efforts to capture all information flows in the system and to track their timing, test the effects of delays, and induce changes to see what their effects will be. Unfortunately, the staffing concept tends to become a mechanistic factor rather than a behavioral one, but this is not inevitable. The simulation mode is ideal for representing behavior, even though it must be either simplistic or overspecified, since we do not know enough about human behavior to represent it properly. But the questions are coming now, more frequently and with increasing cogency.

Does the Matthew effect[48] explain a fundamental flaw in all coordinating systems, which gradually weakens rather than strengthens coordination and synthesis abilities? What are the catalytic factors in coordination? Why does a team have good and bad streaks? Could the character of catalysis change over time? Is Parkinson justified?[49] Is the Peter Principle an accurate statement?[50] Is stability a basic organizational need, or is change demanded by the members to interest them in coordination? Put another way, is the convergence theory (management is hunting toward its best evolutionary state) correct, or is the oscillation theory (there is no absolute best state, only a relative one) more accurate?

Perhaps we shall have to know more about personal needs and group behaviors; more about planning, decision-making, and policy formulation; more about information and value systems before the theory of synthesis—that is, the theory of organizations—can emerge. Or perhaps, after learning more and more, we shall find that synthesis is like the "nothing" from which the universe was formed in six days.

SUMMARY

The person is the basic unit of the group. Membership in a group is not likely to change the individual's motivations, but it does affect the actions he takes. As a result, the group cannot be treated simply as a sum of its members. Groups emerge as real entities, which have their own special behaviors. An organization is composed of many groups, with each individual participating in one or more of them.

Individuals belong to a group for common purposes. The strength of their affiliation can vary, but it is always fair to say that a group is characterized by strong interpersonal relations. Although machines may be important to group functions, they are seldom a real part of the group. Nevertheless, machines are playing ever larger organizational roles, and it is likely that future organization

---

[48] "For unto every one that hath shall be given, and he shall have abundance; but from him that hath not shall be taken away even that which he hath." (Matthew 25:29). See also Robert K. Merton, "The Matthew Effect in Science," *Science,* Vol. 159 (January 5, 1968), pp. 56–63.

[49] "Work expands . . . to fill the time available for its completion." C. Northcote Parkinson, *Parkinson's Law* (Boston: Houghton Mifflin, 1957).

[50] "In a hierarchy every employee tends to rise to his level of incompetence." L. J. Peter and R. Hull, *The Peter Principle* (New York: Morrow, 1969).

charts will include particular computer functions that are responsible for major decisions and critical aspects of planning, policy enforcement, and coordination. The computer is becoming a cyborg (cybernetic organism) and, in this sense, extends itself to automated and self-adaptive systems that can have significant organizational roles. The concept of cyborgs as fully participating members of an organization is not difficult to support.

Groups within the organization are characterized by size and by their alterations in size over time. Size stability is discussed in terms of organizational policies concerning growth. Further, the life span of a group is related to its organizational purpose. An additional group characterization is the degree to which its members belong to one or many groups. Through common memberships, overlaps occur, and measures of the overlap between several groups further distinguish the nature of an organization.

The aggregation of individuals into groups and the interaction between groups raise questions of communication flows. Leaders emerge, in part as a result of their own qualities, but also as a result of environmental factors that affect the organization's purposes and stability. Such complexity is difficult to handle, so a mechanistic model of the group can be tolerated as an approach to understanding. The mechanistic view requires that many intangibles be neglected. An input-output framework is converted to an interaction analysis, which records the patterns of communications both to and from the various individuals who belong to overlapping groups within the total organization. A who-to-whom matrix for analyzing communication patterns is developed. By analyzing communications in this way, we can identify leaders, recognize subgroups, and reveal the pecking order of the organization's members.

The pecking order concept, derived from studies of status relations among chickens, can be extended to the status hierarchy of all animals. When formalized, pecking order is "the organization;" informally, it is "the establishment." In either case, it is still a dimensionally weak description of organizational complexity.

To achieve greater enrichment, we examine the roles of individuals in groups. Role-playing is not intended to represent the acting or playing of a part. Rather, it is an individual's ability to adapt to circumstances that he believes will enable him to become an accepted member of a group. Role-playing considerations lead to the notion of a sequence of actions and reactions, called chain relations. Such chains were described by Eric Berne, who studied various two-person interaction chain systems. Berne's approach is to analyze the dynamic components of interaction patterns and the action content of the components. Certain habitual action-reaction patterns emerge that may not be advantageous to either party.

Within organizations, a leader emerges in the pattern of chain relations. The characteristics of leadership are not well understood; ideas range from traditional concepts concerning born leaders through psychoanalytic notions of the need to be led. Ultimately, it has come to be recognized that many factors operate in large interpersonal systems to determine both who will lead and what his leadership style will be.

Leadership and group functioning can also be studied by examining communication networks of groups set up in various configurations from which marked differences in performance result. Less rigid definitions of organization provide additional viewpoints. For example, by treating the ecology of the system, the organization is seen as responsive to its environments. Even mechanistic views of an organization rapidly aggregate into highly complicated systems of interrelated components.

Notions of authority and responsibility are developed. Various attempts are made to define these terms in relatively unambiguous ways, but it is clear that few significant properties of authority and responsibility are measurable. Consequently, there is always ambiguity in the assignment of authority. To obtain better understanding of these terms, we suggest a normative interaction model. The model approximates the assignments of authority to individuals. Such a model is purely conceptual and highlights the fact that the assignment of authority requires complicated specification. Measures of hierarchical distance between individuals (as suggested by Graicunas or as set down on an organizational chart) are hardly a sufficient basis for interpreting authority and responsibility. Yet, in many organizations, managers present their organization's chart as the company's statement of the formal assignment of authority.

Misinterpretation of what is known about organizations encourages the development of bureaucratic organizations. Whereas Max Weber, in the early twentieth century, praised the ability of bureaucracy to improve performance, Erich Fromm warns today of the destructive effects of bureaucracy. With the knowledge of group dynamics and informal groups, the organization can accept mechanistic views as useful guides and yet understand and expect the myriad intangible qualities of human behavior.

Privilege pay is defined as the freedom with which holders of authority permit their subordinates to interact (in real terms) with them. Privilege pay is one of the major motivational factors for the group, often as important as or more important than monetary pay. Douglas McGregor stressed the importance of such intangibles as they affect the performance of the organization. His Theory X describes the belief of authoritarian management that employees work only for money and fundamentally dislike work, avoiding it if they can. Such a management, McGregor suggests, is far less effective than one practicing Theory Y, which assumes that individuals can enjoy what they are doing if they are permitted to participate realistically in the group's performance. Theory Y may not go far enough, however; new distinctions have been emerging in organizations over the past fifty years. In this regard, sensitivity training, wherein individuals *learn to relate* to one another as individuals and not as job descriptions, is discussed. Job description interrelationships are insufficiently described in Theory *Y*. Therefore, without having been so named, Theory *Z* is now being practiced by many organizations in which the goal is to help individuals relate to each other.

The design of organizational excellence is viewed as unapproachable without knowledge of how to achieve synthesis. Certain managerial styles support synthesis; others undermine it. Fundamentals of staffing—training, promoting, hiring, and so on—can contribute to or hinder achievement of a fully coordinated organization.

EXERCISES

1. How do the structure and purpose of a group differ from those of an organization? Would you characterize a major-league baseball team as a group or as an organization? How would you describe the structure of the league?

2. Are there any thoughts that you would now like to add to the discussion of management language on p. 18 in Chapter 1?

3. Try to set up the necessary conditions for Eric Berne-type games such as "Empire-Building," "Paternalism for Stability," "The Union-Management Strike Game," and "Perfectionism Keeps Inventions from the Marketplace" (an R & D game). Can you name any other organizational games?

4. How does Eric Berne's form of interaction analysis differ from the quantitative methods described earlier on pp. 656–60?

5. In the movie *2001,* the computer called HAL was given a leadership role in navigating and maintaining the spaceship that was headed for Jupiter. For reasons that are never clearly explained, the computer develops an abnormal behavior pattern with grave consequences for all concerned. Could a present-day computer be given a leadership role? Discuss.

6. How do you feel about the idea that a leader is not born but the product of an interactive situation?

7. How do you think the two communication networks, circle and wheel, would compare with one another for the operation of: a project group, a committee set up to consider workers' suggestions, an in-plant infirmary, a company library? Design some new communication-network configurations and discuss the properties you think they might exhibit. Join the central hub of a wheel communication configuration to the apex of a chain with a single link. How would such a group operate?

8. Discuss McGregor's Theory X and Theory Y in terms of the changes that have taken place in society over the past seventy-five years. Could a Theory Z be developed that would be consistent with these changes?

9. In what sense is bureaucracy the antithesis of what is hoped to be achieved by sensitivity training?

10. Instead of using five-man communication systems, increase the number of group members to twenty. Are there any changes in performance that you might expect to result?

11. For the transportation Matrix 3 on p. 659, make the allocation change to F_1, T_3, which we have shown in Table 15–7 (p. 660) is inferior in terms of total hierarchical distance but which might be superior in other ways. Comment on this point, comparing the two allocation patterns. Is either of them satisfactory to you?

12. How can the objective of achieving organizational synthesis be affected by staffing? Does a centralized organization possess any advantages, or suffer any disadvantages, in this regard?

Bibliography

Ackoff, R. L. *A Concept of Corporate Planning.* New York: Wiley, 1970.

Albers, H. H. *Principles of Management: A Modern Approach.* 3rd ed. New York: Wiley, 1969.

Allen, L. A. *Management and Organization.* New York: McGraw-Hill, 1958.

Allport, G .W. *Personality: A Psychological Interpretation.* New York: Holt, Rinehart and Winston, 1937.

Andrews, F.; Morgan, J.; and Sonquist, J. *Multiple Classification Analysis: A Report on a Computer Program for Multiple Regression Using Categorical Predictors.* Ann Arbor: Institute for Social Research, The University of Michigan, 1967.

Ansoff, H. I., ed. *Business Strategy.* Middlesex, Eng.: Penguin Books, 1969.

Arensberg, C. M., *et al.,* eds. *Research in Industrial Human Relations.* New York: Harper & Row, 1957.

Argyris, C. *Interpersonal Competence and Organizational Effectiveness.* Homewood, Ill.: Dorsey, 1962.

————, *et al. Social Science Approaches to Business Behavior.* Homewood, Ill.: Dorsey, 1962.

Arrow, K.; Karlin, J.; and Suppes, P., eds. *Mathematical Methods in the Social Sciences.* Stanford, Calif.: Stanford University Press, 1959.

Asch, S. E. *Social Psychology.* Englewood Cliffs, N.J.: Prentice-Hall, 1952.

Ashby, W. R. *An Introduction to Cybernetics.* New York: Wiley, 1956.

Atkinson, J. W., and Feather, N. T., eds. *A Theory of Achievement Motivation.* New York: Wiley, 1965.

Attneave, F. *Applications of Information Theory to Psychology.* New York: Holt, Rinehart and Winston, 1959.

Barfield, R., and Morgan, J. N. *Early Retirement: The Decision and the Experience.* Ann Arbor: Institute for Social Research, The University of Michigan, 1969.

Barnard, C. I. *The Functions of the Executive.* Cambridge, Mass.: Harvard University Press, 1938.

Bass, B. M. *Organizational Psychology.* Boston: Allyn and Bacon, 1965.

Bauer, R. A., and Gergen, K. J., eds. *The Study of Policy Formation.* New York: The Free Press, 1968.

Baughman, J. P., ed. *The History of American Management: Selections from the Business History Review.* Englewood Cliffs, N.J.: Prentice-Hall, 1969.

Baumhart, S. J. *Ethics in Business.* New York: Holt, Rinehart and Winston, 1968.

Beckhard, R. *Organization Development: Strategies and Models.* Reading, Mass.: Addison-Wesley, 1969.

Bell, D. *"The End of Ideology": On The Exhaustion of Political Ideas in the Fifties (1960).* New York: The Free Press, 1965.

Bennis, W. G. *Changing Organizations.* New York: McGraw-Hill, 1966.

————. *Organization Development: Its Nature, Origins, and Prospects.* Reading, Mass.: Addison-Wesley, 1969.

————; Benne, K. D.; and Chin, R., eds. *The Planning of Change.* New York: Holt, Rinehart and Winston, 1962.

Berelson, B., and Steiner, G. A. *Human Behavior: An Inventory of Scientific Findings.* New York: Harcourt Brace Jovanovich, 1964.

Berg, I., ed. *The Business of America.* New York: Harcourt Brace Jovanovich, 1969.

Bergen, G. L., and Haney, W. V. *Organizational Relations and Management Action: Cases and Issues.* New York: McGraw-Hill, 1966.

Berne, E. *The Structure and Dynamics of Organizations and Groups.* Philadelphia: Lippincott, 1963.

Berrien, F. K. *General and Social Systems.* New Brunswick, N.J.: Rutgers University Press, 1968.

Berscheid, E., and Walster, E. *Interpersonal Attraction.* Reading, Mass.: Addison-Wesley, 1969.

Bethel, L. L., *et al. Essentials of Industrial Management.* 2nd ed. New York: McGraw-Hill, 1959.

————; Smith, G. H. E.;& Stackman, H. A.,Jr. *Industrial Organization and Management.* 4th ed. New York: McGraw-Hill, 1962.

Birch, D., and Veroff, J. *Motivation: A Study of Action.* Belmont, Calif.: Brooks/Cole, 1966.

Bishir, J. W., and Drewes, D. W. *Mathematics in the Behavioral and Social Sciences.* New York: Harcourt Brace Jovanovich, 1970.

Black, M., ed. *The Social Theories of Talcott Parsons.* Englewood Cliffs, N.J.: Prentice-Hall, 1961.

Blake, R. R., and Mouton, J. S. *Building a Dynamic Corporation Through Grid Organization Development.* Reading, Mass.: Addison-Wesley, 1969.

Blough, R. *International Business: Environment and Adaptation.* New York: McGraw-Hill, 1966.

Blumenthal, S. C. *Management Information Systems: A Framework for Planning and Development.* Englewood Cliffs, N.J.: Prentice-Hall, 1969.

Boddewyn, J. *Comparative Management and Marketing.* New York: Wiley, 1968.

Boguslaw, R. *The New Utopians: A Study of System Design and Social Change.* Englewood Cliffs, N.J.: Prentice-Hall, 1965.

Bonini, C. P.; Jaedicke, R. J.; and Wagner, H. M. *Management Controls: New Directions in Basic Research.* New York: McGraw-Hill, 1964.

Borko, H., ed. *Computer Applications in the Behavioral Sciences.* Englewood Cliffs, N.J.: Prentice-Hall, 1962.

Boulding, K. E. *Conflict and Defense.* New York: Harper & Row, 1962.

————. *The Image: Knowledge in Life and Society.* Ann Arbor: The University of Michigan Press, 1956.

Bowman, D. M. *Management—Organization and Planning.* New York: McGraw-Hill, 1963.

Bright, J., ed. *Technological Planning.* Cambridge, Mass.: Harvard University Press, 1962.

Bronowski, J. *Science and Human Values.* New York: Harper & Row, 1956.

Brown, R .E. *Judgment in Administration.* New York: McGraw-Hill, 1966.

Buckley, W., ed. *Modern Systems Research for the Behavioral Scientist.* Chicago: Aldine, 1968.

Bunge, M. *Intuition and Science.* Englewood Cliffs, N.J.: Prentice-Hall, 1962.

Burns, T., and Stalker, G. M. *The Management of Innovation.* London: Tavistock, 1961.

Campbell, A., et al. *Elections and the Political Order.* New York: Wiley, 1966.

Cannon, J. T. *Business Strategy and Policy.* New York: Harcourt Brace Jovanovich, 1969.

Cartwright, D. P., ed. *Studies in Social Power.* Ann Arbor: Institute for Social Research, The University of Michigan, 1966.

————, and Zander, A., eds. *Group Dynamics: Research and Theory.* New York: Harper & Row, 1960.

Carzo, R., Jr., and Yanouzas, J. N. *Formal Organization: A Systems Approach.* Homewood, Ill.: Irwin, 1967.

Champion, J. M., and Bridges, F. J. *Critical Incidents in Management.* Rev. ed. Homewood, Ill.: Irwin, 1969.

Chapple, E. D., and Sayles, L. R. *The Measure of Management.* New York: Macmillan, 1961.

Chardin, P. T. de. *The Future of Man.* Translated by N. Denny. New York: Harper & Row, 1964.

Cherry, C. *On Human Communication.* New York: Wiley (Science Editions), 1961.

Chruden, H. J., and Sherman, A .W., Jr. *Personnel Management.* 3rd ed. Cincinnati: South-western, 1968.

Clynes, M., and Halacy, D. S., Jr. *Cyborg: Evolution of the Superman.* New York: Harper & Row, 1965.

Coleman, J. S. *Introduction to Mathematical Sociology.* Glencoe: The Free Press, 1964.

Cooper, W. W.; Leavitt, H. J.; and Shelley, M. W., eds. *New Perspectives in Organization Research.* New York: Wiley, 1964.

Costello, T. W., and Zalkind, S. S. *Psychology in Administration: A Research Orientation Text with Integrated Readings.* Englewood Cliffs, N.J.: Prentice-Hall, 1963.

Cotton, D. B. *Company-Wide Planning: Concept and Process.* New York: Macmillan, 1970 .

Dale, E. *Management, Theory and Practice.* 2nd ed. New York: McGraw-Hill, 1969.

————, ed. *Readings in Management: Landmarks and New Frontiers.* 2nd ed. New York: McGraw-Hill, 1970.

————, and Michelon, L. C. *Modern Management Methods.* Cleveland: World, 1966.

Dankert, C. E.; Mann, F. C.; and Northrup, H. R., eds. *Hours of Work.* New York: Harper & Row, 1965.

Darden, B. R., and Lucas, W. H. *The Decision Game.* New York: Appleton-Century-Crofts, 1969.

Davis, J. H. *Group Performance.* Reading, Mass.: Addison-Wesley, 1969.

Davis, K. *Human Relations at Work: The Dynamics of Organizational Behavior.* 3rd ed. New York: McGraw-Hill, 1967.

————, and Blomstrom, R. *Business and Its Environment.* New York: McGraw-Hill, 1966.

De Bono, E. *New Think.* New York: Basic Books, 1968.

De Solla, D. J. *Little Science, Big Science.* New York: Columbia University Press, 1963.

Drucker, P. F. *The Age of Discontinuity: Guidelines to Our Changing Society.* New York: Harper & Row, 1969.

————. *The Practice of Management.* New York: Harper & Row, 1954.

Dun & Bradstreet, Inc. *Human Values in Management.* New York: Dun & Bradstreet (Business Education Division), 1968.

Duncan, H. D. *Communication and Social Order.* New York: Oxford University Press, 1968.

Ebbinghaus, H. *Memory.* New York: Teachers College Press, Columbia University, 1913.

Eells, R., and Walton, C. C. *Conceptual Foundations of Business.* Rev. ed. Homewood, Ill.: Irwin, 1969.

Emery, D. A. *The Compleat Manager.* New York: McGraw-Hill, 1970.

Emery, F. E. *Systems Thinking.* Middlesex, Eng.: Penguin Books, 1969.

Erikson, E. H. *Insight and Responsibility*. New York: Norton, 1964.

Etzioni, A., ed. *Complex Organizations*. New York: Holt, Rinehart and Winston, 1961.

Evans, C. R., and Robertson, A. D. J., eds. *Cybernetics*. Baltimore: University Park Press, 1968.

Famularo, J. J. *Supervisors in Action*. New York: McGraw-Hill, 1961.

Farmer, R. N. *International Management*. Belmont, Calif.: Dickenson, 1968.

————. *Management in the Future*. Belmont, Calif.: Wadsworth, 1969.

————; Richman, B. M.; and Ryan, W. G. *Incidents in Applying Management Theory*. Belmont, Calif.: Wadsworth, 1969.

Fayerweather, J. *Management of International Operations: Text and Cases*. New York: McGraw-Hill, 1960.

Feigenbaum, E. A., and Feldman, J., eds. *Computers and Thought*. New York: McGraw-Hill, 1963.

Ferkiss, V. C. *Technological Man: The Myth and the Reality*. New York: Braziller, 1969.

Festinger, L. *A Theory of Cognitive Dissonance*. Evanston, Ill.: Row, Peterson, 1957.

————, and Katz, D. eds. *Research Methods in the Behavioral Sciences*. New York: Holt, Rinehart and Winston, 1953.

Fiedler, F. E. *Theory of Leadership Effectiveness*. New York: McGraw-Hill, 1967.

Filley, A. C., and House, R. J. *Managerial Process and Organizational Behavior*. Glenview, Ill.: Scott, Foresman, 1969.

Flippo, E. B. *Principles of Personnel Management*. 2nd ed. New York: McGraw-Hill, 1966.

Forrester, J. W. *Industrial Dynamics*. New York: Wiley, 1961.

Frank, J. D. *Persuasion and Healing*. New York: Schocken, 1963.

Fraser, J .T., ed. *The Voices of Time*. New York: Braziller, 1966.

Fromm, E. *The Revolution of Hope: Toward a Humanized Technology*. New York: Harper & Row, 1968.

Fuller, R. B. *Ideas and Integrities*. Englewood Cliffs, N.J.: Prentice-Hall, 1963.

Furnas, C. C. *The Next Hundred Years*. Baltimore: Williams & Wilkins, 1936.

Gabor, D. *Inventing the Future*. New York: Knopf, 1963.

Galbraith, J. K. *The New Industrial State*. Boston: Houghton Mifflin, 1967.

Gardner, J. W. *Self-Renewal*. New York: Harper & Row, 1964.

Gass, S. I. *Linear Programming: Methods and Applications*. 3rd ed. New York: McGraw-Hill, 1969.

Gellerman, S. W. *The Management of Human Relations*. New York: Holt, Rinehart and Winston, 1966.

Gergen, K. J. *The Psychology of Behavior Exchange*. Reading, Mass.: Addison-Wesley, 1969.

Ghiselli, E. E., and Brown, C. W. *Personnel and Industrial Psychology*. 2nd ed. New York: McGraw-Hill, 1955.

Ginzberg, E., ed. *The Negro Challenge to the Business Community*. New York: McGraw-Hill, 1964.

————, ed. *Technology and Social Change*. New York: Columbia University Press, 1964.

————, and the Conservation of Human Resources Staff. *Manpower Strategy for the Metropolis*. New York: Columbia University Press, 1968.

————; Hiestand, D. L.; and Reubens, B. G. *The Pluralistic Economy*. New York: McGraw-Hill, 1965.

Glans, T. B.; Meyers, W. E.; and Schmidt, R. N. *Management Systems*. New York: Holt, Rinehart and Winston, 1968.

Goldman, T. A., ed. *Cost-Effectiveness Analysis*. New York: Praeger, 1967.

Good, I. J. *Probability and the Weighing of Evidence*. London: Griffin, 1950.

Gordon, W. J. J. *Synetics*. New York: Harper & Row, 1961.

Gouldner, A. *Patterns of Industrial Bureaucracy*. New York: The Free Press, 1954.

Green, B. *Digital Computers in Research: An Introduction for Behavioral and Social Scientists*. New York: McGraw-Hill, 1963.

Greenberger, M., ed. *Computers and the World of the Future*. Cambridge, Mass.: The M.I.T. Press, 1962.

Greenwood, W. T. *Management and Organizational Behavior Theories: An Interdisciplinary Approach*. Cincinnati: Southwestern, 1967.

Gregory, C. E. *The Management of Intelligence: Scientific Problem Solving and Creativity*. New York: McGraw-Hill, 1967.

Gross, B. M. *Organizations and Their Managing*. New York: The Free Press, 1968.

Guest, R. *Organizational Change, the Effect of Successful Leadership*. Homewood, Ill., Dorsey, 1962.

Guetzkow, H., ed. *Simulation in Social Science: Readings*. Englewood Cliffs, N.J.: Prentice-Hall, 1962.

Gutenberg, A. W., and Richman, E. *Dynamics of Management*. Scranton, Pa.: International Textbook, 1968.

Hadley, G. *Linear Programming*. Reading, Mass.: Addison-Wesley, 1962.

Haimann, T. *Professional Management: Theory and Practice*. Boston: Houghton Mifflin, 1962.

Hampton, D. R., ed. *Behavioral Concepts in Management*. Belmont, Calif.: Dickenson, 1968.

————; Summer, C. E., Jr.; and Webber, R. A. *Organizational Behavior and the*

Practice of Management. New York: Wiley, 1968.

Harary, F.; Norman, R. Z.; Cartwright, D. *Structural Models*. New York: Wiley, 1965.

Hare, V. C., Jr. *Systems Analysis: A Diagnostic Approach*. New York: Harcourt Brace Jovanovich, 1967.

Hastorf, A. H.; Schneider, D.; and Polefka, J. *Person Perception*. Reading, Mass.: Addison-Wesley, 1970.

Haynes, W. W., and Massie, J. L. *Management: Analysis, Concepts, and Cases*. 2nd ed. Englewood Cliffs, N.J.: Prentice-Hall, 1969.

Hersey, P., and Blanchard, K. H. *Management of Organizational Behavior: Utilizing Human Resources*. Englewood Cliffs, N.J.: Prentice-Hall, 1969.

Hertz, D. B. *New Power for Management, Computer Systems and Management Science*. New York: McGraw-Hill, 1969.

Herzberg, F. *The Motivation to Work*. 2nd ed. New York: Wiley, 1967.

Hicks, H. G. *The Management of Organizations*. New York: McGraw-Hill, 1967.

Hill, W. A., and Egan, D. M. *Readings in Organizational Theory: A Behavioral Approach*. Boston: Allyn and Bacon, 1967.

Hodge, B., and Hodgson, R. N. *Management and the Computer in Information and Control Systems*. New York: McGraw-Hill, 1969.

Holden, P. E.; Pederson, C. A.; and Germane, G. E. *Top Management*. New York: McGraw-Hill, 1968.

Homans, G. C. *The Human Group*. New York: Harper & Row, 1950.

————, ed. *Sentiments and Activities*. New York: The Free Press, 1962.

Hull, C. L. *A Behavior System*. New Haven, Conn.: Yale University Press, 1952.

Jaques, E. *The Changing Culture of a Factory*. New York: Dryden Press, 1952.

Johnson, R. A.; Kast, F. E.; and Rosenzweig, J. E. *The Theory and Management of Systems*. 2nd ed. New York: McGraw-Hill, 1967.

Jouvenel, B. de. *The Art of Conjecture*. New York: Basic Books, 1967.

Juran, J. M. *Managerial Breakthrough: A New Concept of the Manager's Job*. New York: McGraw-Hill, 1964.

Kahn, D. *The Codebreakers: The Story of Secret Writing*. New York: Macmillan, 1967.

Kahn, H., and Wiener, A. J. *The Year 2000; A Framework for Speculation on the Next Thirty-Three Years*. New York: Macmillan, 1967.

Kahn, R. L., *et al. Organizational Stress: Studies in Role Conflict and Ambiguity*. New York: Wiley, 1964.

Kast, F. E., and Rosenzweig, J. E. *Organization and Management: A Systems Ap-*

proach. New York: McGraw-Hill, 1970.

Katona, G. *The Mass Consumption Society*. New York: McGraw-Hill, 1964.

Katz, D., and Kahn, R. L. *The Social Psychology of Organizations*. New York: Wiley, 1966.

Kaufmann, A. *The Science of Decision-making* New York: McGraw-Hill, 1968.

Kazmier, L. J. *Principles of Management: A Program for Self-Instruction*. 2nd ed. New York: McGraw-Hill, 1969.

Kelly, J. *Organizational Behaviour*. Homewood, Ill.: Irwin, 1969.

Kepner, C. H., and Tregoe, B. B., *The Rational Manager*. New York: McGraw-Hill, 1965.

Kiesler, C. A. and S. B. *Conformity*. Reading, Mass.: Addison-Wesley, 1969.

Kolasa, B. J. *Introduction to Behavioral Science for Business*. New York: Wiley, 1969.

Koontz, H., ed. *Toward a Unified Theory of Management*. New York: McGraw-Hill, 1964.

————, and O'Donnell, C. J. *Principles of Management: An Analysis of Managerial Functions*. 4th ed. New York: McGraw-Hill, 1968.

Krupp, S. *Pattern in Organization Analysis*. New York: Holt, Rinehart and Winston, 1961.

Kuhn, J. W., and Berg, I. *Values in a Business Society: Issues and Analyses*. New York: Harcourt Brace Jovanovich, 1969.

Landers, R. R. *Man's Place in the Dybosphere*. Englewood Cliffs, N.J.: Prentice-Hall, 1966.

Langer, S. K. *Philosophy in a New Key: A Study in the Symbolism of Reason, Rite and Art*. New York: New American Library, 1942.

Lansing, J. B., and Mueller, E. L. *The Geographic Mobility of Labor*. Ann Arbor: Institute for Social Research, The University of Michigan, 1968.

Lawrence, P. R., and Lorsch, J. W. *Developing Organizations: Diagnosis and Action*. Reading, Mass.: Addison-Wesley, 1969.

Lazarus, H., and Warren, E. K. *The Progress of Management*. Englewood Cliffs, N.J.: Prentice-Hall, 1968.

Learned, E.; Christensen, C. R.; Andrews, K. R.; and Guth, W. D. *Business Policy: Text and Cases*. Rev. ed. Homewood, Ill.: Irwin, 1969.

Leavitt, H., ed. *The Social Science of Organizations*. Englewood Cliffs, N.J.: Prentice-Hall, 1963.

Le Breton, P. P. *General Administration: Planning and Implementation*. New York: Holt, Rinehart and Winston, 1965.

————, and Henning, D. A. *Planning Theory*. Englewood Cliffs, N.J.: Prentice-Hall, 1961.

Levin, R. I., and Kirkpatrick, C. A. *Man-*

agement Planning and Control with PERT-CPM. New York: McGraw-Hill, 1966.

Levi-Strauss, C. The Savage Mind. London: Weidenfeld & Nicolson, 1966.

Lewin, K. A Dynamic Theory of Personality. New York: McGraw-Hill, 1935.

————. Field Theory in Social Science. New York: Harper & Row, 1951.

Libo, L. M. Measuring Group Cohesiveness. Ann Arbor: Institute for Social Research, The University of Michigan, 1968.

Likert, R. L. The Human Organization: Its Management and Value. New York: McGraw-Hill, 1967.

————. New Patterns of Management. New York: McGraw-Hill, 1961.

Lindzey, G., and Aronson, E., eds. Handbook of Social Psychology. 2nd ed. 5 vols. Reading, Mass.: Addison-Wesley, 1970.

Litterer, J. A., ed. Organizations: Structure and Behavior, Vol. I. 2nd ed. New York: Wiley, 1969.

————, ed. Organizations: Systems, Control, and Adaptation, Vol. II. 2nd ed. New York: Wiley, 1969.

Longenecker, J. G. Principles of Management and Organizational Behavior. 2nd ed. Columbus, Ohio: Merrill, 1969.

Luria, A. R. The Nature of Human Conflicts. New York: Simon & Schuster, 1967.

Luthans, F. Cases, Readings, and Review Guide for Principles of Management. New York: Wiley, 1969.

McArthur, J. H., and Scott, B. R. Industrial Planning in France. Cambridge, Mass.: Division of Research, Harvard Business School, 1969.

McClelland, D. C. The Achieving Society. New York: Van Nostrand, 1961.

McDonough, A. M. Information Economics and Management Systems. New York: McGraw-Hill, 1963.

McGregor, D. The Human Side of Enterprise. New York: McGraw-Hill, 1960.

————. The Professional Manager. Edited by W. G. Bennis and C. McGregor. New York: McGraw-Hill, 1967.

McHale, J. The Future of the Future. New York: Braziller, 1969.

McLuhan, M. Understanding Media: The Extensions of Man. New York: McGraw-Hill, 1966.

Magee, J. F., and Boodman, D. M. Production Planning and Inventory Control. 2nd ed. New York: McGraw-Hill, 1967.

Maier, N. R. Problem-Solving Discussions and Conferences. New York: McGraw-Hill, 1963.

Mann, F. C., and Hoffman, L. R. Automation and the Worker. New York: Holt, Rinehart and Winston, 1960.

————; Indik, B. P.; and Vroom, V. H. The Productivity of Work Groups. Ann Arbor: Institute for Social Research, The University of Michigan, 1963.

March, J. G., ed. Handbook of Organizations. Chicago: Rand McNally, 1965.

————, Simon, H. A. Organizations. New York: Wiley, 1958.

Marcus, S. Competition and the Law. Belmont, Calif.: Wadsworth, 1967.

Marrow, A. J.; Bowers, D. G.; and Seashore, S. E. Management by Participation: Creating a Climate for Personal and Organizational Development. New York: Harper & Row, 1967.

Martino, R. L. Critical Path Networks. Wayne, Pa.: Management Development Institute, 1967.

Maslow, A. H. Motivation and Personality. New York: Harper & Row, 1954.

Megginson, L. C. Human Resources: Cases and Concepts. New York: Harcourt Brace Jovanovich, 1969.

Meier, R. C.; Newell, W. P.; and Pazer, H. L. Simulation in Business and Economics. Englewood Cliffs, N.J.: Prentice-Hall, 1968.

Merrihue, W. V. Managing by Communication. New York: McGraw-Hill, 1960.

Merton, R. K. Social Theory and Social Structure. New York: The Free Press, 1957.

————; Broom, L.; and Cottrell, L. F., eds. Sociology Today. New York: Basic Books, 1959.

Metcalf, H. C., and Urwick, L., eds. Dynamic Administration: The Collected Papers of Mary Parker Follett. New York: Harper & Row, 1941.

Michael, D. N. The Unprepared Society: Planning for a Precarious Future. New York: Basic Books, 1968.

Miller, D. W., and Starr, M. K. Executive Decisions and Operations Research. 2nd ed. Englewood Cliffs, N.J.: Prentice-Hall, 1969.

Miller, R. W. Schedule, Cost, and Profit Control with PERT. New York: McGraw-Hill, 1963.

Mills, C. W. The Power Elite. New York: Oxford University Press, 1956.

Minskey, M. L., ed. Semantic Information Processing. Cambridge, Mass.: M.I.T. Press, 1968.

Moore, F. G. Manufacturing Management. 5th ed. Homewood, Ill.: Irwin, 1969.

Morse, P. M. Queues, Inventories, and Maintenance. New York: Wiley, 1958.

Mott, P. E., et al. Shift Work: The Social, Psychological, and Physical Consequences. Ann Arbor: The University of Michigan Press, 1965.

Mowrer, O. H. Learning Theory and Behavior. New York: Wiley, 1960.

————. Learning Theory and the Symbolic Process. New York: Wiley, 1960.

Mumford, L. The Transformations of Man. New York: Collier Books, 1956.

Musselman, V. A., and Hughes, E. H. Introduction to Modern Business: Analysis *and Interpretation.* 5th ed. Englewood Cliffs, N.J.: Prentice-Hall, 1969.

Neuschel, R. F. *Management by System.* 2nd ed. New York: McGraw-Hill, 1960.

Newman, W. H., and Logan, J. P. *Business Policies and Central Management.* 5th ed. Cincinnati: South-western, 1965.

————; Summer, C. E., Jr.; and Warren, E. K. *The Process of Management: Concepts, Behavior, and Practice.* 2nd ed. Englewood Cliffs, N.J.: Prentice-Hall, 1967.

Novick, D. *Program Budgeting: Program Analysis and The Federal Budget.* New York: Holt, Rinehart and Winston, 1969.

Orcutt, G. H.; Greenberger, M.; Korbel, J.; and Rivlin, A. M. *Micro-Analysis of Socio-Economic Systems: A Simulation Study.* New York: Harper & Row, 1961.

Owens, R. N. *Management of Industrial Enterprises.* 6th ed. Homewood, Ill.: Irwin, 1969.

Pavlov, I. P. *Conditioned Reflexes.* London: Oxford University Press, 1927.

Payne, B. *Planning for Company Growth.* New York: McGraw-Hill, 1963.

Pelz, D. C., and Andrews, F. M. *Scientists in Organization: Productive Climates for Research and Development.* New York: Wiley, 1966.

Perrow, C. *Organizational Analysis: A Sociological View.* Belmont, Calif.: Wadsworth, 1970.

Peters, L. H. *Management and Society.* Belmont, Calif.: Dickenson, 1968.

Petrullo, L., and Bass, B. M., eds. *Leadership and Interpersonal Behavior.* New York: Holt, Rinehart and Winston, 1961.

Pigors, P., and Myers, C. A. *Personnel Administration.* 5th ed. New York: McGraw-Hill, 1965.

————, and Pigors, F. *Case Method in Human Relations: The Incident Process.* New York: McGraw-Hill, 1961.

Poe, J. B. *The American Business Enterprise (Introductory Text and Cases).* Homewood, Ill.: Irwin, 1969.

Proshansky, H., and Seidenberg, B., eds. *Basic Studies in Social Psychology.* New York: Holt, Rinehart and Winston, 1965.

Quinn, R. P., *et al. The Chosen Few: A Study of Discrimination in Executive Selection.* Ann Arbor: Institute for Social Research, The University of Michigan, 1968.

————; Tabor, J. M.; and Gordon, L. K. *The Decision to Discriminate: A Study of Executive Selection.* Ann Arbor: Institute for Social Research, The University of Michigan, 1968.

Raiffa, H. *Decision Analysis: Introductory Lectures on Choices Under Uncertainty.* Reading, Mass.: Addison-Wesley, 1968.

Rapoport, A. *N-Person Game Theory, Concepts and Applications.* Ann Arbor: The University of Michigan Press, 1970.

Ready, R. K. *The Administrator's Job: Issues and Dilemmas.* New York: McGraw-Hill, 1967.

Reichenbach, H. *Experience and Prediction: An Analysis of the Foundations and the Structure of Knowledge.* Chicago: The University of Chicago Press, 1938.

Report from Iron Mountain. New York: Dial Press, 1967.

Rescher, N. *Introduction to Value Theory.* Englewood Cliffs, N.J.: Prentice-Hall, 1969.

Richards, M. D., and Nielander, W. A., eds. *Readings in Management.* 3rd ed. Cincinnati: South-western, 1968.

Riesman, D.; Glazer, N.; and Denney, R. *The Lonely Crowd.* New Haven, Conn.: Yale University Press, 1950.

Robinson, J. P.; Athanasiou, R.; and Head, K. B. *Measures of Occupational Attitudes and Occupational Characteristics.* Ann Arbor: Institute for Social Research, The University of Michigan, 1968.

Roethlisberger, F. J. *Man-in-Organization: Essays of F. J. Roethlisberger.* Cambridge, Mass.: Harvard University Press, 1968.

————, and Dickson, W. J. *Management and the Worker.* Cambridge, Mass.: Harvard University Press, 1939.

Rubenstein, A. H., and Haberstroh, C. J., eds. *Some Theories of Organization.* Homewood, Ill.: Dorsey, 1960.

Sayles, L. R. *Individualism and Big Business.* New York: McGraw-Hill, 1963.

————. *Managerial Behavior.* New York: McGraw-Hill, 1964.

Schein, E. H. *Organizational Psychology.* Englewood Cliffs, N.J.: Prentice-Hall, 1965.

Schell, E. H. *Technique of Administration.* 2nd ed. New York: McGraw-Hill, 1951.

Schlender, W. E.; Scott, W. G.; and Filley, A. C., eds. *Management in Perspective: Selected Readings.* Boston: Houghton Mifflin, 1965.

Schon, D. A. *Technology and Change.* New York: Delacorte Press, 1967.

Seashore, S. E. *Group Cohesiveness in the Industrial Work Group.* Ann Arbor: Institute for Social Research, The University of Michigan, 1968.

Seidenberg, R. *Post-Historic Man: An Inquiry.* Boston: Beacon Press, 1950.

Seiller, K., III. *Introduction to Systems Cost Effectiveness.* New York: Wiley, 1969.

Shannon, C. E., and Weaver, W. *The Mathematical Theory of Communication.* Urbana: University of Illinois Press, 1949.

Sherif, M. and C. W. *Reference Groups.* New York: Harper & Row, 1964.

Sielaff, T. J., and Aberle, J. W. *Introduction to Business.* 3rd ed. Belmont, Calif.: Wadsworth, 1969.

Simon, H. A. *Models of Man.* New York: Wiley, 1957.

Simon, H. A. *The New Science of Management Decision.* New York: Harper & Row, 1960.

——. *The Sciences of the Artificial.* Cambridge, Mass.: The M.I.T. Press, 1969.

Sisk, H. L. *Principles of Management: A Systems Approach to the Management Process.* Cincinnati: South-western, 1969.

Siu, R. G. H. *The Tao of Science.* New York: Wiley, 1957.

Smith, H. C. *Sensitivity to People.* New York: McGraw-Hill, 1966.

Sofer, C. *Organization from Within.* London: Tavistock, 1961.

Sokal, R. R., and Sneath, P. H. A. *Principles of Numerical Taxonomy.* San Francisco, Calif.: W. H. Freeman and Co., 1963.

Stagner, R., and Rosen, H. *Psychology of Union-Management Relations.* Belmont, Calif.: Wadsworth, 1965.

Steiner, G. A. *Top Management Planning.* New York: Macmillan, 1969.

——, ed. *The Creative Organization.* Chicago: The University of Chicago Press, 1965.

——, ed. *Management Long-Range Planning.* New York: McGraw-Hill, 1963.

Steinmetz, L. L. *Managing the Marginal and Unsatisfactory Performer.* Reading, Mass.: Addison-Wesley, 1969.

Stockton, R. S. *Introduction to PERT.* Boston: Allyn and Bacon, 1964.

Strauss, G., and Sayles, L. R. *Personnel: The Human Problem of Management.* Englewood Cliffs, N.J.: Prentice-Hall, 1967.

Strong, E. P., and Smith, R. D. *Management Control Models.* New York: Holt, Rinehart and Winston, 1968.

Summer, C. E., Jr., and O'Connell, J. *The Managerial Mind.* Rev. ed. Homewood, Ill.: Irwin, 1968.

Swanson, L. A., and Pazer, H. L. *Pertism: Text and Simulation.* Scranton: International Textbook, 1969.

Tannenbaum, A. S. *Social Psychology of the Work Organization.* Belmont, Calif.: Wadsworth, 1966.

——, ed. *Control in Organizations.* New York: McGraw-Hill, 1968.

Tannenbaum, R.; Weschler, I. R.; and Massarik, F. *Leadership and Organization: A Behavioral Science Approach.* New York: McGraw-Hill, 1961.

Taylor, F. W. *The Principles and Methods of Scientific Management.* New York: Harper & Row Publishers, 1911.

Taylor, J. W. *How to Select and Develop Leaders.* New York: McGraw-Hill, 1962.

Theil, H. *Economics and Information Theory.* Chicago: Rand McNally, 1967.

——. *Optimal Decision Rules for Government and Industry.* Amsterdam: North-Holland, 1964.

Thompson, J. D. *Organizations in Action.* New York: McGraw-Hill, 1967.

Thorndike, E. L. *Human Learning.* New York: Appleton-Century-Crofts, 1931.

Trist, E. L., et al. *Organizational Choice.* London: Tavistock, 1963.

Ullman, J. E., and Cluck, S. E. *Manufacturing Management: An Overview.* New York: Holt, Rinehart and Winston, 1968.

Vickers, G. *Towards a Sociology of Management.* London: Chapman and Hall, 1967.

Vroom, V. H., ed. *Methods of Organizational Research.* Pittsburgh: University of Pittsburgh Press, 1967.

Wadia, M. S. *Management and the Behavioral Sciences.* Boston: Allyn and Bacon, 1968.

——. *The Nature and Scope of Management.* New York: Wiley, 1966.

Wagner, H. M. *Principles of Operations Research.* Englewood Cliffs, N.J.: Prentice-Hall, 1969.

Walton, C. C. *Corporate Social Responsibilities.* Rev. ed. Belmont, Calif.: Wadsworth, 1967.

——, and McGuire, J. W. eds. *Problems in a Business Society Series.* Belmont, Calif.: Wadsworth, 1969.

Warren, E. K. *Long Range Planning: The Executive Viewpoint.* Englewood Cliffs, N.J.: Prentice-Hall, 1966.

Washburne, N. F., ed. *Decisions, Values, and Groups.* New York: Pergamon Press, 1962.

Weber, C. E., and Peters, G., eds. *Management Action: Models of Administrative Decision.* Scranton: International Textbook, 1969.

Wiest, J. D., and Levy, F. K. *A Management Guide to PERT/CPM.* Englewood Cliffs, N.J.: Prentice-Hall, 1969.

Whyte, W. F. *Money and Motivation.* New York: Harper & Row, 1955.

——. *Organizational Behavior: Theory and Application.* Homewood, Ill.: Irwin, 1969.

——. *Pattern for Industrial Peace.* New York: Harper & Row, 1951.

Wilensky, H. L. *Organizational Intelligence.* New York: Basic Books, 1967.

Withington, F. G. *The Real Computer: Its Influence, Uses and Effects.* Reading, Mass.: Addison-Wesley, 1969.

——. *The Use of Computers in Business Organizations.* Reading, Mass.: Addison-Wesley, 1966.

Yoder, D. *Personnel Management and Industrial Relations.* 6th ed. Englewood Cliffs, N.J.: Prentice-Hall, 1970.

Young, S. *Management: A Decision/Making Approach.* Belmont, Calif.: Dickenson, 1968.

——. *Management: A Systems Analysis.* New York: Wiley, 1966.

Index